Managerial Accounting in Canada
Revised Edition

Managerial Accounting in Canada
Revised Edition

FRANK P. DOUGHERTY
Saint Mary's University

SAMUEL H. JOPLING
Saint Mary's University

ARTHUR J. FRANCIA
University of Houston

MATTIE C. PORTER
University of Houston

ROBERT H. STRAWSER
Texas A&M University

1986

dame publications, inc.
P.O. Box 35556
Houston, Texas 77235-5556

© **dame publications, inc.—1986**

Canadian Cataloguing in Publication Data:

Dougherty, Frank P. (1928-   )

  Management Accounting in Canada (Revised Edition)
        p. 571   cm 24
        Includes Index
        1.   Managerial Accounting   2.   Cost Accounting

I. Jopling, Samuel H. (1928-   ); II. Francia, Arthur J. (1942-   ); III.   Title: Managerial Accounting in Canada (Revised Edition).

HF 5635.D, 1986, 658.1'511, L86-

ISBN 0-87393-037-1

Library of Congress Catalog Card No. 82-73436

Printed in the United States of America

Preface

THIS TEXT, like its predecessor, was written as an integrated work in management accounting. Emphasis is placed upon those aspects of accounting with which all business students should be familiar. If an overall theme were used to describe this text, it would focus on five key areas: cost accumulation and analysis; accounting aspects of planning; accounting aspects of control; accounting aspects of performance evaluation; and, relevant internal uses of managerial accounting information for many different management needs. These key areas were selected as the underlying theme for this text because we believe they best describe the "core" of management accounting theory and practice. We felt that if the core material were covered, the student would find the subject matter relevant in other business courses and, more importantly, in practice throughout his or her career.

This book may be used as a basic text for the student who has completed a first course in financial accounting at either the undergraduate or graduate level. The perspective is balanced and where optional treatments or approaches exist, these are identified and discussed.

The text employs a continuous example to maintain and illustrate the continuity of management information flows within an organization. This continuous example permits the student to consider each topic separately while recognizing that the topic is not a separate subject, but is interrelated and maintains its specific role in the total information system available to management for decision making.

Organization of the Text

Following each chapter are numerous questions, exercises and problems. Most of the material adapted from the Uniform Examinations of the Society of Management Accountants of Canada, the National Examinations of The Certified General Accountants Association of Canada and the Uniform Final Examinations of the Institutes and Order of Chartered Accountants in Canada have been placed at the end of the problems. This permits the instructor to select assignments that range from easy-to-follow illustrative exercises and problems to difficult, thought-provoking problems that may be used for further class discussion.

Content

While based on the American *Managerial Accounting* by Arthur J. Francia, Mattie C. Porter and Robert H. Strawser, this text is specifically designed for Canadians. As such we hope that it will spare students from those minor but nevertheless annoying irritations which are the unavoidable by-product of using a text designed for those who are subject to different laws and regulations and whose commerical practices, customs and economic system, though recognizably similar are not the same.

This is not to infer that the basic principles of managerial accounting differ between countries. Rather, it is to give recognition to the fact that national differences do affect the application of universal principles. For example, a failure to appreciate some of the more important differences between the income tax laws of Canada and the United States could have a serious effect on the outcome of certain capital budgeting decisions.

With respect to spelling, we have in general chosen to use the shorter version of those words such as labor (labour), enrolment (enrollment) and airplane (areoplane) for which more than one acceptable spelling exists. Exceptions to this policy exist where Canadian useage is overwhelmingly in favor of the longer form. (For example, cheque rather than check, as in the United States.) In cases where the different versions of a word are of the same length, such as centre and litre, the more traditional (British) useage is followed. Quotations, to include questions taken from nationwide examinations, retain their original spelling.

Acknowledgements

During the preparation of this text we have benefited not only from the efforts of the authors of the original work but also from the comments and constructive criticism rendered by students and colleagues. For this assistance we are grateful.

We also wish to express our appreciation to the Society of Management Accountants of Canada, The Canadian Institute of Chartered Accountants, the Certified General Accountants Association of Canada, the American Institute of Certified Public Accountants and the National Association of Accountants for their kind permission to use problem material from their respective nation-wide examinations.

Obviously any defects in this text are the responsibility of the authors.

Halifax
July, 1986

Frank P. Dougherty
Samuel H. Jopling
Arthur J. Francia
Mattie C. Porter
Robert H. Strawser

Contents

Managerial Accounting in Canada
Revised Edition

Chapter 1

Chapter 1 introduces management and cost accounting systems. Studying this chapter should enable you to:

1. Understand the nature and purpose of both financial and management accounting.
2. Trace the information flows in a typical management accounting system.
3. Identify the basic uses of budgets and budgeting.
4. Discuss how cost accounting is related to both financial and management accounting.
5. Identify the different cost classifications.
6. Distinguish between product costs and period costs, and explain the importance of this distinction in determining income.
7. Distinguish between line and staff functions.
8. Determine the general role of the controller in an organization.

Management Accounting: An Introduction

ACCOUNTING as defined by the Oxford English Dictionary[1] is a generic word "the action or process of reckoning, counting or computing." An accountant is defined as giving or liable to give account." Society, however, has narrowed the scope of the terms *accounting* and *accountant* to deal with the financial events of business and non-business organizations. From these definitions we can see that many individuals and organizations account for events and transactions that are not what we interpret in society as accounting. Accountants and accounting are involved with the financial stewardship function of organizations.

Contemporary society considers accountants as the recordkeepers of and communicators of financial information about these organizations. From a cross section of the texts, monographs and the literature written, the definition best suited for the study of the subject is "accounting is the art of identifying, classifying, measuring, recording, certain economic transactions and exchanges, and communicating to interested parties financial information about the organization." Another view of the function of accounting and the accountant, very similar to that stated above, is that "accounting can be described as the measurement and communication of relevant economic events of individual units. . . . Ideally speaking, the accountant's job is to observe the behaviour of an organization, to measure events that are significant to the individuals concerned with the activities of that organization, and then communicate the data to them."[2]

Implicit in any definition of accounting is the importance of the accountant's role in the reporting function. In fact, the primary role of the accountant is reporting and communicating information which will aid various

[1] The Compact Edition of the Oxford English Dictionary, Vol. I, Oxford University Press, 1971.

[2] Jerry Dermer and Joel Amernic, *Financial Accounting, A Canadian Perspective* (Toronto: The MacMillan Company of Canada Limited, 1979), p.2.

3

users in the financial community in making economic decisions. These users of accounting information include current and potential owners, managers, creditors, and others. Skinner states "one use of accounting data is to assist the management of an enterprise to make business decisions."[3] In the past, when businesses were less complex than they are today, there were usually only a very limited number of users of accounting information. For example, at the turn of the century most businesses in Canada were managed and operated by their owners. Since these owners were intimately involved in the day-to-day operations of their businesses there was little or no need for accounting reports. The owner or decision-maker already had firsthand knowledge of the information he required in order to operate the business effectively. Today, however, the situation is quite different. Many organizations have increased in both size and complexity. In many instances, the ownership and the management of a business have been separated. Firms are frequently managed by professional managers for their absentee owners who exercise a minimal amount of formal control over the operations of the business except in the most general sense. These owners often have virtually no involvement in the day-to-day activities of the business. Even professional managers (at all but the most basic levels of authority in the firm) have little *firsthand* involvement in the most fundamental of these activities. Their decisions are, more often than not, made on the basis of reports and summaries which are prepared by their subordinates. Although the above discussion might overstate the case just a bit (the corner pizza parlor may still be owner-operated, but then again, it could well be a franchise operation), the basic point is that most decisions are made on the basis of summary-type reports rather than firsthand information.

What then is the role of accounting and the accountant in this process? One observation that has been made is that the task of the accountant is to observe, interpret, summarize, and communicate information in a form which will enable the user of the data to evaluate, control, plan, and even predict performance. It is essential to note the importance of the term "user" in this context. A user could be a manager involved in the evaluation and direction of the continuing operations of the business; a present or a potential shareholder (owner) seeking information for an impending investment decision; a bank officer in the process of reviewing a loan application; a supplier making a decision with regard to a credit application; a federal, or provincial revenue officer evaluating the propriety of a tax return; or even a citizen attempting to assess the performance of some governmental unit. In each of the circumstances mentioned above, and in countless other situations as well, user needs are met, at least in part, by a report prepared by an accountant.

---

[3] R.M. Skinner, *Accounting Principles, A Canadian Viewpoint* (Toronto: The Canadian Institute of Chartered Accountants, 1972), p. 25.

ACCOUNTING AS A PROCESS OF COMMUNICATION[4]

Accounting may be regarded as a process of communication in a very real sense. Events occur on a continuing basis which affect the operations of an organization. The accountant acts as an observer-reporter, observing events or transactions as they take place, evaluating the significance of these events, then recording, classifying, and summarizing the events in an accounting report. The user receives the report, analyzes its content, and utilizes the information in making economic decisions. Of course, these decisions made by the user cause new events to take place setting the chain in process again through another cycle.

Two factors are of major importance in this communication. First, there should be mutual understanding and agreement between the accountant preparing the report and the persons using the report on the basis of its preparation and content. The accountant must know the user's needs and perceptions and prepare the report so that what the user understands the report to express will indeed correspond with what the accountant intended to express in the report. Bedford and Baladouni call this fidelity— the correspondence between what is understood by the user of accounting statements and what the accountant intended to express in his report.

The second factor is that the accountant's report show a reliable and relevant relationship to the events it attempts to summarize. The report should, to the degree possible and/or practicable, include and describe all the significant events which did, in fact, take place. In the ideal situation, a user would make the same decision based on the analysis of a report that would have been made if firsthand information obtained on a personal basis was used. Bedford and Baladouni refer to this factor as significance— the relationship between the events which take place and the accounting report which attempts to summarize these events.

FINANCIAL ACCOUNTING AND MANAGEMENT ACCOUNTING

Although there is considerable overlap between the two, accounting may be thought of as consisting of two basic segments, financial accounting and management accounting. The basic difference between these two segments or divisions of accounting lies in their orientation. Financial accounting is primarily concerned with users who are *external* to the firm and management accounting is concerned with *internal* users. Financial accounting attempts to provide external user groups such as current or potential owners, creditors, government agencies, and other interested parties with information concerning the status of the firm and the results of its operations. The objective of financial accounting is to provide these users with the information they require for making decisions. Management accounting attempts to provide the information which is necessary for internal decision making to those who are charged with this responsibility within the firm.

---

[4] This discussion is based on Norton M. Bedford and Vahe Baladouni, "A Communication Theory Approach to Accountancy," *The Accounting Review*, October 1962, pp. 650–59.

One definition of managerial or management accounting and the key terms found in that definition is: [5]

> Management accounting is the process of identification, measurement, accumulation, analysis, preparation, interpretation, and communication of financial information used by management to plan, evaluate, and control within an organization and to assure appropriate use of and accountability for its resources. Management accounting also comprises the preparation of financial reports for non-management groups such as shareholders, creditors, regulatory agencies, and tax authorities.

To facilitate comprehension, the most significant terms used in the definition are defined as follows:

Management Accounting is the process of:

Identification—the recognition and evaluation of business transactions and other economic events for appropriate accounting action.

Measurement—the quantification, including estimates, of business transactions or other economic events that have occurred or may occur.

Accumulation—the disciplined and consistent approach to recording and classifying appropriate business transactions and other economic events.

Analysis—the determination of the reasons for, and the relationships of, the reported activity with other economic events and circumstances.

Preparation and Interpretation—the meaningful coordination of accounting and/or planning data to satisfy a need for information, presented in a logical format, and, if appropriate, including the conclusions drawn from those data.

Communication—the reporting of pertinent information to management and others for internal and external uses.

Management Accounting is used by management to:

Plan—to gain an understanding of expected business transactions and other economic events and their impact on the organization.

Evaluate—to judge the implications of various past and/or future events.

Control—to ensure the integrity of financial information concerning an organization's activities or its resources.

Assure accountability—to implement the system of reporting that is closely aligned to organizational responsibilities and that contributes to the effective measurement of management performance.

Many of the activities constituting the field of management accounting are interrelated and thus must be coordinated, ranked, and implemented by the management accountant in such a fashion as to meet the objectives of the organization as perceived by him or her. A major function of the management accountant is that of tailoring the applica-

---

[5] *Definition of Management Accounting, Statements on Management Accounting, Statement Number 1A* (New York, National Association of Accountants, 1981), pg. 4-5.

tion of the process to the organization so that the organization's objectives are achieved effectively.

A further distinction in accounting is between managerial accounting and cost accounting. But in today's complex business environment the nature and purpose of the different accounting systems are difficult to distinguish. Management uses cost accounting and cost accumulating systems for gathering data and for making management decisions. In addition, cost accounting also serves the purposes of financial accounting by providing a system for accumulating cost information. This cost information is used as the basis for much of the financial information needed for financial reports to shareholders, compliance with government requirements for financial information, and many other users' needs. In a sense then, cost accounting may be regarded as a subdivision of both financial and managerial accounting.

BASIC DIFFERENCES BETWEEN FINANCIAL AND MANAGEMENT ACCOUNTING— FURTHER COMMENTS

Financial and management acccounting methods were developed for different purposes and for different users of financial information. There are, however, numerous similarities and areas of overlap between financial and managerial accounting methods. It is difficult to classify a particular technique or approach as belonging exclusively to financial or managerial accounting.

Financial accounting is primarily intended to provide external user groups with information concerning the current status of the firm and the results of its operations. The accounting system of a company, therefore, accumulates and communicates financial information that is basically historical in nature. Of course, this information is usually presented in the form of financial statements, tax returns, and other formal reports distributed to various external users. The same information may also be used internally to provide a basis for financial analysis by management.

Financial accounting is required for most firms organized as corporations because all firms must apply for either a federal or a provincial charter to operate. All jurisdictions have corporation acts which require the issuance of an annual audited financial report. Federal corporations come under the purview of the Canada Business Corporations Act and provincially incorporated firms under that of the various Provincial Corporation Acts. Except in the case of so-called private companies, those companies whose shares are fully transferable are also required to meet the financial accounting requirement of the Provincial Securities Acts, in the province where their securities are traded, regardless of jurisdiction of incorporation.

Revenue Canada Taxation also requires financial accounting information for compliance with the tax laws. Because the provinces of Alberta, Ontario and Quebec also tax corporations directly, financial data is also required for compliance with their tax laws. Information based on financial accounting is required by all firms in both cases without regard to their size.

Interested third parties without substantial influence over the firm, such as individual shareholders of a large corporation, must use the general purpose financial statements made available to them by management. Financial statements prepared for users (other than governmental regulatory agencies that are authorized to establish their own disclosure laws by legislation) must be prepared in accordance with what are known as generally accepted accounting principles. Generally accepted accounting principles serve as guidelines which are used by accountants in disclosing the financial information which is made available to the general public. Knowledgeable users of general financial information can then interpret the data presented in financial statements with some assurance as to consistency of methodology underlying the data. The auditors' report also adds to the reliability of general purpose financial statements.

Managerial accounting has developed over time to meet the need of management for quantitative information to be used internally for planning, control, performance evaluation and internal decision making. The emphasis of management accounting is then directed toward the internal user of information; therefore, the structure of the managerial accounting system is not nearly as rigid as that of the financial accounting system. The best data available are used as the basis for the information which management relies upon to make its decisions. It is important to note that management accounting is by no means separate and distinct from financial accounting. Financial accounting data are used in the managerial accounting system. Management decisions made today will affect the financial statements of future periods. Managerial accounting does not utilize generally accepted accounting principles per se, but there are general practices that should be followed to maximize the benefits of planning, control and performance evaluation. There is no requirement or legislation that mandates the format or use of managerial accounting. Rather, managerial accounting methods are tools that are available for use to management.

Financial accounting attempts to present some degree of precision in reporting historical information while at the same time emphasizing verifiability and freedom from bias in the information, relevance to the general user and some element of timeliness in reporting. The presentation of historical financial information which is precise, verifiable and free from bias is not as critical for managerial accounting. The timing of information and its relevance to the decision at hand has greater significance to the internal decision maker. If the information is useful in making a good internal decision, management is not *primarily* concerned with precision, verifiability or the bias which might be built into the data on hand. Obviously, management cannot wait until tomorrow for information that is required for today's decision.

Theoretically, a managerial accounting system could provide individualized or tailor-made information which is relevant for each user or for each decision. As a practical matter, however, this simply cannot be done because of the high cost involved. The accounting reports that are prepared should include relevant information for that user's segment of the organization.

The measuring base used in management accounting does not necessarily have to be restricted to dollars. Various bases may be appropriate to report managerial information. Examples include: (1) an economic measure such as dollars, (2) a physical measure such as kilograms, litres, tons, or units, and (3) a relationship measure such as ratios. If all of these and other measures are appropriate to management's needs, then this information should be presented in the same report. Relevance to the decision or to the user is a primary consideration when deciding which measurement technique to use.

THE MANAGEMENT ACCOUNTING CYCLE

defn.

Management accounting may be regarded as having a forward-looking emphasis. A decision is made; the plan is implemented; and the actual results are measured, recorded and communicated. Illustration 1–1 presents a logical format which is used in viewing the information flows in a typical managerial accounting system from an overall perspective.

The sequential nature of the steps included in this illustration may give an impression that a firm could complete the planning cycle at the beginning of an accounting period and then simply follow the steps indicated. This may not be possible, however, since the economic environment in which a firm operates is changing continuously and management wishes to utilize the best and most current information available in its decision-making process. If the economic climate changes for a segment of the firm, it may then be necessary or desirable to alter plans accordingly. Planning, control, performance evaluation and the related decision-making processes must, therefore, take place simultaneously and continuously as economic conditions change.

GATHERING DECISION-MAKING INFORMATION— STEP ONE

Two general categories of decisions in which accounting information is frequently helpful are: (1) routine or recurring decisions and (2) special or nonrecurring decisions. A business may develop its management accounting system to provide information useful in making routine decisions since the need for this type of information usually may be anticipated.

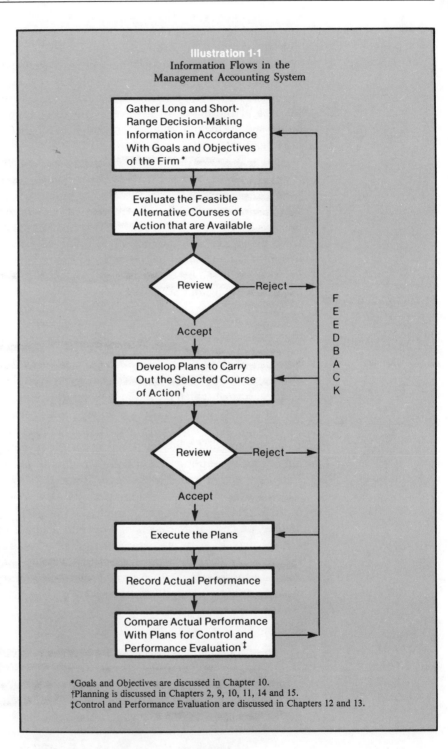

Illustration 1-1
Information Flows in the
Management Accounting System

*Goals and Objectives are discussed in Chapter 10.
†Planning is discussed in Chapters 2, 9, 10, 11, 14 and 15.
‡Control and Performance Evaluation are discussed in Chapters 12 and 13.

Nonrecurring decisions, however, will frequently require input of specific information that must often be obtained by a special study. The planning for these special decisions is discussed in Chapter 14.

A management accounting system does not always provide all the information which is required for decision-making purposes. Management should, of course, utilize the best information currently available in making a particular decision at any point in time. In addition to the data obtained from the financial accounting system, management should also utilize any other information which may be available. This "other" information may include subjective estimates made by qualified personnel as well as information from other sources both internal and external, that is pertinent for evaluating the alternative courses of action under consideration.

EVALUATING THE FEASIBILITY OF ALTERNATIVES— STEP TWO

When sufficient information has been accumulated to evaluate the alternative courses of action, the data are analyzed and the course of action is selected which is considered by management to be the best alternative available consistent with the goals and objectives of the organization. If the data are analyzed and no acceptable course of action is found, the information gathering process begins again.

DEVELOPING PLANS— STEP THREE

defn.

The formulation of plans, a process often referred to as budgeting, is necessary if all of the various segments of the firm are to work together efficiently and effectively. Comprehensive budgeting includes both long and short-term planning. From the perspective of top management, the budgeting process should produce projected financial statements as well as other necessary supplementary budgets, such as a cash budget. From the viewpoint of lower level management, budgets must be prepared in adequate detail to provide the manager with a realistic framework from which his or her segment of the firm can be operated on a current or day-to-day basis.

After the plans made for the various segments of the firm and for the firm as a whole have been reviewed, if management finds a segment budget or the total budget unacceptable, then the management accounting process must begin again with appropriate changes made in the budget. Short-range planning is discussed in Chapters 10 and 11 while long-range planning is considered in Chapter 15.

Budgeting may also be regarded as a process of communication, control, and motivation. Budgeting, as a communications process, reaches all relevant levels or segments of the organization—each with its own plan or target—and coordinates them with the plans of all other segments of the firm. Budgeting is necessary for control purposes because both the firm as a whole and individual segments of the firm must be able to assess their comparative positions at selected points in time. Moreover, budgets can show both meaningful and timely comparisons or variances of actual and planned performances. Budgets are also useful in providing a stimulus to assist in motivating managers and other employees of the firm. In certain instances, incentives such as bonuses may be used in this regard. If managers or other employees actively participate in the setting of goals, they are more likely to attempt to meet the challenge of attaining these goals and performing at the planned levels.

EXECUTION OF THE PLANS— STEP FOUR

Budgets are prepared by each segment of the organization, and all segments and department managers are responsible for carrying out the plans of the budget to the best of their ability. These managers need sufficient detail in their budgets to operate in accordance with the plans and to provide the basic data required for control and performance evaluations. Therefore, it is necessary to segment the firm by economic function for planning purposes. For example, budgets may be developed by: (1) organizational lines such as departments, divisions, branches, or legal entities; (2) business activity such as product lines, sales territories geographic markets, industries, domestic activities or foreign activities; and (3) elements of managerial responsibility such as costs, profits or a return-on-investment.

RECORDING PERFORMANCE— STEP FIVE

As plans are translated into performance, actual operating results are entered in the accounting system. The accounting records used for management accounting purposes include additional detailed information not generally required for financial accounting. For example, a management accounting system may include such information as data regarding the physical units of products purchased or shipped, regular and overtime hours worked, and accounts of key customers visited by salesmen.

COMPARING ACTUAL PERFORMANCE WITH PLANNED PERFORMANCE— STEP SIX

In addition to the budget's other uses, the budgeting process provides a means for delegating responsibility to managers of the various segments within the organization. If the firm's planning process is to be meaningful and if managers are expected to operate in an efficient responsible manner, then an effective system of control must be established.

Uses of Budgets and Budgeting Methods

Management accounting contributes to establishing a control system by providing what is usually referred to as financial control. Financial control — *defn* is the formal process of measuring the performance of segments of the organization to determine if the plan which was adopted has been attained and to analyze any differences or variances between the planned and the actual results.

Financial control is established within the firm to provide management with the appropriate information regarding planned versus actual results for segments of the organization at defined points in time. Effective feedback in the reporting process is established to allow management to take effective action on a problem at the earliest possible time.

The procedure for reporting planned performance versus actual performance and the analysis of any differences or variances is referred to as performance evaluation and variance analysis. These topics are discussed in depth in Chapters 7, 8, 12 and 13.

THE ROLE OF COST ACCOUNTING IN FINANCIAL AND MANAGEMENT ACCOUNTING

The function of cost accounting is to serve both external financial reporting purposes and the internal needs for management information. For external financial reporting purposes, cost accounting provides a cost accumulation system. This is used, for example, in determining the cost of goods manufactured for the accounting period and, therefore, the inventory values and the cost of goods sold. From the standpoint of inventory costing, the cost accounting system accumulates all of the elements of manufacturing cost for a given accounting period and converts these costs into inventory production cost on a per unit, per kilogram, per litre or some other basis of physical measurement. Cost accounting systems for product cost accumulation are discussed in Chapters 3 through 7.

Cost accounting is closely related to management accounting in that it provides a system of cost accumulation which is used in planning, control, performance evaluation and decision making. The cost accountant is involved in cost accumulation problems that management encounters during the normal course of operating the business.

COST CLASSIFICATIONS

— defn.

The cost classifications which are used in accounting are generally determined by the purpose for which the cost information is intended. Four major cost classification categories defined by purpose are discussed in this text:[6]

1. Income determination
2. Planning
3. Control and performance evaluation
4. Special decisions requiring accounting information

For purposes of income determination, costs are normally classified on a functional basis, that is, according to the type of function, i.e., salaries, rent, depreciation etc. The general functional cost classifications which are used for income determination purposes are product costs and period costs.

PRODUCT COSTS: FOR INCOME DETERMINATION

— defn.

Product costs are those costs that can be directly identified with the purchase or production of those goods made available for sale by the firm. These costs are recorded and inventoried as assets until the goods are sold. For example, the inventory purchased by a retailer is considered an asset until the time that it is sold. When the sale takes place, the cost of the asset (inventory) becomes an expense (cost of goods sold) and is reported as such on the income statement.

The cost flows of a manufacturing firm differ substantially from those of a retail business. In a manufacturing company, the process of producing a marketable product for sale causes the accounting process to be somewhat more complex than it is for the retailer. The manufacturer acquires raw materials and converts these materials into a finished product. During this production process, the manufacturer purchases labor and services, utilizes manufacturing facilities, and usually employs a unique process. Thus, value is added to the raw materials by the manufacturing process which ultimately results in a product that is marketable at a price in excess of its cost. The manufacturer must accumulate all of the production costs incurred, along with the cost of raw materials used during a period, in order to determine the cost of goods manufactured during that period.

---

[6] Cost classifications for income determination are discussed in this chapter; planning in Chapter 2; control and performance evaluation in Chapter 12; and special decisions requiring accounting information in Chapter 14.

PRODUCT COST: FLOWS IN MANUFACTURING

defn.

As shown in Illustration 1-2, the three basic elements of product cost incurred by a manufacturing company are: (1) direct materials, (2) direct labor, and (3) manufacturing overhead. *Direct materials* are those raw materials used in the production process which can be directly identified with the finished products. For example, lumber is a direct material used in the production of furniture. *Direct labor* includes the wages of production employees who work directly with a product and whose efforts may be directly traced to specific units or batches of production output. Thus, the wages of an employee who applied paint or varnish to furniture would be a direct labor cost in the production of that furniture. Manufacturing costs which are associated with the production process but which are not directly traceable to specific units of output either as direct materials or direct labor are classified as *manufacturing overhead.* Examples of manufacturing overhead include depreciation on plant, building, and equipment; maintenance costs; indirect labor costs; costs of factory supplies; salaries of production foremen; etc.

As a product is manufactured, the direct materials, direct labor and manufacturing overhead costs used in the process are accumulated and combined in a special inventory account called work-in-process. When the production process is completed, the costs associated with the resulting goods are transferred from the work-in-process inventory account to the finished goods inventory account. These costs remain as assets in this inventory account until the goods are sold. When the sale is made, the cost of the inventory is transferred to the cost of goods sold account for income determination purposes. Product cost accumulation is discussed in detail in Chapters 3 through 7.

PERIOD COSTS: FOR INCOME DETERMINATION

defn.

Those expenses incurred by the company which are associated with the passage of time are normally referred to and classified as period costs. In contrast to product costs, period costs are costs which generally cannot easily be traced to either the purchase or the manufacture of a particular product. Period costs are not considered to be assets because these expenses normally do not yield benefits to the firm beyond the current accounting period or because the possibility of such benefits is not readily measureable. For these reasons, period costs are treated as expenses of the period in which they are incurred. Examples of period costs include such costs as interest expense, salaries of administrative employees, depreciation on non-manufacturing facilities, salesmen's salaries, advertising expense, and insurance expense for non-manufacturing facilities.

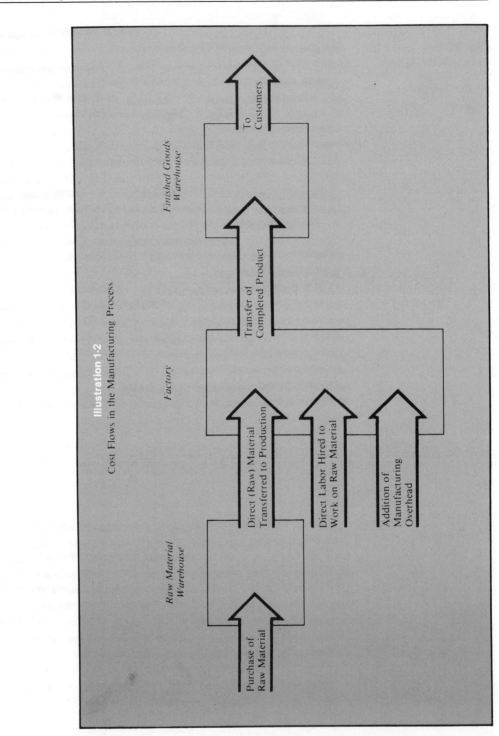

Illustration 1-2
Cost Flows in the Manufacturing Process

IMPORTANCE OF THE DISTINCTION BETWEEN PRODUCT AND PERIOD COST

The distinction between product costs and period costs is essential for purposes of income determination. A brief example may add insight to this important distinction.

Ron Carter and Tom Rogers are both employed by Expo Manufacturing Company, and each earns an annual salary of $25,000. Carter works as a salesman while Rogers is employed as a department head in a manufacturing area. Last year, Expo Manufacturing Company produced a single product. In all, 10,000 units of this product were manufactured and, of these, 8,000 units were sold. Under these circumstances, Carter's salary is considered a period cost and is classified as an expense on the income statement. Roger's salary is considered to be a cost of manufacturing the product, since he is directly involved with producing the product. Only $20,000 of Roger's earnings is considered a part of the cost of goods sold included on the income statement, since Rogers is involved in the manufacturing process and only 80 percent (8,000 of the 10,000 units produced) of the current period's production was sold. The remaining portion of Roger's salary ($5,000 or 20 percent) is considered a part of the ending inventory asset value. Therefore, the importance of the distinction between product costing and period costing is obvious in that the classification of costs directly impacts on the reported profitability of the firm.

see p.22 summary

AUTHORITY AND RESPONSIBILITY IN ORGANIZATIONS

Illustration 1-3 represents a partial organization chart of the Sax Company. Sax Company includes three production divisions: Yuke Chemical Division, Avalon Chemical Division and the Power Turbine Shaft Division. Only the Power Turbine Shaft Division is represented in the partial organization chart presented in Illustration 1-3. Each division employs its own salesmen because the products of each division are sold in different markets. Sax Company's corporate headquarters is responsible for coordinating the efforts of the three divisions.

An organization chart identifies the major decision-making centers of a firm, as well as the formal lines of authority and responsibility within an organization. These lines of authority can be followed in the organization chart in Illustration 1-3. For example, the Machining Department Manager reports to the Production Manager who reports to the General Manager. The General Manager reports to the Manufacturing Vice President who reports to the President. The President reports to the Board of Directors. The Board of Directors is chosen by the shareholders to represent their interest, and the Board's responsibility is to act according to the best interests of the shareholders. The directors discharge their responsibility by reviewing, approving, and/or disapproving the major activities of management.

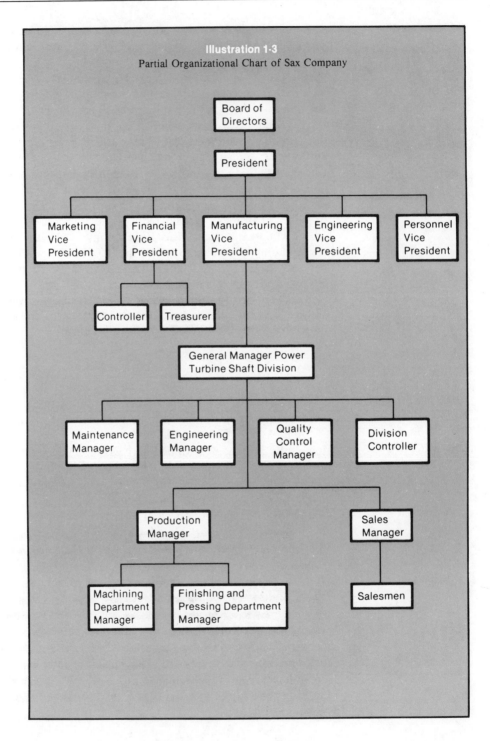

Illustration 1-3
Partial Organizational Chart of Sax Company

The lines of authority and responsibility within an organization usually follow the same path as does the reporting function. Supervisors are usually responsible for the efficiency and effectiveness of the personnel who report to them.

LINE AND STAFF RELATIONSHIPS IN ORGANIZATIONS

defn.

Authority and responsibility within an organization is usually represented by the division of segments and/or individuals into line relationships and staff relationships. Line managers are those operating personnel who produce and sell goods or services. On the other hand, the function of a staff manager is to provide specialized assistance or knowledge to a line manager whenever the line manager needs it.

The distinction between line and staff determines the connecting lines in the partial organization chart presented in Illustration 1-3. The line functions may be traced through the Sax Company by following the vertical lines of authority in the organization chart. Note that a direct line of command extends from the President downward. Operating responsibility also extends down through this line of authority. The respective operating managers are expected to meet their responsibilities in an efficient and effective manner.

In the Power Turbine Shaft Division of the Sax Company, the managers responsible for maintenance, engineering, quality control, and the division controller are all considered to be staff positions. These staff department managers do not have line authority (except over the personnel in their respective departments); no line of command for the staff departments exists outside of their own departments. A staff department manager never attempts to "manage" a line manager. The function of staff positions is limited to providing advice and support to other departments.

THE CONTROLLER

defn.

The corporate controller operates in a staff function, but this position is usually included in the top management of the firm. A major responsibility of the corporate controller is to accumulate and interpret accounting information for use in planning, controlling and evaluating both performance and any special decisions that management is required to make. The corporate controller is also responsible for governmental reporting for tax purposes, and for any other financially oriented reports required by federal and provincial govermental agencies. All accounting and most information processing functions fall under the sphere of responsibility of the corporate controller.

A division controller in a large organization has functions similar to those of the corporate controller; however, this accounting responsibility is limited to a segment of the organization. The division controller usually reports to the corporate controller. These duties and responsibilities are illustrated throughout the text.

PROFESSIONAL MANAGEMENT ACCOUNTANTS

As stated previously, accounting consists of two basic segments: financial and managerial, the former is primarily concerned with external users of financial information and the latter with internal users, i.e., management. Although all professional accounting bodies in Canada, the Canadian Institute of Chartered Accounts, Certified General Accountants' Association of Canada and the Society of Management Accountants of Canada are concerned with and require their members to be knowledgeable in both segments, Chartered Accountants (CA) tend to concentrate in the area of financial accounting, while as implied by their designation Certified General Accountants (CGA) tend to be generalists. Certified Management Accountants (CMA)[7] concentrate in the area of management accounting.

CMA studies encompass three broad subject areas: financial accounting, management accounting and management studies. Courses are offered and uniform examinations are given in a five level program as follows:

I.   Introductory Accounting, Commercial Law, Organizational Behaviour;

II. Management Accounting I, Intermediate Accounting I, Economics, Computerized Information Systems;

III. Management Accounting II, Intermediate Accounting II, Quantitative Methods, Taxation;

IV. Management Accounting III, Financial Management. Internal Auditing, Accounting Information Systems; and

V.   Management Accounting IV, Advanced Financial Accounting, Management: Processes and Problems.

---

[7] Prior to 1985 the Certified Managements Accountant (CMA) designation was known as Registered Industrial Accountants (RIA).

As explained by the Society of Management Accountants:[8]

> The financial status of operations is one of their fundamental capabilities, but it is the direct involvement in the day-to-day and long-term management of an organization that sets the CMA apart. The management accountant aids in the determination of financial objectives; implements and administers operational control systems; effectively manages financial and human resources; and contributes to the decision-making process of the management team.

Certified Management Accountants have a proven record of integrity, proficiency, and dedication. Much of the respect earned by CMAs can be attributed to the rigorous accreditation process administered by The Society of Management Accountants. The Society, incorporated in 1920, is recognized for the comprehensive training it provides, not only in accounting studies, but in such areas as organizational behaviour, economics, systems and management processes. In addition to its high academic standards, the Society requires all professional candidates to demonstrate their expertise during a two year period of appropriate work experience before the CMA designation is granted.

As a professional, the management accountant must be aware of economic and financial trends and developments which affect the public and private sectors. CMAs acquire information and maintain their expertise through a network of professional services provided by The Society of Management Accountants:

- •Research studies on the latest information and techniques developed by leading financial and management experts.

- •Professional development programs, seminars, conferences and self-study opportunities.

- •An informative and practical professional journal.

- •Direct access to a comprehensive resource centre.

---

[8] CMA Brochure, Hamilton: Society of Management Accountants in Canada, 1986.

SUMMARY

Financial accounting is primarily concerned with accumulating historical data and communicating this data to interested external users that require the data. Management accounting, on the other hand, is primarily concerned with providing information for internal planning, control, performance evaluation, and decision making. Therefore, management accounting information is generally more future-oriented than is financial accounting information.

In a typical management accounting system, information is gathered, feasible alternatives are evaluated, a decision is made, plans are developed and executed, actual performance is recorded, and, finally, a comparison between planned and actual performance is made. The economic environment in which a firm operates provides a significant influence on this entire process. In fact, a given change in the economic environment may require substantial revisions in the plans and/or even the goals and objectives of the firm.

In developing plans to support the decisions of the firm, it is generally necessary for management to engage in both long and short-term budgeting to insure that all segments of the firm will operate together in an efficient and effective manner. Budgets are generally prepared by segments of the organization in sufficient detail to provide lower management with a framework within which to operate. Therefore, the budgeting process is a primary means of communicating the overall goals and corporate objectives to the various levels in the firm. In addition, by comparing actual performance to budgeted performance, the budget becomes a significant factor in the control system of the firm.

Cost accounting is a segment of accounting that accumulates cost information used in external financial reporting (usually as inventory costs) and in managerial decision making and control. The cost classifications which are used in accounting are determined by the purpose for which the cost information is to be used. Four major categories of cost classifications defined by purpose are those for: (1) income determination; (2) planning; (3) control and performance evaluation; and (4) special decisions requiring accounting information.

In a manufacturing firm, those costs used for determining income are further classified into product costs (direct material, direct labor, and manufacturing overhead costs which are directly identifiable with the production or purchase of goods made available for sale) and period costs (costs associated with the passage of time). Distinguishing between product and period costs is necessary for proper income determination. This is because period costs are considered expenses in the period incurred, but product costs are carried in inventory valuations and are charged to expense only as the associated products are sold.

The controller of an organization is the top accounting executive in the firm. The controller's job is a staff function under which all accounting functions and most information processing functions will fall.

The significance of the role of the management accountant has become **increasingly apparent in recent years. The Certified Management Accountants (CMA) designation is one indication of this recognition.**

This chapter serves as an overview to the various elements of management and cost accounting. The remaining chapters in the text provide detailed discussions of these elements.

KEY DEFINITIONS

Budgeting—a process of formulating short-term or long-term plans for the organization. A budget is particularly important for control purposes since the plan for each relevant level or segment can later be compared with actual performance. The budget also provides a means for delegating responsibility within the organization.

Certified Management Accountant (CMA)—a designation earned by passing uniform examinations meeting the education and professional standards prescribed by the Society of Management Accountants of Canada. It recognizes professional competence and educational attainment in the field of management accounting.

Controller—a staff position included in the top management of the firm and is responsible for all accounting and information processing in the organization.

Cost accounting—a system of accumulating cost information for external financial reporting and internal management accounting.

Cost classifications—general classifications of accounting costs used for: (1) Income determination, (2) Planning, (3) Control and performance evaluation, and (4) Special decisions requiring accounting costs.

Direct labor—a product cost which includes the wages of production employees whose effort may be traced directly to specific units or batches of output.

Direct materials—a product cost which includes the cost of raw materials used in the production process and directly identified with the finished products.

Financial accounting—a method of accounting which provides external user groups with information concerning the status of the firm and the results of its operations.

Financial control—the formal process of measuring the performance of segments of the organization to: (1) Determine if the plan which was adopted has been followed, and (2) Analyze and explain differences between the planned and actual results.

Finished goods—a special inventory account where the production costs of goods already completed but not yet sold remain as assets until the point of sale.

Line manager—a manager who supervises operating personnel who produce and sell goods or services.

Management or managerial accounting—a type of accounting which is concerned with providing information for internal uses of management such as planning, control, performance evaluation and other decision-making activities. Management accounting utilizes financial accounting data as well as other internal and external information which may be available.

Management accounting cycle—a system of information flows including: (1) Gathering decision-making information, (2) Evaluating alternative courses of action, (3) Developing plans and budgets, (4) Executing plans, (5) Recording performance, and (6) Comparing actual results with budgeted results.

Manufacturing overhead—a product cost that includes manufacturing costs associated with the production process, but not directly traceable to specific units of output either as direct materials or direct labor.

Organization chart—identifies the major decision-making centers as well as the formal lines of authority and responsibility within an organization.

Period costs—costs that are associated with the passage of time and are usually not easily identified with either the purchase or the manufacturing of products. Period costs are recorded as expenses in the period incurred.

Product costs—all costs that can be directly identified with the purchase or production of goods made available for sale by the firm. These costs are inventoried and carried as assets and then expensed as cost of goods sold when the product is sold.

Staff manager—a staff manager's function is to provide specialized assistance or knowledge to a line manager when the line manager needs it.

Work-in-process—a special inventory account where the costs of direct materials, direct labor and manufacturing overhead are accumulated as the product is manufactured.

QUESTIONS

1-1 What differences exist between financial accounting and management accounting? Is management accounting separate and distinct from financial accounting?

1-2 How does management accounting serve both external financial reporting purposes and the internal needs for management information?

1-3 Define product cost. What three general elements make up a product cost? Define them.

1-4 How are the costs used in accounting classified for purposes of income determination and planning?

1-5 Define period cost. Give examples.

1-6 Why are period costs not inventoriable?

1-7 What are the two general categories of decisions in which accounting information may be helpful? Explain.

1-8 Of what importance is budgeting to the corporation—from the perspective of top management and lower management?

1-9 Define financial control. Distinguish financial control from accounting control.

1-10 What basic assumption underlies the thinking in management accounting with respect to analyzing costs?

1-11 Briefly explain the operation of a typical management accounting system.

1-12 Budgeting may be regarded as a process of communication, control, and motivation. Explain how each of these processes is served.

1-13 Why is management accounting information more "future-oriented" than financial accounting? (i.e. What purpose does this orientation serve?)

1-14 Which pieces of information do we take from cost accounting and use to determine cost of goods manufactured in an accounting period?

1-15 Define manufacturing overhead. Give examples.

1-16 What is the purpose of an organizational chart?

1-17 What is the difference between line and staff managers?

1-18 What function does the corporate controller serve?

EXERCISES AND PROBLEMS

1-19 The following management accounting cycle steps are not in order. Place the appropriate number beside each to indicate the proper place of the step in the cycle.

_____ Developing Plans 3
_____ Gathering Decision-Making Information 1
_____ Comparing Actual Performance with Planned Performance 6
_____ Evaluating the Feasibility of Alternatives 2
_____ Recording Performance 5
_____ Executing Plans 4

1-20   Classify each of the following items as either a period cost (P) or a product cost (PR).

a.   Direct materials   PR
b.   Depreciation on office building   P
c.   Property taxes on office building   P
d.   Direct labour   PR
e.   Salesmen's salaries   P
f.   Indirect materials for manufacturing   PR
g.   Rent on administrative building   P
h.   Power for manufacturing machines   PR
i.   5Administrative salaries   P
j.   Office building maintenance   P

1-21   The Small Manufacturing Company employs only six people. There are Max Small, President; Tony Brown, salesman; Bill Russel, foreman; and three people on the assembly line. The salaries for these people in 19x6 were $28,000, $16,000, $17,000, and $10,000, respectively. In 19x6 the company produced 20,000 units of product and sold 18,000 units.

Required:

Determine whether each person's salary is a period cost or a product cost. If it is a product cost, determine how the salary should be allocated.

1-22   Classify each of the following accounts of the Baker Manufacturing Company as to product cost or period costs:

a.   Direct materials   PR
b.   Raw materials used in production   PR
c.   Depreciation on manufacturing machinery   PR
d.   Production manager's salary   PR
e.   Salesmen's salaries   P
f.   Rent expense on administrative building   P
g.   Advertising expense   P
h.   Maintenance on factory machines   PR
i.   Salary of company president   P

1-23   The following are employed by the Randolph Manufacturing Company.

	Annual Salary
John Smith—President	$50,000 P.C.
Lewis Clark—Vice President	30,000 s.e.
David Jones—Manufacturing Department Head	20,000 C.OGS
Paul Frey—Manufacturing Department Head	20,000 COGS
Jerry Lawson—Sales Manager	15,000 s.e.
James Ryan—Salesman	10,000 s.e.
Joe Phillips—Production Foreman	10,000 COGS

Last year the Randolph Manufacturing Company produced a total of 100,000 units of their product of which 60,000 units were sold.

Required:

How would each of the above salaries be recorded on the income state-ment? In other words, which would be classified as cost of goods sold and which as salary expense. — period costs

1-24   Classify each of the following manufacturing costs incurred by the the Jones Desk Manufacturing Company as follows:

1.   Direct Material (DM)
2.   Direct Labor (DL)
3.   Manufacturing Overhead (OH)
     a.   Wood   DM
     b.   Sandpaper   DM
     c.   Paint   DM
     d.   Salary of plant manager   OH
     e.   Heat, light and power   OH
     f.   Depreciation of machinery   OH
     g.   Maintenance   OH
     h.   Salary of manufacturing supervisor   OH
     i.   Salary of employee who paints desk   DL
     j.   Salary of employee who paints desk   DL

1-25   Indicate which of the costs below are product costs and which are period costs for the Toy Manufacturing Company:

a.   Salaries of salespeople
b.   Christmas party for employees
c.   Entertainment expenses
d.   Depreciation of manufacturing equipment
e.   Toy materials
f.   Salaries of production employees
g.   Supplies for manufacturing department

1-26   Classify each of the following positions as either a line position (L) or a staff position (S).

a.   Controller
b.   Manufacturing Vice President
c.   Sales Manager
d.   Personnel Vice President
e.   Treasurer
f.   Production Manager
g.   Machining Department Manager
h.   Salespeople
i.   Finishing and Pressing Department Manager
j.   Marketing Vice President

T   **1-27**   The following information is available from the records of the Raleigh Paint Company:

Salespeople salaries... $50,000
Administrative costs... 1,000
Maintenance costs...   500
Paint & varnish... 5,000
Production employees' salaries..................................... 10,000
Raw materials... 4,000
Indirect labour... 1,000
Supervisor's salary... 1,000
Depreciation on equipment...   500
Heat, light & power (manufacturing facilities).....................   500
Advertising costs (administrative)................................   200

Required:

Classify each of the above costs (if applicable) as direct materials, direct labor or manufacturing overhead. Give a total for each classification.

T   **1-28**   Jeff Sims and Jim Ryan are employed by the Ace Manufacturing Company. Mr. Sims, the production manager, and Mr. Ryan, the sales manager, each earn an annual salary of $30,000. During the year, 10,000 units of the Company's product were produced of which 6,000 units were sold and 4,000 units remained in inventory as finished goods.

Required:

Using only the above data, calculate the following:

BALANCE SHEET
Finished Goods Inventory . . . . (*a*)

INCOME STATEMENT
Cost of Goods Sold . . . . (*b*)

Expense . . . . (*c*)

T   **1-29**   John and Frank Ryan are both salesmen for the Brown Manufacturing Corporation. They each make a salary of $20,000. Bill Snow, the production manager, has a salary of $22,000; John Adams, a production foreman, makes $10,000. During the year of 1979, the corporation produced 100,000 units of its product and sold 75,000 units.

Required:

Which of the salaries above would be classified as product costs and which as period costs? Give the total amount of product costs and the total period costs that would appear on the income statement.

T   **1-30**   During the year the Tonie Plastics Company produced 20,000 units of the company's product. Of this amount, 12,000 units were sold with 8,000 units remaining in the finished goods inventory. The following information shows the components of major cost items for the company:

```
Salaries & Wages
    Executive salaries . . . . . . . . . . . . . . . . . .   $ 50,000
    Sales salaries and commissions . . . . . . . . . . .     30,000
    Office salaries . . . . . . . . . . . . . . . . . . .     21,000
    Production employees wages . . . . . . . . . . . .      65,000
    Factory maintenance employee wages . . . . . . . .     15,000
                                                          $181,000

Depreciation Expense
    On office building and equipment . . . . . . . . . .   $ 15,800
    On factory building and equipment . . . . . . . . .      9,500
                                                          $ 25,300

Supplies Expense
    Supplies used in offices . . . . . . . . . . . . . . .   $  2,200
    Supplies used in production . . . . . . . . . . . .      1,600
                                                          $  3,800
```

Required:

Using the above information only (ignoring direct materials), calculate the finished goods inventory, cost of goods sold and operating expenses for Tonie Plastics.

A 1-31   Nikki Antl, chief accountant for Fashion Girl Cosmetics, Inc. was in the process of determining Christmas bonuses to be paid to officers and employees. To do this she organized the following list of employees, job descriptions and annual salaries to help her in her work:

Name	*Job Description*	*Annual Salary*
Nick Russo	President	$ 40,000
Nikki Antl	Chief accountant	30,000
Jane Thomas	Production manager	20,000
Larry Wilmer	Sales manager	20,000
Jim Wright	Production employee	16,000
Jerry Stern	Production employee	16,000
Chris Jones	Production foreman	19,000
Dick Scott	Production maintenance	15,000
Ann Garvey	Secretary	15,000
John Doe	Delivery truck driver	10,000
		$201,000

The company produced 90,000 units and sold 60,000 units during the year.

Required:

Which of the above salaries would be classified as product costs and which as period costs? Give the total amount of each that would appear on the income statement as the cost of goods sold or as period expense. Also, classify each of the product costs as direct or indirect costs.

Chapter 2

**LEARNING
OBJECTIVES**
Chapter 2 discusses the fundamental patterns of cost behavior and certain
of the basic techniques which may be used to determine and analyze
these patterns. Studying this chapter should enable you to:

1. Define a cost behavior pattern and discuss the
    relationship of cost behavior to a relevant range of
    activity.
2. Identify, discuss, and give examples of each of the
    primary and related cost behavior patterns.
3. Distinguish between the various categories of
    costs, such as committed fixed costs and managed
    fixed costs.
4. Identify and apply the common accounting and
    statistical techniques which may be used to
    determine and analyze cost behavior patterns.

Costs for Planning: Cost Behavior Patterns

PLANNING Is, by its very nature, essentially a future-oriented process. A basic objective of management is to employ the available resources of the firm in the most efficient and effective manner possible. In order to achieve this objective, management must utilize the best information available, irrespective of the source of the data, in making its plans for the future. Some of the most important information used in the planning process is concerned with the behavior of costs.

THE RELEVANT RANGE

In any analysis of cost information, management accounting makes the basic assumption that most cost behavior may be associated with measures of activity within a relevant range. For our purposes, the relevant range may be defined as that operating range or span over which a firm finds it practical to operate in a short-run time period. There is, of course, an upper limit of operating capacity when some short-run constraining factor prevents the firm from operating at a higher level. There is also a lower limit of operating capacity below which it would be impractical for the firm to operate.

Generally, the total cost function for a given range of output is not linear (See Illustration 2–1). The economic nature of costs suggests that at some point in time economies of scale occur. These economies occur when the firm is able to produce higher quantities of output without a proportionate increase in costs. In the relevant range of a firm's operating capacity, the curve representing total cost is approximately equal to a

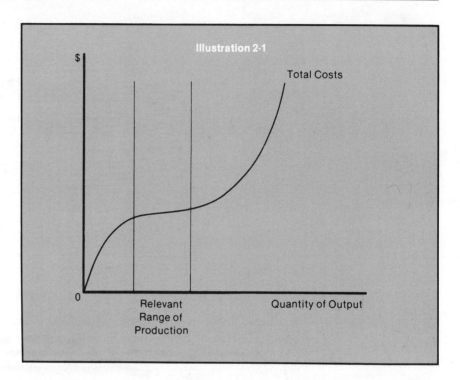

linear curve. Therefore, for planning convenience, managerial accounting frequently assumes linear cost functions within the relevant range of activity. Of course, the estimate of the linear cost function is not precise, but then neither is the planning process.

The activity base or quantity of output within the relevant range depends on the particular cost being measured. A few selected examples may help to illustrate and explain the concept of activity measures.

1. The total cost of raw materials in a manufacturing process is directly related to the number of units which are produced. The activity measure in this instance would be units produced.
2. The total cost of gasoline for a truck is directly related to the number of kilometers driven. The activity measure in this case would be kilometers driven.
3. The total cost of meals in a hospital is directly related to the number of beds occupied by patients. The activity measure in this circumstance would be the number of beds occupied.
4. If the firm uses a billing service to mail out its accounts receivable billings and the charge is twenty-five cents per billing, the total cost is related to the number of customers billed. The activity measure in this situation would be the number of customers billed.

In establishing an activity base, a firm attempts to identify those causal relationships that explain fluctuations in costs. In this regard, it is important to note that certain costs will not appear to change in relation to any particular activity measure. For example, rent or interest costs are normally related to the passage of time rather than to some level of activity.

VARIABLE COSTS

Variable costs are those costs which vary directly and proportionately with some measure of activity within the relevant range. If, for example, the base activity increases by five percent, the *total* variable cost will also increase by five percent. Total variable costs increase and decrease as the level of activity changes within the relevant range. Illustration 2–2 provides a graphic example of two different variable costs.

In Example 1 of Illustration 2–2, the indicated relevant range of production is from 75,000 to 150,000 units, and the variable cost of raw materials is $4 for each unit produced. If the production for the period was scheduled at a level of 100,000 units, the planned raw material cost would total $400,000 (100,000 × $4). At a production level of 120,000 units, the anticipated raw material cost would total $480,000 (120,000 × $4). At production levels of fewer than 75,000 units or more than 150,000 units, the total variable cost cannot be as readily estimated since these levels of output are outside the relevant range of activity.

The relevant range of kilometers driven in Example 2 of Illustration 2-2 is from 20,000 to 50,000 kilometers. The variable cost of gasoline is assumed to be $.10 per kilometer driven. If it were anticipated that the truck would be driven a total of 30,000 kilometers, the projected gasoline cost would be $3,000 (30,000 × $.10). At 40,000 kilometers, the planned gasoline cost would total $4,000 (40,000 × $.10).

Of course, the variable costs per unit could change over time due to such factors as inflation or evolving technology. Naturally, any changes which may be foreseen should be taken into consideration in formulating the budget plan.

FIXED COSTS

Fixed costs are those costs which are not related to activity within the relevant range. As the name implies, fixed costs are those expenditures which remain fixed or constant for a given period of time. Changes in fixed costs may be expected, however, and do occur either over long periods of time or outside the relevant range of activity. Fixed costs provide the capacity required to sustain a planned volume of activity within a

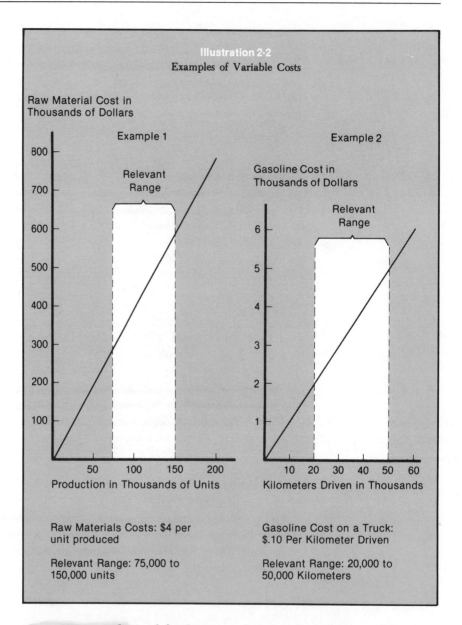

Illustration 2-2
Examples of Variable Costs

Raw Material Cost in Thousands of Dollars

Example 1

Relevant Range

Production in Thousands of Units

Raw Materials Costs: $4 per unit produced

Relevant Range: 75,000 to 150,000 units

Gasoline Cost in Thousands of Dollars

Example 2

Relevant Range

Kilometers Driven in Thousands

Gasoline Cost on a Truck: $.10 Per Kilometer Driven

Relevant Range: 20,000 to 50,000 Kilometers

given time period. Total fixed costs and their relationship to activity are presented graphically in Illustration 2–3.

The fixed costs identified in Illustration 2–3 will remain at $1,500,000 at production levels anywhere within the relevant range, which is assumed to be from 75,000 to 150,000 units. Below 75,000 units or above 150,000 units, the total fixed cost may change.

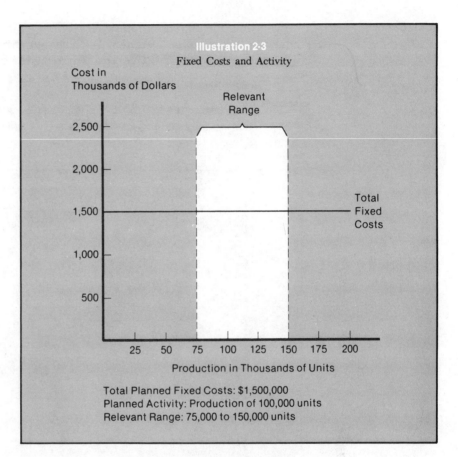

Illustration 2-3
Fixed Costs and Activity

Total Planned Fixed Costs: $1,500,000
Planned Activity: Production of 100,000 units
Relevant Range: 75,000 to 150,000 units

**Per Unit
Fixed Cost**

The fixed cost per unit of activity is an amount which must be considered and used with some degree of caution. In the previous discussions of variable cost included in this chapter, it was noted that the variable cost per unit was constant, and that the total variable cost within the relevant range increased and decreased according to the level of activity.

Total fixed costs, by definition, remain constant within the relevant range for a given time period, irrespective of the level of activity. At higher levels of activity, the fixed cost per unit will be lower than the fixed cost per unit at lower levels of activity simply because the identical amount of cost is being allocated or spread over additional units of activity. For example, in Illustration 2–3, at 75,000 units of production the fixed cost is $1,500,000 or $20 per unit ($1,500,000 ÷ 75,000). At 100,000 units of production, the total fixed cost remains at $1,500,000, but the fixed cost per unit is reduced to only $15 per unit ($1,500,000 ÷ 100,000).

Total Costs   Economics identifies the traditional cost function as being very similar to the one presented in Illustration 2–4. The component parts of total cost include fixed costs plus variable costs. Therefore the total cost equation is:

Total Cost = Total Fixed Costs + Total Variable Costs

Within the relevant range of production capacity, total cost and its component parts—fixed costs and variable costs—are assumed to be linear.

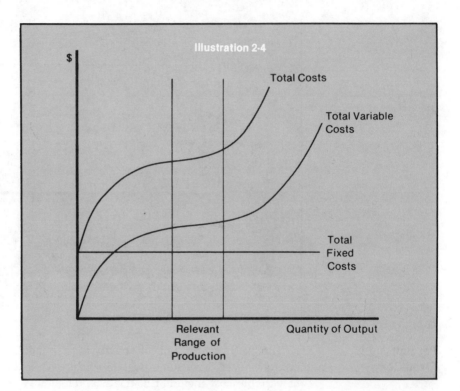

Illustration 2-4

COMMITTED AND MANAGED FIXED COSTS   For purposes of planning, fixed costs may be conveniently classified into two distinctly different categories. These categories are committed fixed costs and managed fixed costs.

Commited Fixed Costs   Committed fixed costs represent those fixed costs which the firm will incur because of the past decisions or commitments made by management. This type of fixed cost relates to the capacity of the firm to engage in its operations at a planned volume or level of activity. Of the two classifications of fixed costs, committed fixed costs are less responsive than are managed costs to the short-term decision-making process.

Committed fixed costs essentially represent the long-term costs of maintaining a given capacity to produce. It is therefore expected that these costs will be associated with the ownership of an organization as well as the related long-term resources or assets that are required to operate the business. Committed fixed costs are those costs which are related to acquiring and maintaining the organization and its long-term assets. Costs such as depreciation on fixed assets, lease or rental costs of buildings, equipment or other assets, property taxes, salaries of key personnel, and insurance are all examples of committed fixed costs.

Managed Fixed Costs

Managed fixed costs (also referred to as discretionary, programmed or planned fixed costs) are those fixed costs incurred on a short-term basis in accordance with an established objective of management. This type of fixed cost does not necessarily relate to the anticipated level of activity. Rather, management will decide on the expenditures it considers necessary to attain a specific objective at some future date. The funds are then spent, unless the objective or economic climate varies and causes a change in management plans.

Examples of managed fixed costs include research and development costs, product improvement costs, public relations costs, advertising costs, sales promotion costs, major plant rearrangement costs, outlays for cost reduction programs, costs of employee training programs and charitable donations. Theoretically, managed fixed costs could be substantially reduced by management decisions in any given period and the profits for that period would be increased (since expenses would have been decreased without a corresponding reduction of revenues). Any adverse impact of reducing a managed fixed cost would probably not be realized until some future time period, assuming that the expenditure would, in fact, have ultimately yielded future benefits.

Illustration 2–5 identifies the two major fixed cost classifications and the relationship of each to production levels. Total fixed costs are projected in the amount of $1,500,000, consisting of a committed cost element of $1,000,000 and a managed cost element of $500,000. Assuming a level of production within the relevant range of 75,000 to 150,000 units, the total fixed cost could be any amount between $1,000,000 (committed costs only) and $1,500,000 (committed costs plus all managed costs), depending on which managed fixed costs management chooses to incur.

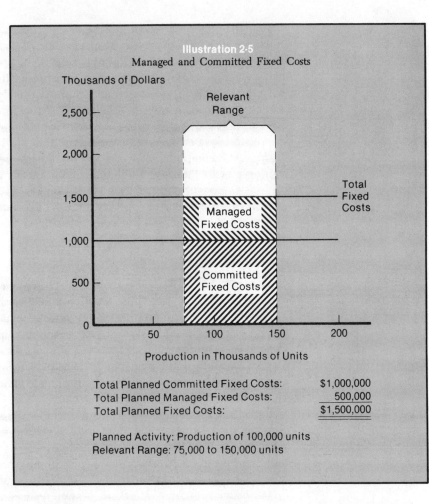

Illustration 2-5
Managed and Committed Fixed Costs

Total Planned Committed Fixed Costs:	$1,000,000
Total Planned Managed Fixed Costs:	500,000
Total Planned Fixed Costs:	$1,500,000

Planned Activity: Production of 100,000 units
Relevant Range: 75,000 to 150,000 units

SEMIVARIABLE COSTS

Semivariable costs, also referred to as mixed costs, are those costs which are comprised of both a fixed and a variable component. As the level of activity increases, the total cost will also increase, but the increase will be less than proportional in amount. A typical example of the variation which occurs with this type of cost is a rental car.

The cost for a short-term rental car has two components. There is a basic charge, usually a daily or weekly amount. The total rental charge can never fall below this fixed base even if the vehicle is not used. A charge on a per kilometer driven basis plus this basic per day or week charge are the components of the total charge. The total cost for the car for the time period used will therefore be a semivariable cost, a cost which is comprised of both a fixed (the basic per day or per week charge) and a variable (the charge on a per kilometer driven basis).

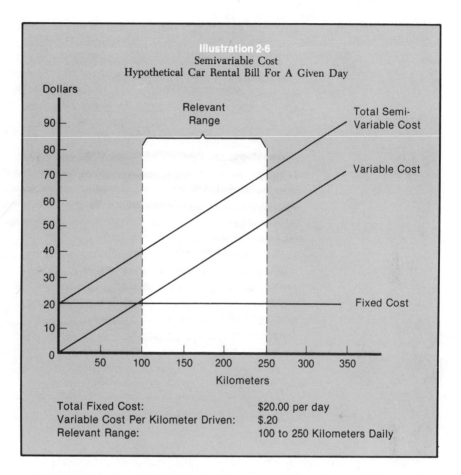

Illustration 2-6
Semivariable Cost
Hypothetical Car Rental Bill For A Given Day

Total Fixed Cost:	$20.00 per day
Variable Cost Per Kilometer Driven:	$.20
Relevant Range:	100 to 250 Kilometers Daily

A hypothetical rental charge is presented graphically in Illustration 2-6. To simplify this illustration, assume that the basic charge for the car is $20.00 per day with an additional charge of $.20 per kilometer for every kilometer driven. In other words, the basic charge of $20.00 simply makes the use of the car available to the renter and does not entitle the renter to drive any kilometers (without paying the additional charge of $.20 per kilometer for each kilometer driven).

As indicated above, the rental charge for any given day can never be less than $20.00. If a hundred kilometers were driven in one day the total bill for that day would be $40.00 [$20.00 + (100 kilometers × $.20)]; and if 200 kilometers were driven in a day the bill would be $60.00 [$20.00 + (200 × $.20)].

Graphically, the slope of the total semivariable cost line is identical to the slope of the variable cost line portion of the semivariable cost. These two lines are parallel because the slope of the lines is based entirely on the variable cost component of the total charge. Each kilometer driven would cause the variable cost component of the semivariable cost to increase in total by $.20. Consequently, the total semivariable cost would also increase by $.20 for every kilometer driven in a given day.

Other possible examples of semivariable costs include repair costs for most types of equipment (normally the greater the usage, the higher the cost), power costs, clerical costs, telephone costs, and delivery costs.

STEP COSTS

Step costs are those costs which must be incurred in a series of fixed amounts. Generally, a cost behaving as a step cost remains constant over a given range of activity and then increases or decreases in a fixed incremental amount. Although step costs are said to vary according to the level of activity, it should be noted that their relationship to activity is not necessarily a proportionate one.

The salary of a supervisor, such as a foreman, is a typical example of a step cost. The cost of supervisory personnel will remain fixed over a broad range of activity; but when a certain level of production is reached, it will be necessary to hire an additional supervisor and the total cost will increase to a new level. The cost will then remain fixed at this new level for another range of activity.

Illustration 2–7 presents an example of a step cost. In this illustration, the total cost of the salaries of production foremen, within the relevant range, will be $60,000 per year for production levels from 75,000 to 100,000 units, $70,000 per year for output between 100,001 to 125,000 units and $90,000 per year for levels of production from 125,001 to 150,000 units.

ANALYZING COST BEHAVIOR PATTERNS

Ideally, for both planning purposes and for making certain types of decisions, all costs would be classified as either fixed or variable, with semivariable costs being separated into their fixed and variable components. Although this optimal classification usually cannot be attained in practice, cost behavior patterns may be and are often approximated for use in planning and decision-making.

Two general approaches which may be used in studying or analyzing historical cost behavior patterns include the accounting approach and the statistical approach.[1] Neither of these approaches should be considered "the best method." They are complementary methods which are most effective if used in conjunction with one another.

---

[1] The statistical technique discussed in this text is the method of least squares. It should be noted that the accounting measures for cost estimation do not provide a measure of probable error in the cost analysis while statistical techniques can provide measures of probable error.

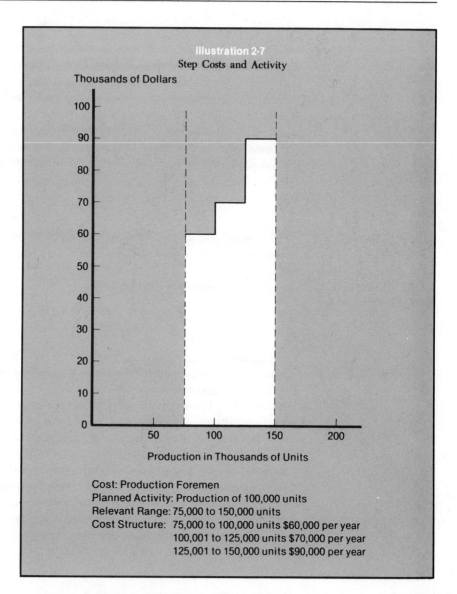

Illustration 2-7
Step Costs and Activity

Cost: Production Foremen
Planned Activity: Production of 100,000 units
Relevant Range: 75,000 to 150,000 units
Cost Structure: 75,000 to 100,000 units $60,000 per year
                 100,001 to 125,000 units $70,000 per year
                 125,001 to 150,000 units $90,000 per year

Certain basic assumptions are made in analyzing the behavior of costs. Three major assumptions often made are:

1. Costs will be linear within the relevant range.
2. There is a single factor that causes a variable cost, or the variable portion of a semivariable cost, to fluctuate in total.
3. Historical cost behavior patterns will continue to be valid in the future.

The final assumption requires further comment. Costs are analyzed in order to aid management in its future decision-making. Many of the cost analysis tools that assist management in its future planning and decision-making activities employ historical cost as a starting point. However, factors such as technological advances, inflation, changes in management policy, the addition of new product lines, or changes in the equipment used could—and often do—alter cost behavior patterns. At a minimum, any use of the analysis of past costs for future cost estimation should be viewed with caution and attention to the inherent limitations of the process.

ACCOUNTING TECHNIQUES FOR DETERMINING COST BEHAVIOR PATTERNS

The techniques which may be classified as accounting approaches used to measure cost behavior patterns include: (1) account analysis, (2) the high–low method, and (3) the semi–averages method. All three of these techniques are based on historical costs.

Account Analysis

Account analysis is accomplished by visually inspecting the details of specific accounts and identifying those amounts or costs which are clearly variable and those which are clearly fixed. The past experience of the firm with regard to those costs clearly variable and those clearly fixed may be tested by further analyzing the details of the appropriate ledger balances for a selected period of time. The semivariable costs, or any other costs, which cannot be clearly defined as to behavior pattern by inspection would, of course, require further analysis using other techniques.

The other accounting and statistical techniques presented in this chapter which are used for analyzing cost behavior patterns may be used to analyze either fixed or variable costs. These approaches are formulated so as to separate the fixed costs from the variable costs in the analysis of semivariable costs, but may also be used to analyze costs that are either solely fixed or variable.

High-Low Method

The high-low method uses accounting data selected from two extreme points for both the amount of cost and for the level of activity; it then assumes a linear behavior of costs between these two points. As the name of this technique implies, the points selected are the highest level of activity with the highest cost amount and the lowest level of activity with lowest cost amount. These figures are taken from the recent operating records of the firm. For purposes of illustrating this method of analysis, the cost of the power required to operate a machine has been accumulated for one year. The results of this analysis are presented in Illustration 2-8.

Illustration 2-8

Power Cost

Month	Hours Used	Power Cost
January	40	$14
February	60	18
March	60	18
April	50	16
May	30	12
June	90	24
July	80	20
August	80	19
September	60	18
October	80	20
November	80	19
December	70	18

The month of June shows the highest level of activity with 90 hours of machine running time and an associated total power cost of $24. May is the lowest activity month with 30 hours of running time and a total power cost of $12. When using the high-low technique, the formula for determining the variable cost component of the total cost to be analyzed may be expressed as follows:

$$\frac{\text{High Cost} - \text{Low Cost}}{\text{High Activity} - \text{Low Activity}} = \text{Variable Cost Per Unit of Activity}$$

Using the data from our example, the calculation would be as follows:

$$\frac{\$24 - \$12}{90 \text{ Hours} - 30 \text{ Hours}} = \frac{\$12}{60 \text{ Hours}}$$

$$= \$.20 \text{ Variable Cost Per Hour}$$

In order to identify the fixed component of the total cost, either the high or low point may be used to determine the total variable cost; any remaining amount is, of course, the fixed cost component.

	90 Hours High Point	30 Hours Low Point
Total Cost	$24	$12
Less: Variable Cost	18 (a)	6 (b)
Fixed Cost Component	$ 6	$ 6

(a) 90 X $.20 variable cost per hour = $18.
(b) 30 X $.20 variable cost per hour = $6.

The high-low formula determines the slope of a straight line which extends between the two points selected. The slope of this line represents the variable cost per unit of activity.

Method of Semi-Averages

The method of semi-averages is a slightly more sophisticated version of the high-low technique described above. A period of time is selected for historical cost analysis. The high activity periods are averaged for both levels of activity and related or corresponding costs, and the low activity periods are averaged for these same factors. The averages are then used in the high-low formulation. Illustration 2–9 was prepared using the same power cost data originally presented in Illustration 2–8 in order to demonstrate the difference between the method of semi-averages and the high-low technique.

Illustration 2-9
Method of Semi-Averages

Month	High Six Months Hours Used	Cost	Month	Low Six Months Hours Used	Cost
June...........	90	$ 24	January.........	40	$14
July...........	80	20	February........	60	18
August.........	80	19	March..........	60	18
October........	80	20	April..........	50	16
November.......	80	19	May............	30	12
December.......	70	18	September.......	60	18
	480	$120		300	96
Divided by	÷ 6	÷ 6	Divided by	÷ 6	÷ 6
Averages........	80	$ 20	Averages........	50	$16

Applying the high-low technique to the averages presented in Illustration 2-9, the average variable cost per hour may be determined as follows:

$$\frac{\$20 - \$16}{80 \text{ Hours} - 50 \text{ Hours}} = \frac{\$4}{30 \text{ Hours}}$$

$$= \$.133 \text{ Variable Cost Per Hour}$$

In order to identify the fixed cost component, again either the average high point or the average low point may be used to substitute the variable cost per unit in the formula for total variable cost; any remaining cost would be classified as fixed costs.

	80 Hours High Average	50 Hours Low Average
Total Average Cost.............	$20.00	$16.00
Less: Variable Cost.............	10.64 (a)	6.65 (b)
Fixed Cost Component.........	$ 9.36 (c)	$ 9.35 (c)

(a) 80 X $.133 variable cost per hour = $10.64.
(b) 50 X $.133 variable cost per hour = $6.65.
(c) Difference caused by rounding.

Recall that the comparable cost components which were determined using the high-low technique were $.20 for each variable cost per hour worked and $6 for the fixed cost component of the semi-variable cost.

BASIC STATISTICAL TOOLS FOR DETERMINING COST BEHAVIOR PATTERNS

There are numerous statistical tools available which may be used for analyzing cost behavior patterns. In general, these tools rely on historical accounting data but are more sophisticated than the accounting tools; they provide management information that may be used with a greater degree of reliability.

Two basic statistical techniques often used for the analysis of cost data are the scattergraph method and the method of least squares. As was the case with the accounting approaches described previously, these two techniques assume: (1) costs are linear within the relevant range; (2) a single causal factor is responsible for the variable cost component of a semivariable cost; and, (3) cost behavior patterns of the past are indicative of those of the future.

The Scattergraph

A scattergraph requires the plotting of both cost and activity observations on a graph. The vertical scale of the graph is normally used to represent dollars of cost, and the horizontal scale represents the activity measure that is causing a change in the total cost amount. This graphical illustration should provide insight into "how well" the cost observations are related (correlated) to the activity measure which has been identified on the horizontal scale.

The scattergraph technique may be used as an initial indicator of the behavior of a specific cost factor. Since all of the numerical techniques described previously will provide an answer in terms of fixed and variable costs, it may seem that a scattergraph is unnecessary. However, remember that the mathematics of these techniques "force" an answer even though the relationship between the cost and activity may be weak or, in some instances, nonexistent. Hence, the determination of an implied cost behavior pattern by means of a scattergraph adds strength to a numerical solution which defines the same cost behavior.

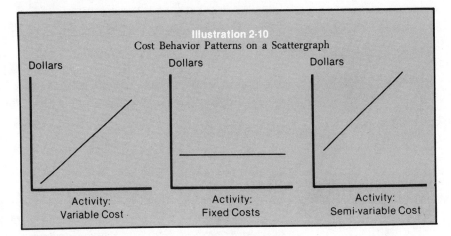

Illustration 2-10
Cost Behavior Patterns on a Scattergraph

The basic cost behavior patterns that would imply a specific cost categorization on a scattergraph are presented in Illustration 2–10. If the relationship between the activity and cost may be defined in some meaningful pattern, a trend line (or a regression line as it is referred to in statistics) can be fitted to the graph by inspection. (This trend line may also be calculated mathematically using the method of least squares which will be discussed in the next section of this chapter.)

The power cost data from Illustration 2–8 are plotted on a scattergraph in Illustration 2–11. The pattern of the observations in the graph implies that the power cost is a semivariable cost. The trend line depicted in Illustration 2–11 was drawn with a straight-edge. In drawing this line, an attempt was made to minimize the total deviations of the observations from the trend line. The line intersects the vertical axis at a level of $6. This $6 represents the fixed cost portion of the power cost as determined using the scattergraph approach. The total variable component of the semi-variable cost at a given level of activity may be determined by subtracting the fixed cost from the total cost at that level of activity. To determine the variable cost per unit of activity, the total variable cost would be divided by the level of activity.

At 35 hours of power usage, the total cost is $13. The fixed cost component is $6. Total variable cost is therefore $7 ($13 — $6) or $.20 per hour of power usage ($7 ÷ 35). To calculate the variable cost per hour, the total variable cost is divided by the activity, that is, $7 ÷ 35 hours.

Total Cost at 35 Hours......................	$13
Less: Fixed Cost Component..................	6
Total Variable Cost.........................	$ 7
Variable Cost Per Hour $7 ÷ 35 hours =	$.20

The pattern of the observations in the graph implies that the power cost is a semivariable cost which consists of fixed cost of $6 and variable cost of $.20 per hour.

Method of Least Squares

The method of least squares may be used to mathematically calculate the trend line that was drawn by inspection with the scattergraph tech-

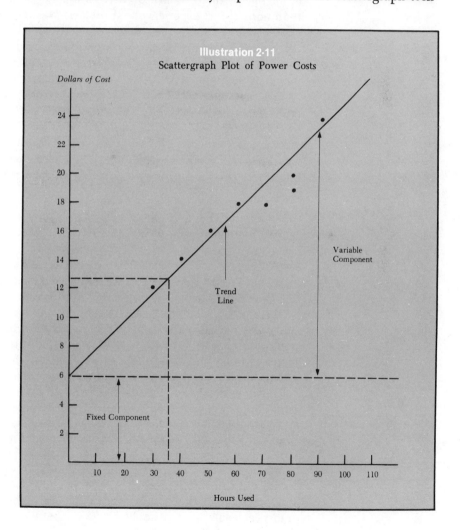

Illustration 2-11
Scattergraph Plot of Power Costs

nique. It should be noted that this technique fits a trend line to cost data even if no relationship actually exists. Therefore, this method must be used with caution; in fact, the method of least squares should only be used if a relationship is believed to exist.

The scattergraph technique presented evidence that the data in Illustration 2–8 are representative of a semivariable cost. This data is used again to calculate the trend line using the method of least squares. If the scattergraph is studied and there are levels of activity for which the costs appear to be somewhat out of line, a statistician might wish to further investigate these observations to ascertain whether or not some event out of the ordinary occurred that might have caused the higher than normal cost experienced. If the cost was indeed caused by unusual circumstances, then the observation should be excluded from the calculations. For the purposes of the following discussion, it is assumed that there were no unusual circumstances so all of the observations are included in the analysis.

The method of least squares linear regression which minimizes the total deviations in the cost data is simply one technique used to estimate the equation of a line. As stated in the initial section of this chapter, total costs equal fixed costs plus variable costs. The least squares method estimates the values of 'a'—fixed costs (in mathematical terms, slope intercept) and 'b'—variable costs (slope of the line) per unit of activity (x) or:

$$Y = a + b(x)$$

Here 'Y' represents total costs. Illustration 2–12 shows the method and presents the equation used to estimate fixed and variable costs. Recall that the original data were presented in Illustration 2–8.

Therefore variable costs are $.16 per hour and fixed costs are $7.60, as indicated by the calculations made and presented in Illustration 2-12. At this point, the student may wish to work through this least squares method example carefully and then compare this method to those which were described previously and which were based upon the same data.

The large number of calculations required by the least squares solution does not present a problem. Almost every computer system has a program in its library that will perform the calculations. Inexpensive regression programs are also available for microcomputers and many pocket calculators will also perform the calculations.

While regression analysis is only introduced in this text, you should be aware that many books have been written about statistical methods and the interpretation of the results. And until you become more familiar with statistical analysis you should be very careful about drawing inferences from the results of regression analysis.

Illustration 2-12

Method of Least Squares

Activity (X)	Cost (Y)	Deviations from Average Activity (X-X̄)	Deviations from Average Cost (Y-Ȳ)	Deviations from Average Activity Squared (X-X̄)²	Deviations of X Multiplied by Deviations of Y (X-X̄) (Y-Ȳ)
40	$ 14	− 25	$ − 4	625	$100
60	18	− 5	0	25	0
60	18	− 5	0	25	0
50	16	− 15	− 2	225	30
30	12	− 35	− 6	1,225	210
90	24	+ 25	+ 6	625	150
80	20	+ 15	+ 2	225	30
80	19	+ 15	+ 1	225	15
60	18	− 5	0	25	0
80	20	+ 15	+ 2	225	30
80	19	+ 15	+ 1	225	15
70	18	+ 5	0	25	0
780	$216	0	$ 0	3,700	$580

Average: $\overline{X} = 780 \div 12 = 65$
$\overline{Y} = \$216 \div 12 = \$18$

$Y = a + b(X) \qquad \hat{Y} = \hat{a} + \hat{b}(X) \qquad \hat{a}$ and $\hat{b}$ are estimates of the cost parameters.

Estimated Variable Cost per unit of activity ° $= \hat{b} = \dfrac{\Sigma(X\text{-}\overline{X})(Y\text{-}\overline{Y})}{\Sigma(X\text{-}\overline{X})^2} = \dfrac{\$ \ 580}{3,700} = \$.16$ (rounded)

Estimated Fixed Costs ** $= \hat{a} = \overline{Y} - \hat{b}(\overline{X}) = \$18 - \$.16 \ (65) = \$7.60$
Estimated Total Cost Equation: $\hat{Y} = \$7.60 + \$.16 \ (X)$

° An alternative equation for estimating the variable cost $\hat{b}$ is:

$$\hat{b} = \frac{n(\Sigma XY) - (\Sigma X)(\Sigma Y)}{n(\Sigma X^2) - (\Sigma X)^2}$$

** An alternative equation for estimating the fixed cost $\hat{a}$ is:

$$\hat{a} = \frac{(\Sigma X^2)(\Sigma Y) - (\Sigma X)(\Sigma XY)}{n(\Sigma X^2) - (\Sigma X)^2}$$

SUMMARY

Effective planning for the future requires that a firm accumulate certain basic information regarding the behavior patterns of its costs. A cost behavior pattern is the typical manner in which a particular cost behaves in relation to a change in a given level of activity. Cost behavior is generally associated with activity within a relevant range; that is, the operating range over which the firm finds it practical to operate in the short-run. In establishing an activity base for a particular cost, the firm attempts to identify those causal relationships that explain the fluctuations in the cost under consideration.

For planning purposes, costs are commonly classified into two major categories according to behavior patterns. These classifications are fixed costs and variable costs. Variable costs are those costs that vary directly and proportionately with the associated activity measure. Fixed costs, on the other hand, generally do not vary according to activity, but instead remain fixed or constant within the relevant range over a given period of time. Fixed costs may be further classified into committed fixed costs (those costs that must be incurred because of past management decision) and managed fixed costs (those costs over which management has the short-run ability to change).

Although the variable and fixed dichotomies are the major categories used for cost classification according to cost behavior patterns, many costs simply cannot be identified as either entirely variable or entirely fixed. Therefore, other related cost categories are required to accurately describe all of the cost behavior patterns of a firm. Semivariable costs are those costs that include both a fixed and a variable component. A step cost is a cost that must be incurred in a series of fixed amounts.

In analyzing cost behavior patterns, it is generally assumed that costs are linear within the relevant range, that a single factor causes the variable portion of a cost to fluctuate, and that past cost behavior patterns will remain valid in the future. A number of techniques are commonly used for determining cost behavior patterns.

Accounting techniques for cost behavior determination generally use the historical data provided by the accounting information system. These techniques include account analysis, the high-low method and the method of semi-averages. Account analysis is simply a visual inspection of the accounts made to determine obvious behavior patterns. The high-low method assumes a linear relationship between the highest and lowest activity levels and the costs associated with those levels. The method of semi-averages employs the high-low technique, but uses an averaging process to obtain the relevant data points.

Two of the basic statistical techniques available for determining cost behavior patterns are the scattergraph and the method of least squares. The scattergraph method requires the graphical plotting of both cost and activity data, and the visual fitting of a trend or regression line to the resulting graph. The method of least squares goes a step further by mathematically calculating the trend line that was previously drawn by inspection.

This chapter has provided a detailed discussion of the primary classifications of costs used for planning purposes. An understanding of these classifications and how they are determined is essential to obtain a further insight into the planning process.

KEY DEFINITIONS

Account analysis—an accounting approach used to determine cost behavior patterns by visually inspecting the accounts and identifying those costs which are clearly variable or clearly fixed.

Committed fixed costs—fixed costs which the firm will incur because of the past decisions or commitments made by management, such as those costs related to acquiring and maintaining the organization and its long-term assets.

Fixed costs—costs which do not change in relationship to an activity within a relevant range and which are fixed or constant for a given period of time.

High-low method—accounting method of determining cost behavior which assumes a linear behavior of costs between the highest level of activity and its related cost and the lowest level of activity and its related cost. These figures are taken from the recent operating records of the firm for a selected period of time.

Managed fixed costs—discretionary, programmed, or planned fixed costs. These are fixed costs incurred on a short-term basis in accordance with an established management objective.

Method of least squares—statistical approach used to determine cost behavior patterns by mathematically calculating the variable and fixed components of the costs, and the trend line that best fits the cost observations.

Method of semi-averages—a more sophisticated version of the high-low method of determining cost behavior patterns. This method assumes a linear behavior of costs between the average of the high activity period and corresponding costs, and the average of the low activity period and corresponding costs over a selected period of time.

Relevant range—range of operating capacity where the firm finds it practical to operate in the short-run. Total fixed costs remain constant within this range.

Scattergraph—a statistical approach used to determine cost behavior patterns and which requires the plotting of both cost and activity observations on a graph.

Semi-variable costs—costs which have both a fixed and a variable component so that as the level of activity increases the total cost will increase, but in a less than proportional amount.

Step costs—costs which are constant over a given range of activity, but which increase or decrease in a fixed incremental amount as the level of activity changes.

Variable costs—costs which vary directly and proportionally with the level of activity.

QUESTIONS

2-1 Define relevant range.

2-2 List two examples which help to explain the concept of activity measures.

2-3 Define variable costs. Give examples.

2-4 (*a*) Define fixed costs. (*b*) Give two categories into which fixed costs may be classified. Define each and give examples.

2-5 Define semi-variable costs. Give examples.

2-6 Define step costs. Give examples.

2-7 What assumptions are made in analyzing cost behavior?

2-8 "Past cost behavior patterns will continue to be valid in the future." Why should this assumption be viewed with caution?

2-9 What are the accounting techniques that may be classified as accounting approaches for determining cost behavior patterns? On what are they based?

2-10 Discuss account analysis.

2-11 Describe the high-low method for determining cost behavior patterns.

2-12 Describe the method of semi-averages.

2-13 What are the two basic statistical techniques that are often used for the analysis of cost data? On what are they based?

2-14 Since the numerical techniques for calculating the fixed and variable components of a cost always provide some answer, why is a scattergraph necessary?

2-15 Why must the method of least squares be used with caution?

EXERCISES AND PROBLEMS

2-16 From the following scattergraphs, state the type of cost each represents.

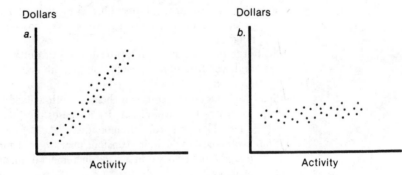

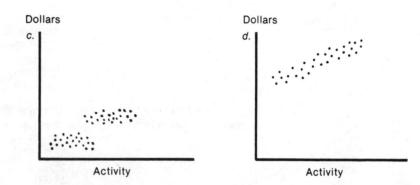

2-17 The Weinberg Company is in the process of developing and marketing a new product. From the list of fixed costs listed below, categorize each cost according to whether it is a committed or managed fixed cost as relates to this new product.

    a. Research and development costs
    b. Building modifications
    c. Depreciation on existing building
    d. Market tests
    e. Initial training expenses of salesmen
    f. Salary of the vice president of the new product department
    g. Product samples distributed by salesmen

2-18 Angus, Inc. has found that the maintenance of its machine costs $300 per month plus $.19 per hour the machine is run. Within a relevant range of 2,800 to 9,000 hours, compute the maintenance costs if the machine is run 3,000, 3,600, 4,100 and 4,250 hours.

2-19 The power for the Evans Company costs $.02 for every unit used. There is a minimum charge of $20 per month. Determine the bill for each of the following months:

	Units Used
January	1,500
February	1,720
March	1,200
April	860
May	1,070
June	1,440

2-20 Given the following, you are to approximate the variable and fixed cost behavior of the monthly repairs for the delivery truck using the high-low method.

Kilometers Traveled	Monthly Maintenance Costs Incurred
1,000	$250
3,000	350
6,000	500

2-21   Using the method of semi-averages, determine the fixed and variable components of the following costs for the past year.

		Hours Worked	Cost
Quarter	1	20,000	$41,000
	2	28,000	55,000
	3	32,000	67,000
	4	30,000	57,000

2-22   Given the following, determine the fixed and variable components of the maintenance costs using the method of least squares.

Quarter	Hours Worked	Cost
1	19,500	$69,000
2	17,600	62,300
3	21,200	74,500
4	25,700	90,100

2-23   Johnson Company would like to determine the variable rate per direct machine hour in order to estimate the electricity costs for the months of May and June. Below is listed relevant information.

Months	Machine Hours Worked	Electricity Cost
January	1,200	$50
February	1,300	53
March	1,400	56
April	1,500	60

Estimated units to be produced:

Months	Units
May	1,067
June	1,134

Each unit requires 1.5 machine hours.

Required:

a.   Compute the variable and fixed electricity cost components of the total electricity cost using the high-low method.

b.   Using the rates calculated above, estimate the electricity for the months of May and June.

T 2-24 The Simpson Company wants to estimate their gross profit for the first two quarters of next year. The price per unit is $50 and the historical costs are listed below.

	Units Produced	Cost
1	2,000	$ 84,000
2	2,500	102,500
3	2,800	112,000
4	3,400	129,200

It is estimated that 3,600 and 4,000 units will be produced and sold in the first and second quarters.

Required:

Using the method of semi-averages, calculate the fixed costs and variable cost per unit and the expected gross profit for each of the first two quarters.

A 2-25 Given below are the sales figures and several related expense figures for six years for the Deckett Company. You are to decide whether the costs are variable, fixed, semi-variable, or step costs by using a graphical analysis.

Year	1	2	3	4	5	6
Sales (in units)	6,000	8,000	8,500	10,000	10,100	10,250
Direct materials	$18,000	$24,000	$25,500	$30,000	$30,300	$30,750
Rent	1,000	1,000	1,000	1,000	1,000	1,000
Selling expense	17,000	22,000	23,250	27,000	27,250	27,625
Electricity	15,000	19,000	20,000	23,000	23,200	23,500
Maintenance	2,000	2,500	2,500	3,000	3,000	3,000

T 2-26 The Royal Corporation has just added a new product and wants to know what it should charge for the product. They will have $250,000 fixed costs and $5.25 per unit in variable costs. The marketing research department feels that Royal can expect the sales volume given below by using the suggested prices.

Expected sales (in units)	450,000	625,000	730,000	1,000,000
Unit sales price	$12.00	$10.30	$8.25	$5.50

Required:

Using the information given above, what should Royal use as its selling price? (Base your answer on the highest expected profit.)

A 2-27 Terry Company has collected the following production cost data:

	0 Units Produced	100 Units Produced	200 Units Produced
Depreciation	$500	$700	$ 900
Supplies	0	950	1,900
Property Taxes	600	600	600
Labor	0	425	850

In addition, the company has found that maintenance expense exhibits the following "step" behavior:

For   0–75 units, maintenance costs = $ 800
For   76–150 units, maintenance costs =   1,600
For 151–225 units, maintenance costs =   2,400

Required:

What would you expect the total production costs to be if Terry Company produced 125 units?

2-28   The Huff Company is trying to estimate its costs for the first three months of next year. It estimates production to be 30,000 units for January; 31,500 units for February; and 35,000 units for March. Given the following data, estimate the costs for these months.

Kilograms of material per unit	2
Cost per kilogram of material	$ 1.50
Direct labor hours per unit	1.5
Cost per direct labor hour	$ 4.25
Fixed maintenance within relevant range of	
0 units–25,000 units	$140.00
25,001 units–31,000 units	$180.00
31,001 units–50,000 units	$220.00
Power costs—minimum	$100.00
Variable cost per direct labor hour	$ .02
Heating cost—basic charge	$ 25.00
Plus, charge per direct labor hour	$ .015

A 2-29   Given below are the hours used and the maintenance costs incurred for the production machinery of the Lawrence Company. The company wants to know what the variable and fixed components are for the maintenance costs. Use (a) the high-low technique, (b) the method of semi-averages, and (c) the method of least squares to determine the cost components. Compare all three methods and give reasons for using the method you feel is best.

Month	Hours Used	Cost
January	3,200	$1,590
February	3,560	1,820
March	3,800	1,890
April	4,050	2,000
May	3,900	1,930
June	3,650	1,825
July	3,740	1,890
August	3,460	1,760
September	3,400	1,700
October	3,550	1,775
November	3,800	1,910
December	4,200	2,050

Chapter 3

Chapter 3 describes job order cost accounting and illustrates how job order costing systems are used to accumulate inventory costs. Studying this chapter should enable you to:

1. Discuss and give examples of each of the basic elements of product costs.
2. Describe a "full" product cost and explain its derivation.
3. Calculate a predetermined overhead rate.
4. Explain the basics of job order cost accounting and job order costing systems.
5. Identify and illustrate alternative methods of handling overapplied and underapplied manufacturing overhead.
6. Discuss the cost of goods manufactured statement.

Cost Accounting
for Inventories:
Job Order Costing

THIS CHAPTER and Chapters 4, 5, and 7 emphasize manufacturing cost accumulation systems used for inventory costing purposes. Inventory costing, on either a per unit or a per batch basis, is necessary to determine a valuation for inventory which is used for planning and control purposes. This inventory is also used as an input in preparing the balance sheet, and in determining the cost of goods sold for income statement purposes.

There are two fundamental systems of cost accumulation: job order costing and process costing. Each of these cost systems provides a product cost for inventory on a physical measure basis. Examples of physical measures used as bases for product costing purposes include units, kilograms, litres, and tons. Job order costing is considered in this chapter and process costing will be discussed in Chapter 4.

THE ELEMENTS OF PRODUCT COST

The basic elements of product cost for a manufacturing firm were identified in Chapter 1 as direct materials, direct labor, and manufacturing overhead. Accounting for product costs is based on the assumption that each of these basic elements of product cost attaches to, or can be matched or identified with, specific units or batches of production.

For income determination purposes, the product cost to be used will, of course, represent the full or total cost of manufacturing. The use of this full or total cost implies that the total manufacturing costs for a given accounting period are allocated or assigned to those units produced during that period. The full costing method requires that a portion of the manufacturing overhead costs incurred during the period, as well as the costs of direct labor and direct materials used in the production process, be allocated or assigned to each unit or batch of products produced.

Direct Materials Cost

As previously indicated, direct materials are those materials which are used in the production process and which can be directly traced to, or identified with, specific units of product or batches of production. In certain instances, direct materials may include certain materials acquired in a semi-finished state from a supplier as well as those materials normally regarded as raw materials. By definition, the total cost of the direct materials introduced and used in the production process will be proportional to the number of units produced, i.e., the amount of goods manufactured. Therefore, the cost of direct materials is, by its very nature, a variable cost of production.

In practice, certain raw materials may be traced directly to units of product or batches of production. However, the cost of doing so exceeds the additional benefits or accuracy which would be derived from this allocation process. The cost of the raw materials which fall into this category are usually classified as indirect materials simply as a matter of convenience. Examples of indirect materials include: lubricants, sandpaper, wiping rags, packing materials, etc. The costs of indirect materials are considered to be a part of manufacturing overhead costs and are allocated to production as such.

Direct Labor Cost

Direct labor costs include expenses incurred for, and related to, the activities of those employees who are involved in the production process and whose efforts may be directly traced to the manufacturing of specific units of product or batches of production. Direct labor cost is a variable manufacturing cost. As is the case for materials, it may not be efficient to trace certain types of labor costs related to production (such as the salaries of foremen, maintenance personnel, janitors, etc.) to units of product or batches of production. Therefore, such expenditures are normally classified as indirect labor costs. Consistent with the treatment suggested for indirect materials costs, indirect labor costs are considered to be a part of manufacturing overhead costs and are accounted for as such as a matter of convenience.

Manufacturing Overhead Cost

Manufacturing overhead includes all manufacturing costs *other* than direct materials and/or direct labor costs which are incurred in order to manufacture the product. Examples of cost items considered part of manufacturing overhead include: depreciation on plant and equipment; heat, light and power pertaining to the factory; factory supplies; insurance and property taxes on the plant; costs of service departments such as maintenance for the plant; and indirect materials and labor.

Any other costs incurred by the firm not related to the production process are considered to be period costs, not manufacturing overhead. Expenses such as depreciation on the administrative and sales facilities, salaries of salesmen, utilities expense for administrative and sales facilities, office supplies expense, rental expense for administrative or sales facilities, and property taxes on administrative buildings are all examples of expenditures classified as period costs. As such, they are included as expenses in the income statement in the time period in which they were incurred. Period costs are not included in computing the cost of manufacturing the product.

Manufacturing overhead includes both fixed and variable cost components. The fixed component of overhead normally includes such costs as insurance, property taxes, and depreciation on plant facilities. Variable cost components usually include costs such as indirect materials, indirect labor, and utilities.

FLOW OF MANUFACTURING COSTS

Manufacturing costs are accumulated for purposes of inventory costing on what is referred to as a full cost basis. The use of "full costing" indicates that the cost of the products produced during a period should include the costs of all direct materials and direct labor used as well as a *normal* share of both variable and fixed manufacturing overhead incurred. The overhead that should be included as a portion of the cost of the products manufactured is that overhead which is incurred under normal operating conditions. (The treatment of "abnormal" or excess costs are considered in Chapters 7 and 8).

The product cost flows generally experienced by a manufacturing firm may be traced in the following diagram:

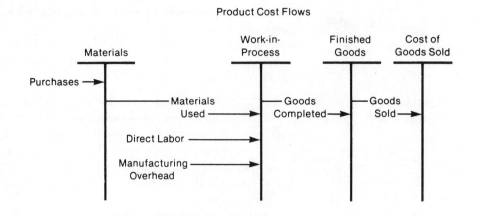

Product Cost Flows

These cost flows may also be summarized in the form of a statement referred to as the cost of goods manufactured and sold statement, as follows:

Cost of Goods Manufactured and Sold Statement

Raw Materials
   Beginning Inventory . . . . $ xx
   Add: Purchases   x

   Raw Material Available for Use . . . . $xxx
   Less: Ending Inventory . . . . (xx)

   Cost of Raw Materials Used . . . . $xxx
Direct Labor   xx
Manufacturing Overhead   xx

Total Manufacturing Costs . . . . $xxx
   Add: Beginning Work-in-Process Inventory   xx

Total Cost of Work-in-Process During Period . . . . $xxx
   Less: Ending Work-in-Process Inventory . . . . (xx)

Total Cost of Goods Manufactured, Completed and
   Transferred during the Period . . . . $xxx
   Add: Beginning Finished Goods Inventory   xx

Goods Available for Sale . . . . $xxx
   Less: Ending Finished Goods Inventory . . . . (xx)

Cost of Goods Sold During the Period . . . . $xxx

The cost of the direct materials, direct labor, and manufacturing overhead incurred are combined and accumulated in a work-in-process inventory account. As goods are completed, the production costs of these goods are determined and transferred to a finished goods inventory account. It is important to note that the raw materials, work-in-process, and finished goods accounts are *all* inventory accounts. The raw materials inventory account reflects the cost of all direct materials on hand which are available for use in the manufacturing process, but which have not yet been used in production during the period. The work-in-process inventory represents the cost of partially completed products on hand at the close of the period and, as such, is composed of transfers from the direct materials, direct labor, and manufacturing overhead accounts. The finished goods inventory indicates the cost of the inventory which has been completed, but which is unsold and remains on hand at the end of the period. These three inventory accounts are all classified as current assets on the balance sheet. As sales are made from the finished goods inventory, the related cost of the products sold is transferred from the asset account to the cost of goods sold expense account.

PREDETERMINED OVERHEAD RATES

As previously indicated, overhead cost includes both variable and fixed cost components. The benefits which may be derived from a precise or exact accounting for certain of the variable components of overhead are usually not justified in terms of the cost of doing so. The fixed cost component of overhead represents, in general, the long-range commitment that management has made to both obtain and retain the firm's ability to produce. These fixed costs are incurred whether production is at the lower or at the upper end of the relevant range.

For example, if the actual fixed overhead costs of $1,000 incurred during January were assigned by a firm to the production of that month when a total of 200 units of product were manufactured, then the fixed overhead per unit would be $5 ($1,000 divided by 200 units). If the production during June increased to 500 units while the fixed overhead remained constant at $1,000, then fixed overhead per unit would be only $2 ($1,000 divided by 500 units). Under these circumstances, this firm would experience fluctuating monthly production costs per unit (product costs) because a constant amount of fixed overhead ($1,000 per month) is allocated to a different number of units produced each month. The variable cost per unit is normally relatively constant within the relevant range since variable costs, by definition, are incurred in proportion to activity.

To eliminate certain problems which might be encountered in the direct allocation of fixed overhead over a short time span, a *predetermined overhead rate* may be established and used. The use of this rate is implemented under the concept of *normal costs*. The overhead rate used for product costing purposes is determined before the production process is completed, thus the rate is identified as predetermined. This rate is based on the total normal overhead cost expected to be incurred for the time period under consideration assuming usual operating conditions.

The time period chosen for "normalizing" overhead should be sufficiently long to eliminate the effects of any seasonal aspects of production. Even if no seasonal fluctuations exist, the time period chosen must be long enough to eliminate any unusual events which might occur during a given period. For purposes of illustration in this text, a year will normally be considered a sufficient period for use in establishing an overhead rate. One should note that both the fixed and the variable overhead cost components are included in the predetermined rate. For example, assume that a firm anticipates the production of 40,000 units for 19x1 and that total overhead costs (i.e., both fixed and variable overhead) of $100,000 are expected for the year. The predetermined overhead per unit is calculated as follows:

$$\frac{\text{Planned Total Overhead Costs}}{\text{Planned Production}} = \frac{\$100,000}{40,000 \text{ units}} = \$2.50 \text{ of Overhead Per Unit Produced}$$

Each unit produced during 19x1 includes the actual costs of the direct materials and direct labor used and, in addition, an allocation of $2.50 per unit produced for manufacturing overhead. This $2.50 allocation for overhead is considered the normal overhead cost applied to each unit without regard to the actual level of production that may take place within any given period—for example, a week or month during the year.

It should be noted that units of production are not always the best measure or denominator for calculating a predetermined overhead rate. In fact, the use of units as a base frequently poses certain problems, as in the case of a firm which produces a number of different products. If the production process for each product differs in such a firm, then the firm might wish to use different overhead rates for each of its products or product groups.

APPLICATION BASES FOR OVERHEAD RATES

There are many bases that may be used for *allocating, absorbing* or *applying* overhead costs to the production of a period. The criteria for selecting a base should emphasize ease of measurability and a causal relationship to the incurrence of variable overhead.

Planned production was used as the application base in calculating the predetermined overhead rate in the previous illustration. Direct labor hours could also have been used. If the firm were a multiple product company, and if the incurrence of variable overhead were related to the number of direct labor hours worked, then the rate could have been established on the basis of planned direct labor hours. Under these circumstances, the product costs for each unit or batch of units produced would absorb an amount of predetermined overhead based on the actual number of direct labor hours worked. Thus, in order to calculate the predetermined overhead rate, the direct labor hours per unit must be computed.

The predetermined rate could also have been based on other factors which have a causal relationship to overhead. If direct labor cost is closely related to the incurrence of overhead, it is not uncommon to use a percentage of this labor cost as a basis for the application of overhead, rather than using an overhead rate based on labor hours. In a firm where there is limited use of labor and extensive use of equipment, machine hours used might be an appropriate base for applying or allocating overhead costs to products. Whatever basis is used for applying overhead, the concept is to have each unit of product produced absorb into its cost its proportional share of the predetermined manufacturing overhead cost.

INVENTORY COST ACCUMULATION: JOB ORDER COSTING USING NORMAL COSTS

As the title "job order costing" implies, costs are accumulated by individual jobs or job lots under a job order costing system. A job is defined as either a single unit or as a batch of units. The costs of direct materials and direct labor traced to the specific job become a part or component of the cost of that job. Normal overhead is assigned to the job using a predetermined overhead rate.

The application of normal overhead is the basis for the term normal costs. Actual costs of direct labor and direct materials are charged to each job, but a normal or a "fair share" of overhead costs is also allocated to the individual jobs. If the causal basis of variable overhead is also the application base for product costing, then normalization is related to the fixed portion of overhead. The projected portion of overhead which is fixed is usually allocated over the projected activity base to develop a cost per unit of activity. Through the use of a predetermined overhead rate, the allocated cost is charged to individual jobs as if it were a variable cost. The total or full cost overhead application rate will be comprised of both the fixed and variable components of overhead.

INVENTORY LEDGERS

The inventory records used in a job order costing system include both the control and the underlying subsidiary ledger accounts. The control accounts used include the following general ledger accounts: raw materials inventory, work-in-process inventory, and finished goods inventory. The subsidiary accounts include the detail which underlies or supports the control account balances. Illustration 3–1 presents the inventory account relationships in "T" account format. Illustration 3–2 is a typical example of the format of the subsidiary ledger inventory accounts.

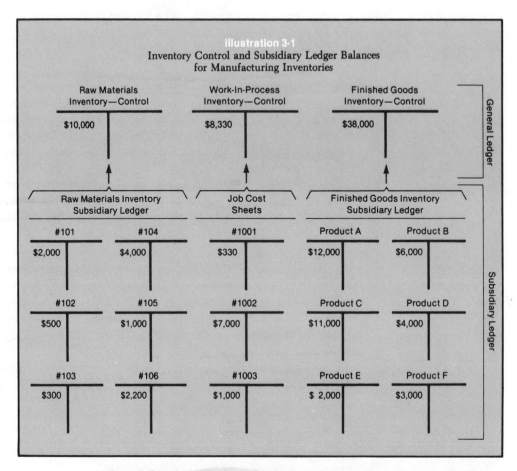

Illustration 3-1
Inventory Control and Subsidiary Ledger Balances
for Manufacturing Inventories

The relationships of the subsidiary and control accounts in the manufacturing inventory accounting system do not differ either in purpose or in use from those used in a retailing concern. In both cases, subsidiary accounts are updated on a periodic basis and the balances of the subsidiary accounts are posted to the control accounts at appropriate intervals.

JOB COST SHEET

The basis of a job order cost system is the job cost sheet. This subsidiary ledger is the cost accumulation device for each job. In other words, each job has its own job cost sheet which serves as the subsidiary ledger account on which costs are accumulated for that specific job. Direct material and direct labor costs are traced to the individual job, and overhead costs are applied or allocated to that job. Per unit costs are calculated directly from the job cost sheet.

Illustration 3-2
Sax Company
Subsidiary Ledger Accounts for Manufacturing Inventories
Raw Materials Inventory Card in Subsidiary Ledger

Material __101   Copper Bushing__   Reorder Point __2,000__
Location ____Aisle 29____   Maximum Order __7,000__

Date	Issue Requisition Number	Quantity Received	Quantity Issued	Unit Cost	Balance Quantity	Balance Total Cost
1/1 Bal.				.25	2,000	500
2/10		7,000		.25	9,000	2,250
2/16	1704		1,000	.25	8,000	2,000

JOB COST SHEET

Manufactured For
Customer ____John Doe____   Job No. ____1001____
Stock _____✓_____   Due Date ____2/26____
Product _____E_____   Date Started____2/16____
Quantity in Job __500 units__   Date Finished __2/26__

Date	Requisition Number	Direct Material Amount Q	Direct Material Amount $	Date	Hours	Cost	Overhead Rate 100% of Direct Labor Cost
2/16	1704	1,000	250	2/16	10	40	40
Totals							

Cost Summary
Direct Material ____$250____   Total Cost____$330____
Direct Labor____40____   Units ____500____
Overhead ____40____   Cost Per Unit ____$.66____
Total ____$330____

Finished Goods Inventory Card in Subsidiary Ledger

Product____A____   Restock Point __3,000__
Location ____Aisle 51____   Production Run __6,000__

Date	Order Number	Job Cost Number	Quantity Received	Quantity Shipped	Unit Cost	Balance Quantity	Balance Total Cost
1/1 Bal.					3.00	6,000	18,000
1/15	1055			4,000	3.00	2,000	6,000
1/25		760	6,000		3.00	8,000	24,000
1/28	2,010			4,000	3.00	4,000	12,000

If you have had your automobile repaired, you have no doubt dealt with a job cost sheet, perhaps without realizing it. The garage prepares a cost sheet which also serves as your bill. Generally, this cost sheet includes the cost of both parts and labor. In the case of a garage, the overhead charge is usually included in the labor charge for billing purposes. The profit earned by the garage is added to the cost of the parts and the combined labor and overhead rate. In this case, the job cost sheet also serves as a pricing mechanism and invoice for the customer.

MANUFACTURING OVERHEAD CONTROL ACCOUNT

The predetermined overhead rate is assigned to jobs as they are completed or as the accounts are closed. In order to achieve a full cost valuation of work-in-process inventory accounts for reporting purposes, it is necessary to maintain the overhead on the job cost sheets on a current basis.

The amount of overhead applied to a particular job is recorded by a debit to the work-in-process control account and a credit to the manufacturing overhead control account. This entry is normally made when the control accounts are updated.

The actual overhead costs for the period are recorded in the accounts by debits to the manufacturing overhead control account and credits to the other appropriate accounts. For example, if the depreciation expense related to the manufacturing equipment is $1,000 for a particular month, then the manufacturing overhead control account is debited $1,000, and accumulated depreciation—manufacturing equipment is credited $1,000. If actual factory supplies of $200 are used during the month, then the manufacturing overhead control account is debited $200, and factory supplies inventory is credited $200.

The inflows and outflows associated with the manufacturing overhead control account are presented in Illustration 3–3. Any balance remaining in the manufacturing overhead control account at the end of an accounting period represents either an *over* or an *under application* of predetermined overhead. If the overhead applied to the production for the period is greater than the actual overhead incurred, the firm will have overapplied its overhead and the manufacturing overhead control account will have a credit balance at the end of the period. If the overhead applied to production is less than the actual overhead incurred, then the firm will have underapplied overhead and the manufacturing overhead control account will have a debit balance at the end of the period.

Theoretically, the amount of actual overhead incurred during a period should be equal to the overhead applied during that period. In practice, this perfect matching will rarely, if ever, be the case and will only occur

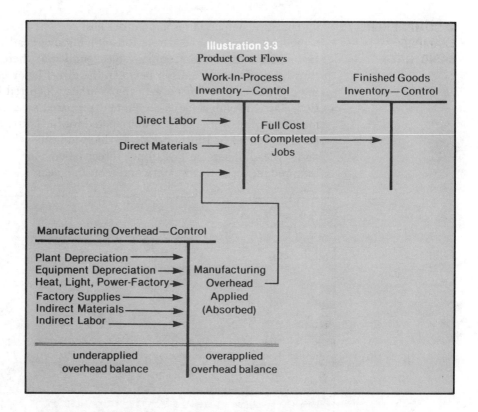

if the predetermined overhead rate is exactly equal to the actual overhead rate for the period and if actual production is exactly equal to planned production. Of course, this equality is extremely unlikely. If the over or underapplied overhead is an immaterial amount, then an adjustment is made to cost of goods sold in order to close out the overhead account and adjust the cost of goods sold amount. A debit balance in the manufacturing overhead control account (actual overhead costs exceed the overhead applied to the jobs) indicates an increase (debit) in the cost of goods sold, because the manufacturing overhead account must be credited in order to close the account. Alternatively, a credit balance in the manufacturing overhead control account represents overapplied overhead and therefore a decrease in cost of goods sold for the period.

If the balance of over or underapplied overhead for the period is considered to be a significant amount, this balance should be allocated to or prorated among the cost of goods sold, finished goods, and work-in-process accounts. The pro rata allocation to these accounts is necessary to eliminate a distortion of the reported income for the period and the financial position of the company at the end of that period.

A COMPREHENSIVE EXAMPLE: BASIC DATA

The Sax Company uses a job order cost system. The company also uses a predetermined overhead rate for applying overhead costs to its manufactured products. Sax Company has found that there appears to be a cause and effect relationship between the direct labor hours worked during a period and the manufacturing overhead incurred for that same period. Last November, Sax's accountant prepared an estimate of the total manufacturing overhead costs anticipated for the current year. This analysis is presented in Illustration 3–4 which indicates that Sax will include an overhead allocation of $10 per direct labor hour worked as a part of the product cost of each job worked on this year.

Illustration 3-4

Sax Company
Projected Manufacturing Overhead Rate

Projected Activity: 60,000 Direct Labor Hours
Projected Total Manufacturing Overhead Costs: $600,000

	Variable Costs Per Direct Labor Hour	Fixed Costs	Total Costs
Indirect Material and Supplies	$3.10	$ 14,000	$200,000
Indirect Labor	1.00	40,000	100,000
Electricity	.10	34,000	40,000
Heat	0	8,000	8,000
Equipment Depreciation	0	48,000	48,000
Plant Depreciation	0	144,000	144,000
Factory Property Taxes	0	60,000	60,000
	$4.20	$348,000	$600,000

Predetermined Manufacturing Overhead Rate:

$$\frac{\text{Total Projected Manufacturing Overhead Cost}}{\text{Total Projected Activity}} = \frac{\$600,000}{60,000 \text{ hours}} = \frac{\$10 \text{ Per Direct}}{\text{Labor Hour}}$$

➤ direct labour hours – causal reln.

January is an ideal time to follow a job through Sax's manufacturing process and accounting records since the firm closes for two weeks at the end of December for employee vacations. Each January, the firm begins its operations without any work-in-process inventory since all jobs are completed during December prior to the shut-down of the plant. The company uses a perpetual inventory system for all of its inventories. Indirect materials and factory supplies are accounted for in terms of dollars only, and not units.

Sax's production schedule for January consists of a single production run of metal shafts for power turbines, a standard inventory product for the company. Normally, Sax would also engage in other transactions during January, but for purposes of illustration we will focus on tracing Job Number 3032, a production run of 7,000 power turbine shafts, through the manufacturing process and the accounts. We will assume that the transactions which are identified and discussed in this example are the only transactions which occurred in January.

A summarized post-closing trial balance as of December 31, 19x0 for Sax Company is presented in Illustration 3-5.

Illustration 3-5
Sax Company
Post-Closing Trial Balance
December 31, 19x0

	Debit	Credit
Cash	$ 60,000	
Accounts receivable	20,000	
Indirect materials and factory supplies	30,000	
Raw materials inventory	40,000	
Work-in-process inventory	0	
Finished goods inventory	10,000	
Equipment	300,000	
Accumulated depreciation—equipment		$ 184,000
Plant	1,082,000	
Accumulated depreciation—plant		600,000
Accounts payable		34,000
Income taxes payable		0
Property taxes payable		0
Long-term debt		400,000
Common stock		190,000
Retained earnings		134,000
Total	$1,542,000	$1,542,000

The normal cost to produce a power turbine shaft is $19, calculated as follows:

One direct Labour hour	$ 5
One round steel billet (shaft)	4
Overhead applied (one hour @ $10.00)	10
Total cost of one shaft	$19

The transactions of the Sax Company for the month of January, 19x1 are presented and discussed in the remainder of this chapter.

A COMPREHENSIVE EXAMPLE: MANUFACTURING JOURNAL ENTRIES

During the month of January, 19x1, the Sax Company planned to begin and complete Job Number 3032, which consisted of 7,000 power turbine shafts. A summary of the manufacturing transactions that occurred during the month of January follows:

January 2.   Materials with a cost of $49,000 were issued to production. Of this amount, $28,000 (representing the cost of 7,000 units of materials) was direct materials and was issued from raw materials. The balance, $21,000, was the cost of indirect materials and factory supplies and was issued from that account. The raw materials requisition number was 1012, and the indirect materials and factory supplies requisition number was 1013.

Work-In-Process Inventory—Control 28,000
Manufacturing Overhead—Control 21,000
    Raw Materials Inventory—Control   28,000
    Indirect Materials and Factory Supplies   21,000

The issue of direct materials to the production process was recorded by a debit of $28,000 to the work-in-process inventory—control account and a corresponding credit to the raw materials inventory—control account. The indirect materials and supplies represent *actual* overhead costs so the manufacturing overhead—control account is increased to reflect these costs. The normal costs of these indirect materials and supplies have been considered in determining the overhead rate, and are therefore components of the rate applied to Job Number 3032 when this job is completed. If a separate inventory account is not maintained for the inventory or indirect material and supplies, the raw materials account is also credited for the $21,000 cost of the indirect material and supplies which were transferred to the work-in-process inventory, thus making the total credit $49,000.

January 15.   Paid wages to manufacturing employees totaling $25,000. Of this amount, $20,000 (representing the cost of 4,000 hours of direct labor) was incurred for direct labor and the balance, $5,000 was for indirect labor.

Work-In-Process Inventory—Control 20,000
Manufacturing Overhead—Control 5,000
    Cash   25,000

All Sax Company employees are paid on the fifteenth and on the final day of each month. The direct labor cost for the first fifteen days of January was $20,000, while indirect labor costs for the same period totaled $5,000. The indirect labor cost represents an actual overhead cost and is recorded as a debit in the manufacturing overhead—control account, just as indirect materials and supplies were recorded in the entry made on January 2.

January 31.   Paid wages of $19,000 to manufacturing employees. Of this amount, $15,000 (for 3,000 hours of direct labor) was for the cost of direct labor incurred and the balance, $4,000, was incurred for indirect labor.

Work-In-Process Inventory—Control 15,000
Manufacturing Overhead—Control 4,000
    Cash 19,000

This entry represents the cost of employee wages for the latter half of January. Again, the indirect labor costs are recorded by a debit to manufacturing overhead—control and not to work-in-process inventory—control, because these indirect costs are part of the predetermined manufacturing overhead rate which is applied to the job upon its completion.

January 31.   Manufacturing overhead of $70,000 (7,000 direct labor hours multiplied by the overhead rate of $10 per direct labor hour) was applied to the production of 7,000 power turbine shafts.

Work-In-Process Inventory—Control 70,000
    Manufacturing Overhead—Control 70,000

This journal entry recognizes the normal overhead for January using the predetermined overhead rate of $10 per direct labor hour for each hour worked on Job Number 3032. The normal portions of all of the manufacturing overhead costs identified in Illustration 3-4 are included in the overhead rate of $10 per direct labor hour.

January 31.   The units that were completed were transferred to finished goods.

Finished Goods Inventory—Control 133,000
    Work-In-Process Inventory—Control . . 133,000

The full cost of the completed inventory includes the direct material cost of $28,000 (January 2), direct labor cost of $35,000 (January 15 and 31), and the manufacturing overhead applied of $70,000 (January 31). The preceding journal entry transferred the accumulated costs of Job Number 3032 from the work-in-process—control account to the finished goods inventory—control account.

January 31.   The plant electricity bill of $3,700 for the month of January was paid.

```
Manufacturing Overhead—Control . . . . . . . 3,700
     Cash  . . . . . . . . . . . . . . . . . . . .          3,700
```

This journal entry records the electricity expense incurred for the month, at its actual cost, as a component of manufacturing overhead. The anticipated cost of electricity had been used in establishing the predetermined manufacturing overhead rate just as the indirect labor and indirect materials and supplies were considered. Therefore, the normal cost of electricity had already been absorbed as a part of the cost of the job when the overhead was applied.

January 31.   The plant heating bill of $2,000 for the month of January was paid.

```
Manufacturing Overhead—Control . . . . . . . 2,000
     Cash  . . . . . . . . . . . . . . . . . . . .          2,000
```

This entry recognizes the actual factory heating cost for January. As was the case with indirect materials and supplies, indirect labor costs, and electricity costs, the normally expected costs of heating were considered in determining the predetermined overhead rate and were thus absorbed into the job. Consequently, the actual heating expense for January is recorded by a debit to the manufacturing overhead—control account.

January 31.   Sold 2,000 of the power turbine shafts which were produced during January at a sales price of $50 per shaft. The proceeds of the sale were received in cash. The entry for cost of goods sold was made.

```
Cash  . . . . . . . . . . . . . . . . . . . . . 100,000
     Sales Revenue . . . . . . . . . . . . . .          100,000
```

Sax sold 2,000 of the power turbine shafts produced during January at a sales price of $50 per shaft for a total selling price of $100,000. The proceeds of the sale were received in cash.

```
Cost of Goods Sold . . . . . . . . . . . . . . 38,000
     Finished Goods Inventory . . . . . . . . .          38,000
```

Sax uses a perpetual inventory system. Therefore, the cost of goods sold is recognized at the time the sale is made. Cost of goods sold, as may be seen in the following calculation, is $19 per unit for 2,000 units or a total of $38,000. A total of $133,000 was transferred to the finished goods—control account on January 31. This amount represented the full cost of the 7,000 units completed during January. The full cost per unit would be $19 ($133,000 divided by 7,000 units).

January 31. The selling and administrative expenses for January totaled $28,000 and were paid in cash.

Selling and Administrative Expenses 28,000
     Cash   28,000

The total selling and administrative costs for January were $28,000, and these amounts were paid in cash.

January 31. Depreciation expense for the month (from Illustration 3-4) is calculated as follows (assuming the straight-line method of depreciation is used):

Equipment: $ 48,000 × $\frac{1}{12}$ = $ 4,000
Plant: $144,000 × $\frac{1}{12}$ = $12,000

Accrued property taxes on the factory for January (from Illustration 3-4) are as follows:

$ 60,000 × $\frac{1}{12}$ = $ 5,000

Manufacturing Overhead—Control 21,000
    Accumulated Depreciation—Equipment .   4,000
    Accumulated Depreciation—Plant   12,000
    Accrued Property Taxes Payable   5,000

Other actual overhead costs, which have not yet been recognized but which were included in the job as part of the overhead applied, include depreciation expense of $4,000 on equipment and $12,000 on plant. Accrued property taxes of $5,000 on the plant also have not previously been recognized in the accounts. The above adjusting journal entry brings the manufacturing overhead—control account up to date as of January 31.

The depreciation expense and accrued taxes are considered as a part of the overhead costs which were included in determining the predetermined overhead rate. Even if this entry were not made—and in most cases it is likely that it would not be made for purposes of the monthly management reports—the inventory values would reflect the normal cost of depreciation and property taxes. These costs are reflected in the inventory values because they are included as a part of the predetermined manufacturing overhead application rate which was used to apply overhead to production.

A COMPREHENSIVE EXAMPLE: GENERAL AND SUBSIDIARY LEDGERS

The general ledger accounts are presented in "T" account format in Illustration 3–6, and the related subsidiary ledger inventory accounts are presented in Illustration 3–7. All beginning balances were taken from the post-closing trial balance which was included in Illustration 3–5. To fully understand the concept of manufacturing cost flows, the reader should trace the general journal entries through both the general ledger and the subsidiary ledger accounts.

The manufacturing overhead—control account included in the general ledger and the job cost sheet in the subsidiary ledger deserve special attention. Manufacturing overhead—control serves as an account that is used to accumulate the actual overhead costs as a debit amount. When overhead is allocated or applied to jobs, the application of the overhead is recorded by a credit to the manufacturing overhead—control account. A credit balance in the manufacturing overhead account at the end of an accounting period represents overapplied overhead, while a debit balance represents underapplied overhead.

The job cost sheet, which is the subsidiary ledger account for the work-in-process—control account, deserves special consideration because of the important role it plays in accumulating costs by specific jobs. This cost sheet is the basic cost accumulation instrument used in the job order costing system.

A COMPREHENSIVE EXAMPLE: THE MANUFACTURING OVERHEAD— CONTROL ACCOUNT

The manufacturing overhead—control account used in Illustration 3–6 reflects the overhead applied or absorbed into production (the credit entry of $70,000) and actual overhead costs for January (the debit entries totaling $56,700). In this example, manufacturing overhead for the month was *overapplied* by a total of $13,300. The $70,000 of manufacturing overhead costs accumulated for inventory valuation purposes using the predetermined overhead rate exceeded the actual costs of $56,700 incurred during January by $13,300.

This overapplication of manufacturing overhead may have been caused by a change in the anticipated volume of activity during January when manufacturing overhead was applied to production. Alternatively, the actual costs of the various components of manufacturing overhead may have differed from the costs which were planned for by the Sax Company when it computed its predetermined overhead rate. The overapplication could also have been the result of a combination of these, as well as other

Illustration 3-6
Sax Company
General Ledger Accounts

Cash

1/1	60,000	25,000	1/15
1/31	100,000	19,000	1/31
		3,700	1/31
		2,000	1/31
		28,000	1/31
1/31	82,300		

Indirect Materials and Factory Supplies

1/1	30,000	21,000	1/2
1/31	9,000		

Raw Materials Inventory—Control

1/1	40,000	28,000	1/2
1/31	12,000		

Work-In-Process Inventory—Control

1/1	–0–	133,000	1/31
1/2	28,000		
1/15	20,000		
1/31	15,000		
1/31	70,000		
1/31	–0–	–0–	

Finished Goods Inventory—Control

1/1	10,000		
1/31	133,000	38,000	1/31
1/31	105,000		

misstated because you should have product in inventory

Manufacturing Overhead—Control

1/1	–0–	–0–	
1/2	21,000	70,000	1/31
1/15	5,000		
1/31	4,000		
1/31	3,700		
1/31	2,000		
1/31	21,000		
		13,300	1/31

overapplied manufacturing overhead

Accumulated Depreciation—Equipment

		184,000	1/1
		4,000	1/31
		188,000	1/31

Accumulated Depreciation—Plant

		600,000	1/1
		12,000	1/31
		612,000	1/31

Property Taxes Payable

		–0–	1/1
		5,000	1/31
		5,000	1/31

Sales Revenue

		–0–	1/1
		100,000	1/31
		100,000	1/31

Cost of Goods Sold

1/31	38,000		
1/31	38,000		

Selling and Administrative Expenses

1/31	28,000		
1/31	28,000		

Illustration 3-7
Sax Company
Subsidiary Ledger Accounts for Manufacturing Inventories

Material __Round Steel Billet__   Reorder Point ____500____
Location __Aisle 84__   Maximum Order __9,000__

Date	Issue Requisition Number	Quantity Received	Quantity Issued	Unit Cost	Balance Quantity	Balance Total Cost
1/1 Bal.				4	8,000	32,000
1/2	1012		7,000	4	1,000	4,000

Material __Ind. Mat. & Fac. Supp.__   Reorder Point __Visual Inspection__
Location __Aisle 29: Bins 40-50__   Maximum Order __Marked in Bin__

Date	Issue Requisition Number	Received	Issued	Balance
1/1 Bal.				30,000
1/2	1013		21,000 _to set 9,000_	9,000

Job Cost Sheet

Manufactured for
Customer ____John Doe____   Job No. ____3032____
Stock ____✓____   Due Date ____1/31____
Product _____   Date Started ____1/2____
Quantity in Job ____7,000____   Date Finished ____1/31____

	Direct Material				Direct Labor		Overhead Rate $10 Per Direct Labor Hour
Date	Requisition Number	Amount Q	Amount $	Date	Hours	Cost	
1/2	1012	7,000	28,000	1/15	4,000	20,000	7,000 hours
				1/31	3,000	15,000	X $10
							$70,000
Totals		7,000	28,000		7,000	35,000	70,000

Cost Summary
Direct Material ____$28,000____   Total Cost ____$133,000____
Direct Labor ____35,000____   Units ____7,000____
Overhead ____70,000____   Cost Per Unit ____$19____
Total ____$133,000____

Product __Power Turbine Shafts__   Restock Point ____500____
Location __Aisle 76__   Production Run ____7,000____

Date	Order Number	Job Cost Number	Quantity Received	Quantity Shipped	Unit Cost	Balance Quantity	Balance Total Cost
1/1 Bal.					19	526	10,000
1/31		3032	7,000		19	7,526	143,000
1/31	2051			2,000	19	5,526	105,000

factors. The analysis of this difference is discussed in Chapter 8.

Theoretically, assuming a reasonable prediction is made for the overhead rate, at the end of each year the difference between actual and applied overhead should be negligible. This is because overapplications in some months will be offset in other months when overhead is underapplied. In our example, Sax Company must now decide how to treat the overapplied manufacturing overhead of $13,300 in its January financial reports. Remember that the predetermined rate is based on normal overhead for an entire year, so that one would usually expect either an overapplied or underapplied amount in any given month.

A COMPREHENSIVE EXAMPLE: TREATMENT OF OVERAPPLIED OR UNDERAPPLIED OVERHEAD

When a periodic closing of the accounts occurs, the over or underapplied overhead is normally immaterial in amount if the costs and level of anticipated activity for the period have been reasonably forecasted. If indeed the amount is immaterial, the procedure usually accepted as most expedient in general practice is to adjust the amount of cost of goods sold by the amount necessary to close out any debit or credit balance in the manufacturing overhead—control account. If overhead were overapplied, using the 13,300 from the illustration of Sax's January operations, this adjusting entry would be made as follows:

Manufacturing Overhead—Control 13,300
    Cost of Goods Sold   13,300

The effect of this entry would be to close out the manufactured overhead—control account and to decrease the cost of goods sold for the period by the amount of the overapplied overhead.

Alternatively, if manufacturing overhead were underapplied, the following adjusting entry would be required:

Cost of Goods Sold XX
    Manufacturing Overhead—Control   XX

The effect of this entry would be to increase the cost of goods sold by the amount of the underapplied overhead and to close out the balance in the manufacturing overhead—control account.

The normal treatment of over or underapplied overhead used by the Sax Company at its year-end is to make a direct adjustment to cost of goods sold assuming that the amount is not significant. In view of this annual treatment, we will assume for purposes of illustration that management has provided for the use of a monthly worksheet closing that is equivalent to the annual closing process. In practice, this procedure may cause a distortion of income on a monthly basis, but we will assume that management uses the financial reports only for internal purposes and is aware of this potential distortion.

Sax's management has also provided for an optional treatment of over or underapplied manufacturing overhead which has theoretical appeal and which should be used when the difference between the actual manufacturing overhead and the applied manufacturing overhead is considered to be a significant amount. This optional treatment is to apportion the over or underapplied amount of overhead among the ending work-in-process inventory, finished goods inventory and cost of goods sold accounts. In the normal situation, the largest portion of the difference will usually be closed to the cost of goods sold account because of the magnitude of this amount in relation to the inventory accounts on an annual basis. This apportionment approach or procedure is illustrated as follows. The data are taken from Sax Company's general ledger accounts as of January 31. (Illustration 3–6).

	Account Balance	Percent of Total	Amount of Overapplied Overhead Apportioned
Ending Work-In-Process......................	$ 0	0%	$ 0
Ending Finished Goods Inventory..............	105,000	79	10,500
Cost of Goods Sold*........................	28,000	21	2,800
Total	$133,000	$100%	$13,300

*From this months production (i.e., $38,000 − $10,000 beginning inventory = $28.000).

The amount of the overapplied manufacturing overhead for the period was determined to be $13,300 ($70,000 applied − $56,700 actual). Since there was no ending work-in-process inventory, none of this overapplied overhead would be closed to this account. The ending finished goods inventory represents 79 percent of the total amount ($105,000 ÷ $133,000). Therefore 79 percent, or $10,500, of the overapplied overhead (.79 × $13,300) is closed to the finished goods inventory account. Cost of goods sold is 21 percent of the total ($28,000 ÷ $133,000). This 21 percent, or $2,800, of the overapplied overhead (.21 × $13,300) is closed out to the cost of goods sold account. The resulting entry which is necessary to dispose of the overapplied overhead for the period is as follows:

Manufacturing Overhead—Control..................	13,300	
Finished Goods Inventory........................		10,500
Cost of Goods Sold............................		2,800

The adjusting entry for overhead made for Sax Company for January is recorded only on the worksheet. Cost of goods sold is then adjusted to reflect the overapplied manufacturing overhead. In either case (the direct write-off to cost of goods sold or the apportionment of the over or underapplied overhead), the impact of closing the manufacturing overhead—control account is to reflect an allocation of the total actual overhead to the appropriate accounts. If the predetermined overhead rate had been totally accurate and the total actual cost had been applied to the production of the accounting period, no adjustment would have been necessary. A worksheet adjustment made on an interim basis is still necessary, however, because of seasonal fluctuations in production.

A COMPREHENSIVE EXAMPLE: THE WORKSHEET FOR FINANCIAL STATEMENT PREPARATION

Illustration 3–8 presents the worksheet used by Sax Company at the end of January. The adjusted trial balance was developed from the post-closing trial balance at December 31 (Illustration 3–5), and from the general ledger accounts (Illustration 3–6). The general ledger accounts included in Illustration 3–6 reflect the January 31 balances for all accounts that were affected by the transactions for January. If an account is not found in Illustration 3–6, it is because the January 31 ledger account balance is unchanged from the December 31 balance presented in Illustration 3–5.

The only adjusting entry required on the worksheet at the end of January, besides the closing of the manufacturing overhead-control account, is the accrual of income taxes assuming a rate of 48 percent. The calculations for this accrual are presented in Illustration 3-9. The adjusting entry is as follows:

Income Taxes..22,704
    Income Taxes Payable..22,704

COST OF GOODS MANUFACTURED STATEMENT

Sax Company maintains its inventories on a perpetual system so that a Cost of Goods Manufactured Statement can be prepared for the month of January from these records. If this were year-end, a physical inventory of work-in-process and finished goods might also be taken in order to verify and, if necessary, adjust the inventory records to reflect the cost of the goods that are actually on hand.[1]

A cost of goods manufactured statement may be regarded as an analysis of the work-in-process—control account, or, alternatively, as a summary of the job cost sheets for the accounting period. The usual format employed in the cost of goods manufactured statement is a chronological analysis of the work-in-process—control account. Illustration 3–9 presents the cost of goods manufactured statement for the Sax Company for January.

----

[1] Alternatively, physical inventories may be taken throughout the year and the accounts adjusted as considered necessary to reflect any differences detected.

Illustration 3-8

Sax Company

Worksheet

For the Month Ended January 31, 19x1

	Trial Balance Before Adjustments	Adjustments	Trial Balance After Adjustment	Income Statement	Statement of Capital	Balance Sheet
Cash	82,300		82,300			82,300
Accounts receivable	20,000		20,000			20,000
Indirect materials and factory supplies	9,000		9,000			9,000
Raw materials inventory	12,000		12,000			12,000
Work-in-process inventory	–0–		–0–			–0–
Finished goods inventory	105,000		105,000			105,000
Equipment	300,000		300,000			300,000
Accumulated depreciation—equipment *	188,000		188,000			188,000
Plant	1,082,000		1,082,000			1,082,000
Accumulated depreciation—plant *	612,000		612,000			612,000
Accounts payable	34,000		34,000			34,000
Income taxes payable	–0–	(b) 22,704	22,704			22,704
Property taxes payable *	5,000		5,000			5,000
Long-term debt	400,000		400,000			400,000
Common stock	190,000		190,000			190,000
Retained earnings 1/1	134,000		134,000		134,000	
Manufacturing Overhead	13,300	(a) 13,300	–0–	–0–		
Sales revenue	100,000		100,000	100,000		
Cost of goods sold	38,000	(a) 13,300	24,700	24,700		
Selling and administrative expenses	28,000		28,000	28,000		
Income taxes (48%)		(b) 22,704	22,704	22,704		
	1,676,300 1,676,300	36,004 36,004	1,685,704 1,685,704	75,404 100,000		1,610,300
Net income after taxes				24,596	24,596	
				100,000 100,000	158,596	
Retained earnings 1/31					–0– 158,596	158,596
					158,596 158,596	1,610,300

Key to Adjustments:
* Adjustments were made in the example directly to facilitate discussing overapplied and underapplied manufacturing overhead.
(a) To adjust cost of goods sold for overapplied manufacturing overhead.
(b) To adjust for income taxes. The before tax income was 47,300. The income tax rate used by Sax's management is forty-eight percent.

[handwritten note: "figuring until end of year" near Manufacturing Overhead / Sales revenue rows]

OTHER FINANCIAL STATEMENTS

The cost of goods sold statement, the income statement, the statement of retained earnings for January and the balance sheet as of January 31 for Sax Company are also presented in Illustration 3-9. These statements were prepared directly from the worksheet in Illustration 3-8, except as noted on the statements.

SUMMARY

Job order costing is one of two fundamental systems of cost accumulation employed by manufacturing firms. Inventory values provided by the cost accounting system of a firm are used to determine inventory valuation on the balance sheet and the cost of goods sold on the income statement. They are, therefore, instrumental in determining the financial position and the profitability of the firm. It follows, then, that the total or full cost of manufacturing the product must be used as the product cost. This "full" cost includes the total costs of the direct materials and direct labor used as well as an allocated share of manufacturing overhead including indirect costs incurred in the period.

Overhead costs are allocated using a predetermined overhead rate. This rate is determined by relating the expected or planned normal overhead costs to a planned level of activity. In this "normalizing" process, a time period is selected which is sufficiently long to avoid the effect of seasonal fluctuations in activity or cost levels. There are many activity bases that may be used to allocate costs. The basis selected should be easily measurable and should be the primary factor related to the incurrence of variable overhead. Some of the common bases used include: units of production, direct labor hours used, and machine hours used.

Under a job order costing system employing normal costs, product costs are usually accumulated in the work-in-process inventory account and transferred to the finished goods inventory account upon completion of the job. The costs are expensed and included as cost of goods sold when the products are sold. The same product cost information contained in the work-in-process inventory account is generally reflected in a specialized subsidiary ledger known as the job cost sheet. Each job will have its individual job cost sheet, and unit costs for inventory costing are often calculated directly from this sheet.

Since manufacturing overhead under a normal cost system is applied using a predetermined rate, it is necessary to accumulate actual overhead costs in a manufacturing overhead control account. Unless the actual costs incurred during a period coincide exactly with the costs used in calculating the predetermined application rate for that period (assuming the planned level of activity is achieved), then the firm will have either over or underapplied overhead at the end of the period. If the over or under-

Illustration 3-9

Sax Company
Cost of Goods Manufactured
For the Month Ended January 31, 19x1

Raw materials used:	
Beginning raw materials inventory	$40,000
Add: Purchases	–0–
Raw materials available for use	$40,000
Less: Ending raw materials inventory	12,000
Raw materials used in production	$ 28,000
Direct labor used in production	35,000
Manufacturing overhead costs applied	70,000
Total manufacturing costs	$133,000
Add: Work-in-process inventory, January 1	–0–
Less: Work-in-process inventory, January 31	–0–
Cost of goods manufactured in January	$133,000

handwritten note: — must include this adjusted once... because no W.I.P.

Sax Company
Cost of Goods Sold Statement
For the Month Ended January 31, 19x1

Beginning finished goods inventory (from Illustration 3–5)	$ 10,000
Cost of goods manufactured (from above)	133,000
Goods available for sale	$143,000
Ending finished goods inventory (from Illustration 3–6)	105,000
Cost of goods sold before over or underapplied manufacturing overhead	$ 38,000
Less: Overapplied manufacturing overhead (adjusting entry) . . .	13,300
Cost of goods sold for January	$ 24,700

handwritten note: ...once COGS... produce... statet etc.

Sax Company
Income Statement
For the Month Ended January 31, 19x1

Sales Revenues	$100,000
Less: Cost of goods sold (from cost of goods sold statement) . . .	24,700
Gross margin	$ 75,300
Less: Selling and administrative expenses	28,000
Operating income before taxes	$ 47,300
Less: Income Taxes (at 48%—adjusting entry)	22,704
Operating income after taxes	$ 24,596

Illustration 3-9 Continued:

Sax Company
Statement of Retained Earnings
For the Month Ended January 31, 19x1

Retained earnings balance, January 1	$134,000
Add: Operating income after taxes	24,596
	$158,596
Less: Dividends	–0–
Retained earnings balance, January 31	$158,596

Sax Company
Balance Sheet
January 31, 19x1

ASSETS

Current Assets:

Cash		$ 82,300
Accounts receivable		20,000
Indirect materials and factory supplies		9,000
Raw materials inventory		12,000
Work-in-process inventory		–0–
Finished goods inventory		105,000
Total Current Assets		$228,300

Long-Term Assets:

Equipment	$ 300,000	
Less: Accumulated depreciation—equipment . .	188,000	$112,000
Plant	$1,082,000	
Less: Accumulated depreciation—plant	612,000	470,000
Total Long-Term Assets		$582,000
TOTAL ASSETS		$810,300

LIABILITIES AND SHAREHOLDERS' EQUITY

Current Liabilities:

Accounts payable		$ 34,000
Income taxes payable		22,704
Property taxes payable		5,000
Total Current Liabilities		$ 61,704

Long-Term Liabilities:

Long-term Debt		400,000
Total Liabilities		$461,704

SHAREHOLDERS' EQUITY

Common stock		$190,000
Retained earnings		158,596
Total Shareholders' Equity		$348,596
TOTAL LIABILITIES AND SHAREHOLDERS' EQUITY		$810,300

application is immaterial in amount, a direct adjustment can be made to the cost of goods sold on the income statement. However, if the amount is significant, then the balance in the control account should be prorated to the cost of goods sold, finished goods, and work in process accounts.

The cost of goods manufactured statement is a specialized financial statement prepared by manufacturing firms. This statement can be regarded as an analysis of the work-in-process control account for the reporting period. It is usually presented along with the firm's regular cost of goods sold statement, income statement, statement of retained earnings, and balance sheet.

This chapter has discussed the basic elements and procedures involved in a job order cost accumulation system. The next chapter discusses process costing, which is the other fundamental system of cost accumulation employed by manufacturing firms.

KEY DEFINITIONS

Cost of goods manufactured statement—a statement which summarizes total manufacturing costs for the period. As such, the statement is regarded as an analysis of the work-in-process control account or as a summary of the job cost sheets for the accounting period.

Full cost basis—full costing of the products produced during a period includes the costs of direct materials, direct labor, and a normal share of both variable and fixed overhead incurred.

Job cost sheet—the job cost sheet serves as the subsidiary ledger account for each job. All cost applicable to the job are accumulated on the job cost sheet.

Job order costing system—under this system, costs are accumulated by individual jobs or job lots. These costs include actual costs of direct materials and direct labor and a normal or fair share of overhead costs applied to each job.

Manufacturing overhead-control account—a subsidiary ledger asset account which accumulates actual overhead costs. When overhead is applied or allocated to a job, the application of the overhead is recorded by a credit to this account.

Overapplied overhead—occurs when more overhead costs are allocated to production during a period than were actually incurred. Overapplied overhead is indicated by a credit balance in the manufacturing overhead control account at the end of the period.

Predetermined overhead rate—an overhead burden rate used to apply overhead costs to production. The predetermined overhead rate is based on the total normal overhead cost that is expected to be incurred for the time period (normally a year) in which the rate is to be used. The base selected for calculating the rate should be easily measurable and should be the factor which causes or is related to the incurrence of variable overhead.

Underapplied overhead—occurs when more overhead costs are actually incurred by the firm than were allocated to production during the period. Underapplied overhead is indicated by a debit balance in the manufacturing overhead-control account at the end of the period.

QUESTIONS

3-1 Why is inventory costing necessary?

3-2 What is a product cost? Why is full or total cost of manufacturing for product costs used in explaining income?

3-3 Define the components of product cost.

3-4 Explain the difference between fixed and variable costs of manufacturing.

3-5 Give some examples of fixed and variable manufacturing overhead costs.

3-6 What is meant by "full costing"?

3-7 What are the three inventory accounts of a manufacturing firm? What functions do they serve?

3-8 Describe the flow of product costs for a manufacturing firm.

3-9 What is meant by "normalizing" overhead?

3-10 How are application bases for overhead selected? Name three bases.

3-11 What do the control and subsidiary ledger accounts include when accounting for the inventories in manufacturing?

3-12 What is the importance of a job cost sheet?

3-13 What is the effect on net income if overhead is underapplied and the balance in the manufacturing overhead account is closed out to cost of goods sold?

3-14 How is an unallocated balance in an overhead control account at the end of an accounting period accounted for?

EXERCISES AND PROBLEMS

3-15 The work-in-process account for the Starnes Company has the following balances:

> Beginning Balance, May 1 = $24,000
> Ending Balance, May 31 = $28,000

During May, the Starnes Company added $134,000 of labor, $64,000 of material and applied $60,000 of overhead to the production process.

Required:

What is the cost of goods manufactured for May?

⊤ ✳ **3-16** The Johnson Company incurred the following costs in producing 40,000 units during April:

1. Raw materials purchased on account $50,000
2. Raw materials used $40,000
3. Direct labor $30,000
4. Indirect labor $10,000
5. Supplies purchased on account . . . . $ 3,000
6. Supplies used . . . . $ 2,400
7. Electricity purchased on account and
    consumed in production . . . . $ 3,600
    Units sold in April 32,000
8. Manufacturing overhead is applied on the basis of $.50 per unit produced.

Johnson Company has no beginning inventories in work-in-process or finished goods, and no ending inventory in work-in-process.

Required:

Set up the following "T" accounts and record the costs. Transfer the costs through the appropriate inventory accounts and into cost of goods sold.

Raw Material Inventory—
  Control
Accrued Payroll
Direct Labor
Indirect Labor
Cost of Goods Sold
Supplies Inventory

Work-In-Process Inventory—Control
Electricity
Finished Goods Inventory—Control
Accounts Payable
Supplies Used
Manufacturing Overhead—Control

3-17   The following "T" accounts are from the Martin Manufacturing Company on November 30:

Raw Materials Inventory—Control		
11/1 Bal. 150	11/30 180 (b)	
(a) 11/16 350		

Wages Payable		
11/30 300	11/30 300 (c)	

Manufacturing Overhead—Control		
(c) 11/30 15	11/30 250 (d)	
(f) 11/30 240		

Work-In-Process Inventory—Control		
11/1 Bal. 50	11/30 675 (e)	
(b) 11/30 180		
(c) 11/30 285		
(d) 11/30 250		

Finished Goods Inventory—Control		
11/1 Bal. 80	11/30 700 (g)	
(e) 11/30 675		

Required:

Prepare a cost of goods manufactured and a cost of goods sold statement for November.

3-18   The following items may be classified as either (a) direct materials, (b) direct labor, (c) factory overhead, or (d) selling and administrative expense. Place the appropriate letter in the blank before each item.

_____ 1. Depreciation on factory equipment
_____ 2. President's salary
_____ 3. Materials used in production
_____ 4. Salaries of production workers
_____ 5. Power bill for production plant
_____ 6. Sales commissions
_____ 7. Salary of factory foreman
_____ 8. Boxes used for shipping product

3-19 Schneider, Inc. has budgeted overhead for next year of $5,640,000. They have 1,880,000 budgeted annual direct labor hours. What will their overhead rate be for next year?

3-20 You are presented with the inventory ledger accounts for one year of the ABC Company. You are called upon by the president of ABC Company to help determine what the various entries in the ledger accounts pertain to.

Materials & Supplies		Work-In-Process		Finished Goods	
30,000	35,000	50,000	76,000	40,000	90,000
40,000	4,000	(1) 35,000		(4) 76,000	
31,000		(2) 40,000		26,000	
		(3) 22,000			
		71,000			

Manufacturing Overhead	
(5) 4,000	22,000
(6) 8,000	
(7) 6,000	
(8) 10,000	
6,000	

The president tells you that indirect labor during the year was 20% of direct labor and that factory supervision costs were 60% of other factory costs.

Required:

a. What do the entries (1)—(8) represent in the inventory ledger accounts?

b. What was the amount of cost of goods sold for the year?

3-21 Following are the ledger accounts of the Dull Manufacturing Company. Complete the posting of the manufacturing cost flow entries. The ending finished goods inventory is $8,500, work-in-process is $12,000, and raw materials is $4,500. The credit to factory wages payable represents direct labor costs.

Raw Materials	Work-In-Process	Finished Goods
Bal. 8,600	Bal. 15,500	Bal. 21,000
7,900		
10,000		

Factory Wages Payable	Cost of Goods Sold
23,000 Bal. 1,000	80,000
24,000	

3-22 The Fixit Company has projected manufacturing overhead costs during June of $55,200. The basis for allocations to individual jobs is direct labor hours. The company is projecting 24,000 direct labor hours for June.

Required:

a. Compute the overhead application rate per direct labor hour for June.

b. 1,000 direct labor hours were used on Job #53, how much of the manufacturing cost should be allocated to this job?

c. Fixit Company has decided to change its allocation base from direct labor hours to direct labor costs. If the hourly wage rate is $1.50, how much manufacturing overhead should be applied to Job #53?

3-23 A job order cost system is used by the Poland Company. The company has no beginning or ending inventory in work-in-process or finished goods, and manufacturing overhead is applied at $4.50 per direct labor hour. Actual results for this year are:

Indirect labor	$ 120,000
Direct labor cost	600,000
Direct labor hours used	225,000
Raw materials used	300,000
Electricity used in factory	210,000
Indirect supplies used	37,500
Miscellaneous overhead	240,000
Cost of goods sold	$1,230,000

Required:

a. How much manufacturing overhead was applied to production during the year?

b. How much manufacturing overhead was actually incurred during the year?

c. Was manufacturing overhead under or overapplied during the year and by how much?

3-24 Below are the balances in selected accounts of the Mustang Company:

Direct labour used in production............................	$ 38,000
Finished goods inventory, January 1, 19x6.....................	10,200
Finished goods inventory, December 31, 19x6..................	3,200
Manufacturing overhead used in production...................	41,000
Raw materials inventory, January 1, 19x6.....................	2,000
Raw materials inventory, December 31, 19x6..................	4,000
Raw materials purchased.................................	23,000
Sales...	200,000
Selling expenses..	60,000
Work-in-process inventory, January 1, 19x6..................	4,800
Work-in-process inventory, December 31, 19x6................	8,800

Required:

Prepare: (*a*) a statement of cost of goods manufactured; and, (*b*) an income statement.

3-25 The Lowell Company uses an apportionment approach in allocating over or underapplied overhead among the ending work-in-process inventory, finished goods inventory, and cost of goods sold accounts. Below are the balances in selected accounts for the year.

Beginning work-in-process	$ 10,600
Ending work-in-process	10,654
Beginning finished goods inventory	195,000
Ending finished goods inventory	245,042
Cost of goods sold	809,704
Manufacturing overhead applied	345,000
Actual manufacturing overhead	467,000

Required:

a. What over or underapplied overhead was incurred for the year?
b. Journalize the allocation of the over or underapplied overhead among the appropriate accounts.

3-26 The following data pertain to the operations of the Misteak Corporation. You are required to prepare the necessary journal entries.

1. $30,000 of raw materials were placed into production.
2. $1,600 of supplies were used; $1,100 for production and $500 for general purposes.
3. Depreciation for the month was $20,000 of which 70 percent was for production and 30 percent was on equipment used by the marketing department for selling goods to customers.

3-27 During its first month of operation, the Phoenix Company had the following transactions:

1. Purchased raw materials for $20,000.
2. $15,000 of raw materials were transferred to production.
3. Direct labor costs totaling $10,000 were paid in cash and total manufacturing overhead costs incurred and applied to work-in-process was $5,000.

4.   Total cost of goods completed was $25,000.

5.   Total cost of the goods sold was $17,000.

Required:

a.   Make journal entries for the above transactions.

b.   Determine the cost of the work-in-process inventory at the end of the month and the cost of the finished goods inventory at the end of the month.

3-28   The following information is available from the records of the Park Manufacturing Company for the month of December:

Work-in-process, December 31	$ 2,000
Raw materials, December 1	1,000
Labor	5,000
Purchases of raw material	10,000
Manufacturing overhead applied and actual . . .	2,000
Raw materials, December 31	2,000
Work-in-process, December 1	1,000

Required:

Determine the cost of goods manufactured for December.

3-29   Determine the cost of goods sold during the period from the following information.

Raw materials, January 1, 19x6.	$ 40,000
Raw materials, December 31, 19x6.	43,000
Finished goods, January 1, 19x6.	128,000
Finished goods, December 31, 19x6.	105,000
Direct labour.	48,500
Purchases of raw material.	75,000
Work-in-process, January 1, 19x6.	87,000
Work-in-process, December 31, 19x6.	69,000
Manufacturing overhead applied and actual.	72,500

3-30   The Vice President of Park Manufacturing Corporation has given you the following information:

1.	Sales	$130,000
2.	Raw materials, Jan. 1	12,000
3.	Raw materials, Dec. 31	20,000
4.	Work-in-process, Jan. 1	18,000
5.	Work-in-process, Dec. 31	14,000
6.	Finished goods, Jan. 1	20,000
7.	Finished goods, Dec. 31	28,000
8.	Raw materials purchased	30,000
9.	Direct labor	32,000
10.	Manufacturing overhead applied and actual . .	26,000
11.	Administrative expenses	16,000
12.	Selling expenses	24,000

Required:

You have been asked to obtain the answers to the following questions for the December Board meeting.
What is:

a.   the cost of raw materials available?
b.   the cost of raw materials used?
c.   the cost of goods manufactured during the year?
d.   the cost of goods sold during the year?
e.   the net profit on sales?

3-31   From the information below, prepare (a) a cost of goods manufactured statement, and (b) an income statement.

Drippy Pipe Company
Before Closing Trial Balance
December 31, 19x6

Assets	$1,800	
Inventory—raw materials (Beginning)	100	
Inventory—Work-in-process (Beginning)	300	
Inventory—Finished goods (Beginning)	500	
Liabilities		$ 100
Capital stock		600
Retained earnings		550
Sales		3,000
Expenses	550	
Raw materials purchases	1,000	
	$4,250	$4,250

December 31, 19x6
Ending inventories:
    Raw materials—$200
    Work-in-process—$400
    Finished goods—$600
Direct labour costs for 19x6 was $800.
Manufacturing overhead actual and applied for 19x6 was $400.

3-32   You are given information concerning the production cost accounts of Which Company for 19x6.

Raw materials purchased.	$ 75,000
Direct factory labour.	35,000
Factory overhead applied.	28,000
Raw materials inventory, December 31, 19x6.	5,500
Cost of goods sold.	143,000
Finished goods inventory, January 1, 19x6.	21,000
Finished goods inventory, December 31, 19x6.	19,600
Work-in-process, January 1, 19x6.	10,000
Work-in-process, December 31, 19x6.	11,500

(Hint: Construct a cost of goods sold statement before attempting to answer the questions. Assume that there is not any over or under applied overhead.)

Required:

Compute the following:

a. The maximum amount of finished goods that could have been sold during 19x6.
b. The amount of goods manufactured during 19x6.
c. The total production costs incurred in 19x6.
d. Raw materials used during 19x6.
e. Raw materials inventory on 1/1/x6.

A 3-33 The Do-Little Company manufactures scratch pads using a job order cost system. It assigns actual factory overhead to individual jobs at the end of each month in proportion to the direct machine hours required of each job during the month.

The August 1 inventories consist of the following:

Materials and supplies inventory $3,400
Work-in-process inventory (Job #203)   200
Finished goods inventory (Job #202) 4,500

Given below is information pertaining to the jobs worked on in August.

Job #	Materials Issued from Inventory	Labor	Machine Time (hrs.)
203	$ 200	$ 300	50
204	1,100	1,450	500
205	980	1,200	450
	$2,280	$2,950	1,000

Other costs incurred during the month were:

Factory maintenance salaries $1,200
Factory heat, light and power expense 2,300
Factory supplies   850
Depreciation of factory equipment   900
                                                    $5,250

Job #202 was shipped to the customer. He was billed $5,260.
Job #203 and #204 were completed on August 28 and transferred to finished goods.

Required:

Fill in the following:

a. The gross margin on Job #202 was $_____.
b. The work-in-process inventory as of August 31 was $_____.
c. The finished goods inventory as of August 31 was $_____.

3-34 Sneed, Inc., a construction company, uses a job order cost accounting system. The company's transactions for the month of July were as follows:

July 2 Company purchased materials for cash with an invoice cost of $2,000.
  5 Materials were issued to individual jobs as follows:
  #10–$800; #11–$600; #12–$200; #13–$150
  9 An analysis of the payroll indicated that direct labor charged to the jobs was as follows:
  #10–$200; #11–$300; #12–$100; #13–$50
  10 The overhead incurred during the month was $500.
  15 The application of overhead was made using the same rate as in June. The application rate is based on direct labor cost.
  25 Jobs #10 and #11 were completed and transferred to finished goods.
  30 Job #10 was sold for cash at a price which included a profit of 10%.

Additional data:

The June 30 inventory balances were as follows:

Finished goods	$1,600
Materials	840
Materials work-in-process	1,100
Labor work-in-process	400
Overhead work-in-process	240

Subsidiary records for work-in-process were as follows:

	Job #10	Job #11
Materials	$600	$500
Labor	280	120
Overhead	168	72

Required:

Prepare all the general journal entries for the month of July to record the above transactions.

3-35 The factory of the Loser Company was completely destroyed by a tornado on December 31, 19x5. You have been asked to assist in reconstructing the accounting records in order to prepare an insurance claim for the inventories lost. With the help of the company's bookkeeper, you were able to obtain the following information for the period December 1 to December 31.

Sales	$180,000
Purchases of materials	30,000
Direct labor	36,000
Indirect labor	10,000
Other overhead costs	20,000
Cost of goods manufactured	90,000

The inventory balances at November 30, 19x5 were as follows:

Raw materials	$ 20,000
Work-in-process	30,000
Finished goods	40,000

The overhead rate used during December was $2.00 per dollar of direct materials used. The amount of underabsorbed overhead which was in the overhead control account at the date of the tornado was $2,000. Cost of goods sold was two-thirds of sales (before any adjustment for under or overabsorbed overhead was made).

Required:

Compute the cost of the raw materials, work-in-process and finished goods destroyed in the tornado.

3-36   The following income summary "T" account was given to you by the bookkeeper of Backwards, Inc. for May.

Income Summary

Raw materials purchases	$15,000	Sales	$51,000
Direct labor	15,000	Gain on the sale of land	4,000
Manufacturing overhead	10,000	Closing inventories:	
Selling expenses	25,000	Raw materials (at cost)	3,000
Loss on fire	1,000	Work-in-process (at	
Opening inventories:		cost)	5,000
Raw materials (at cost)	4,000	Finished goods (at	
Work-in-process (at		selling price)	27,000
cost)	4,000	Net loss to balance for	
Finished goods (at		the year	2,000
selling price)	18,000		
	$92,000		$92,000

Required:

a.   Prepare a statement of cost of goods manufactured (in *proper* form).
b.   Prepare an income statement (in *proper* form).

Hint: Use the ratio of cost of goods manufactured at cost and at sales price in your calculations to arrive at the cost of goods sold.

3-37   The Sorry Manufacturing Company manufactures a single commodity. A summary of its activities for the year is:

```
Sales . . . . . . . . . . . . . . . . . . . . . . . $245,000
Raw materials inventory 1/1 . . . . . . . . . .    24,500
Work-in-process inventory 1/1 . . . . . . . . .    23,200
Finished goods inventory 1/1 . . . . . . . . . .   38,000
Raw materials inventory 12/31 . . . . . . . . .    17,500
Work-in-process inventory 12/31 . . . . . . . .    31,000
Finished goods inventory 12/31 . . . . . . . . .   35,400
Raw materials purchases . . . . . . . . . . . .    75,000
Direct labor . . . . . . . . . . . . . . . . . . .  62,000
Manufacturing overhead actual and applied . .      48,000
Selling, general and administrative expenses . .   65,000
```

Required:

a. Prepare a cost of goods manufactured statement for the year.
b. Prepare an income statement for the year.

3-38   The inventory accounts of the King Company at July 1 are as follows:

```
Raw materials inventory-control . . . . . . . . $40,000
Work-in-process inventory-control . . . . . . .  30,000
Finished goods inventory-control . . . . . . . .  25,000
```

The following transactions occurred during July:

1. Raw materials were purchased on account in the amount of $20,000.
2. Raw materials issued to production amounted to $30,000.
3. Indirect materials amounting to $3,000 were issued.
4. Wages amounting to $35,000 were paid. They were distributed as follows:

```
Direct  labor . . . . . . . . . $25,000
Indirect labor . . . . . . . . .   5,000
Selling . . . . . . . . . . . . .  3,000
Administrative . . . . . . . . .   2,000
```

5. Manufacturing overhead is applied to production at 35% of direct labor cost.
6. Units completed and transferred to the warehouse cost $75,000.
7. Sales amounted to $100,000 and the units sold cost $70,000.

Required:

a. Prepare journal entries for the above.
b. Prepare all closing entries.

3-39   For 19x6, the Luker Manufacturing Company expected to produce 95,000 units. They also expected to incur $114,000 in overhead costs. Actual production was 95,000 units. During the year they had the following expenses which were related to manufacturing overhead:

Indirect materials $20,000
Indirect labor 25,000
Depreciation—plant 12,500
Depreciation—equipment 9,000
Property taxes 5,500
Electricity 27,000
Heating 18,000

Required:

a. Compute the predetermined overhead rate.
b. Prepare journal entries for manufacturing overhead.
c. Close any under or overapplied manufacturing overhead to cost of goods sold.

3-40   Below is the post-closing trial balance for the Micro Company for the month ended July 31.

	Debits	Credits
Cash	$ 142,000	
Accounts receivable	11,000	
Raw materials inventory	8,000	
Work-in-process inventory	2,000	
Finished goods inventory	87,000	
Plant and equipment	1,000,000	
Accumulated depreciation		400,000
Accounts payable		17,000
Notes payable		10,000
Long-term debt		215,000
Common stock		225,000
Retained earnings		383,000
	$1,250,000	$1,250,000

The following transactions occurred during the month of August:

1. Raw materials of $17,000 were purchased for cash, and $13,000 of raw materials were purchased on account.
2. Raw materials costing $28,000 were issued to production.
3. Indirect materials worth $12,000 were purchased on account.
4. Direct labor of $90,000 and indirect labor of $19,000 were paid in cash.
5. Electricity bill was received but not paid. It totaled $1,500.
6. Indirect materials worth $10,500 were issued to production.
7. Depreciation amounts to 1 percent of the cost of plant and equipment per month.
8. The bill for heating was received but not paid and amounted to $3,400.
9. Manufacturing overhead is applied to production at a rate of 50 percent of direct labor cost.

10. Units completed and transferred to finished goods totaled $125,000.

11. Sales were $255,000 on account. The units sold cost $146,000. Fifty percent of this month's sales and 90 percent of accounts receivable as of July 31 were collected in August.

12. Selling and administrative expenses of $25,000 were paid in cash.

13. Income taxes amounting to $42,000 were accrued.

Required:

a. Journalize each of the above transactions.

b. Post the beginning balances and journal entries to "T"-accounts.

c. Prepare a worksheet like that in Illustration 3-8 for the month ended August 31.

3-41 The Aye-Bea-Sea Corporation manufactures large wooden whales using a job order costing system. Job order number 2,468 is summarized below:

> Raw materials $4,960
> Labor 6,740
> Overhead . . . .   ?

Assuming that overhead is 50 percent of labor costs and that the job is now totally complete, show in ledger account format the effect of job order number 2,468 on the raw materials inventory, the work-in-process inventory, the manufacturing overhead control, and the finished goods inventory account.

3-42 On January 1 the records of the Jones Manufacturing Company showed the following balances:

> Cash $65,000
> Raw materials inventory   5,000
> Work-in-process inventory   3,000
> Finished goods inventory 10,000

During the year the following transactions occurred:

1. Raw materials were purchased for $20,000 cash.

2. A total of $22,000 of raw materials was transferred to work-in-process.

3. A total of $30,000 direct labor costs was incurred during the year of which $25,000 was paid in cash by the end of the year.

4. Total manufacturing overhead costs incurred and applied to work-in-process were $10,000.

5. Cost of goods manufactured was $60,000.

6. Total costs of goods sold was $55,000.

Required:

Prepare journal entries for the above transactions and set up "T" accounts for each account.

3-43 Balances of selected accounts of the Baker Toy Company for the year ended December 31, 19x6 are given below:

Factory supervision..	$12,000
Depreciation on production equipment........................	5,000
Direct labour...	55,000
Heat, light and power.....................................	12,000
Finished goods, January 1, 19x6...........................	25,000
Finished goods, December 31, 19x6.........................	21,500
Raw materials, January 1, 19x6............................	8,500
Raw materials, December 31, 19x6..........................	5,500
Purchases of raw materials................................	27,000
Work-in-process, January 1, 19x6..........................	14,000
Work-in-process, December 31, 19x6........................	11,000
Other manufacturing overhead expenses.....................	30,000

Required:

Using the information given above, calculate:

a. Cost of goods manufactured
b. Cost of goods sold

3-44 Determine and fill in the missing amounts:

Raw materials, January 1.....................	$ 4,000
Raw materials, December 31..................	*(a)*
Raw materials used..........................	29,000
Raw materials available for use..............	34,000
Raw materials purchased.....................	*(b)*
Manufacturing overhead......................	80,000
Direct labor used...........................	*(c)*
Total manufacturing costs....................	159,000
Cost of goods manufactured..................	154,000
Work-in-process, January 1..................	*(d)*
Work-in-process, December 31................	10,000
Cost of goods sold..........................	151,000
Finished goods, December 31.................	6,000
Finished goods, January 1...................	*(e)*

3-45 During August the Bryan Furniture Company recorded the following transactions:

1. Lumber was purchased for $5,000.
2. Lumber costing $4,000 was transferred from raw materials to other accounts. Of this transferred lumber, 80 percent was used to make the furniture while the remaining 20 percent of the lumber was used to make some signs for sales advertising.
3. 90 percent of the furniture in work-in-process was completed during August and was transferred to finished goods.
4. 75 percent of the completed furniture in finished goods was sold in August.

5. Assume that all inventory balances were zero at the beginning of the month.

Required:

Using the information given above, give the balances at August 31 for the following accounts:

a. Raw materials
b. Work-in-process
c. Finished goods
d. Cost of goods sold
e. Selling expenses

3-46   Use the following information to answer the questions below:

Finished goods on hand, January 1, 19x0	$ 16,500
Work-in-process, January 1, 19x0	9,250
Total production costs during the year	85,000
Cost of production completed during the year	88,300
Cost of goods sold during the year	85,900
Sales	170,000
Selling expenses	30,700
General expenses	13,400
Retained earnings, January 1, 19x0	42,000
Dividends	19,000
Allowance for uncollectible accounts	2,550

Required:

Determine the:

a. Work-in-process on hand, December 31, 19x0.
b. Finished goods on hand, December 31, 19x0.
c. Gross margin on sales.
d. Net operating income.
e. Retained earnings, December 31, 19x0.

3-47   The beginning and ending inventories of Stapleton, Inc. for 19x1 are:

Inventories	1/1/x1	12/31/x1
Raw materials	$38,600	$36,500
Work-in-process	9,800	10,600
Finished goods	18,000	23,400

The cost of goods sold for 19x1 is $216,300. Direct labour for the year is $83,200 and factory overhead costs are $60,700.

Required:

Compute the following:

a. Cost of goods manufactured
b. Total manufacturing costs incurred this period
c. Cost of raw materials used this period
d. Cost of raw materials purchased this period

T ✗ 3-48 The Swifty Manufacturing Company manufactures office machines to consumer's specifications using a job order cost system.

On August 31, 19x0, their raw materials inventory was $27,600; work-in-process inventory was $7,300; and finished goods inventory for Job #1284 was $10,500. The work-in-process inventory consisted of Job #1285 which had the following accumulated costs:

Direct materials	$3,400
Direct labor	2,700
Manufacturing overhead	1,200
Total	$7,300

During the month of September, Jobs # 1286, 1287, and 1288 were begun. Direct materials used during September were:

Job #1285–$500; Job #1286–$4,250; Job #1287–$2,600; Job #1288–$5,700

Direct labor costs during September were:

Job #1285–$300; Job #1286–$3,200; Job #1287–$1,800; Job #1288–$3,500

Manufacturing overhead costs for September totaled $4,300; these were applied in proportion to the direct labor dollars used on each job. Jobs # 1285, 1286, and 1287 were completed and transferred to finished goods inventory. Jobs # 1284, 1285, and 1286 were shipped to the customers who were billed $11,200, $9,150, and $10,870, respectively.

Required:

a. Cost of Job #1285 $_____; #1286 $_____; #1287 $_____; and #1288 $_____.
b. Cost of goods sold, in September $_____.
c. Work-in-process inventory on September 30 $_____.
d. Gross margin on Job #1284 $_____; #1285 $_____; and #1286 $_____.

A 3-49 During the year the Summo Company produced 87,520 units and incurred the following costs:

Indirect materials	$ 14,100
Direct materials	98,600
Property taxes on plant	6,300
Plant depreciation	36,000
Selling expense	18,600
Indirect labor	34,000
Electricity for plant	22,350

Office equipment depreciation	. . . .	5,200
Manufacturing equipment depreciation	. . . . .	28,000
President's salary	. . . .	80,000
Direct labor	. . . .	275,000
Heating for plant	. . . .	16,500

The company had predicted an overhead cost of $153,000 and the production of 90,000 units.

Required:

a. Compute the predetermined overhead rate.
b. Prepare the journal entries for manufacturing overhead.
c. Determine the amount of any under or overapplied manufacturing overhead and close it out to cost of goods sold.

A   **3-50**   On January 1, 19x6 the Shipper Skateboard Manufacturing Company was formed to produce and sell skateboards. During 19x6 the following transactions occurred:

1. The company issued capital stock for $550,000.
2. Raw materials were purchased on account for $75,000.
3. A total of $45,000 in raw materials was transferred to work-in-process during the year.
4. The company incurred $80,000 in direct labor costs and $25,000 in indirect labor costs. Only $100,000 of this amount was paid by the end of the year.
5. Supplies were purchased for $5,000 in cash. Of this amount, $2,000 was used in production during the year and $1,000 was used for general purposes.
6. Total depreciation expense on plant and equipment was $20,000. Of this amount, 75 percent was applicable to factory buildings and equipment. The other 25 percent was applicable to non-production plant and equipment.
7. All actual manufacturing overhead costs incurred were applied to work-in-process.
8. The cost of units completed and transferred to finished goods inventory was $90,000.
9. All sales for the period were made in cash. Sales for 19x6 totaled $200,000. The cost of the units sold was $80,000.

Required:

a. Prepare journal entries for each of the above transactions.
b. Calculate the ending balances in raw materials, work-in-process and finished goods inventory accounts.

T ⋇ **3-51**   The following T-accounts are shown for the Acme Bubble Gum Company during the month of January, 19x6.

Cash	
1/1/x6 100,000	25,000 (b)
(j) 38,000	1,500 (d)
	30,000 (e)

Raw Materials	
1/1/x6 20,000	20,000 (c)
(a) 50,000	

Supplies	
1/1/x6 1,800	1,000 (f)
(d) 1,500	

Manufacturing Overhead	
(f) 800	3,400 (h)
(g) 4,500	

Supplies Expense	
(f) 200	

Accounts Payable	
(e) 30,000	25,000 1/1/x6
	50,000 (a)

Work-in-Process	
1/1/x6 69,000	
(b) 30,000	34,000 (i)
(c) 20,000	
(h) 3,400	

Accumulated Depreciation	
	22,500 1/1/x6
	7,500 (g)

Sales	
	38,000 (j)

Finished Goods	
1/1/x6 52,000	19,000 (j)
(i) 34,000	

Depreciation Expense	
(g) 3,000	

Cost of Goods Sold	
(j) 19,000	

Wages Payable	
	5,000 (b) 1/1/x6

Required:

Prepare brief explanations for each of the above transactions (*a*) through (*j*) which occurred during January.

Chapter 4

**LEARNING
OBJECTIVES**

Chapter 4 discusses process cost accounting and illustrates the use of a process costing system for accumulating costs. Studying this chapter should enable you to:

1. Discuss a process costing system and give examples of situations in which its use may be desirable.
2. Describe the format and purpose of the production cost report.
3. Explain and illustrate the concept of equivalent units and calculate equivalent units of production.
4. Derive unit costs in given situations.
5. Calculate inventory costs under both the weighted average and the first-in, first-out methods of inventory valuation.

Cost Accounting for Inventories: Process Costing

A PROCESS costing system is normally used for the accumulation of costs in those manufacturing situations characterized by the continuous production of a uniform product. Typical examples of industries where a process costing system may be appropriately used include petroleum refining, chemical manufacturing, paint manufacturing, flour milling and cement manufacturing.

Recall from Chapter 3 that in a job order costing system, manufacturing costs are accumulated by individual jobs or job lots. In a process cost accounting system, costs are accumulated by process rather than by individual job or job lots. At the conclusion of each reporting period, usually a month, a *production cost report* is prepared for each manufacturing department or process. The total output or production for the period is determined, and the costs of the direct materials and direct labor used as well as the overhead applied are accumulated and summarized. The unit cost of the production for the period is then calculated by dividing the total manufacturing costs (direct materials, direct labor and overhead applied) for the period by the number of units produced during that period.

At this point, it should be noted that a job order costing system could also be used under process costing conditions. In practice, however, the expense of maintaining a job order cost system under such circumstances would probably be prohibitive since job order costing requires numerous supporting source documents and extensive detail. These sources and details are normally considered unnecessary in a typical process costing situation. For example, accumulating costs by individual jobs or job lots requires maintaining detailed records of the direct labor applicable to each job; therefore, employee time tickets for each job are necessary. Also, materials must be requisitioned for a specific job and accounted for accordingly.

In a process cost system, however, direct labor cost is simply accumulated and assigned to the work in that particular process or department. Therefore, daily timecards for payroll are usually considered to be sufficient documentation for use in establishing and accumulating the cost of the direct labor incurred in that process. Since the production process is both continual and repetitive in a process costing situation, raw materials flow into the process continuously. Thus, the need for multiple purpose requisitions for materials, such as those required for job order costing, is substantially reduced. The resultant input-output relationships of raw materials to the finished product can usually be fairly well defined and documented in a process costing situation. A degree of control over materials is also available because of the well defined input-output production relationships.

All of these economies are directly related to the nature of the production process. Job order cost systems are established to account for the production of a number of different products with varying inputs of raw materials, direct labor, and overhead. Process costing is used in those circumstances where a limited number of products are produced in large volume by continuous production runs.

THE PRODUCTION COST REPORT

The production cost report serves as the basic document for inventory cost accumulation in a process costing system. A production cost report may be prepared and presented in the same general format as the Cost of Goods Manufactured Statement. The beginning work-in-process inventory plus the additions (materials, labor and overhead) made to work-in-process during the period, less the ending balance in the work-in-process inventory—is the cost of goods manufactured for the period. This relationship or flow is valid for the accountant working with either dollar amounts of cost or units of production. For purposes of process costing, this relationship must be defined in terms of units in order to derive the number of units which were produced during the period. The number of units produced is then divided into the total manufacturing costs for that period to arrive at a cost-per-unit figure. Of course, if there is neither a beginning nor an ending work-in-process inventory, the procedure is greatly simplified. All of the units started during the period would also have been completed. No partially completed units would exist to com-

See p. 113

plicate the computation of number of units produced during the period.

In actual practice, however, the problem of accounting for beginning and ending work-in-process inventories exists in most, if not all, manufacturing situations. In order to deal with this problem, the accountant must calculate the production for the period in terms of the number of *equivalent units* produced. Thus, the work which is done on both the beginning and the ending work-in-process inventories must be considered in order to determine the total production for the period.

EQUIVALENT UNITS OF PRODUCTION

Equivalent units of production are measured in terms of the number of whole or completed units of product that could have been produced at the expended cost if every unit worked on had been started and worked on until it was completed. The assumption is made that the effort and cost required to complete one unit, for example, is *equivalent* to that which is necessary to have three units which are each one-third complete, hence the term equivalent units. For example, assume that the Regan Manufacturing Company began its January, 19x1 operations with no work-in-process inventory. During January it started and completed a total of 100 units and had an ending work-in-process inventory of 10 units at January 31. The ending work-in-process inventory was fully complete as to materials (all materials are added at the beginning of the process) but only 60 percent complete as to labor and overhead. The equivalent production for the month of January would be calculated as follows:

	Total	Materials	Labor and Overhead
Units Completed............	100	100	100
Add: Ending Work-in-Process..	10	10 (10 × 100%)	6 (10 × 60%)
Total Equivalent Units........	110	110	106

Note that the equivalent units of the ending work-in-process inventory were added to the units which were started and completed (which were, of course, 100 percent completed as to materials, labor and overhead since these units were finished) in order to determine the total equivalent units for the month. Note also that the number of equivalent units for materials (110) differs from that for labor and overhead (106). This is not at all unusual and is to be expected. In our example, all material is added at the time a unit is put into production, so all units will be 100 percent complete as to materials. On the other hand, it is to be expected that units will be at various stages of completion as to labor and overhead. At the end of each period, estimates will be made as to the completion status of the inventories on hand and still in process, and these estimates will be used to determine the equivalent units of production in the ending work-in-process inventories.

To continue our example, assume that Regan Manufacturing completed a total of 200 units during the month of February. Its ending work-in-process inventory at the end of February consisted of 20 units which were 100 percent complete as to materials and 40 percent complete as to labor and overhead. The equivalent production for the month of February would be calculated as follows:

	Total	Materials		Labor and Overhead	
Units Completed.............	200	200		200	
Add: Ending Work-in-Process..	20	20	(20 × 100%)	8	(20 × 40%)
Total Equivalent Units........	220	220		208	

Again, note that the number of units completed were combined with the equivalent units of the ending work-in-process inventory in order to determine the total equivalent units of production for the month. Note also that the equivalent units included in the beginning work-in-process inventory (which is, of course, the ending work-in-process inventory for January) was ignored in this computation. This is because we used the *weighted average* technique for calculating equivalent units; beginning equivalent units are not used with this method.

An alternative to the use of the weighted average method is the first-in, first-out (FIFO) method. We will now illustrate the calculation of equivalent units under the FIFO technique using the data for the Regan Manufacturing Company for February.[1]

	Total	Materials		Labor and Overhead	
Units Completed.................	200	200		200	
Less: Beginning Work-in-Process....	10	10	(10 × 100%)	6	(10 × 60%)
Units Started and Completed........	190	190		194	
Add: Ending Work-in-Process......	20	20	(20 × 100%)	8	(20 × 40%)
Total Equivalent Units.............	210	210		202	

Using the FIFO method, we start with the units completed, deduct the equivalent units included in the beginning work-in-process inventory to obtain the number of units which were started and completed. We then add the equivalent units included in the ending work-in-process inventory to the units started and completed to obtain the total equivalent production for the period, in this case the month of February.

The purpose of calculating equivalent units of production is to measure in terms of the number of completed units of product the number of units that

---

[1] Since there was no beginning work-in-process inventory at January 1, the total equivalent units for January will be the same for the weighted average and FIFO methods.

could have been produced during a period if every unit started had been worked on until it was fully completed. Again, the assumption that we make is that the effort and cost required to fully complete one unit is the same as that required to have five units which are each 20 percent complete, ten units which are each 10 percent complete, etc. Equivalent unit calculations are used for such purposes as evaluating production activities and determining costs of production.

In order to further illustrate the calculation of equivalent units and the determination of production costs, we will assume that the Jackson Company completed a total of 500 units during a period and had 100 units in its ending work-in-process inventory. We will also assume that there was no work-in-process inventory at the beginning of the period, and that sufficient materials had been applied those units included in the ending work-in-process inventory to manufacture exactly 100 complete units of a product (in other words all units were fully complete as to materials). Also assume that if the labor and overhead which was applied to all 100 units included in the ending work-in-process inventory had been used to fully complete units at the normal cost for the period, 40 complete units could have been produced. Given these two assumptions, we can now calculate the number of equivalent units and the production cost per unit for this period.

To calculate these unit costs, we must first determine the equivalent number of units of production which were included in the ending work-in-process inventory. The number of equivalent units in the ending work-in-process inventory is then added to the number of fully-completed units of production for the period to arrive at the total production for the period stated in terms of equivalent whole units of production.

Therefore, in the example cited above, the equivalent units that would be used for the ending work-in-process inventory cost calculation for inventory valuation are 100 units for raw materials, 40 units for direct labor and 40 units for manufacturing overhead calculated as follows:

Manufacturing Cost Component	Number of Units That Could Be Completed	×	Percent of Completion in Terms of Cost Incurred at the End of the Period	=	Number of Equivalent Units
Raw Materials................	100	×	100%	=	100 Units
Direct Labor.................	100	×	40	=	40
Manufacturing Overhead......	100	×	40	=	40

Remember, there are a total of 100 units in the ending work-in-process that could have been completed. To date, however, these units are fully complete only as far as materials are concerned. In terms of direct labor and manufacturing overhead, the 100 units are only 40% complete.

To illustrate the complete calculation of both the equivalent units of production and the cost per unit produced during the period, assume that the following costs were incurred during the current accounting period.

Cost Calculation

Total Direct Material Costs . . . . $ 6,000
Total Direct Labor Costs   4,320
Manufacturing Overhead Applied   2,160
    Total Costs of Production $12,480

Data regarding the units produced are as follows:

Unit Calculation	*Equivalent Units*
Beginning Work-In-Process	–0–
Units Completed During the Period	500
Ending Work-In-Process:	
Direct Material 100 Units, 100% Complete	100
Direct Labor 100 Units, 40% Complete	40
Manufacturing Overhead 100 Units, 40% Complete	40

The calculation of cost per unit is presented below:

Per Unit Cost Calculation

(a) Costs	Direct Materials	Direct Labour	Manufacturing Overhead	Total Costs
Totals.	$6,000	$4,320	$2,160	$12,480
Equivalent units calculations				
Finished units.	500	500	500	
Add: Equivalent units included				
Ending work-in-process (100 units)				
Direct material (100% complete).	100			
Direct labour (40% complete).		40		
Manufacturing				
overhead (40% complete).			40	
b) Equivalent units.	600	540	540	
Unit cost a/b.	$10.00 +	$8.00 +	$4.00	= $22.00

Cost of Goods Completed (500 Units @ $22) $11,000
Cost of Ending Work-In-Process:
    Raw Materials (100 Units @ $10) $1,000
    Direct Labor (40 Units @ $8)   320
    Manufacturing Overhead (40 Units @ $4)   160   1,480
Total Cost Accounted For $12,480

The calculations which are made under a process costing system to compute the number of equivalent units included in the work-in-process inventory are usually not complex. Remember, the intent is to arrive at a unit cost for the production of an equivalent number of fully completed units.

In many firms, manufacturing overhead is applied using some predetermined base, such as direct labor hours or direct labor cost. In this situation, the costs associated with direct labor and manufacturing overhead are usually combined and referred to as *conversion costs.* Under these circumstances, the equivalent units for both direct labor and manufacturing overhead are identical.

A COMPREHENSIVE EXAMPLE: PROCESS COSTING

The production cost report serves as the basic document which is used in a process costing system for developing the inventory cost per equivalent unit. Several factors must be known in order to develop the cost per equivalent unit: (1) the cost and the number of equivalent units associated with the beginning work-in-process inventory; (2) the total manufacturing costs incurred during the period; (3) the number of equivalent units of product associated with the ending work-in-process inventory; and (4) the number of units which were produced during the period. The beginning equivalent units do not need to be calculated when using the weighted average technique because both the costs and units are averaged with the current period's units and costs. The formats which may be used for accumulating costs and calculating equivalent units are developed and presented in the example in the following paragraphs.

Beginning Work-in-Process Inventories

By definition, the beginning inventories of work-in-process under a process costing system consist of only partially completed units. The number of equivalent units and the related costs are identified at the end of the prior accounting period. It is, of course, possible that these costs may vary from one accounting period to the next.

Any inventory valuation method can be applied to the flow of costs under a process costing system. This chapter illustrates two basic methods: the weighted average method and the first-in, first-out (Fifo) method.[2]

More Than One Processing Department

If more than a single department is involved in the processing of products, those departments that work on products transferred from other de-

---

[2] The Fifo method is illustrated assuming a clearly identifiable Fifo flow. In practice, the typical use of the Fifo method would include an averaging of the cost of goods transferred into a processing department. Cost of goods transferred out of a processing department would be on a Fifo basis.

partments must account for an additional input factor; that is, the costs accumulated in and transferred from a prior department or departments.

The initial department (i.e., the one that begins the manufacturing process) accounts for its inputs of raw materials, direct labor, and manufacturing overhead. Subsequent departments may also use additional raw materials, direct labor, and manufacturing overhead as they process the product further. However, all departments other than the one beginning the manufacturing process must consider an additional cost factor—the cost of the inventory which was transferred in from the preceding department. The flow of manufacturing costs is such that the last department that works on the product transfers the *total* cost of the completed products to the finished goods inventory. The cost transferred to the finished goods inventory, then, includes the total cost of the direct materials, direct labor, and manufacturing overhead incurred by all departments in the plant, less any costs associated with the ending work-in-process, plus any costs carried forward from the prior period in the beginning work-in-process. This flow of total costs is the same as was the case in job order systems.

COMPREHENSIVE EXAMPLE: THE BASIC DATA

The Yuke Chemical Division of Sax Company produces a number of chemicals which require similar general processing techniques. One of these chemicals is Floo. Floo is relatively simple to manufacture and store and, therefore, it is produced whenever it is expedient to do so in order to take up any slack in production. Floo is normally manufactured in production runs varying from 1,000 to 20,000 litres, depending on the storage space available.

Floo is processed in two departments. The first department mixes the raw materials while the second department bleaches the mixed chemical transferred to it from the mixing department. The normal cost incurred to produce one litre of Floo is presented in Illustration 4-1.

All direct materials used in the mixing and bleaching departments are added at the beginning of each process. The actual quantity and cost data worksheets for both the mixing and the bleaching operations in January are presented in Illustration 4-2.

Reviewing the Data

The data included in Illustration 4-2 are used to calculate a unit cost for Floo using (1) the weighted average cost inventory technique and (2) the Fifo inventory technique. The most difficult aspect of these calculations is usually interpreting the available data so as to accurately compute the number of equivalent units, the total cost, and the cost per

Illustration 4-1

Normal Cost to Make One Litre of Floo

Mixing Department

Raw Materials (½ Kilogram @ $.50 Per Kilogram)	$ .25
Direct Labor (½ Hour @ $4.00 Per Hour)	2.00
Manufacturing Overhead (Applied on a Direct Labor	
Hour Basis. Predetermined Rate is $6.00 Per Hour)	3.00
Total Normal Cost of Mixing	$ 5.25

Bleaching Department

Raw Materials (½ Kilogram @ $1.00 Per Kilogram)	$ .50
Direct Labor (1 Hour @ $4.00 Per Hour)	4.00
Manufacturing Overhead (Applied on a Direct Labor	
Hour Basis: Predetermined Rate is $6.00 Per Hour)	6.00
Total Normal Cost of Bleaching	$10.50
Total Normal Cost of Producing One Litre of	
Floo ($5.25 Mixing Cost + $10.50 Bleaching Cost)	$15.75

equivalent unit. The worksheets included in Illustration 4-2, therefore, require further explanation.

Quantity Data for Mixing

The quantity data worksheet summarizes, in terms of the number of units, the work-in-process inventory account. The beginning inventory of 500 litres, plus the 2,000 litres started during the period, less the 1,600 litres completed and transferred to the mixing department gives the ending work-in-process inventory of 900 litres (500 + 2,000 − 1,600 = 900). Note that the beginning work-in-process inventory of 500 litres is 100 percent complete as to raw materials (since all materials are added at the beginning of the process), but that this inventory is only 50 percent complete as to direct labor and manufacturing overhead. This is because only half of the necessary labor and overhead costs to complete the units were incurred in the prior period. The same interpretation of percentage of completion may be applied to the ending work-in-process inventory using the information included on the worksheet. This inventory is also 100 percent complete as to materials, and 50 percent complete as to direct labor and manufacturing overhead.

Cost Data for Mixing

The cost data worksheet is used to summarize the costs of each of the three basic elements of manufacturing cost (materials, labor and over-

Illustration 4-2

Yuke Chemical Division Worksheets

Product: *Floo*   Month: *January*

Quantity (Litres) Data for Mixing

	Litres	Percentage of Direct Material	Percentage of Direct Labor	Percentage of Manufacturing Overhead Application
Beginning Work-In-Process..........	500	100%	50%	50%
Add: Litres Started.................	2,000			
Total That Could Be Completed......	2,500			
Less: Litres Completed.............	1,600			
Ending Work-In-Process...........	900	100%	50%	50%

(handwritten: transferred from bleachy dept)

Cost Data For Mixing

	Direct Material	Direct Labor	Manufacturing Overhead Application	Total Costs
Beginning Work-In-Process..........	$125	$ 500	$ 750	$ 1,375
Cost Added This Month.............	500	3,600	5,400	9,500
Totals.........................	$625	$4,100	$6,150	$10,875

Quantity (Litres) Data for Bleaching

	Litres—All Transferred From Mixing	Percentage of Direct Material	Percentage of Direct Labor	Percentage of Manufacturing Overhead Application
Beginning Work-In-Process...........	800	100%	25%	25%
Add: Litres Transferred From Mixing This Month.......................	1,600			
Total That Could Be Completed....................	2,400			
Less: Litres Completed.............	1,800			
Ending Work-In-Process...........	600	100%	40%	40%

Cost Data for Bleaching

(handwritten: cost from prev. period; from previous month that had it but transferred out)

	Costs Transferred from Mixing	Direct Materials Added	Direct Labor Added	Manufacturing Overhead Applied	Total Costs
Beginning Work-In-Process.....	$4,800	$ 200 °	$ 800	$ 1,200	$7,000
Cost Added This Month.........	?	800	7,040	10,560	?
Totals.......................	?	$1,000	$7,840	$11,760	?

°Note that the 800 litres included in the beginning work-in-process inventory in the Bleaching Department have an associated direct materials cost of only $200 although they are 100 percent complete as to materials. Normally, this cost is $400, but the company made a low cost purchase of its normal quality materials in the prior period. This bargain purchase accounts for the reduced cost of the beginning work-in-process inventories as to direct materials.

head) which are described in the quantity worksheet and which have been accumulated in the work-in-process inventory account. In our example, the costs accumulated for the 500 litres of beginning inventory consist of $125 for direct materials, $500 for direct labor, and $750 for manufacturing overhead. The costs which were added by the mixing department in January included $500 for direct materials, $3,600 for direct labor, and $5,400 for manufacturing overhead (See Illustration 4–2). Direct labor and direct material are actual costs and manufacturing overhead is the normal (applied) cost.

Quantity Data for Bleaching

The bleaching operation takes place in the second department in the production process. Therefore, all of the bleaching department's inventory is initially obtained by transfer from the mixing department. The bleaching department receives the inventory transferred to it from the mixing department and adds additional raw materials, direct labor and manufacturing overhead to this inventory in its processing operations.

The 800 litres of beginning work-in-process inventory in the bleaching department had been processed by the mixing department in a prior period. All of the raw materials that are to be added to this beginning work-in-process inventory in the bleaching process have already been added, so it is fully complete as to materials from both departments. However, the beginning work-in-process is only 25 percent complete as to the direct labor and manufacturing overhead input factors. The ending work-in-process inventory is 100 percent complete as to direct materials, but only 40 percent complete with regard to both direct labor and manufacturing overhead.

Cost Data for Bleaching

The 800 litres of beginning work-in-process inventory in the bleaching department had accumulated costs totaling $7,000 as of January 1. The breakdown of this $7,000 cost into its components is given on the worksheet in Illustration 4–2. The $7,000 beginning inventory consists of $4,800 in costs transferred from the mixing department, and $2,200 in costs of direct materials, direct labor and manufacturing overhead applied by the bleaching department in the prior period.

The cost factors which were added to this inventory by the bleaching department during the current month should be carefully reviewed. Note that there is a question mark inserted in the Illustration for those costs which were transferred from the mixing department during the current month (January). The unit cost for the 1,600 litres which were completed by the mixing department during January and transferred to the bleaching department cannot be entered on the worksheet until the cost calculations for the mixing department are completed. The direct material and direct labor costs added to the product as a result of the bleaching process are actual costs incurred by the bleaching department during January. The cost accumulations for the 1,600 litres transferred from the mixing department must be completed to arrive at the unit cost per litre for Floo.

MIXING PRODUCTION COST REPORT: USING THE WEIGHTED AVERAGE TECHNIQUE

The production cost report for the mixing department is prepared using the data included in the worksheets in Illustration 4–2. These data are necessary to prepare this report and could be incorporated as a part of the report. For management purposes, however, this detail is usually unnecessary. The production cost report for the mixing department is presented in Illustration 4–3.

Illustration 4-3
Yuke Chemical Division
Production Cost Report—Mixing Department
Weighted Average Technique

Product: *Floo*   Month: *January*

(a) Costs	Direct Materials	Direct Labour	Manufacturing Overhead Applied	Total Costs
Totals	$ 625	$4,100	$6,150	$10,875
Equivalent unit calculations (litres)				
Units completed (litres)	1,600	1,600	1,600	
Ending work-in-process (900 litres)				
Direct material (100% complete)	900			
Direct labour (50% complete)		450		
Manufacturing overhead (50% complete)			450	
b) Equivalent units	2,500	2,050	2,050	
Unit cost a/b	$0.25 +	$2.00 +	$3.00 =	$5.25

For inventory costing purposes, each unit of inventory transferred from the mixing department to the bleaching department in January carries with it an associated inventory cost of $5.25. In total, the transfers to the bleaching department and the ending work-in-process inventory in the mixing department should equal a total production cost of $10,875. This amount represents the cost of the beginning work-in-process in the mixing department, plus those costs which were added to the production process during January.

Completed (1,600 Litres @ $5.25).................	$ 8,400
Ending Work-In-Process:	
Direct Material (900 Litres @ $.25)..................	225
Direct Labor (450 Litres @ $2.00)...................	900
Manufacturing Overhead (450 Litres	
@ $3.00)...................................	1,350
Total..	$10,875

The total costs for the bleaching department for January may now be computed. The cost data for the bleaching department from Illustration 4–2, with the costs transferred from mixing for January ($8,400), are presented in Illustration 4–4.

Illustration 4-4

Yuke Chemical Division Worksheets
Weighted Average Technique

Product: *Floo* Month: *January*

Cost Data For Bleaching

	Costs Transferred From Mixing	Direct Materials Added	Direct Labor Added	Manufacturing Overhead Applied	Total Costs
Work-in-Process— Beginning	$ 4,800	$ 200	$ 800	$ 1,200	$ 7,000
Costs Added This Month	8,400	800	7,040	10,560	26,800
Totals	$13,200	$1,000	$7,840	$11,760	$33,800

BLEACHING DEPARTMENT PRODUCTION COST REPORT: USING THE WEIGHTED AVERAGE TECHNIQUE

The production cost report for the bleaching department shown in Illustration 4–5 is prepared using the data included in the worksheets presented in Illustrations 4–2 and 4–4. Again, this data could be incorporated as a part of the report, but for management purposes, this detail is usually considered unnecessary.

Illustration 4-5
Yuke Chemical Division
Production Cost Report—Bleaching Department
Weighted Average Technique

Product: *Floo*

Month: *January*

(a) Costs	Liters All Transferred From Mixing	Direct Materials	Direct Labour	Manufacturing Overhead Applied	Total Costs
Totals (Illustration 4-4)...........	$13,200	$1,000	$7,840	$11,760	$33,800
Equivalent units calculations (litres)					
Units completed (litres)...........	1,800	1,800	1,800	1,800	
Ending work-in-process (600 litres)					
Transferred in..............	600				
Direct material (100% complete).....		600			
Direct labour (40% complete)......			240		
Manufacturing overhead (40% complete).......				240	
(b) Equivalent units.............	2,400	2,400	2,040	2,040	
Unit cost a/b...............	$5.50 +	$0.42 +	$3.84* +	$5.76 =	$15.52

* Rounded

The transfers to finished goods from the bleaching department plus the ending work-in-process in bleaching should equal the total production cost for the period of $33,800.

```
Completed . . . . . . . . . . . . ( 1,800  Litres  @ $15.52 ). . . . . . . . . $27,936.00
Work-In-Process—Ending:
    Transferred in . . . . . . . . ( 600  Litres  @ $ 5.50 ). . . . . . . . . . . . 3,300.00
    Direct  Material . . . . . . . ( 600    „     @ $  .42 ). . . . . . . . . . .   252.00
    Direct  Labor . . . . . . . . . ( 240    „     @ $ 3.84 ). . . . . . . . . . .   921.60
    Manufacturing  Overhead . . ( 240    „     @ $ 5.76 ). . . . . . . . . . 1,382.40
        Total. . . . . . . . . . . . . . . . . . . . . . . . . . . . . . . . . . . . . . . . . . . . . . . $33,792.00 °
```
° Difference of $8.00 due to rounding.

As is implied by the title, the weighted average technique averages the costs of the beginning work-in-process inventory and the costs added to production during the accounting period on a weighted basis in order to arrive at a cost for the current period.

The costs which were transferred from the mixing department to the bleaching department will be used as an example to illustrate the averaging technique. The beginning work-in-process inventory in the bleaching department (Illustration 4-2) included 800 litres of Floo that were transferred from the mixing department during a prior period. The cost of the Floo totaled $4,800 or $6.00 per litres (slightly higher than the normal cost of $5.25). A total of 1,600 litres was transferred to the bleaching department from the mixing department during January at a cost of $5.25 per litre. The ending work-in-process inventory in the bleaching department consisted of 600 litres. The average cost of the 600 litres transferred to bleaching from the mixing department which is included in the ending work-in-process on the Production Cost Report—Bleaching Department, is $5.50 per litre. The calculations which were necessary to arrive at the weighted average figure of $5.50 per litre are included on the production cost report for the bleaching department (Illustration 4-5).

PRODUCTION COST REPORTS: USING THE FIFO TECHNIQUE

The production cost reports using the Fifo technique of process costing are prepared using the same worksheets presented in Illustration 4–2. In applying the Fifo technique, a clearly identifiable first-in, first-out flow of costs is assumed, and the production costs and related production are accounted for in terms of specific batches of production. The Fifo concept in process costing is best illustrated in this manner. [3]

[3] The actual use of Fifo does not require the detailed records that one might initially expect because transfers to a department are averaged and only transfers out are made on a Fifo basis.

Illustration 4-6

Yuke Chemical Division
Production Cost Report—Mixing Department
First-In, First-Out Technique

Product: *Floo*   Month: *January*

(a) Costs

	Direct Materials	*Direct Labour*	*Manufacturing Overhead Applied*	*Total Costs*
Added this month..............................	$ 500	$3,600	$5,400	$9,500
Equivalent unit calculations (litres)				
Units completed (litres)......................	1,600	1,600	1,600	
Ending work-in-process (900 litres)				
Direct material (100% complete)...........	900			
Direct labour (50% complete)..............		450		
Manufacturing overhead (50% complete)....			450	
Total processed...............................	2,500	2,050	2,050	
Less: Beginning work-in-process (500 litres)				
Direct material (100% complete)...........	500			
Direct labour (50% complete)..............		250		
Manufacturing overhead (50% complete)....			250	
(b) Total equivalent units processed this month...	2,000	1,800	1,800	
Unit cost added this month (a/b)............	$0.25 +	$2.00 +	$3.00 =	$5.25

Illustration 4-6 (Continued):
Production Cost of Inventory

	Direct Materials	Direct Labor	Manufacturing Overhead	Total
Beginning Work-in-Process	$ 125	$ 500	$ 750	$1,375
Cost Added to Complete This Month				
Direct Materials	-0-			-0-
Direct Labor 250 Litres @ $2		$ 500		$ 500
Manufacturing Overhead 250 Litres @ $3			$ 750	$ 750
Total Cost Accumulation for Beginning 500 Litres				$2,625

Cost per Litre $2,625 ÷ 500 = $5.25

Inventory Costs under Fifo				
Completed and Transferred (1,600 Litres)				
First: 500 Litres @ $5.25	$2,625			
Second: 1,100 Litres @ $5.25	5,775			$ 8,400
Ending Work-in-Process—(900 Litres)				
Direct Material 900 Litres @ $ .25	$ 225			
Direct Labor 450 Litres @ 2.00	900			
Manufacturing Overhead 450 Litres @ 3.00	1,350			2,475
Total Cost Accounted for				$10,875[1]

[1] Beginning work-in-process $1,375 + costs added $9,500 = $10,875.

Illustration 4-7

Yuke Chemical Division
Production Cost Report—Bleaching Department
First-In, First-Out Technique

Product: *Floo*   Month: *January*

(a) Costs

	Litres All Transferred From Mixing	Direct Materials	Direct Labour	Manufacturing Overhead	Total Costs
(a) Costs added this month...............	$8,400	$ 800	$7,040	$10,560	$26,800
Equivalent unit calculations to which cost of this month apply					
Units completed (litres)............	1,800	1,800	1,800	1,800	
Add: Ending work-in-process (600 litres)					
Material transferred from mixing......	600				
Direct material (100% complete).......		600			
Direct labour (40% complete).........			240		
Manufacturing overhead (40% complete).....				240	
Total units processed................	2,400	2,400	2,040	2,040	
Less: Beginning work-in-process (800 litres)					
Direct material (100% complete).......		800			
Direct labour (25% complete).........			200		
Manufacturing overhead (25% complete).....				200	
(b) Total equivalent units processed this month......	1,600	1,600	1,840	1,840	
Unit cost added this month (a/b)......	$5.25 +	$0.50 +	$3.83* +	$5.74* =	$15.32

*Rounded

Illustration 4-7 (Continued):
Production Cost of Inventory

	Transferred from Mixing	Direct Materials	Direct Labor	Total Manufacturing Overhead	Total
Beginning Work-in-Process	$4,800	$200	$ 800	$1,200	$ 7,000
Costs Added to Complete this Month					
Direct Materials	0				
Direct Labor 600 Litres @ $3.83			$2,298		$ 2,298
Manufacturing Overhead 600 Litres @ $5.74 . .				$3,444	$ 3,444
Total Cost Accumulation for Beginning 800 Litres . . .					$12,742

Cost Per Litre $12,742 ÷ 800 = $15.93 (Rounded)

Inventory Costs Under Fifo
Completed and Transferred (1,800 Litres)
First: 800 Litres @ $15.93 . . . . $12,742
Second: 1,000 Litres

Transferred from Mixing	$ 5.25	
Current Costs in Bleaching	10.07	
	$ 15.32 × 1,000 Litres	15,320

Ending Work-In-Process (600 Litres)

Transferred from Mixing 600 Litres @ $5.25 . . .	$3,150.00	
Direct Material 600 Litres @ .50 . . .	300.00	
Direct Labor 240 Litres @ 3.83 . . .	919.20	
Manufacturing Overhead 240 Litres @ 5.74 . . .	$1,377.60	5,746.80

Total Cost Accounted for . . . . $33,808.80 *

*Difference of $8.80 due to rounding. Beginning work-in-process $7,000 + costs added $26,800 = $33,800.

The Production Cost Reports for the Mixing and Bleaching Departments using the Fifo method are presented in Illustrations 4–6 and 4–7. These reports are more complex than those required for the weighted average technique because the Fifo method requires that individual batches of inventory be accounted for separately. It is assumed that the first costs which were incurred during a period are those which are applicable to the beginning inventory. Any additional costs of the current period are attached to the units started or transferred during this period on a Fifo basis. Any ending work-in-process inventory consists of the units started or transferred in on a Fifo basis.

The key to these calculations lies in determining the cost which was incurred by a department during the current period and in determining the equivalent units to which these costs are attached. Consider the flow of information which is presented in Illustration 4–6.

1. The costs added in January are determined from the worksheet included in Illustration 4–2.
2. The number of equivalent units to which *January's costs* apply is then determined.
3. The production cost of the inventory is calculated. The order of the calculations should be noted. The beginning work-in-process inventory is considered first in terms of the current costs which were necessary to complete that specific batch of inventory.
4. Any inventory completed beyond the beginning work-in-process absorbs or carries the current period's cost per equivalent finished unit.
5. The cost of the ending work-in-process inventory is based on the number of finished equivalent units.
6. The total costs accounted for are calculated to ascertain that all costs incurred have, in fact, been absorbed into the inventory costs.

SUMMARY

Process costing systems are used to accumulate costs in those firms that manufacture uniform products in continuous production runs. Costs are normally accumulated for each process and a production cost report is then prepared at the end of the accounting period for each process. Unit costs are generally calculated using information from these reports.

The basic format of the production cost report resembles the cost of goods manufactured statement. Where no beginning or ending work-in-process inventories exist, the unit cost calculation simply involves dividing total costs by units completed. However, in most process manufacturing systems, beginning and ending inventories do exist and this fact complicates the unit cost calculation significantly.

In calculating the unit cost in a process costing system, it is normally necessary to determine the equivalent units of production. This represents the number of whole or completed units that could have been entirely processed with the materials, labor, and overhead that were actually expended or used up. This computation involves adding the equivalent units in the ending work-in-process to the equivalent units of completed production. The equivalent units of completed production are equal to the actual units completed less the equivalent units in the beginning work-in-process inventory.

Generally, it is necessary to calculate equivalent units for each element of product cost (i.e., direct material, direct labor, and manufacturing overhead). The total cost for each element is then divided by the number of equivalent units for that element to determine the unit element cost. The three unit element costs are then summed to yield a unit cost per equivalent unit of product.

Once the unit cost per equivalent is derived, the firm's normal inventory valuation method is employed to arrive at ending inventory values. The two primary inventory valuation methods used by process manufacturing firms are the weighted average method and the first-in, first-out method.

When more than one production department is involved in manufacturing a product, each department (except the initial processing department) must account for all costs previously incurred in the manufacture of the product. These costs from prior departments are generally referred to as "transferred" costs. The final department involved in the manufacture of the product will then transfer the total cost of the completed product to the finished goods inventory.

This chapter has discussed and illustrated the second of the fundamental cost accumulation systems used for product costing in manufacturing firms. At this point it may be beneficial to review and compare these two basic systems: job order costing and process costing.

KEY DEFINITIONS   Conversion costs—the costs of direct labor and manufacturing overhead incurred in a production process.

Cost data worksheet—summarizes the costs which are accumulated in the work-in-process account for each element of manufacturing cost described in the quantity data worksheet.

Equivalent units of production—a measure in terms of the number of whole or completed units of a product which could have been produced at the actual expended cost.

Process costing system—a cost accounting system in which costs are accumulated by the production process. This system is normally used in manufacturing situations characterized by continuous productions runs of a uniform product.

Production cost report—a report prepared at the end of an accounting period for each production process. It summarizes the amounts of production, total costs of direct materials, direct labor and applied overhead so that the unit cost of production may be calculated.

Quantity data worksheet—summarizes, in terms of units, the work-in-process account and the percentage of completion of each element of manufacturing cost for beginning and ending inventories.

QUESTIONS

4-1 When is is most appropriate to use a process costing system? May a job-order cost system be used under process costing conditions?

4-2 What is the purpose of a production cost report and what does it generally include?

4-3 In relation to requisitioning material, how does a job-order cost system differ from a process costing system?

4-4 How does the production cost report resemble the cost of goods manufactured statement? How do they differ?

4-5 Define equivalent units of production. Why are the costs associated with direct labor and manufacturing overhead usually combined when calculating equivalent units?

4-6 How does the process costing method handle the flow of costs if there is more than a single processing department?

4-7 What is the purpose of the cost data worksheet?

4-8 How does the weighted-average technique treat beginning work-in-process?

4-9 Transferred-in costs are costs which were incurred in a previous department and are now being transferred to another department. How may these transferred-in costs be treated in the latter department?

4-10 Which of the process costing techniques is the more difficult to apply, weighted-average or Fifo, and why?

4-11 How can one verify that the correct amount of production costs has been allocated to finished goods?

4-12 What three factors must be known in order to develop the cost per equivalent unit?

EXERCISES AND PROBLEMS

4-13 Compute the equivalent units produced using the Fifo technique in each of the following independent situations.

		Units
a.	Beginning inventory—50% complete	15,000
	Ending inventory—50% complete	15,000
	Units started	120,000
b.	Beginning inventory—30% complete	72,000
	Ending inventory—75% complete	90,000
	Units transferred out	300,000
c.	Ending inventory—75% complete	42,000
	Units transferred out	78,000
	Units started	102,000
	Beginning inventory—80% complete	?

    d.   Units transferred out 108,000
         Beginning inventory—75% complete 33,000
         Units started 90,000
         Ending inventory—45% complete . . . . . .   ?

4-14   Compute the equivalent units of production for each element of cost (material, labor, and overhead) in each of the following UNRELATED instances: Assume Fifo cost flow.

    a.   Started into production–12,000 units (no beginning work-in-process); finished and transferred–10,500 units. Ending work-in-process 35%, complete as to direct labor and overhead, 100% complete as to materials.

    b.   Beginning work-in-process–9,000 units (fully complete as to materials, ⅓ complete as to labor and overhead); started into process–25,000 units; finished and transferred–23,000 units. (The ending work-in-process is ½ complete as to materials; ⅘ complete as to labor and overhead.)

    c.   Beginning work-in-process–6,000 units (¾ complete as to materials, ½ complete as to labor and overhead); started into production–60,000 units; finished and transferred–50,000 units. (Ending work-in-process is complete as to materials and ⅜ complete as to labor and overhead.)

4-15   The Keyso Company, a manufacturing firm, begins the month of March with 5,000 units in work-in-process. These units are 50% complete as to direct labor and 75% complete as to factory overhead. All raw materials are added at the beginning of the cycle. During the month, 15,500 units are started and 17,000 units are transferred to finished goods. Ending work-in-process is 30% complete as to direct labor and 60% complete as to factory overhead. Compute the equivalent units in ending work-in-process.

4-16   During 19x9 the Ace Company completed and transferred to finished stock 100 wigets. The inventory of wigets in process at January 1, 19x9 totaled 40—they were 75 percent complete as to materials, 50 percent complete as to labour and overhead. The company began work on 80 new wigets in 19x9; at the end of the year the wigets on hand were 80 percent complete as to materials; 50 percent complete as to labour and 40 percent complete as to overhead. Calculate the equivalent production of wigets (as to materials, labour and overhead) for 19x9. Assume Fifo.

4-17   During 19x0 the Diamond Company completed and transferred to finished goods a total of 100 wigets. The inventory of wigets-in-process on January 1, 19x0 was 20 wigets; they were 60 percent complete as to conversion costs (all materials are added at the beginning of the process). The company began work on 130 new wigets in 19x0. At the end of the year, the wigets on hand were 40 percent complete as to conversion costs. Assume Fifo cost flow.

Required:

Compute the equivalent units for 19x0.

4-18   During April, the Brandon Manufacturing Company incurred the following costs:

Direct materials $24,000
Direct Labor 35,984
Manufacturing overhead 29,904

Production for April was as follows:
  Beginning work-in-process—0 units
  Units completed—4,000 units
  Ending work-in-process
    Direct materials—2,000 units, 100% complete
    Direct labor—2,000 units, 60% complete
    Manufacturing overhead—2,000 units, 40% complete

Required:

Compute the cost per equivalent unit.

4-19   Womsley Company has 400 units in beginning work-in-process for May. These units are 60% complete as to direct labor and factory overhead. All materials are added at the beginning of the process. During the month, 1,200 units are put into production for the first time. On May 31, there are 300 units still in work-in-process, 35% complete as to direct labor and overhead. Assuming the weighted average technique, compute the equivalent units of production for material, labor, and overhead for May.

4-20   Given the following information, compute the cost of finished goods manufactured.

	Direct Materials	Direct Labor	Manufacturing Overhead
Total cost	$126,000	$132,000	$99,000
Total equivalent units . .	12,600	8,250	8,250

Beginning finished goods inventory . . . . .   4,000 units
Number of units sold . . . . 10,200 units
Ending finished goods inventory . . . . 1,600 units

4-21   Simpson Company produces shoes. It takes two departments to produce these shoes, the Stitching and the Polishing departments. From the information listed below, calculate the total cost per pair of shoes for July (assume weighted average technique).

Polishing Department

Pairs of shoes transferred from Stitching Department 500
Beginning work-in-process (60% complete labor and overhead) . . . 100
Ending work-in-process (40% complete labor and overhead) 200
Material is added at the beginning of the process.

	Costs		
	Transferred from Stitching	Direct Materials	Direct Labor and Overhead
Total costs	$2,628	$1,350	$1,560

4-22 Assuming the Fifo technique, calculate the total equivalent units that relate to this period's cost under each of the following unrelated assumptions for each element of production cost:

a. Beginning work-in-process—1,500 units (materials are added at the *end* of the process; 60% of labor and 40% of overhead have been added); 8,000 units were put into production during the period. Ending work-in-process inventory consists of 3,500 units (70% complete as to both labor and overhead).

b. Beginning work-in-process—800 units (materials are added at the beginning of the process; 30% of labor and 50% of overhead have been added); 7,000 units were put into production during the period. There is no ending work-in-process inventory.

c. No beginning work-in-process inventory. 1,200 units were put into production during the period. 600 units are still in work-in-process inventory at the end of the period. (Material is added at the *end* of the period, 55% of both labor and overhead have been added.)

4-23 From the information listed below, calculate the total cost per equivalent unit.

	Direct Material	Direct Labor	Overhead Applied
Ending work-in-process:			
Direct material (100% complete)	650		
Direct labor (80% complete)		520	
Manufacturing overhead (80% complete)			520
Units completed	2,200	2,200	2,200
Cost incurred for each area	$1,425	$8,160	$12,240
There is no beginning work-in-process.			

4-24 Using the following division worksheet for the Stick-em Glue Corporation, prepare a production cost report using the weighted average technique.

Quantity Data for Glue Processing

	Litres	% of Direct Material	% of Direct Labor	% of Manufacturing Overhead Application
Beginning work-in-process . .	200	100%	60%	50%
Add: Litres started	3,500			
Total which could be completed	3,700			
Less: Litres completed . . .	3,300			
Ending work-in-process	400	100%	30%	25%

Cost Data for Glue Processing

	Direct Material	Direct Labor	Manufacturing Overhead Applied	Total Costs
Beginning work-in-process . .	$ 40	$ 240	$ 300	$ 580
Actual costs added this month	700	6,600	9,900	17,200
Totals	$740	$6,840	$10,200	$17,780

4-25   Given the following information for Stacy, Inc., compute the equivalent units and the cost per equivalent unit for the month of June using the weighted average technique.

Production:
Beginning—work-in-process . . . . 20 units
   Direct materials . . . . 80% complete
   Direct labor . . . . 50% complete
   Manufacturing overhead . . . . 40% complete
Units completed . . . . 4,000 units
Ending—work-in-process . . . . 40 units
   Direct material . . . . 60% complete
   Direct labor . . . . 30% complete
   Manufacturing overhead . . . . 25% complete

Costs:
Beginning—work-in-process
   Direct material $96.00
   Direct labor 40.00
   Manufacturing overhead 24.00
Cost added this month:
   Direct material $24,048
   Direct labor 16,008
   Manufacturing overhead 12,006

4-26   On December 31, 19x0, Drippy Pipe, Inc., a manufacturer of plumbing supplies, had an ending work-in-process inventory in Department 1 of 60 faucets. These faucets are 100% complete as to materials, 80% complete as to labor, and 80% complete as to manufacturing overhead with costs of $150, $144, and $60 respectively. During the year, 1,500 faucets were completed and transferred to finished goods. On December 31, 19x1, there were 70 units in work-in-process which were 40% complete as to materials, 20% complete as to labor, and 10% complete as to manufacturing overhead. During 19x1, costs added to the production process were direct materials of $3,816.80, direct labor of $4,691.20, and manufacturing overhead of $1,896.70. Determine the cost of the inventory transferred to finished goods using the first-in, first-out method.

4-27   The Frey Company uses a process cost system. At the beginning of the period they had 200 units in process. These units were 25 percent complete as to labor and overhead (all material is added at the beginning of the process). The costs associated with the beginning work-in-process are $180 for materials and $75 for labor and overhead. During the period 1,000 units were completed and transferred to finished goods. The current period costs were $720 for materials and $1,375 for labor and overhead. The ending work-in-process consisted of 400 units which were 75% complete as to labor and overhead.

Required:

Complete the following using Fifo.

a. The equivalent units produced during the period as to materials totaled . . . . _____.

b. The equivalent units produced during the period as to labor & overhead . . . . _____.

c. The total unit cost for the period was (per unit) . . . _____.

d. The total unit cost for the preceding period was (per unit) . . . . _____.

e. The unit cost of the units finished and transferred to finished goods during the period was (per unit) . . . . _____.

f. The number of units started during the period totaled _____.

4-28　Joyce Company uses a process cost system. At January 1 it had 10 units in process. These units were 60% complete as to labor and overhead. (All material is added at the beginning of the process.) The costs associated with the beginning work-in-process are $90 for materials, $60 for labor and $30 for overhead. During the period 90 units were completed and transferred to finished goods. The current period costs were $1,010 for materials, $900 for labor and $450 for overhead. The ending work-in-process consisted of 20 units which were 30% complete as to labor and overhead.

Required:

Calculate the following, for both the average and the Fifo method:

	Fifo	*Average*
a. The equivalent units produced during the period as to materials totaled	_____	_____
b. The equivalent units produced during the period as to labor and overhead totaled . .	_____	_____
c. The total unit cost for the period was (per unit)	_____	_____
d. The total unit cost for the preceding period was (per unit)	_____	_____
e. The unit cost of the units finished and transferred to finished goods during the period was (per unit)	_____	_____

f. The number of units started during the
period totaled . . . . _____ _____

4-29   Comfo, Inc., manufactures rocking chairs. These chairs are processed
in two departments. In the first department the wood is cut and put
together. In the second department the finishing work is done. Given
the following information, compute the cost per equivalent unit using
the weighted average inventory technique.

Production Data

	Number of Chairs	Percentage of Direct Materials	Percentage of Direct Labor	Percentage of Manufacturing Overhead Application
Cutting Department:				
Work-in-process—				
beginning	20	100%	50%	50%
Add: Chairs started	480			
Total that could be				
completed	500			
Less: Chairs completed . . .	490			
Work-in-process—ending . .	10	100	40	40
Finishing Department:				
Work-in-process—				
beginning	30	100	10	10
Add: chairs transferred				
from cutting this month . .	490			
Total that could be				
completed	520			
Less: Chairs completed . . .	500			
Work-in-process—ending . .	20	50	25	25

Cost Data

	Cost Transferred from Cutting	Direct Materials	Direct Labor	Manufacturing Overhead
Cutting Department:				
Work-in-process—				
beginning		$ 680	$ 135	$ 80
Cost added this month		16,320	6,534	3,872
Totals		$17,000	$6,669	$3,952
Finishing Department:				
Work-in-process—				
beginning	$1,665	$ 195	$ 54	$ 33
Cost added this month	?	3,120	9,036	5,522
Totals	$?	$ 3,315	$9,090	$5,555

4-30   Using the same information as given in Problem 4-29, compute the cost per
equivalent unit using FIFO.

4-31   From the information listed below calculate the value of the ending work-in-process inventory for October using the Fifo method.

1. Beginning work-in-process—1,750—80% complete for material, 30% complete for labor and 40% complete for overhead. Costs were $3,248, $1,338.75, and $2,205, for material, labor, and overhead respectively.
2. Units started into production during October—9,245. Costs added were $21,480.88, $24,556.50, and $29,783.25, for material, labor, and overhead respectively.
3. Ending work-in-process—1,120 units—70% complete for material, and 25% complete for labor and overhead.

4-32   The Hansen Company uses process cost accounting to determine their cost of goods manufactured. However, the company is undecided as to whether they should use the weighted average or the Fifo method. They prefer the method which gives them the highest cost of goods manufactured for income tax purposes, and they will use this method consistently in the future.

Below is production data for the year ended December 31.

Beginning work-in-process—3,500 units—100% complete for material and 70% complete for conversion costs (labor and overhead).

Finished and transferred to finished goods—32,000 units.

Ending work-in-process—2,100 units—100% complete for material and 60% complete for conversion costs.

Cost Summaries for the Year

Material: Beginning work-in-process	$ 7,350.00	
Current costs	68,160.00	$75,510.00
Conversion: Beginning work-in-process	$ 5,414.50	
Current costs	$73,280.00	$78,694.50

Required:

Compute the cost of goods manufactured under both the weighted average and the Fifo methods in order that the Hansen Company may choose that method which gives the highest value. Carry costs to the nearest cent.

4-33   The Caldor Company would like you to calculate their gross profit for the year ended September 30, 19x0. You are to use the weighted average method to calculate the company's cost of goods manufactured and the Fifo inventory method to determine their cost of goods sold. Cost and sales data for the year are listed below:

1. Sales for the year equals 4,500 units at $18 a unit.
2. Beginning finished goods inventory consisted of 500 units at $10.25 a piece.
3. Beginning work-in-process inventory contained 475 units, 100%

complete as to material, and 52% complete as to labor and over-head. Costs were $1,591.25 for material and $1,712.16 for labor and overhead.

4. Units both *started* and *finished* during the year totaled 5,220 (not including those in beginning work-in-process). Costs added in 19x0 were $18,505.40 for material and $37,431.36 for labor and overhead.

5. Ending work-in-process inventory consisted of 320 units, 95% complete for material and 85% complete for labor and overhead.

4-34 Using the information in Problem 4-33, calculate the gross profit for the Caldor Company using the Fifo method to determine the cost of goods manufactured and the Lifo method to calculate cost of goods sold.

4-35 Using the first-in, first-out method of valuing inventories, determine the total equivalent units produced, the cost per unit of the beginning work-in-process and the total cost per unit produced this month from the following information.

Costs:
    Beginning—work-in-process:
        Direct materials . . . . $ 120.00
        Direct labor . . . . $ 153.00
        Manufacturing overhead . . . . $ 60.00
    Costs added this month:
        Direct materials $2,529.60
        Direct labor $4,275.00
        Manufacturing overhead $2,004.00

Production:
    Beginning—work-in-process . . . . 30 units
        Direct materials . . . . 80% complete
        Direct labor . . . . 60% complete
        Manufacturing overhead . . . . 50% complete
    Units completed . . . . 500 units
    Ending—work-in-process . . . . 20 units
        Direct materials . . . . 100% complete
        Direct labor . . . . 90% complete
        Manufacturing overhead . . . . 80% complete

4-36 On December 31, 19x0, Sudsy Floors, Inc., which manufactures commercial and home floor care products, took an inventory of its Wax Division. In particular, they were interested in the Mixing Department. They found that there were 400 litres of wax in work-in-process. The wax was 100% complete as to materials, 60% complete as to labor, and 60% complete as to manufacturing overhead. Costs accumulated at that time were $200, $144, $72, respectively. During 19x1, 21,000 litres of wax were completed and transferred to the Bottling Department. Costs incurred during 19x1 were $10,520 of direct materials, $12,588 of direct labor, and $6,294 of manufacturing overhead. At the end of the year, the 550 litres in work-in-process were 80% complete as to direct materials and 40% complete as to direct labor and manufacturing overhead.

Required:

Your job is to determine the equivalent units produced in 19x1, the cost per equivalent unit, and the total cost transferred to the Bottling Department using the weighted average method.

A **4-37** Your job, as accountant for a blue jean manufacturer, is to determine the cost of one pair of blue jeans produced in April. The jeans go through three departments before they are sold to retail clothing stores throughout Canada. In the first department, the jeans are cut out; in the second department, they are sewn; in the third department any labels are attached and the jeans are packaged for shipping since the jeans are sold in standard lots of one dozen jeans of the same size.

Required:

From the following information, compute the cost per equivalent unit using the weighted average inventory technique.

Production Data

	Number of Pairs of Blue Jeans	Percentage of Direct Materials	Percentage of Direct Labor	Percentage of Manufacturing Overhead Application
Cutting Department:				
Work-in-process— beginning	15	100%	80%	80%
Add: Jeans started	560			
Total that could be completed	575			
Less: Jeans completed	555			
Work-in-process—ending . . .	20	100	90	90
Sewing Department:				
Work-in-process— beginning	30	50	50	50
Add: Jeans transferred from cutting this month . . .	555			
Total that could be completed	585			
Less: Jeans completed	570			
Work-in-process—ending . . .	15	40	20	20
Packaging Department:				
Work-in-process— beginning	10	70	80	80

Add: Jeans transferred
  from sewing this month . . . 570

Total that could be
  completed 580
Less: Jeans completed 576

Work-in-process—ending 4		25	50	50

Cost Data

	Transferred Costs	Direct Materials	Direct Labor	Manufacturing Overhead
Cutting Department:				
Work-in-process— beginning		$ 37.50	$ 24.00	$ 5.40
Costs added this month		1,400.00	1,122.00	252.45
Totals		$1,437.50	$1,146.00	$257.85
Sewing Department:				
Work-in-process— beginning	$148.50	$ 1.70	$ 63.00	$ 17.00
Costs added this month	?	55.90	2,400.90	556.00
Totals	?	$ 57.60	$2,463.90	$573.00
Packaging Department:				
Work-in-process— beginning	$103.50	$ .35	$ 9.20	$ 3.90
Costs added this month	?	28.50	626.60	285.10
Totals	?	$ 28.85	$ 635.80	$289.00

4-38   Using the information given in Problem 4-37, compute the cost per equivalent unit using Fifo.

4-39   This problem is for the instructor that wants to introduce both normal and abnormal spoilage. Ranka Company manufactures high quality leather products. The company's profits have declined during the past nine months. Ranka has used unit cost data which were developed eighteen months ago in planning and controlling its operations. In an attempt to isolate the causes of poor profit performance, management is investigating the manufacturing operations of each of its products.

    One of Ranka's main products is fine leather belts. The belts are produced in a single, continuous process in the Bluett Plant. During the process leather strips are sewn, punched, and dyed. Buckles are attached by rivets when the belts are 70 percent complete as to direct labor and overhead (conversion costs). The belts then enter a final finishing stage to conclude the process. Labor and overhead are applied continuously during the process.

    The leather belts are inspected twice during the process: (1) right before the buckles are attached (70 percent point in the process) and (2) at the conclusion of the finishing stage (100 percent point in the process). Ranka uses the weighted average method to calculate its unit costs.

The leather belts produced at the Bluett Plant wholesale for $9.95 each. Management wants to compare the current manufacturing costs per unit with the prices which exist on the market for leather belts. Top management has asked the Bluett Plant to submit data on the cost of manufacturing the leather belts for the month of October. This cost data will be used to evaluate whether modifications in the production process should be initiated or whether an increase in the selling price of the belts is justified. The cost per equivalent unit which is being used for planning and controlling purposes is $5.35 per unit.

The work-in-process inventory consisted of 400 partially completed units on October 1. The belts were 25 percent complete as to conversion costs. The costs included in the inventory on October 1 were as follows:

Leather strips.......	$1,000
Conversion costs....	300
	$1,300

During October 7,600 leather strips were placed in production. A total of 6,800 good leather belts were completed. A total of 300 belts were identified as defective at the two inspection points—100 at the first inspection point (before buckle is attached) and 200 at the final inspection point (after finishing). This quantity of defective belts was considered normal. In addition, 200 belts were removed from the production line when the process was 40 percent complete as to conversion costs because they had been damaged as a result of a malfunction during the sewing operation. This malfunction was considered an unusual occurrence, and consequently, the spoilage was classified as abnormal. Defective (spoiled) units are not reprocessed and have zero salvage value. The work-in-process inventory on October 31 consisted of 700 belts which were 50 percent complete as to conversion costs.

The costs charged to production during October were as follows:

Leather strips.......	$20,600
Buckles............	4,550
Conversion costs....	20,700
	$45,850

Required:

a. In order to provide cost data regarding the manufacture of leather belts in the Bluett Plant to the top management of Ranka Company, determine for the month of October:

1. The equivalent units for each factor of production.
2. The cost per equivalent whole unit for each factor of production.
3. The assignment of total production costs to the work-in-process inventory and to goods transferred out.

4.   The average unit cost of the 6,800 good leather belts completed and transferred to finished goods.

b.   If Ranka Company decided to repair (rework) the 300 defective belts which were considered normal spoilage, explain how the company would account for the rework costs.

(CMA, adapted)

4-40   In any production process losses are likely from spoilage, waste, defective units and scrap. These losses present a managerial control problem as well as a product costing problem.

"Spoilage" refers to units of product (partly or fully processed) the defects in which cannot be physically corrected at all, or cannot be corrected economically.

"Defective units" consist of those that are only partly spoiled and which may be economically reworked to improve their quality, thus allowing them to be offered for sale.

Required:

a.   Briefly indicate the essential features of a control system to monitor production spoilage.
b.   Outline the acceptable accounting treatment for the cost of spoiled goods in a process costing situation.
c.   In a job order costing situation, to what acounts should the cost of reworking defective units be charged?

(SMA, adapted)

Chapter 5

LEARNING OBJECTIVES

Chapter 5 examines the methods and procedures used in allocating joint product costs. Studying this chapter should enable you to:

1. Differentiate between joint products and by-products.
2. Discuss and apply the methods of allocating joint costs to products.
3. Identify and discuss the methods of accounting for the revenues from the sale of by-products under both certain and uncertain market conditions.

Cost Accounting
for Inventories:
Joint and By-Products

DUE To the nature of a number of products and/or production processes involved, it is impossible to manufacture certain products without obtaining additional products from the production process. For example, when crude oil is processed the refiner obtains a combination of gasoline, kerosene, fuel oil, naptha, lubricating oil and numerous additional products. It is important to note that the refiner does not have a choice in deciding which of these products will be produced; they are all generated in the refining process. Under most circumstances, gasoline is the most profitable of these products, but in order to obtain gasoline, the other products must also be produced. However, the product mix or proportion of the products may be—and is—altered by the refiner within limitations.

When a packing house slaughters a steer, various cuts of meat with different sales values are obtained. These assorted cuts are basically different products. In addition, other products, such as hides, bone meal, glue, and grease, are also obtained from the steer.

The cost accumulation problem which results when more than a single major product is obtained from a manufacturing process is referred to as a joint or common cost problem. It is important to note that, of necessity, joint costs are assigned or allocated to products for inventory costing purposes by the use of an arbitrarily selected basis for the allocation. This allocation process is discussed in this chapter.

NATURE OF THE PRODUCTS OBTAINED FROM A JOINT PROCESS

Outputs of a joint cost manufacturing process, either in the form of joint raw materials, joint processing or both, are categorized for accounting purposes as either joint products or as by-products. Joint products are the *major* products which are obtained from a joint cost production process. It is anticipated that these products will make a significant contribution to the revenues of the firm. In general, joint products are those products usually considered to be the most desirable ones obtained from the production process. If it were possible, only joint products would be produced in most circumstances.

By-products represent those products obtained from the manufacturing process which are not usually of major importance or significance to the firm. Therefore, by definition, by-products are less important than joint products. The production of by-products is the natural result of the process undertaken to obtain the joint products. In comparison to the revenues generated by the sale of the joint products, by-product sales make a relatively minor contribution to revenues. This characteristic is helpful in classifying by-products. Such factors as small quantities of production, low per unit sales prices, or a combination of these and other factors are also measures considered in classifying a by-product. It is possible, however, in some circumstances that the total revenues which are realized from the sale of by-products of the production process may be substantial.

The exact point at which a distinction is made between a joint product and a by-product cannot always be identified or defined with precision. For inventory costing purposes, a manufacturing concern with substantial joint costs must make this distinction using the best judgment available, given the circumstances at hand.

JOINT PRODUCT COSTS

In every joint manufacturing process, there is some point where two or more co-products are physically identifiable as separate and distinct products. This point is usually referred to as the split-off point or the point of separation. In practice, there are numerous split-off points where various products become identifiable at different stages or points in the manufacturing process.

The costs incurred prior to the split-off point cannot be directly traced to any single product. Therefore, they are handled or accounted for as joint costs. Costs incurred after the split-off point which are attributable to the further processing of a physically identifiable product are not considered joint costs. Rather, these costs are treated as separate costs or further processing costs traceable to the specific product involved.

JOINT COST ALLOCATION TO JOINT PRODUCTS

The costs incurred in manufacturing products are *entirely* absorbed by those products produced in the manufacturing process. If all of the output produced from a multiple product process is sold in the period in which it is produced, no allocation of costs is necessary for inventory costing purposes. Because all of the products were sold in the period in which they were produced there are no finished goods inventories on hand at the end of the period. However, this is not usually the case.

The allocation techniques used for distributing costs fall into two major categories: (1) allocation based on physical measures and (2) allocation based on relative sales value measures. Remember that only joint costs are allocated; any separable costs that may be identified with the further processing of a specific product are absorbed into the cost of that particular product.

In order to illustrate the basic considerations which are involved in the allocation of costs to multiple products, we will begin with a simple example. Assume that a manufacturing company is able to produce 2 units of X, 3 units of Y and 10 units of Z by incurring processing costs of $60. The selling price of X is $30 per unit, Y sells at a price of $10 per unit and Z has a selling price of $1 per unit.

As indicated above, one technique which may be used for allocating costs is an allocation based upon physical measures. In our example, 2 units of X, 3 units of Y and 10 units of Z were obtained at a cost of $60. If this $60 in processing cost is allocated to the three products based upon physical measures (in this case, the number of units), the allocation would be as follows:

Product	Units Produced	Proportion to Total Units		Processing Cost		Allocated Joint Cost	Cost Per Unit*
X	2	$2/15$	×	$60	=	$ 8	$4
Y	3	$3/15$	×	60	=	12	4
Z	10	$10/15$	×	60	=	40	4
	15					$60	

*Allocated joint cost divided by number of units.

Note that allocating processing costs to products by the use of physical measures assigns the same cost to each unit of product ($60 divided by 15 units or $4). This technique ignores any differences between and among products, including the relative values of the products.

An alternative method which may be used is to allocate costs based upon the relative sales values of the products. This approach assumes that each product should absorb a share of production costs which is proportionate to the ability of that product to generate revenues. This approach assigns a proportionately higher amount of costs to those products with higher sales values. Using the information presented above, the $60 of processing costs would be allocated to the three products as follows using the relative sales values approach:

Product	Units Produced		Selling Price		Total Sales Value	Sales Value to Total Sales	Processing Cost		Allocated Joint Cost	Cost Per Unit*
X	2	×	$30	=	$ 60	$60/$100	× $60	=	$36	$18.00
Y	3	×	10	=	30	$30/$100	× 60	=	18	6.00
Z	10	×	1	=	10	$10/$100	× 60	=	6	.60
	15				$100				$60	

*Allocated joint cost divided by number of units.

Both of the methods illustrated above assume that all three products are joint products. This assumption may be somewhat unrealistic in this case because of the relatively low selling price and total sales value of product Z, relative to X and Y. A more appropriate allocation might consider X and Y to be joint products and Z a by-product. If Z is considered to be a by-product, one method of allocating costs would be to allocate the processing costs of $60 between the two joint products, X and Y, and consider any revenues from the sale of by-product Z as (1) other income or (2) a reduction of the cost of goods sold for the period. Using the information employed in the examples above, the $60 of processing costs would be allocated as follows:

Product	Units Produced		Selling Price		Total Sales Value	Sales Value to Total Sales	Processing Cost		Allocated Joint Cost	Cost Per Unit*
X	2	×	$30	=	$60	$60/$90	× $60	=	$40	$20.00
Y	3	×	10	=	30	$30/$90	× 60	=	20	6.67
	5				$90				$60	

*Allocated joint cost divided by number of units.

Using this method, all of the $60 in processing costs are allocated to the two joint products, X and Y. Product Z is considered to be a by-product and the revenues received from the sale of Z (10 units × $1) may be considered as either (1) other income or (2) a reduction of the cost of goods sold for the period.

An alternative method of accounting for production costs when there are both joint products and by-products is to consider the sales value of the by-product as a reduction of the processing cost of the joint products. Using this method, the allocation would be made as follows:

Product	Units Produced	Selling Price		Total Sales Value	Sales Value to Total Sales	Net Processing Cost*	Allocated Joint Cost	Cost Per Unit**
X	2	× $30	=	$60	$60/$90 × ($60 − $10)		$33.33	$16.67
Y	3	× 10	=	30	$30/$90 × ($60 − $10)		16.67	5.56
	5			$90		$50	$50.00	

*Total processing cost less the sales value (10 units × $1) of the by-product.
**Allocated joint cost divided by the number of units.

The costs allocated to X, Y and Z under the various methods described above may be summarized as follows:

Method	Allocated Unit Cost		
All Joint Products	X	Y	Z
Physical measures........................	$ 4.00	$4.00	$4.00
Relative sales values.....................	18.00	6.00	.60
Joint and By-Products			
Relative sales values with by-product other income or a reduction of cost of goods sold..........................	20.00	6.67	1.00*
Relative sales values with by-product treated as a reduction of processing costs...............................	16.67	5.56	1.00*

*Under these methods, the unit "cost" of the by-product is its selling price.

As can easily be seen from the above table, the allocated cost per unit varies widely depending upon the techniques used. It should be noted that any method of allocating costs among multiple products is at least somewhat arbitrary. Further, if all of the output produced from a multiple product process is sold, no allocation of cost for inventory costing purposes is necessary since all processing costs will be included in cost of goods sold. Of course, it is rare that all production will be sold every period, so some method of allocation must be selected and used for inventory costing purposes. The various methods of allocation which were summarized above will be described and discussed in greater detail in the remaining sections of this chapter.

JOINT COST ALLOCATION BY PHYSICAL MEASURES

As indicated above, joint costs may be allocated to joint products using a physical measure such as kilograms, tons, or litres. This method of allocation assumes that all units of the product, irrespective of the physical measure used, have identical manufacturing costs.

To illustrate the physical measure basis of joint cost allocation to joint products, assume that the Avalon Division of Sax Company has a manufacturing process from which a maximum of four chemicals may be obtained. Assume also that these chemicals are all considered to be joint products. Avalon has calculated the costs for this process for the month of February. These costs and the resultant outputs are presented and described in the diagram included in Illustration 5-1.

Avalon does not have a choice with regard to the production of either Chemical A or Chemical B. These two chemicals are the natural outputs of Process One, the initial production process. Chemical A is not processed further by Avalon. Chemical B may be further processed to yield Chemical C and Chemical D. Once Process Two is begun for Chemical B, Chemicals C and D are the natural outputs of this second production process.

In Illustration 5-1, the mathematical relationships between the inputs, outputs, costs and sales values remain proportionately the same irrespective of the quantity of inputs introduced into the production process (within the relevant range). Not all of Chemical B will always be processed further, although under most circumstances it is normally more profitable for the firm to undertake the additional processing. The sales value of Chemical B in the illustration is $200. The combined sales value of Chemicals C and D is $250[(50 × $2) + (50 × $3)]. Therefore, for an additional expenditure of $10 made in Process Two, an additional $50($250 − $200) in revenue is obtained. A major reason Chemical B may not be processed further is the market demand for Chemicals C and D. If the demand for Chemicals C and D is considered insufficient, then Chemical B will be sold without further processing. (There is always a demand for Chemical B.) An additional reason for not processing Chemical B further is that the extra profit made possible producing Chemicals C and D may not warrant sacrificing the processing time which could instead be used to produce additional units of Chemicals A and B.

Assume that during February only Chemical A, Chemical C and Chemical D were produced (i.e. All of Chemical B produced was processed into Chemicals C and D.) The joint costs assigned or allocated to Chemical A might be determined at the split-off point of Process One, based on the ratio of the number of litres of A to the total number of litres produced in Process One.

Chemical A absorbs production costs in February totaling $100 or $1 for each litre produced. Chemical A has a sales value of $3 per litre. At this point, if it were not processed further, Chemical B would also have an assigned production cost of $1 per litre. The sales value of Chemical B is only $1 per litre. This allocation of joint production cost is, of course, arbitrary. Avalon cannot obtain Chemical A without also

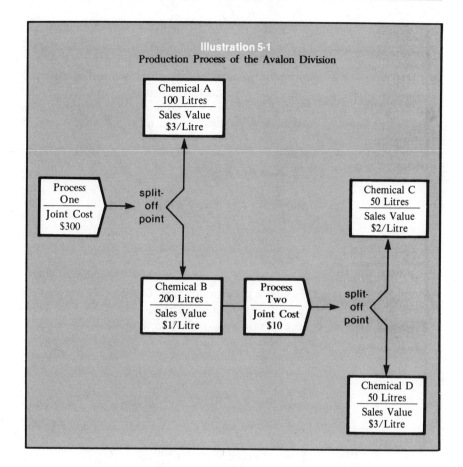

Illustration 5-1
Production Process of the Avalon Division

Chemical	Litres Produced	Proportion to Total Litres		Production Cost		Allocated Joint Cost		Number of Litres		Cost Per Litre
A.......	100	100/300	×	$300	=	$100	÷	100	=	$1
B.......	200	200/300	×	300	=	200	÷	200	=	1
	300					$300				

obtaining Chemical B. Chemical A is carried in the accounts at a cost of $1 for inventory costing purposes, an amount which is only one-third of its sales value. If Chemical B were not processed further, it would have an assigned production cost of $1 per litre which is equal to its selling price. From an accounting standpoint, therefore, Avalon could not sell Chemical B at a profit. The failure to consider a per unit selling price is a major weakness of the physical measure basis of cost allocation in a joint cost situation.

Chemical C and Chemical D are assigned costs based upon February production and the costs which are subsequently incurred in Process Two. Thus, in total they are assigned a cost of $210; this cost is comprised of $200 (the cost of Chemical B determined from Process One) plus $10 (the costs of Process Two which are traceable to Chemicals C and D). From a production standpoint, Chemical B must be produced before Process Two can be initiated to obtain Chemicals C and D.

Chemical	Litres Produced	Proportion to Total Litres		Cost*		Allocated Joint Cost*	Number of Litres		Cost Per Litre
C.......	50	50/100	×	$210	=	$105	÷ 50	=	$2.10
D.......	50	50/100	×	210	=	105	÷ 50	=	2.10
	100					$210			

*Total joint cost consists of $200 from Process One and $10 from Process Two or an aggregate amount of $210.

Under these conditions, Chemical C absorbs a production cost of $2.10 per litre. This product has a sales price of $2.00 per litre. Chemical D has a production cost of $2.10 and a sales value of $3.00 per litre.

The total production costs and sales values of Chemicals A, C, and D for February may be summarized in the following table.

Chemical	Litres Produced	Production Cost Per Litre	Total Production Cost	Sales Value Per Litre	Total Sales Value	Total Gross Profit
A.......	100	$1.00	$100	$3.00	$300	$200
C.......	50	2.10	105	2.00	100	(5)
D.......	50	2.10	105	3.00	150	45
	200		$310		$550	$240

Note that Chemical A has the highest profit margin (unit selling price of $3.00 less unit cost of $1.00 or a profit of $2.00 per unit). Chemical D is much less profitable ($3.00 per unit selling price less $2.10 per unit cost for a profit of $.90 per unit), and Chemical C sells at a loss of $.10 ($2.00 per unit selling price less $2.10 per unit cost). Remember that it was impossible to obtain any one product without obtaining the others, particularly Chemicals C and D which both result if Chemical B is processed further. Therefore, any managerial analysis of profitability which is made on the basis of cost accumulation data for inventory valuation is useless in a joint cost production process because of the arbitrary nature of the joint cost allocation process. However, it should be emphasized that the *total* gross profit amounting to $240 (total revenues of $550 minus total costs of $310) would not change regardless of the cost allocation method used.

**JOINT COST
ALLOCATION
BY RELATIVE
SALES VALUES**

    The relative sales value approach to the allocation of joint costs assumes that each joint product absorbs a portion of the joint costs proportional to the ability of that product to generate revenues. The result of this approach is to assign to those products with higher sales values a proportionately higher amount of the joint costs. Note that this allocation process results in generating the same percentage of profit for each joint product.

    As long as sales values are known at the split-off points and there are no separable processing costs, the relative sales value method or technique yields proportional profit percentages for joint products. If sales values are not obvious at the split-off points, the accountant, with the assistance of other members of the management team, must estimate a sales value for the joint products in order to make cost allocations using the relative sales value technique.

**Allocation When
Sales Values Are
Known at
Split-Off Points**

    As indicated in Illustration 5-1, the sales values of Chemicals A and B were known at the split-off point. Chemical A has a total sales value of $300 and Chemical B has a total sales value of $200. The joint cost of producing these two Chemicals is $300. The joint cost, using the relative sales value technique, may be allocated in two different ways. Both approaches will yield the same results.

1. Percent of Relative Sales to Total Sales

Chemical	Sales Value	Sales Value to Total Sales	Percent of Sales Value
A	$300	$300/$500	60%
B	200	$200/$500	40
	$500		100%

Joint Cost Allocation

Chemical	Joint Cost Allocation	Litres Produced	Cost Per Litre
A	$180	100	$1.80
B	120	200	.60
	$300	300	

2. Percent of Joint Cost to Total Sales Value

$$\frac{\text{Joint Cost}}{\text{Total Sales Value}} = \frac{\$300}{\$500} = 60\%$$

Chemical	Sales Value	Cost to Sales Value Percentage	Joint Cost Allocation	Litres Produced	Cost Per Litre
A............	$300	60%	$180	100	$1.80
B............	200	60	120	200	.60
	$500		$300	300	

If both Chemicals A and B were sold at this point, they would yield equally profitable gross margins on a percentage basis, as indicated previously. The following computations support this conclusion.

Chemical A	Amount	Percent		Chemical B	Amount	Percent
Sales Value..............	$300	100%	Sales Value..............	$200	100%
Cost of Goods Sold.......	180	60	Cost of Goods Sold.......	120	60
Gross Margin...........	$120	40%	Gross Margin...........	$ 80	40%

If Chemical B were processed further in order to obtain Chemicals C and D, the joint costs that Chemicals C and D would absorb would consist of $120 from Process One and $10 from Process Two. The allocation made to Chemicals C and D, using the relative sales value approach, would follow the same principles which are applied to Chemicals A and B in allocating the joint costs which were incurred in Process One.

Percent of Joint Cost to Total Sales
Chemical C and Chemical D
(assuming that Chemical B was processed further)

$$\frac{\text{Joint Cost } \$120 + \$10}{\text{Total Sales Value*}} = \frac{\$130}{\$250} = 52\%$$

$$
\begin{aligned}
*C &= 50 \text{ Litres @ } \$2.00 &=& \quad \$100 \\
D &= 50 \text{ Litres @ } \$3.00 &=& \quad \underline{150} \\
& & & \quad \underline{\$250}
\end{aligned}
$$

Chemical	Sales Value	Cost to Sales Value Percentage	Joint Cost Allocation	Litres Produced	Cost Per Litre
C............	$100	52%	$ 52	50	$1.04
D............	150	52	78	50	1.56
	$250		$130	100	

If Chemicals C and D were sold at this point, these products would yield the same gross margin on a percentage basis, as demonstrated by the calculations which follow.

Chemical C	Amount	Percent		Chemical D	Amount	Percent
Sales Value..............	$100	100%	Sales Value..............	$150	100%
Cost of Goods Sold.......	52	52	Cost of Goods Sold.......	78	52
Gross Margin...........	$ 48	48%	Gross Margin...........	$ 72	48%

Allocation When Sales Values Are Unknown at Split-Off Point

The accountant must compute the approximate sales values at split-off points when the joint products are not readily marketable at that point in time. If the joint products are marketable, but management chooses to process these products further rather than to sell them at the split-off point, then the actual market (sales) value of the joint products at split-off should be used in allocating the joint cost. This was the procedure followed in the previous example.

Now, let us assume that all of the factors presented in Illustration 5–1 for the Avalon Division are identical, *except* that Chemical B does not have a market value at the split-off point. The information in Illustration 5–1 is presented again in Illustration 5–2 for ease of this analysis. Illustration 5–2 has taken into consideration the fact that there is no current market, and therefore no readily determinable sales value for Chemical B.

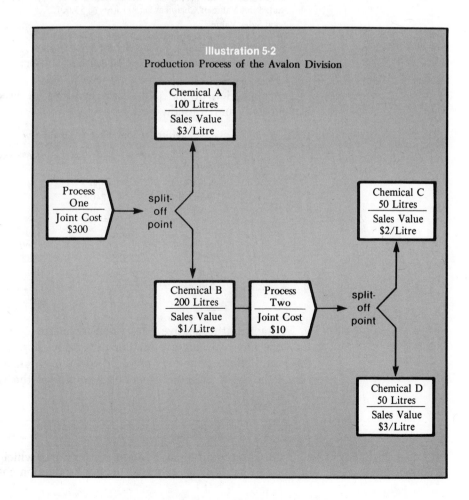

Illustration 5-2
Production Process of the Avalon Division

Since the relative sales value for Chemical B at the split-off point is not known, the allocation process requires two steps.

1. Estimating the sales value for Chemical B.
2. Allocating the joint cost of $300 for Chemical A and Chemical B using the relative sales value technique for product costing.

For product costing purposes, the approximate sales value of Chemical B at the split-off point is determined by working backwards from the point at which Chemical B does become marketable due to additional processing. For the Avalon Division, this is the point at which Chemicals C and D become marketable as finished products. The calculations necessary to compute the approximate sales value for Chemical B are as follows:

Sales Value of Chemical C (50 Litres @ $2.00)	$100
Add: Sales Value of Chemical D (50 Litres @ $3.00)	150
Total Sales Value	$250
Deduct: Further Processing Costs Beyond Split-Off Point (Process Two)	10
Approximate Market Value of Chemical B at Split-Off Point	$240

The allocation of the joint costs incurred in Process One between Chemicals A and B follows.

Percent of Joint Cost to Total Sales

$$\frac{\text{Joint Costs}}{\text{Total Sales Value*}} = \frac{\$300}{\$540} = 55.6\% \text{ (rounded)}$$

* Chemical A	=	$300
Chemical B	=	240
		$540

Chemical	Sales Value	Cost to Sales Value Percentage	Joint Cost Allocation	Litres Produced	Cost Per Litre
A	$300	55.6%	$167	100	$1.67
B	240	55.6	133	200	.67
	$540		$300	300	

In practice, the relative sales value technique is used more frequently than the physical measure methods. Possibly, this is due to a desire on the part of the accountants involved to value the inventory so as to represent the relative income-generating ability of the various items of inventory.

ACCOUNTING FOR BY-PRODUCTS

From an accounting standpoint, by-products which are not processed further are not usually allocated by any production costs. The production costs are normally allocated to and absorbed by the joint products. Thus, by-products may not have an associated accounting cost in the sense that joint products do. However, any revenue from by-product sales is recognized for accounting purposes.

There are numerous methods used in accounting for the revenues realized from the sale of by-products. Three approaches are:

1. The treatment of by-product revenues as a reduction of cost of goods sold.
2. The treatment of by-product revenues as other income.
3. The treatment of by-product revenues as a reduction of the cost of joint products.

In the cases mentioned above, the net revenues to be received from the sale of by-products are treated as a reduction of the cost of goods sold, as other income for income statement purposes or, in the third case, as a reduction of the cost of the joint products. When the benefits will be recognized under any alternative will depend on the potential demand for the by-products.

By-Products With a Ready Market

If by-products have a known market price, the cost of goods sold for a given accounting period may be reduced by the *expected* net revenues which will be obtained or realized from the sale of the by-products which were *manufactured* during that period. Alternative treatments are to recognize the net revenues to be realized from the sale of the by-products produced during the period as other income of that period or as a reduction of the cost of the joint-products.

To illustrate the accounting treatment of by-products with a ready market, assume that the Avalon Division decided to produce only Chemicals A and B during the month of February. The output of the production process includes 50 litres of a marketable by-product, Chemical X, which may be sold at a price of $.80 per litre. The costs of selling Chemical X are approximately $.10 per litre. Avalon uses the relative sales value technique in order to allocate the joint costs to its joint products, Chemical A and Chemical B. There are no beginning inventories of either the joint products or the by-products. Three-fourths of February's production of Chemicals A, B, and X were sold during February. The data for the allocation of the $300 in joint costs which were incurred to produce the joint products, Chemicals A and B, was presented in Illustration 5-2.

The important points to note in Illustration 5-3 are the alternative income statement treatments and the related inventory values for balance sheet purposes at the end of February.

Illustration 5-3
Avalon Division
By-Products With a Ready Market

		Actual Production			Actual Sales	
	Litres	Production Cost Per Litre	Production Cost in Total	Litres Sold	Sales Price Per Litre	Total Sales
Chemical A ..	100	$1.80	$180	75.0	$3.00	$225
Chemical B ..	200	.60	120	150.0	1.00	150
Chemical X ..	50	0	0	37.5	.80	30
	350		$300	262.5		$405

Anticipated Net Revenues *from By-Product Produced*

Anticipated Revenues..............	50 X	$.80	=	$40	
Less: Selling Costs.................	50 X	.10	=	5	
Net Revenues Anticipated..........	50 X	$.70	=	$35	

Income Statement for February

	By-Product Net Revenues Treated as Reduction of Cost of Goods Sold	By Product Net Revenues Treated as Other Income
Sales (Joint Products from *Actual Sales*).............	$375	$375
Income from the Sale of By-Products*..............	0	35
Total Sales and Other Income.....................	$375	$410
Less: Cost of Goods Sold		
Chemical A $1.80 × 75 = $135		
Chemical B $ .60 × 150 = 90		
$225		225
Net Revenues from Chemical X Production (35)	190	
Gross Margin..................................	$185	$185

Ending Inventory Values On the February 28 Balance Sheet

	Litres	Production Cost Per Litre	Valuation at Net Revenue	Total
Chemical A	25.0	$1.80		$45.00
Chemical B	50.0	.60		30.00
Chemical X	12.5	0	$.70	8.75
				$83.75

*The income from the sale of by-products would normally appear after income from operations on a multiple step income statement.

In arriving at the net revenues anticipated from by-product sales in Illustration 5–3, note that selling costs were deducted from the anticipated revenues. It is not uncommon for a firm to incur further processing costs, as well as handling, storage and delivery charges for its by-products, and any costs that can be specifically identified with the by-products are deducted from the anticipated revenues in order to arrive at net revenues.[1]

By-Products With an Uncertain Market

If by-products do not have a ready market, the cost of goods sold for a given accounting period is reduced by the *actual* net revenues obtained from the *sale* of the by-products during that period. Once again, an alternative treatment is to recognize the net revenues from the sale of by-products as other income in the period of sale. Any ending inventory of by-products has no associated cost, i.e. carrying value for balance sheet purposes. The uncertainty of marketability requires that the accountant wait until the by-product is actually sold before any formal recognition of revenue is made in the accounts. The alternate income statement treatments and the related inventory values for the February balance sheet (assuming that Chemical X is considered to be a by-product with an uncertain market) are presented in Illustration 5–4.

The difference in accounting for those by-products with a ready market and accounting for those by-products with an uncertain market is significant. With a ready market value for the by-products, revenue is recognized as the by-products are produced. Inventories of the by-products are carried in the accounts at their net realizable value. With an uncertain by-product market value, revenues are recognized only as the by-products are actually sold. In this latter case, the inventories of by-products do not absorb any costs of production and, therefore, have no accounting values for balance sheet purposes. These differences can be identified by comparing Illustration 5–3 with Illustration 5–4.

By-Products Treated as a Reduction of the Cost of Joint Products

If by-products have a known market price, the production costs of the joint products may be reduced by the expected net revenues which will be obtained or realized from the sale of the by-products which were manufactured during that period. To illustrate, we will use the following data from Illustration 5-3:

Total Production Cost of Chemicals A and B ($180 + $120)........	$300
Anticipated *Net* Revenues from By-Product Produced.............	35
Production in Litres of Chemicals:	
A...	100
B...	200
X...	50
Sales Price Per Litre of Chemicals:	
A...	$ 3
B...	1

[1] The net revenues anticipated represent what is also referred to as the net realizable value.

Illustration 5-4
Avalon Division
By-Products With an Uncertain Market

		Actual Production			Actual Sales	
	Litres	Production Cost Per Litre	Production Cost in Total	Litres Sold	Sales Price Per Litre	Total Sales
Chemical A ...	100	$1.80	$180	75.0	$3.00	$225
Chemical B ...	200	.60	120	150.0	1.00	150
Chemical X ...	50	0	0	37.5	.80	30
	350		$300	262.5		$405

Actual Revenues *from By-Product Sold*

Actual Revenues..............	(37.5 X $.80)	=	$30.00
Less: Selling Costs............	(37.5 X .10)	=	3.75
Actual Net Revenues...........................			$26.25

Income Statement for February

	By-Product Net Revenues Treated as Reduction of Cost of Goods Sold	By Product Net Revenues Treated as Other Income
Sales (Joint Products from *Actual Sales*)..........	$375.00	$375.00
Income from the Sale of By-Products.............	0	26.25
Total Sales and Other Income...................	$375.00	$401.25
Less: Cost of Goods Sold		
Chemical A $1.80 × 75 = $135		
Chemical B $ .60 × 150 = 90		
$225		225.00
Net Revenues from Chemical X Sales (26.25)	198.75	
Gross Margin...............................	$176.25	$176.25

Ending Inventory Values on the February 28 Balance Sheet

	Litres	Production Cost Per Litre	Total
Chemical A.......	25.0	$1.80	$45
Chemical B.......	50.0	.60	30
Chemical X.......	12.5	0	0
			$75

Chemical	Litres Produced	Sales Price	Sales Value	Sales Value to Total Sales	Net Production Cost*	Joint Cost Allocation	Cost Per Litre
A	100	$3	$300	$300/$500	$265	$159	$1.59
B	200	1	200	$200/$500	265	106	.53
			$500			$265	

* Total production cost of the two joint products ($300) less the anticipated *net* revenues from the by-product, Chemical X, produced ($35).

Using this method, the production cost to be allocated to the joint products is reduced by the anticipated *net* revenues from the by-product. The "cost" per unit of the by-product is its selling price, reduced by selling expenses.

SUMMARY

Because of their very nature, certain manufacturing processes result in the production of more than a single product. When this occurs, it is necessary to allocate the common costs of production on some arbitrary basis in order to arrive at inventory costs for the various products. The manner in which these costs are allocated depends, in part, on the nature of the products produced.

The two basic types of products produced in a joint cost manufacturing process are joint products and by-products. Joint products are the main objectives of the production process and as such are the desirable products that normally make a significant contribution to the revenues of a firm. By-products, on the other hand, are inadvertent results of the production process. They are, therefore, generally of little importance to the firm and make only a nominal contribution to the firm's revenues.

The common costs that must be allocated are referred to as joint product costs and include all costs incurred prior to the split-off point or point of separation. In the case of joint products, joint costs are usually allocated on the basis of physical measures or relative sales value measures. When the physical measures allocation method is used, the costs are distributed uniformly according to some common physical unit, such as litres, kilograms or tons. Alternatively, with the relative sales value approach, each product is assigned a cost proportionate to its ability to generate revenues.

When the relative sales value of each joint product is known at the split-off point, the allocation process is as follows: assign to each product the percentage of the total joint costs to the total sales value at split-off, times the relative sales value of the given product. Alternatively, each product can be assigned joint costs equal to the total joint costs multiplied by the ratio of relative sales value of each product to the total sales value of all products.

When the relative sales values at the split-off point are unknown, the accountant must work backwards from the point at which relative sales values are known in order to approximate the value at the split-off point. This is generally accomplished by subtracting further processing costs from the relative sales values at the latter point and then assuming that the result is equal to the relative sales values at the split-off point.

From an accounting standpoint, it is assumed that by-products are not allocated any production costs (all such costs are normally absorbed by the major or joint products). The accounting treatment of revenues from the sale of by-products differs according to whether or not a ready market exists for the product and whether the firm wishes to account for the revenues on the income statement as a reduction of the cost of goods sold for the accounting period, as other income for the period or as a reduction of the cost of the joint products.

The primary difference in the treatments discussed lies in the timing of the recognition of the revenues. In the case of ready markets, the expected net revenues to be generated by the sale of the by-products are recognized as a reduction of the cost of goods sold, as other income as the products are produced or as a reduction of the cost of the joint products. Where no ready market exists, net revenues are recognized as a reduction of the cost of goods sold or as other income only as the by-products are actually sold.

Finally, the various inventory cost accounting methods for joint products and by-products are of great significance to management. Since pricing policies are partially a function of cost, the cost accounting method used may significantly affect a firm's potential revenues and profits.

KEY DEFINITIONS   **By-products**—products produced by the production process as a natural result of obtaining the more desirable joint products. By products are not the main objectives of the production process and are not a major revenue source for the firm.

Joint costs—costs of the production process which are incurred prior to the split-off point and which cannot directly be traced to any single product.

Joint products—major products which are the output of a single production process and which are normally expected to make a significant contribution to revenues of the firm.

Net realizable value—revenue which is anticipated or estimated for the sale of a product less any expense associated with the sale.

Separable or further processing costs—costs incurred after the split-off point which are attributable to the further processing of a physically identifiable product. These costs are traceable to the specific product for which they were incurred.

√ **Split-off point or point of separation**—the point during a joint manufacturing process where two or more products are physically identifiable as separate and distinct products.

QUESTIONS

5-1 Define joint products and by-products.

5-2 Explain the split-off point.

5-3 How are costs treated before and after the split-off point?

5-4 What allocation techniques can be used for distributing joint costs?

5-5 Explain what is meant by allocating joint costs using a physical measure.

5-6 Explain what is meant by allocating joint costs using relative sales value.

5-7 What is required when the relative sales value for a product is not known at the split-off point?

5-8 Which technique, the relative sales value or the physical method, is more frequently used in practice to allocate joint costs? Why?

5-9 What three approaches are used in accounting for the revenues realized from the sale of by-products?

5-10 What is the effect on the income statement if by-products have a ready market?

5-11 What is the effect on the income statement if by-products do not have a ready market?

EXERCISES AND PROBLEMS

5-12 Stevenson Company produces three products; Alpha, Beta, and Gamma. All three products are initially put into process at the same time in Department A, and in this process, joint costs of $5,600 are incurred. Alpha is further processed in Department B, incurring $2,400 in additional costs. Beta and Gamma are further processed in Department C, incurring joint costs of $3,200. Beta and Gamma are then finished in separate departments (Departments D and E) where they incur additional costs of $300 and $500 respectively. In the month of April, 2,000 units of Alpha, 2,500 units of Beta, and 3,200 units of Gamma were produced. Alpha sells for $1.50 per unit; Beta, $3.25 per unit; and Gamma $2.75 per unit.

Required:
Diagram the costs and outputs of this total process for the month of April.

5-13 ABC Company produces two joint products, Alpha and Beta, and a by-product Gamma. Alpha sells for $20,000, Beta sells for $30,000 and Gamma sells for $1,000. The production process costs $15,000.

Required:

Using the relative sales value, allocate the joint costs.

5-14 Samson Oil, Inc. uses a manufacturing process from which three products are obtained. The joint costs incurred to produce 24,000 units of Product One, 18,000 units of Product Two, and 18,000 units of Product Three are $141,000. The products sell for $2.80, $3.60, and $2.30, respectively.

Required:

Allocate the joint costs using the physical measures. Is this a good method of allocation? Why?

5-15   Gree-Dee, Inc. has two products, Gamma and Sigma which sell for $28 and $35, respectively. These two products are the natural result of one production process. The company incurs joint cost of $22,400 to produce 5,000 units of Gamma and 4,000 units of Sigma.

Required:

Allocate the joint cost using the relative sales value method.

5-16   Yason and Sons Chemical Company has two joint products, XYZ and JXL, and a by-product ABC. During 1980, 25,000 units of XYZ, 30,000 units of JXL and 400 units of ABC were produced. Allocated joint costs for XYZ were $3.30 per unit and $4.80 for JXL. Selling prices were $5.50, $8.00, and $.75, respectively. Selling costs for ABC were $.12 per unit. During 1980, 18,900 units of XYZ, 26,200 units of JXL, and 400 units of ABC were sold.

Required:

Determine the gross margin by treating the net revenues from the by-product as (a) a reduction of cost of goods sold, and (b) other income.

5-17   The Starnes Chemical Company has two products, R and S, which are the natural output of their production process. This process, which costs $42,000, produces 10,000 tons of R and 11,000 tons of S. They sell for $35,000 and $49,000, respectively.

Required:

a.   Allocate the production costs to R and S using the relative sales value.
b.   If S can be further processed for $15,000 to produce T and U which sell for $40,000 and $70,000 respectively, use the relative sales value approach to allocate these costs.

5-18   The Cogwell Company produces two products in a joint process. Material, labor, and overhead for the month of October in this process were $2,025, $2,592, and $2,349 respectively. Product J sold for $4,500 and Product N sold for $3,600.

Required:

Allocate material, labor, and overhead joint costs to products J and N using the relative sales value method.

5-19   Consider the data listed below involving joint product costs.

1. Two products produced from the same process, Pro and Con.
2. Joint costs were $366,400.
3. 6,000 pecks of Pro and 8,800 bushels of Con were produced during the period.
4. Pro sells for $25 per peck and Con sells for $33 per bushel.
5. Beginning inventory included 200 pecks of Pro costing $18.00 per peck and 616 bushels of Con costing $23.00 per bushel.
6. There are no ending inventories.

Required:

Compute the gross margin for Pro and Con using the relative sales value method to allocate costs.

5-20   Jones Lumber Company produces plywood and lumber with shavings as a by-product. In May, 850 sheets of plywood and 4,125 board feet of lumber were produced at a total cost of $55,000. Joint costs included in this cost were $32,000. Separate costs to produce the plywood and lumber consisted of $13,000 and $10,000 respectively. The plywood sells for $50 a sheet and the lumber sells for $8 per board foot. There are 50 sheets of plywood in ending inventory. There were no beginning inventories. All of the lumber was sold. Two tons of shavings were the result of this process and they sold for $20 a ton. Costs incurred in selling the shavings included $3 per ton for transportation and $3.50 per ton for storage.

Required:

Using the relative sales value method, find the gross margin for the month of May, treating the revenue from the shavings as additional income from by-products.

5-21   As the accountant for the Beverly Company, you are to determine the price that should be charged next year for each of their joint products, Tic and Tac. During the year ending September 30, 3,000 units of Tic and 2,000 units of Tac were produced. Joint costs in the production of these items totaled $8,850. Allocate the joint costs using a physical measure basis.

Required:

If Beverly Company would like to have a 30% mark-up on costs as its selling price per unit, what would be that price for both Tic and Tac?

5-22   The Amsden Company allocates joint costs according to the number of litres of each of the joint products produced. Three products are produced and $36,000 worth of joint costs are incurred monthly. In the production process, 4,000 litres of product E are produced and 6,000 litres of products F and G are produced. E is sold for $3.00 per litre, F is sold for $2.50 per litre and G is sold for $2.25 per litre. Allocate the joint costs using a physical measure.

Required:

a. What is the gross margin per product assuming all litres produced are sold?

b. If the price of G goes down to $1.80 per litre due to market conditions, should the Amsden Company continue to produce product G assuming the joint costs would decrease by only $1,500 if production of G ceased (due to a savings in handling and separation costs)?

5-23   The Lectronics Company began operations in January. They produce two products, Timer and Tinkers, in a joint process, and allocate joint costs using the relative sales value method. However, they cannot decide whether to use Fifo or Lifo to cost their ending inventories and cost of goods sold. Below cost data are presented for the first two months of the year.

	January	February
Units of Timers produced	250	280
Units of Tinkers produced	230	290
Joint costs	$1,180.00	$2,000.00
Additional costs to produce Timers	$ 650.00	$ 655.00
Additional costs to produce Tinkers	$ 840.00	$ 825.00
Units of Timers sold	210	260
Units of Tinkers sold	180	270
Price of Timers per unit . . . . $	7.10	$ 7.15
Price of Tinkers per unit . . . . $	7.90	$ 8.10

Required:

Calculate the ending inventories for January and February under the Fifo and Lifo methods.

5-24   The Ames Company must make a decision concerning the further processing of a product produced in a joint process. The process produces three chemicals, AA, BB, and CC. AA and BB must be produced further in order to be salable. CC, however, may be produced further or may be sold after the joint process. From the information listed below, decide whether to produce CC further or to sell it in its initial form.

Joint costs per month	$12,000
Additional costs to produce AA	$10,000
Additional costs to produce BB	$16,000
Additional costs to produce CC	$14,000
Selling price of AA	$69
Selling price of BB	$85
Selling price of CC after joint process	$18
Selling price of CC after produced further . . .	$95
Tons of AA produced per month	250
Tons of BB produced per month	300
Tons of CC produced per month	200

The Ames Company uses relative sales values to allocate joint costs. Assume all units produced can be sold.

5-25   The Rite-cut Co. is a slaughter house which must allocate costs to the different cuts of beef.

Cuts	Amount Per Animal	Wholesale Selling Price
1. High quality steaks	180 kilos	$1.65/kilo
2. Medium quality steaks	220 kilos	1.40/kilo
3. Low quality steaks	240 kilos	1.20/kilo
4. Hamburger	300 kilos	.95/kilo
5. Roasts	200 kilos	1.80/kilo
6. Liver	50 kilos	.90/kilo
7. Other (by-products)	150 kilos	1.00/kilo

It takes 3 union butchers 5 hours each to carve the animal at a cost of $16 per man per hour. (These are joint costs.)

Required:

Calculate the per kilo cost for labor for each of the above cuts using (a) relative sales value method, and (b) physical units method (one kilo = 1 unit). Which method is preferable? Why?

5-26   The Temper-Tone Steel Company produces two major products, a stainless steel sheet called Flextin and stainless steel silverware. Both products go through the same initial production process where the costs are inseparable. The total cost of this process last period was $550,000. The silverware goes through a second process for completion and the cost of this process is $10,000. The resulting volume is 500,000 pieces of silverware and 45,000 sheets of Flextin. The market value of the Flextin is $2,250,000 while the market value of the silverware is $250,000.

Required:

Using the relative sales value method, determine the unit cost of each product.

5-27   The King Chemical Company produces two chemicals, A and B. They use a joint process, but are unable to decide on the best allocation method. You have been asked to compare allocation methods and make your recommendations to the King Company. The necessary information follows:

Joint processing cost $60,000

At Split-off:	Units made	Volume (Ltr.)	Market Value
Chemical A	15,000	30,000	$75,000
Chemical B	30,000	90,000	$15,000

Required:

a. Allocate the joint costs to each chemical by the following methods:
   1. Units made
   2. Relative volume
   3. Market value
b. Make your recommendations as to the best method.

5-28 In February, the Berna Company spent $50,000 in production costs for three joint products, G, H, and I and a by-product Z up to the split-off point. There were 10,000 units of G produced, 15,000 units of H, 25,000 units of I, and 500 units of Z. G sells for $2.50 per unit, H for $1.75 per unit, I for $1.25 per unit, and Z for $.70 per unit. The company incurs selling costs of $.15 per unit of Z sold. The company had no beginning or ending inventories in February.

Required:

a. Allocate the production costs using relative sales value.
b. Find the gross margin by treating the net revenues of the by-product as a reduction of cost of goods sold.
c. Find the gross margin by treating the net revenues of the by-product as other income.

5-29 Jerry Company began operations on January 1. By processing raw material X, Jerry Company obtains two products: 1,000 units of A and 2,000 sheets of B. A may be sold at $3 per unit and B's selling price is $1 per sheet. The total processing cost for the year is $4,000.

Required:

a. If all of the production is sold, how should the processing cost be allocated to A & B?
b. If the ending inventory at December 31 consists of 500 units of A and 1,000 sheets of B, what would be the total cost of the inventories at year-end? (Use the relative sales value method.)
c. If the ending inventory is 100 units of A and 200 sheets of B, what would be the total carrying value of each inventory item at December 31 for balance sheet purposes? (Use the relative sales value method.)
d. If A is considered a major product and B is considered a by-product, what would be the total carrying value of 100 units of A at December 31 for balance sheet purposes? Is it logical to assume that B, is in fact, a by-product? Why or why not?

5-30 The Blatz Chemical Company makes Chemicals A, B, and D in its production process with Chemical C as a by-product. It takes 600 litres of raw material, X, at a cost of $800, to make 200 litres of each of the chemicals

(A, B, C, and D). 200 litres of A sells at $800, 200 litres of B sells at $200 and 200 litres of D sells at $200. There is a market available for the 200 litres of Chemical C which sells at $40.

Required:

What is the allocated cost of these joint products and by-products under the relative sales value method and the anticipated net revenues from the by-product if there is a selling cost of $.10 per litre? (Assume no beginning or ending inventories.)

A   **5-31**   The Stooges Chemical Company has three products (Larry, Moe and Joe) which are the natural outputs of their production. This process, which costs $12,000, produces 2,000 tons of Larry, 1,500 tons of Moe and 2,500 tons of Joe.

Required:

a.   What would be the allocation of production costs to Larry, Moe and Joe under physical measures?
b.   If Larry retails at $7,000, Moe at $6,000 and Joe at $5,000, what would be the allocation by the relative sales value method?

5-32   Dixie Chemical Corporation produces two products Y and X up to the split-off point; 7,500 barrels of each chemical are produced at a cost of $30,000. Y has a sales value at this point of $4.00 per barrel. The sales value of X is not known at this point.

X will be processed further to make chemicals M & N. The cost of this process is $22,500. In the process, 5,000 barrels of M and 2,500 barrels of N are produced. M has a sales value of $4.50 per barrel while N sells for $6.00 per barrel.

Required:

Using the relative sales value method, allocate the joint costs to Y and X and to M and N.

5-33   The Sharon Company produces the three products listed below in a joint process:

	Ham	*Cain*	*Abel*
Units produced in May	2,125	1,500	2,000
Units sold in May	1,500	1,500	1,500
Price per unit	$12.00	$3.00	$9.50
Direct costs incurred in addition to joint costs	$8,000	$4,500	$19,000

Joint costs incurred up to split-off were $15,000. Each product is a natural output of this joint process.

Required:

Calculate the allocation of joint costs to Ham, Cain, and Abel using the relative sales value method. Cain and Abel are sold to provide a complete product line.

A **5-34** The McMillon Company produces three products, Plain and Barbecued Potato Chips and French Fries. 10,000 kilograms of raw potatoes used in producing these products were put into production in May at a total cost of $7,000. These material and conversion costs are incurred in Department 1. In Department 2, 5,000 kilograms of the potatoes were used to make 5,000 kilograms of French Fries at a total cost of $700 for the month. The remaining 5,000 kilograms of potatoes were cut-up in a form in Department 3 which could be used to produce both Plain and Barbecued Potato Chips. In Department 3, total costs for May were $250. In Department 4, 2,500 kilograms of the cut-up potatoes were used to make Barbecued Potato Chips at an additional cost of $650; and in Department 4, the remaining 2,500 kilograms were made into Plain Potato Chips at an additional cost of $550.

The French Fries sell for $.90 a kilogram, the Barbecued Potato Chips sell for $1.50 a kilogram, and the Plain Potato Chips sell for $1.40 a kilogram.

Required:

Calculate the total cost per kilogram of each product using the relative sales value method. It may be helpful to first draw a diagram of the flow of costs and outputs.

5-35 The Robert Company uses the relative sales value method to allocate the joint costs of their two products, Chit and Chat. Costs incurred in this joint process for July were $12,000. From this cost, 2,000 units of Chit and 3,500 units of Chat were produced. Chit sells for $3.00 a unit and Chat sells for $3.25 a unit. Beginning and ending inventories for the month of July are as follows:

	Chit	Chat
Beginning inventory:		
Units	110	360.
Cost per unit	$1.90	$2.20
Ending inventory:		
Units	215	320
Cost per unit	?	?

Required:

Calculate the gross margin of each product using the average cost method to determine the cost of goods sold.

5-36 The Smith Company is in its first year of business. The company produces four products in a joint process, H, I, J and K. The joint costs incurred for the first year ending December 31 were $87,500. Below is listed production and sales data for this year:

Product	Units Produced	Kilograms Produced	Price per Unit	Total Sales Value
H	2,000	4,000	$5.00	$ 10,000
I	4,000	6,000	$5.50	22,000
J	6,000	8,000	$5.25	31,500
K	8,000	10,000	$5.75	46,000
	20,000	28,000		$109,500

Required:

a. Assuming 100 units of each product are in ending inventory, allocate costs for the Smith Company using allocation by units, kilograms, and relative sales values.

b. Continuing from requirement *a.*, find the gross margin under each method for product I, and select that method to be used for reporting purposes this year and consistently in the future which gives the highest gross margin for product I.

5-37   In August, the Intac Co. incurred $196,000 of production costs for four joint products, S, T, U, V and one by-product Zap. There were 24,500 units of S, 49,000 units of T, 39,200 units of U, 98,000 units of V produced, and 12,000 units of Zap. (There was no beginning inventory.) In September, $187,000 of production costs were incurred. There were 22,000 units of S, 46,000 units of T, 35,000 units of U, 90,000 units of V produced, and 10,000 units of Zap. The selling price of S is $3.00 per unit, T is $1.90 per unit, U is $2.40 per unit, and V is $1.50 per unit. Zap has a ready market at $.15 per unit. Selling and transportation costs for Zap total $.08 per unit. August sales in units were: S = 19,500, T = 38,700, U = 36,080, V = 97,800, Zap = 11,300. September sales in units were: S = 21,500, T = 44,800, U = 31,100, V = 88,100, Zap = 8,500.

Required:

a. Allocate the production costs using relative sales values for each month.

b. Calculate the September ending inventory and cost of goods sold using Fifo and Lifo.

5-38   Farmer Brown spends much of the winter indoors. He realizes that idle hands are the devil's workshop and therefore occupies his time by whittling. In one hour he can whittle down five blocks of wood. Realizing that this would be a waste of time unless he could produce something worthwhile, he decided to carve out pencils, matches and toothpicks. He discovered that from each block he could produce 100 pencils, 500 matches and 1,000 toothpicks. Farmer Brown also obtains 1 kilo of wood shavings from each block as a by-product. In the past month, he has whittled 200 hours and he considers an hour of his time worth $4. Other pertinent information is as follows:

Cost of a wood block . . . . . $.80
Sales value of a pencil   . . . . $.02
Sales value of a match   . . . . $.005
Sales value of a toothpick   . . . $.001
Sales value of 1 kilo of
      shavings . . . . $.05

Required:

a. Calculate the joint costs incurred by Farmer Brown during the past month.
b. Allocate the joint costs using relative sales values.
c. Find the gross margin by treating the net revenues of the by-product as a reduction of cost of goods sold.

5-39   The Howaya Perfume Company manufactures four types of perfume: W, X, Y and Z. Total joint processing costs were $195,200 in 19x0. An activity report revealed the following information:

Product	Production (in grams)	Price per Gram	Sales	Additional Processing Costs
W	1,000,000	$ .2300	$230,000	$60,000
X	20,000	1.0000	20,000	12,000
Y	10,000	.8000	8,000	—
Z	18,000	3.3333	60,000 °	2,000

° Rounded

Required:

Calculate the gross margin for each product using the relative sales value method.

5-40   The Oddball Company is a producer of a synthetic plastic. The initial mixing process yields two joint products, Plastex and Rubberoid, as well as a residual or by-product, Glue-all. The production costs for Oddball for the month of May were $60,000. There were 12,000 tons of Plastex and 8,000 tons of Rubberoid produced in May as well as 700 tons of Glue-all. Plastex has a market value of $4 per ton, Rubberoid has a market value of $6 per ton, and Glue-all is sold for $2 per ton. Selling costs for Glue-all consist solely of salesmen's commissions of 10%.

Required:

a. Allocate costs under the physical measure method.
b. Allocate costs under the relative sales value method.
c. How would you treat the by-product? Show figures.

5-41   The Scalding Sport Company produces balls used in various athletic contests. The products of the manufacturing process are basketballs, soccerballs, and volleyballs. The manufacturing process costs total $50,000. Details concerning the output are as follows:

2,000 basketballs selling at $9.00 each
3,000 soccerballs selling at $8.00 each
5,000 volleyballs selling at $6.00 each

Required:

a. Allocate the joint cost according to physical output.
b. Allocate the joint cost according to relative sales value.

5-42 Lafferty Ltd. has three products derived from the same manufacturing operation. However, each product requires additional processing beyond the split-off point. The main products are X and Y. The by-product is ZZ.

Cost incurred before the split-off point is $320,000. Costs incurred beyond the split-off point were recorded as follows:

Product X.................................. $300,000
Product Y.................................. 250,000
By-Product ZZ..............................   11,200

During a review of costs, it is ascertained that Product Y was overcharged with an amount of $50,000 representing direct labour.

The following additional information was obtained:

	Weight	Selling Price Per Pound	Anticipated Net Profit (% of Sales)
Product X............	200,000 pounds	$4.00	15%
Product Y............	200,000 pounds	2.20	15%
By-Product ZZ.......	30,000 pounds	1.20	15%

Selling and administrative expense amounts to 20% of sales.

Required:

a. Prepare a schedule of production costs showing the allocation of costs incurred prior to the split-off point. Use the net realizable value less a normal profit margin method.

b. Assuming all three products are joint products, present a schedule of profits for each product using the relative sales value method as the cost allocation basis.

c. List and briefly describe two different methods of accounting for by-products.

(SMA, adapted)

5-43 A pharmaceutical company manufactures two products: A and B, in a common process. The joint costs amount to $12,000 per batch of finished goods. Each batch amounts to 10,000 litres, of which 25 percent are Product A and 75 percent are Product B. The two products are processed further, but without any gain or loss in volume. The costs of additional processing are $0.30 per litre for Product A and $0.40 per litre for Product B. After the additional processing, the selling price of Product A is $2.10 per litre, and the selling price of Product B is $1.60 per litre.

Required:

a. If the joint costs are to be allocated on the basis of the net realizable value of each product at the split-off point, what amount of joint costs will be allocated to each product?

b. Prepare a schedule of gross profit by product and by batch using the preceding allocation and assuming that 80 percent of Product A and 60 percent of Product B were sold, with no opening inventories of either product.

c. The company has discovered an additional process by which Product A can be transformed into Product AA which could be sold for $6 per litre. On the other hand, this additional processing would increase costs by $2.10 per litre. Assuming that there is no other change in costs, should the company use the new process? Show supporting calculations.

(SMA, *adapted*)

5-44 The Abson Chemical Company produces two joint products A and B from the same raw materials. Also during the processing, a by-product "X" emerges which has a market value if processed further.

The following information is available for the annual budget for the coming year:

Estimated Sales:	Product A—240,000 lbs. @ $2.50............	$ 600,000
	Product B—720,000 lbs. @ $1.50............	1,080,000
	By-Product X—sells for $0.60 a pound.	

Estimated Costs:	Processing Department:	
	Material.............................	$ 312,000
	Labour..............................	198,000
	Overhead............................	330,000

Cost after separation:

Product A	Packaging	$.80 per lb.
Product B	Finished	$.45 per lb.
By-Product X	Mixing	$.44 per lb.

| Selling and Administrative Expenses: | 10 percent of sales dollars |

Out of 9 pounds of raw materials started in the processing department, only 8 pounds can be processed further for Products A and B. The remaining pound is of inferior quality and is set aside for Product X.

The director of marketing was concerned about measuring future profit contribution by-products and maintained that:

1. Sales of by-product X should be treated separately; assigning costs before separation from the processing department and allowing for selling and administrative expenses but no profits (Reversal Cost Method).
2. A cost per pound should be established for products A and B from the processing department before adding costs for packaging and finishing, respectively. This cost should be such that each product contributes the same net profit percentage per sales dollar.

(SMA, adapted)

Chapter 6

LEARNING OBJECTIVES

Chapter 6 discusses the development of departmental manufacturing overhead rates. It illustrates the direct method of allocation and the step method of allocation of the costs of service or support departments to producing departments. Studying this chapter should enable you to:

1. Discuss the concept of a plant-wide manufacturing overhead application rate.
2. Discuss the concept of departmental manufacturing overhead application rates.
3. Discuss the development of a departmental overhead rate.
4. Explain the logic and use of the direct method of allocation.
5. Explain the logic and use of the step method of allocation.

Allocation of Service Department Costs to Producing Departments

IN CHAPTERS 3, 4, and 5, a plant-wide manufacturing overhead rate for the application of overhead to those products produced was used. The plant-wide rate is developed by projecting total overhead for the manufacturing plant, and dividing the *total* overhead by an application basis. This application basis might be machine hours, direct labor hours, direct labor cost, or any other basis that will provide an equitable application of overhead to the products produced.

$$\text{Plant-Wide Manufacturing Overhead Rate} = \frac{\text{Projected Total Factory Overhead Cost}}{\text{Projected Application Base}}$$

A plant-wide rate applies the same cost per unit of the application base to all products produced without regard to the unique production resource uses of the individual products.

For example, if the application basis was direct labor hours, all products would absorb the same overhead charge per direct labor hour worked in each department without regard to any differences in resource uses that would otherwise cause a different overhead rate to be applied to the production of each department. If direct labor hours were the basis for applying manufacturing overhead and one product used many direct labor hours but few machine hours to complete, this product would be absorbing a greater proportional cost of power to run equipment than a product that used many machine hours and few direct labor hours. The labor intensive product should actually be absorbing a minimal allocation of power cost since it uses little power in the production process. If a plant-wide rate is used, all of the projected overhead costs will be allocated to products produced without regard to the specific mix of overhead factors used to make the different products. Obviously, if products follow similar production processes, little or no cost inequities would occur in product costing with a plant-wide rate. The inequity occurs when the nature and amount of overhead is different across the producing departments, and different products use the resources of the production departments in different ways.

Plant-Wide versus Departmental Manufacturing Overhead Rates

When a firm makes diverse products that pass through more than one producing department and utilize the services of those departments differently, a departmental overhead rate is necessary if the different products are to absorb their equitable share of total factory overhead. A departmental overhead rate will permit the individual products to absorb overhead costs of the department based on the product's utilization of the resources of the department.

The departmental overhead rate is developed by projecting total overhead for that department and dividing the cost projection by the appropriate projected application basis.

$$\text{Departmental Manufacturing Overhead Rate} = \frac{\text{Projected Total Departmental Overhead Cost}}{\text{Appropriate Projected Application Basis for that Department}}$$

Different departments will have different application bases. A labor intensive department would use direct labor hours or, possibly, direct labor cost. A machine intensive department might use machine hours as the basis. These different departments would have different manufacturing overhead rates.

Even if the application base is the same, such as direct labor hours, the rate per direct labor hour may be substantially different. If different products spend varying amounts of time in different departments, an equitable application of overhead may only be possible with different overhead rates in each department.

Illustration 6-1 is an example of two producing departments with different projected manufacturing overhead application rates. Both departments will apply overhead on a direct labor hour basis with a plant-wide rate because direct labor is the only common basis that both departments share.

Illustration 6-1

**Plant-Wide Overhead Rate versus
Departmental Overhead Rate**

	Plant-Wide Rate	
	Producing Department A	Producing Department B
Projected Annual Overhead	$10,000	$ 2,000
Projected Direct Labor Hours	1,000	2,000

Plant-Wide Overhead Rate:

$$\frac{\$10,000 + \$2,000}{1,000\ \text{Hours} + 2,000\ \text{Hours}} = \$4.00\ \text{Per Direct Labor Hour}$$

	Departmental Rate	
	Producing Department A	Producing Department B
Projected Annual Overhead	$10,000	$ 2,000
Projected Overhead Application Basis	5,000 Machine Hours	2,000 Direct Labor Hours

Departmental Overhead Rates:

$$\frac{\$10,000}{5,000\ \text{Machine Hours}} =$$ $2 Per Machine Hour

$$\frac{\$ 2,000}{2,000\ \text{Hours}} =$$ $1 Per Direct Labor Hour

Producing Department A is machine intensive and Producing Department B is labor intensive. If a plant-wide overhead rate is used, overhead will be applied at the rate of $4 per direct labor hour. Alternatively, if a departmental overhead rate is used, every job that passes through Department A will absorb $2 per machine hour used. If a departmental manufacturing overhead rate based on direct labor hours was used in Department A, the rate would be $10 per direct labor hour.

If a departmental overhead rate is used, every job that passes through Department B will absorb $1 per direct labor hour used. In the Illustration, if a plant-wide rate were used, overhead charges to the products produced would be shifted from the machine intensive department to the labor intensive department. The projected total overhead in Department B is $2,000, but the products passing through Department B would have absorbed $8,000 (2,000 hours × $4 per hour) if the projections were correct and the application of overhead was based on a plant-wide overhead rate.

The implications for product costing are substantial in Illustration 6–1. If two specific jobs, Jobs 101 and 102, were started and completed in a given time period and Job 101 was machine intensive and Job 102 was labor intensive, the amount of overhead charged to each job would be substantially different under the plant-wide overhead rate versus the departmental overhead rate. Assume that the following direct labor and machine hours were used on the two jobs:

		Department A		Department B	
Job		Labor Hrs.	Machine Hrs.	Labor Hrs.	Machine Hrs.
Machine Intensive . . 101		1	10	2	8
Labor Intensive 102		3	1	4	2

If a plant-wide overhead rate is used, the overhead charge to each job would be as follows:

	Job 101		Job 102	
	Department A	Department B	Department A	Department B
Direct Labor Hours	1	2	3	4
Manufacturing Overhead Rate	× $4	× $4	× $4	× $4
Applied Manufacturing Overhead	$4	$8	$12	$16

Job 101 would absorb $12 and Job 102 would absorb $28 with a plant-wide rate. Job 102 is labor intensive and with direct labor hours as the basis for manufacturing overhead application to products, a greater absorption of overhead would be expected.

If the departmental overhead rates from Illustration 6–1 are used to apply overhead to each job, the overhead absorbed would be as follows:

	Job 101		Job 102	
	Department A	Department B	Department A	Department B
Machine Hours	10		1	
Direct Labor Hours		2		4
Manufacturing Overhead Rate	× $2	× $1	× $2	× $1
Applied Manufacturing Overhead	$20	$2	$2	$4

Job 101 would absorb $22 and Job 102 would absorb $6 using a departmental overhead rate. Each job would absorb that overhead which reflects the use of the resource assumed to be the causal factor in incurring the overhead in each department. If the plant-wide and the departmental overhead applications were compared, the absorption by the two jobs is different.

— spreading overhead based on a cfor causal factor in dept

	Job 101	Job 102	Total
Plant-Wide Rate	$12	$28	$40
Departmental Rate . . .	22	6	28

The difference in absorption of overhead by the jobs is caused by the difference in the basis for application under the two different approaches for applying overhead. The difference in the totals is not meant to imply that a departmental rate in some way reduces overhead. It just means that some other jobs will be absorbing more overhead by using the departmental rate than they would have by using the plant-wide rate.

Service Department Costs

— needed but required for production

All manufacturing overhead costs should be allocated to products produced under the full or absorption costing approach to product costing. For purposes of simplicity, the prior chapters assumed a plant-wide overhead rate and ignored service departments and the allocation of the costs of the service departments to the producing departments. The allocation of service department costs to producing departments is necessary if the departmental manufacturing overhead rate applied to products is to reflect the *full* or *total* manufacturing overhead costs. Some general examples of service departments in a manufacturing plant that would serve as support for production departments are as follows:

Cost Accounting	Maintenance
General Building Services	Power Plant
General Supervision	Production Planning
Plant Cafeteria	Purchasing
Plant Engineering	Toolroom

Allocating Service Department Costs— General Concepts

Any allocation of the costs of the service departments to producing departments in an equitable manner is complicated by the fact that some service departments will serve other service departments. The basis for the allocation of the costs of the service departments to the producing departments should be that basis which best reflects the services rendered to the producing departments. This basis will usually be different for different service departments. The interrelationship of the service departments in rendering service to each other would distort the allocation because some of the cost of service is caused by the needs of other service departments and not the producing departments.[1]

The concept of reciprocal services between service departments and

---

[1] This problem of reciprocal services can be solved using linear algebra or simultaneous equations. The step method of allocation, which is covered in this chapter, is an approximation of the linear algebra solution when reciprocal services are involved.

the allocation of the costs of the departments to the producing departments in establishing an overhead rate is presented in Illustration 6–2.

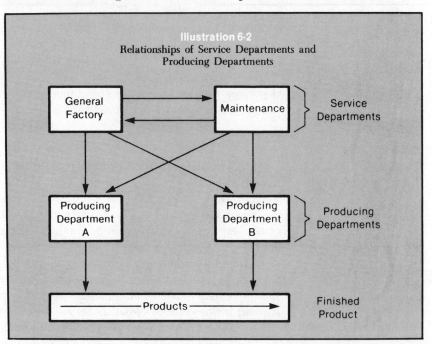

Illustration 6-2
Relationships of Service Departments and
Producing Departments

In Illustration 6–2, there are two service departments, Maintenance and General Factory. To keep the example simple, assume that the General Factory Department does everything associated with service except maintenance. General Factory and Maintenance provide service to each other and to the producing departments. In order to pass the total overhead cost on to the products which are produced, the service department costs will have to be allocated in total to the producing departments. The service department allocations will be added to the overhead costs in the producing departments to arrive at the total overhead projection for each producing department. These overhead projections and the basis for the allocations will serve to establish the predetermined overhead rate to be used in applying overhead costs to production. As the products pass through the producing departments, the manufacturing overhead will be applied using the predetermined overhead rate.

METHODS FOR ALLOCATING COSTS OF SERVICE DEPARTMENTS TO PRODUCING DEPARTMENTS

The two methods covered in this chapter for allocating the costs of the service departments to the producing departments are the direct method of allocation and the step method of allocation. The major difference between the two approaches is the recognition given to reciprocal services between service departments.

The basic data that will be used in illustrating both the direct method of allocation and the step method of allocation is presented in Illustration 6–3.

Illustration 6-3
Projected Overhead Costs for Service Departments and Producing Departments

	Service Departments		Producing Departments		
	General Factory	Maintenance	Machining	Finishing and Pressing	Total
Departmental Identifiable (Traceable) Overhead Costs	$5,000	$4,000	$3,500	$2,500	$15,000
Services Furnished:					
1. General Factory Based on Area	–0–	400	1,000	1,000	2,400
2. Maintenance Based on Projected Maintenance Hours Worked in Each Department	1,000	–0–	3,000	1,000	5,000
Basis For Allocation To Production:					
Projected Machine Hours			2,000		
Projected Direct Labor Hours				1,000	

(handwritten annotations: "how do you allocate \$4,000" and "how do you allocate \$5,000 to Prod. Dept")

In the example in Illustration 6–3, there are two service departments, General Factory and Maintenance, and two producing departments, Machining and Finishing and Pressing. The projected overhead costs for the General Factory Department are $5,000. This would be the total projected cost of this department for the period under consideration. The basis for the allocation of the $5,000 will be square meters of plant used in the other departments. This is the basis that is the most common denominator that can be used to measure the services provided by the General Factory Department to all other service departments and producing departments.

The projected cost of the Maintenance Department is $4,000. The basis of allocation of maintenance costs for the projected overhead rate will be projected maintenance hours to be worked in each service and production department. Maintenance hours are considered to be the common denominator in the other departments that provides a causal relationship with costs in the maintenance department.

The overhead directly identifiable with the producing departments is $3,500 for Machining and $2,500 for Finishing and Pressing. The basis that will be used to apply overhead to production in the Machining Department is machine hours. The basis in Finishing and Pressing will be direct labor hours. These bases for application are felt to be the most meaningful because of their relationship to overhead cost incurrence. The final predetermined manufacturing overhead rates will include the total $15,000 of projected costs when the rates for both producing departments are considered. That is, the combined application rates will attempt to pass the $15,000 of overhead to the products produced during the time period under consideration.

The Direct Method of Allocation

The direct method of allocation of service department costs allocates the projected costs of each service department directly to the producing departments. The interaction between service or support departments and the related costs that are incurred in one service department because of the needs of another service department is ignored.

The $5,000 of the costs of the General Factory Department will be allocated directly to the producing departments on a square meter basis. The $4,000 of projected costs of the Maintenance Department will be allocated to the producing departments on the basis of projected maintenance hours to be worked in each producing department. The $9,000 of the projected costs of all the service departments, therefore, will be allocated to the producing departments and included in the final predetermined overhead rate.

The direct method of allocation using those projected overhead costs for service departments and producing departments from Illustration 6–3, is presented in Illustration 6–4. Using the direct method of allocation, the order of the allocation of the costs of the service departments to the producing departments does not make any difference. Each of the producing departments uses 1,000 square meters of factory and the Maintenance Department uses 400 square meters. The Maintenance Department's use will be ignored in the allocation because the costs of the General Factory Department will be allocated directly to the producing department. The Machining Department and the Finishing and Pressing Department both use equal amounts of square meters of factory space; therefore, each will be allocated one-half of the cost of the General Factory Department or $2,500.

The costs of the Maintenance Department are allocated on the basis of projected maintenance hours to be worked in each department. Total projected maintenance hours are 3,000 hours for the Machining Department

Illustration 6-4

Direct Method of Allocation of
Projected Service Department Costs

	Service Departments		Producing Departments		
	General Factory	Maintenance	Machining	Finishing and Pressing	Total
Overhead Costs Before Allocation	$5,000	$4,000	$3,500	$2,500	$15,000
Allocation:					
1. General Factory Based on Area $\frac{1,000}{2,000}$ $\frac{1,000}{2,000}$ °	(5,000)		2,500	2,500	
2. Maintenance Based on Projected Maintenance Hours Worked in Each Department $\frac{3,000}{4,000}$ $\frac{1,000}{4,000}$ †		(4,000)	3,000	1,000	
Total Overhead to be Applied to Production			$9,000	$6,000	$15,000

Predetermined Departmental Overhead Rates:

Projected Overhead Costs in Machining	$9,000	
Projected Machine Hours in Machining	2,000	=
Overhead Application Rate Per Machine Hour	$4.50	

Projected Overhead Costs in Finishing and Pressing	$6,000	
Projected Direct Labor Hours in Finishing and Pressing	1,000	=
Overhead Application Rate Per Direct Labor Hour	$6.00	

° Each producing department uses 1,000 square meters (from Illustration 6-3).
† The projected maintenance hour usage is 3,000 hours for Machining and 1,000 hours for Finishing and Pressing (from Illustration 6–3).

and 1,000 hours for the Finishing and Pressing Department. The appropriate allocation of the projected costs of the Maintenance Department are three-quarters (3,000 hours ÷ 4,000 hours) of the $4,000 projected costs to Machining and one-quarter (1,000 hours ÷ 4,000 hours) of the $4,000 projected costs to Finishing and Pressing. Therefore, $3,000 will be allocated to the Machining Department and $1,000 to the Finishing and Pressing Department. The projected manufacturing overhead rate that will be applied to products produced in the two production departments will include the allocated costs of the service departments and the manufacturing overhead costs of the production departments.

The predetermined manufacturing overhead rate for the Machining Department will include $3,500 of manufacturing overhead identified directly with the Machining Department, $2,500 allocated from the General Factory Department, and $3,000 allocated from the Maintenance Department, or $9,000 in manufacturing overhead in total. The manufacturing overhead application basis for the Machining Department in Illustration 6-4 is machine hours. Two thousand machine hours are projected; therefore, the predetermined overhead rate for the Machining Department will be $9,000 ÷ 2,000 hours or $4.50 per machine hour worked on a job. If a job uses 2 hours of machine time, the applied overhead on that job will be $4.50 × 2 hours or $9.00.

The Finishing and Pressing Department has $2,500 of manufacturing overhead identified directly with itself (Illustration 6-4). Twenty-five hundred dollars of manufacturing overhead is allocated from the General Factory Department. The Maintenance Department allocation is $1,000. In total, the projected manufacturing overhead that will be applied to products being worked on in the Finishing and Pressing Department is $6,000 ($2,500 + $2,500 + $1,000). The basis for the application of overhead in the Finishing and Pressing Department is direct labor hours. There are 1,000 direct labor hours projected. The predetermined manufacturing overhead rate will be $6.00 ($6,000 ÷ 1,000 direct labor hours) per direct labor hour worked. If a job uses two direct labor hours in Finishing and Pressing, that job will absorb $6.00 × 2 hours or $12.00 in manufacturing overhead. If a job used 5 hours of machine time in the Machining Department and 3 hours of direct labor time in the Finishing and Pressing Department, the job would absorb ($4.50 × 5 hours) + ($6.00 × 3 hours) or $40.50 in manufacturing overhead.

The Step Method of Allocation

Direct allocation of the costs of the service department to the production departments is the most popular approach for service department cost allocations. Some accountants would argue that cost inequities result when using the direct method if there are reciprocal services between service departments. If some service departments serve other service departments, and if the use of service departments is different for different production departments, an unequitable allocation of service department costs, and thus overhead allocation to products, could result.

For example, a maintenance department would normally provide more service to a producing department that is machine intensive than to one that is labor intensive. If another service department is a large user of the Maintenance Department but provides a greater proportion of its resources to the labor intensive production department, that production department may be getting the benefits of maintenance expenditures without a proportional share of the maintenance costs if a direct method of allocation is used. The maintenance-using machine intensive department would be allocated a share of the maintenance cost based on its proportional use of the maintenance department. However, a large part of maintenance cost would be caused by the other service department that provides a greater share of its resources to the labor intensive production department.

Where reciprocal relationships between departments exist, simultaneous equations may be used to make an equitable allocation. If done manually, this could be quite time consuming, particularly if more than a few service departments are involved. The task can be made somewhat easier by applying matrix algebra and making use of a computer. However, it is questionable whether such mathematically precise solutions are necessary in view of the arbitrary nature of any system of allocation.[2] Fortunately an approximation of an equitable solution using simultaneous equations can be achieved by using the step method of allocation. The step method of allocation is only an approximation to the extent that costs are allocated on a sequential basis starting with the service department that provided the most service to other service departments. The costs of this service department will be allocated to the remaining service departments and all production departments. Then, in turn, all costs of the service department that provided the next most service are allocated to the remaining service and production departments. The costs of the second service department would include an allocated portion of the costs of the first service department. This sequential system will continue until all service department costs are allocated to the production departments. Once a service department's costs are allocated, that service department will not be allocated any costs from the subsequent cost allocations of other service departments.

The Step Method of Allocation— An Illustration

Illustration 6–5 is an example of the step method of allocation using the data presented in Illustration 6–3. Assume that the costs of the General Factory Department will be allocated first because it provides more services to the Maintenance Department than the Maintenance Department provides to it. The General Factory Department costs will be allocated to the Maintenance Department, the Machining Department, and

---

[2] These approaches will not be covered in this text. The practical application of service department allocations using simultaneous equations is not common.

Illustration 6-5

Step Method of Allocation of
Projected Service Department Costs

| | Service Departments | | Producing Departments | | |
	General Factory	Maintenance	Machining	Finishing and Pressing	Total
Overhead Costs Before Allocation	$5,000	$4,000	$3,500	$2,500	$15,000
Allocation:					
1. General Factory Based on Area 400 / 2,400 1,000 / 2,400 1,000 / 2,400 °	(5,000)	834	2,083	2,083	
2. Maintenance Based on Projected Maintenance Hours Worked in Each Department 3,000 / 4,000 1,000 / 4,000 †		(4,834)	3,625	1,209	
Total Overhead to be Applied to Production			$9,208	$5,792	$15,000

Predetermined Departmental Overhead Rates:	
Projected Overhead Costs in Machining	$9,208
Projected Machine Hours in Machining	$\dfrac{}{2,000}$ =
Overhead Application Rate Per Machine Hour	$4.60
Projected Overhead Costs in Finishing and Pressing	$5,792
Projected Direct Labor Hours in Finishing and Pressing	$\dfrac{}{1,000}$ =
Overhead Application Rate Per Direct Labor Hour	$5.79

*Maintenance uses 400 square meters, Machining 1,000 and Finishing and Pressing 1,000 (from Illustration 6-3).

† The projected maintenance hour usage is 3,000 hours for Machining and 1,000 hours for Finishing and Pressing (from Illustration 6–3).

Handwritten annotations (left margin and within table):

MAINTENANCE DEPT.
1,000 / 5,000 HRS IN GEN FACTORY
= 1/5 × 4,000 = $8,000

GEN. FACTORY
400 / 2,400 × 5100 = 834
ALLOCATE TO MAIN

FACTORY PROVIDES
MOST SERVICE

(400/2400+500)

(1,000/5,000 × 5,000)

(300/400 × 4834)   (1,000/4,000 × 4834)

the Finishing and Pressing Department on the basis of area.

The Maintenance Department will be allocated $834 [(400 square meters ÷ 2,400 square meters) × $5,000] of the General Factory Department's costs. Each of the producing departments will be allocated an equal amount of the remaining General Factory Department's costs based on their proportional square meters of use (1,000 square meters ÷ 2,400 square meters) × $5,000, or $2,083.

The second step in the sequential allocation will be to allocate the Maintenance Department's costs to the producing departments. The Maintenance Department's costs to be allocated are $4,834 which is the cost of providing $4,000 of manufacturing overhead directly identifiable with the Maintenance Department in Illustration 6-5 plus the $834 of costs allocated from the General Factory Department. The Maintenance Department's costs of $4,834 will be allocated based on the projected usage of maintenance hours by the producing departments. No maintenance costs will be allocated back to the General Factory Department.

The projected usage of maintenance hours is 3,000 hours for the Machining Department and 1,000 hours for the Finishing and Pressing Department. The allocation of the $4,834 will be three-fourths to the Machining Department (or $3,625) and one-fourth (or $1,209) to the Finishing and Pressing Department.

The total projected manufacturing overhead to be applied to production in the Machining Department is $9,208 of the $15,000 of manufacturing overhead for the entire plant. The basis for manufacturing overhead application for the Machining Department of Illustration 6-5 is 2,000 hours of projected machine usage. The appropriate application rate for applying manufacturing overhead to production will be $9,208 ÷ 2,000 projected machine hours, or $4.60 per machine hour worked on a job.

The total projected manufacturing overhead that will be applied to production in the Finishing and Pressing Department is $5,792. The basis for manufacturing overhead application for the Finishing and Pressing Department is the projected 1,000 hours of direct labor time usage. The manufacturing overhead rate per direct labor hour will be $5,792 ÷ 1,000 projected direct labor hours, or $5.79 per direct labor hour.

SUMMARY

A plant-wide manufacturing overhead rate provides one overhead rate to be used for applying manufacturing overhead to all of the products produced. If a plant-wide rate is used, all of the projected overhead costs will be allocated to the products produced without regard to the specific mix of overhead factors used to make the different products.

A departmental overhead rate is developed by projecting total overhead for each producing department and dividing the cost projection by the appropriate projected application base. Different production departments may have different manufacturing overhead rates and different overhead application bases.

The allocation of service department costs to producing departments is necessary if the departmental manufacturing overhead rate applied to products is to reflect the projected full or total manufacturing overhead costs. The two methods covered in this chapter for allocating the costs of the service departments to the producing departments are the direct method of allocation and the step method of allocation. The major difference between the two approaches is the recognition given to reciprocal services between service departments.

The direct method of allocation of the costs of service departments allocates each service department's projected costs directly to the producing departments. The interaction between service departments (reciprocal services) and the related costs incurred in one service department because of another service department's needs are ignored.

The step method of allocation of the costs of the service departments to the producing departments gives some recognition to reciprocal services between service departments. Costs of the service departments are allocated sequentially, starting with the service department that provided the most service to other service departments. That department's costs are allocated to the remaining service and production departments. Then the costs of the service department that provided the next most service are allocated to the remaining service and producing departments. This sequential system continues until the costs of all the service departments are allocated to the producing departments. Once a service department's costs are allocated, that service department is not assigned any costs in subsequent cost allocations. The final result of either the direct method or the step method of allocation is to include all projected manufacturing overhead costs of the plant in the departmental overhead rates so that full costs of manufacturing will be absorbed by the production of the time period under consideration.

KEY DEFINITIONS   Allocation of service department costs—the process of assigning the costs of service departments to production departments so that the total manufacturing overhead of the plant will be reflected in the departmental overhead rates. The basis for the allocation of the costs of the service departments to the producing departments should be the basis which best reflects the services rendered to the producing departments.

Departmental manufacturing overhead rate—a rate is established for each department in a plant based on the unique overhead factors in that department. The overhead application basis will be the basis which is the causal factor for incurring manufacturing overhead in that department.

Direct method of allocation—the allocation of each service department's projected costs directly to the producing departments. The basis to be used for this allocation is the basis that best reflects the services used by the producing departments. Reciprocal services between service departments are ignored.

Plant-wide manufacturing overhead rate—one overhead rate that is established for the entire plant. Every department applies the same overhead rate on the same basis to its production as every other department. The same basis for overhead application would be used throughout the plant.

Reciprocal services—the services rendered by service departments to each other.

Service or support departments—the departments in a manufacturing plant that supply needed services to producing departments. The service departments do not produce products. The maintenance department and production planning would be examples of service departments.

Step method of allocation—the allocation of the projected costs of the service departments, on a sequential basis, starting with the service department that provided the most service to other service departments. This first department's costs are allocated to all the remaining service and producing departments. Then the costs of the service department that provided the next most service, in turn, is allocated to the remaining service and production departments. This process continues until all service department costs are allocated to the production departments.

QUESTIONS

6-1 Why might a departmental rather than a plant-wide manufacturing overhead rate be used?

6-2 Describe the development of a departmental overhead rate for a production department.

6-3 Why might different departments use different bases of application in developing their respective departmental overhead rates?

6-4 Why might the departmental overhead rates of two departments differ even though both departments use an identical basis for the application of overhead?

6-5 Why are the costs of service departments allocated to the producing departments in a manufacturing company?

6-6 Discuss the concept of reciprocal services. How may reciprocal services present a problem in the allocation of service department costs?

6-7 Identify and briefly describe two approaches for allocating the costs of several service departments to more than one producing department.

6-8 What does the step method of allocation specifically take into account that the direct method does not?

6-9 Which department has its costs allocated first in the step method of allocation? Which department is allocated next? Last?

EXERCISES AND PROBLEMS

6-10 Production Departments A and B have the following budgeted amounts:

	Department A	Department B
Budgeted Overhead	$100,000	$100,000
Budgeted Direct Labor Hours	25,000	40,000
Budgeted Machine Hours	40,000	25,000

Department A is machine intensive and Department B is labor intensive. Determine the appropriate manufacturing overhead rates for these two departments.

6-11 Jobs 21 and 22 required the following input from Production Departments X, Y, and Z.

	Dept. X		Dept. Y		Dept. Z	
Job	Labor Hrs.	Mach. Hrs.	Labor Hrs.	Mach. Hrs.	Labor Hrs.	Mach. Hrs.
21 . .	½	1½	2	1	1	3
22 . .	1	½	1½	1	2	1¾

The wage rate is $3 per hour. Departments X, Y, and Z respectively apply overhead at the rates of $4.00 per machine hour, $6.00 per direct labor hour, and 70% of direct labor cost. Determine the amounts of overhead absorbed by Jobs 21 and 22 in production.

6-12 Service Department 1 provides maintenance to Production Departments 2 and 3. Service department costs are allocated according to projected usage of direct labor hours. Given the following information:

Department 1 projected costs $100,000
Department 2 projected usage is 2,500 hours of Department 1 labor
Department 3 projected usage is 3,500 hours of Department 1 labor

How much of the projected service department costs are to be allocated to each production department?

6-13 Ajax Company has two service departments, Maintenance and Power, and two production departments, Powders and Liquids. Budgeted costs for Maintenance and Power are $60,000 and $200,000 respectively. Service costs are allocated to production according to the number of labor hours of maintenance and the number of machine hours of power used. Powders and Liquids are expected to use the following:

	Expected Usage of *Labor Hours of Maintenance*	*Expected Usage of* *Machine Hours of Power*
Powders	500 Hours	2,500 Hours
Liquids	750 Hours	7,500 Hours

Allocate the service costs to the production departments.

6-14 Atlas Corporation has two service departments (A and B) providing services to three production departments (I, II, and III). All service department costs are allocated to the production department based on the projected amount of labor cost expected to be incurred by the respective service departments for each of the production departments. Expected service department costs are $10,000 for A and $20,000 for B. The wage rate for A is $5.00 per hour and for B is $4.00 per hour. The service departments are expected to be needed as follows:

Expected Departmental Requirements for Service Labor Hours

Dept.	A	B	I	II	III
A		10	20	30	40
B	50		60	70	80

By using a direct method of allocation, determine the amount of service costs allocated to each production department.

6-15 Redetermine the amount of service costs allocated to each production department in exercise number 6-14 by using a step method of allocation. Allocate A first.

6-16 The Accounting Department services two production departments, Food and Toys. The projected manufacturing overhead costs for Food and Toys are $5,000 and $10,000 respectively. The basis for application in each production department is machine hours. The projected number of machine hours for Food is 2,000 hours and for Toys is

2,500 hours. The Accounting Department, with expected costs of $1,500, allocates its costs according to the number of its labor hours used by the production departments. For the next period, it is expected that Accounting will spend 100 hours in Food and 200 hours in Toys. What are the appropriate predetermined departmental overhead rates for each of the production departments?

6-17 Given the following information:

	Service Departments		Production Departments	
	1	2	1	2
Application Basis	Area Used	Direct Labor Hours Used	Machine Hours Used	Units Finished
Expected use of Service Dept. 1		100 Sq.M.	2,000 Sq.M.	1,200 Sq.M.
Expected use of Service Dept. 2	10 Hours		120 Hours	130 Hours
Expected Machine Hours	55 Hours	75 Hours	2,000 Hours	370 Hours
Expected Number of Units Finished				4,000 Units
Expected Service Costs	$15,000	$40,000		
Expected Manufacturing Overhead			$200,000	$350,000

Service Department 1 provides more service to Service Department 2 than Service Department 2 does to Service Department 1. Determine the amount of service cost allocated to each of the production departments from Service Department 2 if a direct allocation method is used.

6-18 Redetermine the amount of service cost allocated to each of the production departments from Service Department 2 in exercise number 6-17 if a step method of allocation is used.

6-19 If a step method of allocation is used in exercise number 6-17 to allocate the costs of the service departments to the production departments, what are the appropriate predetermined manufacturing overhead rates for Production Departments 1 and 2? Assume that Department 1 applies overhead on the basis of machine hours and Department 2 uses finished units.

6-20 The Dire Company has one service department which serves three production departments. The projected annual costs are $143,000 in the service department. The annual services provided are expected to be apportioned among the production departments according to one of the following bases:

Production Departments	Area Square Meters	Direct Labor Hours	Total Revenue of each Prod. Dept.
X	283,000	350,000	$150,000
Y	250,000	180,000	$300,000
Z	375,000	30,000	$250,000
Total	908,000	560,000	$700,000

Required:

Allocate the service departments expected annual costs to the production departments using the following allocation bases:

a.   Area
b.   Direct labor hours
c.   Total revenue

6-21   The Abbott Co. has two service departments, maintenance and research and development, and two production departments, assembly and finishing. Projected overhead costs in the various departments are $500,000 in maintenance, $320,000 in research and development, $816,000 in assembly and $467,000 in finishing. Overhead in assembly is allocated in accordance with the number of machine hours used; the average annual amount is 37,000 hours. Finishing allocates overhead according to the number of direct labor hours worked; the average annual amount is 29,000 hours. Maintenance allocates overhead according to total projected labor hours which are 55,000, of which 13,000 are in research and development, 21,000 in assembly and 16,000 in finishing. Research and development allocates overhead in accordance with the number of projected direct labor hours worked for each department. These hours total 29,000, of which 7,000 are for maintenance, 19,000 for assembly, and 3,000 for finishing.

Required:

Using the direct method, allocate the projected service departments' overhead to the production departments and compute the predetermined overhead rate for each production department.

6-22   The Clinton Company has two Production Departments, X and Y, and two Service Departments, I and II. Projected overhead amounted to $305,000 for X, $428,000 for Y, $298,000 for I and $367,000 for II. Overhead in Department X is allocated in accordance with the number of physical units of projected production, which is 350,000. Department Y allocates overhead based upon projected direct labor hours which totaled 293,000. Department I allocates its overhead based upon the projected number of machine hours used for other departments which amounted to 30,000 for X, 47,500 for Y and 20,450 for II. Department II allocates overhead based upon the projected units of direct materials that it handles for the various departments. These amounted to 29,000 units for X, 56,000 units for Y and 13,000 units for I.

Required:

Using the direct allocation method, allocate the overhead of the service departments to the production departments and compute the predetermined overhead rate for each production department.

6-23   The Sched Manufacturing Company is made up of two production departments, A and B, and three service departments, I, II, and III. The projected fixed overhead of each department is: $578,000 for A; $479,000 for B; $323,000 for I; $289,000 for II; and $239,000 for III. The overhead allocation bases used by each department are direct labor hours for A, machine hours for B, pounds of materials handled for I, total labor hours for II, and units of finished product handled for III. The projected allocation bases are 48,000 direct labor hours for A and 67,000 machine hours for B. Department I handles 96,500 pounds of materials. Approximately 25% of the materials is handled for Department A, 46% for Department B, 15% for II and 14% for III. Department II has projected 60,000 total labor hours. The allocation of the labor hours is: 39% to A; 34% to B; 13% to I; and, 14% to III. Department III has projected handling 48,000 units of finished product. This amount is allocated 43% to A, 34% to B, 12% to I and 11% to II.

Required:

Using the direct method of allocation, redistribute the overhead of the service departments to the production departments and compute the predetermined overhead rates for each production department.

6-24   The Trend Company manufactures calculators. It is made up of three production departments: the component, assembly and the testing departments. There are two service departments: engineering and materials handling. The overhead of the various departments amounted to $768,000 for component, $533,000 for assembly, $324,000 for testing, $993,000 for engineering, and $289,000 for materials handling. The component department's allocation base is units produced. The number of units projected is 239,000. The assembly department's allocation base is direct labor hours. The projected direct labor hours are 388,000. The testing department's projected allocation base is 387,000 direct labor hours. The engineering department's allocation base is total labor hours. The projected total labor hours of 248,500 have been allocated 34% to components, 37% to assembly, 21% to testing and 8% to materials handling. The materials handling department's allocation base is kilograms of materials handled which is projected at 304,000: 42% for the component department; 21% for assembly; 18% for testing; and, 19% for engineering.

Required:

Using the direct method of allocation for service department costs, compute the predetermined overhead rates for each of the production departments.

6-25 The Continental Company produces brass lamps, and is made up of two production and two service departments. The production departments are the electrical department and the finishing department, and the service departments are the maintenance department and the research department. The electrical department's overhead is $845,000 allocated on a direct labor hour basis. The finishing department's overhead is $920,000 allocated on the basis of units finished. The maintenance department's overhead is $803,000 allocated on the basis of labor hours worked. The research department's overhead is $700,000 allocated on the basis of labor hours. The projected annual direct labor hours of the electrical department are 190,000. The projected annual number of units finished by the finishing department are 109,000 units. The direct labor hours projected by the maintenance department are 172,000. Projected incurrence is: 30% by electrical; 40% by finishing; and 30% by research. The direct labor hours projected by the research department are 240,000 and are allocated 55% to electrical and 45% to finishing.

Required:

Using the direct method of allocation, assign service department costs to the production departments and compute a predetermined overhead rate for each department.

6-26

	Service Departments		Production Departments		
	I	II	X	Y	Total
Overhead	$320,000	$510,000	$780,000	$405,000	
Number of Labor Hours of Dept I allocated to other Departments		38,000	60,000	70,000	168,000
Number of Pounds of Materials handled by Dept. II for the other Departments	87,000		285,000	190,000	562,000

The allocation base used by Department X is 250,000 projected labor hours. The allocation base for Department Y is projected production of 180,000 units.

Required:

Using the step method of allocation of service department costs, compute the predetermined overhead rate for each production department:

a. Assume Department I provides Department II with the greater amount of service.

b. Assume Department II provides Department I with the greater amount of service.

6-27   The Zepher Company has two service departments and two production departments. The costs of operating the various departments are as follows:

| | Service Departments | | Production Departments | | |
	A	B	Y	Z	Total
Overhead	$30,000	$44,000	$75,000	$51,000	$200,000
Dept. A (allocation base is area) Proportion allocable to each of the other Depts.		16%	39%	45%	100% of 350,000 Sq.M.
Dept. B (allocation base is direct labor hours) Proportion allocable to each of the other Depts.	20%		45%	35%	100% of 210,000 direct labor hours

Department Y's allocation base is labor cost. The projected labor cost is $390,000. Department Z's allocation base is direct labor hours. The projected direct labor hours are 130,000.

Required:

Assuming Department A provides the greater amount of services to B, compute the predetermined overhead rate for each department using the step method of allocation for service department overhead.

6-28   The Clark Company has three service departments which provide services to two factory departments. The following annual costs have been budgeted for the various departments:

| | Service | | | Production | | |
	I	II	III	Y	Z	Total
Overhead	$30,000	$50,000	$90,000	$25,000	$55,000	$250,000

The following amounts have been budgeted with regard to the services expected to be provided by the three service departments to the other departments:

| Dept. | Allocation Base | Departments | | | | | |
		I	II	III	Y	Z	Total
I	Machine Hrs.		70,000	80,000	100,000	100,000	350,000
II	Sq.M. of Space	40,000		60,000	80,000	120,000	300,000
III	Labor Cost	$100,000	$100,000		$250,000	$350,000	$800,000

Required:

Using the step method, allocate the budgeted costs of the service departments to the factory departments, assuming III renders the greatest service to the other service departments, followed by I and then II.

6-29   The Birdsong Company manufactures cuckoo clocks. It has three service departments which serve three production departments. Annual fixed overhead of the various departments is budgeted as follows:

	Service			Production			
	I	*II*	*III*	*X*	*Y*	*Z*	*Total*
Overhead	$200,000	$300,000	$100,000	$500,000	$400,000	$600,000	$2,100,000

The following proportional breakdowns have been budgeted to the various departments:

Service Department	Allocation Base	Departments					
		I	*II*	*III*	*X*	*Y*	*Z*
I	Labor Hours		10%	5%	30%	25%	30%
II	Machine Hrs.	15%		15%	20%	30%	20%
III	Number of Orders	10%	12%		28%	25%	25%

Required:

Using the step method, allocate service department overhead to the various production departments assuming Department II provides services to the greatest number of other service departments, followed by I and then III.

6-30   The Monday Co. has two service departments, design and maintenance, and two production departments, assembly and finishing. Projected overhead costs in the various departments are $3,000 in design, $4,800 in maintenance, $7,000 in assembly and $10,000 in finishing. Overhead in assembly is allocated in accordance with the number of machine hours used; the average annual amount is 1,000 hours. Finishing allocates overhead according to the number of direct labor hours worked; the average annual amount is 2,000 hours. Design allocates overhead according to total projected labor hours which are 5,500, of which 500 are in maintenance, 2,000 in assembly and 3,000 in finishing. Maintenance allocates overhead in accordance with the number of projected labor hours worked for each department which total 7,000, of which 1,000 are for design, 3,500 for assembly, and 2,500 for finishing.

Required:

Using the direct method, allocate the projected service departments' overhead to the production departments and compute the predetermined overhead rate for each production department.

6-31 The Brasso Company has a maintenance department which serves three production departments. The projected annual costs are $250,000 in the maintenance department. The annual services provided are expected to be apportioned among the production departments according to one of the following bases:

Production Departments	Area Square Meters	Direct Labor Hours	Total Revenue of Each Prod. Dept.
A	40,000	52,500	$120,000
B	70,000	75,000	$160,000
C	90,000	22,500	$120,000
Total	200,000	150,000	$400,000

Required:

Allocate the service departments' expected annual costs to the production departments using the following allocation bases:

a. Area
b. Direct labor hours
c. Total revenue

6-32 The Rosen Company has three service departments which provide services to two factory departments. The following annual costs have been budgeted for the various departments:

	Service			Production		
	M	N	P	X	Z	Total
Overhead	$50,000	$60,000	$100,000	$60,000	$80,000	$350,000

The following amounts have been budgeted with regard to the services expected to be provided by the three service departments to the other departments:

Dept.	Allocation Base	M	N	P	X	Z	Total
I	Machine Hrs.		3,000	10,000	6,000	21,000	40,000
II	Sq. M. of Space	20,000		10,000	30,000	20,000	80,000
III	Labor Cost	$10,000	$10,000		$60,000	$120,000	$200,000

Required:

Using the step method, allocate the budgeted costs of the service departments to the factory departments assuming P renders the greatest service to the other service departments, followed by M and then N.

6-33 The Sharon Company has two service departments and two production departments. The manufacturing overhead costs are as follows:

	Service Depts.		Production Depts.		
	1	2	Y	Z	Total
Overhead	$20,000	$10,000	$40,000	$50,000	$120,000
Dept. 1 (allocation base is sq. m. of area) Proportion allocable to each of the other Depts.		15%	45%	40%	100% of 200,000 sq. m.
Dept. 2 (allocation base is direct labor hours) Proportion allocable to each of the other Depts.	10%		45%	45%	100% of 2,000 direct labor hours

Department Y's allocation base is labor cost. The projected labor cost is $16,000. Department Z's allocation base is direct labor hours. The projected direct labor hours are 5,000.

Required:

Assuming Department 1 provides the greater amount of services to Department 2, compute the predetermined overhead rate for each department using the step method of allocation for service department overhead.

6-34

	Service Depts.		Production Depts.		
	I	II	A	B	Total
Overhead	$20,000	$15,000	$40,000	$80,000	$155,000
Number of Labor Hours of Dept. I allocated to other Departments		1,500	5,500	3,000	10,000
Number of Pounds of Materials handled by Dept. II for the other Departments	4,000		12,000	4,000	20,000

The allocation base used by Department A is 8,000 projected labor hours. The allocation base for Department B is projected production of 2,500 units.

Required:

Using the step method of allocation of service department costs, compute the predetermined overhead rate for each production department:

a. Assume Department I provides Department II with the greater amount of service.

b. Assume Department II provides Department I with the greater amount of service.

6-35   The Gatler Company is made up of two production and two service departments. The production departments are the cylinder department and the finishing department, and the service departments are the maintenance department and the research department. The cylinder department's overhead is $130,000 allocated on a direct labor hour basis. The finishing department's overhead is $250,000 allocated on the basis of units finished. The maintenance department's overhead is $26,000 allocated on the basis of labor hours worked. The research department's overhead is $100,000 allocated on the basis of labor hours. The projected annual direct labor hours of the cylinder department are 10,000. The projected annual number of units finished by the finishing department are 20,000 units. The direct labor hours projected by the maintenance department are 3,000. Projected incurrence is: 30% by cylinder; 35% by finishing; and 35% by research. The direct labor hours projected by the research department are 4,000, and are allocated 70% to cylinder and 30% to finishing.

Required:

Using the direct method of allocation, assign service department costs to the production departments and compute a predetermined overhead rate for each department.

6-36   The Light Company manufactures headlights. It is made up of three production departments: the wiring, hooking and the hitting departments. There are two service departments: engineering and materials handling. The overhead of the various departments amounted to $200,000 for wiring, $200,000 for hooking, $50,000 for hitting, $34,400 for engineering, and $48,000 for materials handling. The wiring department's allocation base is units produced. Forty thousand units are projected. The hooking department's allocation base is direct labor hours. The projected direct labor hours are 20,000. The hitting department's projected allocation base is 10,000 direct labor hours. The engineering department's allocation base is total labor hours. The projected total labor hours of 2,500 have been allocated 20% to wiring, 35% to hooking, 31% to hitting and 14% to materials handling. The materials handling department's allocation base is kilograms of materials handled, which is projected at 15,000 kilograms; 40% for the wiring department; 10% for hooking; 30% for hitting; and 20% for engineering.

Required:

Using the direct method of allocation for service department costs, compute the predetermined overhead rates for each of the production departments.

Chapter 7

Chapter 7 discusses and illustrates the use of a standard cost system. Studying this chapter should enable you to:

1. Distinguish between standard costs and normal costs.
2. Discuss the uses and advantages of a standard cost system.
3. Identify and explain the basic types of standards in general use.
4. Calculate the standard manufacturing overhead cost per unit.
5. Explain the sources of the direct materials and direct labor variances and how these variances are calculated.
6. Describe the alternative methods of treating variances that may be used at the end of the accounting period.

Cost Accounting
for Inventories:
Standard
Costs

P RIOR To this chapter, the inventory costing systems used by manufacturing firms have been discussed and illustrated using actual historical costs for the accounting for both direct materials and direct labor. In these examples, manufacturing overhead was applied or absorbed into production using a predetermined overhead rate. Therefore, the inventory produced, absorbed or included a normal amount of overhead without regard to the actual level of production. These procedures are used in an attempt to smooth out the expected overhead costs over a sufficiently long time period in order to eliminate any distortions of cost. For example, distortions in per unit costs could be caused by fluctuations in the production schedule. These distortions are possible because the allocated fixed overhead remains relatively constant for each period, while the number of units produced varies according to production which is scheduled considering the anticipated demand for products.

It should be noted, however, that the inventory cost determined using the predetermined overhead rate introduced in Chapter 3 is not a standard cost. Rather, the overhead rate is a measure based upon the *expected* future costs that are allocated over the anticipated production and expressed per a selected unit of activity. The activity base chosen was used as the basis for applying or allocating the anticipated overhead costs to the production for the period. Standard costs, on the other hand, are based on the level of costs which *should* be incurred under efficient and effective operations. Thus standard costs do not necessarily reflect the costs which are expected to occur or actually do occur in a particular period. Standard costs are regarded as cost guidelines, or benchmarks, for the input factors of production and the related outputs resulting from the processing of these inputs.

When standard costs are used in accounting for the factors of production, the inventory cost system is referred to as a standard cost system. Standard costs may be used with either a job-order or a process cost system or with a combination and/or variation of these two basic methods for accumulating the costs of production.

PHYSICAL STANDARDS AND STANDARD COSTS

Physical standards for the production process relate to the standard requirements necessary to manufacture a product. These standards are stated or expressed in terms of quantities of raw materials, hours of direct labor, hours of processing time and similar measures. There is a general relationship between these input factors and the quantity or amount of output that may be expected or anticipated at standard levels of production. The standard costs of manufacturing are these physical standards expressed in terms of dollars of costs.

TYPES OF STANDARDS

The types of standards in general use in standard cost systems fall into three basic categories or classifications:

1. Standards based on historical or past performance.
2. Standards based on ideal performance.
3. Standards based on attainable performance.

Any standard based on historical or past performance will, by definition, include the efficiencies and inefficiencies of the period(s) of time used as the base in determining the standard. At best, this type of standard can be considered only a very rough benchmark or estimate of what may be anticipated or expected in the future. However, this does not indicate that historical performance should be ignored, but rather that it should not be used as the sole basis for establishing a standard cost for a specific cost factor for future periods.

Any standard based on ideal or engineering performance may not consider factors such as waste, downtime, fatigue, breakdowns, reworking, idle time or other similar inefficiencies. An "ideal" standard, therefore, represents perfection. All factors in the production process are assumed to interact perfectly. This type of standard cannot be ignored completely because it does represent what is possible under ideal or optimum conditions. In actual practice, an ideal standard is usually impossible to attain for all of the input factors of production for any sustained time period.

An attainable standard is an ideal or engineering standard which has been modified or adjusted for tolerable inefficiencies. Attainable standards represent a level of efficiency and effectiveness that can be attained over a sustained production period if all of the factors of production are operating and interacting at a satisfactory level. Theoretically, attainable standards are normally considered the proper standards to be applied to the many facets of management accounting.

AN IMPORTANT ADVANTAGE OF STANDARD COSTS FOR INVENTORY COSTING

For inventory costing purposes, a simple yet important advantage realized by using standard costs is clerical convenience. The raw materials inventory subsidiary ledgers can be maintained in terms of physical quantities, but without pricing these quantities at actual input prices. Material requisitions may be costed at their standard cost. When the manufacturing process is completed, the finished goods are costed and recorded at their standard cost. Historical costs are not traced to either specific units or to batches of product. Although it may seem to be somewhat unusual at first, these record keeping conveniences may make a standard cost system worthwhile even without considering the other advantages which the use of a standard cost system affords.

OTHER USES OF STANDARD COSTS

A standard cost system usually is not limited to a single primary use. Rather, standards have many and varied applications in any type of organization. Standards are useful aids to management in planning, control, performance evaluation, cost reduction programs, pricing studies, cost interpretation studies, and other types of special studies made to assist management in the decision-making process. Well designed and accepted standards enhance employee motivation, because practical guidelines or benchmarks for performance measurement are identified, communicated, and may be attained under efficient and effective operating conditions.

A SIMPLE EXAMPLE: USING STANDARD COSTS

In order to illustrate the use of standard costs, a simple example will be used. We will assume that the Sherrill Manufacturing Company produces a single product that requires the use of 2 kilograms of material (at a cost of $3 per kilogram) and 3 hours of direct labor (at a cost of $5 per hour). During the month of January, 19x1, Sherrill purchased and used 23 kilograms of materials (at $2 per kilogram) and employed 26 hours of direct labor (at a cost of $6 per hour). A total of 10 units of product were produced during the month. Sherrill uses a standard cost system.

Standard cost data for a unit of product for the Sherrill Manufacturing Company may be summarized as follows:

Standard cost of one unit of product:
Materials: 2 kilograms @ $3................... $ 6
Labor: 3 hours   @ $5................... _15_
Standard Cost Per Unit................... $21

Based upon this standard cost data, Sherrill's cost of producing 10 units during January should have been $210 (10 units @ $21). The actual cost of the 10 units produced by Sherrill during January was $202 (23 kilograms of materials × $2 + 26 hours of labor × $6). The comparison of standard and actual costs for January may be summarized as follows:

Cost of producing 10 units of product:

	at Standard	at Actual		Difference
Materials (10 units × 2 kilos × $3)..	$ 60	(23 × $2)	$ 46	$(14)
Labor (10 units × 3 hrs. × $5)......	150	(26 × $6)	156	6
Total........................	$210		$202	(8)

The actual costs of production for January ($202) were $8 less than the standard costs; this $8 difference ($202 vs. $210) is referred to as a variance. Variances are due to two factors (1) the actual prices paid for materials and labor may differ compared to the standard prices established for these inputs and (2) the actual quantities of materials (kilograms) and labor (hours) used may differ from the standard quantities allowed for these items. For example, the price variance experienced by Sherrill Manufacturing Company during January, 19x1 would be calculated as follows:

$$\begin{matrix} Price \\ Variance \end{matrix} = \left(\begin{matrix} Standard \\ Price \\ Per \\ Unit \end{matrix} - \begin{matrix} Actual \\ Price \\ Per \\ Unit \end{matrix} \right) \times \begin{matrix} Actual \\ Number \\ of\ Units \end{matrix}$$

Using this approach, the material price variance is:

$$\$23 = (\$3 - \$2) \times 23 \text{ kilograms}$$

This variance is favorable since the actual price paid per kilogram was less than the standard price per kilogram.

The labor price variance would be calculated as follows:

$$(\$26) = (\$5 - \$6) \times 26 \text{ hours}$$

This variance is unfavorable because the actual price paid per labor hour was more than the standard price per direct labor hour.

Note that in calculating both the material price variance and the labor price variance, the total *actual* number of units (kilograms of materials purchased and hours of labor paid) for the period was used. Actual units are used because the objective of a price variance is to isolate the entire effect (for all inputs acquired) of any differences between the standard cost and the actual cost during the period.

The quantity variance experienced by Sherrill Manufacturing Company for the month of January would be computed as follows:

Using this approach, the material quantity variance would be calculated as follows:

$$(\$9) = [(10 \times 2) - 23] \times \$3$$

The material quantity variance is unfavorable since the actual quantity of materials used during January (23 kilograms) exceeded the standard quantity that should have been used in order to produce 10 units of product (10 units @ 2 kilograms).

The labor quantity variance would be:

$$\$20 = [(10 \times 3) - 26] \times \$5$$

The labor quantity variance for January is favorable since the actual hours worked (26) were less than the standard hours allowed for January production (10 units $\times$ 3 hours).

Note that in calculating the quantity variances for both materials and labor the difference between the standard quantity allowed for the number of units produced and the actual quantity used is multiplied by the *standard* price per unit. The standard, rather than actual, price is used in calculating the quantity variance in order to isolate the effect of the quantity difference only (the difference between standard and actual prices were already isolated when the price variances were computed).

The variances between standard cost and actual cost for Sherrill Manufacturing Company for the month of January may be summarized as follows:

| | Cost for January | | | Variance Due to | |
	Standard	Actual	Variance	Price	Quantity
Materials	$ 60	$ 46	$14	$23	$(9)
Labor	150	156	(6)	(26)	20
Total	$210	$202	$ 8	$(3)	$11

Note that the $8 difference between the standard costs of $210 and the actual costs of $202 is explained by the calculation of the variances. The total price variance was $3 (unfavorable) — consisting of a $23 favorable material price variance and a $26 unfavorable labor price variance. The total quantity variance was $11 (favorable) — consisting of a $9 unfavorable material quantity variance and a $20 favorable labor quantity variance. Likewise, the $14 favorable variance for materials may be explained by the combination of the $23 (favorable) materials price variance and the $9 (unfavorable) materials quantity variance. The unfavorable labor variance of $6 consists of the $26 (unfavorable) labor price variance and the $20 (favorable) labor quantity variance.

A COMPREHENSIVE EXAMPLE: USING STANDARD COSTS

In September 19x0, the management of Sax Company decided that a standard cost system would assist the company in its planning, control, performance evaluation, and inventory costing activities. Prior to this time, the management of Sax Company had no experience in implementing a standard cost system. Therefore, it was decided that standard costs should first be introduced in the manufacturing area where the firm had the greatest production experience—the production of power turbine shafts. Power turbine shafts had become such a high volume item for Sax Company that the firm was scheduled to move into new production facilities for this product line during November. The company wished to have its standard cost job order inventory system on-line as of January 1, 19x1.

Sax Company established a team for developing its standard cost system that included at least one representative from each of the basic areas involved: production management, engineering, personnel, purchasing and cost accounting. The task of this group was to develop physical standards for manufacturing from which the company's cost accounting department could determine standard costs for inventory costing and control purposes.

The team viewed its assignment as being comprised of four distinct steps:

1. Developing a standard operations routing sheet.
2. Developing a standard bill of materials.
3. Developing manufacturing overhead standards at a defined level of capacity.
4. Converting all of the manufacturing cost factors into a format that the cost accounting department could use in developing a standard cost sheet.

Operations Routing Sheet

The new facility has modern equipment and the capacity for manufacturing almost any type of turbine shaft. However, Sax's management anticipates a demand for only power turbine shafts which have been manufactured from a six-centemeter diameter steel shaft or billet. Sax Company also presses ball bearings onto the ends of the turbine shafts to conform to the orders of specific customers. Since the difference in size is minor, there is no difference in the cost of the bearings because of this added feature.

Two departments were established in the new facility. The machining department is charged with the responsibility for all of the initial machining work performed on the shafts. The finishing and pressing department does all of the finishing work and presses on the bearings as ordered by customers. Although many different turbines can be produced, separate operations are not necessary for the production of any of the versions currently manufactured.

The initial decision required of the standards team was to determine whether or not rework time, waiting time and setup time should be included in the operations routing sheet. After careful consideration and study, it was decided that these cost factors should be considered in determining the manufacturing overhead rate that is charged to specific jobs. There are simply too many uncontrollable variables to assume that these factors are associated with or caused by any one specific job. By including rework time, waiting time, and setup time in the manufacturing overhead charge, these costs would be allocated or spread over all of the production of any given time period instead of affecting just a few units or batches of production.

The final operations routing sheet developed by Sax's standards team is presented in Illustration 7–1.

The standard time required for processing a power turbine shaft in the machining department is 20 minutes. Sax Company wishes to use attainable standards; therefore, based on their prior experience, an 11 percent allowance for delays is built into the standard time. Remember, all rework time, waiting time, and setup time is included in the manufacturing overhead rate.

The standard time for the finishing and pressing operation is 10 minutes. Again, based on prior experience, an 11 percent allowance for delays is built into the standard time to arrive at an attainable standard.

Standard Bill of Materials

Sax Company employs two basic materials in manufacturing its power turbine shafts: a six-centemeter diameter steel billet and various sizes of ball bearings. As previously indicated, the ball bearings are fitted to order, but most of the production is accomplished using off-the-shelf items with standard size ball bearings. There is little or no cost differential for the materials. However, because of market conditions, Sax Company commands a higher selling price for its made-to-order power turbine shafts.

Certain indirect materials and supplies are also used in producing the power turbine shafts. The standards team felt that these items should be included in the manufacturing overhead standard, because the cost of accounting for these indirect materials and supplies probably exceed any benefits that might be derived from a separate accounting for these items as direct materials.

Illustration 7–2 presents the standard bill of materials that was prepared for the power turbine shaft production.

After preparing the standard bill of materials, the standards team had to decide on an appropriate capacity measure to be used for developing the standard manufacturing overhead rate. It was also necessary to select a base for applying the overhead to the products produced.

Manufacturing Overhead Costs

The standards team decided to use the practical capacity of the new facility in determining a standard for overhead. Practical capacity is that capacity that can be attained under efficient and effective operating conditions. The practical output that can be expected from the new production facility is 1,800 power turbine shafts per month. Standard direct

Illustration 7-1
Sax Company
Operations Routing Sheets

Operations Routing Sheet

Department Machining
Product Name Power Turbine Shafts
Materials Round Steel Billet 6cm. Diameter

Operation	Minutes	Tools
Initial materials handling	2	
Put into lathe	3	Lathe
Machining	3	Lathe
Check machining	2	Micrometer
Machining	1	Lathe
Check machining	2	Micrometer
Final machining	3	Lathe
Materials handling	2	
Allowance for delays (11%)	2	
Standard Time	20	

Operations Routing Sheet

Department Finishing and Pressing
Product Name Power Turbine Shafts
Materials Round Steel Billet from Machining
           Ball Bearings

Operation	Minutes	Tools
Initial materials handling	2	
Finishing	3	Lathe and Polisher
Pressing	2	Hydraulic Press
Materials handling	2	
Allowance for delays (11%)	1	
Standard Time	10	

labor hours were chosen as the base to be used for the application of overhead. Direct labor hours were considered the factor most closely related to the variable portion of manufacturing overhead in the past, and management anticipates that this relationship will hold in the new

Illustration 7-2
Sax Company
Standard Bill of Materials

Standard Bill of Materials		
Product Power Turbine Shafts		
Location	Required Number	Description
Aisle 84	1	Round Steel Billet 6 cm. Diameter
Aisle 85	2	Ball Bearings — Size Varies by Order

facilities. The standards team estimated that 900 direct labor hours are required to produce a total of 1,800 power turbine shafts.

The standards team made an analysis of the overhead factors and related costs that are anticipated in the new facility during 19x1. The results of this study are presented in Illustration 7-3.

The standards team based its analysis of overhead costs on an output measure, the production of 1,800 units, which represents the practical capacity of the new facilities. Standard manufacturing overhead at this level of production is determined to be $3.40 per unit produced. As previously indicated, standard direct labor hours were the input measure chosen and used as the basis for applying manufacturing overhead to the products produced. The relationship between the input and output measures is known. Two power turbine shafts can be produced, at standard, for each direct labor hour worked. Overhead per direct labor hour is twice the overhead rate per unit produced since one direct labor hour is required to produce every two units of product. The standard variable manufacturing overhead rate per standard direct labour hour is $2.80, and the standard fixed manufacturing overhead per standard direct labour hour totals $4.00.

The Standard Cost Sheet

After the standards team prepared a standard operations routing sheet, a standard bill of materials, and the manufacturing overhead cost standards, the entire study was forwarded to the cost accounting department. The cost accounting department made a further analysis of the data and developed the standard cost sheet for power turbine shaft production that is presented in Illustration 7-4.

Illustration 7-3
Sax Company
Developing the Standard Manufacturing Overhead

Projected Practical Capacity: 1,800 Units
Standard Direct Labor Hours at Practical Capacity: 900 Hours

Standard Manufacturing Overhead Per Unit

	Variable per Unit Produced	Fixed	Total
Rework Time................................	$ .10	0	$ 180
Waiting Time................................	.06	0	108
Setup Time................................	.08	0	144
Indirect Materials and Supplies............	.60	$ 88	1,168
Indirect Labor................................	.46	272	1,100
Electricity................................	.10	240	420
Heat................................	0	100	100
Equipment Depreciation................	0	600	600
Plant Depreciation................	0	1,500	1,500
Factory Property Taxes................	0	800	800
Totals................................	$1.40	$3,600	$6,120

Standard Manufacturing Overhead per Unit:

Standard Variable Manufacturing Overhead per Unit................. $1.40
Standard Fixed Manufacturing Overhead per Unit........ $3,600 / 1,800 units = 2.00

Standard Total Manufacturing Overhead per Unit.................. $3.40

A COMPREHENSIVE EXAMPLE: ACCOUNTING FOR STANDARD COSTS

The actual process of record keeping for standard costs varies from company to company. To illustrate both the accounting for standard costs for purposes of inventory costing and the analysis of the related variances, assume that Sax Company wishes to integrate its standard costing system into its accounts as of January 1, 19x1.

Sax Company decided that its standard cost system should be developed such that:

1. All inventories (raw materials, work-in-process, and finished goods) are accounted for at standard costs in preparing its internal monthly financial reports.

2. Any variances from standard costs are analyzed on a monthly basis, but the inventories will remain at standard costs. Variances are also analyzed and closed to the cost of goods sold account, provided that

Illustration 7-4
Sax Company
Standard Cost Sheet

Standard Cost Sheet
Product: Power Turbine Shafts
Basis for Cost Sheet: One Unit

Materials

Location	Standard Quantity	Standard Price per unit	Total
Aisle 84	1	$4.00	$4.00
Aisle 85	2	1.00	$2.00
			$6.00

Labor

Department	Standard Hours	Standard Hourly Rate	Total
Machining	1/3	$6.00	$2.00
Finishing and Pressing	1/6	6.00	$1.00
			$3.00

Manufacturing Overhead

Variable Overhead Per Unit	$1.40
Fixed Overhead Per Unit	2.00
Total Overhead Per Unit	$3.40

Cost Summary Per Unit

Materials @ Standard	1 Steel Billet @ $4.00	=	$ 4.00
	2 Ball Bearings @ 1.00	=	2.00
Direct Labor @ Standard	½ hour @ $6.00/hour	=	3.00
Variable Manufacturing Overhead @ Standard*		=	1.40
Fixed Manufacturing Overhead @ Standard*		=	2.00
Total Manufacturing Cost @ Standard			$12.40

*Basis of Application to Product is Standard Direct
Labor Hours. Application Rate is $6.80 Per Standard
Direct Labor Hour.

in so doing, the financial position and results of operations of Sax Company will not be materially distorted.

At this point, Sax Company feels that it lacks both the personnel and the expertise to make a thorough analysis of variances for control and cost reduction purposes. Sax does plan to introduce a more comprehensive system in the future.

Sax Company plans to test its standard cost system for at least a year before attempting to undertake any major modifications or refinements of the system. Recall that the company closes down for employee vacations during the last two weeks in December, so it will have sufficient time to modify the system if it appears necessary to do so.

During January 19x1, Sax Company entered into numerous transactions with regard to its power turbine shaft manufacturing operation. For purposes of this comprehensive example, these transactions are presented in summarized form along with the corresponding general journal entries. The related ledger accounts are also presented in "T" account format.

Recording Raw Material Purchases

Since Sax Company wishes to maintain all of its inventory balances at standard costs, any inventory increases or withdrawals that affect raw materials, work-in-process, or finished goods must be recorded in the accounts at standard costs. This procedure permits all of the subsidiary accounts to be maintained in terms of physical units without including the corresponding dollar amounts in these records.

As raw materials are purchased, an unfavorable price variance is recognized if the price actually paid for the materials exceeds the standard price. Alternatively, if the price paid is less than the standard price, a favorable price variance is recognized at the point of the purchase.[1]

Transaction 1. During the month, Sax Company purchased a total of 1,850 steel billets at an average price of $4.02 per billet. Assuming that all of these purchases were paid for in cash during the year, the summary journal and "T" account entries necessary to record the steel billet purchase transactions are as follows:

Raw Materials Inventory—Steel Billets ($4.00 X 1,850)....   7,400
Raw Materials Price Variance [($4.02-$4.00) X 1,850].....   37
  Cash ($4.02 X 1,850)...............................   7,437

Cash		Raw Materials Inventory Steel Billets		Raw Materials Price Variance	
1/1 Bal. 20,000	7,437 (1)	(1) 7,400		(1) 37	

The raw materials price variances can also be calculated at this point using the following formula:

---

[1] In some instances, companies record their raw material inventories at actual cost. Under such a system, price variances are not recognized until the raw materials are introduced into the production process.

$$\begin{array}{l} \textit{Raw Materials} \\ \textit{Purchase Price} \\ \textit{Variance} \end{array} = \left(\begin{array}{c} \textit{Standard Price} \\ \textit{Per Unit} \end{array} - \begin{array}{c} \textit{Actual Price} \\ \textit{Per Unit} \end{array} \right) \times \begin{array}{c} \textit{Number of} \\ \textit{Units} \\ \textit{Purchased} \end{array}$$

$$= (\$4.00 - \$4.02) \times 1,850$$
$$= \$37 \text{ Unfavorable Price Variance}$$

Another method which may be used to calculate this variance is one which utilizes the total purchases of steel billets as follows:

Actual Purchases at Standard Prices (1,850 X $4.00)...........	$7,400
Actual Purchases at Actual Prices (1,850 X $4.02)..............	7,437
Excess of Total Actual Prices over Standard Prices.............	($ 37)

Both methods arrive at the identical answer.

Since all inventories are carried in the accounts at standard cost, the price variance is determined entirely within the accounting system. The debit to raw materials inventory or purchases will be at standard cost and the credit to accounts payable or cash will be at actual cost. The offsetting debit or credit will be the raw materials price variance. If the Sax Company had used actual costs in their accounting records, the formula approach could have been used for an analysis of the raw materials price variance. Both standard and actual costs must be analyzed in order to determine if the variance is favorable or unfavorable. In this case, an average price of $4.02 was actually paid for the steel billets. The standard price is $4.00. The price differential between the actual price ($4.02) and the standard price ($4.00) caused the price variance. If the standard price had been paid, any quantity could have been purchased and a price variance would not have been incurred. When standard costs are incorporated in an accounting system, an unfavorable variance is always recorded by a debit to a variance account while a favorable variance is indicated by a credit to a variance account. An unfavorable variance indicates that actual costs exceeded standard costs, while a favorable variance indicates that actual costs were less than standard costs.

Transaction 2. Sax Company purchased 4,000 ball bearings during the month and paid an average price of $.98 per ball bearing. These purchases of ball bearings caused a favorable material price variance since the price paid ($.98) was less than the standard price ($1.00).

Raw Materials Inventory—Ball Bearings ($1.00 X 4,000)...	4,000	
Raw Materials Price Variance [($1.00-$.98) X 4,000]......		80
Cash ($.98 X 4,000)................................		3,920

Cash		Raw Materials Inventory— Ball Bearings	Raw Materials Price Variance	
1/1 Bal. 20,000	7,437 (1)	(2) 4,000	(1) 37	80 (2)
	3,920 (2)			

Again, the raw materials price variance could have been calculated using the formula as follows:

$$\begin{array}{c} \text{Raw Materials} \\ \text{Purchase Price} \\ \text{Variance} \end{array} = \left(\begin{array}{c} \text{Standard Price} \\ \text{Per Unit} \end{array} - \begin{array}{c} \text{Actual Price} \\ \text{Per Unit} \end{array} \right) \times \begin{array}{c} \text{Actual Number} \\ \text{of Units} \\ \text{Purchased} \end{array}$$

$$= (\$1.00 - \$.98) \times 4,000$$
$$= \$80 \text{ Favorable Price Variance}$$

If the total ball bearing purchases were used in the calculation, the variance would be computed as indicated below:

Actual Purchases at Standard Prices (4,000 X $1.00)	$4,000
Actual Purchases at Actual Prices (4,000 X $.98)	3,920
Excess of Standard Prices over Actual Prices	$ 80

Again, both of these methods will provide the same answer since the only difference is that the first calculation is made on a per unit basis while the second uses total figures.

When standard costs are incorporated into the accounting system, a favorable variance is reflected by a credit balance in a variance account. The term favorable when used in this regard indicates that the standard cost anticipated exceeded the actual cost incurred.

Recording Raw Material Transfers to Work-in-Process

Before a production run is initiated, a requisition is prepared for the standard amount of raw materials required to produce the goods. If the production run ultimately requires the use of additional raw materials, the foreman or other supervisory personnel in the production department must make a formal request for the additional raw materials needed. This request would, of course, ultimately cause an unfavorable raw materials quantity or usage variance. If less than the standard quantity of raw materials is used, then the excess materials are returned to the raw materials inventory. This return causes a favorable raw materials quantity or usage variance.

During January, Sax had formal production runs totaling 1,760 power turbine shafts. The materials requisitions, at standard quantities, were for 1,760 steel billets and 3,520 ball bearings. Additional requests for raw materials made by production foremen totaled 40 steel billets and 30 ball bearings. Therefore, the usage or quantity variances for both steel billets and ball bearings were unfavorable since the actual quantities used during the period exceeded the standard amounts.

Transaction 3.   A total of 1,800 steel billets was transferred from the raw materials inventory to the work-in-process inventory. Of these billets, 1,760 were transferred by standard materials requisitions and 40 were transferred by excess materials requisitions. The summary journal entry necessary to record the transfer of all of the steel billets (both regular and excess) to work-in-process is as follows:

Work-in-process ($4.00 X 1,760)......................	7,040	
Raw Materials Quantity Variance ($4.00 X 40)..........	160	
Raw Materials Inventory—Steel Billets ($4.00 X 1,800)..		7,200

Raw Materials Inventory Steel Billets		Work-In-Process	Raw Materials Quantity Variance
(1) 7,400	7,200 (3)	(3) 7,040	(3) 160

As was the case with raw materials, the work-in-process inventory account is recorded at standard costs. The raw materials quantity or usage variance can be calculated using the following formula:

$$\begin{matrix} Raw \\ Materials \\ Quantity \\ Variance \end{matrix} = \left(\begin{matrix} Standard \\ Quantity \\ Allowed \end{matrix} - \begin{matrix} Actual \\ Quantity \\ Used \end{matrix} \right) \times \begin{matrix} Standard \\ Price \\ Per \\ Unit \end{matrix}$$

$$= (1,760 - 1,800) \times \$4.00$$
$$= \$160 \text{ Unfavorable Materials Quantity Variance}$$

Alternatively, if total amounts are used, the variance calculation is made as follows:

Standard Quantity Allowed at the Standard Price	
(1,760 X $4.00)...	$7,040
Actual Quantity Used at the Standard Price (1,800 X $4.00).........	7,200
Excess of Quantity Used at the Standard Price....................	($ 160)

Again, both methods yield the identical result.

A quantity variance measures the deviation of actual from standard usage. The variance experienced by Sax Company in January was caused by the fact that an excess of 40 steel billets over the standard quantity was used during the year. The standard price is employed in calculating the variance for both the actual quantities used and the standard quantities that should have been used. Of course, a variance is introduced into the analysis only if the standard and actual quantities differ.

Transaction 4.   A total of 3,550 ball bearings was transferred from raw materials inventory to the work-in-process inventory. Of these, 3,520 ball bearings were transferred by standard materials requisitions and 30 by excess materials requisitions. The summary transaction for the month would be recorded as follows:

Work-in-Process ($1.00 X 3,520)........................ 3,520
  Raw Materials Quantity Variance ($1.00 X 30)...........   30
    Raw Materials Inventory—Ball Bearings ($1.00 X 3,550).   3,550

Raw Materials Inventory Ball Bearings		Work-in-Process	Raw Materials Quantity Variance
(2) 4,000	3,550 (4)	(3) 7,040 (4) 3,520	(3) 160 (4) 30

Again, both the raw materials account and the work-in-process account are maintained at standard cost. The transfer to work-in-process can be calculated at standard in either of two ways. Since 1,760 power turbine shafts were produced in January, the amount of the standard inventory transfer should have been $2.00 X 1,760 or $3,520. Alternatively, as was presented in the previous journal entry, 3,520 bearings should have been transferred at the standard price of $1.00.

The variance is calculated using the following formula:

$$\text{Raw Materials Quantity Variance} = \left(\text{Standard Quantity Allowed} - \text{Actual Quantity Used} \right) \times \text{Standard Price Per Unit}$$

$$= (3,520 - 3,550) \text{ X } \$1.00$$
$$= \$30 \text{ Unfavorable Materials Quantity Variance}$$

If total amounts are used, the variance calculation is made as follows:

Standard Quantity Allowed at the Standard Price
(3,520 X $1.00)... $3,520
Actual Quantity Used at the Standard Price (3,550 X $1.00)...... 3,550
Excess of Quantity Used at the Standard Price................. ($ 30)

This unfavorable material quantity variance was caused by the fact that 30 ball bearings in excess of the standard amount were used in the production process during the month.

Recording Direct Labor Costs

All direct labor costs are charged to jobs at the standard labor rate using the standard time established for performing a particular job or operation. However, employees are paid based on their actual pay rate and the actual amount of time that they work. Given these two statements, it is apparent that two types of direct labor variances are possible. A rate of pay either greater or lesser than the standard wage rate may be paid. This would cause Sax Company to recognize a rate variance for direct labor. In addition, the amount or quantity of direct labor worked may be more than or less than the standard amount. This would cause an efficiency or usage variance for direct labor.

Transaction 5. *During January, a total of 890 direct labor hours was used by Sax Company to produce the 1,760 power turbine shafts.* This amount, as per standard, *should* have been 880 hours. The actual payroll for this direct labor totaled $5,251. This amount represented an average cost of $5.90 for each direct labor hour worked. There were no wages payable at the end of the year.

When the standards team developed the standard for labor time (Illustration 7–1), it established the basis for recording the standard labor on the job cost sheets. As jobs progress through the factory, the actual time for each job is also recorded on the job cost sheets. The standard time at the standard rate is recorded by a debit to the work-in-process inventory account. Remember, all manufacturing inventory accounts are maintained at standard costs by Sax Company. Any difference between the standard time (recorded at the standard rate) and the actual time (recorded at the standard rate) is reflected in the labor efficiency or usage variance. The difference between the actual labor rates which were paid and the standard rates is multiplied by the actual hours worked to determine the labor rate variance.

The summary entry for January to record direct labor costs is as follows:

Work-in-Process ($6.00 X 880)	5,280	
Direct Labor Efficiency Variance [$6.00 X (890-880)]	60	
Cash		5,251
Direct Labor Rate Variance [($6.00-$5.90) X 890]		89

Cash		**Work-in-Process**	
1/1 Bal. 20,000	7,437 (1)	(3) 7,040	
	3,920 (2)	(4) 3,520	
	5,251 (5)	(5) 5,280	

Direct Labor Efficiency Variance		**Direct Labor Rate Variance**	
(5) 60			89 (5)

The debit to the work-in-process account reflects the standard rate per hour ($6.00) multiplied by the standard number of hours (880) allowed to produce 1,760 power turbine shafts.

The debit to the direct labor efficiency variance account reflects the difference between the actual direct labor hours worked (890) and the standard hours that should have been worked (880) at the standard rate ($6.00). Since actual hours worked exceeded the standard established for hours worked, the direct labor efficiency variance is unfavorable. The credit to cash of $5,251 represents the actual direct labor wages paid to employees. The standard wage rate is $6.00 per hour, and employees were paid an average rate of $5.90 per hour for the 890 hours worked during January. Therefore, the direct labor rate variance was favorable and is recorded by a credit of $89 [($6.00 — $5.90) X 890] to the direct labor rate variance account.

Alternatively, the labor efficiency and rate variances could have been calculated using the following formulas:

$$\begin{matrix} \text{Direct} \\ \text{Labor} \\ \text{Efficiency} \\ \text{Variance} \end{matrix} = \left(\begin{matrix} \text{Standard} \\ \text{Hours} \\ \text{Allowed} \end{matrix} - \begin{matrix} \text{Actual} \\ \text{Hours} \\ \text{Used} \end{matrix} \right) \times \begin{matrix} \text{Standard} \\ \text{Wage} \\ \text{Rate} \\ \text{Per Hour} \end{matrix}$$

$$= (880 - 890) \times \$6.00$$
$$= \$60 \text{ Unfavorable Direct Labor Efficiency Variance}$$

Or, if total amounts are used, the calculation is:

Standard Hours Allowed at the Standard Rate (880 X $6.00) $5,280
Actual Hours Used at the Standard Rate (890 X $6.00)   5,340
Excess of Quantity Used at the Standard Price . . . .   ($ 60)

$$\begin{matrix} \text{Direct} \\ \text{Labor} \\ \text{Rate} \\ \text{Variance} \end{matrix} = \left(\begin{matrix} \text{Standard} \\ \text{Rate} \end{matrix} - \begin{matrix} \text{Actual} \\ \text{Rate} \end{matrix} \right) \times \begin{matrix} \text{Actual} \\ \text{Quantity} \\ \text{of Labor} \\ \text{Used} \end{matrix}$$

$$= (\$6.00 - \$5.90) \times 890$$
$$= \$89 \text{ Favorable Direct Labor Rate Variance}$$

Or, if total amounts are used:

Standard Rate at the Actual Hours Worked (890 X $6.00) $5,340
Actual Rate at the Actual Hours Worked (890 X $5.90)   5,251
Excess of Standard Rate at the Actual Hours Worked . . . . $ 89

The above computations indicate that the method for calculating the labor efficiency or usage variance follows the same principles used to calculate the raw materials usage variance. The principles underlying the computation of the labor rate variance and the raw materials price variance are also identical.

Applying Manufacturing Overhead to Production

Sax Company has decided to use standard direct labor hours as a basis for applying manufacturing overhead to its products. At this point it should be noted that since all inventories are carried at standard costs, Sax Company uses standard direct labor hours rather than actual direct labor hours because to do otherwise would allow the efficiencies or in-efficiencies of labor to affect the amount of overhead absorbed by a specific job. By using standard direct labor hours, the inventories are maintained at standard costs. The use of standard direct labor hours provides the same absorption of overhead by products as the output measure, units finished, would provide. Standard direct labor hours are relatively easy to calculate and are homogeneous in that one standard direct labor hour is identical to all other standard hours.

The manufacturing overhead applied at standard for Sax Company is determined by multiplying the total standard direct labor hours for January (880) by the manufacturing overhead rate at standard (obtained from the standard cost sheet presented in Illustration 7-4). The standard manufacturing overhead rate is $6.80 per standard direct labor hour.

Transaction 6. The manufacturing overhead applied to the 1,760 power turbine shafts produced in January totaled $5,984 ($6.80 × 880). The summary journal and "T" account entries required to record the overhead for January are as follows:

Work-in-Process ($6.80 X 880)............................ 5,984
    Manufacturing Overhead—Control ($6.80 X 880)..........   5,984

Work-in-Process		Manufacturing Overhead—Control	
(3) 7,040			5,984 (6)
(4) 3,520			
(5) 5,280			
(6) 5,984			

Recording Transfers From Work-in-Process

As goods are completed, they are transferred from the work-in-process inventory to the finished goods inventory at their standard cost.

Transaction 7. During January, a total of 1,760 power turbine shafts were completed and transferred to the finished goods inventory. The standard cost of one power turbine shaft is $12.40, according to Sax Company's standard cost sheet (Illustration 7-4). The total transferred to finished goods is therefore 1,760 X $12.40 or $21,824. The summary journal and "T" account entries required to recognize the transfers from work-in-process to finished goods are:

Finished Goods Inventory ($12.40 X 1,760).................. 21,824
    Work-in-Process ($12.40 X 1,760)........................   21,824

Work-in-Process		Finished Goods	
(3) 7,040	21,824 (7)	(7) 21,824	
(4) 3,520			
(5) 5,280			
(6) 5,984			

For any goods sold during January, the cost of goods sold associated with these sales would also be recognized at standard cost. (Sales for the period will be recorded in Transaction 9.)

Recording Actual Manufacturing Overhead Costs

Sax Company's actual manufacturing overhead costs for January totaled $6,320. An analysis of the subsidiary records revealed the following components of the actual manufacturing overhead for January.

Rework Time	$ 160
Waiting Time	100
Setup Time	140
Indirect Materials and Supplies	1,100
Indirect Labor	1,160
Electricity	700
Heat	60
Equipment Depreciation	600
Plant Depreciation	1,500
Factory Property Taxes	800
	$6,320

The rework time, waiting time, setup time and indirect labor were all labor costs which were paid but which were not reflected in the direct labor payroll recorded in Transaction 5. The indirect materials and supplies were obtained from the materials and supplies inventory. The electricity, heat, and property taxes were all paid. The total cash outlay for the manufacturing overhead items for the period was $3,120.

Transaction 8. Actual manufacturing overhead costs incurred during the period are $6,320. The summary entry necessary to record the actual manufacturing overhead for January is as follows:

Manufacturing Overhead—Control	6,320	
Cash		3,120
Indirect Materials and Supplies Inventory		1,100
Accumulated Depreciation—Equipment		600
Accumulated Depreciation—Plant		1,500

Manufacturing Overhead— Control		Cash	
(8) 6,320	5,984 (6)	1/1 Bal. 20,000	7,437 (1)
			3,920 (2)
			5,251 (5)
			3,120 (8)

Indirect Materials and Supplies Inventory	
1/1 Bal. 2,000	1,100 (8)

Accumulated Depreciation— Equipment		Accumulated Depreciation— Plant	
	600 (8)		1,500 (8)

Manufacturing overhead of $5,984 at standard cost was applied to the products during the month in Transaction 6. As indicated in Transaction 8, however, the actual manufacturing overhead for the year was $6,320. Manufacturing overhead costs were, therefore, underapplied by a total of $336. This difference will be analyzed in Chapter 8.

Recording Cost of Goods Sold at Standard

The finished goods inventory is recorded and accounted for at standard cost. As the goods are sold, any cost of goods sold is also recognized at standard cost.

Transaction 9. A total of 1,600 power turbine shafts were sold during January at an average selling price of $50 per shaft. All but $2,000 of these sales had been collected by month-end.

The summary entry to record this transaction is as follows:

Cash [($50 X 1,600)—$2,000].......................... 78,000
Accounts Receivable................................... 2,000
    Sales Revenue ($50 X 1,600)......................... 80,000

Cash			
1/1 Bal. 20,000		7,437	(1)
(9) 78,000		3,920	(2)
		5,251	(5)
		3,120	(8)

Accounts Receivable	
(9) 2,000	

Sales Revenue	
	80,000 (9)

The cost of goods sold for January is recorded by the following entry:

Cost of Goods Sold ($12.40 X 1,600)...................... 19,840
    Finished Goods Inventory ($12.40 X 1,600)............. 19,840

Cost of Goods Sold	
(9) 19,840	

Finished Goods Inventory	
(7) 21,824	19,840 (9)

The cost of goods sold account represents the standard cost of the goods sold during the period. For income statement purposes, the management of Sax Company wishes to close out all of the variance accounts to the cost of goods sold account at the end of the month.

Closing the Variance Accounts

At the end of January, Sax Company decided to adjust the amount of cost of goods sold used for income statement purposes to include the net effect of all of the variances from standard costs which were experienced during the month. This means that the cost of goods sold account will absorb all of the differences between standard and actual costs that were recognized during the month. In effect, closing all the variance accounts to the cost of goods sold account will convert Sax's standard cost system to an actual cost system for income statement purposes.[2]

The balances in the cost of goods sold account and the individual variance accounts at the end of January are as follows:

Raw Materials Price Variance			Raw Materials Quantity Variance	
(1) 37	80 (2)		(3) 160	
			(4) 30	
	43		190	

Direct Labor Efficiency Variance			Direct Labor Rate Variance	
(5) 60				89 (5)
60				89

Manufacturing Overhead— Control			Cost of Goods Sold	
(8) 6,320	5,984 (6)		(9) 19,840	
336			19,840	

Transaction 10. ***The variance accounts should be closed to the cost of goods sold account.*** The following journal entry is necessary:

Cost of Goods Sold.........................	454	
Raw Materials Price Variance...............	43	
Direct Labor Rate Variance.................	89	
Raw Materials Quantity Variance..........		190
Direct Labor Efficiency Variance..........		60
Manufacturing Overhead—Control........		336

Raw Materials Price Variance			Raw Materials Quantity Variance	
(1) 37	80 (2)		(3) 160	
			(4) 30	
(10) 43	43		190	190 (10)

[2] As discussed in Chapter 3, the variances, if material in amount, should be apportioned on a weighted average basis among the ending inventories of work-in-process, finished goods and the cost of goods sold. All accounts would approximate actual costs via this apportionment.

Direct Labor Efficiency Variance	
(5) 60	
60	60 (10)

Direct Labor Rate Variance	
	89 (5)
(10) 89	89

Manufacturing Overhead— Control	
(8) 6,320	5,984 (6)
336	336 (10)

Cost of Goods Sold	
(9) 19,840	
(10) 454	
20,294	

By adopting this procedure, the management of Sax Company is assuming that the net variance of $454 is immaterial for purposes of financial reporting. This does not imply, however, that the individual variances are immaterial or insignificant for purposes of managerial analysis. Management will decide which variances to investigate in detail.

SUMMARY

A standard cost system is often used in conjunction with a job order or process costing system to facilitate the costing of inventory. In a standard cost system, products are costed at that cost which should have been incurred under efficient and effective operations. Any deviations from the standard cost are reflected as variances at the end of the period.

Standard costs differ from normal costs in that normal costs are a combination of actual and expected costs, whereas standard costs are entirely based on costs expected under a given set of conditions. In addition to the obvious clerical convenience resulting from their use, standard costs are useful aids in planning, control, performance evaluation, and other management activities. If well-designed, standard costs may also be an effective means of employee motivation.

Standard costs are based on the physical standards of production. Physical standards relate to the quantities of materials, labor, processing time, etc. that are required under standard conditions to produce the product. Several types of standard costs are in general use. These types include standards based on (1) historical or past performance, (2) ideal or engineering performance, and (3) attainable performance. Of these, standard costs based on attainable performance are preferred for management accounting purposes.

The variance in direct materials cost and in direct labor cost can usually be explained by two factors: (1) the actual price paid differing from the standard price (referred to as the price or rate variance) and (2) the actual quantity used differing from the standard quantity (referred to as the quantity or efficiency variance) When variance accounts are incorporated in the accounting system, the variance accounts will be closed at the end of the accounting period. If immaterial in amount, the variances are generally closed directly to the cost of goods sold for the period. However, if material in amount, the balances should be apportioned on a weighted average basis to the ending work-in-process, finished goods inventories, and to the cost of goods sold.

Following is a summary of the equations for your reference of the standard cost variances listed in this chapter.

1.
$$\text{Material Price Variance} = \left(\begin{array}{c} \text{Standard} \\ \text{Price} \\ \text{Per} \\ \text{Unit} \end{array} - \begin{array}{c} \text{Actual} \\ \text{Price} \\ \text{Per} \\ \text{Unit} \end{array} \right) \times \begin{array}{c} \text{Actual} \\ \text{Number of} \\ \text{Units} \\ \text{Purchased} \end{array}$$

2.
$$\text{Material Quantity Variance} = \left(\begin{array}{c} \text{Standard} \\ \text{Quantity} \\ \text{Allowed} \end{array} - \begin{array}{c} \text{Actual} \\ \text{Quantity} \\ \text{Used} \end{array} \right) \times \begin{array}{c} \text{Standard} \\ \text{Price} \\ \text{Per} \\ \text{Unit} \end{array}$$

or units produced

3.
$$\text{Direct Labor Rate Variance} = \left(\begin{array}{c} \text{Standard} \\ \text{Rate} \\ \text{Per} \\ \text{Hour} \end{array} - \begin{array}{c} \text{Actual} \\ \text{Rate} \\ \text{Per} \\ \text{Hour} \end{array} \right) \times \begin{array}{c} \text{Actual Number} \\ \text{of Hours of} \\ \text{Direct} \\ \text{Labor} \\ \text{Used} \end{array}$$

4.
$$\text{Direct Labor Efficiency Variance} = \left(\begin{array}{c} \text{Standard} \\ \text{Hours} \\ \text{Allowed} \end{array} - \begin{array}{c} \text{Actual} \\ \text{Hours} \\ \text{Used} \end{array} \right) \times \begin{array}{c} \text{Standard} \\ \text{Wage} \\ \text{Rate} \\ \text{Per Hour} \end{array}$$

based on # of units produced at STD hours

KEY DEFINITIONS

Attainable standard—a satisfactory level of efficiency where the ideal standard has been modified to allow for normal tolerable inefficiencies.

Favorable variance—a variance which occurs in a standard cost accounting system when actual costs are less than standard costs. A favorable variance is recorded by a credit to a variance account.

Ideal standard—the highest level of efficiency attainable, based on all input factors interacting perfectly under ideal or optimum conditions.

Labor efficiency or usage variance—a variance occurring in a standard cost accounting system when the actual amount or quantity of direct labor used differs from the standard amount required.

Labor rate variance—a variance which occurs in a standard cost accounting system when the actual pay rate differs from the standard pay rate for direct labor.

Materials price variance—a variance which occurs in a standard cost accounting system when actual prices paid for raw materials differ from the standard prices.

Materials quantity or usage variance—a variance which occurs in a standard cost accounting system when the actual amounts of raw materials used to produce a good differ from the standard amounts required to produce that good.

Practical capacity—that level of production that can be attained under efficient and effective operating conditions.

Standard costs—costs which are assigned to the factors of production based on physical standards under efficient and effective operations required to manufacture the product, and not necessarily the costs which are expected to occur or actually do occur.

Standard cost system—an inventory cost system where standard costs are used in accounting for the factors of production.

Unfavorable variance—a variance which occurs in a standard cost accounting system when actual costs exceed standard costs. An unfavorable variance is recorded by a debit to a variance account.

QUESTIONS

7-1 What is the purpose of using standard costs?

7-2 How does allocating fixed overhead cause distortions in per unit costs from period to period?

7-3 What are the three basic classifications used to determine standard costs? Theoretically, which of these standards should be applied to a standard cost system?

7-4 Is there any one primary use of a standard cost system? If so, what is it?

7-5 What is the rationale behind including rework time, waiting time, and set up time in manufacturing overhead?

7-6 At what two times may a material price variance be recognized, and at which time do you feel it is the more correct for control reasons?

7-7 What are the two possible variances associated with direct labor costs and identify one reason why each could occur?

7-8 Which of the following variances are favorable (F)? Unfavorable (U)?

    a. Debit to direct labor efficiency variance.
    b. Credit to direct labor rate variance.
    c. Debit to raw material price variance.
    d. Credit to material quantity variance.

7-9 If end-of-the-period variances are material in amount, how should they be apportioned?

7-10 In conjunction with what type of cost systems may standard costs be used?

EXERCISES AND PROBLEMS

7-11 The Walters Manufacturing Company has established the following standards for one unit of their product, Alpha.

        Material.......... 6 Kg. @ $8.00/Kg.
        Labor........... 12 hrs. @ $6.00/Hr.

During August, the Walters Manufacturing Company purchased 7,000 kilograms of material at $56,350 and incurred total labor costs of $71,248. 1,000 units of Alpha were produced. They used 6,220 kilograms of material and 11,680 hours of labor.

Required:

    a. Compute the material price and usage variances.
    b. Compute the labor rate and efficiency variances.

7-12 The Goodness Company uses a standard cost system with the following standard costs:

    Material, 5 kilograms @ $6.00/kilogram . . . $30.00
    Labor, 3 hours @ $4.50/hour 13.50
    Overhead, 3 hours @ $7.00/hour 21.00
    Total standard cost per unit $64.50

During the year, 10,000 units were produced. Costs incurred for material and labor were $325,000 and $135,000 respectively.

Required:

Calculate the total material variance and labor variance from standard costs. It is not necessary to calculate price, rate, and efficiency variances.

7-13 You are given the following information about the King Company:

Standard cost of one whatisit:
1 kilogram of material @ $1 . . . . $1
2 hours of direct labor @ $2 per hour 4
                                                $5

Required:

During the month of May, King produces 1 whatisit. Prepare journal entries to record the following transactions which occurred in May. You must use King's standard cost system.

a. Materials purchased and used in May—2 kilograms at $2 per kilogram
b. Labor (Direct) for May—3 hours @ $1.50 per hour

Assume no beginning or ending material inventory.

7-14 You have been given the following information:

Actual labor hours used = 315 hours
Standard materials price = $2.50 per unit
Standard labor hours used = 300 hours
Standard quantity of materials used = 450 units
Actual labor rate per hour = $3.00
Actual quantity of materials purchased and used = 445 units
Standard labor rate per hour = $3.10
Actual materials price = $2.52 per unit

Required:

Prepare a schedule for the following variances:

a. Raw materials price variance
b. Raw materials quantity variance
c. Direct labor efficiency variance
d. Direct labor rate variance

7-15 The Simons Company manufactures bolts in standard batches of 5,000 units. The standard cost for a batch is as follows:

Raw materials 200 Kg. @ $.04 per Kg . . . . $ 8.00
Direct labor 4 hrs. @ $5.15 per hour 20.60
Overhead (including variable overhead of $4.50) 10.00
    Total standard cost $38.60

Data for the month of March is as follows:

Planned production . . . . 240 batches
Actual production . . . . 250 batches
Cost of raw materials purchased (55,000 Kg.) $2,310.00
Cost of raw materials used (51,250 Kg.) $2,152.50
Direct labor cost (998 hours) $5,189.60
Actual overhead cost $2,560.00
Budgeted fixed overhead cost $1,320.00

Required:

Compute the following variances indicating whether favorable or unfavorable.

a. Raw materials price variance
b. Raw materials quantity variance
c. Direct labor rate variance
d. Direct labor efficiency variance

7-16 Given the following information, what is the standard cost per finished unit?

Normal activity—10,000 units

Standard Costs:

Direct materials	$2 per Kg.
Direct labor	$4.20 per hr.
Variable overhead	$2.75 per direct labor hr.
Fixed overhead	$30,000

Standard Quantity:

Direct materials	5 Kg. per unit
Direct labor	3 hrs. per unit

7-17 All of the items listed below are included in the budgeted manufacturing overhead costs of the Ames Company's only product. Projected production is 300,000 units. At standard, the overhead costs are:

	Fixed Costs	Total Costs
Rework time	$ –0–	$ 15,000
Set-up time	–0–	36,000
Indirect materials	10,200	250,200
Indirect supplies	2,000	8,000
Indirect labor	20,000	170,000
Electricity	1,075	1,075
Heat	1,900	1,900
Telephone	350	350
Equipment depreciation	15,000	15,000
Factory property taxes	9,475	9,475
	$60,000	$507,000

Required:

Calculate the standard variable manufacturing overhead per unit, the standard fixed manufacturing overhead per unit, and the total manufacturing overhead per unit.

7-18   The Taylor Company would like you to calculate for them the standard costs per unit for their product, widgets. Each unit must go through two departments, processing and finishing. The hourly employees in the processing department are paid $5.00 an hour and $6.15 an hour in finishing. Materials used in the processing department for making widgets include wids for $20 per kilogram and gets for $6 per kilogram. Practical capacity is expected to be 50,000 units per year. From the additional information listed below provided by various departments in the Taylor Company, calculate the standard cost per unit for material, labor, and overhead. Use the high-low method to calculate the fixed and variable cost components of manufacturing overhead.

Department   *Processing*
Product Name   *Widgets*

Operation	Minutes per widget
Materials handling	5
Machining	6
Check machining	2
Final machining	4
Materials handling	4
Allowance for delays	3
	24

Department   *Finishing*
Product Name   *Widgets*

Operation	Minutes per widget
Materials handling	3
Finishing	6
Final inspection	2
Materials handling	6
Allowance for delays	3
	20

Standard Bill of Materials
Department   *Processing*
Product Name   *Widgets*

Material	Required number
Wids	1 Kilogram
Gets	3 Kilograms

Manufacturing Overhead Costs
Departments   *Processing and Finishing*
Product Name   *Widgets*

Year	Units Produced	Costs
19x5	48,000	249,600
19x6	45,000	240,000

7-19 The Loren Company produces one product with the following standard costs per unit:

```
Materials, 2 kilograms @ $3.25 . . . . . . . . . . . . . . . . $ 6.50
Labor, 5 hours @ $2.05     . . . . . . . . . . . . . . . . .  10.25
Manufacturing overhead:
    Variable $1.00 per hour × 5 hours =        $5.00
    Fixed $120,000 = $.50 per hour × 5 hours = $2.50      7.50
            240,000 (hours practical yearly capacity)
                                                         _____
                                                         $24.25
```

Journalize the following transactions for the Loren Company for June. Units produced during the month totaled 3,000.

a. Purchased 6,400 kilograms of material at a cost of $19,600 on account.

b. Issued 6,300 kilograms of material to production to be used during June.

c. 21,500 labor hours were charged to production during June at a cost of $2.00 per hour.

d. Actual overhead incurred was $22,000 for variable overhead and $9,500 for fixed overhead. The variable overhead was paid for in cash and the fixed overhead was made up entirely of depreciation on plant and equipment.

e. Applied overhead was recorded based on standard direct labor hours.

f. Sales in June totaled 2,900 units at a mark-up of 40% on standard costs.

g. There were no beginning inventories on June 1. Variances are closed to the cost of goods sold at year end, on December 31.

7-20 Given the following balances in the variance accounts, journalize the closing entry.

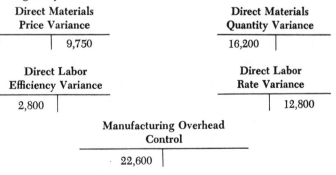

Direct Materials Price Variance	Direct Materials Quantity Variance
9,750	16,200

Direct Labor Efficiency Variance	Direct Labor Rate Variance
2,800	12,800

Manufacturing Overhead Control

22,600

7-21 During December the Strickem Co. produced 4,000 hunting knives which required 12,380 grams of steel and 6,000 litres of plastic (raw material plastic in liquid form). In order to do this, Strickem purchased 15 kilograms of steel for $6,450 and 7,000 litres of plastic for $2,100. The payroll for December amounted to $14,895. Total hours worked were 1,960 hours. The following are the per unit standards for material and labor established by Strickem.

Material
  Steel, 3 g. @ $.40/g.
  Plastic, 1.5 litres @ $.30/litre
Labor
  ½ hour at $7.50/hr.

Required:

a. Calculate the material price and quantity variances.
b. Calculate the labor rate and efficiency variances.

7-22   The following summarizes the standard cost for producing one metal tennis racket frame for McMullian Corp. In addition, the variances for January's production are given. Note that all inventory accounts have zero balances at the beginning of January.

	Standard Costs/Unit	Standard Production Costs
Materials	$4.00	$ 8,400
Direct Labour, ½ hrs. @ $10.40	5.20	10,920
Manufacturing Overhead:		
Variable	1.80	3,780
Fixed	5.00	10,500
		$33,600

Variances

Material price	($222.50) °
Material quantity	(500.00)
Direct labor rate	(750.94)
Direct labor efficiency	(2,096.25)

Required:

Determine the following for a tennis racket frame:

a. Actual direct labor hours.
b. Actual direct labor rate.
c. Actual materials used.
d. Actual per unit price for materials.

° Brackets indicate unfavorable variances.

7-23   In July, fire destroyed the XYZ Company's manufacturing facilities and inventory. The company's accounting records were saved; however, all inventory accounts were kept at standard costs. As an insurance adjustor, you are required to use the available records to determine the actual materials and labor costs for the month of July. The materials price variance is as calculated at the point of transfer into work in process. (Note: Inventory accounts have zero balances at the end of June.)

Per Unit Standard Costs

Materials, 5 Kg. @ $.50/Kg.	$ 2.50
Labor, 2 hrs. @ $2.25/hr.	4.50
Variable manufacturing overhead, 4 hrs. @ $3.00/hr.	12.00
Total standard cost (variable)	$19.00
Standard production and actual production	900 units

Material Price Variance	Material Quantity Variance
$90	$50
Direct Labor Rate Variance	**Direct Labor Efficiency Variance**
$9.40	$177.50

7-24 Because of inflation and a new labor agreement, Miller Thunderbolt Co. is revising its standard costs of producing a toy race car. The new labor agreement increased direct labor rates $.15 per hour. In addition, Thunderbolt Co. is facing a 6 percent increase in the cost of materials. From the available information, calculate the new standard cost for material per unit produced and labor per hour. Raw materials used in production is the amount of raw materials purchased.

1. Normal production = 750 units
2. Actual material purchases = $2,195
3. Actual direct labor wages paid = $6,795
4. Actual production = 723 units
5. Materials price variance = $46.30 Favorable
6. Actual direct labor hours = 2,265
7. Direct labor rate variance = $135.90 Favorable

7-25 The Allen Production Company requires two materials, A and B, to manufacture their product, X. During January they produced 4,500,000 units of X. Allen Company purchased 310,000 litres of material A at the cost of $24,180 and 25,000 kilograms of material B for $3,250. During January, Allen Company used 275,000 litres of material A and 21,000 kilograms of material B. The Allen Company has established the following material standards:

For 1,000 units of X:
    Material A, 30 litres @ $.08/litre . . . .
    Material B, 2.5 kilograms @ $.12/kilogram . . . .

Required:

Compute the material price and quantity variances for materials **A** and **B**.

A **7-26** Dente Company has established the following standard costs for its materials and direct labor:

	Per Finished Unit
Materials, 20 kilograms @ $4.00	$ 80
Direct labor, 10 hours @ $3.00	30
	$110

During the month, purchases amounted to 10,000 kilograms of materials at a total cost of $50,000. The number of finished units budgeted for the period was 500; 480 were actually produced. The actual operating results were as follows:

Materials, 9,500 kilograms used
Direct labor, 4,900 hours at a cost of $19,600

Required:

Show computations for all material and labor variances.

7-27 Wilson Corporation makes one product, tennis rackets. During May, in preparation for the summer season, Wilson produced 500 tennis rackets. The established standard variable costs for one racket follow:

Materials, 10 kilograms @ $.45/kilogram	$ 4.50
Labor, 3 hours @ $2.15/hour	6.45
Variable manufacturing overhead, 3 hours @ $2.75/hour .	8.25
	$19.20

The Wilson Corporation purchased 5,500 kilograms of material at a cost of $2,695. The production department used 5,150 kilograms of material. The payroll for direct labor hours of 1,495 amounted to $3,289.

Required:

Calculate the material and labor variances for the Wilson Corporation.

7-28 Krueger, Inc. uses a standard cost system. Given below is the standard cost information:

For one unit of product: Materials—3 kilograms @ $2 per kilogram
Labor—4 hours @ $3.50 per hour

Additional information:

1. There was no beginning or ending work-in-process inventory. A total of 6,500 units of product were produced during the period.
2. A total of 19,580 kilograms of materials which cost $38,181 were used during the period.
3. Direct labor costs totaling $93,528 were incurred during the period. Actual hours worked were 25,980.

Required:

Compute the variances from standard for materials and labor for the period. Label properly and indicate whether the variances are favorable or unfavorable. The quantity of materials purchased was the same as the quantity used in production.

7-29 The Garner Manufacturing Company produces a single product. Its standard cost is as follows:

Materials, 2 kilograms @ $6.50 . . . . $ 13.00
Labor, 3 hours @ $3.75 . . . . 11.25
Manufacturing expenses, 3 hours @ $2.25
    (including $1.75 of variable overhead) 6.75
                                                    $ 31.00

Standard manufacturing overhead expenses . . . $\dfrac{\$16,875}{7,500} = \$2.25$ per hour
Standard labor hours . . . .

Production (2,500 units) started and completed for the month of June: Production capacity 2,500 units.

1. Purchases of materials, 6,000 kilograms @ $6.60
2. Materials requisitioned, 4,900 kilograms
3. Payroll, 7,560 hours @ $3.90 per hour
4. Manufacturing expenses incurred during June totaled $17,000 (including $4,000 fixed overhead)
5. Sales 2,000 units @ $40

Required:

Journal entries to record the transactions for the month, using a standard cost system, and transferring variances to their proper accounts. (Do not distribute them to the ending inventory.) The Garner Manufacturing Company closes its books at the end of each month.

7-30 A manufacturing firm produces three varieties of a basic product which are manufactured from *two* raw materials.

Finished Product	Standard Usage per Finished Unit Units of Raw Material		Standard Prices
	A	B	
R	1	2	Raw material A $4.00 per unit
S	2	2	Raw material B $3.00 per unit
T	2	3	

Purchases:

Material A 100,000 units $405,000
Material B 140,000 units $415,800

Usage:

Material A 75,600 units
Material B 115,000 units

Finished Units:	Variety	Amount
	R	15,000 items
	S	15,000 items
	T	15,000 items

Required:

Make the journal entries for materials: (*a*) purchases and (*b*) usage as they would appear under an actual cost system and as they would appear under a standard cost system. Assume no previous balances in any of the accounts.

7-31 The Beaulieu Company uses a process cost system and standard costs. Below are the standard costs per unit for their only product, Bangles.

Material, 2 litres @ $3.50/litre	. . . .	$7.00
Labor, 0.2 hours @ $3.00/hour	. . . .	.60
Overhead: Variable @ $2.25/hour = .45		
Fixed ° @ $1.00/hour = .20	. . . . .	.65
Total standard cost per Bangle	. . . .	$8.25

° Fixed overhead is based on a normal capacity of 10,100 Bangles.

Production statistics for January are as follows:

Bangles produced this month—8,000.
Ending work-in-process—3,000; 100 percent complete for material, 70 percent complete for labor, and 70 percent complete for overhead.
There was no beginning work-in-process inventory.
Costs incurred this month were $90,000, $6,900 and $6,600 for material, labor and overhead, respectively.
25,000 litres of material and 3,000 labour hours were actually incurred.
The materials price variance is calculated at the time of transfer into work in process.

Required:

Using the weighted average method to determine the cost flow for January compute:

a. The material price and usage variances.
b. The labor rate and efficiency variances.

7-32 The Scott Company would like to compare material costs in June to material costs in July. Below is relevant information for both months.

Month	Material Costs	Kilograms of Material Used	Units Produced
June	$58,590	18,600	6,200
July	$63,488	19,840	6,400

Required:

Using June material prices and usage as a standard, calculate the material price and usage variances for July. Why can't you add these two variances together to arrive at the total material variance of $4,898 ($63,488 − $58,590)?

7-33 *a.* Which of the items listed below could *not* be considered a use of a standard cost system?

  1. Inventory costing.
  2. Bookkeeping convenience.
  3. Performance evaluation.
  4. Pricing studies.
  5. None of the above.

b. Which of the following is *not* a reason for a material price variance:

  1. Inadequate control over material requisitions.
  2. Seasonal purchases of material.
  3. Cheaper method of transportation.
  4. Volume purchasing of material.
  5. Less expensive sources for raw material.

c. At the end of the period, all variances in the individual variance accounts, theoretically should be

  1. closed to cost of goods sold.
  2. apportioned on a weighted average basis to the ending inventories of work-in-process, finished goods, and cost of goods sold.
  3. closed to the ending inventory of work-in-process.
  4. apportioned on a weighted average basis to the beginning inventories of work-in-process, finished goods, and cost of goods sold.
  5. closed to the ending inventory of finished goods.

A 7-34 The Hanlon Co. manufactures a product called Pattimar which has the following Standard Cost Sheet:

Standard Cost Sheet

Product: Pattimar
Basis for Cost Sheet: One Unit

Materials

#	Location	Standard Quantity	Standard Price/Unit	Total
1	Bin 57	3	$2.00	$6.00
2	Bin 72	5	.60	3.00
				$9.00

Labor

Department	Standard Hours	Standard Hourly Rate	Total
Assembly	2	$4.50	$ 9.00
Finishing	1	5.00	5.00
			$14.00

Manufacturing Overhead

Variable overhead per unit	$ 7.00
Fixed overhead per unit	9.00
Total overhead per unit	$16.00

The company's records indicate the following production and cost figures:

```
Units produced . . . . . . . . .  18,000
Material used
      #1 . . . . . . . . . . . . .  56,800 units
      #2 . . . . . . . . . . . . .  91,200 units
Labor costs
Assembly (35,980 hours) . . . . . $165,508
Finishing (18,200 hours) . . . . . $ 88,270
Materials purchased:
      #1 . . . . . . . . . . . . .  ( 60,000 units ) for $129,000
      #2 . . . . . . . . . . . . .  (100,000 units) for $ 55,000
```

Required:

Calculate materials price and quantity variances for each material and labor rate and efficiency variances for each department.

7-35 You have been hired by Mama Verdi to discover why she is not making as large a profit as she had expected from her famous Italian sauce. The three main ingredients are Thats, Asum, and Asausa. Mama's secret formula calls for 2 parts Asum for every one part Thats for every

3 parts Asausa therefore yielding 6 parts of sauce. The following information was found in the records in Mama's kitchen:

1. 12,000 kilograms of sauce made in August
2. 6,000 kilograms of Thats purchased for $7,200
3. 7,000 kilograms of Asum purchased for $13,800
4. 8,000 kilograms of Asausa purchased for $12,400
5. Standard cost of Thats/kilogram = $1.15
6. Standard cost of Asum/kilogram = $2.00
7. Standard cost of Asausa/kilogram = $1.50
8. 5,000 kilograms of Asum used in August
9. 3,500 kilograms of Thats used in August
10. 6,600 kilograms of Asausa used in August

Required:

Calculate the material price and quantity variance for Thats, Asum, and Asausa for the month of August.

7-36 Nancy Company produced 17,800 footballs during May. Material purchases amounted to 184,000 kilograms at $2.10 per kilogram. Usage of the materials amounted to 92,200 kilograms. The footballs required 53,000 hours of labor at $4.20 per hour. Nancy Company has established the following material and labor standards for one football:

> 5 Kg. of material @ $2.00 per Kg.................. $10.00
> 3 hrs. of labor @ $4.00 per hour................... 12.00

Required:

Compute the material and labor variances for May.

7-37 A clothing company has just switched from an actual cost system to a standard cost system. The following information pertains to the new standard cost system they have just employed.

> Material, 3½ meters @ $3.50 per meter $12.25
> Labor, 4 hours @ $3.00 per hour................. 12.00
> Overhead, $1.50 per direct labor hour............. 6.00
> $30.25

The manager of the plant wants to see the difference between the actual cost system previously employed, and the newly initiated standard cost system.

Required:

Prepare the journal entries as they would appear under *each* system.

a. Purchased 40,000 meters of material—$150,000.
b. Production completed 10,000 units. There was no beginning or ending work-in-process inventory. 37,000 meters of material were used in production.

c. Direct labor hours used totaled 42,500 hours at a total cost of $131,750.

7-38   Simco has established the following standards for its product called Chewies.

Material
Caramel............................ 3 g./bar @ $.02/g.
Nuts.............................. ½ g./bar @ $.02/g.
Labor
Mixing........................... 1/100 hr. @ $3.00/hr.
Caramel purchased.................. 30,000 g. for $1,050.00
Nuts purchased..................... 7,500 g. for $ 240.00
Labor for the period................. 95 hours for $ 280.25
Total bars produced.................. 9,000
Total caramel used.................. 28,125 g.
Total nuts used..................... 4,750 g.

Required:

Calculate materials price and quantity variances for each material and labor rate and efficiency variances.

7-39   The Monkey Precinct Department Store has suffered a fire in its business office. Many of the records were destroyed and you have been called to piece things back together again. The store wants to know the amount and price of materials A, B, and C which were purchased and used during the past year. The following information was available from the records that were not destroyed.

1. Cost of goods sold was $6,030 greater due to variances
2. Total variance of A was $1,000 F
3. Total variance of B was $4,000 U
4. Actual price of A was $3 per unit
5. Actual price of B was $.75 per unit
6. Actual price of C was $2 per unit
7. Standard price of B was $1 per unit
8. Standard amount of A needed 5,000 units
9. Standard amount of B needed 10,000 units
10. Standard amount of C needed 6,000 units
11. 4,000 units of A were purchased
12. 7,000 units of C were purchased
13. Material price variance of A = $1,000 U
14. Material price variance of B = $1,000 F
15. Material price variance of C = $2,030 U
16. Material quantity variance of C = $1,000 U

Required:

a. Determine the standard price of A and C.
b. Determine the actual number of B purchased.
c. Determine the actual quantity of A, B, and C used.

7-40   Edwards Limited produces a single product in one process and costs its inventories using standard costs and the first-in, first-out (FIFO) method of cost allocation.

For the fiscal year ended December 31, 19x9 it anticipated that 20,000 units of the product would be produced based on the following standards:

Per Unit — Variable—	Direct materials	— 11 litres...............	$	33
	— Direct labour	— 8 hours...............		38
	— Manufacturing			
	overhead	— 8 direct labour hours....		40
	Variable standard cost per unit		$	111
Total — Fixed	— Manufacturing overhead per annum.........		$320,000	

On January 1, 19x9, work-in-process consisted of 1,000 units complete as to materials and 80% complete as to labour and overhead. It was shown in the accounts at a total standard cost of $95,000. The raw materials inventory consisted of 10,000 units at a total standard cost of $30,000. During the twelve months ended December 31, 19x9, 18,000 units were placed in production and 17,500 units were completed. The remaining 1,500 units in process were 100% complete as to materials and 20% complete as to labour and overhead.

Actual costs for the year were as follows:

Materials purchased	— 300,000 litres....	$ 867,000
Direct labour	— 130,000 hours...	663,000
Manufacturing overhead	— Fixed.........	318,000
	— Variable........	672,000
		$2,520,000

210,000 litres of material were issued to production.

Required:

Compute the following variances between actual and standard costs. Indicate in each case whether the variance is favourable or unfavourable. Support your computations with appropriate data showing equivalent production, actual costs, etc.

a. Materials efficiency variance
b. Labour price variance
c. Fixed overhead budget variance
d. Variable overhead spending variance
e. Overhead efficiency variance
f. Fixed overhead denominator (volume) variance.

(SMA, adapted)

7-41   A manufacturing company using standard costs as the basis for valuation of its inventories frequently encounters some degree of opposition from financial accountants concerned with rendering a report to shareholders on its financial statements.

Financial accountants generally take the position that standard costs are appropriate only if the variances in the aggregate are insignificant, in which case they must be treated as period charges or credits. If such variances are material they insist on an allocation between inventories and cost of goods sold so that actual costs may be approximated in the statements.

Management accountants, on the other hand, are more concerned with contrasting actual costs with standard costs so that actual performance may be contrasted with expected performance.

Required:

a. Take the position of the management accountant. Distinguish between the relative importance of what costs should have been, from actual costs.
b. Explain briefly, in *point form*, how the financial accountant would respond to the position set forth by the management accountant taken in (a) above?
c. Do you believe that the same standards can serve both management accounting and financial accounting? If your answer is in the affirmative, explain how this may be accomplished; if negative, explain how the difference may be reconciled.

(SMA, adapted)

7-42   Monson Company manufactures a special assembly which requires three different types of labour inputs: E1, E2 and E3. The standard inputs of labour for the assembly units are: 2 hours of E1, 3 hours of E2 and 5 hours of E3. Standard wage rates per hour are $10, $12 and $8 for E1, E2 and E3, respectively.

In the month of February, 1,000 assembly units were produced. Recorded inputs of E1, E2 and E3 were 900 hours, 1,800 hours and 2,100 hours, respectively. Wage rates for E1 and E2 remained at standard, but E3 being in short supply, was paid $8.50 per hour.

Required:

Determine the labour wage rate, mix and yield variances, if any.

(SMA, adapted)

Chapter 8

LEARNING OBJECTIVES

Chapter 8 discusses the cost implications of manufacturing overhead and the analysis of any difference between actual manufacturing overhead costs incurred and standard manufacturing overhead costs applied to production. Studying this chapter should enable you to:

1. Understand the concept of the flexible budget.
2. Understand the underlying concepts of manufacturing overhead variance analysis.
3. Determine why the variances could occur.
4. Calculate the volume, budget, efficiency and spending variances for manufacturing overhead costs.

Analysis of
Manufacturing
Overhead Costs

THIS CHAPTER is an extension of Chapter 7 and focuses on variance analysis of manufacturing overhead costs. The basic data regarding manufacturing overhead developed in the standard cost illustrations from Chapter 7 will be presented in this chapter. The manufacturing overhead variances will be analyzed to review the cost implications of manufacturing overhead, and the differences between actual manufacturing overhead costs incurred and standard manufacturing overhead costs applied to production.

Controlling Manufacturing Overhead When Compared to Other Product Costs

Manufacturing overhead is a major production cost. In fact, the total manufacturing overhead costs may be as large or larger than the direct material or direct labor costs. But the individual cost items in the total overhead cost may not justify the in-depth analysis and control techniques that can be justified for direct materials and direct labor. That is, the amount of cost at risk for the individual items may not be worth an item by item analysis on a continual basis. As a general statement, it can be said that direct material and direct labor costs and the effectiveness and efficiency of their use may be reviewed on a daily or hourly basis, but manufacturing overhead costs are reviewed and analyzed on a basis covering a longer time period such as a week or a month.

Direct materials and direct labor are considered to be variable costs within the relevant range of production. Total manufacturing overhead is a mixed cost (semi-variable) with both a fixed and variable component of cost within the relevant range of production. The directly variable relationship between the financial and physical aspects of both direct materials and direct labor make controlling and analyzing variances from these production costs easier and more meaningful than a similar analysis of manufacturing overhead. Standard costs can be used as a tool in controlling direct materials and direct labor costs on a daily basis. Standard costs in conjunction with departmental overhead budgets are used in controlling manufacturing overhead.

Concept of a Flexible Budget

A major underlying assumption of standard costs for manufacturing is that a known relationship exists between the production inputs and output. This relationship can be expressed in physical measures or in dollars when the physical inputs are multiplied by their respective costs. For example, the standard cost sheet for one power turbine shaft for Sax Company is presented in Illustration 8–1.

It takes one steel billet and two ball bearings to manufacture one power turbine shaft. The quantity of steel billets necessary to meet the January production of 1,760 power turbine shafts is 1,760 steel billets. The input to output relationship at standard is defined. The standard cost of a steel billet is $4.00. The standard cost of the steel billets needed to output 1,760 power turbine shafts is 1,760 billets X $4.00 or $7,040. The input to output relationship for ball bearings in Illustration 8-1 is a standard input of two ball bearings, at a standard cost of $1.00 per ball bearing, for every power turbine shaft produced.

Input to output relationships for labor and overhead from Illustration 8–1 could also be identified. The critical factor in identifying the relationships is a knowledge of the input to output factors and the cost per unit of the input factor. The knowledge of the cost behavior patterns and costs within the relevant range of production permits the use of the *flexible budget* in analyzing both the efficiency and effectiveness of the use of input factors in producing the required output at the required quality and cost. With a flexible budget, a budget can be established for any level of activity.

The Flexible Budget —An Example

If the production standards from Illustration 8-1 are used as the basis for a flexible standard cost budget for power turbine production, a

Illustration 8-1
Sax Company
Standard Cost Sheet

Standard Cost Sheet

Product: Power Turbine Shafts
Basis for Cost Sheet: One Unit

Materials

Location	Standard Quantity	Standard Price per unit	Total
Aisle 84	1	$4.00	$4.00
Aisle 85	2	1.00	$2.00
			$6.00

Labor

Department	Standard Hours	Standard Hourly Rate	Total
Machining	1/3	$6.00	$2.00
Finishing and Pressing	1/6	6.00	$1.00
			$3.00

Manufacturing Overhead

Variable Overhead Per Unit	$1.40
Fixed Overhead Per Unit	2.00
Total Overhead Per Unit	$3.40

Cost Summary Per Unit

Materials @ Standard	1 Steel Billet @ $4.00	=	$ 4.00
	2 Ball Bearings @ 1.00	=	2.00
Direct Labor @ Standard	½ hour @ $6.00/hour	=	3.00
Variable Manufacturing Overhead @ Standard*		=	1.40
Fixed Manufacturing Overhead @ Standard*		=	2.00
Total Manufacturing Cost @ Standard			$12.40

*Basis of Application to Product is Standard Direct
Labor Hours. Application Rate is $6.80 Per Standard
Direct Labor Hour.

budget could be prepared for any level of activity. Illustration 8-2 has
the flexible budget prepared at production levels of 1,700, 1,760, and
1,800 power turbine shafts. Once the output level of power turbine
shafts is determined, the production input factors in Illustration 8-1 are
used to develop the flexible budget.

Illustration 8-2
Sax Company
Flexible Budget for Power Turbine Shaft Production

Input Cost Factors	Budget Formula per Unit of Activity	Fixed Costs	Variable Costs Budgeted Activity Level		
			1,700 Units	1,760 Units	1,800 Units
Direct Material:					
Billets	$ 4.00 per Unit		$ 6,800	$ 7,040	$ 7,200
Bearings	2.00 per Unit		3,400	3,520	3,600
Direct Labor	3.00 per Unit		5,100	5,280	5,400
Manufacturing Overhead:					
Variable Costs	1.40 per Unit		2,380	2,464	2,520
Fixed Costs	-0-	$3,600			
	$10.40 per Unit	$3,600	$17,680	$18,304	$18,720

As can be seen from Illustration 8–2, the flexible portion of the flexible budget for production costs is caused by the variable cost components. The fixed cost component of the flexible budget is the *static* component of the budget. The flexible budget formula for total production cost is:

$$\begin{array}{l}\text{Total} \\ \text{Production} \\ \text{Costs}\end{array} = \begin{array}{l}\text{Standard or} \\ \text{Budgeted Fixed} \\ \text{Production Costs}\end{array} + \left(\begin{array}{l}\text{Standard Variable} \\ \text{Production Cost Per} \\ \text{Unit of Activity}\end{array} \times \begin{array}{l}\text{Level} \\ \text{of} \\ \text{Activity}\end{array}\right)$$

This formula can provide the standard production cost in total for any projected activity level within the relevant range. For an after-the-fact analysis of what production costs should have been given the level of activity attained, the formula can be used by introducing the actual level of activity in the calculations. For example, using the data in Illustration 8-2, if 1,770 power turbine shafts were the projected or actual production, the total manufacturing costs should be or should have been, respectively:

$$\begin{aligned}\text{Total Manufacturing Costs} &= \$3,600 + (\$10.40 \text{ X} \\ &\quad 1{,}770 \text{ Power Turbine Shafts)} \\ &= \$3,600 + \$18,408 \\ &= \$22,008\end{aligned}$$

Each of the individual cost items can also be calculated using the concept of the flexible budget. This concept was implicitly assumed in Chapter 7 when analyzing the variances from direct materials and direct labor.

In this chapter, the flexible budget concept and its use must be explicitly used to perform the necessary calculations in analyzing manufacturing overhead costs.

A COMPREHENSIVE EXAMPLE: THE FLEXIBLE MANUFACTURING OVERHEAD BUDGET

At the close of January, Sax Company knew the actual total overhead for the year was $6,320. The company also knew that the amount of manufacturing overhead that had been applied to production totaled $5,984. The difference between these two amounts, $336, represents the total overhead variance for the month. Sax's management is interested in an analysis of this variance and wishes to identify its underlying causes.

Recall that the standard costs used for the application of overhead were developed for a practical production level of 1,800 units, or 900 standard direct labor hours. Actual production in January totaled 1,760 units, or 880 standard direct labor hours. For any meaningful analysis of overhead, a concept not normally encountered in the accounting records must be introduced, that is, the concept of the flexible budget. With regard to manufacturing overhead, the flexible budget indicates the amount of overhead which should have been incurred at standard rates if Sax Company had known in advance that 1,760 rather than 1,800 units were going to be produced during January.

The total flexible budget for Sax Company may be developed after-the-fact from the information provided in Illustration 8-3. The standard variable manufacturing overhead cost was $1.40 per unit produced for a total of ($1.40 X 1,760 power turbine shafts) or $2,464 in January. Fixed manufacturing overhead *at standard* totaled $3,600. At 1,760 units, or 880 standard direct labor hours, the flexible budget is derived as follows:

$$\begin{array}{lcccc} \text{Flexible} \\ \text{Budget} & = & \begin{array}{c}\text{Standard Fixed}\\\text{Manufacturing}\\\text{Overhead}\\\text{Costs}\end{array} & + & \left(\begin{array}{c}\text{Standard Variable}\\\text{Manufacturing}\\\text{Overhead Cost}\\\text{Per Unit}\end{array} \times \begin{array}{c}\text{Actual}\\\text{Units}\\\text{Produced}\end{array}\right) \end{array}$$

$$= \$3,600 + (\$1.40 \times 1,760 \text{ units})$$
$$= \$3,600 + \$2,464$$
$$= \$6,064$$

If the variable overhead costs are in fact variable and the fixed overhead costs are indeed fixed, at 1,760 units or 880 standard direct labor hours, Sax Company's planned total overhead cost would be $6,064. A flexible budget could have been prepared for each specific overhead

Illustration 8-3

Sax Company
Developing the Standard Manufacturing Overhead

Projected Practical Capacity: 1,800 Units
Standard Direct Labor Hours at Practical Capacity: 900 Hours

Standard Manufacturing Overhead

	Variable per Unit Produced	Fixed	Total
Rework Time	$ .10	0	$ 180
Waiting Time	.06	0	108
Setup Time	.08	0	144
Indirect Materials and Supplies	.60	$ 88	1,168
Indirect Labor	.46	272	1,100
Electricity	.10	240	420
Heat	0	100	100
Equipment Depreciation	0	600	600
Plant Depreciation	0	1,500	1,500
Factory Property Taxes	0	800	800
Totals	$1.40	$3,600	$6,120

Standard Manufacturing Overhead per Unit:
Standard Variable Manufacturing Overhead per Unit................ $1.40
Standard Fixed Manufacturing Overhead per Unit $\frac{\$3,600}{1,800 \text{ units}}$ = 2.00

Standard Total Manufacturing Overhead per Unit.................. $3.40

cost and the total would have remained the same. Illustration 8-4 presents a flexible budget for manufacturing overhead costs at a production level of 1,760 units or 880 standard direct labor hours.

A COMPREHENSIVE EXAMPLE: THE VOLUME VARIANCE FOR MANUFACTURING OVERHEAD

The total underapplied overhead of $336 for Sax Company is caused, in part, by a volume variance. Sax Company based its standard overhead rates for applying manufacturing overhead on an anticipated level of production of 1,800 units or 900 standard direct labor hours (Illustration 8-3). Since the actual production achieved was 1,760 units or 880 standard direct labor hours, a portion of the fixed manufacturing overhead incurred was not applied to production.

An analysis of the resultant volume variance can be made based either on the number of units produced or on the standard direct labor hours.

Illustration 8-4
Sax Company
The Flexible Budget

	Variable* per Unit Produced	Fixed*	Total Budgeted Cost at 1,760 Units or 880 Standard Hours
Rework Time	$ .10	0	$ 176.00
Waiting Time	.06	0	105.60
Setup Time	.08	0	140.80
Indirect Materials and Supplies	.60	$ 88	1,144.00
Indirect Labor	.46	272	1,081.60
Electricity	.10	240	416.00
Heat	0	100	100.00
Equipment Depreciation	0	600	600.00
Plant Depreciation	0	1,500	1,500.00
Factory Property Taxes	0	800	800.00
Total	$1.40	$3,600	$6,064.00

*From Illustration 8-3

Alternatively, the total flexible budget may be compared to the total overhead applied to production. Remember, the volume variance relates to the absorption of fixed manufacturing overhead—*not* variable manufacturing overhead—into the cost of production.

Volume Variance Based on Units Produced

Standard Fixed Overhead per Unit Produced	$ 2	*
Practical Capacity (units)	1,800	
Actual Production (units)	1,760	
	40	
Unfavorable Volume Variance = 40 units X $2.00 =	$ 80	

Volume Variance Based on Standard Direct Labor Hours Used

Standard Fixed Overhead per Standard Direct Labor Hour	$ 4	*
Practical Capacity (Standard Direct Labor Hours)	900	
Actual Production (Standard Direct Labor Hours)	880	
	20	
Unfavorable Volume Variance = 20 Direct Labor Hours X $4.00 =	$ 80	

*See Illustration 7-3 and Illustration 8-1.

Volume Variance Based on Applied Manufacturing
Overhead and the Flexible Budget

Manufacturing Overhead Applied to Products.................	$5,984
Flexible Budget...	6,064
Unfavorable Volume Variance............................	$ 80

Of course, each of these methods provides the identical answer because each examines the same variance. The volume variance for Sax Company is unfavorable because the company did not produce a sufficient number of units to apply all of the fixed manufacturing overhead at standard to its production. Thus, in effect, the company lost the opportunity to produce at a practical capacity level in January.

A COMPREHENSIVE EXAMPLE: THE BUDGET VARIANCE FOR MANUFACTURING OVERHEAD

The budget variance analysis determines the amount by which the total actual overhead deviated from the overhead determined by the flexible budget. For Sax Company, the budget variance represents an attempt to determine the portion of underapplied manufacturing overhead of $336 which was due to a deviation from the amount of manufacturing overhead costs that should have been incurred at standard costs and a production level of 1,760 units. Standard manufacturing overhead costs for this level of production can be determined by using the flexible budget. The actual amount of manufacturing overhead costs are obtained from the accounting records. For Sax Company, the actual manufacturing overhead costs for the year were recorded in Transaction 8 in Chapter Seven.

The budget variance plus the volume variance must equal the total overhead variance. In this case, the total overhead variance is $336 (unfavorable) and the volume variance is $80 (unfavorable); thus, the budget variance must be $256 (also unfavorable). Note that there is absolutely no reason why both components of the overhead variance should be either favorable or unfavorable. One of the variances may be favorable and the other unfavorable. The budget variance is calculated using either the actual units produced or standard direct labor hours, and then determining the difference between the total flexible budget costs and the actual costs incurred.

Budget Variance Based on Units Produced

Actual Manufacturing Overhead Costs......................	$6,320
Flexible Budget $3,600 + (1,760 units X $1.40)...............	6,064
Unfavorable Budget Variance.............................	($ 256)

Budget Variance Based on Standard Direct Labor Hours

Actual Manufacturing Overhead Costs...................... $6,320
Flexible Budget
    $3,600 + (880 Standard Direct Labor Hours X $2.80)....... 6,064
Unfavorable Budget Variance............................. ($ 256)

In this example the budget variance is unfavorable because the actual manufacturing overhead costs were greater than anticipated at the actual level of 1,760 units of production, or 880 standard direct labor hours.

The cost items that caused the unfavorable variance can be identified. If the flexible budget for manufacturing overhead is calculated on an item-by-item basis and compared with the actual item costs, then the individual variances should total the budget variance. Illustration 8–5 presents an item-by-item analysis of the manufacturing overhead costs that caused the budget variance.

Rework time, waiting time, setup time, indirect materials and supplies and heat caused favorable cost variances totaling $106.40. Indirect labor and electricity caused unfavorable cost variances totaling $362.40. The manufacturing overhead budget variance was the net unfavorable variance of the individual items, $256.

Illustration 8-5
Sax Company
Manufacturing Overhead Budget Variance

	Total Budgeted Cost * at 1,760 Units or 880 Standard Hours	Total Actual † Cost at 1,760 Units	Manufacturing ‡ Overhead Budget Variance
Rework Time................	$ 176.00	$ 160.00	$ 16.00
Waiting Time................	105.60	100.00	5.60
Setup Time................	140.80	140.00	.80
Indirect Materials and			
Supplies................	1,144.00	1,100.00	44.00
Indirect Labor..............	1,081.60	1,160.00	(78.40)
Electricity................	416.00	700.00	(284.00)
Heat....................	100.00	60.00	40.00
Equipment Depreciation........	600.00	600.00	0
Plant Depreciation............	1,500.00	1,500.00	0
Factory Property Taxes........	800.00	800.00	0
Totals	$6,064.00	$6,320.00	($256.00)

* From Illustration 8-4
† From information for Transaction 8 in Chapter Seven.
‡ ( )'s indicate an unfavorable variance.

Dividing the under or overapplied overhead into two variances is referred to as two-way analysis of overhead variances. A two-way analysis of overhead variances is presented as follows:

Actual Manufacturing Overhead Costs......... $6,320

Budget Variance   ($256)
(Unfavorable)

Flexible Budget............................ $6,064

Volume Variance   ($ 80)

Applied Manufacturing Overhead Costs........ $5,984

(Unfavorable)

A COMPREHENSIVE EXAMPLE: THE EFFICIENCY AND SPENDING VARIANCES FOR MANUFACTURING OVERHEAD

The budget variance of $256 for the Sax Company may be separated into two additional factors or components that explain the cause of the budget variance. These two factors are: (1) the efficiency or inefficiency of the use of direct labor and (2) whether or not spending for overhead costs was appropriate considering the amount that should have been spent given the *actual* direct labor hours worked.

EFFICIENCY VARIANCE

The efficiency variance requires further explanation. If direct labor is a causal factor in incurring variable manufacturing overhead, the efficiency or inefficiency of direct labor will have an impact on the actual amount of the variable overhead incurred. If direct labor usage is less than standard, the variance will be favorable. If, as in the case of Sax Company, the actual use of direct labor exceeded the standard, the variance will be unfavorable.

The efficiency variance portion of the budget variance is calculated as follows:

$$\text{Efficiency Variance} = \left(\begin{array}{c} \textit{Actual} \\ \textit{Direct} \\ \textit{Labor} \\ \textit{Hours} \\ \textit{Used} \end{array} - \begin{array}{c} \textit{Standard} \\ \textit{Direct} \\ \textit{Labor} \\ \textit{Hours} \\ \textit{Allowed} \end{array} \right) \times \begin{array}{c} \textit{Variable Manufacturing} \\ \textit{Overhead Rate} \\ \textit{Per Standard} \\ \textit{Direct Labor} \\ \textit{Hour} \end{array}$$

= (890 Hours — 880 Hours) X $2.80

= $28 Unfavorable Efficiency Variance

For Sax Company, 10 direct labor hours in excess of the standard amount were used. If variable overhead is related to direct labor hours, this inefficiency would have caused an additional $28 of variable overhead to be incurred. An item-by-item analysis of the overhead efficiency variance is presented in Illustration 8-6.

Illustration 8-6
Sax Company
Manufacturing Overhead Efficiency Variance

	Variable * Per Direct Labor Hour	Total Budgeted Variable Cost at 880 Direct Labor Hours	Total Budgeted Variable Cost at 890 Direct Labor Hours	Efficiency † Variance
Rework Time.............	$ .20	$ 176.00	$ 178.00	($ 2.00)
Waiting Time............	.12	105.60	106.80	(1.20)
Setup Time..............	.16	140.80	142.40	(1.60)
Indirect Materials and				
Supplies	1.20	1,056.00	1,068.00	(12.00)
Indirect Labor...........	.92	809.60	818.80	(9.20)
Electricity	.20	176.00	178.00	(2.00)
Heat...................	0	0	0	0
Equipment Depreciation...	0	0	0	0
Plant Depreciation........	0	0	0	0
Factory Property Taxes.....	0	0	0	0
Totals.............	$2.80	$2,464.00	$2,492.00	($28.00)

* From Illustration 8-3 or 8-4: Remember, the standard variable overhead per direct labor hour is twice the variable standard per unit.
† ( )'s indicate an unfavorable variance.

Note that every variance which is included in Illustration 8-6 is unfavorable. This is appropriate since only the variable manufacturing overhead hours are considered in relation to the standard labor hours. Because actual labor hours exceeded standard hours by 10 hours, each individual variable cost factor exceeds standard cost by its individual cost rate multiplied by this factor of 10 hours.

**SPENDING
VARIANCE**

The spending variance is a measure of the overhead costs that were incurred at the actual level of activity (direct labor hours) as compared to the standard manufacturing overhead costs which should have been incurred at that level of activity. In the case of Sax Company, this variance is the difference between the total actual manufacturing overhead costs at 890 direct labor hours as compared to the standard manufacturing overhead costs at 890 direct labor hours. The spending variance portion of the budget variance is calculated as follows:

$$\text{Spending Variance} = \left[\begin{pmatrix}\text{Budgeted}\\\text{Total}\\\text{Fixed}\\\text{Manufacturing}\\\text{Overhead}\end{pmatrix} + \begin{pmatrix}\text{Actual}\\\text{Direct}\\\text{Labor}\\\text{Hours}\\\text{Used}\end{pmatrix} \times \begin{pmatrix}\text{Standard}\\\text{Variable}\\\text{Manufacturing}\\\text{Overhead}\\\text{Rate}\end{pmatrix}\right] - \begin{pmatrix}\text{Actual}\\\text{Total}\\\text{Manufacturing}\\\text{Overhead}\\\text{Costs}\end{pmatrix}$$

$$= [\$3{,}600 + (890 \times \$2.80)] - \$6{,}320$$
$$= (\$3{,}600 + \$2{,}492) - \$6{,}320$$
$$= \$228 \text{ Unfavorable Spending Variance}$$

An item-by-item analysis of the overhead spending variance is presented in Illustration 8-7.

From the standpoint of spending for overhead costs at the actual level of activity, 890 direct labor hours, Sax Company performed favorably in the area of rework time, waiting time, setup time, indirect materials and supplies, and heat. Unfavorable spending variances were incurred for indirect labor and electricity.

Illustration 8-7
Sax Company
Manufacturing Overhead Spending Variance

	Variable* per Direct Labor Hour	Fixed	Total Budgeted Manufacturing Overhead Costs at 890 Direct Labor Hours	Total † Actual Manufacturing Overhead Costs at 890 Direct Labor Hours	Spending ‡ Variance
Rework Time	$ .20	0	$ 178.00	$ 160.00	$ 18.00
Waiting Time	.12	0	106.80	100.00	6.80
Setup Time	.16	0	142.40	140.00	2.40
Indirect Materials and Supplies	1.20	$ 88.00	1,156.00	1,100.00	56.00
Indirect Labor	.92	272.00	1,090.80	1,160.00	(69.20)
Electricity	.20	240.00	418.00	700.00	(282.00)
Heat	0	100.00	100.00	60.00	40.00
Equipment Depreciation	0	600.00	600.00	600.00	0
Plant Depreciation	0	1,500.00	1,500.00	1,500.00	0
Factory Property Taxes	0	800.00	800.00	800.00	0
Totals	$2.80	$3,600.00	$6,092.00	$6,320.00	($228.00)

* From Illustration 8-3 or 8-4: Remember, the standard variable overhead rate per direct labor hour is twice the variable standard per unit.
† From information for Transaction 8 in Chapter Seven.
‡ ( )'s indicate an unfavorable variance.

The overhead spending variance can be further subdivided into a fixed overhead spending variance and a variable overhead spending variance, because additional expenditures could have been made for *both* fixed and variable manufacturing overhead over those that were anticipated in the flexible budget based on the actual level of activity for that period. This is not the case, however, with the efficiency and volume variances. The overhead efficiency variance is caused entirely by the efficiency or inefficiency of direct labor hours used; therefore the impact is on only the actual amount of *variable* overhead incurred. Alternatively, the volume variance relates to the absorption of fixed manufacturing overhead into the cost of production and nothing else.

The variable overhead spending variance may be calculated as follows:

$$\begin{matrix} Variable \\ Overhead \\ Spending \\ Variance \end{matrix} = \left(\begin{matrix} Actual \\ Direct \\ Labor \\ Hours \\ Used \end{matrix} \times \begin{matrix} Standard \\ Variable \\ Manufacturing \\ Overhead \\ Rate \end{matrix} \right) - \begin{matrix} Actual \\ Variable \\ Manufacturing \\ Overhead \\ Costs \end{matrix}$$

The equation for the fixed overhead spending variance is shown below:

$$\begin{matrix} Fixed \\ Overhead \\ Spending \\ Variance \end{matrix} = \left(\begin{matrix} Budgeted \\ Fixed \\ Manufacturing \\ Overhead \end{matrix} - \begin{matrix} Actual \\ Fixed \\ Manufacturing \\ Overhead \\ Costs \end{matrix} \right)$$

Since the actual manufacturing overhead incurred during January for the Sax Company is not separated into its fixed and variable components, it is not possible to calculate the company's fixed and variable overhead spending variances in this example.

When the budget variance is divided into its efficiency and spending components, the analysis of manufacturing overhead is referred to as a three-way analysis of manufacturing overhead variances. The three variances that are developed and analyzed are:

1. The impact of production volume (manufacturing overhead volume variance).
2. The impact of direct labor efficiency (manufacturing overhead efficiency variance).
3. The impact of spending for overhead costs (manufacturing overhead spending variance).

Below is a comparison showing the manufacturing overhead variances of the Sax Company in the form of both a two-way analysis and a three-way analysis. Notice that the efficiency and spending variances in the three-way analysis total the budget variance in the two-way analysis.

Two-Way Analysis of Overhead Variances

Budget Variance (Unfavorable)..........................	($256)
Volume Variance (Unfavorable)........................	(80)
Unfavorable Manufacturing Overhead Variance........	($336)

(Unfavorable)

Three-Way Analysis of Overhead Variances

Efficiency Variance (Unfavorable).....................	($ 28)
Spending Variance (Unfavorable)........................	(228)
Volume Variance (Unfavorable)........................	(80)
Unfavorable Manufacturing Overhead Variance........	($336)

(Unfavorable)

The spending, efficiency and volume overhead variances may be isolated and accounted for when the journal entry is made to record the manufacturing overhead applied, rather than waiting until the end of the period when the closing entries are made. For example, instead of the journal entry which was made for Transaction 6 in Chapter Seven to record the manufacturing overhead applied without recording any overhead variances, the following journal entry could be made:

Work-in-Process ($6.80 X 880)...........................	5,984	
Manufacturing Overhead Efficiency Variance...............	28	
Manufacturing Overhead Spending Variance..............	228	
Manufacturing Overhead Volume Variance.................	80	
Manufacturing Overhead—Control....................		6,320

Notice that the credit to the manufacturing overhead control account represents the actual amount of overhead incurred during January. Thus, if this entry is made after the actual manufacturing overhead was journalized (Transaction 8 in Chapter 7), then the manufacturing overhead control account is closed out, with any over or underapplied overhead already having been converted into the three overhead variances. At the end of the period, these three overhead variances—spending, efficiency and volume—are closed to cost of goods sold along with the material and labor variances.

SUMMARY

Total manufacturing overhead is a semi-variable cost with both a fixed and variable component. A flexible budget can be used to determine manufacturing overhead at standard costs at any level of production within the relevant range. The flexible portion of the flexible budget is caused by the variable cost components of manufacturing overhead. The fixed cost component of the flexible budget is the static component of the budget.

The analysis of overhead variances can be done using a two or three variance approach. In either case, the difference or total variance being analyzed is the difference between actual manufacturing overhead and manufacturing overhead applied to production. With a two-way analysis, this difference will be analyzed on the presumption that only two factors could have caused the variance: a volume deviation or a budget deviation. The volume variance occurs as the result of attaining a level of production other than the standard or practical capacity level, and over or under applying fixed manufacturing overhead to products produced. The budget variance is the difference between the flexible budget, based on actual activity, and the actual manufacturing overhead costs that were incurred.

A three-way analysis of variance also considers the volume variance, but divides the budget variance into the portion that was caused by the efficiency of the application base and the portion that was caused by spending for overhead costs. The manufacturing overhead efficiency variance and the manufacturing overhead spending variance must, therefore, sum to the budget variance.

Following is a summary of the equations for your reference of the standard cost variances listed in this chapter and Chapter 7.

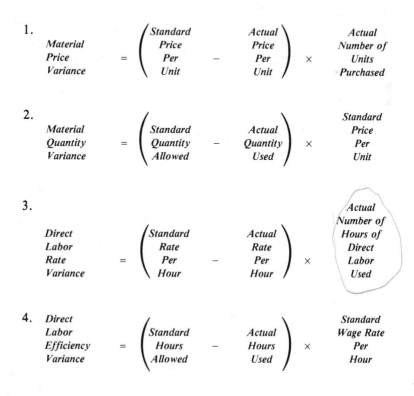

1.
$$\text{Material Price Variance} = \left(\begin{array}{c} \text{Standard} \\ \text{Price} \\ \text{Per} \\ \text{Unit} \end{array} - \begin{array}{c} \text{Actual} \\ \text{Price} \\ \text{Per} \\ \text{Unit} \end{array} \right) \times \begin{array}{c} \text{Actual} \\ \text{Number of} \\ \text{Units} \\ \text{Purchased} \end{array}$$

2.
$$\text{Material Quantity Variance} = \left(\begin{array}{c} \text{Standard} \\ \text{Quantity} \\ \text{Allowed} \end{array} - \begin{array}{c} \text{Actual} \\ \text{Quantity} \\ \text{Used} \end{array} \right) \times \begin{array}{c} \text{Standard} \\ \text{Price} \\ \text{Per} \\ \text{Unit} \end{array}$$

3.
$$\text{Direct Labor Rate Variance} = \left(\begin{array}{c} \text{Standard} \\ \text{Rate} \\ \text{Per} \\ \text{Hour} \end{array} - \begin{array}{c} \text{Actual} \\ \text{Rate} \\ \text{Per} \\ \text{Hour} \end{array} \right) \times \begin{array}{c} \text{Actual} \\ \text{Number of} \\ \text{Hours of} \\ \text{Direct} \\ \text{Labor} \\ \text{Used} \end{array}$$

4.
$$\text{Direct Labor Efficiency Variance} = \left(\begin{array}{c} \text{Standard} \\ \text{Hours} \\ \text{Allowed} \end{array} - \begin{array}{c} \text{Actual} \\ \text{Hours} \\ \text{Used} \end{array} \right) \times \begin{array}{c} \text{Standard} \\ \text{Wage Rate} \\ \text{Per} \\ \text{Hour} \end{array}$$

5. $\text{Volume Variance for Manufacturing Overhead} = \left(\begin{array}{c} \text{Standard Production Capacity in Units} \end{array} - \begin{array}{c} \text{Actual Production in Units} \end{array} \right) \times \begin{array}{c} \text{Standard Fixed Overhead Rate Per Unit Produced} \end{array}$

(This equation may substitute direct labor hours if fixed overhead rate has also been calculated using direct labor hours.)

6. $\text{Fixed Overhead Rate} = \dfrac{\textit{Total Fixed Overhead Costs at Standard}}{\textit{Projected Practical Production Capacity (in Units)}}$

7. $\text{Budget Variance for Manufacturing Overhead} = \begin{array}{c} \text{Flexible Budget} \end{array} - \begin{array}{c} \text{Actual Manufacturing Overhead Costs} \end{array}$

8. $\text{Flexible Budget for Manufacturing Overhead} = \begin{array}{c} \text{Fixed Costs at Standard for Projected Practical Capacity} \end{array} + \left(\begin{array}{c} \text{Actual Level of Production in Units} \end{array} \times \begin{array}{c} \text{Variable Per Unit Costs at Standard} \end{array} \right)$

(This equation may substitute standard direct labor hours allowed if variable costs are related to direct labor hours.)

9.

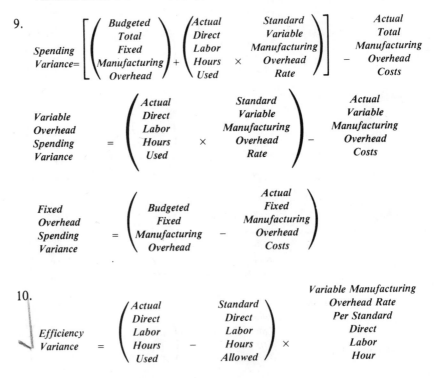

$\text{Spending Variance} = \left[\left(\begin{array}{c} \text{Budgeted Total Fixed Manufacturing Overhead} \end{array} \right) + \left(\begin{array}{c} \text{Actual Direct Labor Hours Used} \end{array} \times \begin{array}{c} \text{Standard Variable Manufacturing Overhead Rate} \end{array} \right) \right] - \begin{array}{c} \text{Actual Total Manufacturing Overhead Costs} \end{array}$

$\text{Variable Overhead Spending Variance} = \left(\begin{array}{c} \text{Actual Direct Labor Hours Used} \end{array} \times \begin{array}{c} \text{Standard Variable Manufacturing Overhead Rate} \end{array} \right) - \begin{array}{c} \text{Actual Variable Manufacturing Overhead Costs} \end{array}$

$\text{Fixed Overhead Spending Variance} = \left(\begin{array}{c} \text{Budgeted Fixed Manufacturing Overhead} \end{array} - \begin{array}{c} \text{Actual Fixed Manufacturing Overhead Costs} \end{array} \right)$

10.

$\text{Efficiency Variance} = \left(\begin{array}{c} \text{Actual Direct Labor Hours Used} \end{array} - \begin{array}{c} \text{Standard Direct Labor Hours Allowed} \end{array} \right) \times \begin{array}{c} \text{Variable Manufacturing Overhead Rate Per Standard Direct Labor Hour} \end{array}$

KEY DEFINITIONS

Budget variance—an overhead variance which results when the actual total manufacturing overhead costs differ from the total manufacturing overhead costs budgeted for the actual level of production.

Flexible budget—a budget used to calculate a total budgeted manufacturing overhead cost for a given level of production.

Three-way analysis of overhead variances—a method which separates total overhead into volume, efficiency and spending variance components. The total of the manufacturing overhead efficiency and spending variances is equal to the budget variance.

Two-way analysis of overhead variances—a method which separates total overhead variance into volume and budget variance components.

Volume variance—an overhead variance which results when actual production differs from the practical capacity so that the total manufacturing overhead is under- or over-applied to the cost of production.

QUESTIONS

8-1 What is the purpose of the flexible manufacturing overhead cost budget?

8-2 Why is fixed cost considered the static component of the flexible budget?

8-3 What is the volume variance for manufacturing overhead cost analyzing?

8-4 What is the budget variance for manufacturing overhead cost analyzing?

8-5 When is a volume variance for manufacturing overhead cost favorable?

8-6 Why does the flexible budget have to be adjusted to the actual level of outputs or standard inputs to analyze manufacturing overhead cost variances?

8-7 When analyzing the volume variance or the budget variance, why must standard activity instead of actual activity be used when the basis for the flexible budget is an input factor such as direct labor hours?

EXERCISES AND PROBLEMS

8-8 The Walters Manufacturing Company has established the following standards for one unit of their product, Alpha.

Material	6 Kg. @ $8.00/Kg.	=	$ 48
Labor	12 hrs.@ $6.00/hrs.	=	72
Variable M.O.H..................	@ $18	=	18
F.M.O.H........................	@ $25	=	25
Total standard cost.............		=	$163

During August, the Walters Manufacturing Company purchased 7,000 kilograms of material at $56,350 and incurred total labor costs of $71,248. 1,000 units of Alpha were produced. They required 6,220 kilograms of material and 11,680 hours of labor. Normal capacity is 1,100 units. Actual manufacturing overhead was $45,000.

Required:

a. Compute the material price and usage variances.
b. Compute the labor rate and efficiency variances.
c. Compute the budget and volume variances for manufacturing overhead.

8-9 The Goodness Company uses a standard cost system with the following standard costs:

Material—5 tons @ $6.00/ton................	$30.00
Labor—3 hours @ $4.50/hour...............	13.50
Overhead—3 hours @ $7.00/hour............	21.00
Total standard cost per unit................	$64.50

During the year, 10,000 units were produced. Costs incurred for material, labor, and overhead were $325,000, $136,000, and $209,000 respectively. Normal capacity is 9,000 units. Variable overhead is $4 per standard direct labor hour.

Required:

a. Calculate the total variation from standard costs of the total costs incurred this year.
b. Calculate the total material variance, labor variance, and the overhead variance from standard costs. It is not necessary to calculate price, rate, and efficiency variances.
c. Calculate the budget and volume variances for manufacturing overhead.

8-10   Given the following balances in the variance accounts:

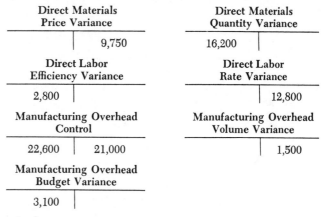

Direct Materials Price Variance	Direct Materials Quantity Variance
9,750	16,200

Direct Labor Efficiency Variance	Direct Labor Rate Variance
2,800	12,800

Manufacturing Overhead Control	Manufacturing Overhead Volume Variance
22,600 21,000	1,500

Manufacturing Overhead Budget Variance
3,100

Required:

Prepare the entry that should have been made to close the manufacturing overhead control account when the overhead variances were recognized. Prepare the entry to close all variance accounts to the cost of goods sold account.

8-11   You have been given the following information:
   Actual labor hours used = 315 hours
   Actual variable overhead = $700
   Standard materials price = $2.50
   Standard labor hours used = 300 hours
   Standard quantity of materials used = 450 units
   Actual labor rate per hour = $3.00
   Actual quantities of materials purchased and used = 445 units
   Standard variable overhead per standard labor hour = $2.25
   Standard labor rate per hour = $3.10
   Actual materials price = $2.52 per unit

Required:

a. Variable overhead spending variance.
b. Variable overhead efficiency variance.
c. Total variable overhead variance.

8-12   Fremont, Inc. uses a standard absorption cost system. During June, 5,000 units were produced and sold. Given below are the standard costs for one unit:

Materials	A, 2 kilograms	@ $1.25	$ 2.50
Materials	B, 3½ kilograms	@ $ .50	1.75
Materials	C, 1¼ kilograms	@ $2.00	2.50
Labor	3 hours @ $4.50		13.50
Variable overhead	$2.00 per labor hour		6.00
Fixed overhead	$1.25 per labor hour		3.75
Total standard costs			$30.00

Additional Data:

There are no beginning inventories. There is no ending work-in-process or finished goods.

Plant capacity	15,500 labor hours	
Purchases	20,000 kilograms of B	@ $ .53
	11,000 kilograms of A	@ $1.23
	8,000 kilograms of C	@ $2.08
Actual material usage	A, 10,200 kilograms	
	B, 17,650 kilograms	
	C, 6,000 kilograms	
Direct labor cost	$70,610	
Direct labor hours	15,350	
Actual variable manufacturing overhead	$31,400	
Actual fixed manufacturing overhead	$20,500	
Selling price	$45.00 per unit	

Required:

a.   Make the general journal entries for June.
b.   Make the general journal entries to close out the variances.
     (Note: Separate the overhead variance into its spending, efficiency and volume variances.)

8-13   Sharon Corporation makes one product, tennis rackets. During May in preparation for the summer season, Sharon produced 500 tennis rackets. The established standard variable cost for one racket follows:

Materials	10 Kg. @ $.45/Kg.	$ 4.50
Labor	3 hrs. @ $2.15/hr.	6.45
Variable manufacturing overhead	3 hrs. @ $2.75/hr.	8.25
Total standard cost		$19.20

The Sharon Corporation purchased 5,500 kilograms of material at a cost of $2,695. The production department used 5,150 kilograms of material. The payroll for direct labor hours of 1,495 amounted to $3,289 and actual variable manufacturing overhead was $4,186.

Required:

Calculate the variable manufacturing overhead variances for the Sharon Corporation.

8-14   Enter the transactions listed for the Kingston Company below into "T" accounts. Record all variances in separate accounts. Analyze any manufacturing overhead variance into its spending, efficiency, and volume variances.

a.   Purchased 2,500 kilograms of material at a cost of $5,875 on account. The standard cost per kilogram is $2.30.

b.   During the period, 2,200 kilograms of material were requisitioned. Assume all material was used efficiently. Each unit is made up of 2.2 kilograms of material.

c.   4,500 hours were charged to production during the month at a cost of $16,875. Standard costs for labor were 4.2 hours per unit at a cost of $3.70 an hour.

d.   Actual overhead incurred included $9,200 variable overhead expenses and $11,000 fixed overhead expenses. (The variable expenses are all included in accounts payable and the fixed are for depreciation on equipment.)

e.   Overhead was applied at a rate of $5.00 per standard labor hour ($2.50 per hour which is variable). Normal production capacity is 1,000 units (or 4,200 hours).

f.   Sales for the period were 900 units at $55 per unit, all sold on account.

g.   Assume Kingston Company is in its first year of operations.

8-15   The Gibson Company would like you to calculate their spending, efficiency, and volume overhead variances for both the fixed and variable portion of their manufacturing overhead costs. Relevant data are listed below.

Normal capacity	8,000 units
Actual production	8,500 units
Standard variable overhead per hour	$2.00
Standard fixed overhead per hour	$1.00
Standard labor hours per unit	2 hours
Actual labor hours	16,500 hours
Actual variable overhead	$32,000
Actual fixed overhead	$16,900

8-16   The Loren Company produces one product with the following standard costs per unit:

Materials, 2 kilograms @ $3.25.				$ 6.50
Labor, 5 hours @ $2.05.				10.25
Manufacturing overhead:				
Variable:	$ 1.00	per hour × 5 hours.	= $5.00	
Fixed:	$120,000 / 240,000	= $.50 per hour × 5 hours.	= 2.50	7.50
		(hours practical yearly capital)		
				$24.25

The company produced 3,000 units last month. A total of 21,500 direct labor hours were charged to production.

Actual overhead incurred was $22,000 for variable overhead and $9,500 for fixed overhead. The variable overhead was paid for in cash and the fixed overhead was made up entirely of depreciation on plant and equipment. Applied overhead was recorded based on standard direct labor hours.

Required:

a. Calculate the volume variance, efficiency variance and spending variance for manufacturing overhead cost.
b. Journalize the application of manufacturing overhead to work in process, the recognition of the actual overhead and the recognition of the variances.

8-17 Nancy Company produced 17,800 footballs during May. Material purchases amounted to 184,000 kilograms at $2.10 per kilogram. Usage of the materials amounted to 92,200 kilograms. The footballs required 53,000 hours of labor at $4.20 per hour while plant capacity is 60,000 labor hours. Manufacturing overhead actually incurred was $35,000 for fixed and $66,250 for variable. Nancy Company has established the following standards for one football:

5 Kg. of material @ $2.00 per Kg	$10.00
3 hrs. of labor @ $4.00 per hour	12.00
Fixed manufacturing overhead	
$1.00 per labor hour	3.00
Variable manufacturing overhead	
$2.00 per labor hour	6.00
	$31.00

Required:

Compute the material, labor, and manufacturing overhead budget and volume variances for May.

8-18 The Monroe Company incorporates standard costs in their process costing system. The standard costs per unit for their only product, trinkets, are listed below:

Material: 2 kilograms @ $4.10/kilogram	$ 8.20
Labor: 0.6 hours @ $6.00/hour	3.60
Overhead: Variable @ $4.60/hour = $2.76	
° Fixed @ $2.00/hour = 1.20	3.96
Total standard cost per trinket	$15.76

° Fixed overhead is based on a normal capacity of 132,000 trinkets.

Production statistics for this year are as follows:

Trinkets finished this year—110,000.
Costs incurred for this year were $1,037,850, $430,500, and

$475,120 for material, labor, and overhead, respectively.
There was no beginning work-in-process inventory.
Ending work-in-process—15,000 trinkets; 100% complete for material, 80% complete for labor and overhead.
255,000 kilograms of material and 70,000 labor hours were actually used. Monroe computes material price variances at the point of transfer to work in process.

Required:

Using the weighted average method of process cost accounting, compute:

a. the material price and usage variances,
b. the labor rate and efficiency variances, and
c. the overhead budget and volume variances.

8-19 Alpha Company produces electronic gadgets. The standard cost of one gadget is:

Direct Material—2 kilograms @ $3.00/kilogram . . .	6.00
Direct Labor—2 hours @ $4.00/hour	$8.00
Manufacturing Overhead—Variable	$2.00
Manufacturing Overhead—Fixed	$1.50
Total Standard Cost per Gadget	$17.50

Overhead is applied to products on a standard direct labor hour basis. Normal capacity for a month is 5,000 gadgets. Last month 4,800 gadgets were produced. The actual direct labor hours used were 9,800 hours. The actual manufacturing overhead costs were $17,500.

Required:

a. Calculate the total manufacturing overhead variance.
b. Calculate the volume variance, budget variance, spending variance and efficiency variance for manufacturing overhead costs.

8-20 The Beaulieu Company uses a process cost system and standard costs. Below are the standard costs per unit for their only product, Bangles.

Material 2 litres @ $3.50/litre	. . . .	$7.00
Labor 0.2 hours @ $3.00/hour		.60
Overhead: Variable @ $2.25/hour = .45		
Fixed ° @ $1.00/hour = .20	. . . . .	.65
Total standard cost per Bangle		$8.25

° Fixed overhead is based on a normal capacity of 10,100 Bangles.

Production statistics for January are as follows:

Bangles produced this month—8,000.

Ending work-in-process—3,000; 100 percent complete for material, 70 percent complete for labor, and 70 percent complete for overhead.

There was no beginning work-in-process inventory.

Costs incurred this month were $90,000, $6,900, and $6,600 for material, labor and overhead, respectively.

25,000 litres of material and 3,000 labor hours were actually incurred.

The materials price variance is calculated at the time of transfer into work in process.

Required:

Using the weighted average method to determine the cost flow for January, compute:

a.   the material price and usage variances,
b.   the labor rate and efficiency variances, and
c.   the overhead budget and volume variances.

8-21   The Barker Corporation has established the following manufacturing overhead standards for one unit of Beta Data:

Variable Manufacturing Overhead . . . . $ 4.00
Fixed Manufacturing Overhead . . . . $ 6.00
Total Manufacturing Overhead per Unit $10.00

The normal capacity per month is 1,000 units of production. Last month, April, 950 equivalent units were produced at a cost of $20,200. The work in process control account and the manufacturing overhead control account contained the following entries:

Work in Process		Manufacturing Overhead Control	
Beg. Bal. 3,000	20,200	11,000	9,500
4,000			
4,700			
9,500			
End. Bal. 1,000			

Required:

a.   Calculate the budgeted fixed cost for April.
b.   Do a two-way analysis of overhead variance.

8-22   Given the information in Problem 8-21: assume that it takes 1.5 standard direct labor hours to make one unit of Beta Data and that 1,500 direct labor hours were actually worked. Calculate the volume variance, the budget variance, the spending variance and efficiency variance for manufacturing overhead cost.

8-23   The Simons Company manufactures bolts in standard batches of 5,000 units. The standard cost for a batch is as follows:

Raw materials 200 Kg. @ $.04 per Kg.   . . . . $ 8.00
Direct labor 4 hrs. @ $5.15 per hour 20.60
Overhead (including variable overhead of $4.50) 10.00

Total standard cost $38.60

Data for March is as follows:

Planned production . . . . 240 batches
Actual production . . . . 250 batches
Cost of raw materials purchased (55,000 Kg.)   . . $2,310.00
Cost of raw materials used (51,250 Kg.) $2,152.50
Direct labor cost (998 hours) $5,189.60
Actual overhead cost $2,560.00
Budgeted fixed overhead cost $1,320.00

Required:

Compute the following variances indicating whether favorable or unfavorable.

a. Raw materials price variance
b. Raw materials quantity variance
c. Direct labor rate variance
d. Direct labor efficiency variance
e. Overhead budget variance
f. Overhead volume variance.

8-24   Given the information in Problem 8-23: prepare a three-way analysis of variance for manufacturing overhead cost.

8-25   The Holbrook Manufacturing Company produces paper boxes. The plant manager has requested an analysis of manufacturing overhead costs for the last month. The standards for manufacturing overhead costs are:

Standard Costs Per Batch

Variable Manufacturing Overhead $5.00
Fixed Manufacturing Overhead $2.00

Total Manufacturing Overhead Per Batch $7.00

The flexible monthly manufacturing overhead cost budget on a direct labor hour basis is:

Standard Direct Labor Hours	*Budgeted Overhead*
1,000	$ 5,500
2,000	8,000
3,000 (Normal Capacity)	10,500
4,000	13,000
5,000	15,500

3,000 ÷ 2

It takes two direct labor hours at standard to make one batch of boxes. Sixteen hundred batches of boxes were made last month. Actual total overhead was $12,000.

Required:

a. Calculate the flexible budget formula.
b. Do a two-way analysis of overhead variance.

8-26   Given the information in Problem 8-25: assume that 3,000 direct labor hours were worked. Prepare a three-way analysis of variance for manufacturing overhead costs.

8-27   The Green Thing Company produces green things. The standard cost of one green thing is:

Direct materials—1 kilogram @ $2.00/kilogram	$2.00
Direct labor—1½ hours @ $3.00/hour	4.50
Manufacturing Overhead—Variable	1.50
Manufacturing Overhead—Fixed	.60
Total Standard Cost per Thing	$8.60

Overhead is applied to things produced on a standard direct labor hour basis. Normal capacity per month is 10,000 things. Last month, 9,800 things were produced. Actual manufacturing overhead was $21,000, of which $15,000 was variable. Fourteen thousand direct labor hours at a total actual cost of $63,000 were used to produce the things. A total of 9,900 kilograms of materials was used. Raw materials purchases of 10,000 kilograms at $2.05 per kilogram were made last month.

Required:

Calculate the materials price and usage variances, the direct labor rate and efficiency variances, and the overhead budget and volume variances.

8-28   The Haywood Company is preparing to close their accounts. They have asked you to: (1) prepare the journal entry that would be made to close the manufacturing overhead control account; and (2) prepare the journal entry to close all variance accounts to the cost of goods sold account.

Direct Materials Price Variance		Direct Materials Quantity Variance	
4,000			2,000

Direct Labor Efficiency Variance		Direct Labor Rate Variance	
	2,200	400	

Manufacturing Overhead Control		Manufacturing Overhead Volume Variance	
27,000	30,000		1,000

Manufacturing Overhead Efficiency Variance		Manufacturing Overhead Spending Variance	
	4,000	2,000	

8-29   Using the following information:

Actual labor hours used   14,000
Standard labor hours allowed   14,700
Actual total overhead $21,000
Actual variable overhead $15,000
Standard variable overhead per standard labor hour $1.00
Standard fixed overhead per standard labor hour . . . . $.40
Normal volume (direct labor hours)   15,000

Required:

Determine the volume variance and the budget variance for manufacturing overhead costs.

8-30   Given the information in Problem 8-29: (1) prepare a three-way analysis of variance, and (2) calculate the variable overhead spending variance and the fixed overhead spending variance.

8-31   Ceramic, Inc. had the following budget for three individual overhead cost items at a normal level of activity of 1,000 barrels for one month.

	Variable	*Fixed*	*Total*
Indirect Materials	$1,000	–0–	$1,000
Setup Time	200	300	500
Equipment Depreciation . . .	–0–	3,000	3,000
			$4,500

Actual production was 1,100 barrels. Direct labor hours, the overhead application basis, was two hours per barrel at standard, but actual hours averaged 1.75 hours per barrel. Actual overhead cost at 1,100 barrels was $1,150 for indirect materials, $500 for setup time and $3,000 for equipment depreciation. The actual cost incurrence for setup time was $150 of variable cost and $350 of fixed cost.

Required:

a.   Calculate the manufacturing overhead applied to production for each of the items.
b.   What was the total volume variance?
c.   What was the volume variance per item?
d.   What was the total budget variance?

e. What was the spending variance per item?

f. What was the efficiency variance per item?

8-32   You have been given the following information:

> Actual labor hours used = 315 hours
> Standard materials price = $2.50
> Standard labor hours allowed = 300 hours
> Standard quantity of materials used = 450 units
> Actual labor rate per hour = $3.00
> Actual quantity of materials purchased and used = 445 units
> Standard labor rate per hour = $3.10
> Actual materials price = $2.52
> Standard variable manufacturing overhead = $1.50 a unit
> Actual variable manufacturing overhead in total = $925
> Standard fixed manufacturing overhead = $3.50 a unit
> Actual fixed manufacturing overhead = $1,900
> Budgeted fixed manufacturing overhead = $1,750
> Normal production = 500 units
> Actual production = 600 units

Required:

Prepare a schedule for the following variances:

a. Raw materials price variance

b. Raw materials quantity variance

c. Direct labor efficiency variance

d. Direct labor rate variance

e. Volume variance for manufacturing overhead cost

f. Budget variance for manufacturing overhead cost

8-33   Given the information in Problem 8-32: prepare a three-way analysis of variance for manufacturing overhead cost.

8-34   Given the information in Problem 8-32: calculate the variable overhead spending variance and the fixed overhead spending variance.

8-35   During the past year Maurstace Limited incurred overhead and labour costs in excess of standard to the extent of several thousand dollars. The company's cost accounting system is based upon standard costs and a flexible budget. The following data pertain to the company's operations for the year:

a.   Actual production for the year was 22,000 units. Standards call for the production of 20,800 units in fifty-two 40-hour weeks.

b.   Due to a strike, there was no production during the first four weeks of the year. During the next thirty-nine weeks, the plant operated 50 hours a week in order to make up production lost during the strike.

Overtime labour rates at 150% of the regular hourly rates were paid for the hours worked in excess of the regular 40-hour week. This overtime ultimately resulted in overproduction so that the plant operated only 20 hours a week during the last nine weeks of the year.

c. Overtime paid to direct labour was charged to the direct labour account, but variable overhead cost should be calculated with reference to regular hourly rates, not overtime rates. Direct labour cost, exclusive of overtime, paid per hour of plant operation was as budgeted.

d. The denominator activity is based upon plant usage in hours.

Actual overhead costs for the year were as follows:

Supervision and indirect labour................	$ 40,000
Sundry supplies............................	44,000
Light, heat and power.......................	15,000
Depreciation...............................	40,000
Property taxes.............................	4,500
	$143,500

Budgeted overhead—on the basis of producing 20,800 units was:

	Fixed	Variable Per Direct Labour Dollar
Supervision and indirect labour.......	$10,400	$0.10
Sundry supplies....................	1,664	0.16
Light, heat and power..............	832	0.05
Depreciation......................	37,440	—
Property taxes....................	4,160	—
	$54,496	$0.31

The budgeted variable overhead to produce 20,800 units totaled $77,376.

Required:

a. i. Calculate the budget (spending) variance from standard for each of the five component parts of overhead.

   ii. *Briefly* explain what the total overhead budget (price) variance indicates.

   iii. Identify the company personnel, if any, who probably should be held responsible for the budget variance for each of the component parts of overhead.

b. Calculate separately the fixed overhead denominator (volume) variance from standard.

c. Calculate separately the overhead efficiency variance from standard.

d. Discuss *briefly* the factors which caused the:

i. Fixed overhead denominator (volume) variance.

ii. Overhead efficiency variance from standard, indicating the company personnel, if any, who should be held responsible for each factor which caused the variances.

(SMA, adapted)

8-36 The Wolib Company Limited produces and sells a single household product called Goofer. The company is a wholly owned subsidiary of a large U.S. firm and became operational on August 31, 19x5. The production and operating procedures were similar to those used by the parent company in order to minimize setup costs and to facilitate comparative reporting.

The standard cost per unit for Wolib Company Limited (Canada) is as follows:

Material..................... 6 parts @ 50¢ each
Labour...................... 2 hours @ $4.00 each
Overhead................... $3.00 per standard labour hour, based on an annual volume of 80,000 units

A flexible budget for total overhead expenses, also adopted from the parent company, shows expense increases of $3,000 for every 1,000 units of volume increase.

At the end of the first quarter, November 30, 19x5, the following actual cost data were accumulated.

Purchases:	140,000 parts for.....................	$ 72,500
Labour:	37,000 hours for.....................	147,300
Overhead:	Variable............................	59,400
	Fixed	72,000

The general ledger showed the following balances as at November 30, 19x5 (all based on standard costs):

Stores..	$ 14,000
Work-in-Process —Materials....................	3,000
—Labour.....................	4,000
—Overhead...................	3,000
Finished Goods..................................	34,000
Cost of Goods Sold.............................	255,000

Required:

a. Determine all standard cost variances for:

Material .... (price and usage)
Labour .... (rate and efficiency)
Overhead .... variable and fixed spending, efficiency and volume)

b. When Wolib Company Limited adopted the standard cost system from the parent company, it changed material price and labour rates standards, but not the hourly overhead rate.

Comment on the usefulness of the standard cost system adopted by Wolib Company Limited.

(SMA, adapted)

8-37 During the budget preparation two major cost items caused concern:

i. The supplier of a high volume part has informed the company that the price is changing in March next year from $68 to $95 each.

ii. Labour rates for the production department which have averaged $3.50 an hour will rise by 20% in May next year, depending on the contract settlement.

Required:

Discuss how each of these cost items should be treated for the purpose of:

a. Setting standard costs for the next year;
b. Establishing a fixed budget for January next year;
c. Preparing a flexible budget for January assuming that the price per part ($68) remained the same, but January volume was up 10%.

(SMA, adapted)

  8-38 The Backward Company uses a standard cost system and reported the following gross profit for November 19x5:

Sales (14,000 units @ $40)...............			$560,000
Cost of goods sold—at standard...........		$350,000	
Adjustments of variances:			
Unfavourable:			
Material price.............	$3,600		
Material usage............	1,600		
Labour efficiency..........	4,800		
Overhead spending.........	1,200		
Overhead efficiency........	2,400		
Total unfavourable......	$13,600		
Favourable:			
Labour rate...............	$ 2,480		
Overhead volume.........	7,500		
Total favourable........	$ 9,980		
Net unfavourable....................		3,620	353,620
Gross margin..........................			$206,380

Additional information for November:

Cost of goods manufactured—November (at standard)

Material........................	$ 64,000	(160,000 parts)
Labour.........................	144,000	(48,000 standard hours)
Overhead Applied..............	192,000	
Total	$400,000	

Required:

a. The number of units produced in November.
b. The number of parts used during November.
c. The actual number of hours worked during November.
d. Actual average labour rate per hour during November.
e. What is the denominator activity (in direct labour hours) per month?
f. What was the flexible budget for overhead expenses at the standard hours worked?
g. What is the spending variance for variable and for fixed overhead separately, assuming that actual variable overhead amounted to $72,900 in November.
h. Assuming that the actual completed production for the month was erroneously understated by 200 units, list those variances which would change and indicate (without calculations) the direction of the change for each variance.

(SMA, adapted)

Chapter 9

Chapter 9 discusses the variable costing format and the various approaches to cost-profit-volume analysis. Studying this chapter should enable you to:

1. Compare and contrast variable costing and absorption costing.
2. Understand the basic elements of short-range profit planning.
3. Distinguish between common and traceable cost factors.
4. Discuss and apply the general approaches to cost-profit-volume analysis.
5. Discuss and apply the basic methods of multiple product cost-profit-volume analysis.

Variable Costing and Cost-Profit-Volume Analysis

Cost Accumulation for inventory valuation using full inventory costs was discussed in Chapters 3, 4, 5 and 7. Full inventory costs include the costs of all direct materials, direct labor, variable manufacturing overhead used in the production process, and an allocated portion of the fixed manufacturing overhead based on normal or practical capacity. This approach stresses the accumulation of full costs in determining the cost of goods manufactured for a given accounting period. The determination of the cost of goods manufactured directly affects both the carrying value of the inventory reported on the balance sheet and the cost of goods sold included on the income statement.

Cost of goods sold is one of two broad cost categories normally included on a traditional full or absorption costing income statement. The amount which is reported as cost of goods sold represents a product cost. The other expenses included on the income statement are classified as period costs, and are normally classified and reported on a functional basis. The absorption costing income statement is generally accepted by the accounting profession for external reporting purposes.

For purposes of internal planning, control, performance evaluation, and decision-making by management, an alternative cost behavior format has developed for the income statement which many accountants feel appears to be superior to the full or absorption costing format, at least for internal decision-making purposes. This alternative method is referred to as the variable costing or direct costing approach to income measurement.[1] The emphasis of this approach is focused on the separation of costs into their fixed and variable components on the income statement. From a managerial point of view, variable costing is considered an internal management tool. Normally a firm must prepare its external reports on an absorption costing basis for third party users. An income statement prepared under the variable costing concept includes separate classifications for variable and fixed costs. Variable costs include expenditures for such items as: raw materials, direct labor, variable manufacturing overhead, and variable selling and administrative expenses. Fixed costs include the fixed portion of manufacturing overhead and fixed selling and administrative expenses. A full absorption income statement summarizes the expenses for the period in traditional product cost and period expenditure form or format. Product costs, including both fixed and variable portions, are incorporated into cost of goods sold while period costs, also including both fixed and variable elements, are included in the expense section. These two income statement formats are shown in Illustration 9–1.

Illustration 9-1

Income Statement Formats

1. **Using Variable Costing Methods**

    Sales Revenue . . . . $xx

    Variable Costs

        Production Costs . . . . $xx

        Selling Expenses xx

        Administrative Expenses xx   xx

    Contribution Margin . . . . $xx

    Fixed Costs:

        Manufacturing Overhead Costs . . . . $xx

        Selling Expenses xx

        Administrative Expenses xx   xx

    Net Income Before Taxes . . . . $xx

2. **Using Absorption Methods**

    Sales Revenue . . . . $xx

    Cost of Goods Sold:

        Direct Labor . . . . $xx

        Direct Materials xx

        Variable Manufacturing Overhead xx

        Fixed Manufacturing Overhead xx   xx

    Gross Margin . . . . $xx

    Expenses:

        Selling Expenses . . . . $xx

        Administrative Expenses xx   xx

    Net Income Before Taxes . . . . $xx

---

[1] Since "variable costing" describes the approach more accurately than "direct costing" we will use the term "variable costing" in this chapter.

In summary, full or absorption costing includes fixed manufacturing overhead costs as a part of the cost of goods manufactured by applying a predetermined or standard rate for fixed manufacturing overhead. Variable costing treats fixed manufacturing overhead as a cost of the time period under consideration, i.e., a period cost. The cost of goods manufactured under absorption costing includes direct labor, direct materials, variable manufacturing overhead, and fixed manufacturing overhead. The cost of goods manufactured under variable costing will include only the variable elements of manufacturing costs: direct labor, direct materials, and variable manufacturing overhead. Fixed manufacturing overhead is a *product cost* under absorption costing, but a *period cost* under variable costing.

In order to illustrate the differences between an income statement prepared under absorption costing and one prepared under variable costing a simple example will be used. Assume that a company manufactures and sells a single product. The selling price of this product is $10 per unit and sales for the first two months of 19x1 were 8 units in January and 11 units in February. There was no beginning inventory of this product at January 1, 19x1 and 10 units were produced in both January and in February. The costs incurred by the company in producing and marketing this product were as follows:

	January	February
Fixed Production Costs (in total)......................	$30	$30
Variable Production Costs (per unit)...................	4	5
Fixed Selling and Administrative Expenses (in total)*.....	10	10

*All selling and administrative expenses are assumed to be fixed in this simplified example.

Using the above information, the income statements prepared under absorption and variable costing for the month of January are as follows:

A Company
Income Statement
For the Month Ending January 31, 19x1

		Absorption Costing		Variable Costing
Sales Revenue (8 units × $10)........................		$80		$80
Beginning Inventory.............................	$ 0		$ 0	
Cost of Goods Manufactured:				
Variable (10 units × $4)......................	40		40	
Fixed	30		—	
	$70		$40	
Ending Inventory:				
($70/10 units × 2 units)......................	$14			
($40/10 units × 2 units)......................			8	
Cost of Goods Sold...............................		56		32
Gross Margin or Contribution Margin................		$24		$48
Selling and Administrative Expenses..................	$10	$10		
Fixed Production Costs...........................	—	10	30	40
Net Income......................................		$14		$ 8

Note that in the absorption costing income statement the fixed production costs of $30 are considered to be a part of the cost of the units manufactured during the period. Alternatively, fixed production costs are considered to be an expense of the period in the variable costing income statement. This difference in the treatment of fixed production costs accounts for the difference ($14 vs. $8) in net income reported in the two alternative income statements. In the absorption costing income statement, these fixed costs were included in the cost of the inventory ($30 divided by 10 units produced = $3 per unit). Since 8 units were sold during the month and 2 units remain in the ending inventory at the end of January, $24 (8 units × $3) of fixed production costs were included in January expenses (as a part of cost of goods sold) and $6 (2 units × $3) were considered a part of the carrying value of the ending inventory at January 31. This $6 of fixed production costs carried as an asset accounts for the difference ($14 vs. $8) in the net income reported under the two methods since, under variable costing, all $30 of fixed production costs was treated as a January expense. The ending inventory at January 31 under variable costing consists of 2 units at a cost of $3 per unit; only variable production costs are included in the inventory carrying value when variable costing is used.

Continuing our example, the income statement for the month of February under absorption and variable costing (using the FIFO method of inventory valuation) are as follows:

A Company
Income Statement
For the Month Ending February 28, 19x1

		Absorption Costing		Variable Costing
Sales Revenue (11 units × $10)......................		$110		$110
Beginning Inventory:				
($70/10 units × 2 units)......................	$14			
($40/10 units × 2 units)			$ 8	
Cost of Goods Manufactured:				
Variable (10 units × $5)......................	50		50	
Fixed	30		—	
	$94		$58	
Ending Inventory (FIFO):				
($80/10 units × 1 unit)......................	8			
($50/10 units × 1 unit)......................			5	
Cost of Goods Sold..............................		86		53
Gross Margin or Contribution Margin................		$24		$57
Selling and Administrative Expenses..................	$10		$10	
Fixed Production Costs...........................	—	10	30	40
Net Income.....................................		$14		$17

Again, in the absorption costing income statement the fixed production costs of $30 are considered a part of the cost of the units produced during

February. These costs are treated as expenses of the month in the variable costing income statement. The difference in the treatment of fixed production costs again accounts for the difference ($14 vs. $17) in net income reported in the two alternative income statements. Since 11 units were sold during the month of February, a total of $33 in fixed production costs was expensed in the absorption costing income statement ($6 included in the 2 units of beginning inventory sold plus $27 included in the 9 units produced and sold during February) while only $30 (the fixed production costs incurred during February) was included as an expense in the variable costing income statement. This difference ($33 vs. $30) is the reason for the difference ($14 vs. $17) in net income for February reported using the alternative methods. In January, production exceeded sales (10 vs. 8) so income calculated using absorption costing ($14) exceeded income using variable costing ($8) by the amount of fixed production cost included in the ending inventory (2 units $\times$ $30/10 units). This will always be true when production exceeds sales because inventories will increase and the carrying value of inventories is always higher under absorption costing since fixed production costs are included in inventory. In February, sales exceeded production (11 vs. 10) so income under variable costing ($17) exceeded income calculated using absorption costing ($14). This will always be the case when sales exceed production because inventories will decrease and the inventories carried under variable costing which are charged to expense will be of a lesser amount since they include no fixed production costs. Of course, if sales and production are exactly equal, income under the two methods will be the same[2] since all costs, variable and fixed, will be expensed under both methods.

Although the example discussed above is a relatively simple one, it does serve to illustrate the basic differences between absorption and variable costing. A more complex illustration will be used later in the chapter to emphasize and reinforce these differences.

THE CONTRIBUTION MARGIN AND VARIABLE COSTING

The contribution margin is defined as the difference between revenues and all variable costs associated with those revenues. The contribution margin may be calculated on a total income statement basis, on a per unit basis, or as a percentage of sales. The contribution margin is a managerial decision-making tool. Moreover, variable costing may be regarded as a contribution margin approach to the measurement of income.

As indicated in Illustration 9–1, the format used in the variable costing income statement first deducts all variable manufacturing costs as well

---

[2] This assumes that there are either no beginning and ending inventories or, if this is not the case, there are no changes in costs.

as all other variable costs (selling and administrative expenses) from total revenues in order to arrive at the contribution margin. The total fixed manufacturing costs and other fixed selling and administrative expenses are then deducted from the contribution margin to arrive at net income before taxes. Since total fixed manufacturing costs are expensed each period, there is no volume variance to consider at the end of each accounting period using variable costing.

EXTERNAL FINANCIAL REPORTING IMPLICATIONS

If inventory levels fluctuate during an accounting period (that is, if the beginning and ending inventory balances differ), then the variable costing and full or absorption costing techniques provide different income amounts for that period due to the different treatment of fixed costs.

The approach normally used to illustrate the different income statements is to prepare a comparative example that has no beginning or ending finished goods inventory. This permits an analysis which illustrates the fact that over the long-run, the two techniques will provide identical total income amounts when the income for all accounting periods is summed. The assumption made is that all other factors are equal. However, this is rarely, if ever, the case.

The three cases that must be considered in order to fully illustrate the impact of the two costing approaches on income are:

1. Production equals sales.
2. Production exceeds sales.
3. Sales exceed production.

AN ILLUSTRATION: ABSORPTION VERSUS VARIABLE COSTING

During January, 19x1, the president of Sax Company decided that the power turbine shaft segment of the business should be established as a separate division with its own division manager, and that a planning, control and performance evaluation system should be added to its standard cost system. The standard cost system for manufacturing costs was discussed in Chapters 7 and 8. The planning, control and performance evaluation system is considered in Chapters 10 through 13.

A variable cost system for cost accumulation appears to be appropriate for internal use. The company uses absorption costing for external financial reporting purposes. The president requested that an analysis be made of the differences between variable costing and absorption costing in terms of the impact that each of these methods has on income. Implicit in his request was the fact that the president did not wish to maintain the accounts on both a variable costing basis for internal purposes and on an absorption costing basis for external financial reporting purposes.

Sax Company's president asked that the standard costs of manufacturing developed in Chapter 7 (Illustration 7-4) be used and, in addition, that a $20,000 budget for fixed selling and administrative costs be assumed. The variable selling costs are approximately $5 per unit sold. The production and sales levels which the president suggested for use in the analysis are rough estimates of the anticipated activity for the months of February, March, April and May and are presented in Illustration 9-2.

Factors other than volume are assumed to be constant for all months under consideration. Selling prices, standard costs of manufacturing, and selling and administrative costs should not change for any month of the time period under observation. For absorption costing purposes, the practical capacity of 1,800 power turbine shafts, or 900 direct labor hours, is used to allocate fixed overhead to production.

Illustration 9-2

Sax Company
Power Turbine Shaft Division
Projected Cost, Sales and Production Data

Per Unit Sales and Production Costs:
Average Sales Price $50.00

Standard Production Cost:
Direct Material @ Standard 6.00
Direct Labor @ Standard 3.00
Variable Manufacturing Overhead @ Standard 1.40

Total Variable Production Cost $10.40
Fixed Manufacturing Overhead @ Standard ° 2.00
                                                                     $12.40

Projected Selling and Administrative Expense:
Variable Selling Costs. . . . . $5 per unit
Fixed Selling and Administrative Expenses. $20,000

President's Estimate of Production and Sales Volumes in Units:

	February	March	April	May	Total
Beginning inventory.	0	0	550	150	—
Production	1,800	2,200	1,250	1,500	6,750
Sales.	1,800	1,650	1,650	1,650	6,750
Ending Inventory.	0	550	150	0	—

°Total fixed overhead is budgeted at $3,600 (Illustration 7-3) or $2.00 per unit.

Illustration 9–2 summarizes the sales, production and cost data which the president of Sax Company wants used in the comparison of income calculations using absorption and variable costing.

The income statements prepared using absorption costing use the full cost of manufacturing, $12.40 per unit, which has been adjusted for any volume variance since Sax Company closes its variances to cost of goods sold at the end of each period. Remember, the basis for developing the fixed manufacturing overhead in Illustration 7-4 in Chapter 7 was 1,800 units of production or 900 standard direct labor hours. At any other level of production, a volume variance would appear in the accounts. The income statements prepared under both conventional absorption costing and variable costing for the four months are presented in Illustration 9-3.

To understand the computations included in Illustration 9-3, the absorption costing and the variable costing income statements should be reviewed for a month in which there is a volume variance. For example, in March projected sales are 1,650 units at $50 per unit or a total sales revenue of $82,500. Under absorption costing, cost of goods sold at standard would be 1,650 units at $12.40 per unit for a total of $20,460. Fixed overhead applied at standard is $2.00 per unit produced, and is based on a practical capacity of 1,800 units. Anticipated production in March is 2,200 units. The favorable volume variance is 400 units at $2.00 per unit or $800. If standard direct labor hours were used in the analysis, then the volume variance would still be projected at $800 (200 hours X $4 per hour). The total selling and administrative expenses would consist of a fixed portion of $20,000 and a variable portion of $5.00 per unit sold or $8,250.

The sales for March in the variable costing income statement would, of course, be identical to the amount of absorption costing sales—$82,500. Under variable costing, the cost of goods sold, however, would include only the variable manufacturing costs of $10.40 per unit (Illustration 9-2) for 1,650 units or a total of $17,160. The variable selling expenses would be $8,250 ($5.00 per unit sold). Total fixed manufacturing overhead is projected at $3,600 per month. The president projected fixed selling and administrative expenses of $20,000 per month. These fixed costs would be considered period, rather than product, costs under variable costing.

A number of observations concerning the two different income statement formats are appropriate:

1. Expense classifications under absorption costing are made on a functional cost basis while variable costing classifications are made on a cost behavior pattern basis (variable vs. fixed).

Illustration 9-3
Sax Company
Power Turbine Shaft Division

Comparison of Absorption and Variable Costing Income Statements (In Units)

	February	March	April	May	Total
Production (Budget).....	1,800	2,200	1,250	1,500	6,750
Sales (Budget).........	1,800	1,650	1,650	1,650	6,750

Projected Income Statements—Absorption Costing

	February	March	April	May	Total
Sales.................	$90,000	$82,500	$82,500	$82,500	$337,500
Less: Cost of Goods Sold After Adjustment*.........	22,320	19,660	21,560	21,060	84,600
Gross Margin...........	$67,680	$62,840	$60,940	$61,440	$252,900
Less: Selling and Administrative Expenses.............	29,000	28,250	28,250	28,250	113,750
Net Income Before Taxes.........	$38,680	$34,590	$32,690	$33,190	$139,150

*Cost of Goods Sold After Adjustment for Volume Variance. Assume the entire variance is included in cost of goods sold.

February. No adjustment
March —($12.40 X 1,650 units sold) + [(1,800 units — 2,200 units) x $2]
       $20,460 — $800 = $19,660
April —$20,460 + [(1,800 units — 1,250 units) X $2]
       $20,460 + $1,100 = $21,560
May —$20,460 + [(1,800 units — 1,500 units) X $2]
       $20,460 + $600 = $21,060

Projected Income Statements—Variable Costing

	February	March	April	May	Total
Sales.................	$90,000	$82,500	$82,500	$82,500	$337,500
Less: Variable Costs Product Costs.......	18,720	17,160	17,160	17,160	70,200
Selling Expenses.........	9,000	8,250	8,250	8,250	33,750
Contribution Margin....	$62,280	$57,090	$57,090	$57,090	$233,550
Less: Fixed Costs Manufacturing Overhead..........	3,600	3,600	3,600	3,600	14,400
Selling and Administrative Expenses.........	20,000	20,000	20,000	20,000	80,000
Net Income Before Taxes.........	$38,680	$33,490	$33,490	$33,490	$139,150

2. The gross margin obtained using the absorption costing format is not
    the same as the contribution margin under variable costing. Sales less
    all product costs equals the gross margin under absorption costing.
    Sales less all variable costs equals the contribution margin under vari-
    able costing.

3. Income under variable costing follows the level of sales. When sales
    increase, income increases; when sales fall, income declines; and
    when sales remain constant, income remains the same
    (March-May). Income under absorption costing is related to *both*
    the level of sales and to the level of production. Sales for the mon-
    ths of March through May are projected at the same level. By in-
    specting production levels shown in Illustration 9-3, we note that
    under the absorption method, income varies in those months in
    relationship to the levels of production.

4. When sales and production are identical, as in February, both costing
    methods yield the same net income before taxes. Under either ap-
    proach, the total fixed manufacturing overhead is considered an ex-
    pense on the income statement when sales and production are equal,
    since there is no change in the beginning or ending inventory balance.
    Classifications within the income statement differ, however. Cost of
    goods sold, including any volume variance, incorporates total fixed
    manufacturing overhead under absorption costing. Under variable
    costing, total fixed manufacturing overhead is reflected as a period
    cost.

5. When production exceeds sales (as is the case in March) absorption
    costing yields a higher net income before taxes, because a portion of
    the fixed manufacturing overhead costs has been allocated to and in-
    cluded in the ending inventory, and thus, deferred to future periods.
    Under variable costing, all fixed manufacturing overhead costs are
    expensed during the period in which they are incurred.

6. When production is less than sales (April and May), variable costing
    yields a higher net income before taxes. Under absorption costing,
    the cost of goods sold, after taking volume variances into considera-
    tion, includes an amount of current and past applied fixed manufac-
    turing overhead costs exceeding the total fixed manufacturing over-
    head costs incurred during the current period. The inventories are
    reduced to match decreased sales demands; therefore, the applied
    fixed manufacturing overhead in ending inventories is less than the
    applied fixed manufacturing overhead in the beginning inventories.
    Using variable costing methods, total fixed manufacturing overhead is
    considered to be an expense in each accounting period in which it is
    incurred; therefore, there is no deferral of fixed costs in the finished
    goods inventory accounts.

7. Over time, assuming that all factors except volume are equal, total income under the two income statement formats is the same. Furthermore, total production could not exceed total sales by a material amount in the long-run. If production did exceed sales over the long-run, the firm would have large quantities of finished goods inventories on hand.

AN ILLUSTRATION: RECONCILING ABSORPTION AND VARIABLE COSTING INCOME STATEMENTS

The differences between absorption costing and variable costing are explained by analyzing the beginning and the ending inventory amounts for each month. Alternatively, the difference in income can be calculated each month by considering the impact of fixed overhead on both production and sales levels.

The finished goods inventory levels under both absorption and variable costing from Illustration 9-2 are as follows:

Month	Beginning Inventory	Ending Inventory	Difference
February	0 units	0 units	0 units
March	0	550	550
April	550	150	(400)
May	150	0	(150)

The inventory values reported on the balance sheets at the end of each month are at the full standard manufacturing cost per unit ($12.40) under absorption costing, and at the variable manufacturing cost per unit ($10.40) under variable costing. The difference between these two values, $2.00, represents the allocated fixed manufacturing overhead cost per unit at standard cost.

In March, the president anticipates that inventory will increase by a total of 550 units. The costs accumulated for these 550 units under absorption costing are $6,820 (550 units X $12.40 per unit). The costs accumulated under variable costing are $5,720 (550 units X $10.40 per unit). The difference between the two inventory costs at the end of March is $1,100. Again, this difference of $1,100 represents the $2.00 per unit of fixed manufacturing overhead allocated to the 550 units which is deferred to future months under absorption costing. Since there is no beginning inventory, absorption costing shows a higher net income before taxes for March than does the variable costing method. As shown in Illustration 9-3, the net income under absorption costing is $34,590 and for variable costing income is $33,490; a difference of $1,100 (550 units @ $2.00 per unit).

If the inventory differences are calculated for April and May, then the same reconciliation can be made. It is not necessary to calculate the costs accumulated for both the beginning and the ending inventories; only the amount and direction of change need to be considered. In April, the president anticipates that the finished goods inventory will decrease by 400 units. The absorption costing income statement will include fixed overhead in cost of goods sold on the income statement in an amount larger than that which was incurred because production was less than sales by 400 units. The fixed overhead at standard included in these 400 units is $800; therefore, net income before taxes under absorption costing is $800 less than the comparable net income before taxes computed using variable costing. In May, the inventory decline is 150 units, and the absorption costing net income before taxes is $300 less than the variable costing net income before taxes.

The same analysis may be used to calculate the impact on inventories and net income before taxes by considering production and sales volumes in each month. As an example of these calculations, the projected April data from Illustration 9-3 are presented below.

$$\text{April Sales} \ldots \ldots \ldots 1{,}650 \text{ units}$$
$$\text{April Production} \ldots \ldots 1{,}250 \text{ units}$$

Net Income Before Taxes Under Variable Costing........		$33,490
Fixed Manufacturing Costs Included in Sales (1,650 X $2.00).................................	$3,300	
Fixed Manufacturing Costs Included in Production (1,250 X $2.00)......................	2,500	
Inventory Level Impact.............................		(800)
Net Income Before Taxes Under Absorption Costing......		$32,690

Since finished goods inventory levels are projected to decrease during April, absorption costing includes fixed costs of manufacturing in cost of goods sold of $800 in excess of that incurred in April.

THE VARIABLE COSTING CONTROVERSY

For external reporting purposes, the concept of absorption costing is well entrenched and represents "generally accepted principles of accounting" as well as being the formally accepted method as required by Revenue Canada Taxation for purposes of income tax determination. There have been many advocates of variable costing for external reporting, but the arguments for acceptance have met with very limited success to date. Generally accepted accounting principles and most, if not all, regulatory bodies require absorption costing income statements for external reporting purposes. For internal planning, control, performance evaluation, and decision-making, the variable costing approach has gained widespread managerial acceptance. For internal use, the concept of variable costing is usually adjusted to meet the particular information needs of the firm.

COST-PROFIT-VOLUME ANALYSIS

4

Cost-profit-volume analysis is a managerial technique which is used for analyzing profit planning information for short-range planning purposes. This technique is a modeling tool which may be used for estimating income or selecting between alternative short-run operating strategies. Cost-profit-volume analysis uses the variable costing concept of income determination, and provides a quick overview of a firm's profit structure which supplies management with estimates of limited accuracy. These estimates, however, are valuable for such purposes as analyzing potential changes in selling prices, sales mix, sales volume, variable costs, and fixed costs. These five elements represent managerial decisions which must be considered in short-range profit planning.

Cost-Profit-Volume Analysis: Common Versus Traceable Factors

Cost-profit-volume analysis may be applied to the entire firm or to one or more segments of the firm. When this technique is applied to the entire firm, all of the revenues and costs are directly traceable to the planning unit. Directly traceable costs and revenues are those costs and revenues that may be attributed to the segment under consideration on a non-arbitrary basis. Theoretically, if the segment were eliminated, the directly traceable costs or revenues would also be eliminated.

Cost-profit-volume analysis is also applied to individual segments of the firm such as product lines, divisions, or sales territories. The smaller the segment of the organization analyzed by this technique, the greater the problem of common cost allocation. Common costs are those costs which benefit more than one segment of the firm. If these costs are allocated, the allocation is usually made on an arbitrary basis. Fixed manufacturing overhead is an example of a common cost that is allocated to production. There are numerous other examples of common cost if one considers only a specific segment of the firm. The president's salary, costs of company production planning, research and development expenditures, market research costs, advertising campaign costs, and the costs incurred in the legal department are all examples of costs common to many segments of an organization.

By definition, a common cost problem does not exist in those circumstances when the unit being analyzed using cost-profit-volume analysis is the entire firm. The firm must generate revenues which are adequate to cover its total costs, but any segment cost-volume-profit analysis should use only those costs and revenues which are traceable to that segment. Furthermore, if all segments of a firm are engaged in cost-profit-volume analysis separately, certain common costs would not be considered in the analyses.

COST-PROFIT-VOLUME ANALYSIS: THE CALCULATIONS

After reviewing the absorption and variable costing income statements presented in Illustration 9-3, the president of Sax Company requested that a graph illustrating the cost-profit-volume relationships per month for the Power Turbine Shaft Division be prepared assuming changes in certain financial factors. These factors were: (1) a reduction in variable production costs to $10 per unit; (2) a reduction in fixed manufacturing overhead costs to $3,000 per month; and (3) a reduction to $18,000 per month in fixed selling and administrative expenses. The costs were reclassified into the following variable and fixed components:

		Amount	Percent
Sales Revenue Per Unit		$ 50	100%
Variable Costs:			
Production Costs	$10		
Selling Expenses	5		
		15	30
Contribution Margin		$ 35	70%
Fixed Costs:			
Fixed Manufacturing Overhead Costs		$ 3,000	
Fixed Selling and Administrative Expenses		18,000	
Total Fixed Costs		$21,000	

Illustration 9–4 presents the profit capabilities of the Power Turbine Shaft Division in a format which indicates areas of loss and profit and the break-even point for this division.

A break-even point is that point where total revenues are exactly equal to total costs. Revenues in excess of the break-even point produce a profit, while revenues in an amount less than that stipulated by break-even analysis indicate a loss. However, the break-even formula or relationship may also be used by the firm to determine the level of profit it wishes to obtain.

Break-Even Relationships:
Total Revenues = Total Costs
or Total Revenues = Variable Costs + Fixed Costs
or Total Revenues = Variable Costs + Fixed Costs + Desired Profit
Level

The president was especially pleased with the margin of safety indicated by the cost-profit-volume graph. The margin of safety is the amount that budgeted sales can decline before the break-even point is reached. In the near future, the president could not foresee a loss in the Power Turbine Shaft Division.

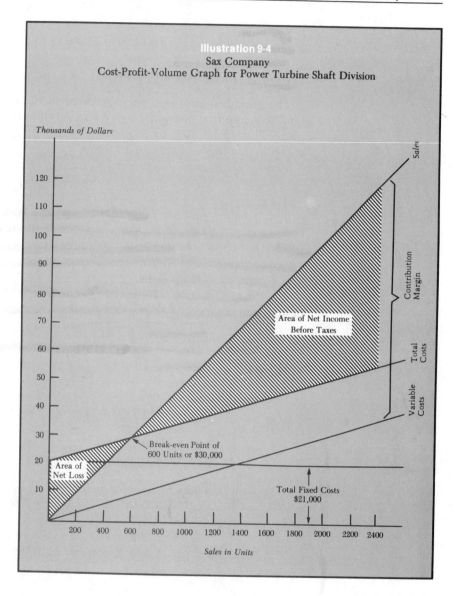

Illustration 9-4
Sax Company
Cost-Profit-Volume Graph for Power Turbine Shaft Division

The next factor that the president wished to consider was the level of sales required to earn $56,000 in before-tax profits each month assuming a reduction in variable production costs to $10 per unit, and a reduction in total fixed costs to $21,000 with all other financial factors remaining constant. Four approaches may be used in cost-profit-volume analysis. Each of these approaches provides the same information, but in a different manner. The four approaches or techniques are:

1. Graphical
2. Equation
3. Contribution Margin
4. Contribution Percentage or Ratio

The graphical approach was presented in Illustration 9-4. The equation, contribution margin, and contribution ratio or percentage approaches may be used to respond to questions raised by management regarding changes in financial factors.

Equation Method ✳

The equation method establishes the mathematical relationships between sales, variable costs, fixed costs, and desired net income before taxes. This approach provides a solution expressed in terms of units, which must be multiplied by the selling price per unit to obtain the solution in terms of sales dollars.

The general form of the equation, with X representing the number of units necessary to yield the desired net income before taxes is:

$$\begin{Bmatrix} \text{Unit} \\ \text{Sales} \\ \text{Price} \end{Bmatrix}(X) = \begin{Bmatrix} \text{Variable} \\ \text{Expenses} \\ \text{per Unit} \end{Bmatrix}(X) + \text{Fixed Expenses} + \begin{Bmatrix} \text{Desired Net} \\ \text{Income Before} \\ \text{Taxes} \end{Bmatrix}$$

1. To break-even

$$\$50\ (X) = \$15\ (X) + \$21,000 + \$0$$
$$\$35\ (X) = \$21,000$$
$$X = 600 \text{ units}$$
$$\text{Sales dollars} = 600 \times \$50 = \$30,000$$

2. To earn $56,000 net income before taxes

$$\$50\ (X) = \$15\ (X) + \$21,000 + \$56,000$$
$$\$35\ (X) = \$77,000$$
$$X = 2,200 \text{ units}$$
$$\text{Sales dollars} = 2,200 \times \$50 = \$110,000$$

Contribution Margin Method ✳

The contribution margin approach rearranges the equation, but also provides a solution in units. The general form of the contribution margin approach is as follows:

$$X = \frac{\text{Fixed Expenses} + \text{Desired Net Income Before Taxes}}{\text{Contribution Margin Per Unit}}$$

1. To break-even

$$X = \frac{\$21,000 + \$0}{\$50 - \$15}$$

$$= \frac{\$21,000}{\$35}$$

$$= 600 \text{ units}$$

$$\text{Sales dollars} = 600 \ X \ \$50 = \$30,000$$

2. To earn $56,000 net income before taxes

$$X = \frac{\$21,000 + \$56,000}{\$50 - \$15}$$

$$= \frac{\$77,000}{\$35}$$

$$= 2,200 \text{ units}$$

$$\text{Sales dollars} = 2,200 \ X \ \$50 = \$110,000$$

The results using the contribution margin approach are, of course, identical to those obtained under the equation approach. The contribution margin approach answers the question, "Given a $35 contribution margin, how many units must be sold in order to attain the desired profit?"

Contribution Percentage or Ratio Method

The contribution percentage or ratio approach provides an answer stated in terms of dollars of sales. If an answer in terms of units is desired, the dollars of sales must be divided by the selling price per unit. The contribution percentage approach uses the contribution margin approach and converts the contribution margin in the denominator to a percentage of contribution margin per sales dollar. The general formulation of the contribution percentage approach is:

Let Y = Necessary dollars of sales to yield the desired net income before taxes.

$$Y = \frac{\text{Fixed Costs} + \text{Desired Net Income Before Taxes}}{(\frac{\text{Contribution Margin Per Unit}}{\text{Sales Price Per Unit}})}$$

1. To break-even

$$Y = \frac{\$21,000 + \$0}{(\frac{\$50 - \$15}{\$50})}$$

$$= \frac{\$21,000}{(\frac{\$35}{\$50})}$$

$$= \frac{\$21,000}{.70}$$

$$= \$30,000$$

In units $= \$30,000 \div \$50 = 600$

2. To earn $56,000 net income before taxes

$$Y = \frac{\$21,000 + \$56,000}{(\frac{\$50 - \$15}{\$50})}$$

$$= \frac{\$77,000}{(\frac{\$35}{\$50})}$$

$$= \frac{\$77,000}{.70}$$

$$Y = \$110,000$$

In units $= \$110,000 \div \$50 = 2,200$

The contribution margin percentage approach asks the question, "Given a contribution margin of $.70 for every $1 of sales, how many dollars of sales are necessary to cover fixed costs and attain the desired profit level?"

Summary of Methods

All of the above approaches provide identical answers because they are merely variations of the same equation and consider identical input factors. In choosing one approach as opposed to another, one must consider such factors as the purpose for which the information is intended, the form in which the information is desired, personal preference, and convenience.

COST-PROFIT-VOLUME ANALYSIS: MULTIPLE PRODUCTS

The analysis of cost-profit-volume relationships made by the Power Turbine Shaft Division was based on a single product. When two or more products are involved in cost-profit-volume analysis, the analysis becomes more complex and even less precise than the analysis of a single product. This is because different products normally have different selling prices, different variable costs, different contribution margins, and different sales forecasts that must be considered to arrive at the product mix.

The president of Sax Company is considering producing two different versions of an electric fan in a manufacturing plant that will become available in the near future. After reviewing the sales forecasts for electric fans, the marketing department feels that three small fans can be sold for every large fan. The manager that is responsible for the feasibility study wishes to calculate the level of sales that would be necessary to break-even each month and the sales level required to earn a net income of $5,200 before taxes each month.

It is anticipated that the small electric fan will sell for $10 per unit and the large electric fan will sell at a price of $20 per unit. The variable costs of production per unit is $4 and $12, respectively. The initial fixed costs per month are projected at $6,400 for manufacturing and $4,000 for selling and administrative expenses.

The Weighted Average Contribution Margin Percentage

There are certain obvious implications uncovered in an examination of the contribution margin percentages of the two products. In this case three small fans can be sold for every large fan.

	Small Electric Fans	Percent	Large Electric Fans	Percent
Selling Price	$10	100	$20	100
Variable Costs	4	40	12	60
Contribution Margin	$ 6	60	$ 8	40

The projected contribution margin percentage on small fans is 60 percent, and the large fans have a projected contribution margin percentage of 40 percent. The weighted average contribution margin percentage for the two products combined must fall somewhere between 40 and 60 percent.

The weighted average contribution margin percentage may be calculated in two ways. An obvious approach is to consider the two products as being sold in a package of three small fans and one large fan. The total contribution margin for this package is the weighted average contribution margin per package when expressed in dollars, and is the weighted average per dollar of projected sales when expressed on a percentage basis.

	Three Small Fans	One Large Fan	Total	Percent of Total
Selling Price	$30	$20	$50	100
Variable Costs	12	12	24	48
Contribution Margin	$18	$ 8	$26	52

The projected weighted average contribution margin is 52 percent for each package of three small fans and one large fan sold. Using the second method, the weighted average contribution margin is calculated by using the contribution margin percentages for each product, 60 percent for small fans and 40 percent for large fans, and weighting the contribution margins by their relative sales proportions.

Weighted Average Contributions:

$$\text{Small Electric Fans} = \frac{\text{Selling Price of Three Fans}}{\text{Total Selling Price for Both Fans}}$$

$$= \frac{\$30}{\$50} \times .60 = .36$$

$$\text{Large Electric Fan} = \frac{\text{Selling Price of Large Fan}}{\text{Total Selling Price for Both Fans}}$$

$$= \frac{\$20}{\$50} \times .40 = .16$$

Total Weighted Average Contribution Margin

$$= .36 + .16 = .52$$

The above analysis indicates that, given the sales mix of three small fans and one large fan, $.36 is the contribution margin per dollar of sales from small fans, and $.16 is the contribution margin per dollar of sales from large fans. The total contribution margin per dollar of sales is $.52.

Multiple Product Cost-Profit-Volume Analysis: Package of Goods Approach

Any of the four general approaches to the cost-profit-volume analysis could be used to answer questions concerning the break-even point and the sales volume necessary to earn net income before taxes of $5,200. For purposes of illustration only, the equation and the weighted average contribution margin percentage approaches are utilized. The equation approach provides a basic solution in units, while the contribution margin percentage approach provides a basic solution in terms of sales dollars. Using the package of goods approach, the answer will be the number of packages of three small fans and one large fan that must be sold, and the total dollars of sales of the two products. The basic data developed for the electric fan analysis are presented in Illustration 9-5.

If the equation approach to cost-profit-volume analysis is used and sales are viewed as packages of three small fans and one large fan, the totals for the package may be used in the analysis as follows:

1. To break-even using the equation approach:

$$\$50 \ (X) = \$24 \ (X) + \$10,400 + \$0$$
$$\$26 \ (X) = \$10,400$$
$$X = 400 \text{ packages}$$

Since a package is comprised of three small fans and one large fan, the number of units of each fan that must be sold in order to break-even is as follows:

Small Fans = 400 packages X 3 units per package
= 1,200 units

Large Fan = 400 packages X 1 unit per package
= 400 units

Illustration 9-5
Sax Company

Basic Data for Electric Fan Cost-Profit-Volume Analysis
Questions to be answered:
1. What is the break-even point?
2. What volume of sales is necessary to earn $5,200 net income before taxes?

Sales Mix (Projected):
  Three small fans to one large fan.
Individual Product Contribution Margins (Projected):

	Small Electric Fans	Percent	Large Electric Fans	Percent
Selling Price	$10	100	$20	100
Variable Costs	4	40	12	60
Contribution Margin	$ 6	60	$ 8	40

Weighted Average Contribution Margins (Projected):

	Three Small Fans	Percent	One Large Fan	Percent	Total	Percent of Total
Selling Price	$30	100	$20	100	$50	100
Variable Costs	12	40	12	60	24	48
Contribution Margin	$18	60	$ 8	40	$26	52

Fixed Costs (Projected):
  Fixed Manufacturing Costs $6,400
  Fixed Selling and Administrative Expenses $4,000

2. To earn $5,200 net income before taxes using the equation approach:

$$\$50 \ (X) = \$24 \ (X) + \$10,400 + \$5,200$$
$$\$26 \ (X) = \$15,600$$
$$X = 600 \text{ packages}$$

The separation of the package would be made on the basis of the composition of the package: three small fans and one large fan per package.

$$\text{Small Fans} = 600 \text{ packages X 3 units per package}$$
$$= 1,800 \text{ units}$$
$$\text{Large Fan} = 600 \text{ packages X 1 unit per package}$$
$$= 600 \text{ units}$$

The contribution margin percentage approach, using the weighted average contribution margin percentage of .52, will yield the identical answers in sales dollars.

1. To break-even using the contribution margin percentage approach:

$$X = \frac{\$10,400 + \$0}{.52}$$

$$X = \$20,000$$

Using the equation approach, the break-even number of packages was 400. If this were multiplied by the selling price of a package, $50, the total sales necessary to break-even would have been $20,000.

The unit sales ratio is three small fans to one large fan, but the contribution margin percentage approach provides an answer in terms of sales dollars. The sales dollars ratio of one package is $30/$50 or 60% for small fans and $20/$50 or 40% for large fans.

```
Small Fans
Sales Dollars   = $20,000 X 60%  = $12,000
Large Fan
Sales Dollars   = $20,000 X 40%  = $ 8,000
```

2. To earn $5,200 net income before taxes using the contribution margin percentage approach:

$$X = \frac{\$10,400 + \$5,200}{.52}$$

$$X = \frac{\$15,600}{.52}$$

$$X = \$30,000$$

The equation approach solution in packages, when multiplied by the selling price of a package, would have provided the same answer. The sales ratios when multiplied by the total projected sales of $30,000 would provide the projected sales of each product.

```
Small Fans
Sales Dollars   = $30,000 X 60%  = $18,000
Large Fan
Sales Dollars   = $30,000 X 40%  = $12,000
```

Multiple Product Cost-Profit-Volume Analysis: Weighted Average Approach

The weighted average approach treats each product as a separate product instead of considering the unit as a package. The sales mix cannot be ignored, however. The sales mix is introduced into the calculations by weighting the individual financial factors included in the formulas. Again, any of the four approaches to cost-profit-volume analysis can be used. The equation approach and the contribution margin percentage approach will be illustrated here. The data presented in Illustration 9-5 are again used in these calculations.

When the cost-profit-volume equation is used, the solution is stated in terms of units. Therefore, the weighting factors are based on the unit sales mix of three small fans to one large fan. Seventy-five percent (3 of 4) of the units sold are small fans, and 25 percent (1 of 4) are large fans.

1. To break-even using the equation approach

$$.75\ (\$10)\ X\ +\ .25\ (\$20)\ X = .75\ (\$4)\ X\ +\ .25\ (\$12)\ X\ +\ \$10,400$$
$$\$7.50\ X\ +\ \$5\ X = \$3\ X\ +\ \$3\ X\ +\ \$10,400$$
$$\$12.50\ X = \$6\ X\ +\ \$10,400$$
$$\$6.50\ X = \$10,400$$
$$X = 1,600\ \text{units}$$

Both the selling prices and variable costs in this equation have been weighted by the projected sales mix. Of the break-even sales volume in units, 75 percent are small fans and 25 percent are large fans.

$$\text{Small Fans} = 1,600\ X\ .75 = 1,200\ \text{units}$$
$$\text{Large Fan} = 1,600\ X\ .25 = 400\ \text{units}$$

2. To earn $5,200 net income before taxes using the equation approach

$$.75\ (\$10)\ X\ +\ .25\ (\$20)\ X = .75\ (\$4)\ X\ +\ .25\ (\$12)\ X$$
$$+\ \$10,400\ +\$5,200$$
$$\$7.50\ X\ +\ \$5\ X = \$3\ X\ +\ \$3\ X\ +\ \$15,600$$
$$\$12.50\ X = \$6\ X\ +\ \$15,600$$
$$\$6.50\ X = \$15,600$$
$$X = 2,400\ \text{total units}$$
$$\text{Small Fans} = 2,400\ (.75)\ = 1,800\ \text{units}$$
$$\text{Large Fan} = 2,400\ (.25)\ = 600\ \text{units}$$

When the contribution margin percentage approach is used, the solution is expressed in terms of sales dollars. The weighting factors must be based on the weighted average sales dollar which is $30/$50 or 60% for small fans and $20/$50 or 40% for large fans.

3. To compute break-even using the contribution margin percentage approach

$$X = \frac{\$10,400 + \$0}{[(.6)(.6) + (.4)(.4)]}$$

$$= \frac{\$10,400}{(.36 + .16)}$$

$$= \frac{\$10,400}{.52}$$

$$X = \$20,000$$

Small Fans Sales Dollars $= \$20,000 \times .6 = \$12,000$

Large Fan Sales Dollars $= \$20,000 \times .4 = \$8,000$

COST-PROFIT-VOLUME ANALYSIS: UNDERLYING ASSUMPTIONS

Conventional cost-profit-volume analysis is a static tool in that it assumes that all factors, with the exception of the single factor that is being analyzed, will remain constant over the relevant range. The equations are mathematical; therefore, any single factor may be computed given that all the other factors are known. The examples included in this chapter have all considered sales volume in units or dollars, which is the conventional approach.

Once the relationship of the following factors to volume are determined, this analysis assumes that the relationships with the following variables do not change over the relevant range of volume.

1. Variable costs
2. Fixed Costs
3. Selling prices
4. Sales mix
5. Efficiency
6. Productivity

Any projected change requires a new analysis. The linearity of the approach forces the user to consider all of the financial factors that affect profit and their relationships to volume. Note that this tool is not a precise planning tool, but it does provide an estimate of projected net income before taxes using the variable costing concept of income determination.

SUMMARY

For external reporting purposes, the use of full or absorption costing is required. However, for management accounting purposes, variable or direct costing is often more useful as a decision-making tool. Variable costing emphasizes the separation of manufacturing costs into their fixed and variable components.

From the standpoint of income determination, the primary difference between the two costing formats is in the treatment of fixed costs. Under the absorption costing format, fixed manufacturing overhead is allocated and inventoried as an element of product cost and is charged to expense only as the associated units of product are sold. In contrast, under the variable costing format, fixed manufacturing overhead is expensed as a period cost as it is incurred and the product cost includes only the variable cost elements.

This difference in the treatments of fixed manufacturing overhead means that net income under the two formats will vary whenever there is a difference between the sales and production for the period. When sales are equal to production, both formats will yield the identical net income figure.

The variable costing approach, although not acceptable for external financial accounting purposes, is instrumental in cost-profit-volume analysis for management purposes. Cost-profit-volume analysis is used as a tool for short-range profit planning purposes. The essential elements that must be considered in such planning include potential changes in selling prices, sales mix, sales volume, variable costs, and fixed costs. Usually such an analysis considers only those costs which are directly traceable to the unit under analysis, but in certain cases common costs are also considered.

Four general approaches to cost-profit-volume analysis include: (1) graphical, (2) equation, (3) contribution margin, and (4) contribution percentage or ratio. All four approaches yield approximately the same results, although in different formats, and all are based on the premise that sufficient sales revenue must be generated to cover both fixed and variable expenses as well as to produce the desired net income.

When more than a single product is involved in the cost-profit-volume analysis, the analysis process becomes more complex. The two primary

approaches in multiple product cost-product-volume analysis are the package of goods approach (where the units sold are considered as a package) and the weighted average approach (where the units sold are considered as individual products). In either approach, the sales mix is a very important factor that must be taken into consideration.

This chapter has introduced short-range planning by discussing one of the tools of such planning, cost-profit-volume analysis. The next chapter continues the topic of short-range planning by illustrating the budgeting process.

KEY DEFINITIONS   **Common costs**—costs which benefit more than one segment of the firm. Any allocation of common costs will be arbitrary.

Contribution margin—the difference between revenues and all variable costs associated with those revenues.

Contribution margin approach—an approach to cost-profit-volume analysis which is similar to the equation approach but which bases its calculations on the contribution margin.

Contribution percentage approach—an approach to cost-profit-volume analysis which uses the contribution margin approach but bases its calculations on the percentage of contribution margin per dollar of sales.

Cost-profit-volume analysis—a technique using the variable costing concept of income determination in analyzing the impact of potential changes in selling prices, sales mix, sales volume, and variable and fixed costs on short-range profits.

Equation approach—the approach to cost-profit-volume analysis which establishes a basic mathematical relationship between sales, variable costs, fixed costs, and desired net income before taxes, and provides a solution in terms of units.

Full or absorption costing—the traditional type of costing generally used for external reporting puroposes where fixed manufacturing overhead costs are included as a part of the cost of goods manufactured according to pre-determined rates of application.

Package of goods approach—a cost-profit-volume analysis for multiple products being sold in a given package or sales mix.

Traceable factors—those costs and revenues which may be directly traced on a non-arbitrary basis to a segment of the firm.

Variable or direct costing—a costing approach which includes only the variable portion of manufacturing overhead as a part of the cost of goods manufactured, while treating the fixed portion of manufacturing overhead as a period cost. Variable costing is not generally used for external financial reporting but is an informative management tool.

Weighted average contribution margin—the contribution margin weighted by the product mix when two or more different products are sold.

QUESTIONS

9-1 What is the major use of a variable costing income statement? An absorption costing income statement?

9-2 From an income determination standpoint, what is the only difference between absorption and variable costing? Explain.

9-3 Explain the contribution margin approach to decision-making. In your explanation concentrate on the actual format of this type of income statement.

9-4 What causes income to vary under absorption costing? How does this differ from variable costing? (That is, what causes income to vary under variable costing?)

9-5 When production is more than sales, which method produces the higher income, variable or absorption costing, and why?

9-6 How is cost-profit-volume analysis used? Give examples.

9-7 What is the difference between traceable and common costs?

9-8 Of the following which would you consider common costs?

  a.   R & D expenditures
  b.   Advertising costs
  c.   Variable overhead costs
  d.   Depreciation of executive office building
  e.   Direct materials costs

9-9 What is the overall purpose of cost-profit-volume analysis?

9-10 Explain the equation approach to cost-profit-volume analysis. Does the answer it gives differ from that given under another approach?

9-11 Why is it difficult to use cost-profit-volume analysis when dealing with a firm which produces multiple products?

9-12 Name the underlying assumption in cost-profit-volume analysis.

9-13 Since the variable costing approach is not acceptable for external financial accounting purposes, why do firms bother with it?

EXERCISES AND PROBLEMS

9-14 The Wax Company has the following operating information:

Production   14,000 units
Sales   11,200 units @ $5/unit
Variable costs $35,000
Fixed costs $14,000

Required:

Prepare an income statement using absorption costing and another using variable costing.

9-15   You are given the following information about the operations of the Queen Company:

Direct labor costs	$19,000
Direct materials purchases	7,000
Overhead (all variable except fixed rent of $1,000 and depreciation of $2,000)	14,000
General and administrative expense	2,000
Selling expenses	9,000
	$51,000

There were no beginning inventories. During the year 10,000 units were produced; 8,000 were sold. There were no inventories of materials or work-in-process at year-end—only finished goods. Prepare statements of cost of goods manufactured under each of the following assumptions:

a.   Full absorption
b.   Variable costing

9-16   Given below is cost information for the Sales Company for the month of June:

Sales	400 units
Variable manufacturing costs	$6 per unit
Total fixed manufacturing costs	$2,400
Total administrative expense (fixed)	$1,200
Finished goods beginning inventory	0 units
Finished goods ending inventory	200 units
Selling price	$25 per unit
Variable selling expense	$ 1 per unit

Required:

a.   What is the net income under absorption costing?
b.   What is the net income under variable costing?

9-17   Given the following break-even chart:

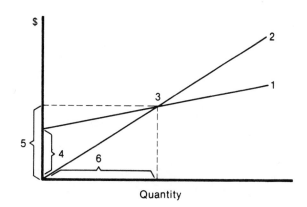

Quantity

Identify the following items by numbers.

a. Total revenue line
b. Total cost line
c. Total fixed cost
d. Break-even volume
e. Break-even sales
f. Break-even point

9-18   The solid lines in the following break-even charts represent the present cost-profit-volume relationships in a firm. The dotted lines represent changes. Explain what financial factors changed the original relationships.

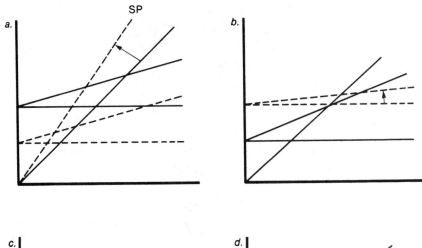

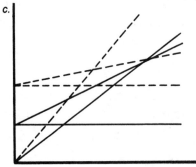
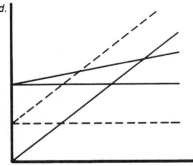

9-19   You are told the following about Jones Company's production costs:

Fixed costs $36,000
Variable costs:
    Materials   . . . . $2.50 per unit
    Labor   . . . . $1.70 per unit
    Other processing . . . . . . $ .80 per unit

Required:

a.   What is the *lowest price* at which you can sell the product and not lose money if you intend to produce and sell 60,000 units? (Use the equation method.)
b.   At what price will you sell the product if you desire to have a 15% profit on sales?

9-20   The A&M Company has just been formed. In their first year of production, they have a plant capacity of 10,000 units which they feel they will be able to sell.

Their costs are:

Direct labor, $2.00 per unit
Direct materials, $1.00 per unit
Other variable costs, $.50 per unit
Fixed costs, $28,000

The company wants to make a profit of $25,000 in the first year. What should their selling price be? (Use the equation method.) What is the contribution margin?

9-21   A company produces a single product to sell for $5.00 per unit. The company incurs $18,000 in fixed costs, and variable costs run $3.00 per unit.

Required:

a.   Compute the contribution margin per unit.
b.   Compute the break-even point using the contribution margin approach.

9-22   The management of the Richards Company has developed the following estimates of costs and sales, assuming the company is able to operate at full capacity:

Total fixed expenses . . . . $ 80,000
Total variable costs 30,000
Total sales revenues 150,000

Fixed expenses are constant at all levels of business activity and variable expenses vary in direct proportion to sales.

Required:

a. Calculate the break-even point of the Richards Company using the contribution margin ratio approach.
b. Calculate the break-even point assuming the above *except* that the total expenses at full capacity are composed of $60,000 fixed and $75,000 variable.

9-23   Soloco Inc.'s chief financial officer has given you the following information:

Fixed costs	$365,000.00
Selling price per unit	16.00
Direct labor per unit	2.20
Direct material per unit	4.00
Other variable costs	5.25

Required:

Calculate (a) the sales in dollars, and (b) the unit sales necessary to acquire a $55,000 profit.

9-24   Prepare a cost of goods manufactured statement and an income statement using: (a) variable and (b) absorption costing from the information given below:

Sales: Product A—3,500 units @ 27.50
   Product B—4,000 units @ $32.00
Direct labor: Cutting: Product A—2 hours @ $2.00
                        Product B—2½ hours @ $2.00
               Finishing: Product A—2 hours @ $2.50
                         Product B—3 hours @ $2.50
Beginning finished goods inventory—0 units
Variable overhead: Cutting: Product A&B—$.50 per direct labor hour
                    Finishing: Product A&B—$1.00 per direct labor hour
Beginning work-in-process—0 units
Ending work-in-process—0 units
Direct materials: Product A—2 units @ $1.50
                 Product B—3 units @ $1.50

Fixed overhead: $18,000 (applied at a rate of $1.50 per unit of A and $2.40 per unit of B)
Ending finished goods inventory: Product A—500 units
                                Product B—1,000 units
Beginning raw materials—4,000 units @ $1.50
Ending raw materials—3,000 units @ $1.50
Fixed selling and administrative expense—$20,000
Purchases of raw materials—22,000 units @ $1.50

9-25   Whodunit, Inc. has given you the following information for 1980 concerning its products. They have hired you to:

a. Compute the selling price per unit.
b. Project an income statement for the year using variable costing.
c. Compute a break-even point expressed in dollars and in units assuming that $20,000 of overhead and the total administrative expenses are fixed but that all other costs are fully variable.

Estimated annual sales . . . . 25,000 units

	Amount	Per Unit
Estimated costs:		
Material	$ 93,750	$3.75
Direct labor	20,000	.80
Overhead	31,250	1.25
Administrative expense	50,000	2.00
Total	$195,000	$7.80

Selling expenses are expected to be 13% of sales and profit is to amount to $1.77 per unit.

9-26   The JKL Company expects the following relationships between its products to exist in 1980:

	Product J	Product K	Product L
Sales	$3.50 per unit	$6.20 per unit	$8.40 per unit
Variable costs	$2.00 per unit	$3.80 per unit	$5.20 per unit
Volume	40,000 units	50,000 units	35,000 units
Fixed costs	$280,000		

Required:

The break-even point for the company in terms of J, K, and L.

9-27   The Rosen Company makes a single product which has the following costs:

Fixed costs—$400 (total)
Variable costs—$.10 (per unit)

The income tax rate is 40%. Rosen will make exactly 1,000 units this period.

Required:

a. How much will Rosen have to charge per unit in order to break-even on the sale of the 1,000 units? (Use the equation method.)
b. In order to make a profit of $120 (after taxes) on the sale of 1,000 units, how much will Rosen have to charge per unit?

9-28   The Sales Company has just been formed to produce Z. The first year, the capacity of the plant will be 12,000 units which they feel they will be able to sell.

> Their costs are: Direct labor, $2.50 per unit
> Raw materials, $1.80 per unit
> Other variable costs, $1.20 per unit
> Fixed costs, $36,000

Required:
a. If the company wishes to make a profit of $30,000 the first year, what should their selling price be? What is the contribution margin?
b. At the end of the first year, they wish to increase their volume. An increase of $15,000 in annual fixed costs will increase their capacity to 30,000 units. They now want a profit of $70,000 and to achieve this end, they also invest $29,000 in advertising. No other costs change. Under these new conditions, how many units will they have to sell to realize this profit, if their new selling price will be $13.00 per unit? How many units will they have to sell to break-even?

9-29   Company T has a relevant production range of 1,500 to 4,000 units. At 1,500 units, the total production cost is $2,500. At 4,000 units, the total production cost is $5,500. The selling price is $2.25 per unit.

Required:

a. What is the variable cost per unit?
b. What is the total fixed cost?
c. What is the break-even volume? (Use the contribution margin approach.)
d. What must variable cost per unit be if the break-even point is to be at 3,000 units.

9-30   Given below is selected information concerning two products sold by the Kilmer Company.

	Rink	Dink
Selling price (per unit)	$10	$15
Variable cost (per unit)	7	5

The fixed costs associated with the manufacture of these two products are $48,000 per year.

Required:

Calculate the break-even point for the sale of Rink and Dink if the sales mix is 2 units of Rink and 1 unit of Dink.

9-31   Following are data relative to the revenues and costs of the Montgomery Company for the calendar year 1980:

Sales		$300,000
Cost of goods manufactured and sold:		
Materials	$45,000	
Labor	50,000	
Variable manufacturing overhead	25,000	
Fixed manufacturing overhead	40,000	160,000
Gross margin		$140,000
Selling Expense:		
Variable	$20,000	
Fixed	18,000	38,000
		$102,000
Administrative expense:		
Variable	25,000	
Fixed	64,000	89,000
Net earnings		$ 13,000

Required:

Find the dollar sales required for Montgomery Company to break-even, using the contribution ratio approach.

9-32   The following is selected information from Melodies Co. which sells two products.

	Sing	Song
Selling price (per unit)	$5.50	$3.75
Direct materials (per unit)	1.20	.80
Direct labor (per unit)	2.00	1.85
Other variable costs	.60	.40

Total fixed costs associated with these two products are $68,530.

Required:

a.   Calculate the break-even point for the sale of Sing and Song if sales mix is 4 units of Sing and 3 units of Song.
b.   Assuming sales of $266,000, prepare a variable costing income statement. Assume no beginning or ending inventories and assume a 48% tax rate. Use the sales mix in part a.

9-33   Farmer Green, your uncle, has decided that he is too old to continue to milk 100 cows each day and has decided, therefore, to purchase a milking machine. He has narrowed his choice down to the Super Milk and Easy Milk models. You have just returned from the big city and want to impress your uncle with some of your recently acquired knowledge. The following information is available concerning the two models.

	Super Milk	Easy Milk
Capacity	150 cows	200 cows
Fixed cost/year	$8,000	$10,000

Each cow can produce 32 litres of milk a day which can be sold for $0.50 per litre. Super Milk will produce a profit of $15,000 and Easy Milk can generate a profit of $19,000 when they are operated at full capacity.

Required:

Calculate sales in dollars and units per year for each machine needed to break even.

9-34   Crash Products has just perfected a rip-proof "rip-a-way" football jersey which it can sell to the Yellowknife Red Jackets football team for $10 per jersey. Crash's economist forecasts that demand for this unique product (fiendishly designed to maim the fingers of enemy tacklers) will be 80 in 19x1 and 110 in 19x2. Product costs are estimated as follows:

	19x1	*19x2*
Fixed (in total)	$100	$100
Variable (per unit)	5	6

Because Crash's production facilities can accommodate only a single worker per shift, only 100 jerseys are turned out annually by the organization's skilled craftsman.

Required:

Prepare an income statement using variable costing and one using absorption costing for 19x1 and 19x2. Crash Products uses Fifo to cost their inventories.

9-35   The Samson Company expects the following relationships to exist between its products:

	Product P	*Product Q*	*Product R*
Sales	$4.80 per unit	$6.30 per unit	$2.50 per unit
Variable costs	$3.00 per unit	$4.60 per unit	$1.50 per unit
Volume	63,000 units	45,000 units	72,000 units

Fixed costs are $300,000.

Required:

Compute the break-even point for the company in terms of P, Q, and R.

9-36   Given below is information concerning the three products sold by Cricket, Inc.

	A	*B*	*C*
Selling price (per unit)	$8	$12	$16
Variable cost (per unit)	4	9	11

The fixed costs associated with the manufacture of these three products are $84,000 per year.

Required:

a. Calculate the break-even point for the sale of A, B, and C if the sales mix is 4 units of A, 3 units of B, and 1 unit of C.

b. Prepare an income statement using variable costing if 3,600 units of the mix are sold.

9-37   Presented below is selected information from the records of Acto Co. concerning its two products, Ping and Pong.

	Ping	*Pong*
Selling price/unit	$220	$162
Variable cost/unit	$170	$124

The fixed costs associated with the manufacture of these products are $180,000.

Required:

a. Calculate the break-even point for the sale of Ping and Pong assuming the sales mix is 1 Ping and 1 Pong. Assume Acto Co. wants to achieve a profit of $84,000. What sales volume is necessary?

b. Present the income statement for the target profit of $84,000.

9-38   The following data relate to a year's budgeted activity for Rickuse Limited, a company manufacturing a single product:

Units

Beginning inventory..............................	30,000
Production	120,000
Available for sale................................	150,000
Sales...	110,000
Ending inventory................................	40,000

Per Unit

Selling price.....................................	$5.00
Variable manufacturing costs......................	$1.00
Variable selling, general and administrative expenses......................................	$2.00
Fixed manufacturing cots (based on 100,000 units)......	$0.25
Fixed selling, general and administrative expenses (based on 100,000 units).................	$0.65

Total fixed costs and expenses remain unchanged within the relevant range of 25,000 units to a total capacity of 160,000 units.

Required:

Calculate the following:

a.   The projected annual break-even sales in units.
b.   The projected net income for the year under direct (variable) costing.
c.   On the assumption that all variances are charged to cost of goods sold, the company's net income for the year under absorption (full) costing.
d.   The price per unit that should be charged for a special order for 10,000 units (to be sold in an unrelated market) in order to increase the company's net income by $5,000.

(SMA, adapted)

9-39   The Martell Company has recently established operations in a very competitive market. Management has been very aggressive in its attempt to establish a market share.

The price of their product was set at $5 per unit, well below the major competition selling price. Variable costs were $4.50 per unit and total fixed costs were $600,000 during the first year.

Required:

a.   Assume the firm was able to sell 1,000,000 units in the first year. What was the profit (loss) for the year?
b.   Assume that variable per unit and total fixed costs do not increase in the second year. Management has been sucessful in establishing its position in the market. What price must be set to achieve a profit of $25,000? Assume output cannot be increased over the first year level.

(SMA, adapted)

9-40   During the peak of last summer's construction period, Trevor Ritchie, the owner/manager of Ritchie Construction Ltd., had prepared the following bid on the construction of a new house for a local merchant:

Materials...................................	$ 36,000
Labour (5,200 hrs. @ $8/hr.).....................	41,600
Overhead ($5 per labour hr.)......................	26,000
Full cost......................................	$103,600
Profit margin @ 20%............................	20,720
Bid price.....................................	$124,320

The overhead charge reflects all overhead costs, including general and administrative expense, and was based on an estimate of $750,000 of overhead for the year related to an estimate of 150,000 labour hours. It was estimated that approximately $450,000 of the overhead costs would not vary with the level of expected activity in the short run.

The local merchant rejected the bid as too high and deferred purchase of a new house.

By November, construction had slowed to the point where Ritchie needed more work in order to avoid laying-off "hard-to-get" tradesmen. He was now willing to cut his margin significantly in order to obtain additional business, therefore, he contacted the merchant and offered him a new bid of $114,000 for constructing the house. The merchant replied with a counter-offer to have the house built for $100,000, much to Mr. Ritchie's disgust!

Mr. Ritchie's son (and understudy) counselled his father not to reject the bid without a little more pencil work because under the concept of the contribution approach to pricing, it might still be wise to accept the counter-offer, under the present circumstances.

Required:

a. What would be the dollar effect, on net income before taxes, of accepting the counter-offer of $100,000?
b. In general, what are the advantages and disadvantages of utilizing the contribution margin approach to pricing?

(SMA, adapted)

9-41 The management of Alvas Limited is concerned with the adequacy of the company's accounting reports, which are presently prepared on the basis of standard absorption (full) costing. It has been suggested that these reports would be more meaningful were they prepared on the basis of standard direct (variable) costing.

Income statements prepared under the present system for the past three months follow:

Alvas Limited
Income Statements
For the Months of

	October	November	December
Sales	$1,105,000	$975,000	$700,000
Cost of goods sold	699,000	669,000	491,000
Gross margin on sales	$ 406,000	$306,000	$209,000
Selling and administrative expenses	152,100	149,500	144,000
Net income before provision for income taxes	$ 253,900	$156,500	$ 65,000

During each of the three months, the following unfavourable standard cost variances have been charged to cost of goods sold:

	October	November	December
Fixed overhead denominator (volume)	$ 29,000	$ 80,000	$ 90,000
Other	7,000	4,000	(19,000)
	$ 36,000	$ 84,000	$ 71,000

Inventory on October 1, consisting of 10,000 units at standard absorption (full) cost, is broken-down by cost elements as follows:

Direct material......................	$0.65	
Direct labour......................	1.20	
Overhead — fixed................	1.00	
— variable.............	0.15	
10,000 ×........................	$3.00	$30,000

Normal production is 260,000 units per month. Selling and general expenses during the three months—which accorded with the budget—were set at $0.60 per unit, of which $0.50 was fixed.

Required:

a. Prepare monthly income statements for each of the three months on a direct (variable) costing basis.

b. Prepare a reconciliation explaining the reported monthly income amounts determined in (a) with those reported above under absorption (full) costing.

c. Compute the number of units which must be sold for the company to earn $364,000, before provision for income taxes.

d. State and explain two disadvantages of using direct (variable) costing.

(SMA, adapted)

9-42   The Speedy Company provides you the following data for the latest operating year:

Sales...	$500,000
Direct labour....................................	117,500
Gross profit.....................................	180,000

Inventories	April 1, 19x5	March 31 19x6
Direct materials................................	$ 9,058	$12,000
Work-in-process................................	Nil	Nil
Finished goods................................	16,520	16,520
Total contribution margin........................	$220,000	
Direct material purchases........................	132,942	
Variable manufacturing overhead....................	22,500	
Break-even point, in sales dollars....................	250,000	
Volume variance, favourable (deducted from cost of sales......................	10,000	

Required:

Provide the following amounts (show your calculations):

a. Direct materials used

b.   Total variable selling and administrative expense
c.   Cost of goods manufactured
d.   Total fixed manufacturing overhead
e.   Total fixed selling and administrative expense
f.   Net income or loss

(SMA, adapted)

9-43   A firm has an assured market for any quantities of two products which are processed on one machine and then finished by hand. The products are not complementary and may be produced independently in varying quantities. Planned output is 1,200 units per week of each product, a combination chosen because it fully utilizes the machine and labour capacities.

Machine capacity is 2,400 units per week of either product or a combination of the two; no time is lost in changing over from one product to the other. Machine operators' wages are included in fixed overhead. Finishing labour supply is limited to 4,800 direct hours per week. Finishing labour is a fixed cost in the short run, as no other work is available if machine output is delayed for any reason. Standard product costs are as follows:

	A	B
Materials	$ 2	$ 2
Finishing labour @ $3 per hour.........	9	3
Fixed overhead @ ⅓ labour cost........	3	1
Standard cost......................	$14	$ 6
Standard profit....................	2	2
Selling price......................	$16	$ 8

Required:

a.   Calculate the optimum production mix.
b.   Last week, the factory manager scheduled production of only 1,000 units of each product, as he wanted to overhaul the machine, reducing available machine capacity to 2,000 units. As a result, the finishing staff was idle for most of one day while the operators carried out the overhaul.

   i.   How many units of each product should have been scheduled to keep the finishing staff occupied (as well as utilizing the available machine capacity) and, on this basis, how much should the overhaul have cost in terms of lower profit?

   ii.   How much profit was lost by the wrong production decision during the overhaul week?

(SMA, adapted)

9-44   The income statement for Francis Company Ltd. for the month of May, 19x0 reads as follows:

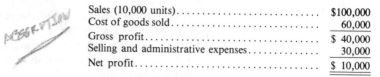

Sales (10,000 units).............................	$100,000
Cost of goods sold.............................	60,000
Gross profit....................................	$ 40,000
Selling and administrative expenses.............	30,000
Net profit.....................................	$ 10,000

The following additional information is obtained:

1. The cost of goods sold is computed according to standard cost:

    — Variable costs (raw materials, direct labour,
        manufacturing overhead)...................... $ 2 per unit
    — Fixed manufacturing costs ($40,000 per month)
        Standard volume is 10,000 units per month....... $ 4 per unit
    — Standard cost................................. $ 6 per unit

2. Selling and administrative expenses are fixed.
3. All production variances are charged to the cost of goods sold in the
    month in which they occur.

Required:

Solve each of the following independently.

a. Prepare a budgeted income statement for the month of June, 19x0
    based on a sales and production volume of 8,000 units. All other
    data are identical to those of May, 19x0. Indicate the amount of fix-
    ed costs and gross profit.

b. Compute the amount of sales (in units and dollars) at the break-even
    point:

    i.   according to the budget forecast for the month of June, 19x0.
    ii.   assuming that fixed costs for June will be reduced by $15,000.

c. The following additional data are obtained:

	Units
Finished goods inventory, May 1, 19x0.............	5,000
May production...............................	10,000
Finished goods inventory, May 31, 19x0...........	5,000
June production..............................	8,000
June sales...................................	12,000
Finished goods inventory, June 30, 19x0...........	1,000

    Entries affecting inventories and cost of goods sold are made at the
    standard cost of $6 per unit (full absorption costing). The income
    statement for the month of May is given above; with the exception of
    the sales volume and production volume, all data were the same for
    June. Since the net profit for May was $10,000, management asks
    you why profits did not increase in spite of the growth in sales.

i. Prepare an income statement, using standard absorption costing, for the month of June.
ii. Name and illustrate a method which would more clearly bring out the effect of sales volume on profits.

(SMA, adapted)

9-45   The L&J Company makes the following data available for 19x5:

	Budget	*Actual* Results
Sales in units:		
Product L........................	45,000	46,000
Product J........................	66,000	65,000
Total Units.....................	111,000	111,000
Sales	$432,900	$430,680
Cost of sales:		
Variable	$206,460	$207,000
Fixed...........................	111,000	111,570
	$317,460	$318,570
Gross profit......................	$115,440	$112,110
Selling and administrative expenses:		
Variable	$ 18,540	$ 20,210
Fixed...........................	9,000	9,100
	$ 27,540	$ 29,310
Net income before taxes..............	$ 87,900	$ 82,800

Required:

a. *Using only the budget data for 19x5* draw a break-even chart for total company sales on the graph paper. Indicated the following areas, lines or points clearly on your chart.

  i.   Net loss area
  ii. Net income area
  iii. Break-even point
  iv. Total variable expenses
  v.   Total fixed expenses
  vi. Total contribution margin

b. Assuming break-even sales were $341,991 [*not* the correct answer for part (a)], compute the margin of safety ratio on budgeted sales.
c. List 6 basic assumptions which underlie cost-volume-profit analysis.
d. Compute the sales mix variance and the quantity variance for 19x5 actual gross profit using budgeted average gross profit as a base.

(SMA, adapted)

9-46   The Wencam Company Ltd. produced and sold 55,000 units during 19x1. The following amounts were obtained from the financial statements for the year ended December 31, 19x1:

Sales	$2,475,000
Direct materials used	467,500
Direct labour costs	805,750
Variable overhead incurred	269,500
Fixed overhead incurred*	347,600
Selling and administrative costs:	
Fixed*	187,200
Variable	129,500

*The relevant range for fixed costs is 10,000 units to 85,000 units.

Expectations for 19x2:

1.   Variable and fixed costs are expected to behave in the same manner as indicated above, but inflation is expected to increase costs in general by 12 percent.
2.   The selling price is expected to be raised by 10 percent.
3.   The company's 19x2 income tax rate is expected to be 35 percent.

Required:

How many units would the company be required to sell in 19x2 in order to earn *net income after taxes* of $211,250? Show all calculations.

(SMA, adapted)

9-47   The condensed income statement of M Ltd., for the month of March, 19x7, is as follows:

Sales (10,000 units)	$100,000
Cost of goods sold	60,000
Gross margin	$ 40,000
Selling and administrative expenses	30,000
Net income	$ 10,000

The following additional information is provided:

1.   Cost of goods sold is calculated at standard cost:

Variable costs (material, labour and overhead)	$2	per unit
Fixed manufacturing costs ($40,000 per month),		
standard volume 10,000 units per month	4	per unit
Standard cost	$6	per unit

2.   Selling and administrative expenses are fixed.

Required:

1.   Prepare a budgeted income statement for April, 19x7 based on sales and production volume of 8,000 units. All other conditions are the same as for March. Show the amount of fixed costs and marginal income.

2.   Compute the break-even dollar volume of sales:

   a.   Budgeted for April, 19x7.
   b.   On assumption that April fixed costs will be reduced by $10,000.

3.   The following additional facts are given:

Finished goods inventory, March 1, 19x7	5,000 units
Production during March	10,000 units
Finished goods inventory, March 31, 19x7	5,000 units
Production during April	8,000 units
Sales during April	12,000 units
Finished goods inventory, April 30, 19x7	1,000 units

   Inventories and cost of goods sold are charged and credited at standard cost of $6 per unit (i.e., using absorption costing). The income statement for March has been given above. With the exception of production and sales volume, all conditions were the same during April. The net income for April is $10,000 and management has asked CA why profits failed to increase when sales were higher in April than they were in March.

   a.   Prepare a statement to explain what has happened.
   b.   How might the company change its accounting procedures to prepare income statements which more clearly reflect the effect of sales volume on profits?

(CA, adapted)

Chapter 10

LEARNING OBJECTIVES

Chapter 10 examines short-range planning and provides a comprehensive example of the budgeting process. Studying this chapter should enable you to:

1. Describe the general budgeting process.
2. Identify and discuss the primary benefits of the budgeting process.
3. Prepare operating and performance budgets and the associated schedules when given the necessary data.
4. Prepare the budgeted income statement that is the final product of the operating and performance budgeting process.
5. Develop the background for the study of the financial and resource budgets presented in Chapter 11.

Short-Range Planning

SHORT-RANGE planning, also referred to as budgeting or profit planning, is a measure of management's financial expectations for the near future, usually the coming year. Often, plans are made on a month-by-month basis. The short-range period is normally considered to be that period in which the firm faces constraining factors. Constraining factors are those factors which cannot be significantly altered in the short-run, such as capacity of equipment, number of employees, or demand for products.

All except perhaps the smallest of firms engage in some type of short-range planning. At a minimum, some analysis of projected cash flows must be considered in order to assure management that the firm will be able to meet its cash requirements during the coming period. If the plans are formalized, then these plans are usually referred to as budgets.

LONG-RANGE VERSUS SHORT-RANGE PLANNING

Long-range planning is also referred to as budgeting. The longer time period involved, however, means that plans developed for the distant future are less reliable and cannot be prepared in as much detail as plans developed for the near future. At the extreme, long-range plans can be considered goals that the firm would like to achieve or attain in the future. Goals are expressed in very general descriptive terms, such as the goal or objective to be the largest firm or the best quality producer in the industry. Intermediate-range plans are considered objectives the firm is striving to achieve in the next three to five years. Examples of intermediate objectives include increasing sales volume, increasing the asset base, and expanding product lines in the next five years.

329

Most short-range budgets must provide sufficient detail to allow day-to-day functioning at operational levels. Generally, the significant planning decisions are made and the formalized plans are prepared on a segment-by-segment basis for a firm. Examples of segments include divisions, product lines, and sales territories. Management participation is an integral part of the successful budgeting process. The management personnel in each segment should be involved in determining budget inputs, and, in return, these individuals should be held responsible for any variances that occur between actual and budgeted performances.

A NORMAL APPROACH TO BUDGET PREPARATION

In large firms, short-range budgeting normally begins with lower management and then progresses upward to the upper levels of management. The managers of the planning segments aid in the preparation of their segment's budget for the next operating period. If the budgeted operating period coincides with the calendar year, then a meeting is usually held late in the year, perhaps in October or November, to formalize the budgets for each segment in the organization and for the entire organization. The actual budget preparation, however, generally begins much earlier, normally in June or July. Top management of the firm, or a formal budget committee composed of selected top managers, receives the proposed budgets for the individual segments and for the total firm. Both the segment plans and the overall plans are reworked in order to provide a realistic and acceptable budget such that each segment of the company and the firm as a whole has operational plans on a month-by-month basis. The annual budget for the entire firm is then submitted to the board of directors for their approval or rejection.

The annual budget is not the end of the planning process. For budgeting purposes, the best information available must be used to constantly revise and update the annual budget. A new budget is prepared by each planning segment for the up-coming month before the current month is over. This revised monthly budget takes into account the additional information that has become available since the formulation of the annual budget.

BENEFITS OF SHORT-RANGE PLANNING

The general benefits of short-range planning in any firm include:

1. Communication and coordination.
2. Before-the-fact control.
3. A basis for after-the-fact control and performance evaluation.
4. Identification of weak areas in the firm.
5. Management motivation.

These are described in the sections which follow.

Communication and Coordination

Profit planning enables a manager to identify the overall short-range plans of the firm and how his or her managerial area fits into this plan. Profit planning also enables a manager to realize before-the-fact what is expected of him and his division.

The efforts of the functional areas of the business are coordinated by planning. For example, a sales forecast is an important consideration in planning production schedules. Advertising campaigns and salesmen's efforts must be coordinated to be fully effective. Raw material purchases must reflect production demand. Short-range financial plans are made in conjunction with projected cash flows.

If the managers of all areas of the business operated independently without a coordinated plan, then each manager would act according to his individual perceptions of the best interests of his department and the firm. The production manager might plan long production runs in order to minimize costs. The purchasing manager would order the largest possible quantities in order to maximize the available discounts. The inventory control manager would minimize inventories in order to reduce the funds committed to inventory and the carrying costs of the inventory. Sales managers would maintain large quantities of finished goods inventories on hand to provide the best possible customer service. To the individual manager, each of these strategies would appear to be in the best interests of the firm. Without studied coordination and assessment of the interaction of the various individual plans and strategies, however, it is possible for any one individual strategy to be counterproductive when considered in light of the firm's overall objectives.

Before-the-Fact Control

The communication and coordination which result from the budgeting process introduce an element of continuous before-the-fact control. Every manager knows what is expected of him in terms of performance in a given budgeting period. The manager then supervises his division and its employees to meet the budgeted goals in the most effective and efficient manner.

In developing budgets, managers must establish and justify a need for resources. This formalization of the segment's needs serves as a control factor in the planning function. Using this method, operating and financial constraints of the firm become obvious to each manager.

A Basis for After-the-Fact Control and Performance Evaluation

Because the budgeting process serves as a basis for measuring a manager's performance, each manager knows that he will be judged by his ability to satisfy the goals of his department budget. Any variations from the budget are analyzed after the performance takes place. If the planning and budgeting process does not take place, control after-the-fact is almost non-existent because of the difficulty in determining what performance should have been attained by a given manager.

Identification of Weak Areas of the Firm

Through formal planning, weak segments of the firm can be identified. Potential operating and financial factors such as an unsatisfactory contribution margin in a segment, a production bottleneck, a poor sales mix, excessive inventories or accounts receivable, and insufficient cash flows can be readily identified. Any imbalance between segments of the firm becomes apparent in the planning process.

Motivation for Management

When lower-level management is involved in the budgeting process, these managers become directly involved with the goals, objectives, problems, and policies of the firm. The budgeting process assists in identifying the importance of a manager's job in the overall performance of the firm. Coordinated action of all employees toward achieving the firm's goals becomes a major objective of the individual managers. Because the goals of each segment have been established in conjunction with the overall goals and policies of the firm through the coordinating aspects of budgeting, the manager's own self-interests should be served by acting in the best interest of the firm.

GENERAL COMPREHENSIVE BUDGETING RELATIONSHIPS

The concept of comprehensive budgeting covers the entire area of planning, control and performance evaluation. Illustration 10–1 presents the skeletal relationships of the general types of budgets. This illustration should be viewed as the "tip of an iceberg," in that more specific budgets and special budgets are prepared for management at all levels using the general budgets as guidelines. Budgets should be sufficiently detailed and specialized to provide plans for the day-to-day operations at the lowest level of management.

Illustration 10–1 identifies the major budget categories, their interrelationships and their ultimate articulation into pro-forma or projected financial statements. All budgets except those involving long-range sales

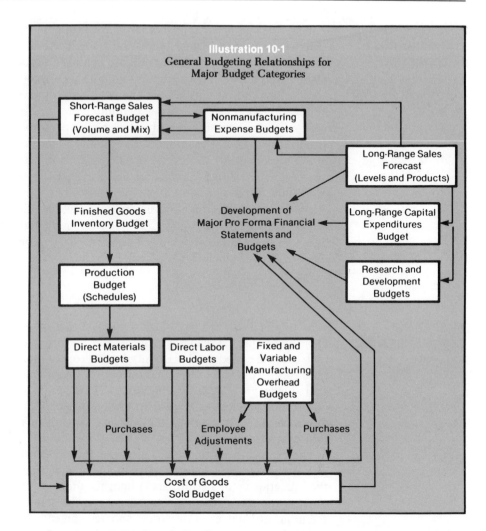

Illustration 10-1
General Budgeting Relationships for
Major Budget Categories

forecasts, research and development expenditures, and long-range capital expenditures are covered in this chapter. Long-range capital budgeting is discussed in Chapter 15.

The major budgets and pro-forma financial statements developed in this text are:

see p 345

1. Budgeted cost of goods manufactured statement
2. Budgeted cost of goods sold statement
3. Budgeted income statement
4. Cash budget
5. Budgeted shareholders' equity statement
6. Budgeted balance sheet

ROLE OF STANDARD COSTS IN BUDGETING

If established attainable standards are available, these standards can serve as the basis for developing the budget. Attainable standards are useful in budget development because standard costs define a series of relationships among various inputs and outputs of production. Once these relationships are established via the standard cost system, sales and/or production forecasts can be expanded into more detailed budgets through the application of the established relationships between the input and output measures. For example, if the standard labor cost for making one unit of a product is two direct labor hours at $4 per hour, then this input measure of two direct labor hours at $4 is equal to the output measure of one unit of product (in terms of a direct labor input measure.) If 500 units of the product are forecast for production, direct labor costs of $4,000 (500 units $\times$ 2 hours $\times$ $4) can be budgeted for that product. Since the standard cost for direct labor is $8 per unit of product, the budgeted direct labor cost is $4,000.

BUDGETING: A COMPREHENSIVE EXAMPLE

In July of 19x0, Sax's president requested that the Power Turbine Shaft Division establish a planning, control and performance evaluation system that could be used in the Division's 19x1 operations. The president requested that the variable costing format for measuring income be used for short-range profit planning purposes. The Division's financial staff was given until November 1, 19x0 to establish a planning system and until December 1, 19x0 to submit the Division's month-by-month plans for the first quarter of 19x1.

The finance department analyzed the Power Turbine Shaft Division's operations and established forecasts and management policies for both the operational (or performance) budgets and the financial (or resource) budgets for 19x1. Management considered the standard costs for manufacturing attainable and realistic and recommended that these costs be used wherever possible in the budgeting process. The management policies and forecasts are separated into two categories: (1) those policies and forecasts which primarily affect the operating budgets and (2) those policies and forecasts which primarily affect the financial budgets. As the operating and financial budgets are fundamentally related, this segregation of policies and forecasts is not strict.

Eighteen management policies and forecasts established by Sax Company are listed. The first six policies are related to income statement items and therefore primarily affect the operating budget. The policies and forecasts numbered seven through eighteen are concerned with various balance sheet accounts and, as such, primarily affect the financial budget. The projected balance sheet for December 31, 19x0 for the Power

Turbine Shaft Division is presented in Illustration 10-2. The beginning balances in the permanent accounts are necessary for financial planning for the first quarter of 19x1.

Income taxes are not considered in the budgeting process for the Power Turbine Shaft Division, as all income tax budgeting is handled by corporate headquarters.

Illustration 10-2
Sax Company
Power Turbine Shaft Division
Projected Balance Sheet as of December 31, 19x0

Assets		*Liabilities and Shareholders' Equity*	
Current Assets:		Current Liabilities:	
Cash	$ 40,000	Accounts Payable	$ 60,000
Accounts Receivable	424,400	Wages Payable	18,000
Direct Materials Inventories:		Total Current	
Steel Billets @ Standard . .	96,000	Liabilities	$ 78,000
Ball Bearings @ Standard .	48,000		
Indirect Materials and			
Supplies	30,000		
Work-In-Process @ Standard			
Variable Cost	300,000		
Finished Goods @ Standard		Long-Term Liabilities:	
Variable Cost	249,600		
Total Current Assets	$1,188,000	Long-Term Debt	1,200,000
		Total Liabilities	$1,278,000
Long-Term Assets:			
Equipment . . . . $ 600,000			
Less: Accumulated			
Depreciation . 60,000			
Net: Equipment $ 540,000		Shareholders' Equity:	
Plant $3,000,000			
Less: Accumulated		Shareholders'	
Depreciation . 150,000		Investment	3,300,000
Net: Plant	2,850,000	Total Liabilities	
Total Long-Term Assets . . .	$3,390,000	and Shareholders'	
Total Assets	$4,578,000	Equity	$4,578,000

Management Policies and Forecasts Affecting the Operating Budget

1. The standard sales price of $50 per power turbine shaft should be maintained during 19x1. New competition has not entered the market, and is unlikely to do so during 19x1. A projected sales forecast, in units, will be developed by the sales manager of the division.

2. The standard variable production cost of $10.40 from Illustration 8-2 will be used for planning purposes. For convenience, the pertinent standards from Illustration 8-2 are presented again in Illustration 10-3.

3. Variable selling costs were $5 per unit sold in 19x0; no change is expected.

4. Fixed manufacturing overhead costs are budgeted at $360,000. These costs are incurred uniformly throughout the year at a rate of $30,000 per month. An individual cost breakdown will be presented in a separate budget. Depreciation is a non-cash expense. (See Policy and Forecast items 13 and 14.)

5. Fixed selling and administrative expenses will be budgeted at $2,004,000 in 19x1.

6. Annual interest expense on long-term debt is $132,000, payable in equal monthly payments of $11,000. (See item 17.)

Illustration 10-3
Sax Company
Power Turbine Shaft Division

Summary of Standard Variable Manufacturing
Costs Per Unit of Production

Materials @ Standard
1 Steel Billet	$ 4.00
2 Ball Bearings	2.00
Direct Labor @ Standard ½ Hour @ $6.00 per hour	3.00
Variable Manufacturing Overhead @ Standard °	1.40
	$10.40

° Basis of application to product is standard direct labor hours. Application rate is $2.80 per standard direct labor hour.

Management Policies and Forecasts Affecting the Financial Budget

7. A minimum cash balance of $40,000 is necessary in order to provide sufficient cash to support day-to-day operations. If the Division needs to borrow cash to maintain the $40,000 balance, it can be borrowed from corporate headquarters. Cash must be borrowed and repaid in $5,000 increments.

8. All sales are made by the sales force on a credit basis. Sax Company provides customers with credit terms of net/30. Customers normally pay within 30 days and bad debts are rare.

9. There should always be sufficient direct (raw) materials on hand to meet the production demands for the next two month period.

10. Indirect materials and supplies inventory should be maintained at a level of $30,000. This inventory account will be replenished monthly to maintain a level of $30,000.

11. The work-in-process inventory should be maintained at a balance of approximately $300,000.

12. The finished goods inventory should be maintained at a level sufficient to meet the next two months' demand for power turbine shafts.

13. The original cost of the equipment in the Power Turbine Shaft Division was $600,000. The equipment has an estimated life of 10 years with no salvage value anticipated. Sax Company uses the straight-line method of depreciation. The equipment was purchased on January 1, 19x0. Depreciation expense for equipment will be $5,000 per month in 19x1.

14. The original cost of the plant was $3,000,000. The estimated life of the plant is 20 years. No salvage value is anticipated. As is the case with the equipment, straight-line depreciation will be used in depreciating the plant. The plant was purchased on January 1, 19x0. Depreciation expense will be $12,500 per month in 19x1.

15. Accounts payable represent credit purchases of direct materials on net/30 terms. Accounts payable are paid on time, but never sooner than necessary. Therefore, payments lag behind actual purchases by 30 days.

16. Wages payable are stabilized at approximately $18,000, because Sax's policy is to hold the first two weeks pay earned by each employee. Wages are paid on the fifteenth and on the last business day of each month.

17. A long-term debt of $1,200,000 is outstanding. Interest payments of $11,000 are made monthly. Principal payments of $30,000 per quarter will be made on the loan for 10 years. The initial principal payment will be made on March 31, 19x1.

18. Sax Company has an investment of $3,300,000 that is traceable to the Power Turbine Shaft Division. This represents the shareholders' equity (corporate investment) in the Division.

DEVELOPMENT OF THE MAJOR OPERATING AND PERFORMANCE BUDGETS
Sales Budget (Budget #1)

The sales budget is usually the starting point for short-range profit planning. If the sales projections are inaccurate, all subsequent budgets will be unreliable because these budgets are based, either directly or indirectly, on the sales budgets.

Sales forecasting is an art that relies upon both external and internal information gathered by the marketing or the sales department of the firm. External information sources such as industry periodicals, trade journals, analyses of general economic conditions, and marketing surveys can be used to aid in the development of a sales forecast. Information available internally, such as the firm's past performance and salesmen's estimates, can assist in projecting sales. Sales management assimilates and assesses all available information regarding sales projections, and then uses this information and their professional judgment to establish a reliable sales forecast.

The management of Sax Company requires a monthly sales forecast for the first quarter of 19x1 and for the months of April and May. Forecasts for April and May are necessary to plan the ending inventories for the first quarter of 19x1 in accordance with management's policies. (See items 9-12 in Management Policies and Forecasts.)

The sales manager reviewed the pertinent estimates of industry demand and the Power Turbine Shaft Division's position in the industry. Each salesperson developed a sales forecast for his or her territory by key (large) customers and in the aggregate for small customers. The sales manager also examined the sales volume for the last three years and checked trends and monthly fluctuations. With the assistance and approval of the other key managers in the Division, the sales manager prepared the following sales budget.

Budget #1
Sales Budget
(January-May, 19x1)

Month	Units	Dollars
January	12,000	$ 600,000
February	12,000	600,000
March	17,000	850,000
Total First Quarter Sales Forecast	41,000	$2,050,000
April	20,000	$1,000,000
May	20,000	1,000,000

Finished Goods Inventory Budget and Production Budget (Budgets #2 and #3)

The production budget is prepared after the sales budget has been finalized. Finished goods inventory serves as the buffer between the level of sales and the level of production. Most firms prefer to maintain a reasonably stable level of production even when faced with fluctuating product demand. Fluctuating production volume causes obvious problems in scheduling and cost control and adversely affects employee morale due to overtime or temporary layoffs.

Most firms maintain some minimum level of finished goods inventory in order to provide satisfactory customer service. There is also a maximum level of inventory that most firms will not exceed because of the cost of carrying inventory, the capital committed to the inventory, and the fear of inventory obsolescence or possible spoilage.

The Power Turbine Shaft Division has a management policy (Item 12 in Management Policies and Forecasts) requiring that the ending finished goods inventory balance be maintained at a level sufficient to meet the next two months' anticipated sales demands. The finished goods inventory balance expected on December 31, 19x0 is 24,000 units. (Illustration 10-2 shows finished goods inventory at standard cost of $249,600 or 24,000 units.) This quantity of finished goods inventory is sufficient to meet the forecasted January 19x1 sales of 12,000 units and February sales of 12,000 units. At the end of January 19x1, the finished goods inventory should be at a level of 29,000 units, which will meet the forecasted sales for February 19x1 (12,000 units) and March 19x1 (17,000 units). The finished goods inventory budget, Budget #2, for the Power Turbine Shaft Division quantifies management's finished goods inventory policy. The sales budget, Budget #1, is the basis used to establish ending finished goods inventory balances.

Budget #2
Finished Goods Budget
(1st Quarter, 19x1)

Date	Units	Dollars at Standard Variable Cost of $10.40
January 1	24,000	$249,600
January 31	29,000	301,600
February 28	37,000	384,800
March 31	40,000	416,000

The production budget is based upon this fundamental accounting inventory relationship: beginning finished goods inventory plus the cost of goods manufactured less the cost of goods sold is equal to the ending inventory of finished goods. After completing the sales budget and the finished goods budget, production requirements (Budget #3) can be calculated to comply with the specified inventory and sales figures.

Budget #3
Production Budget in Units
(1st Quarter, 19x1)

	January	February	March	Quarter Total
Sales (Budget #1)	12,000	12,000	17,000	41,000
Desired Ending Finished Goods Inventory (Budget #2)	29,000	37,000	40,000	40,000
Total	41,000	49,000	57,000	81,000
Less: Beginning Finished Goods Inventory (Budget #2)	24,000	29,000	37,000	24,000
Production Requirements	17,000	20,000	20,000	57,000

Direct Materials Requirements and Purchase Budgets (Budgets #4, #5, and #6)

Once the production budget is prepared, the raw materials budget and the raw materials purchases budget can be developed. The amount of raw materials necessary depends upon both the ending raw materials inventory requirements established by management and the production requirements established in the production budget. Item 9 of the Management Policies and Forecasts requires that the Power Turbine Shaft Division maintain a level of raw materials inventories at the end of each month that is sufficient to meet the next two months' production demands. Management decided that the standard usage and costs of one steel billet at $4 and two ball bearings at $1 each (from Illustration 10-3) were realistic and attainable. The December 31, 19x0 direct (raw) materials inventory from Illustration 10-2 is 24,000 steel billets ($96,000/$4) and 48,000 ball bearings ($48,000/$1). The desired ending raw materials inventories for March 31, 19x1 are large enough to provide for the budgeted April production of 13,000 units and the budgeted May production of 10,000 units as per item 9.

The preparation of the direct materials purchases budget (Budget #5) requires converting the estimated monthly unit purchases of raw materials into a budget expressed in terms of dollars. The monthly purchase requirements are developed in Budget #4 in units. The direct material purchases budget (Budget #5) is then prepared in terms of dollars. The costs or purchase prices assigned to the purchase requirements in Budget #5 are the standard costs for raw materials found in Illustration 10-3. Management believes that the standard costs are the best estimate of the purchase prices that the Power Turbine Shaft Division will have to pay for direct materials. The standard cost of steel billets is $4 and the standard cost of ball bearings is $1.

Budget #4
Direct Materials Requirements Budget (in Units)
(1st Quarter, 19x1)

Steel Billets (One per Finished Unit)

	January	February	March	Quarter Total
Production Requirements (Budget #3)	17,000	20,000	20,000	57,000
Desired Ending Direct Materials Inventory	40,000	33,000	23,000	23,000
Total	57,000	53,000	43,000	80,000
Less: Beginning Direct Materials Inventory	24,000	40,000	33,000	24,000
Purchase Requirements	33,000	13,000	10,000	56,000

Ball Bearings (Two per Finished Unit)

	January	February	March	Quarter Total
Production Requirements (Budget #3)	34,000	40,000	40,000	114,000
Desired Ending Direct Materials Inventory	80,000	66,000	46,000	46,000
Total	114,000	106,000	86,000	160,000
Less: Beginning Direct Materials Inventory	48,000	80,000	66,000	48,000
Purchase Requirements	66,000	26,000	20,000	112,000

The direct materials usage budget (Budget #6) can be prepared at this point, or it can be included as part of the cost of goods manufactured budget (Budget #12). The direct materials usage budget can be prepared using the relationships inherent in the accounting inventory equation: beginning raw materials inventory plus purchases less the amount transferred to work-in-process equals the ending raw materials inventory. An alternative method is to convert the production requirements from the direct materials requirements budget (Budget #4) into dollars. The direct materials usage budget (Budget #5) converts the unit production requirements from Budget #4 into dollars.

Direct Labor Budget (Budget #7)

For the direct labor budget, the Power Turbine Shaft Division uses the standard time of one-half hour per power turbine shaft and a standard direct labor cost of $6 per hour (Illustration 10-3). The production schedule, Budget #3, is the basis for developing the direct labor budget (Budget #7).

Budget #5
Direct Materials Purchases Budget
(1st Quarter, 19x1)

Steel Billets

	January	*February*	*March*	*Quarter Total*
Purchase Requirements (Budget #4)	33,000	13,000	10,000	56,000
Standard Cost per Unit (Illustration 10–3)	$ 4.00	$ 4.00	$ 4.00	$ 4.00
Total Billet Purchases	$132,000	$52,000	$40,000	$224,000

Ball Bearings

	January	*February*	*March*	*Quarter Total*
Purchase Requirements (Budget #4)	66,000	26,000	20,000	112,000
Standard Cost per Unit (Illustration 10–3)	$ 1.00	$ 1.00	$ 1.00	$ 1.00
Total Ball Bearing Purchases . .	$ 66,000	$26,000	$20,000	$112,000
Total Direct Material Purchases	$198,000	$78,000	$60,000	$336,000

Budget #6
Direct Materials Usage Budget
(1st Quarter, 19x1)

Steel Billets

	January	*February*	*March*	*Quarter Total*
Production Requirements (Budget #4)	17,000	20,000	20,000	57,000
Standard Cost per Unit (Illustration 10–3)	$ 4.00	$ 4.00	$ 4.00	$ 4.00
Total Usage	$68,000	$80,000	$80,000	$228,000

Ball Bearings

	January	*February*	*March*	*Quarter Total*
Production Requirements (Budget #4)	34,000	40,000	40,000	114,000
Standard Cost per Unit (Illustration 10–3)	$ 1.00	$ 1.00	$ 1.00	$ 1.00
Total Usage	$34,000	$40,000	$40,000	$114,000

Budget #7
Direct Labor Budget
(1st Quarter, 19x1)

	January	February	March	Quarter Total
Production Requirements—Units (Budget #3)	17,000	20,000	20,000	57,000
Direct Labor per Unit in Hours	.5	.5	.5	.5
Direct Labor Requirements in Hours	8,500	10,000	10,000	28,500
Direct Labor Cost per Hour	$ 6.00	$ 6.00	$ 6.00	$ 6.00
	$51,000	$60,000	$60,000	$171,000

Manufacturing Overhead Budgets (Budgets #8 and #9)

Standard costs for manufacturing overhead, which were computed in Illustration 10-3, are used for planning purposes. The variable manufacturing overhead can be planned on the basis of units of production (Budget #3) or using direct labor hours at standard (Budget #7). The same budgeted cost will result using either basis. Since units of production are used as the basis of activity in the other production related budgets, the activity measure for the variable manufacturing overhead budget (Budget #8) will also be units of production.

The fixed manufacturing overhead costs are budgeted at $360,000 annually (item 4 in Management Policies and Forecasts). Individual items of

Budget #8
Variable Manufacturing Overhead Costs Budget
(1st Quarter, 19x1)

	January	February	March	Quarter Total
Production Requirements—Units (Budget #3)	17,000	20,000	20,000	57,000
Variable Manufacturing Overhead per Unit Produced:				
Rework Time . . . . $ .10	$ 1,700	$ 2,000	$ 2,000	$ 5,700
Waiting Time 06	1,020	1,200	1,200	3,420
Setup Time 08	1,360	1,600	1,600	4,560
Indirect Materials and Supplies 60	10,200	12,000	12,000	34,200
Indirect Labor 46	7,820	9,200	9,200	26,220
Electricity 10	1,700	2,000	2,000	5,700
Total $1.40	$23,800	$28,000	$28,000	$79,800

Budget #9
Fixed Manufacturing Overhead Costs Budget
(1st Quarter, 19x1)

	January	February	March	Quarter Total
Indirect Materials and Supplies . .	$ 750	$ 750	$ 750	$ 2,250
Indirect Labor	2,200	2,200	2,200	6,600
Electricity	2,000	2,000	2,000	6,000
Heat	800	800	800	2,400
Equipment Depreciation	5,000	5,000	5,000	15,000
Plant Depreciation	12,500	12,500	12,500	37,500
Factory Property Taxes	6,750	6,750	6,750	20,250
	$30,000	$30,000	$30,000	$90,000

the fixed overhead costs for the Division were updated to reflect current changes in costs. Management considers the breakdown of fixed manufacturing overhead costs reflected in Budget #9 to be reasonable approximations of 19x1 expenditures for overhead. Because fixed manufacturing overhead costs are linked primarily to the passage of time, management decided that an equal amount should be budgeted for each month of 19x1.

Non-Manufacturing Expense Budgets (Budgets #10 and #11)

The budgeted non-manufacturing expenses include variable selling costs of $5 per unit sold, $2,004,000 annually in fixed selling and administrative expenses, and annual interest expense on long-term debt of $132,000. These expenses were discussed in Management Policies and Forecasts, Items 3, 5, and 6, respectively. The activity basis for establishing the variable selling costs budget is the sales budget (Budget #1), because sales volume determines the amount of variable selling costs.

Over half of the fixed selling and administrative expenses budgeted are for monthly salaries. All other fixed selling and administrative expenses are also prorated into equal monthly installments for budgeting purposes, even though actual expenditures may be considerably more erratic.

DEVELOPMENT OF THE MAJOR OPERATING OR PERFORMANCE BUDGETED FINANCIAL STATEMENTS

The major operating or pro-forma budgeted financial statements can be prepared using the Management Policies and Forecasts, and Budgets #1 through #11. The major operating budgeted financial statements are the cost of goods manufactured statement, the cost of goods sold statement, and the income statement.

Budget #10
Variable Selling Costs Budget
(1st Quarter, 19x1)

	January	February	March	Quarter Total
Forecast Unit Sales (Budget #1)	12,000	12,000	17,000	41,000
Variable Selling Cost per Unit	$ 5.00	$ 5.00	$ 5.00	$ 5.00
Total Variable Selling Cost	$60,000	$60,000	$85,000	$205,000

Budget #11
Fixed Non-Manufacturing Costs Budget
(1st Quarter, 19x1)

	January	February	March	Quarter Total
Selling and Administrative Expenses:				
Salaries	$ 96,000	$ 96,000	$ 96,000	$288,000
Advertising	28,000	28,000	28,000	84,000
Office Supplies	3,000	3,000	3,000	9,000
Travel	8,500	8,500	8,500	25,500
Telephone	5,000	5,000	5,000	15,000
Insurance	1,500	1,500	1,500	4,500
Research and Development	25,000	25,000	25,000	75,000
Total Selling and Administrative Expenses . .	$167,000	$167,000	$167,000	$501,000
Interest Expense	11,000	11,000	11,000	33,000
Total Non-Manufacturing Expenses	$178,000	$178,000	$178,000	$534,000

Budgeted Cost of Goods Manufactured Statement (Budget #12)

The budgeted cost of goods manufactured statement is a projection and analysis of the changes occurring in the work-in-process account during the budgeted period. The work-in-process account at January 1, 19x1 is projected to have a balance of $300,000 (Illustration 10-2). Management expects to maintain this $300,000 balance in work-in-process throughout the year (item 11 of Management Policies and Forecasts). The variable manufacturing costs which are added to work-in-process each month can be determined from the budgets previously prepared for direct materials, direct labor, and variable manufacturing overhead. The budgeted cost of goods manufactured statement is presented in Budget #12.

Budget #12
Budgeted Cost of Goods Manufactured Statement
For the Quarter Ending March 31, 19x1

	January	February	March	Quarter Total
Beginning Work-In-Process . .	$300,000	$300,000	$300,000	$300,000
Add: Manufacturing Costs				
Direct Materials:				
Steel Billets (Budget #6)	68,000	80,000	80,000	228,000
Ball Bearings (Budget #6)	34,000	40,000	40,000	114,000
Direct Labor (Budget #7)	51,000	60,000	60,000	171,000
Variable Manufacturing				
Overhead (Budget #8)	23,800	28,000	28,000	79,800
Total Available	$476,800	$508,000	$508,000	$892,800
Less: Ending				
Work-In-Process	300,000	300,000	300,000	300,000
Cost of Goods Manufactured	$176,800	$208,000	$208,000	$592,800

Budgeted Cost of Goods Sold Statement (Budget #13)

The budgeted cost of goods sold statement is a projection and an analysis of the changes occurring in the finished goods account during the budget period. The beginning finished goods inventory is budgeted for $249,600 (Budget #2 or Illustration 10-2). The additional forecast data are taken from the budgeted cost of goods manufactured statement and the finished goods budget. The budgets are prepared on a variable costing basis; therefore, only variable costs are considered in the cost of goods sold.

Budgeted Income Statement (Budget #14)

Budget #14, the budgeted income statement, is the forecasted results of operations for the budget period using the variable costing format for income determination. Note that Budget #14 shows two contribution margins—one after variable manufacturing costs are deducted from sales revenues and one after *all* variable costs are deducted from sales revenues. This refinement of the contribution margin approach reveals the source of the various contribution margins. The contribution margin computed by deducting *all* variable costs is the contribution margin available to cover fixed costs and profits. Therefore, it is the more significant of the two contribution margins. The budgeted income statement is presented on an accrual basis, not on a cash flow basis.

Budget #13
Budgeted Variable Cost of Goods Sold Statement
(1st Quarter, 19x1)

	January	February	March	Quarter Total
Beginning Finished Goods Inventory (Budget #2) . .	$249,600	$301,600	$384,800	$249,600
Add: Budgeted Cost of Goods Manufactured (Budget #12)	176,800	208,000	208,000	592,800
Total Available	$426,400	$509,600	$592,800	$842,400
Ending Finished Goods Inventory (Budget #2) . .	301,600	384,800	416,000	416,000
Cost of Goods Sold	$124,800	$124,800	$176,800	$426,400

Budget #14
Budgeted Income Statement
For the Quarter Ending March 31, 19x1

	January	February	March	Quarter Total
Sales Revenues (Budget #1)	$600,000	$600,000	$850,000	$2,050,000
Less: Variable Cost of Goods Sold (Budget #13) . . .	124,800	124,800	176,800	426,400
Contribution Margin from Manufacturing	$475,200	$475,200	$673,200	$1,623,600
Less: Variable Selling Costs (Budget #10)	60,000	60,000	85,000	205,000
Contribution Margin	$415,200	$415,200	$588,200	$1,418,600
Less:				
Fixed Manufacturing Overhead Costs (Budget #9)	$ 30,000	$ 30,000	$ 30,000	$ 90,000
Fixed Selling and Administrative Costs (Budget #11)	167,000	167,000	167,000	501,000
Interest Expense (Budget #11)	11,000	11,000	11,000	33,000
Total Fixed Expenses	$208,000	$208,000	$208,000	$ 624,000
Budgeted Income Before Taxes	$207,200	$207,200	$380,200	$ 794,600

SUMMARY

Most firms employ some form of routine annual budgeting process resulting in segment-by-segment monthly budgets for the coming year. The process normally begins with the development of company objectives and lower management's projection of needs to meet those objectives. The budgeting process culminates in a formal integration of all divisional budgets into a corporate budget. The monthly budgets are updated at given intervals to reflect any new or additional information that may be pertinent.

Short-range planning or budgeting has several general benefits. One primary benefit is that a budget communicates the short-range plans of the firm to each manager and thereby facilitates coordination of the efforts and activities of all segments of the company. The budget process also serves as an element of *before-the-fact* control because each manager must justify his requests for resources. In addition, the budget serves as a basis for *after-the-fact* control by providing a benchmark against which actual performance can be measured. Formal budgeting can identify weak areas of the firm by pinpointing unsatisfactory contribution margins, production bottlenecks, etc. Finally, by involving various personnel in the budgeting process, the budget becomes an effective motivational tool for employees and management.

The basic end-product of the budgeting process is a set of budgeted or pro-forma financial statements. In developing these statements, a firm generally finds it necessary to produce numerous specialized budgets and schedules. The starting point in the budgeting process is generally a projection of sales in units for the budget period. Estimates are then made to determine the level of finished goods inventory and production requirements necessary to meet this anticipated demand for the product. Information from the production budget is then used to forecast direct material requirements and to prepare the purchases budget. The direct labor and manufacturing overhead budgets are also prepared based on the production budget.

The budgets for non-manufacturing expenses are completed and the major budgeted operating statements are then prepared. These statements include the budgeted cost of goods manufactured statement, the budgeted cost of goods sold statement, and the budgeted income statement. The major financial or resource budgets are presented in Chapter 11.

This chapter introduced the use of budgeting as a basis for performance evaluation. The following three chapters provide additional information regarding the reporting of performance for the segments of a firm.

KEY DEFINITIONS

Budget—formalized plans prepared by management, generally on a segment-by-segment basis, for a specified period in the near future. Budgets may be prepared for a wide range of operating and financial factors such as sales, production and manufacturing expenses. These factors are the basis for the major operating or performance and financial or resource budgeted (pro-forma) financial statements. They may be long or short-term (most firms use both).

Budgeted cost of goods manufactured statement—a projection and analysis of the changes occurring in the work-in-process account during the budget period.

Budgeted cost of goods sold statement—a projection and analysis of the changes occurring in the finished goods account during the budget period.

Budgeted income statement—the forecasted results of operations for the budget period.

Comprehensive budgeting—a system encompassing and integrating the areas of planning, control and performance evaluation for the entire company.

Intermediate-range planning—planning to achieve objectives for which the firm is striving in the next three to five years.

Long-range planning—planning for the distant future.

Major financial resource budgeted statements—cash budget, shareholders' equity or corporate investment statement, and budgeted balance sheet.

Short-range planning—also known as budgeting or profit planning, this planning consists of management's financial expectation for the near future, a period in which the firm faces factors which cannot be altered in the short-term.

QUESTIONS

10-1 What is the definition of constraining factors and how do they relate to short-range planning?

10-2 Name two specific ways in which long-range planning differs from short-range planning.

10-3 Briefly describe the normal procedure for preparing a budget.

10-4 Is the approved annual budget the end of the planning process and if not, what follows?

10-5 Two of the benefits of short-range planning are communication and co-ordination. Why are these two factors important to the firm?

10-6 How can short-range planning act as a motivator for management?

10-7 How does short-range planning yield a basis for after-the-fact control?

10-8 At what stage in the short-range budgeting process is the sales budget formulated? What external sources are used to establish a reliable sales forecast?

EXERCISES AND PROBLEMS

10-9 The Downhill Ski Company has forecasted sales in February to be 38,500 pairs of skis. The company has three areas for sales, Eastern, Central and Western. The Eastern area captures about 35% of the sales and the price is $90. The Central and Western areas sell 28% and 37%, respectively. The price is $120 in the Central and $165 in the Western areas.

Required:

Prepare a sales budget for February showing quantity and dollar sales in each area as well as a total for the company.

10-10 The Foolery Company has requested the construction of an income budget for sales of $7,200, $6,300, and $7,680. The company accountant has estimated that variable costs are 67% of sales and fixed costs are $2,400 per year.

Required:

Prepare the three budgets the Foolery Company has requested.

10-11 The Nelson Company produces two products: standard and custom. Next year the company plans to produce 4,000 units of each product. These products require the raw materials given below:

	Cost/Unit	Standard	Custom
X......................	$2.00	2 units	
Y......................	2.50	1 unit	1 unit
Z......................	1.25		3 units

Required:

Prepare a material usage budget for next year.

10-12   Given below is the beginning inventory and the desired ending inventory of raw materials for Jones, Inc.

| | Beginning | | Ending | |
Material	No. Units	Cost Per Unit	No. Units	Cost Per Unit
A...............	400	$.50	300	$.50
B...............	2,000	.40	2,000	.40
C...............	600	.90	750	.90

The company plans to produce 40,000 units of Product X and 37,500 units of Product Z. Product X requires 2 units of A, 1 unit of B, and 1 unit of C. Product Z requires 1 unit of B and 3 units of C.

Required:

Prepare a purchases budget in units and dollars for raw materials.

10-13 You have been asked to prepare a sales budget broken down by month for the first quarter of next year.

Required:

Prepare the requested sales budget from the information given below. Your answer should show the sales budget in units and dollars.

> Sales price, $10 per unit.
> Sales for December, this year, 5,000 units.
> Sales are expected to increase by 3 percent each month.

10-14 Gamma, Inc. plans to produce 25,000 units of Alpha and 29,000 units of Beta. The units go through cutting and finishing processes. Alpha requires 2 hours cutting and ¾ hour in finishing at direct labor rates of $2 and $3.50, respectively. Beta requires 1 hour in cutting and 2 hours in finishing at the same rates.

Required:

Prepare a direct labor budget for Gamma, Inc.

10-15 Rite, Inc. manufactures pencils. For next year they predict a sales volume of 25,240,000 pencils. At the present time, their finished goods inventory has 1,500,000 pencils. Rite hopes to increase this inventory by 15 percent at the end of the year. At the present time, there is no work-in-process inventory.

Required:

Prepare a production budget by units.

10-16   The sales budget of Wackie Toy Co. projects the following level of sales for the second quarter: April 20,000 units, May 22,000 units and June 19,000 units. The finished goods budget shows desired ending inventories as follows: April 30,000 units, May 35,000 units and June 25,000 units. The ending desired inventory for March was 28,000 units.

Required:

Prepare a production budget in units for the second quarter.

10-17   Vandergelder, Inc. produces hockey sticks with a standard cost of material of $1.75 per stick. The raw materials production requirements for the last quarter of 19x0 are as follows: October = 27,000 units, November = 35,000 units and December = 40,000 units. It requires $\frac{1}{10}$ hours of direct labor per stick at a cost of $3 per hour. Rework costs amount to $.05 per unit. Waiting time is zero and set-up time is $.02 per unit. Indirect materials and supplies total $.40 per unit. Indirect labor is $.15 per unit and electricity is $.08 per unit.

Required:

Prepare the direct materials usage budget, the direct labor budget, and the variable manufacturing overhead budget for the last quarter.

10-18   Lazyman, Inc., a producer of mattresses, has predicted total sales of 190,500 mattresses in 19x6. The company has three outlets for the product: the East Coast, the West Coast, and Central Canada. The mattresses sell for $180, $200, and $215, respectively. The East Coast captures 40 percent of the market with the other two areas dividing the remainder equally.

In 19x6, it took 40 kilograms of stuffing at $2.00 per kilogram and 20 meters of material at $1.50 per meter to make one mattress. Lazyman expects the cost of stuffing to go up 15 percent and the material to go up 8 percent. It takes 1½ hours of direct labour, which cost $6.50 per hour in 19x6, to make one mattress. Due to a new labour contract, labour costs per hour will rise 20 percent in 19x7. Because of improved machinery, it will only take 1¼ hours to make one mattress in 19x7. Variable costs will be applied at a rate of $4.50 per direct labour hour. This is the same rate as was used in 19x6. Fixed overhead costs are expected to be $200,000 and administrative costs to be $150,000.

At the end of 19x6, the inventory consisted of 620 finished mattresses, no work-in-process, 800 kilograms of stuffing, and 600 meters of material. They plan to increase all of their inventories except work-in-process by 30 percent at the end of 19x7. Lazyman uses Fifo and variable costing for inventory costing purposes.

Required:

a.   Production budget in units
b.   Direct material requirements budget (in units)

c.   Direct material purchase budget (in dollars)
d.   Direct material usage budget
e.   Direct labour budget
f.   Variable manufacturing overhead budget
g.   Cost of goods manufactured statement
h.   Cost of goods sold statement
i.   Income statement

10-19   The Highlight Company, a subsidiary of a large furniture manufacturer, produces and sells a single product called Sibo. The company prepares monthly income statements under the full absorption costing method. Each month the Highlight Company also prepares a budgeted income statement for the next month.

Actual results for the month of March have been prepared and are shown below:

Income Statement
For the Month of March

Sales (11,000 units @ $12).....................		$132,000
Cost of goods sold:		
Finished goods, March 1,		
4,000 units...........................	$ 31,200	
Production—13,000 units		
Material ($1.30 per unit) $16,900		
Labour ($1.70 per unit) 22,100		
Overhead ($4.80 per unit) 62,400........	101,400	
	$132,600	
Finished goods, March 31..................	46,800	
	$ 85,800	
Less: overhead over-absorption due		
to volume only........................	3,000	82,800
Gross margin...........................		$ 49,200
Selling and administrative (fixed		
and variable).........................		40,500
Profit before income taxes...................		$ 8,700

Additional Information:
—   All costs behaved normally during the month.
—   During a normal month (normal = 12,000 units monthly activity) the company expects a profit of $8,400 before taxes.

Required:

a.   Prepare a budgeted income statement for the month of April (use the same format as the March statement). Anticipated sales are 13,000 units, and production is cut back to 11,000 to reduce the ending finished goods inventory for April.

b.   Another subsidiary of the parent company requested 1,000 units for a special sale. This special sale will have no effect on the domestic market or on the normal business of the Highlight Company. What price per unit should be quoted, assuming that this order is in addition to the normal expected volume, that there is sufficient plant capacity (without any extra outlay for fixed costs), and that the parent company requested that only half of the normal profit per unit should be charged?

c.   What are the monthly break-even sales in units?

(SMA, adapted)

10-20   The Arch Company is having budgets prepared for the first time. To facilitate budget preparation for January and February, the following data were assembled:

a.   Sales forecasts (selling price per unit is $3.20).

	Units
January	8,000
February	10,000
March	12,000
April	9,000

b.   Inventories on January 1 were:

Raw materials.................... 4,200 lbs.
Finished goods.................... 1,600 units

c.   Inventories are maintained at the following levels:

Raw materials — 25 percent of the estimated production requirements for the following month.
Finished goods — 20 percent of the estimated sales for the following month.

d.   The standard cost of one unit at a normal volume of 10,000 units per month is:

Materials—2 pounds.................... $ .80
Labour................................ .70
Variable overhead..................... .30
Fixed overhead........................ .20
  Cost per unit........................ $2.00

e.   Administrative expenses, including depreciation, will be $4,000 per month.

f.   Selling expenses will be 10 percent of gross sales.

Required:

$ 36,000

Prepare the following, showing separate amounts for each of the months of January and February:

a. A sales budget
b. A production budget in units
c. A raw material purchases budget
d. A projected income statement (show any expected over- or under-applied overhead as an adjustment to cost of sales).

(SMA, adapted)

10-21   Barcelana, Inc. produces two products, A and B. The company plans to produce 5,000 units of A and 6,000 units of B. Production requirements for raw material are given below

	Cost/unit	A	B
X	$2.60	3 units	2 units
Y	$4.20	2 units	
Z	$1.80		4 units

It takes 3½ hours of direct labor to produce one unit of A and 3 hours to produce one unit of B. It costs $4.00 for one hour of direct labor. Variable costs are applied at $2.90 per direct labor hour. Assume variable costing and no beginning or ending inventories.

Required:

Determine the cost of goods manufactured for Barcelana, Inc. Prepare the necessary budgets used to arrive at this answer.

10-22   The Lamb Company has asked you to supply them with a budgeted cost of goods manufactured statement covering the first quarter. Work-in-process inventory on January 1 is $30,000. It is expected that this inventory will be increased by 2 percent in each of the budgeted months.

There are to be 2,500 units produced in January and this will be increased by 500 units in each of the next two months. It took 3 kilograms of raw material at $2 per kilogram to produce one unit last year. On January 1, the price of raw material increased by $.05 per kilogram. On January 1, there is no raw material inventory.

It takes 15 minutes to produce one unit and employees are paid $6.00 an hour. Variable manufacturing overhead is applied at $5.50 an hour. Fixed manufacturing overhead is $20,000 per month.

Required:

A budgeted cost of goods manufactured statement for the first quarter.

10-23   Stanfield Manufacturing Co. produces two products, Good and Better. It takes 1½ hours of direct labor to produce one unit of Good and

3 hours to produce one unit of Better. Direct labor costs $5.00 per hour. Variable overhead is applied at a rate of $1.70 per direct labor hour.

Stanfield plans to produce 8,000 units of Good and 5,000 units of Better. Requirements for direct materials are as follows:

	Cost/unit	Good	Better
A	$1.00	3	3
B	.95	2	3
C	2.20		2

Required:

Determine the budgeted cost of goods manufactured for Stanfield Manufacturing Co. Prepare the necessary supporting budgets used to arrive at this answer.

10-24   The Stuko Co. has budgets prepared incorporating ideal standards. Management feels that the use of ideal standards motivates employees positively. The following data apply to the upcoming budget year:

a.   Production (scheduled evenly over the year):

400,000 units of Product I

b.   Raw materials standard costs per unit:

I—5 quarts at $.50

c.   Direct labour standard costs per unit:

I—.4 hours at $8.00

Management expects that material costs will rise by 20% starting with raw materials put into production after the first day of the seventh month. Labour negotiations for next year's contract are incomplete, but management anticipates an increase of $1 per hour for direct labour to be effective for the whole budget year.

Raw material standards make no allowance for a normal expected loss of 10% of output. Labour performance can be expected to require .1 hours longer per unit for each product.

Required:

(Do not adjust the standards given in the question)

a.   Prepare a raw materials budget for the next year showing:

i.   the total standard costs
ii.   the total expected cost

b. Prepare a direct labour budget for the next year showing:

   i. the total standard costs
  ii. the total expected cost

c. Prepare two expected or budgeted variances (indicate whether favourable or unfavourable) for each of:

   i. raw materials
  ii. direct labour

(SMA, adapted)

10-25 The Jones Company manufactures only one product, trinkets. In the second quarter, it is expected that 10,000 units will be produced in April; 12,000 in May; and 9,480 in June. The work-in-process inventory on March 31 was valued at $2,500. This inventory is expected to increase or decrease in the same proportion as production. 8,000 trinkets were produced in March.

It took 5 ounces of raw material at $0.08 an ounce to produce one trinket in the first quarter. The price of raw material used is expected to go up $0.02 in each month in the second quarter. There is no beginning raw materials inventory.

Employees can make one trinket every ten minutes and they are paid $2.50 an hour. Variable manufacturing overhead is applied at $1.00 an hour and there is no fixed manufacturing overhead.

Required:

A budgeted cost of goods manufactured statement for the second quarter.

10-26 A sales budget for the first five months is given for a particular product line manufactured by Arthur Guthrie Co. Ltd.

	Sales Budget in Units
January	10,800
February	15,600
March	12,200
April	10,400
May	9,800

The inventory of finished products at the end of each month is to be equal to 25 percent of the sales estimate for the next month. On January 1, there were 2,700 units of product on hand. No work is in-process at the end of any month.

Each unit of product requires two types of materials in the following quantities:

Material A.............................. 4 units
Material B.............................. 5 units

Materials equal to one-half of the next month's production are to be on hand at the end of each month. This requirement was met on January 1.

Required:

Prepare a budget showing the quantities of each type of material to be purchased each month for the first quarter.

(SMA, adapted)

10-27 R Ltd. manufactured 900,000 units annually which took up 90 percent of the plant capacity. Each unit sold for $8.00.

Due to increased competition, a reduction in volume of 50,000 units was forecast for 19x6 and subsequent years, but no reduction in the sales price was anticipated.

Direct material costs are $2.50 and direct labour costs are $2.00 per unit. The variable factory service expense is $0.75 per unit while fixed factory service expense is $950,000. Selling and administrative expenses for 19x6 are estimated to be fixed—$400,000 and variable—$425,000.

An offer has been received from C Ltd. to purchase 250,000 units at $6.00 per unit. These units are to be marketed under the customer's brand name at prices somewhat lower than the $8.00 charged by R Ltd.

To produce the additional 250,000 units, $120,000 would have to be invested in additional production facilities. Variable factory service expense at the new level of production would be reduced to $0.70 per unit, but there will be no change in administrative expenses.

The president of R Ltd., who has asked you to prepare a budget for 19x6, feels that he should refuse the offer on the basis that the direct costs per unit total $6.17 (material and labour of $4.50, plus variable costs of $0.70 and fixed factory service costs of $0.97); and thus there would be a loss of $0.17 on each unit sold at $6.00.

Required:

a.   Prepare a comparative statement of budgeted profit and loss for 19x6, showing the effect of the acceptance of the offer from C Ltd.
b.   What is the break-even sales volume at 19x6 regular selling prices?
c.   What other factors should be considered before accepting or rejecting the offer?

(CA, adapted)

10-28   X Co. Ltd. is engaged in a process manufacturing industry in which all operations are completed in one department. On completion of the manufacturing operations the goods are transferred to a finished goods warehouse. The inventory records are maintained on a first-in, first-out basis.

The inventories at January 1, 19x2 were:

Finished goods..........................	150,000 units at $1.10
Work-in-process..........................	30,000 units
Material................................	80% complete
Direct labour and factory service expense......	40% complete

The following information applies to production at the present capacity:

Material cost............................	$0.30 per unit
Direct labour............................	$0.20 per unit

	Fixed Per Quarter	Variable
Factory service expense.........................	$45,000	$0.30 per unit processed
Selling expense................................	30,000	.15 per unit sold
Administrative expense........................	15,000	.05 per unit sold

The sales manager has suggested that, in order to increase sales, the fixed selling expense be increased by $10,000 during each of the three-month periods ending March 31 and June 30, 19x2. At the same time, selling prices should be decreased.

This would have the following estimated results as compared with present operations:

	3 Months Ended March 31	3 Months Ended June 30
Sales..................................	200,000 units @ $1.70	225,000 units @ $1.60
Fixed expenses:		
Factory service expense..................	No change	Increase $7,640
Selling expense........................	$40,000	$40,000
Administrative expense..................	No change	Increase $5,000
Variable—based on present capacity:		
Factory service expense..................	10% decrease	20% decrease
Selling expense........................	20% decrease	20% decrease
Administrative expense..................	20% decrease	20% decrease
Production:		
Started in-process......................	160,000 units	200,000 units
Work-in-process at end of month..........	40,000 units	50,000 units
Material............................	60% complete	40% complete
Direct labour and factory service expense..	30% complete	20% complete

Required:

Prepare budgeted profit and loss statements for each of the three-month periods ended March 31, 19x2 and June 30, 19x2. Submit details of your calculations.

(CA, adapted)

Chapter 11

LEARNING OBJECTIVES

Chapter 11 continues the examination of short-range planning and completes the comprehensive example of the budgeting process. Studying this chapter should enable you to:

1. Prepare financial and resource budgets and the associated schedules when given the necessary data.
2. Prepare the pro-forma financial statements that are the final products of the budgeting process.
3. Understand how quantitative decision models can aid in the short-range planning process.

Short-Range Planning: Financial and Resource Budgets

IN CHAPTER 10 the short-range planning process leading to the preparation of the operating and performance budgets was examined. In this chapter we continue the comprehensive budgeting illustration in the preparation of the financial and resource budgets.

This chapter also contains an appendix which examines some quantitative models that may aid in short-range planning and decision making. Because Chapters 10 and 11 use much of the same information, the reader needs to refer to Chapter 10 for relevant management policies and data.

DEVELOPMENT OF THE MAJOR FINANCIAL OR RESOURCE BUDGETS

Once the operating or performance budgets are prepared, the financial or resource budgets can be prepared. The financial budgets rely mainly on the data included in the beginning balance sheet as presented in Illustration 10–2, the performance budgets and the Management Policies and Forecasts.

All balance sheet accounts are permanent accounts in which the accounting relationship (beginning balance in the account plus additions to the account less withdrawals from the account equals the ending balance) must be maintained. The ending account balances appear on the budgeted balance sheet. A number of ending balances for the permanent accounts have already been established by the performance budgets or by the Management Policies and Forecasts. Each account on the balance sheet is budgeted individually and then combined with other permanent accounts to develop the budgeted balance sheet. The ending cash balance cannot be ascertained until all other March 31, 19x1 budgeted account balances have been determined because data developed in the other budgeted permanent accounts are necessary in order to develop the cash budget. The accounts are considered in their order on the balance sheet.

Accounts Receivable Budget (Budget #15)

Collections of accounts receivable lag one month behind sales. The ending accounts receivable balance on March 31, 19x1 is equal to sales of $850,000 which are budgeted for March (Budget #1). The beginning accounts receivable for 19x1 is forecasted at $424,400 (Illustration 10-2).

Budget #15
Accounts Receivable Budget
(1st Quarter, 19x1)

	January	February	March	Quarter Total
Beginning Accounts Receivable (Illustration 10–2) .	$ 424,400	→$ 600,000	→$ 600,000	$ 424,400
Sales for the Month (Budget #1)	600,000	600,000	850,000	2,050,000
Total	$1,024,400	$1,200,000	$1,450,000	$2,474,400
Ending Accounts Receivable	600,000—	600,000—	850,000	850,000
Collection of Accounts Receivable	$ 424,400	$ 600,000	$ 600,000	$1,624,400

Inventory Budgets (Budgets #16 and #17)

For the most part, inventory budgets are developed from operating budgets, because the ending inventory balance is dictated by management policy. The direct materials inventory budget is developed using the information provided in the direct materials purchases budget (Budget #5) and the budgeted cost of goods manufactured statement (Budget #12).

The indirect materials and supplies budget is to be maintained at a level of $30,000 (item 10 in Management Policies and Forecasts). Purchases each month are therefore equal to the amount of indirect materials and supplies used. These data are found in the manufacturing overhead budgets (Budgets #8 and #9).

Budget #16
Direct Materials Budget
(1st Quarter, 19x1)

Steel Billets

	January	*February*	*March*	*Quarter Total*
Beginning Inventory (Illustration 10–2)	$ 96,000	→$160,000	→$132,000	$ 96,000
Add: Purchases (Budget #5)	132,000	52,000	40,000	224,000
Total Materials Available	$228,000	$212,000	$172,000	$320,000
Less: Transfers to Work-in-Process (Budget #6)	68,000	80,000	80,000	228,000
Ending Inventory	$160,000	$132,000	$ 92,000	$ 92,000

Ball Bearings

	January	*February*	*March*	*Quarter Total*
Beginning Inventory (Illustration 10–2)	$ 48,000	→$ 80,000	→$ 66,000	$ 48,000
Add: Purchases (Budget #5)	66,000	26,000	20,000	112,000
Total Materials Available	$114,000	$106,000	$ 86,000	$160,000
Less Transfers to Work-in-Process (Budget #6)	34,000	40,000	40,000	114,000
Ending Inventory	$ 80,000	$ 66,000	$ 46,000	$ 46,000

The work-in-process inventory account is to be maintained at a level of $300,000 in order to insure relatively stable production volume requirements (Item 11 in Management Policies and Forecasts).

The finished goods inventory balances are determined by the sales forecast and the requirement that a quantity of finished goods sufficient to meet demand for two months in advance be on hand (Item 12 in the Management Policies and Forecasts). The monthly ending inventory balances required for finished goods are developed in Budget #2. A budget for finished goods inventory levels is also developed by using the budgeted cost of goods manufactured statement (Budget #12) and the budgeted variable cost of goods sold statement (Budget #13).

Budget #17
Finished Goods Budget
(1st Quarter, 19x1)

	January	February	March	Quarter Total
Beginning Inventory of Finished Goods (Illustration 10–2)	$249,600	→$301,600	→$384,800	$249,600
Add: Cost of Goods Manufactured (Budget #12)	176,800	208,000	208,000	592,800
Total Goods Available	$426,400	$509,600	$592,800	$842,400
Less: Cost of Goods Sold (Budget #13)	124,800	124.800	176,800	426,400
Ending Inventory of Finished Goods	$301,600—	$384,800—	$416,000	$416,000

Fixed Asset Budgets (Budget #18)

The Power Turbine Shaft Division does not anticipate buying, selling, or trading any fixed assets in 19x1. The original cost of the equipment was $600,000. The estimated life of the equipment is 10 years, no salvage value is anticipated and straight-line depreciation is used to depreciate the equipment. Only one year's depreciation (19x0) has been recognized on the equipment prior to the preparation of the 19x1 budget.

The original cost of the plant was $3,000,000. A 20-year life is anticipated with no salvage value and straight-line depreciation is used as the basis for depreciating the plant. Both the equipment and plant depreciation were included in the fixed manufacturing overhead costs budget (Budget #9). The calculation of net book values is presented in Budget #18.

Accounts Payable and Wages Payable Budget (Budget #19)

Accounts payable represent direct material purchases; therefore, the accounts payable budget is based upon the direct material purchases budget (Budget #5). Credit terms in the industry and for the Power Turbine Shaft Division are net/30. The payments of accounts payable lag behind the purchases schedule by 30 days (item 15 of Management Policies and Forecasts). The beginning accounts payable balance of $60,000 (Illustration 10-2) will be paid in January of 19x1. The January purchases of $198,000 will be paid in February.

Wages are paid on the fifteenth and on the last business day of each month. The outstanding wages payable at the end of any month is

Budget #18
Fixed Asset Budget
(1st Quarter, 19x1)

Equipment

	January	February	March	Quarter Total
Original Cost	$600,000	$600,000	$600,000	$600,000
Less: Beginning Accumulated Depreciation	60,000	65,000	70,000	60,000
Less: Depreciation for the Period (Budget #9)	5,000	5,000	5,000	15,000
Accumulated Depreciation to Date	$ 65,000	$ 70,000	$ 75,000	$ 75,000
Net Book Value	$535,000	$530,000	$525,000	$525,000

Plant

	January	February	March	Quarter Total
Original Cost	$3,000,000	$3,000,000	$3,000,000	$3,000,000
Less: Beginning Accumulated Depreciation	150,000	162,500	175,000	150,000
Less: Depreciation for the Period (Budget #9)	12,500	12,500	12,500	37,500
Accumulated Depreciation to Date	$ 162,500	$ 175,000	$ 187,500	$ 187,500
Net Book Value	$2,837,500	$2,825,000	$2,812,500	$2,812,500

Budget #19
Accounts Payable Budget
(1st Quarter, 19x1)

	January	February	March	Quarter Total
Beginning Accounts Payable (Illustration 10–2)	$ 60,000	→$198,000	→$ 78,000	$ 60,000
Add: Purchases of Direct Materials (Budget #5) . .	198,000	78,000	60,000	336,000
Total	$258,000	$276,000	$138,000	$396,000
Less: Payments on Accounts Payable	60,000	198,000	78,000	336,000
Ending Accounts Payable . .	$198,000	$ 78,000	$ 60,000	$ 60,000

$18,000; this represents the wages earned by employees for the first two weeks that they are employed (item 16 in Management Policies and Forecast). The budgeted wages paid are the monthly wages determined in the direct labor budget (Budget #7).

Long-Term Debt Budget (Budget #20)

The Power Turbine Shaft Division does not foresee any additional borrowing in 19x1. A current long-term debt of $1,200,000 is outstanding and requires monthly interest payments of $11,000 and principal payments of $30,000 per quarter beginning March 31, 19x1 (item 17 of Management Policies and Forecasts). The current payment schedule is projected in Budget #20.

Budget #20
Long-Term Debt Budget
(1st Quarter, 19x1)

Loan Payments

	January	February	March	Quarter Total
Interest Payments . . .	$ 11,000	$ 11,000	$ 11,000	$ 33,000
Principal Payments . .	–0–	–0–	30,000	30,000
Total	$ 11,000	$ 11,000	$ 41,000	$ 63,000

Balance of Principal

	January	February	March	Quarter Total
Beginning Principal (Illustration 10–2) .	$1,200,000	→$1,200,000	→$1,200,000	$1,200,000
Less: Principal Payments	–0–	–0–	30,000	30,000
Net Principal	$1,200,000	$1,200,000	$1,170,000	$1,170,000

DEVELOPMENT OF THE MAJOR FINANCIAL OR RESOURCE BUDGETED FINANCIAL STATEMENTS

The next step in the budgeting process is the preparation of three major budgeted resource financial statements:

1. A cash budget
2. A shareholders' equity (corporate investment) statement
3. A budgeted balance sheet

Cash Budget (Budget #21)

A cash budget is an analysis of the cash account in terms of cash receipts and disbursements, and as such can facilitate the planning and control of cash flows. One intent of a cash budget is to establish minimum balance requirements so that normal cash needs can be met without borrowing. Determination of a minimum balance also frees surplus cash for investment. Cash budgeting is also necessary in order to anticipate possible cash shortages and thus allow adequate time to arrange borrowing. Cash budgeting is usually planned for very short periods (i.e., weekly or bi-weekly) in order that the budget be as responsive as possible to the cash needs of the company, for there can be drastic financial implications when a firm runs out of cash.

The primary source of cash for the Power Turbine Shaft Division is customer receipts (Budget #15). The cash balance and company borrowing policies (Item 7 of Management Policies and Forecasts) require a minimum cash balance of $40,000 to sustain the operations of the division. Any necessary cash can be borrowed from corporate headquarters, but only in increments of $5,000.

A number of factors affect cash disbursements:

1. The payment schedule for accounts payable for direct material purchases is presented in the accounts payable budget (Budget #19).
2. Wages payable are paid in the month earned and can be determined from the direct labor budget (Budget #7).
3. The long-term debt repayment schedule is found in the long-term debt budget (Budget #20).
4. All variable (Budget #8) and fixed manufacturing overhead costs (Budget #9) are paid in the month incurred except for the semiannual property taxes in Budget #9. The property taxes are paid on June 30 and December 31. (Remember, depreciation is a non-cash expense and therefore is not considered in the cash budget.)
5. All non-manufacturing costs (Budgets #10 and #11) are paid in the month incurred.

Budgets for cash receipts and cash disbursements could be prepared separately. A complete cash budget is then prepared which incorporates both receipts and disbursements and reconciles the beginning and ending cash balances. Budget #21, the cash budget, includes all the budgeted factors which affect the cash position.

Budgeted Shareholder's Equity Statement (Budget #22)

The budgeted shareholder's equity statement, Budget #22, is the projected analysis of the change in Sax Company's investment in the Power Turbine Shaft Division. Corporate headquarters plans no increase or decrease in the investment in the division for the first quarter.

Budget #21
Cash Budget
(1st Quarter, 19x1)

	January	February	March	Quarter Total
Cash Receipts:				
Collections of Accounts Receivable (Illustration 10–2, Budget #15) . .	$424,400	$600,000	$600,000	$1,624,400
Cash Disbursements:				
Accounts Payable (Illustration 10–2, Budget #19)	$ 60,000	$198,000	$ 78,000	$ 336,000
Payments for Direct Labor (Budget #7)	51,000	60,000	60,000	171,000
Long-Term Debt Principal Repayment (Budget #20)	–0–	–0–	30,000	30,000
Long-Term Debt Interest Payment (Budget #11 or 20)	11,000	11,000	11,000	33,000
Variable Manufacturing Overhead (Budget #8)	23,800	28,000	28,000	79,800
Fixed Manufacturing Overhead (Budget #9)[a]	5,750	5,750	5,750	17,250
Variable Selling Costs (Budget #10)	60,000	60,000	85,000	205,000
Fixed Selling and Administrative Costs (Budget #11)[b]	167,000	167,000	167,000	501,000
Total Disbursements	$378,550	$529,750	$464,750	$1,373,050
Excess (Deficit) of Cash Receipts Over Disbursements	$ 45,850	$ 70,250	$135,250	$ 251,350
Beginning Cash Balance .	40,000	85,850	156,100	40,000
Ending Cash Balance Before Borrowing or Repayment	$ 85,850	$156,100	$291,350	$ 291,350
Borrowing from Corporate Headquarters . . .	–0–	–0–	–0–	–0–
Repayment to Corporate Headquarters . . .	–0–	–0–	–0–	–0–
Ending Cash Balance	$ 85,850	$156,100	$291,350	$ 291,350

[a] Equipment and plant depreciation is not a cash outflow. The monthly cash outflows for fixed manufacturing overhead must be adjusted accordingly. For example, January—[$30,000-$6,750 (property taxes) — $17,500 (depreciation)] = $5,750 net cash outflow.

[b] Interest expense was considered separately in this cash budget. The January through March cash outflows are $178,000 — $11,000 (interest) = $167,000.

Budget #22
Budgeted Stockholders' Equity Statement
(1st Quarter, 19x1)

	January	February	March	Quarter Total
Beginning Corporate Investment (Illustration 10–2)	$3,300,000	→$3,507,200	→$3,714,400	$3,300,000
Add: Income (Budget #14) . . .	207,200	207,200	380,200	794,600
Less: Withdrawals by Corporate Headquarters	–0–	–0–	–0–	–0–
Ending Corporate Investment . .	$3,507,200	$3,714,400	$4,094,600	$4,094,600

Budgeted or Pro Forma Balance Sheet (Budget #23)

The budgeted or pro forma balance sheet in Budget #23 is the result of all budgets developed which involved assets, liabilities, or shareholders' equity. Management Policies and Forecasts have an added impact on the budgeted balance sheet. The function of management is to establish guidelines for obtaining and utilizing resources. If management requires certain balances in given accounts in order to attain the goals and objectives of the firm, then the budget should be prepared in light of these policies. For example, the budgeted balances in indirect materials and supplies, work-in-process, and wages payable were established by Management Policies and Forecasts. All other accounts were affected, either directly or indirectly, by management policies designed to utilize the resources of Sax Company in the most efficient and effective manner.

THE COMPREHENSIVE BUDGET, SIMULATION AND FINANCIAL PLANNING MODELS

The comprehensive or master budget is the backbone of the planning process which defines the organization's objectives and then attempts to measure the related inputs and outputs. Perhaps most important, objectives for the coming period are often reassessed and changed during the budgeting process. In this way the comprehensive budget is similar to a formal model of the total organization.

Budget #23
Budgeted Monthly Balance Sheets
(1st Quarter, 19x1)

	January 31	February 28	March 31
ASSETS			
Current Assets:			
Cash (Budget #21) . . . . $	85,850	$ 156,100	$ 291,350
Accounts Receivable (Budget #15)	600,000	600,000	850,000
Direct Materials Inventories:			
Steel Billets @ Standard			
(Budget #16)	160,000	132,000	92,000
Ball Bearings @ Standard			
(Budget #16)	80,000	66,000	46,000
Indirect Materials and Supplies . . .	30,000a	30,000a	30,000a
Work-in-Process @ Standard			
Variable Cost	300,000b	300,000b	300,000b
Finished Goods @ Standard			
Variable Cost (Budget #17) . . .	301,600	384,800	416,000
Total Current Assets	$1,557,450	$1,668,900	$2,025,350
Long-Term Assets:			
Equipment (Budget #18) . . . . . $	600,000	$ 600,000	$ 600,000
Less: Accumulated Depreciation			
(Budget #18)	65,000	70,000	75,000
Net: Equipment (Budget #18) . .	535,000	530,000	525,000
Plant (Budget #18)	3,000,000	3,000,000	3,000,000
Less: Accumulated Depreciation			
(Budget #18)	162,500	175,000	187,500
Net: Plant (Budget #18)	2,837,500	2,825,000	2,812,500
Total Long-Term Assets	3,372,500	3,355,000	3,337,500
Total Assets	$4,929,950	$5,023,900	$5,362,850
LIABILITIES AND SHAREHOLDERS' EQUITY			
Current Liabilities:			
Accounts Payable (Budget #19) . . $	198,000	$ 78,000	$ 60,000
Wages Payable	18,000c	18,000c	18,000c
Deferred Factory Property Taxes			
(Budget #9)	6,750d	13,500d	20,250d
Total Current Liabilities . . . . $	222,750	$ 109,500	$ 98,250
Long-Term Debt (Budget #20) . . .	1,200,000	1,200,000	1,170,000
Total Liabilities	$1,422,750	$1,309,500	$1,268,250
Shareholders' Equity			
Corporate Investment			
(Budget #22)	3,507,200	3,714,400	4,094,600
Total Liabilities and Shareholders'			
Equity	$4,929,950	$5,023,900	$5,362,850

a Item 10, Management Policies and Forecasts
b Item 11, Management Policies and Forecasts
c Item 16, Management Policies and Forecasts
d Deferred factory property taxes are $6,750 per month. The property taxes are paid on June 30 and December 31.

Increasing attention has been given to the use of mathematical simulation models in the budgeting process. These are also called financial planning models. The key to financial planning models are the mathematical formulas that describe the relationships between the various activities within the organization. The relationships between the sales activity and the operating and financial activities have to be reduced to equations that can be fed into the formal models. These relationships often involve lead-time and lag-time functions. Production activities usually lead the sales activity while accounts receivable collections usually lag the sales activity. One advantage to the formal decision model is that mathematical probabilities can be explicitly introduced into the decision process.

While the financial planning models can be extremely useful in the preparation of short-range planning budgets, they may also be used in long-range planning or capital budgeting. One company, for example, uses a formal model and simulation to study proposed new restaurant sites. The demographics of the proposed location are fed into the model which projects customer demand and the probable success or failure.

While a complete study of formal models is beyond the scope of this text, the Appendix to this chapter examines some quantitative decision models that may aid planning.

SUMMARY

Chapter 10 introduced the use of budgeting as a basis for performance evaluation and planning. The major operating and performance budgets were then developed. This chapter continues the study of the comprehensive or master budget by developing the major financial and resource budgets.

When the organization's objectives are reassessed and changed during the budgeting process, the comprehensive budget is a formal decision model. Increasing attention has been given to the use of financial planning models and simulation in the budgeting process. One advantage is that mathematical probabilities can be explicitly considered in the decision process.

APPENDIX:
THE ROLE OF
QUANTITATIVE
TECHNIQUES IN
SHORT-RANGE
PLANNING
AND DECISIONS

In this appendix we examine some quantitative techniques that may be useful in short-range planning and decisions. While the in-depth study of formal decision models and risk or uncertainty is usually considered part of other fields or disciplines, the managerial accountant needs the knowledge and ability to utilize these techniques in the proper circumstances. This includes the ability to recognize when the techniques may be used incorrectly.

Objective vs.
Subjective Probabilities

Many formal models require a schedule of probable demand, commonly called a probability distribution. This schedule describes the chance that a possible event will occur out of all possible events. In gaming strategy, where engineered gadgets perform according to natural or physical laws, this is quite simple. We know that from a randomly shuffled deck of cards the probability of drawing a heart is $13 \div 52 = 0.25$. If we draw five cards from the deck, and they are four hearts and one spade, the probability of the next card being a heart is $9 \div 47 = 0.19$ (there are only nine hearts in the remaining forty-seven cards). If several people independently calculated the chance of drawing the card they would all arrive at the same answer, hence, the term objective probability.

In most business situations we are unable to determine the actual probability that an event will occur or even to determine all of the possible events. Because of this, the probability distributions used in the formal models are of necessity only subjective estimates of the underlying probabilities. And as such, we should always be aware that the use of formal models may lead to incorrect decisions if the subjective probabilities do not represent reality.

Determination of
Single Point
Sales Estimates

When using a single point sales estimate in budgeting, the sales level selected is usually the level having the highest probability of occurrence or the modal event. Because the actual probability distribution is not known, the decision maker assumes a normal distribution which makes the mean and the mode identical and no further calculations are necessary.

When the probability distribution of possible sales levels is skewed the expected value (mean) might be a better estimation than the mode. The mode does not consider the effect of the extreme events while the expected value does. The expected value is the weighted average mean value of all of the possible outcomes. The expected value is computed by multiplying each possible outcome (conditional value) by the probability of its occurrence. Consider the following illustration:

Illustration 11-1
Weighted Average Expected Value

	Possible Sales Levels	Subjective Probabilities	Expected Value
	$700,000	.20	$140,000
	750,000	.30	225,000
(mode)	800,000	.35	280,000
	850,000	.10	85,000
	900,000	.05	45,000
	Weighted Average Expected Value (mean)		$775,000

Example of Decision Making Under Uncertainty

Each Thursday a storekeeper buys boxes of fresh strawberries. The strawberries cost $1 and sell for $1.75. Because of their perishable nature, any unsold strawberries are worthless. The storekeeper wants to know how many boxes should be purchased each week in order to maximize profits. Based upon past experience, the demand for strawberries is estimated as follows:

Illustration 11-2
Demand for Strawberries

Demand	Estimated Probability
0	0.00
100 boxes	0.05
150 boxes	0.10
200 boxes	0.20
250 boxes	0.35
300 boxes	0.20
350 boxes	0.10
400 boxes	0.00
	1.00

The strategies to be examined are 100 through 350 boxes. Zero or 400 boxes are not considered because there is no demand at these levels. The solution to the problem is presented in Illustration 11-3. There is a 75¢ profit on each box sold and a $1 loss on each unsold box.

Illustration 3

Payoff Table Solution

Possible Events / Probability of Event / Strategies	100	150	200	250	300	350	Expected Value
	.05	.10	.20	.35	.20	.10	
100	$ 75	$ 75	$ 75	$ 75	$ 75	$ 75	$ 75
150	25	112.50	112.50	112.50	112.50	112.50	108.125
200	− 25	62.50	150	150	150	150	132.50
250	− 75	12.50	100	187.50	187.50	187.50	139.375
300	− 125	− 37.50	50	137.50	225	225	115.625
350	− 175	− 87.50	0	87.50	175	262.50	74.375

The strategy of buying 250 boxes produces the largest expected value. The expected value (EV) for the 250 box strategy is:

$$EV = .05(-75) + .10(12.50) + .20(100) + .35(187.50) + .20(187.50) + .10(187.50) = \$139.375$$

The Value of Perfect Information

In the previous illustration, because the demand was uncertain, the solution was to use the optimum strategy each week; buy 250 boxes. If, however, the demand for strawberries was known with certainty, a different number of boxes would be purchased each week. With perfect information the storekeeper would never lose a sale nor would he ever have to throw away spoiled strawberries. The weighted average weekly profit with perfect information is calculated as follows:

Illustration 4

Average Weekly Profit with Perfect Information

Demand (Boxes)	Conditional Value	×	Probability of Event	=	Expected Value
100	$ 75		.05		$ 3.75
150	112.50		.10		11.25
200	150		.20		30.00
250	187.50		.35		65.625
300	225		.20		45.00
350	262.50		.10		26.25
					$181.875

With perfect information the storekeeper could increase the expected weekly profit by $42.50 ($181.875 − $139.375). The problem, obviously, is that perfect information is not available. If management believes that better information is available, the calculation of the value of perfect information does provide a maximum price that could be paid for such information.

Management of Inventory Costs

The management of inventories involved three types of cost: (1) the fixed costs of setting up for a production run or placing an order, (2) the carrying costs of warehousing, insuring, interest, spoilage, etc., and (3) the stock-out opportunity costs of lost sales and customers.

Illustration of Inventory Management

Peter Ruplinger, Inc. imports diamonds from abroad and sells them in the Vancouver area. Ruplinger is trying to determine the economic order quantity and reorder point for a one carat "D" quality diamond. The following data is available:

Cost of placing an order..................	$ 500
Purchase price of a diamond..............	$1,000
Selling price of a diamond................	$1,100
Cost of borrowed money..................	20%
Annual demand.........................	500
Average time to receive an order...........	3 months

Based on this data, the economic order quantity of 50 diamonds is presented in Illustration 7.

Illustration 5

Economic Order Quantity

Order Quantity	C_s Annual Cost of Placing an Order	C_i Annual Carrying Cost	C Total Annual Cost
$\left(\dfrac{SD}{Q} = C_s\right)$		$+ \left(\dfrac{IQ}{2} = C_i\right)$	$= \left(C = \dfrac{IQ}{2} + \dfrac{SD}{Q}\right)$
40	$6,250	$4,000	$10,250
50	5,000	5,000	10,000
60	4,167	6,000	10,167

EOQ = Economic order quantity
Q = Size of order in units
D = Annual demand in units
I = Cost of carrying one unit for one year
S = Set up or cost of placing an order

The graphic solution is presented in Illustration 11-6. A mathematical solution to the economic order quantity can be obtained by setting the first derivative of the total cost function equal to zero.

$$EOQ = \sqrt{\frac{2 \times D \times S}{I}} = \sqrt{\frac{2 \times 500 \times 500}{200}} = 50$$

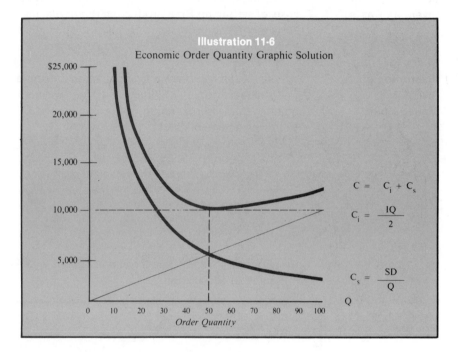

Illustration 11-6
Economic Order Quantity Graphic Solution

$$C = C_i + C_s$$
$$C_i = \frac{IQ}{2}$$
$$C_s = \frac{SD}{Q}$$

The recorder inventory level consists of two parts:

Reorder Point = Lead time stock + Safety stock

The lead time stock is determined by the average demand during the average time that it takes to receive an order:

Lead time stock = 3/12 × 500 = 125

The optimal safety stock will minimize the total cost of carrying safety stock and the opportunity cost of lost sales (stock out costs). In order to analyze the need for safety stock, we need to know what the possible demands might be during the reorder period and the probability of those demands occuring (see Illustration 11-7).

Illustration 11-7
Probability of Demand

Demand	Probability	Possible Safety Stock
125	.05	125 − 125 = 0
135	.10	135 − 125 = 10
145	.25	145 − 125 = 20
155	.35	155 − 125 = 30
165	.20	165 − 125 = 40
175	.05	175 − 125 = 50
	1.00	

We can now construct a decision table (Illustration 11-8). One very important point; there is no cost of running out of stock unless customers are turned away. For example, if Ruplinger reorders when the inventory level is 165 diamonds and 165 customers come in before the new order arrives no sales will be lost. But if 175 customers want diamonds, ten sales will be lost. Because the contribution margin is $100, the loss of ten sales has an opportunity cost of $1,000. With a probability of occurrence of 5%, this strategy has an expected loss of $50 per order or a $500 annual stock out cost. The Company will be ordering ten times a year $\left(\dfrac{D}{Q} = \dfrac{500}{50} = 10 \right)$

Illustration 11-8
Decision Table for Safety Stock

Safety Stock	Annual Carrying Cost	Annual Stock-out Cost	Total
0	$ 0	$27,000	$27,000
10	2,000	17,500	19,500
20	4,000	9,000 [1]	13,000
30	6,000	3,000 [2]	9,000
40	8,000	500	8,500
50	10,000	0	10,000

[1][((30 × 100) .05)10 + ((20 × 100).20)10 + ((10 × 100).35)10] = 9,000
[2][((20 × 100) .05)10 + ((10 × 100).20)10] = 3,000

With a safety stock of 40 diamonds, the appropriate time to reorder is:

Reorder point = 125 + 40 = 165 diamonds

LINEAR PROGRAMMING

Linear programming is a mathematical approach to allocating scarce resources in order to maximize profit or reduce cost.

Since its development, linear programming has been applied to a number of production problems. Examples include product mix, raw material mix, capacity allocation problems, make or buy problems, and shipping problems.

Example of Scarce Resource Problem

A small business makes two products, A and B. These products must be machined in department D1 and assembled in department D2. There are 200 hours available in D1 and 300 hours available in D2. While the company can sell all the product B that they produce, the demand for product A is limited to 80 units. Product A requires 2 hours of machining in D1 and 2 hours of assembly in D2. Product B requires 1 hour of machining in D1 and 3 hours of assembly in D2. Product A has a contribution margin of $2.50 per unit. Product B has a contribution margin of $3 per unit.

The objective function in this example is to maximize the contribution margin, where:

$$\text{Total Contribution Margin} = \$2.50A + \$3B \qquad (1)$$

Since the total time required in each department cannot exceed available capacity, we have the following constraints:

Department D1	$2A + 1B \leq 200$	(2)
Department D2	$2A + 3B \leq 300$	(3)

Since the demand for A is limited to 80 units, we have the additional constraint:

For Product A	$A \leq 80$	(4)

These constraints are represented by the three solid lines in Illustration 11-9.

It should be observed that the optimum solution must always be one of the corners of the area of possible solutions in Illustration 11-9. These corners are analyzed in Illustration 11-10. The optimum solution is to produce 75 units of product A and 50 units of product B. This combination provides a total contribution margin of $337.50 which is larger than any of the other possible solutions.

Since our example was very simple and uncomplicated, the graphical approach was easy to apply and understand. Most companies use a mathematical approach, the simplex method, in practice.

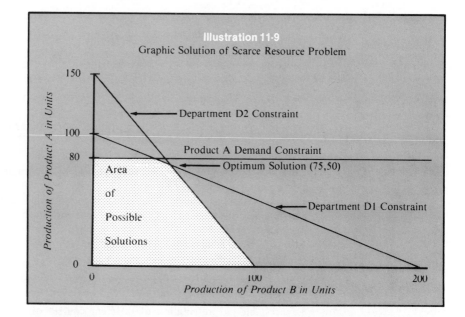

Illustration 11-9
Graphic Solution of Scarce Resource Problem

Production of Product A in Units

Department D2 Constraint

Product A Demand Constraint

Optimum Solution (75,50)

Area
of
Possible
Solutions

Department D1 Constraint

Production of Product B in Units

Illustration 11-10
Analysis of Corners Solution

Possible Solutions	Contribution Margin			
A, B	A	+	B	=	Total
0,0	0	+	0	=	0
80,0	200	+	0	=	200
80,40[1]	200	+	120	=	320
75,50[2]	187.50	+	150	=	337.50
0,100	0	+	300	=	300

[1] From equation (2):

$$2(80) + 1B = 200; B = 40$$

[2] From equation (2) and (3):

$$
\begin{array}{rr}
2A + 3B = & 300 \\
-2A - 1B = & -200 \\
\hline
0 + 2B = & 100
\end{array}
\quad ; B = 50 \text{ and } A = 75
$$

KEY DEFINITIONS

Budgeted balance sheet—the projected balance sheet of the firm showing the expected financial position of the firm at a given point in time during or at the conclusion of the budget period.

Budgeted shareholders' equity statement—a projected analysis of investment changes in the firm during the budget period.

Budgeted owner's equity statement—a projected analysis of investment change in the firm during the budget period.

Cash budget—an analysis of the cash account in terms of anticipated cash receipts and disbursements in order to establish cash balances over the budget period for the planning and control of cash.

Economic order quantity—the order quantity that minimizes the annual cost of ordering and carrying inventory.

Financial planning models—simulation models based on mathematical formulas that describe the relationships between the various activities within the organization.

Linear programming—a mathematical approach to allocating scarce resources in order to maximize profit or reduce cost.

Major financial resource budgeted statements—cash budget, shareholders' equity or corporate investment statement, and budgeted balance sheet.

Payoff table—a presentation of different courses of action and the conditional values that might result based on the events that could affect the results of the actions. The payoff table is used to present the expected values of the various courses of actions or strategies.

Subjective probability—the estimated chance that a certain event may occur if a certain action is undertaken.

QUESTIONS

11-1 What is the definition of constraining factors and how do they relate to short-range planning?

11-2 Why do firms maintain a minimum and a maximum level of inventory?

11-3 What is a cash budget and what is its purpose?

11-4 What factors do the normal operating cash receipts of a firm depend on?

11-5 What is the last budget which is usually made in the short-range profit planning procedure and why is it the last?

11-6 What is a formal decision model and what is its purpose?

11-7 What distinguishes a decision made under conditions known with certainty from a decision made under conditions of risk or uncertainty?

11-8 What are the two types of inventory costs that the economic order quantity attempts to minimize?

11-9 What two types of inventory costs are analyzed in the safety stock decision?

11-10 What is lead time stock?

11-11 How might linear programming help in the allocation of scarce resources?

11-12 Why are subjective probabilities often used in business decisions instead of objective probabilities?

EXERCISES AND PROBLEMS

11-13 The Task Company is to begin operations in January. They have budgeted January sales of $34,000, February sales of $40,000, March sales of $42,000 and April sales of $38,000. Prepare a budget of cash receipts from sales for the first five months of the year if 75% of sales are collected the month following sale, 16% the second month, 6% the third month, and the balance is bad debts.

11-14 During December, the Burns Co. sold 40,000 litres of charcoal lighter. In the first quarter of the new year, the company expects sales to increase 20 percent each month. The company normally collects 30 percent of the sales price in the month of the sale, 50 percent in the second month, and the remainder in the next month. Sales for November totaled 35,000 litres. A litre of charcoal lighter sold for $0.60 this year, but the company plans to raise the price to $0.68 per litre in the new year due to increasing costs.

Required:

You are to prepare a sales budget and an accounts receivable budget for the first quarter of the new year.

11-15   Jenkins, Inc., makes two products G and X. G sells for $8.00 per unit and X sells for $10.00 per unit.

The company's expected production schedule for the fourth quarter is:

	G	X
October	5,000	6,000
November	6,000	6,500
December	5,200	7,000

Raw materials needed for production are:

	Cost/unit	G	X
A	$ .75	3	3
B	.90	2	1
C ....,..	2.00		2

There are 200 units of A, 150 units of B, and 100 units of C in beginning inventory. They plan to increase the ending inventories by 15 units at the end of each month.

Jenkins pays for 60% of their purchases in the month of the purchase and the remainder in the next month. Beginning accounts payable are $23,250.

Required:

You are to prepare a direct material purchases budget and an accounts payable budget for the fourth quarter.

11-16   Below are given the condensed financial statements of the Flophouse Hotel:

Flophouse Hotel
Balance Sheet
as of December 31

Cash...............................	$ 10,000	
Accounts receivable (net)..............	25,000	
Other current assets...................	5,000	$ 40,000
Fixed assets..........................	$120,000	
Less: Accumulated depreciation........	36,000	84,000
Total Assets......................		$124,000
Accrued payables.....................		$ 20,000
Mortgage payable....................		40,000
Flophouse, capital...................		64,000
Total Liabilities and Equities.........		$124,000

Flophouse Hotel
Income Statement
Year 19x5

Revenues...........................	$250,000
Expenses...........................	200,000
Income...........................	$ 50,000

Other data:

a.   Revenues for 19x6 are expected to increase by 20 percent.

b.   Fixed expenses will remain constant at $100,000; the remaining expenses will continue to vary directly and proportionally with revenue.

c.   Accounts receivable at December 31, 19x6 are expected to be 10 percent of 19x6 revenue.

d.   The hotel plans a fixed asset addition on July 1, 19x6, costing $50,000. All fixed assets have a useful life of 10 years and no salvage value.

e.   Accounts payable at December 31, 19x6, are expected to aggregate 10 percent of total expenses.

f.   The 19x6 mortgage principal payment is $2,000.

g.   The owner plans to withdraw $25,000 during the year.

Required:

Prepare the following for the Flophouse Hotel for 19x6:

1.   Operating budget (budgeted income statement).
2.   Cash budget.
3.   Pro-forma balance sheet as of December 31, 19x6.

11-17   In 19x1, Sammy, Inc., sold 80,500 units of its product for $65 each. Of these sales, 80 percent were for cash. On December 31, 19x0, accounts payable totaled $26,870 and accounts receivable totaled $22,560, both of which were paid or received during 19x1. Seventy-five percent of direct materials were purchased for cash.

Sammy paid all of its direct labour and overhead in cash. Direct labour costs $4.25 per hour and variable overhead is $2.30 per direct labour hour. It takes 2½ hours to make one unit of the product. Direct materials total $10.65 per unit. There are no beginning or ending work-in-process inventories. Beginning and ending finished goods totaled 670 units and 950 units, respectively. Beginning raw material inventories were $8,524 and ending raw material inventories were $9,056.50. Total fixed overhead was $35,960 with depreciation totaling $9,840.

Variable selling costs are $.18 per unit. Fixed selling and administrative expenses are $150,000. The company pays $1,000 per month on long-term debt. The company's beginning cash balance in 19x1 was $32,645.

Required:

Prepare a cash budget for 19x1.

11-18 The Supply Company intends to expand in the last quarter of the year. In order to accomplish this expansion, they must purchase two new pieces of machinery and a used warehouse. On October 1, they plan to purchase the warehouse at a cost of $45,000. The warehouse will have no salvage value and is to be depreciated on the straight-line basis over a period of 20 years.

On November 1, they will purchase the first of the two machines at a cost of $27,450. This machine is to be depreciated using the sum-of-the-years' digits over a 7-year life. A $5,000 salvage value is expected at the end of its life.

On December 1, the last machine is to be purchased at a cost of $12,000. This machine is expected to have a $1,500 salvage value at the end of 5 years. It is to be depreciated on the straight-line basis.

Total fixed assets for the Suppy Company on September 30 were $1,500,650. Accumulated depreciation to that date was $800,000. These assets are all depreciated on the straight-line basis over a period of 10 years.

Required:

Prepare a fixed asset budget for the last quarter. Round to the nearest whole dollar.

11-19 You have been asked to assist in the preparation of a cash budget for the Fairley Co. Ltd.

Fairley sells one item only at a price of $100. Budgeted unit sales are as follows:

> January............................ 5,000 units
> February........................... 4,000 units
> March.............................. 3,000 units

All of Fairley's customers buy on account. Of these, 75% take advantage of a cash discount of 3%. Fairley's terms are 3/10; n/30. Fairley's bad debts average 2% on account.

Required:

Budgeted cash receipts for March.

(CGA, adapted)

11-20   Presented below is the income statement and balance sheet for the Lane Ax Company.

Lane Ax Co.
Income Statement
For the Year 19x5

Revenues	$770,000
Cost of goods sold	(530,000)
Contribution margin	$240,000
Operating expenses (including depreciation)	(40,000)
Fixed expenses	(90,000)
Selling and administrative expense	(40,000)
Net income	$ 70,000

Lane Ax Co,
Balance Sheet
19x5

Assets

Cash		$ 32,000
Accounts receivable		57,500
Other current assets		47,000
Total current assets		$136,500
Property, plant & equipment	$180,000	
Less: Accumulated depreciation	(54,000)	126,000
Total assets		$262,500

Liabilities

Accounts payable	$ 21,000
Long-term liabilities	127,000
Owners' capital	114,500
Total liabilities and owners' capital	$262,500

Additional Information:

1. Revenues should increase by 15 percent in 19x6.
2. Cost of goods sold will increase by 12 percent in 19x6 and selling and administrative expenses will increase by 10 percent.
3. 19x6 payment on long-term debt is $30,000.
4. The property, plant & equipment are depreciated over 10 years using the straight-line method and zero salvage value.
5. Ending accounts receivables are expected to be $53,130.
6. Capital will be reduced by $96,000 from withdrawals by the owners.
7. Fixed expenses will increase by 10 percent in 19x6.
8. Ending accounts payable will be $18,000.
9. Operating expenses (other than depreciation) will increase by 15%.

Required:

a. Prepare a projected income statement for 19x6.
b. Prepare a projected balance sheet as of December 31, 19x6.
c. Prepare a cash budget for 19x6.

11-21 During February and March, the Farm Fresh Egg Co. sold 110,000 and 90,000 dozen eggs, respectively. The eggs sell for $.49 per dozen for the small eggs, $.56 for medium eggs, $.60 for large eggs, and $.68 for extra large eggs. The ratio of eggs from small to extra large is 1-3-4-2 respectively. Sales for the second quarter are expected to increase 20% each month. Collections on sales are 50% in the month of the sale, 40% the next month, and 10% the third month.
Required:

Your joþ is to prepare a sales budget for February through June and an accounts receivable budget for April through June.

11-22 In 19x0, Lincaln, Inc. sold 95,460 units of its product. Each unit sells for $59.00. Seventy-five percent of these sales were for cash; the remainder were not paid by the end of the year.

Beginning finished goods inventory totaled 5,250 units; at the end of the year there were 7,860 units on hand. The company had no beginning or ending work-in-process inventories.

Direct material costs are $14.25 per unit. Ninety percent of the direct material purchases are paid in the year of the purchase. On January 1, 19x0, direct materials on hand totaled $14,250. On January 1, 19x1 they totaled $12,825.

It takes $3\frac{1}{4}$ hours of direct labor at $4.00 per hour to produce one unit of the product. Variable overhead is applied at $4.80 per direct labor hour. Fixed overhead is $89,500 per year. Plant depreciation is $19,400 per year, and equipment depreciation is $12,300 per year. All of the direct labor and factory overhead is paid in the year incurred.

Variable selling costs are $.27 per unit sold. Fixed selling and administrative expenses are $160,000 per year. The company has a debt of $200,000 of which 20% is paid per year. Interest of 6% is paid on the total debt outstanding at the beginning of the year. On January 1, 19x0, 60 percent of the debt was still outstanding.

On January 1, 19x0, accounts receivable were $53,260 and accounts payable were $84,250, all of which were received or paid during the year. The beginning cash balance was $380,226.

Required:

Prepare a cash budget for 19x0.

11-23   The following information has been obtained by the UVW Co. Ltd. during its budgeting process:

Inventory policy is to have in stock at the end of each month 25% of next month's requirements providing this does not exceed 4,000 units.
    Purchases are spread evenly throughout the month.
    All our suppliers offer a discount of 2/10; n/30. We take advantage of all cash discounts.
    Average sales price per unit is $50.00.
    Our average mark-up is 40% (of sales).

	Sales in Units
April	20,000
May	18,000
June	14,000
July	8,000
August	9,000

Required:

Compute the cash required for payments on account in June.

(CGA, adapted)

11-24   The Layton Co. Ltd. is in the process of preparing its budget for the coming year. The sales forecast includes the following:

June	— 6,000 units
July	— 10,000
August	— 9,000
September	— 5,000

    Ending inventories of finished goods are expected to be one-quarter of the following month's projected sales.
    Each unit of finished product includes 5 square feet of Material A and 2 gallons of Material B. Projected prices are $3.00/sq. ft. for Material A and $1.00/gal. for Material B. Ending inventories of materials are expected to be 20% of the following month's production requirements.
    Accounts payable for materials are eligible for a 2/10; n/30 discount. Layton plans to take advantage of all purchase discounts. Assume that one-third of the purchases of any month are due for discount and are paid for in the following month.
    No work-in-process is budgeted for.

Required:

Cash disbursements related to Material A for the month of July.

(CGA, adapted)

11-25 You are preparing net year's cash budget for the Balaclava Co. Ltd. and have collected the following information:

1. Balaclava manufactures one product having standard variable costs as follows:

Materials 5 sq. ft. @ $2,00.....................	$10.00
Direct labour 3 hr. @ $3.00....................	9.00
Variable overhead...........................	3.00

2. Depreciation per month is $3,000.
3. Sales price per unit is $40.
4. The only variable selling expenses are salesmen's commissions at 10%.
5. Fixed selling and administrative expenses are $2,000 per month.
6. Normal monthly production is 1,500 units.
7. Budgeted monthly sales in units:

March.....................................	1,100
April......................................	1,000
May.......................................	1,200
June	1,800

8. The economic order quantity for materials is 20,000 sq. ft. An order must be placed and paid for in the month before it is required.
9. Inventory of material on March 31 will be 11,000 sq. ft.
10. Cash balance on March 31 will be $10,000.
11. Assume that payroll, variable overhead and fixed costs are paid for in the month that they are incurred.
12. All sales are made on account. All customers pay within 30 days.

Required:

Prepare the cash budget for April. Indicate if any financing will be required.

(CGA, adapted)

11-26 You have been asked to prepare a flexible overhead budget for January, 19x1. You are to base this budget on the actual costs incurred during two representative months of 19x0. July and October have been selected as appropriate for this purpose. In addition, you have been advised that indirect materials costs are expected to be 5 percent higher in 19x1 than in 19x0, and indirect labour costs are expected to increase by 10 percent. No increase is predicted for other overhead costs.

	July	*October*
Units produced	10,000	20,000
Direct labour hours	5,000	10,000
Units sold	12,000	17,000
Direct materials used	$30,000	$60,000
Heat, light and power	800	1,100
Foremen's salaries	4,000	4,000
Direct labour cost	25,000	50,000
Depreciation of machinery	1,300	1,300
Maintenance supplies	1,000	2,000
Factory rent	1,800	1,800
Advertising expense	13,000	15,000
Wages of maintenance men	15,000	30,000
President's salary	5,000	5,000

Required:

a.   Prepare a flexible overhead budget in good form for the month of January, 19x1, when production is expected to be 16,000 units.

b.   What is the company's monthly flexible overhead budget formula for 19x1?

(CGA, adapted)

11-27   The Montreal Co. Ltd. has developed the following costs and other data pertaining to one of its materials:

Normal use per day	— 400 units
Maximum use per day	— 600 units
Minimum use per day	— 100 units
Working days per year	— 250
Lead time	— 8 days
Cost of placing one order	— $20
Carrying cost per unit per year	— $0.25

Required:

Compute the following:

a.   Safety stock
b.   Reorder point
c.   Economic order quantity
d.   Normal maximum inventory
e.   Absolute maximum inventory
f.   Average inventory

(CGA, adapted)

11-28   The Saskatoon Co. Ltd. manufactures a product for which the following sales forecast has been prepared.

	Number of Units
January	12,000
February	10,000
March	13,000
April	11,000

Saskatoon has a policy of producing enough units so that there will be a beginning inventory each month equal to 20 percent of the month's predicted sales.

The standard cost per unit is as follows:

Materials 3 lbs. @ $5.00	$15.00
Direct labour 1 hr. @ $6.00	6.00
Variable overhead	2.00
Fixed overhead	7.00
	$30.00

Materials inventories at the beginning of each month are to be equal to 40 percent of that month's production requirements.

All materials are purchased on account with terms of 2/10; n/30. Purchases are made evenly throughout the month. For convenience assume that all months have 30 days.

Required:

Compute the amount of cash required in February for payment of accounts payable related to the purchase of materials.

(CGA, adapted)

11-29   The following chart is a graphic solution to a company's production problem. The company has two departments and makes two products; each product requires processing in each of the two departments. Severe raw material shortages for one of the products will limit its production.

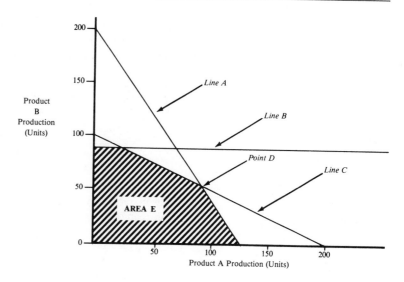

Required:

a. Referring to the graphic solution, indicate the significance of the following:

    i.   the line A
    ii.   the line B
    iii. the line C
    iv. the point D
    v.   the area E

b. Define operations research, name two OR techniques and give an example of a problem to which each technique could be applied.

(SMA, adapted)

11-30   The Fleury Company, a manufacturer of plastic containers is attempting to forecast inventory requirements and cash flow for the month of March. The following information is available:

    i.   Sales were budgeted at $150,000 for the month of March (15,000 units). The accounts receivable at the end of February are $135,000, (February sales totaled $120,000). The collection pattern is as follows:

% of Sales	Collected
20%	During the month of sale
50%	During month after month of sale
30%	During second month after month of sale

ii.   Inventory plans calls for a basic stock of 5,000 finished units plus 50% of the next month sales requirements to be on hand at the month-end. Expected sales for April, May and June are 18,000 units a month and units on hand at February 28 totaled 13,000. (500 units more than planned).

iii. Production costs per unit are:

Materials	(½ lb. @ $3.00)	=	$1.50
Labour	½ hr. @ $4.00)	=	2.00
Overhead	(½ hr.@ $5.00)	=	2.50
Total cost per unit			$6.00

iv.   Raw materials inventory is to be maintained at the expected production requirements for the next two months, to avoid any shortage. The inventory of raw materials at February 28 was 16,000 lbs. During February a total of 6,500 lbs. were purchased. The terms of purchase are net 30 days.

v.   The overhead rate of $5.00 per hour is based on an annual budget of:

Variable Overhead:
Indirect materials	$ 49,000
Indirect labour	143,000
	$192,000

Fixed overhead:
Salaries	$204,000
Services (heat, light, etc.)	36,000
Taxes (accrued, payable in May and November)	18,000
Insurance (prepaid in January)	9,000
Depreciation expenses	21,000
Total	$288,000
All totaled	$480,000
Expected hours (192,000 units)	96,000 hrs.
Overhead rate per hour	$5

vi.   Variable manufacturing overhead costs are paid in the month of incurrence.

vii. Marketing and administrative expenses are estimated as 30% of sales, ⅔ of which is payable during the month and ⅓ payable in the month following the sale.

Required:

a.   Determine the number of pounds of raw materials to be purchased during the month of March.

b.   Prepare a cash forecast statement for the month of March. The statement should show the amount of cash generated from operations during the month, and the amount available for other expenditures at month-end, assuming a cash balance of $4,500 at February 28.

(SMA, adapted)

11-31 Mourmark Limited is a large and rapidly expanding concern, which has grown very quickly from a local operation to a multi-plant organization operating in five provinces.

The Executive Vice-President has engaged you as a consultant because of both his concern over rising manufacturing costs and his feeling that the company's control techniques are no longer adequate. In your preliminary discussions with him, he has presented you with questions with respect to the use of budgets as a control device.

Required:

Briefly answer the following: (point form is acceptable)

a. What is meant by "budgetary control"?
b. Discuss the impact of budgets on the control of costs.
c. What limitations do budgets have in controlling costs?
d. What four main budgets should be prepared?

(SMA, adapted)

11-32 The Big Boy Company is in a seasonal business, and prepares quarterly budgets. Its fiscal year runs from July 1 through June 30. Production occurs only in the second quarter (October to December) while sales take place throughout the year. The forecast for the coming year shows sales as:

1st quarter	$390,000
2nd quarter	750,000
3rd quarter	390,000
4th quarter	390,000

There are no cash sales, and the beginning balance of receivables is expected to be collected in the first quarter. Subsequent collections are made two-thirds in the quarter in which sales takes place and one-third in the quarter following.

Material purchases valued at $360,000 are made in the first quarter and none in the last three quarters. Payment is made when materials are purchased.

Direct labour of $350,000 is incurred and paid only in the first quarter. Factory overhead of $430,000 is also incurred and paid in the first quarter. Factory overhead is at a standby level of $100,000 during the other three quarters. Selling and administrative expenses are paid at $50,000 per quarter throughout the year. Big Boy maintains an operating line of credit with its bank at an interest rate of 6% per annum. The company plans to maintain at least $8,000 at all times, and borrows in *multiples of $5,000*. All borrowings are made at the beginning of a quarter, and all payments are made at the end of a quarter.

The company plans to purchase equipment in the second and fourth quarters in the amounts of $150,000 and $50,000, respectively. Cash balance on July 1 is $23,000 and accounts receivable is $130,000.

Required:

Prepare a cash budget for the first two quarters showing receipts, disbursements, ending cash balance before borrowing, amounts borrowed, repaid, interest payments, and ending cash balance. Round interest payments to the nearest $1,000.

(SMA, adapted)

A 11-33   The partners of Constructo Company are concerned about the adequacy of cash flow in their business during the coming two months. In their zest for getting contracts they made generous performance guarantees which must be met before payments from customers become due. Unfavourable weather conditions and material shortages combined have frustrated their ability to meet deadlines.

The following data pertain to the company's cash position for the period June 1 to July 31:

	June	July
Revenue...........................	$125,000	$175,000

Purchases of goods and services

	June	July
On credit...........................	$124,000	$155,000
By cash............................	800	800

The following opening balances are estimated:

	Accounts Receivable	Accounts Payable
June 1..........................	$ 70,000	$ 67,000

The estimated opening cash balance on June 1 is $14,000. The partners wish a minimum cash balance of $10,000 at the end of each month.

All revenue is subject to credit terms as specified in various contracts. No cash discounts are offered. Cash collections are expected to be as follows:

	June	July
From the total opening balance of accounts receivable of each month	25%	20%
From current revenue.................	20%	20%

Purchases on credit are paid 50% in the month of purchase and the balance in the following month.

The partners may borrow from a financial institute specializing in high risk financing at the short-term rate of 12%. They expect to complete several major contracts by mid-September and to liquidate the outstanding loan by September 30th. Interest is paid at the beginning of the following month.

Required:

Prepare a cash budget for each of the months of June and July. Show loans, in multiples of $10,000 as necessary to preserve the minimum cash balance. Loans must be made at the start of the month in which the cash will be needed.

(SMA, adapted)

11-34 The chief accountant of ABC Limited requires a cash budget for the month of July. He has given you the following information:

Planned cash balance, July 1st:................	$20,000
Payrolls due in July:........................	$13,000
Depreciation for month of July:..............	$ 3,000
Merchandise purchases: (all made before the 15th day of a month)	
June	$40,000
July............................	35,000

— terms 2/10, n/30
— 50 percent paid within the discount period
— 30 percent paid within the month of purchase
— 20 percent paid in the next month

Accrued taxes for July, payable December.............................	$ 4,000
Other expenses for July, payable in July:.......	$ 900
Premium on a two-year insurance policy, due and payable in July:..................	$ 1,000

All credit sales incurred during a month are billed at the very beginning of the next month.

The record of accounts receivable collection reflects the following:

1% Uncollectible
99% Collectible:

60%	in month of billing
25%	in the next month
10%	in the second next month
5%	in the third next month
100%	

Estimated sales for July and actual sales for the four preceding months are as follows:

	Sales	
	Cash	*Credit*
March	$34,000	$62,000
April	36,000	61,000
May	30,000	64,000
June	35,000	54,000
July	33,000	58,000

July administrative expenses are estimated as follows:

Fixed expenses (exclusive of depreciation)	$5,000 per month
Variable expenses	10% of sales

Required:

Prepare a cash budget showing expected cash receipts, disbursements and ending cash balance for the month of July. Show all supporting calculations.

(SMA adapted)

11-35 The following information concerning Stanley Limited has been made available to you, for the development of cash and other budget information for the months of July, August and September:

a. Balances at July 1 are expected to be as follows:

Cash	$ 5,500
Accounts receivable	$437,000
Inventories	$309,400
Accounts payable	$133,055

b. The budget is to be based on the following assumptions:

   i. Each month's sales are billed on the last day of the month.
   ii. Customers are allowed a 3% discount if payment is made within ten days after the billing date. Receivables are booked at gross.
   iii. Sixty percent of the billings are collected within the discount period, 25% are collected by the end of the month after the date of sale, 9% are collected by the end of the second month after the date of sale and 6% prove uncollectible.
   iv. Fifty-four percent of all purchases of material and selling, general and administrative expenses are paid in the month purchased. The remainder is paid in the following month.
   v. Each month's units of ending inventory are equal to 130% of the next month's units of sales.
   vi. The cost of each unit of inventory is $20.

vii. Selling, general and administrative expenses, of which $2,000 is depreciation, are equal to 15% of the current month's sales.

c. Actual and projected sales are as follows:

	Sales	Units
May	$354,000	11,800
June	363,000	12,100
July	357,000	11,900
August	342,000	11,400
September	360,000	12,000
October	366,000	12,200

Required:

Calculate the following:

a. Budgeted cash disbursements during the month of August.
b. Budgeted cash collections during the month of July.
c. Budgeted number of units of inventory to be purchased during the month of September.

(SMA, adapted)

11-36 A company sets the price for its product at $300 per unit. Predicted variable costs are $175 per unit and fixed costs are expected to be $600,000 per year. Sales for the year are expected to be 8,000 units.

The company has the capacity to produce 10,000 units per year. Expansion of capacity is not feasible at present. Assume that the beginning inventory was zero.

Required:

(Solve each part independently of the other.)

a. Determine the cost of prediction error if actual variable costs were $190 per unit. All other predictions were correct.
b. All predictions were correct, except that 11,000 units could have been sold at the $300 price if enough had been available. However, only 8,000 units were produced and sold. Determine the cost of prediction error.

(SMA, adapted)

11-37 The controller of the Rustler Company recently attended a seminar on linear programming and feels that some of the concepts may be useful in planning operations for the coming year. The Rustler Company produces two models (Standard and Deluxe) of its basic product. The company operates in a competitive market and hence, can sell as many of each unit as it can produce.

The controller has prepared the following estimates of prices and costs (per unit) for the coming year.

	Standard	Deluxe
Selling price........................	$112.00	$152.00
Direct material A.....................	54.00	108.00
Direct material B.....................	18.75	18.75
Direct labour.......................	18.00	9.00
Variable overhead...................	6.25	6.25

Direct material A costs $9 per kilogram and the company can purchase up to 60,000 kilograms from its supplier. Direct material B is in short supply and Rustler Company can only acquire 90,000 litres at a price of $1.25 per litre. Direct labour is paid $4.50 per hour and the capacity of the factory is 20,000 direct labour hours.

Required:

Calculate the number of Standard and Deluxe units that should be produced in the coming year. What will be the resulting contribution?

(SMA, adapted)

11-38 The Malden Company Limited produces units which sell for $50 each. Each unit requires four pounds of raw materials at a cost of $4 per pound. Management policy is to have the following inventory levels on hand at the end of each month:

Finished goods: 15 percent of next month's budgeted sales.
Raw materials: 2,000 pounds plus 15 percent of next month's production requirements.

The company qualifies for a 1 percent discount by paying all accounts in the month following all monthly purchases. Management has always followed the inventory guidelines and has now budgeted the following sales:

January......... $1,600,000
February........ 2,000,000
March.......... 2,400,000
April.......... 1,800,000

Required:

How much money should the company budget for disbursement in February for payment of purchases? Show all calculations.

(SMA, adapted)

11-39 Luper Co. produces two products, A and B, in its Winnipeg plant. Unit selling prices and standard costs are as follows:

	Product A		Product B	
Selling price.............................		$280		$370
Standard cost:				
Direct materials.........................	$ 60		$ 80	
Direct labour..........................	120		150	
Variable overhead.......................	40		50	
Fixed overhead.........................	20	240	25	305
Profit margin.............................		$ 40		$ 65

The production departments and their capacities are as follows:

Department	Capacity
Machining	1,800 machine hours
Assembly	4,500 direct labour hours
Finishing	1,600 direct labour hours

Both products utilize the same facilities. Demand is strong for both products; prices and costs are stable. Luper Co. can sell all of the product it can manufacture. The two products require the following inputs per unit as they proceed through the entire production cycle:

Product	Machine Hours	Assembly Hours	Finishing Hours
A	5	9	4
B	4	18	5

Required:

Using linear programming, develop a production plan that will make the most beneficial use of current plant capacity. Clearly identify all calculations.

(SMA, adpated)

11-40 The ABC Company Limited expected to be able to sell 10,000 units at $100 per unit, with variable costs of $38 per unit and fixed costs of $420,000. The company stocked the 10,000 units, but was able to sell only 9,000 units at $100 per unit, with the remainder being perishable and therefore of no value. The variable costs were actually $43 per unit.

Required:

What was the company's cost of prediction error? Show all calculations.

(SMA, adpated)

11-41 The sales budget is instrumental in determining all other budgets (such as the production and cash budgets) as well as the pro-forma financial statements. Therefore, in cases where it is impossible to precisely estimate future sales, all other budgets and the pro-forma financial statements will be correspondingly different from actual. Thus, the entire budget process is not only expensive, but fails to provide any benefit to the company. The company would be better off to evaluate performance by comparing actual results to historical results.

Required:

Give specific criticisms of the above statement. Include in your reply a discussion of the benefits that could be obtained in the above situation through budgeting.

(SMA, adapted)

11-42 As part of the company's overall planning program, the controller of the So Good Blueberry Packing Co. Ltd. prepares a cash budget by quarters each year.

The company's operations consist solely of processing and canning the yearly crop of blueberries. As this is a seasonal commodity, all manufacturing operations take place in the quarter of October through December. Sales are made throughout the year and the company's fiscal year ends June 30.

The sales forecast for the coming year indicates (all figures in thousands):

1st quarter:	(July—September, 19x1)........	$ 780
2nd quarter:	(October—December, 19x1).....	1,500
3rd quarter:	(January—March, 19x2)........	780
4th quarter:	(April—June, 19x2)...........	780

All sales are on account. The beginning balance of receivables is expected to be collected during the first quarter. It is anticipated that subsequent collections will follow the pattern of two-thirds collected in the quarter of sales, the remaining one-third in the quarter following.

Purchases of blueberries are scheduled as follows: $240,000 in the 1st quarter and $720,000 in the 2nd quarter. Payment is made in the quarter of purchase.

Direct labour of $700,000 is incurred and paid in the second quarter.

Manufacturing overhead cost (paid in cash during quarter it is incurred) is $860,000 in the second quarter. The standby amount in each of the other three quarters is $200,000.

Selling and administrative expenses, incurred and paid, amount to $100,000 per quarter during the year.

To finance its seasonable working capital needs, the company has obtained a line of short-term credit with the Royal Toronto Bank. The company maintains a minimum cash balance of $8,000 and borrows and repays only in multiples of $5,000. It repays as soon as it is able without impairing the minimum cash balance. Interest is at 8 percent and is paid at time of loan repayment. It is assumed that all borrowing is made at the beginning of a quarter, and the repayments are made at the end of a quarter (round interest calculations to the nearest $1,000).

The company plans to spend the following amounts on fixed assets:

3rd quarter....................	$150,000
4th quarter....................	50,000

Account balances as of July 1, 19x1 were:

Cash.........................	$ 8,000
Accounts receivable.............	25,000

Required:

a. Prepare a schedule to show the cash budget and financing requirements for the year ended June 30, 19x2.
b. Comment briefly on the nature and purpose of cash budgets for managerial planning.

(SMA, adapted)

11-43 The Barnes Company budgeted the data for certain months in 19x5 and 19x6, as shown below:

	December	January	February	March	April
Sales on account—					
gross.........	$1,500,000	$1,600,000	$1,700,000	$1,700,000	$1,600,000
Cash sales.......	200,000	210,000	220,000	220,000	210,000

Merchandise is marked up at 20 percent of the gross sales price. All purchases of merchandise are on account with terms of 2/10, net/30. All purchase discounts are taken, and normally two-thirds of each month's purchases are paid during the month of purchase, whereas the other one-third is paid during the first month after purchase. Merchandise inventories at the beginning of each month are kept at 30 percent of that month's projected cost of goods sold. Even though all purchase discounts are taken; purchases, inventories, and cost of goods sold are all recorded gross.

Terms for sales on account are 1/10, net/30. Fifty percent of each month's sales on account are collected during that month, whereas 45 percent are collected in the succeeding month. The remainder is normally uncollectible. Only 50 percent of the collections in the month of sale and in the following month are made early enough to receive cash discounts.

Required:

Prepare schedules showing cash receipts from sales and cash disbursements on merchandise purchases for the months of January, February, and March.

11-44 The Rapids Manufacturing Company had the following trial balance as of January 1, 19x6:

Cash	$ 280,000	
Accounts receivable	440,000	
Raw material X (70,000 lb,)	140,000	
Raw material Y (80,000 gal.)	120,000	
Work-in-process	100,000	
Finished goods (25,200 units)	340,200	
Prepaid insurance	5,800	
Property, plant, and equipment	1,500,000	
Property, plant, and equipment—depreciation		$ 550,000
Accounts payable—materials		280,000
Accrued expenses		130,000
Federal income taxes payable		240,000
Notes payable—bank		800,000
Common stock		700,000
Retained earnings		226,000
	$2,926,000	$2,926,000

Sales for the coming year were estimated at 150,000 units at $20 per unit. The standard cost of each unit of output consisted of the following:

Standard Cost Per Unit

Material:	
2 lb. of X @ $2.00	$ 4.00
2 gal. of Y @ 1.50	3.00
Labor:	
¼ hr. @ $10.00	2.50
Factory overhead—variable:	
1 hr. @ $1.80	1.80
Factory overhead—fixed:	
1 hr. @ $2.20	2.20
Total unit cost	$13.50

The company was highly dissatisfied with its inventory levels, except in the case of work-in-process. It was decided to cut all inventories 50 percent by the end of the year except for work-in-process which was to remain stable. Only December purchases of 30,000 pounds of X and 40,000 gallons of Y are to remain unpaid as of the year end. All purchases are anticipated to be made at standard prices.

One-third (2,500 units) of November sales (7,500 units) and two-thirds (7,000 units) of December sales (10,500 units) are expected to be uncollected as of December 31. Of the accounts collected during each year, 80 percent are normally subject to a cash discount of 2 percent.

The estimate of factory overhead for the year is as follows:

Estimated Manufacturing Overhead

Variable:

Indirect labor....................................	$115,000
Supplies...	73,200
Power	59,120
Total variable.............................	$247,320

Fixed:

Salaries...	$125,000
Depreciation.....................................	150,000
Insurance..	18,000
Property taxes...................................	57,000
Total fixed.................................	$350,000
Total manufacturing overhead..................	$597,320

Selling and administrative expenses are estimated as follows for the years activities:

Estimated Selling and Administrative Expense

Salaries...	$245,000
Supplies...	18,000
Sales promotion..................................	190,000
Telephone and telegraph..........................	16,000
Depreciation.....................................	40,000
Insurance..	4,000
Interest	25,000
Property taxes...................................	9,000
Total	$547,000

Accrued expenses at the end of the year are estimated at $110,000, which will include unpaid payroll, supplies, power, etc. Depreciation is, of course, a non-cash item, and all insurance bills amounting to $23,000 will be prepaid.

No variances are expected in the prices of materials, labor, or overhead elements. However, direct labor inefficiency of 10 percent is expected because of the addition of inexperienced workers. This 10 percent variance and any overhead variances are to be treated as additions to cost of goods sold.

The minimum desired cash balance is $280,000. Amounts needed to achieve this minimum can be borrowed from the bank in multiples of $1,000. Amounts in excess of this minimum can be used to repay bank notes in multiples of $1,000. Ignore the possibility of interest expense (for the purpose of simplification).

Required:

a. A profit budget for the year—assume a Federal income tax rate of 50 percent.

b. A cash budget for the year, including any changes in bank notes.

c. A budgeted balance sheet as of December 31, 19x6.

Hint: Before attempting a solution to this problem, the student would be wise to calculate production required, materials required, materials purchases, labor required, and overhead required.

11-45   Pointer Furniture Company manufactures and sells office furniture. In order to compete effectively in different quality and price markets it produces several brands of office furniture. The manufacturing operation is organized by the item produced rather than by the furniture line. Thus, the desks for all brands are manufactured on the same production line. For efficiency and quality control reasons the desks are manufactured in batches. For example, 10 high quality desks might be manufactured during the first two weeks in October and 50 units of a lower quality desk during the last two weeks. Because each model has its own unique manufacturing requirement, the change from one model to another requires the factory's equipment to be adjusted.

The management of Pointer wants to determine the most economical production run for each of the items in its product lines. The manager of the cost accounting department is going to adapt the economic order quantity (EOQ) inventory model for this analysis.

One of the cost parameters that must be determined before the model can be employed is the setup cost incurred when there is a change to a different furniture model. The cost accounting department has been asked to determine the setup cost for the desk (Model JE 40) in its junior executive line as an example.

The equipment maintenance department is responsible for all of the changeover adjustments on production lines in addition to the preventive and regular maintenance of all the production equipment. The equipment maintenance staff has a 40 hour work week; the size of the staff is changed only if there is a change in the workload that is expected to persist for an extended period of time. The equipment maintenance department had 10 employees last year, and they each averaged 2,000 hours for the year. They are paid $9.00 an hour and employee benefits average 20% of wage costs. The other departmental costs, which include such items as supervision, depreciation, insurance, etc., total $50,000 per year.

Two men from the equipment maintenance department are required to make the change on the desk line for Model JE 40. They spend an estimated five hours in setting up the equipment as follows:

Machinery Changes..................	3 hours
Testing...........................	1 hour
Machinery Readjustments............	1 hour
Total...........................	5 hours

The desk production line on which Model JE 40 is manufactured is operated by five workers. During the changeover these workers assist the maintenance workers when needed and operate the line during the test run. However, they are idle for approximately 40 percent of the time required for the changeover.

The production workers are paid a basic wage rate of $7.50 an hour. Two overhead bases are used to apply the indirect costs of this production line because some of the costs vary in proportion to direct labor hours while others vary with machine hours. The overhead rates applicable for the current year are as follows:

	Based on Direct Labor Hours	Based on Machine Hours
Variable.............	$2.75	$ 5.00
Fixed................	2.25	15.00
	$5.00	$20.00

These department overhead rates are based upon an expected activity of 10,000 direct labor hours and 1,500 machine hours for the current year. This department is not scheduled to operate at full capacity because production capability currently exceeds sales potential at this time.

The estimated cost of the direct materials used in the test run totals $200. Salvage material from the test run should total $50.

Required:

A. Prepare an estimate of Pointer Furniture Company's setup cost for desk Model JE 40 for use in the economic production run model. For each cost item identified in the problem, justify the amount and the reason for including the cost item in your estimate. Explain the reason for excluding any cost item from your estimate.

B. Identify the cost items which would be included in an estimate of Pointer Furniture Company's cost of carrying the desks in inventory.

(CMA adapted)

11-46 The Jessica Co. has been searching for more formal ways to analyze its alternative courses of action. The expected value decision model was among those considered. In order to test the effectiveness of the expected value model a one-year trial in a small department was authorized.

This department buys and resells a perishable product. A large purchase at the beginning of each month provides a lower cost than more frequent purchases and also assures that Jessica Co. can buy all of the item it wants. Unfortunately, if too much is purchased the product unsold at the end of the month is worthless and must be discarded.

If an inadequate quantity is purchased, additional quantities probably cannot be purchased. If any should be available, they would probably be of poor quality and be overpriced. Jessica chooses to lose the potential sales rather than furnish poor quality product. The standard purchase arrangement is $50,000 plus $0.50 for each unit purchased for orders of 100,000 units or more. Jessica is paid $1.25 per unit by its customers.

The needs of Jessica's customers limit the possible sales volumes to only four quantities per month—100,000, 120,000, 140,000 or 180,000 units. However, the total quantity needed for a given month cannot be determined prior to the date Jessica must make its purchases. The sales managers are willing to place a probability estimate on each of the four possible sales volumes each month. They noted that the probabilities for the four sales volumes change from month to month because of the seasonal nature of the customers' business. Their probability estimates for December, 1978 sales units are 10% for 100,000, 30% for 120,000, 40% for 140,000, and 20% for 180,000.

The following schedule shows the quantity purchased each month based upon the expected value decision model. The actual units sold and product discarded or sales lost are shown also.

		Quantity (in units)		Sales Units
	Purchased	Sold	Discarded	Lost
January........	100,000	100,000	—	20,000
February.......	120,000	100,000	20,000	—
March.........	180,000	140,000	40,000	—
April..........	100,000	100,000	—	80,000
May...........	100,000	100,000	—	—
June	140,000	140,000	—	—
July...........	140,000	100,000	40,000	—
August	140,000	120,000	20,000	—
September	120,000	100,000	20,000	—
October........	120,000	120,000	—	20,000
November......	180,000	140,000	40,000	—

Required:

A. What quantity should be ordered for December 1978 if the expected value decision model is used?
B. Suppose Jessica could ascertain its customers' needs prior to placing its purchase order rather than relying on the expected value decision model. How much would it pay to obtain this information for December?
C. The model did not result in purchases equal to potential sales except during two months. Is the model unsuitable in this case or is this a characteristic of the model? Explain your answer.

(CMA adapted)

Chapter 12

Chapter 12 introduces the concept of responsibility accounting and the role it plays in management accounting systems. This chapter also discusses performance reporting for cost centers. Studying this chapter should enable you to:

1. Distinguish between controllable costs and direct costs and explain why this distinction is important to responsibility accounting.
2. Discuss the general types of responsibility centers.
3. Explain how a typical responsibility accounting system functions.
4. Describe a performance report and explain how it is used in a responsibility accounting system.
5. List and evaluate the guidelines which have been developed for assigning controllability.
6. Recognize the problems created by the existence of service department costs.
7. Discuss how the use of a responsibility accounting system might result in suboptimization of organizational goals.

Responsibility Accounting and Performance Reporting for Cost Centers

RESPONSIBILITY accounting is an accounting system which emphasizes the human element of the firm and its effect on operations. Responsibility accounting stresses the control or influence that a manager can exert within the segment of the organization which operates under his direction. Ideally, the manager's participation in establishing the budget for his segment and his responsibility for its operations is based on those economic factors that he can control or at least influence. The manager is held responsible for attaining the performance level which was budgeted for his segment.

Responsibility accounting aids in the delegation of authority by permitting the various levels of management within the firm to make decisions regarding those economic factors which they can control. Accounting information is collected and classified on the basis of the responsibility structure of the organization. This information, in part, is the same information which is collected for planning and financial accounting purposes, but is reclassified to meet responsibility accounting needs.

CONTROLLABLE ECONOMIC FACTORS

The controllable economic factors which are found in any firm include revenues, costs, assets, liabilities, and shareholders' equity. Somewhere in the management hierarchy, decisions regarding all of these factors are made. Responsibility accounting identifies the individuals who are making these decisions and aids in holding these individuals accountable for their decisions and actions.

Two classifications or definitions of costs are appropriate for responsibility accounting purposes: controllable costs and noncontrollable costs. These concepts of controllable and noncontrollable may also be applied to revenues, assets, liabilities, and owners' equity as will be explained later in this chapter.

CONTROLLABLE VERSUS NONCONTROLLABLE COSTS

Responsibility accounting requires that costs be classified in terms of the ability of individuals to influence costs in a given time period. The following definition of controllable costs, while more stringent than need be for responsibility accounting, is nonetheless applicable: A controllable cost is a cost which can be traced to a specific responsibility center on a nonarbitrary basis and which can be directly influenced by the manager of that center in a given time period. A noncontrollable cost cannot be directly influenced by the responsibility center manager. Thus it is the managers who influence specific costs who should participate in planning those costs and who should be held accountable for those costs during the operating period. If the entire firm is considered to be a responsibility center, all costs are considered controllable by someone at some level in the organization. Therefore, in assigning costs to a responsiblity center, the controllability of costs by someone in that center is a primary consideration.

There are certain common misconceptions regarding controllable costs, fixed costs, variable costs, direct or traceable costs, and indirect or common costs. It is important to note that the dichotomy of fixed and variable costs has no relationship to controllable and noncontrollable costs. All costs within a given responsibility center can be classified either as direct or indirect costs. Direct costs are those costs that can be traced to a given segment of the organization (in this case, a responsibility center) on a non-arbitrary basis. Theoretically, if a responsibility center was eliminated, the direct cost would also be eliminated. All controllable costs are direct costs, because controllable costs can be traced to a specific cost center. However, all direct costs in a responsibility center may not be controllable by the manager of that center. For example, depreciation on equipment might be traceable to a production foreman's responsibility center, even though the foreman cannot control that particular cost.

Indirect or common costs are those costs which are common to more than one segment of the organization (in this case, the responsibility center). Any cost assignment is based on some arbitrary method of allocation. Therefore, all indirect costs are noncontrollable costs for any specific responsibility center.

At each level within the organization, a manager is held directly responsible for the controllable costs of his operation. In addition, he is also responsible for the controllable costs of those segments which are headed by his subordinates. This structure of responsibility provides for the delegation of authority at the lowest possible level of management and recognition of the chain of command and span of control principles.

FORMS OF RESPONSIBILITY CENTERS

Responsibility centers can be classified based on the financial factors which the manager in charge of the responsibility center can influence. A common method of classification is to consider a responsibility center as either a cost center, a profit center or an investment center. Each of these forms of responsibility centers is discussed below.

Cost Centers

The difference between a cost center and an expense center is related to the concept of period versus product costs. The costs of an expense center are usually period costs, while the costs of a cost center normally relate to product costs which are inventoried until the goods are sold. The terms cost and expense center are often considered to be interchangeable in practice.

In a production department where output can be measured objectively in dollars and a specific output is associated with a given cost level, the term cost center is usually used in describing the segment. The segment manager is then held accountable for a specific dollar output at a given cost level.

Cost centers or expense centers are established when conditions are such that the responsible manager can influence only costs. For a cost to be incurred in a given cost center, that cost center should be required to produce a specified amount of output. Since, in certain cases, output cannot feasibly be measured in terms of dollars, the term expense center may be appropriate. Examples of such cases are the accounting department's and purchasing department's contributions to the firm.

Profit Centers

Profit centers are established in those situations where the responsibility center manager can influence both the expenses and revenues of his center. In practice, all or part of the revenues reported by many profit centers are actually the result of sales to other segments of the firm. The price attached to these "intersegment" sales is called a transfer price and is discussed in Chapter 13. For managerial accounting purposes, a profit center must have measurable outputs if a transfer price is to be used to measure intersegment sales. Of course, for financial accounting purposes, only sales to third parties are considered in determining income. The profit center concept is useful, however, in that it allows the manager to make decisions concerning costs and revenues in attaining the expected profit for his segment.

Investment Centers

The investment center concept places the responsible manager in a situation that is analogous to running his own business. The investment center manager is held responsible for producing a future planned income by utilizing a certain amount of invested capital. In other words, the investment center manager can influence revenues, expenses, and the capital invested in his segment. This manager must utilize all resources available to him in order to acquire the best overall results possible. Most divisions of large corporations are actually investment centers, but the term is not widely used in practice. Instead, investment centers are usually referred to as profit centers.

ORGANIZATION STRUCTURE AND RESPONSIBILITY ACCOUNTING

To be effective, responsibility accounting systems are developed along the decision-making lines of authority. If the organizational structure is developed on the basis of authority and decision-making responsibilities, then planning, control and performance reporting can be developed using the same organizational structure.

The job descriptions for the managers in the various responsibility centers should identify the functions, responsibilities, and authority of the manager with respect to his position. Each manager should be concerned with the controllable economic factors that fall within his sphere of responsibilities. In addition, the integration provided by the planning function should assure that the responsibility centers will all act in the best interests of the entire firm. In other words, the ideal situation is for a manager to act in the best interests of his segment while also simultaneously acting in the best interests of the firm as a whole.

ILLUSTRATION OF RESPONSIBILITY ACCOUNTING COST CENTERS

As was previously stated, the responsibility accounting system should be related to the general lines of accountability and authority found in the company's organization chart, if at all possible. A partial organization chart of Sax Company is presented in Illustration 12-1. Only the segment which is related to the Power Turbine Shaft Division is included in detail.

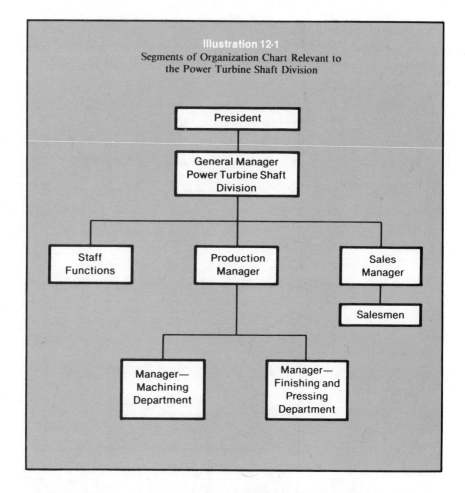

Illustration 12-1
Segments of Organization Chart Relevant to
the Power Turbine Shaft Division

The budgets found in Chapters 10 (Short-Range Planning) and 11 (Short-Range Planning: Financial and Resource Budgets) are developed for the entire division on an accrual accounting basis. For responsibility accounting purposes, these budgets have limited usefulness because the format and detail does not permit the assignment of specific managerial responsibility. To be useful for responsibility accounting purposes, the forecast budgets would have to be recast according to the responsibility format, starting at the lowest level of management where controllable factors can be identified and where the decision-making process takes place. Illustration 12-2 is an example of a responsibility forecast budget for the manager of the machining department for the month of February.

The forecast budget, and ultimately, the entire performance report for the machining department is based on those factors subject to the control of the machining department manager. Illustration 12-2 is only one po-

Illustration 12-2
Responsibility Budget
Machining Department

Manager—Machining Department
Month *February*

Forecast Production 20,000
Actual Production

	Per Unit	(1) Forecast Budget at Standard a	(2) Flexible (Control) Budget at Standard	(3) Actual This Month	(4) Actual Year To Date b	Variances (Unfavorable) (5) This Month	(6) Year To Date c
Controllable Costs:							
Direct Labor	$2.00	$ 40,000			$ 33,500		$500
Direct Materials	4.00	80,000			68,000		–0–
Rework Time	.05	1,000			500		350
Setup Time	.04	800			1,020		(340)
Indirect Materials & Supplies	.30	6,000			4,900		200
Total Controllable Costs	$6.39	$127,800			$107,920		$710

a This column refers to the budget for one month only. In this case, it represents the forecast for the month of February.
b This column pertains to January performance only. None of the performance in February is yet included in the actual to date.
c This column is explained in the text.

tential format for such a responsibility budget. A firm generally uses that format which best meets the needs of its management.

The forecast budget (column 1) for the machining department is prepared using established standards for the controllable costs at a level of 20,000 units of production. Last month's (January) production of 17,000 units represents the year-to-date production costs at the beginning of February. The actual controllable costs incurred in producing the 17,000 units are given in column four of Illustration 12-2. The flexible (control) budget for the year-to-date is developed by considering the year-to-date variances (column 6), and the actual controllable costs (column 4). For example, the direct labor cost at standard that should have been used to date is the actual cost of $33,500 plus the favorable variance of $500, for a total cost of $34,000.

During February, the machining department completed 21,000 units of the product. This department had the same dollar amount of work-in-process inventory at the end of the month as it had at the beginning of the month. The forecast budget was developed on the basis of 20,000 units of production, but 21,000 units were actually produced. To prepare a performance report when there are variable controllable costs involved, a flexible budget or a control budget must be prepared after-the-fact, but before any variances can be calculated. The control budget considers the actual activity that took place at the standard cost of producing that activity. Actual costs accumulated in the records are then compared with the standard costs at the same level of activity (21,000 units for February). Illustration 12-3 shows the completed responsibility report for the machining department.

The performance report presented in Illustration 12-3 for the machining department manager includes more detail than is necessary for a variance analysis of the controllable costs. All six columns of Illustration 12-3 should be reviewed in order to understand the use of responsibility accounting for planning, control, and performance evaluation purposes.

The forecast budget (column 1) included in the responsibility report presented in Illustration 12-3 is not needed for variance analysis purposes. The basis of performance reporting for a cost center is the comparison of budgeted costs and actual costs for the output produced. Measures other than cost factors, such as percentage of volume attained, efficiency ratios, and cost ratios are also usually developed. In certain situations, these measures may be more important than cost variances.

The actual collection of costs and related information for responsibility accounting takes place on a regular basis. Actual performance reporting for financial control takes place as frequently as management deems nec-

Illustration 12-3
Responsibility Report
Machining Department

Manager—Machining Department
Month *February*

Forecast Production 20,000
Actual Production 21,000

	Per Unit	(1) Forecast Budget at Standard a	(2) Flexible (Control) Budget at Standard b	(3) Actual This Month c	(4) Actual Year To Date d	Variances (Unfavorable) (5) This Month e	(6) Year To Date f
Controllable Costs:							
Direct Labor	$2.00	$ 40,000	$ 42,000	$ 43,000	$ 76,500	($1,000)	($ 500)
Direct Materials	4.00	80,000	84,000	84,400	152,400	(400)	(400)
Rework Time	.05	1,000	1,050	800	1,300	250	600
Setup Time	.04	800	840	700	1,720	140	(200)
Indirect Materials & Supplies	.30	6,000	6,300	5,500	10,400	800	1,000
Total Controllable Costs .	$6.39	$127,800	$134,190	$134,400	$242,320	($ 210)	$ 500

a Column one is the original forecast budget for 20,000 units of production at the standard cost.
b Column two is the flexible or control budget prepared at the end of the reporting period. The basis for this budget is actual activity, 21,000 units, at the standard cost.
c Column three is the actual controllable costs incurred at the actual production level of 21,000 units.
d Column four is actual production costs for the year-to-date (for January and February). When column four from Illustration 12-2 is added to column three from Illustration 12-3, the sum of the two equals the actual year-to-date, column four, in Illustration 12-3.
e The variances from the budgeted amounts for the month of February represents the difference between columns two and three—the control budget costs at 21,000 units and the actual costs at 21,000 units. These variances are presented in column five.
f Column six shows the variances between the control budget and actual costs for the year-to-date. To develop column six in Illustration 12-3, the year-to-date variances on February 1 (from Illustration 12-2) and the variances for February from column five in Illustration 12-3 must be summed.

essary to evaluate a given cost center. The performance report should be viewed as an additional cost control tool for the use of the responsible manager as well as a performance evaluation tool for the use of his superiors.

THE RESPONSIBILITY ACCOUNTING SYSTEM

Performance reports are integrated by responsibility levels. If a subordinate is responsible for a given financial factor, the subordinate's superior is also responsible for that same factor. The organization chart presented in Illustration 12-1 outlines the levels of responsibility in the Power Turbine Shaft Division. Performance reporting, both within the Division and to the President of Sax Company, follows the lines of authority and responsibility established by the organization chart.

The reporting relationships established for responsibility accounting are identified in Illustration 12-4. Each of the reports is condensed at the next level of management by reporting only the "bottom line" of subordinates' performance reports.

The total controllable costs which were included on the performance report of the manager of the machining department become a single line on the report of the production manager. The production manager's performance report also includes the bottom line from the finishing and pressing department manager's report. The production manager is also held responsible for the other costs of production which neither the manager of the machining department nor the manager of the finishing and pressing department can influence. As the production manager can influence only costs, his sphere of responsibility is a cost center.

The bottom line on the production manager's performance report becomes one line of the general manager's performance report. The controllable cost totals of the sales manager and division staff are also a part of the general manager's performance report. All Power Turbine Shaft Division costs which are controllable by the general manager appear on the general manager's performance report. In addition, the general manager has controllable revenues from the sales manager's performance report. Therefore, at a minimum, the general manager's sphere of responsibility may be considered a profit center. If the general manager can also influence capital investment, then his sphere of responsibility is an investment center.

The controllable income for the Power Turbine Shaft Division can be traced to a single line item included on the company president's performance report. The company president is held responsible for all of the subordinates within the firm. His sphere of responsibility is obviously an investment center because the president can control revenues, costs, and capital investments.

Illustration 12-4
Responsibility Accounting Performance Reports
President—Sax Company
Month February

	Budget		Variances (Unfavorable)	
	This Month	Year To Date	This Month	Year To Date
Controllable Income:				
Power Turbine Shaft Division	$119,100	$ 300,700	($6,200)	($2,480)
Other Divisions °	256,000	552,000	2,000	4,500
Total Controllable Income . . .	$375,100	$ 852,700	($4,200)	$2,020
Controllable Costs:				
Other Corporate Costs ° . . .	150,000	300,000	(5,000)	(6,000)
Controllable Income	$225,100	$ 552,700	($9,200)	($3,980)

General Manager—Power Turbine Shaft Division
Month February

	Budget		Variances (Unfavorable)	
	This Month	Year To Date	This Month	Year To Date
Controllable Revenues:				
Sales Manager	$575,000	$1,175,000	($5,000)	($3,000)
Controllable Costs:				
Sales Manager	134,000	270,500	500	2,000
Production Manager	219,250	396,800	(250)	720
Division Staff	73,500	147,000	(1,500)	(1,600)
Other Division Costs °	29,150	60,000	50	(600)
Controllable Income	$119,100	$ 300,700	($6,200)	($2,480)

Production Manager
Month February

	Budget		Variances (Unfavorable)	
	This Month	Year To Date	This Month	Year To Date
Controllable Costs:				
Machining Department	$134,190	$ 242,320	($ 210)	$ 500
Finishing and Pressing Department	71,190	128,820	190	900
Other Costs °	13,870	25,660	(230)	(680)
	$219,250	$ 396,800	($ 250)	$ 720

Manager—Machining Department
Month February

Forecast Production This Month   20,000
Actual Production This Month   21,000
Actual Production Year to Date   38,000

	Budget		Variances (Unfavorable)	
	This Month	Year To Date	This Month	Year To Date
Controllable Costs:				
Direct Labor	$ 42,000	$ 76,500	($1,000)	($ 500)
Direct Materials	84,000	152,400	(400)	(400)
Rework Time	1,050	1,300	250	600
Setup Time	840	1,720	140	(200)
Indirect Materials and Supplies	6,300	10,400	800	1,000
Total Controllable Costs	$134,190	$ 242,320	($ 210)	$ 500

° These numbers are condensed. In an actual report, detail would be presented.

MANAGEMENT BY EXCEPTION

After the forecast budgets are developed with the participation of management, it is up to the managers to meet or achieve the plans as stated in their budgets. When actual results are recorded and the performance reports are prepared, management need only consider the significant variances from the budget. The performance report should place major emphasis on variances, because variances should be the focus of management's attention. The reports in Illustration 12-4 contain the minimum information necessary for the month or year-to-date variances. The emphasis on variances assists management in concentrating its attention on the exceptions from the budget. This is called management by exception. In order to increase the emphasis on variances, many firms express variances both in dollars and as percentages of the budget. The budgeted amounts found in the performance reports are dependent on the emphasis of management and on the type of responsibility center producing the report (i.e., cost center, profit center, or investment center).

THE REPORTING CYCLE

The timing of reporting is crucial because reports must meet the needs of management. If the nature of a responsibility center's operations are such that a daily report is necessary for control purposes, then that center should receive the performance report on a daily basis. Remember, responsibility reporting is considered a tool for management use, not a threat. Variances are early warnings to management that something needs attention. The more important the item is to management, the more critical the time factor becomes.

Each manager should receive only those reports he needs. Again, a sensitive area may warrant daily reporting. However, a manager whose operations do not require daily or weekly reports should not be included on the same reporting cycle as a manager of a more sensitive area. Typically, the longest internal reporting cycle is about one month.

Non-current information is of little value in identifying problem areas. Managers need up-to-date information in order to correct current problems. A performance report delivered today which presents an analysis of the operations which is three months old has limited usefulness in correcting current problems or measuring current performance.

IDENTIFYING RESPONSIBILITY

Controllability is not always easy to identify due to the fact that very few cost items fall under the decision-making sphere of a single individual.

Responsibility accounting requires that the individual with the most influence over costs be responsible and be held accountable for those costs. One group of knowledgeable accountants has identified guidelines that could be used, along with good judgment, in making the controllability decisions.[1]

1. If a person has authority over both the acquisition and the use of the service, he should be charged with the cost of such service.
2. If the person can significantly influence the amount of cost through his own action, he may be charged with such cost.
3. Even if the person cannot significantly influence the amount of cost through his own direct action, he may be charged with those elements with which management desires him to be concerned, so that he will help to influence those who are responsible.

The first two guidelines are workable, but implementing the third can cause difficulties. The interrelationships of decisions also pose certain difficult, but solvable, problems in assigning cost responsibility.

For example, production planning may plan the number of units to be produced and the quantity and quality of the raw materials to be purchased. The purchasing department then acquires the raw materials. A number of events can occur that could affect variances from the point of purchase to the warehousing of the finished goods:

1. There may be a variance from the standard price. If this is the case, the purchasing manager will be held responsible for this variance.
2. It is possible that the material price variance would be favorable, but the materials could be of substandard quality. A production foreman requisitions the materials, rejects them due to their low quality, and, as a result, has an idle work force on his hands. If the foreman accepts the materials, with or without knowledge of their low quality, a host of other variances can arise. Because of the low quality of the materials, an unfavorable materials usage variance is probable. The labor usage variance could well be unfavorable due to the difficulty involved in working with low quality materials. Scrap and rework variances will be unfavorable. The obvious solution for the foreman is to reject the materials. However, if the favorable materials price variance were greater than all of the production related unfavorable variances, and if the final product were of the quality desired by the firm, the materials should be used. This would be to the over-all advantage of the firm.

---

[1] "Report of Committee on Cost Concepts and Standards," *The Accounting Review*, April 1956, p. 189.

3. Suppose that the materials price variance was unfavorable because a higher quality material was purchased. The purchasing manager will show the unfavorable variance on his performance report. The production foreman's performance report will not be affected by the price of the raw materials used, but the high quality raw materials may have a favorable impact on a number of the production variances. The overall favorable or unfavorable impact can only be measured by considering all of the variances produced by using the higher priced, higher quality materials.

Responsibility for Service Department Costs

Service departments also present problems in responsibility accounting. If a maintenance department is responsible for the upkeep of production equipment, maintenance costs are still affected by the degree of care exercised by production personnel. Although maintenance is held responsible for the costs of maintaining equipment, production personnel can certainly influence the total maintenance costs incurred.

An approach to solving this problem of "dual responsibility" is to charge each department a standard price per hour for every hour of maintenance the department uses. This charge appears as an expense on the performance report of the department using the service. If maintenance costs exceed the department's maintenance budget, then the user department's manager will incur an unfavorable cost variance.

The maintenance department is responsible for staffing its work force in order to meet both scheduled maintenance and any emergencies which may arise. Maintenance users are then billed at a standard rate for maintenance services with a separate billing for any costs for materials or parts. Theoretically, the maintenance department could make a "profit" in the sense that its billings could exceed its costs. The attempt of this internal pricing scheme is to reduce excessive requests for services. The services will no longer be viewed as *free* by the user departments. Cost reponsibility is placed with managers who can influence the costs.

Responsibility Accounting and Human Behavior

Decisions are made by managers at all levels of an organization. Top management develops the goals and objectives of the firm and all management should work together to attain these goals and objectives. Individual managers also have their own personal goals which they are striving to attain. Professional goals are generally only one aspect of personal goals. Any aspect of control should result in decisions which are both in the best interest of the firm's goals and objectives and in the best personal interest of the manager.

If responsibility accounting is to be a useful tool in planning, control, and performance evaluation, then the entire system must be designed to eliminate or reduce the potential of a manager making decisions that appear to be in his own best interest, but are not in the best interest of the firm. The responsibility accounting system must be useful and provide performance measures based on controllable factors. Some reward structure must be developed, even if it is only verbal, to provide incentives for management and employees to act in the best interests of the firm.

SUMMARY

Under a responsibility accounting system, a manager participates in establishing the budget for the economic factors over which he has control or influence. He is then held responsible for reaching that budget. The responsibility system is generally integrated into the regular accounting system and includes information regarding controllable economic factors.

Responsibility centers are normally classified according to the economic factors that the manager of the center can influence. In the most common type of responsibility center, the cost or expense center, only costs are considered controllable by the manager of the center. The manager is generally held responsible for a specified amount of output given the costs incurred. Only those costs which are under the control of the manager are considered in evaluating his performance. A cost center typically refers to the control of the manager over product costs whereas an expense center refers to a manager's control over non-manufacturing costs. A profit center exists in those circumstances where the manager can influence both revenues and expenses associated with his segment. In the most comprehensive form of responsibility centers, the investment center, the manager is similar to a sole proprietor in that he has control over capital investments as well as revenues and expenses.

The responsibility accounting system is generally developed along lines of organizational authority. Managers at each level are responsible for their own individual financial factors as well as those of their subordinates. The system typically uses a performance report that emphasizes variances from the budget. These reports are prepared at intervals which permit the timely and effective correction of deviations from the budget.

Since control is often difficult to identify with any given individual, controllability must at times be delegated for responsibility accounting purposes. Guidelines have been established in order to assist in the controllability decision. In addition, service department costs may create problems and require the use of an allocation process, for example the charge of an internal "expense" for each hour of service consumed by a department.

One danger in using a responsibility accounting system is that a manager may take actions or make decisions that optimize his segment's performance but which are not beneficial to the firm as a whole. If possible, the system should be designed to eliminate every possibility of this occurring and should provide incentives for management at all levels to act in the best interests of the firm.

This chapter has introduced the concept of responsibility centers and illustrated the performance reporting for a cost center. The following chapter discusses performance reporting for the remaining types of responsibility centers: profit and investment centers.

KEY DEFINITIONS

Controllable cost—a cost that can be traced to a specific responsibility center on a non-arbitrary basis and is influenced by the manager of that center in a given time period.

Cost center—a type of responsibility center where the manager influences only costs and is held accountable for a specific output at a given cost level.

Direct costs—costs which can be traced to a given segment or responsibility segment of the organization on a non-arbitrary basis. All direct costs may not necessarily be controllable costs of a specific responsibility center.

Indirect costs—costs which are common to more than one segment or responsibility center of the organization. All indirect costs are non-controllable costs for any particular responsibility center.

Investment center—a type of responsibility center where the manager can influence revenues, expenses, and capital invested in his center to attain the best performance possible.

Management by exception—when variances from the budgets are emphasized in reporting procedures so that management concentrates its attention on these variances or exceptions from the budget.

Non-controllable cost—a cost which cannot be directly influenced by the manager of the responsibility center.

Profit center—a type of responsibility center where the manager can influence both revenues and expenses for his center.

Responsibility accounting—an accounting system in which the accountability for costs is assigned to a segment manager of the firm based on the amount of control or influence he possesses over those costs.

Responsibility performance reports—reports concerning the performance of various responsibility centers of the firm with respect to controllable costs. They report variances that result from a comparison of budgeted and actual controllable costs.

QUESTIONS

12-1 What is responsibility accounting? What additional accounting costs are added by responsibility accounting?

12-2 What is a controllable cost? How are controllable costs related to direct costs?

12-3 What is the relationship between indirect costs and noncontrollable costs?

12-4 When is the term "expense center" the more appropriate description of a responsibility center? When should the term "cost center" be used?

12-5 What is a profit center and what does it accomplish?

12-6 Where should management's attention be focused after performance reports have been prepared? What is the term for this?

12-7 In what two ways is the timing of responsibility reporting crucial?

12-8 What criteria are used in setting responsibility in a center? Briefly outline some guidelines that have been identified for this purpose.

12-9 In what manner may the problem of dual responsibility among service departments possibly be solved?

12-10 How can managers be shown that decisions made in the best interest of the firm are also in the best interest of the manager?

EXERCISES AND PROBLEMS

12-11 The manager of Department 1 is responsible for costs incurred by his department. As a manager, he is responsible for the purchase of supplies, maintenance and repair costs, and labor costs. Following are costs identifiable to his department:

Departmental supplies	$1,500
Manager's salary	1,000
Direct labor	5,000
Indirect materials	800
Repairs and maintenance	550
Depreciation of equipment	1,000
Heat, light and power	350

Required:

Identify the costs which are controllable by the manager.

12-12 Determine whether each of the following costs is controllable or non-controllable by a manufacturing department manager.

a. Depreciation on building and equipment
b. Supplies and indirect materials
c. Rent on building
d. Heat, light and power
e. Maintenance and repair costs
f. Salary of salesmen
g. Direct labor
h. Rework time

12-13   You have been hired by the Par Golf Company to look into its cost system to determine the cause of the increased costs in making golf clubs. In touring the factory you have learned that to make a wood club, certain materials are required. Jack Palmer, the president of Par Golf, had required that some system for standards be established and you have found them to be:

1 head @ $4.00
1 shaft @ $1.00
1 grip @ $2.00

During the past year, you have discovered that 10,000 woods were produced at a total cost of $71,800. Mr. Palmer said that this was an unfavorable variance of $1,800 and he wants to know where to lay the blame. Your investigation shows that Joe Duffer was the purchasing agent for shafts. Since Joe considered all shafts to be equal, he got the cheapest shaft possible at $.90. Unfortunately this required the assembly department to use 12 shafts to successfully complete 10 clubs. Other information showed actual costs of:

10,100 heads at a total cost of $40,000
10,200 grips at a total cost of $21,000

Required:

a.   Calculate the total material quantity and price variances.
b.   Who should be given the shaft variance?

12-14   The following data are taken from the records of a specific cost center which is controlled by a manager. Furthermore, a plant Vice President supervises the manager.

Raw materials and supplies	$10,000
Depreciation on equipment	500
Repair and maintenance costs	600
Direct labor	15,000
Heat, light and power	1,000
Salary of manager	12,000
Rental for floor space	200
Rework time	500
Salary of Vice President	20,000

Required:

Which of the above costs are controllable by the manager? Which are controllable by the plant Vice President?

12-15   Given below are the controllable costs for the assembly division of the Hays Manufacturing Company for October.

Budgeted production was 4,000 units.
Actual production was 5,000 units.
Standard costs:
   Direct labor—$5 per unit
   Direct material—$3 per unit
   Supplies—$0.75 per unit
   Other—$0.10 per unit
Actual costs for the month were as follows:

Direct labor	$25,850
Direct material	14,600
Supplies	3,500
Other	500

Required:

Prepare a responsibility accounting performance report showing variances for the assembly division for October.

12-16   The Love Tennis Company has been experiencing dissension between its purchasing and manufacturing divisions. The division that has the largest favorable variance has been promised a free tennis lesson with the company pro, Rod Connors. Your job is to determine the material and labor variances and assign them to the competing divisions.

The standard racket is comprised of:		
String, 80 meters @ $.05 per meter.	=	$ 4.00
Frame @ $6.00.	=	6.00
Grip @ $1.00.	=	1.00
Total standard material cost per racket.	=	$11.00

The standard time required to construct a racket is 1 hour at $5.00 per hour. The standard string used is a high quality catgut. In an attempt to win the contest for the purchasing division, Billy Riggs, a real hustler, purchased a cheaper nylon string at 4 cents a meter. Unfortunately, 100 meters of string per racket was required and this also increased the direct labour time per racket to 1.1 hours.

During the past month, 5,000 rackets were completed. The following data were available:

5,100 frames used—total cost = $30,400
5,200 grips used—total cost = $ 5,400
         direct labor—total cost = $25,000

Required:

a.   Calculate material quantity and price variances. Calculate direct labor efficiency and rate variances.

b.   Assign the variances previously calculated to the division responsible.

12-17   The ABC Department of the Fox Company budgeted 1,000 units of production for April and allowed 3,000 direct labor hours for this production at a standard rate of $5.00 per hour. During March a mandatory pay raise was established which increased the labor rate to $5.75 per hour. There was no labor efficiency variance.

Required:

a. Compute the variance.
b. If the variance is unfavorable, is it fair to charge the departmental supervisor with the variance? In other words, was this specific situation controllable or noncontrollable by the supervisor?

12-18   The general foreman of Department I is responsible for the purchase of supplies, the hiring of employees and for repairs and maintenance. The following information shows all costs traceable to Department I during November.

a. Direct materials
b. Direct labor
c. Supplies and indirect materials
d. Salary of foreman
e. Salary of production manager
f. Depreciation of equipment
g. Depreciation of building
h. Rental of building
i. Advertising expense
j. Repairs and maintenance

Required:

Prepare a list of all the costs controllable by the foreman.

12-19   The following data indicate various costs traceable to the machinery department of Star Manufacturing Company for April:

	Budgeted	*Actual*
Direct materials	$12,000	$11,000
Direct labor	15,000	17,500
Salary of department manager	15,000	15,000
Heat, light and power	1,000	850
Repairs and maintenance	1,200	1,500
Supplies	800	600
Depreciation on equipment	500	500

Ken Fargo, the manager, is responsible for various costs incurred by the machinery department except for his own salary, which is established by upper management and for any allocated costs. Both budgeted and actual costs are at 10,000 units of production.

Required:

Prepare a responsibility accounting report for April, showing all costs controllable by Mr. Fargo. Show all variances.

12-20　The organization chart given below shows the lines of responsibility for the Stacy Manufacturing Company:

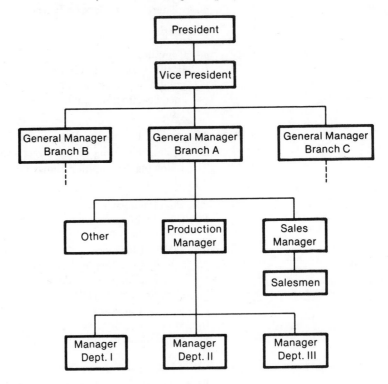

Determine whether the responsibility center for each of the following is most likely a cost, profit or investment center.

a.　Manager, Dept. III
b.　President
c.　Vice President
d.　Production manager
e.　General manager, Branch A
f.　Sales manager
g.　Salesmen on commission and with expense accounts

12-21　The production manager of Department II is responsible for various costs incurred by his department. Production planning determines the quantity and quality of raw materials to be purchased. The Purchasing Department is responsible for acquiring the raw materials ordered by the production manager.

Assume that the standard price per unit of raw material is $5.00. 2,000 units of raw material are to be ordered. Due to an increase in price, the purchasing department acquires the 2,000 units of raw material at $5.50 per unit.

Required:

a. Calculate the variance.

b. Which department should be charged with this variance?

12-22   Bob Smart is general manager of the Production Division of the Model Auto Company. One of his responsibilities is the acquisition of raw materials from the purchasing department which orders them from an outside supplier.

Assume that the standard price per unit of raw material is $2.50. 1,000 units of raw material are ordered by the purchasing department at a price of $1.50 per unit, but the materials ordered are of sub-standard quality. If the production division works with the inferior raw material, the following variances are anticipated: a $500 unfavorable material usage variance and a $700 unfavorable labor usage variance.

Required:

Should the production manager accept or reject the shipment of sub-standard raw material? Support your answer.

12-23   The production manager, Mr. Jones, is responsible for the Production Division of the Harris Tool Manufacturing Company. He is unable to influence the amount of raw material used to produce a given number of units. He is also responsible for hiring and firing his employees. He is authorized to establish the rates at which his employees will be paid. He is responsible for the purchase of all supplies and indirect materials and for repairs and maintenance. Mr. Jones is not held responsible for costs allocated to his department.

From the list of costs given below, select those controllable by the production manager and those noncontrollable by him. Give a list and total for each type.

Raw materials	$ 5,500
Depreciation on machinery	1,000
Heat, light and power	700
Maintenance and repairs	500
Direct labor	10,000
Rework time	600
Supervision of factory by guards	400
Lease rental on building	1,000
Supplies	500

12-24   The Marshall Door Corporation is organized on a functional basis and uses a responsibility accounting system. The production division, one of the five main divisions, is supervised by a general manager. The production division consists of three producing departments and three service departments.

During July, 10,000 units were produced by the production division. Given below are the controllable costs incurred by the six departments and the manager. Also shown in the first column are the budgeted totals.

	Budget Totals	Direct Material	Direct Labor	Manufacturing Overhead	Total
Producing Departments					
1	$187,000	$25,000	$65,000	$100,000	$190,000
2	122,000	15,000	40,000	65,000	120,000
3	66,500	8,000	22,000	37,000	67,000
Service Departments					
A	10,000	–	–	7,500	7,500
B	8,000	–	–	10,000	10,000
C	4,500	–	–	5,000	5,000
Production manager	13,000	–	–	13,000	13,000

Required:

Prepare a cost responsibility accounting report showing all controllable costs for the production manager of the production division for July. Show all variances.

12-25   Given below are data for the production department of the Morris Manufacturing Company for the month of September.

Forecast production . . . . 10,000 units
Actual production . . . . 12,000 units
Standards for controllable costs:
  Direct labor . . . . $3.00 per unit
  Direct material . . . . 5.00 per unit
  Rework and set up time . . . . . . 0.10 per unit
  Supplies and indirect materials . . . 0.50 per unit
Actual costs for month:
  Direct labor $37,000
  Direct material 59,500
  Rework time 1,000
  Supplies 5,500

Required:

Prepare a responsibility accounting performance report for the production department for September. Make your report similar to the one in Illustration 11-3. Show forecast and control budgets, actual costs and all variances.

12-26   The Mitchell-Parks Corporation uses responsibility reporting (performance reports) for its various departments. Given below is a comparison of actual costs with control budgeted costs for Production Department A for May. The department manager is held responsible for various costs incurred by his department such as the purchase of materials, the hiring of employees and the requisition of repairs and maintenance. Although the manager's salary is listed under "production salaries and wages," his salary is not controllable by him. The Vice President of production determines the manager's salary.

Assume that 10,000 units of production were budgeted and 11,000 were actually produced during May. The manager's salary is $1,200 per month.

	Budgeted	Actual
Departmental costs		
Direct material ($5 per unit)	$ 50,000	$ 51,000
Production salaries and wages		
($1,200 plus $4 per unit)	41,200	48,000
Repairs and maintenance (fixed)	1,000	850
Indirect materials and supplies (fixed)	15,000	14,700
Depreciation on machinery (fixed)	500	500
Salary of superintendent (fixed)	20,000	20,000
Heat, light, and power ($500 plus		
$.05 per unit)	1,000	1,100
Total costs	$128,700	$136,150

Required:

Prepare a revised reponsibility accounting performance report for Production Department A showing the actual variances from the budget for May. Show only the costs that are controllable by the manager.

A✓12-27   John Able is the manager of the Finishing and Processing Division at the Scotian Plant of the Morgan Company. His responsibility report for March is as follows:

	Flexible Budget	Actual	Variances (unfavorable)
Controllable Costs:			
Direct materials	$10,000	$12,500	($2,500)
Direct labor	5,000	6,900	(1,900)
Supplies	850	600	250
Repairs and maintenance	1,000	1,200	(200)
Total controllable costs	$16,850	$21,200	($4,350)

Additional data:

1. 5,000 tons of raw material at a price of $2.00 per ton were budgeted for March ($10,000). During March the purchasing department could not obtain the materials at $2.00 per ton. The price increased to $2.50 per ton. Therefore, 5,000 tons of raw material were obtained at a price of $2.50 per ton ($12,500).

2. When the budget was prepared in January, the labor rate was $5.00 per hour. However, the labor rate was increased to

$6.00 per hour when a union contract was signed in February. Also, 100 hours of overtime were authorized during March even though no amount of overtime had been approved by the budget. Overtime was paid at a rate of 1½ times the regular rate ($9.00 per hour). This overtime was incurred during an emergency in which Mr. Able's department aided another department. The budget allowed 1,000 hours; the actual hours worked conformed to the budgeted hours plus the 100 authorized overtime hours.

Required:

a. Is the given responsibility report for Mr. Able's department a fair one? Mr. Able argues that he should not be charged with the unfavorable variances resulting from direct materials and direct labor. Do you agree with Mr. Able's argument?

b. Prepare a revised responsibility report showing only those costs controllable by Mr. Able and variances chargeable to him.

12-28 Baker and Carr Enterprises consists of four divisions which are supervised by the manufacturing Vice President; the four divisions are the assembly division, the finishing and processing division, the machining division and the packing division. Each division is supervised by a manager and each division consists of several departments. Each department is supervised by a department head. Responsibility accounting performance reports are prepared monthly for each department head, the division manager and the Vice President.

The finishing and processing division consists of two departments. The following data for the finishing and processing division for December show the controllable costs of the manager:

	Department X		Department Y	
	Budgeted	Actual	Budgeted	Actual
Controllable Costs:				
Direct materials	$12,000	$12,500	$ 9,500	$ 9,400
Direct labor	25,000	27,500	18,000	16,500
Supplies	2,000	1,600	1,200	1,350
Repairs and maintenance .	1,000	950	700	850
Total controllable costs . .	$40,000	$42,550	$29,400	$28,100

Additional data:

Total controllable costs for the other three divisions for December were as follows:

	Budgeted	Actual
Assembly division	$135,000	$132,600
Machining division	117,500	120,200
Packing division	175,600	172,050

Required:

a. Prepare a performance report for the division manager of finishing and processing assuming that "Other Costs" for this division are:

Budgeted—$100,000
Actual   —$ 99,000

b. Prepare a performance report for the manufacturing Vice President assuming that "Other Costs" for his segment are:

Budgeted—$ 55,000
Actual   —$ 57,100

12-29 Following is a simplified organizational chart showing the lines of responsibility for the Carter Company:

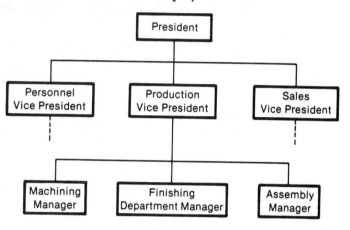

Prepare a chart like the one shown below. Determine whether each given account is a cost controllable by the four officers shown on the chart. Give answers as "Yes" or "No."

	Controllable Costs			
	By Manager of Machining Department	By Vice President of Production	By Vice President of Sales	By President
Production-direct materials				
Salary of sales Vice President				
Salesmen salaries				
Direct labor—assembly				
Supplies—finishing				
Repairs and maintenance— machining				
Salary of manager				
Depreciation— machinery				

12-30   The following data indicate the standard material, quantity and cost per unit of the product produced by the manufacturing department:

2 kilograms of material X @ $2.00 per kilogram
2 kilograms of material Y @ $1.50 per kilogram
1 kilogram of material Z @ $1.00 per kilogram

Due to an error in the purchasing department, an insufficient amount of material Y was ordered. Therefore, material X was substituted for material Y. Furthermore, the price of material Z increased to $1.25 per kilogram. The manufacturing department produced 5,000 units of the product at the actual quantities used and the actual costs:

14,000 kilograms of material X@ $2.00 per kilogram.....	=	$28,000
6,000 kilograms of material Y@ $1.50 per kilogram.....	=	9,000
5,000 kilograms of material Z@ $1.25 per kilogram.....	=	6,250
Total cost for material for production of 5,000 units......		$43,250

As a result, the manufacturing department was charged with unfavorable material variances.

Required:

a.   Compute the amount of material variance charged to the department. Separate the material variance into quantity and price variances.

b.   Should the unfavorable material variance be charged to the manufacturing department? If not, who should probably be charged with it?

12-31   Assuming that this applies to a Production Department, classify each of the following items into: Controllable (C) and Noncontrollable (NC) costs, Direct (D) and Indirect (I) costs.

a.   Advertising expense
b.   Direct materials
c.   Depreciation on equipment
d.   Direct labor
e.   Supplies used
f.   Depreciation on building
g.   Salary of department head
h.   Heat, light, and power
i.   Rental of plant
j.   Indirect materials.

12-32   The Sutton Company consists of three divisions—the sales division, production division, and personnel division. Each division is supervised by a manager who is held responsible for various costs. The approved budgets (flexible) for each division are as follows:

	Sales Manager	Production Manager	Personnel Manager
Controllable Costs:			
Direct materials	–	$10,000	–
Direct labor	–	25,000	–
Salaries	$50,000	–	$35,000
Supplies	1,000	2,000	1,500
Repairs and maintenance	500	1,500	500
Total	$51,500	$38,500	$37,000

The actual costs incurred by each division are as follows:

	Sales	Production	Personnel
Controllable Costs:			
Direct materials	–	$12,000	–
Direct labor	–	23,800	–
Salaries	$51,000	–	$34,000
Supplies	800	1,700	1,450
Repairs and maintenance	300	1,100	350
Total	$52,100	$38,600	$35,800

Required:

a. Prepare a responsibility accounting performance report for the production division showing budget, actual and variances. (Period is June.)

b. Prepare a performance report for the Vice President who is responsible for all three divisions. In preparing the report, use only "Total Controllable Costs" for each division. It is not necessary to itemize each cost. Also assume that "Other Costs for Vice President" are: Budgeted—$35,000; Actual—$34,400.

12-33   Robin Smith is the regional sales manager for International Fragrances, Inc. As such, she is responsible for the management of sales personnel in her area, including the determination of sales salaries. Company policy, however, requires that a minimum salary of $12,000 per year be paid to each sales person.

As a sales manager, Ms. Smith is also responsible for budgeting and arranging for all local and regional advertising and other selling expenses in her area. National advertising is handled by the corporate offices of International Fragrances with total annual costs allocated to each regional area.

Cost information for Ms. Smith's region follows below:

Total sales salaries: (13 sales personnel)	$215,000
Local advertising and promotion	78,000
Regional advertising and promotion	155,000
National advertising	200,000
Display, set-up costs	12,000
Miscellaneous expenses	7,500

Required:

Given the above information, prepare a schedule of controllable and non-controllable costs for Ms. Smith.

12-34   Slack is often incorporated in budgets. This is because of the dual role of budgets in the planning and performance evaluation processes in any organization. Answer the following unrelated questions with respect to the impact of people on budgets.

Required:

a.   i.   Which two goals are managers motivated to achieve in an organization?
     ii. Give two examples of each type of goal.
     iii. How can a manager achieve both these goals?

b.   Define slack and clearly explain how it can be distributed giving one example of each type of distribution.

c.   i.   How does the budget system affect an employee's aspiration and his willingness to accept the system?
     ii. Organizationally, how does the reward structure affect the creation of slack?

d.   Briefly suggest a procedure to minimize slack.
e.   In a multi-divisional company, how does the degree of decentralization affect the creation of slack?

(SMA, adapted)

12-35   "The budget can be a powerful tool for motivating people to achieve the organization's objectives or it can be a positive hindrance."

Required:

Analyze extensively the effects of budgeting on people and show how it can lead to either bad or good consequences according to the way it is applied in various types of organizations.

12-36 The Priester Company Limited is divided into three separate departments which share common facilities although each produces and sells its own distinctive product. In order to control and evaluate the performance of the department and the department's manager, the company has prepared the following performance report for department "A":

	Budgeted	Actual	Variance
Sales ($120 per unit)...............	$1,260,000	$1,176,000	$84,000 (U)
Cost of goods sold:			
Raw materials..................	$ 367,500	$ 343,000	$24,500 (F)
Direct labour..................	441,000	426,500	14,500 (F)
Variable overhead			
(square footage)*..............	68,000	67,000	1,000 (F)
Fixed overhead			
(square footage)*..............	127,500	129,200	1,700 (U)
Total cost of goods sold.........	$1,004,000	$ 965,700	$38,300 (F)
Gross profit on sales.............	$ 256,000	$ 210,300	$45,700 (U)
Operating expenses:			
Selling—variable	$ 100,800	$ 94,080	$ 6,720 (F)
Selling—fixed			
(square footage)*.............	35,000	35,000	0
Administrative—fixed			
(square footage)*.............	47,600	52,500	4,900 (U)
Total operating expenses.........	$ 183,400	$ 181,580	$ 1,820 (F)
Net income....................	$ 72,600	$ 28,720	$43,880 (U)

*Allocation base used.

When Mr. Corbett, the manager of department "A", was presented with this performance report, he responded by pointing out that sales had decreased because of an overall slowdown in the economy which was beyond his control. This decrease in sales was the cause of the overall unfavourable variance in the department's profitability, and Mr. Corbett pointed out that he had obviously done an excellent job in controlling the department's costs as shown by the number of favourable variances. The only cost showing unfavourable variances were ones which were incurred for the benefit of all three departments and over which he had no control.

Additional data:

1. Budgeted direct labour costs for the three departments together totalled $1,455,000.
2. Department "A" occupied 40 percent of the total factory space and 35 percent of the total selling space.

Required:

a.   Evaluate the company's present methods of performance appraisal for both the department and the department manager.

b.   Comment on the validity of Mr. Corbett's response to the initial performance report.

c.   Prepare a performance report which would give a better evaluation of both the department and the department manager.

(SMA, adapted)

12-37   The Noton Company has operated a comprehensive budgeting system for many years. This system is a major component of the company's program to control operations and costs at its widely scattered plants. Periodically the plants' general managers gather to discuss the overall company control system with the top management.

At this year's meeting the budgetary system was severely criticized by one of the most senior plant managers. He said that the system discriminated unfairly against the older, well-run and established plants in favor of the newer plants. The impact was lower year-end bonuses and poor performance ratings. In addition, there were psychological consequences in the form of lower employee morale. In his judgment, revisions in the system were needed to make it more effective. The basic factors of Noton's budget include:

1.   Announcement of an annual improvement percentage target established by top management.

2.   Plant submission of budgets implementing the annual improvement target.

3.   Management review and revision of the proposed budget.

4.   Establishment and distribution of the final budget.

To support his argument, he compared the budget revisions and performance results. The older plants were expected to achieve the improvement target but often were unable to meet it. On the other hand, the newer plants were often excused from meeting a portion of this target in their budgets. However, their performance was usually better than the final budget.

He further argued that the company did not recognize the operating differences which made attainment of the annual improvement factor difficult, if not impossible. His plant has been producing essentially the same product for its 20 years of existence. The machinery and equipment, which underwent many modifications in the first five years, have had no major changes in recent years.

Because they are old, repair and maintenance costs have increased each year, and the machines are less reliable. The plant management team has been together for the last ten years and works well together. The labor force is mature, with many of the employees having the highest seniority in the company. In his judgment, the significant improvements have been "wrung out" of the plant over the years and that merely keeping even is difficult.

For comparison he noted that one plant opened within the past four years would have an easier time meeting the company's expectations. The plant is new, containing modern equipment that is in some cases still experimental. Major modifications in equipment and operating systems have been made each year as the plant management has obtained a better understanding of the operations. The plant's management, although experienced, has been together only since its opening. The plant is located in a previously nonindustrial area and therefore has a relatively inexperienced work force.

Required:

a. Evaluate the manufacturing manager's views.
b. Equitable application of a budget system requires the ability of corporate management to remove "budgetary slack" in plant budgets. Discuss how each plant could conceal "slack" in its budget.

(CMA, adapted)

Chapter 13

**LEARNING
OBJECTIVES**

Chapter 13 discusses performance reporting for both profit centers and investment centers. Studying this chapter should enable you to:

1. Identify those financial factors considered controllable in each type of responsibility center.
2. Explain the concept of decentralization and discuss how decentralization is related to responsibility accounting.
3. Identify the usual types of transfer prices and discuss the advantages and disadvantages of each.
4. Describe the types of variances typically used in the performance evaluation of a profit center.
5. Know and apply the basic return on investment formula.
6. Discuss the problems involved in defining the concept of assets utilized.

Performance Reporting for Profit Centers and Investment Centers

RESPONSIBILITY accounting for profit centers and investment centers encompasses many controllable factors in addition to costs. The performance report for a cost center, discussed in Chapter 12, is based on the capability of the manager of that cost center to produce the required output at the specified quality at the standard cost of producing that output. A profit center is evaluated on both its controllable costs and its revenues. A major objective of a manager in a profit center is to realize the budgeted income for the center within the budget period.

An investment center manager is responsible for earning a budgeted return on the assets used by the center. The investment center manager should be able to make those decisions that affect revenues, costs, and invested assets for the responsibility center.

DECENTRALIZATION AND RESPONSIBILITY ACCOUNTING

As a financial tool, responsibility accounting permits a performance evaluation of the manager who makes decisions with regard to the factors under his influence and within the limits established by the top management of the firm. Responsibility accounting permits the decentralization of decision making in that the manager of each responsibility center is charged with making decisions with regard to that operation. The efforts of the individual managers are coordinated by top management, company policy, planning and any other methods for coordination that may be established by the firm.

In effect, decentralization places each profit or investment center manager in a position similar to an independent entrepreneur operating under a minimum set of constraints or policies. This procedure provides incentives for managers because performance, and therefore bonuses, are measured as if an individual manager were a sole proprietor with that segment of the firm as his own business.

The definition of the financial components of income and invested assets for both profit centers and investment centers poses certain problems from an accounting standpoint. Among these problems are: (1) determining the appropriate measure of revenues when intracompany sales are made between segments or divisions of the firm, and (2) defining assets invested in a center for purposes of calculating the return on investment for investment centers.[1]

TRANSFER PRICING FOR INTRACOMPANY SALES

A transfer price is the price that one segment of an organization pays to another segment within the same organization for the output or service of the supplying segment. In determining the performance of each unit, a transfer price is the basis for: (1) interunit sales from the viewpoint of the selling unit, and (2) variable costs to the buying unit. For financial reporting purposes, the firm recognizes a sale only when goods or services are sold to buyers external to the firm and not when one segment or division of a company sells to another. However, for purposes of performance measurement by segments, an internal sale is considered in calculating segment income; otherwise, the responsible manager would be encouraged to make only external sales in order to maximize income. Of course, top management wishes to establish transfer prices which will maximize the objectives of the firm as a whole.

Generally, the manager of a responsibility center attempts to operate his unit in such a manner as to maximize the profits of the center. Establishing a fair transfer price permits segment managers to make decisions that are in the best interest of the segment as well as in the best interests of the entire firm. These transfer prices are usually market-based, cost-based and/or negotiated. In most cases a transfer price is a combination of these bases.

Market-Based Transfer Prices

If a competitive market price is available for a product also sold internally, then the equitable transfer price, from both a theoretical and prac-

---

[1] The problem of common costs discussed in Chapter 12 and the problems involved in the allocation of these costs could have been included in this discussion and should be considered by the reader.

tical viewpoint, is the external competitive market price adjusted for any savings in cost, such as selling expenses. If savings are realized as a result of the ability of a unit to sell its product within the firm, then those savings should be fairly distributed or allocated between the buying and selling units. Examples of factors resulting from intersegment sales which may cause cost savings include improved planning, more efficient production runs or the elimination or reduction of selling and distribution expenses. A market-based transfer price for intersegment sales is the closest approximation to an "arm's length" transaction.

Any shortcomings of a market-based transfer price are usually related to the operations or uncertainties concerning the market place. Few markets are truly competitive in an economic sense and any price may be affected by the presence of a few large buyers or sellers. Market prices are also influenced by such factors as supply and demand, quantity discounts and product quality. All of these factors must be considered when an internal transfer price based on market price is established for internal company use.

Cost-Based Transfer Prices— Full Cost

Transfer prices for intersegment sales based on full cost or full cost-plus are common for the following reasons:

1. Certain products have limited or nonexistent outside markets.
2. The full cost transfer price concept is understandable to both the buyer and the seller.
3. Cost accumulations are made for inventory costing purposes so a "cost figure" is readily available.

If the transfer price is based on the actual costs incurred, then the supplying segment may have little incentive to control its costs because the full cost will be recovered by the transfer price. On the other hand, if a normal or standard cost transfer price is used, then this measure of costs which *should* have been incurred by the supplying segment provides an incentive to control costs. The use of a normal or standard cost is also consistent with the basic concepts of responsibility accounting because any efficiencies or inefficiencies are identified with the responsibility center where the cost is incurred.

Cost-Based Transfer Prices— Variable Cost

A variable cost or variable cost-plus transfer price may be justified on a theoretical basis since this transfer price is consistent with the traditional "short-run" economic decision model of a firm. A "short-run" economic decision model assumes that the manager of the supplying segment cannot influence the fixed costs of the segment in the short-run. Therefore the manager is accountable for only the variable costs of the segment and the interunit sales price should be determined using only variable costs as a base.

Negotiated Transfer Prices

Most transfer pricing approaches are negotiated in practice because an equitable price for both the selling and buying segments must be established if the price is to be meaningful. When transfer prices are based on negotiation, both the supplying and the buying segment managers arrive at a fair transfer price considering any information concerning costs and market conditions available to them. A truly negotiated transfer price assumes that neither manager involved in the negotiations has an unfair bargaining position.

In any negotiated transfer price, some arbitration procedure may be necessary in order to neutralize friction or unreasonable positions assumed by one or both of the managers. For all practical purposes, if the buying segment *must* purchase the goods or services internally or the selling segment *must* sell to the buying segment, an unfair bargaining situation may develop. In these cases, company policy or company transfer price formulas may be used to establish the price.

RETURN ON INVESTMENT AS A MEASURE OF PERFORMANCE

When a manager is able to influence revenues, costs and capital investments in a segment, that manager is said to be responsible for an investment center. Performance measures for an investment center should consider the profit element in relation to the size of the asset base used to earn that profit. A performance measure that attempts to relate income (from the income statement) to the assets utilized (from the balance sheet) is the concept of return on investment. The general formula for return on investment (ROI) is as follows:

$$ ROI = \frac{Income}{Assets\ Utilized} $$

The exact definitions for both income and assets utilized may vary from firm to firm. The two elements in the equation, income and assets utilized to earn that income, may be analyzed in terms of their respective components:

$$\text{ROI} = \text{Profit Margin on Sales} \times \text{Sales Turnover of Assets}$$

$$= \frac{\text{Income}}{\text{Sales}} \times \frac{\text{Sales}}{\text{Assets Utilized}}$$

The profit margin on sales is a measure of the profitability of a firm while the turnover of assets is an indication of the assets used in relationship to the sales level achieved during the same accounting period. These ratios identify two of the factors that a manager in an investment center should be able to control or influence. The return on investment for a center may be improved by increasing sales, reducing expenses, reducing the level of the assets utilized or by some combination of these three factors. The relationship of the profit margin on sales and the turnover of assets describes the relationship between profit planning and asset (or capital) management. A firm that experiences a two percent profit margin and an asset turnover of ten times in a given accounting period provides the same return on investment as a firm with a ten percent profit margin and an asset turnover of two times per period. In both of these cases, the return on investment is 20 percent.

<table>
<tr><td style="text-align:center">Firm A</td><td style="text-align:center">Firm B</td></tr>
<tr><td style="text-align:center">$\text{ROI} = 2\% \times 10 = 20\%$</td><td style="text-align:center">$\text{ROI} = 10\% \times 2 = 20\%$</td></tr>
</table>

PROBLEMS IN DEFINING ASSETS UTILIZED

In order to effectively use the ROI measure to evaluate the performance of an investment center manager, a consistent definition of assets utilized must be established. Responsibility accounting for investment centers requires that the investment center manager be able to influence the "package" of assets for which he is held responsible. Most managers of an investment center have inherited the majority of the fixed assets of their center from the prior manager. The age and condition of the assets, the depreciation policy in use and the original cost of the assets all play a significant role in the measurement of the appropriate asset base to be used. These factors must be considered in developing a planned or target return on investment. A commonly accepted measure of assets used is total net assets (total original cost of assets less any accumulated depreciation on those assets).

Joint assets pose an additional problem. Many large corporations have established centralized cash, accounts receivable, and long-term debt management; therefore, investment centers in these firms do not have control over cash, accounts receivable or long-term debt. These financial factors are managed by corporate headquarters. In these instances, the centrally-managed financial factors are allocated to the various investment centers involved. An attempt is made to impute the values (including interest expense and interest payable for long-term debt) that would be reported in the financial statements of the investment center if the segment could control these financial factors. This procedure forces the investment center manager to consider and control the factors used as the basis for the allocation of the joint assets if he is to maintain control of ROI for his investment center.

PERFORMANCE EVALUATION OF PROFIT CENTERS

The analysis of variances of a profit center should explain why actual income differed from the forecast budgeted income for the accounting period under consideration. The general types of variances that can be used to analyze and explain the reasons for the difference between the forecasted income and the actual income are:

1. Sales volume variance [2]   3.   Price variance
2. Sales mix variance [3]   4.   Expense variance

Illustration 13-1 presents the variance worksheet that will be used in preparing the performance report for Mr. Gess, the manager of the Industrial Filter Division of Sax Company.. The division produces and sells over 100 different filters all with different contribution margins.

The controllable revenues and costs of this division are used to illustrate performance evaluation and reporting for a profit center even though Sax Company considers the Industrial Filter Division to be an investment center. In a later section of this chapter, Mr. Gess's controllable assets and income statement information will be considered in an illustration of the performance evaluation of an investment center.

Illustration 13-1 includes only controllable revenues and costs in order to be consistent with the concept of responsibility accounting. Each of the columns included in the variance worksheet should be reviewed prior to the preparation of the profit center performance report.

The forecast budget is based on the anticipated sales volume and mix of filters for the Industrial Filters Division. The selling prices and costs included in the budget are the standard prices and costs for the Division. This budget was prepared prior to the start of the accounting period.

The control budget is prepared after the end of the accounting period. At that point, the actual quantities of filters sold are known. The control budget is a flexible budget prepared after-the-fact using the actual quantity and mix sold at the standard selling prices and costs. Any differences between the individual price or cost factors found on the forecast and

---

[2] There are other methods of calculating sales volume and mix variances in addition to the approaches used in this text. A contribution margin approach is used here to analyze these two variances.

[3] *Ibid.*

Illustration 13-1

Sax Company
Industrial Filter Division
Variance Worksheet

	Forecast Budget (Forecast volume and mix at standard prices and costs) (1)		Control Budget (or Flexible Budget) (Actual volume and mix at standard prices and costs) (2)		Actual (Actual volume and mix at actual prices and costs) (3)		Variances* Volume/Mix (2-1)	Price/Expense (Cost) (3-2)
	Budget	Budget	Budget	Budget	Actual	Actual		
Sales Revenue	$1,500	100%	$1,400	100.0%	$1,500	100%	($100)	$100
Less: Variable Costs								
Cost of Goods Sold	810	54	700	50.0	840	56.0	110	(140)
Salesmen's Commissions	150	10	140	10.0	150	10.0	10	(10)
Contribution Margin	540	36	$ 560	40.0	$ 510	34.0	$ 20	($ 50)
Less: Fixed Costs								
Manufacturing Overhead	$ 270	18	$ 270	19.3	$ 283	18.9	0	($ 13)
Selling & Administrative	195	13	195	13.9	122	8.1	0	73
Total Fixed Costs	$ 465	31%	$ 465	33.2%	$ 405	27.0%	0	$ 60
Income Before Taxes	$ 75	5%	$ 95	6.8%	$ 105	7.0%	$ 20	$ 10

*Stated as favorable or (unfavorable) as to the impact on income.

control budgets are caused by changes in the volume or mix of products sold since both budgets use standard prices and costs in their preparation. Therefore this variance can be broken down into two component parts: the sales volume variance and the sales mix variance.

The column on the variance worksheet headed "actual" is taken directly from the accounting records of the Division. Actual costs and prices at actual volume and mix are shown in these accounts. If the actual data are compared with the data in the control budget, variances can be identified as either selling price or expense (cost) variances because the actual volume and mix of products sold are used in preparing the control budget.

The performance report should identify the impact of the variances on income since a profit center manager is held responsible for achieving an established budgeted income figure. Variances are calculated in order to isolate specific impacts on profits when all other factors are held constant. For example, the sales volume variance should provide an explanation of the impact of sales volume on profits. The impact of product mix, sales prices and costs are separated from the sales volume variance.

Sales Volume Variance

If the actual volume of products sold at standard prices differs from the forecasted volume of products sold at standard prices, then the result is a sales volume variance. The formula for calculating the sales volume variance is as follows:

$$\begin{matrix} \text{Sales} \\ \text{Volume} \\ \text{Variance} \end{matrix} = \left(\begin{matrix} \text{Forecasted Volume} \\ \text{of Sales at} \\ \text{Standard Prices} \end{matrix} - \begin{matrix} \text{Actual Volume} \\ \text{of Sales at} \\ \text{Standard Prices} \end{matrix} \right) \times \begin{matrix} \text{Forecasted} \\ \text{Contribution} \\ \text{Margin} \\ \text{Percentage} \end{matrix}$$

The forecasted sales volume at the standard price is $1,500. The actual sales volume at the standard price is $1,400. Sales volume at standard prices decreased; therefore, the variance is unfavorable. The forecast contribution margin is 36 percent. If the results for the Industrial Filter Division are substituted in the formula, the sales volume variance is:

$$\begin{aligned} \text{Sales Volume Variance} \ &= \ (\$1,500 - \$1,400) \times .36 \\ &= \ \$36 \text{ unfavorable variance} \end{aligned}$$

If all financial factors except sales volume had occurred as forecasted, actual income would have been $36 less than budgeted income as a result of the decline in sales volume.

**Sales
Mix Variance**

If the contribution margin percentage for the forecasted mix and standard prices and costs (forecast budget) differs from the contribution margin percentage for the actual mix and standard prices and costs (control budget), then a sales mix variance results. The forecast budget contribution margin percentage from Illustration 13-1 is 36 percent ($540/$1,500). The contribution margin percentage from the control budget is $560/$1,400 or 40 percent. The formula for calculating the sales mix variance is:

$$\text{Sales Mix Variance} = \left(\begin{array}{l} \text{Contribution Margin} \\ \text{Percentage from the} \\ \text{Forecast Budget} \end{array} - \begin{array}{l} \text{Contribution Margin} \\ \text{Percentage from the} \\ \text{Control Budget} \end{array} \right) \times$$

Sales on the
Control (Flexible) Budget

If the contribution margin percentage used in the control budget is greater than the contribution margin percentage in the forecast budget, the resulting sales mix variance is favorable. This is because the actual mix of products sold at the standard prices and costs represents a more profitable mix than was originally forecasted or anticipated. Sales volume does not affect the contribution margin percentage. Even if the forecast budget sales volume had doubled, the control contribution margin percentage would be the same as the forecasted contribution margin so long as the sales mix remained constant.

If the results from the Industrial Filter Division are used in the formula, the sales mix variance is calculated as follows:

$$\text{Sales Mix Variance} \quad = (.36 - .40) \times \$1,400$$
$$= \$56 \text{ favorable variance}$$

The impact on actual income as compared to forecasted income as a favorable $56 because the actual mix of products sold was a more profitable mix than was originally anticipated and budgeted.

**Sales
Price Variance**

The sales price variance is taken directly from the variance worksheet. This variance is the difference between standard prices at actual volume and mix (control budget) and actual prices at actual volume mix (actual). In the case of the Industrial Filter Division, sales revenue at actual volume and mix and standard price totaled $1,400. Actual sales revenues are $1,500 (from Illustration 13-1). Actual revenues exceeded control budget revenues by $100; therefore, the sales price variance is a favorable $100.

Salesmen's commissions increased by $10 due to an increase in actual prices charged customers over the standard prices. It could be argued that the actual sales price variance was $90 ($100 increase in revenues less $10 increase in commissions) because of the impact of salesmen's commissions.

Expense Variances

The expense variances or cost variances are taken directly from the variance worksheet presented in Illustration 13-1. Variable cost variances represent the traditional approach to variance analysis. Standard costs at actual volume and mix (control budget) are compared with actual costs at actual volume and mix (actual amounts). If actual amounts are less than standard, the variance is favorable. The variable cost expense variances include an unfavorable cost of goods sold variance of $140 and, as indicated above, an unfavorable salesmen's commissions expense of $10. The variance in salesmen's commissions was caused by the favorable sales price variance and, as previously stated, may be considered a reduction in the sales price variance on a performance report.

Fixed cost variances may also be taken directly from the variance worksheet presented in Illustration 13-1. There are no volume or mix variances for fixed costs because the budgeted fixed costs are not affected by volume or mix changes within the relevant range. [4] The fixed cost variances are caused by spending. Manufacturing overhead has exceeded the budgeted amount by $13. The selling and administrative expense variance is a favorable variance of $73. The impact of these expense variances on actual before-tax income is on a one-to-one basis, that is, for every dollar of favorable expense variance, actual income increases by a dollar over budgeted before-tax income.

PERFORMANCE REPORTS FOR PROFIT CENTERS

The performance report for the Industrial Filter Division of Sax Company presented in Illustration 13-2 is based on the worksheet presented in Illustration 13-1. A performance report, such as the one shown in Illustration 13-2, explains the major reasons for achieving $105 in profit instead of the forecasted profit of $75. The format of the performance report for the Industrial Filter Division begins with the forecasted budgeted income and then analyzes the volume and mix variances in

---

[4] Remember that Sax Company uses the variable costing approach for internal planning, control and performance evaluation. Fixed manufacturing costs are treated as period costs

order to arrive at the control budgeted income. The impact of the sales price variances and the expense variances on the control budget income is then computed in order to arrive at the actual income before taxes.

The net effect of the operations of the current period results in an income amount in the Industrial Filter Division that is $30 more than the amount originally budgeted. Illustration 13-2 summarizes the combination of factors that caused the net $30 favorable variance from budgeted income before taxes.

Illustration 13-2
Sax Company
Industrial Filter Division
Performance Report
Manager: Mr. Gess
( ) = Unfavorable

Forecast Budgeted Income Before Taxes.............................	$ 75
Sales Volume Variance ($1,500 — $1,400) X .36 = ...	(36)
Sales Mix Variance:	
Forecast Budget Contribution Margin $ 540 = .36	
$1,500	
Control Budget Contribution Margin $ 560 = .40	
$1,400	
Change in Contribution margin caused	
by Change in Mix........................ = .04	
Sales Mix Variance $1,400 X .04 = ...	56
Control Budgeted Income Before Taxes............................	$95
Sales Price Variances:	
Increased Prices to Customers $1,500 — $1,400 = ...	100
Less: Increase in Salesmen's Commissions $100 X .10 = ...	(10)
Cost of Goods Sold Cost Variances................................	(140)
Fixed Cost Spending Variances:	
Manufacturing Overhead.....................................	(13)
Selling and Administrative.................................	73
Actual Income Before Taxes....................................	$105

PERFORMANCE EVALUATION OF INVESTMENT CENTERS

The management of Sax Company views the Industrial Filter Division as an investment center. The balance sheet used to determine the assets or capital employed in this Division is based on the traceable assets, liabilities and corporate investment. In other words, only those balance sheet factors which are directly traceable to the Industrial Filter Division are used to determine the capital utilized in the Division.

Management recognizes that a measure of return-on-investment (ROI) is only one indication of overall performance. Since no single correct means of calculating return on investment exists, all divisions of the firm that are considered investment centers may be held responsible for two different budgeted rates of return: a rate-of-return on total traceable assets and a rate-of-return on traceable corporate investment. In these measures, the budgeted assets or the budgeted corporate investment at the end of the year is used as the basis for the ROI calculation. The use of the budgeted assets utilized provides the division managers with a target asset package or corporate investment.

The rate of return on total traceable assets is important because it provides a measure of how well the responsible manager utilized the resources that were available to him. Return on corporate investment traceable to the division is used to provide a measure of the financial performance of the firm's capital investment in that division. Each division may borrow money externally and, through the use of leverage, increase its return on corporate investment. Cash could also be borrowed internally from corporate headquarters. When cash is borrowed from corporate headquarters, corporate investment in that division is increased. When cash is sent to corporate headquarters, corporate investment is reduced.

Sax Company has established and maintains a monthly reporting system. Rates of return are calculated on a monthly basis to assure the adherence of a division to its budgets and to encourage the responsible manager to attempt to attain the budgeted returns on investment. Illustration 13-3 presents the budgeted and actual balance sheets for the past year for the Industrial Filter Division.

The worksheet analyzing the income statement variance was presented in Illustration 13-1.

BUDGET ROI VERSUS ACTUAL ROI

The budgeted returns for the year using budgeted end-of-year total assets and corporate investment from Illustration 13-3 and the forecast budgeted income from Illustration 13-1 are as follows:[5]

$$\text{ROI on Total Assets} = \text{Profit Margin} \times \text{Asset Turnover}$$

$$= \frac{\text{Profit}}{\text{Sales}} \times \frac{\text{Sales}}{\text{Assets Utilized}}$$

$$= \frac{\$75}{\$1,500} \times \frac{\$1,500}{\$600}$$

---

[5] It is common to use average total assets and average corporate investment for the accounting period instead of end-of-year totals. End-of-year totals could be influenced by last minute decisions and could present a distorted perspective when compared to averages.

$$= \quad .05 \text{ X } 2.5$$

$$= \quad .125 \text{ or } 12\frac{1}{2}\%$$

$$\text{ROI on Corporate Investment} = \frac{\text{Profit}}{\text{Sales}} \text{ X } \frac{\text{Sales}}{\text{Corporate Investment}}$$

$$= \quad \frac{\$75}{\$1,500} \text{ X } \frac{\$1,500}{\$300}$$

$$= \quad .05 \text{ X } 5$$

$$= \quad .25 \text{ or } 25\%$$

The results for the year using actual end-of-year total assets and corporate investment from Illustration 13-3 and the actual income from Illustration 13-1 are as follows:

$$\text{ROI on Total Assets} = \frac{\$105}{\$1,500} \text{ X } \frac{\$1,500}{\$500}$$

$$= \quad .07 \text{ X } 3$$

$$= \quad .21 \text{ or } 21\%$$

$$\text{ROI on Corporate Investment} = \frac{\$105}{\$1,500} \text{ X } \frac{\$1,500}{\$200}$$

$$= \quad .07 \text{ X } 7.5$$

$$= \quad .525 \text{ or } 52\frac{1}{2}\%$$

Mr. Gess, the manager of the investment center, was able to exceed the budgeted return on total assets by increasing both the actual profit margin and asset turnover compared to budget. The budgeted profit margin was 5 percent and the budgeted asset turnover was 2.5 times. The actual profit margin and budgeted asset turnover was 7 percent and 3 times, respectively.

An analysis of the increased profit margin can be made from Illustration 13-2. The sales volume, sales commissions, cost of goods sold and manufacturing overhead variances were all unfavorable, but were less in total than the favorable variances for sales mix, sales prices, and selling and administrative expenses. Thus a net favorable variance resulted in a 2% increase in the profit margin.

Illustration 13-3

Sax Company
Industrial Filter Division
Budgeted and Actual Balance Sheets
Manager: Mr. Gess

ASSETS	Budget	Actual	Variances
Current Assets:			
Cash	$ 20	$ 20	$ 0
Accounts Receivable	100	60	(40)
Direct Materials Inventories	50	20	(30)
Indirect Materials and Supplies	10	5	(5)
Work-in-Process Inventories	30	30	0
Finished Goods on a Variable			
Costing Basis	90	65	(25)
Long-Term Assets:			
Equipment (Net of Accumulated			
Depreciation)	100	100	0
Plant (Net of Accumulated			
Depreciation)	200	200	0
Total Assets	$600	$500	($100)

LIABILITIES AND SHAREHOLDERS' EQUITY

	Budget	Actual	Variances
Current Liabilities:			
Accounts Payable	$ 75	$ 80	$ 5
Wages Payable	50	40	(10)
Long-Term Liabilities:			
Long-Term Debt	175	180	5
Shareholders' Equity:			
Corporate Investment	300	200	(100)
Total Liabilities and Shareholders'			
Equity	$600	$500	($100)
Return on Total Assets (Income from			
Illustration 13-1)	12½ %	21 %	
Return on Corporate Investment			
(Income from Illustration 13-1)	25 %	52½ %	

Budgeted and actual total revenues were the same. To increase asset turnover, Mr. Gess reduced assets by $100. This reduction may, in fact, represent only a short-run improvement in the utilization of resources if the budgeted amounts in Illustration 13-3 are assumed to be the amounts necessary to fund the operations of the Division over a long-run period.

The actual return on corporate investment exceeded the budgeted return by 27.5 percent. Mr. Gess accomplished the increased return by increasing the profit margin by 2 percent and decreasing corporate investment by $100. The decrease in corporate investment was sufficient to increase the turnover of corporate investment from a budgeted 5 times to an actual turnover of 7.5 times.

In addition to the cash transfers made to corporate headquarters (which reduced corporate investment in the Division by $100), Mr. Gess reduced accounts receivable by $40, direct materials inventories by $30, indirect materials and supplies by $5 and finished goods inventory by $25. He increased accounts payable by $5 and long-term debt by $5. Wages payable was reduced by $10. The variances from budget for these balance sheet accounts must be considered in view of the Division's needs before any statements or conclusions may be made regarding Mr. Gess's management approach.

If the performance report presented in Illustration 13-2 and the budgeted and actual balance sheets and other analyses included in Illustration 13-3 are all considered, the following statements can be made concerning Mr. Gess's management of the Industrial Filter Division.

1. The sales volume variance was an unfavorable $36 because budgeted sales were not attained.
2. The sales mix variance was a favorable $56. The actual mix included a greater proportion of the more profitable filters than was originally budgeted.
3. The sales prices charged to some or all customers were higher than standard. This enabled the division to make an additional $100 in gross sales revenues or $90 net after the increased salesman's commissions.
4. The production cost variances charged to the cost of goods sold for the year were unfavorable and thus decreased the division's income by $140.
5. The fixed cost spending variances totaled $60 favorable. This increased the income of the division by $60.
6. The division's actual income before taxes was $105. This was $30 above the forecast budget income.

A selected measure of income is used as the numerator in all return-on-investment equations. The denominator will always be based on a selected measure of resources utilized. By controlling or influencing either the numerator or the denominator (or both) the manager can influence ROI. The denominators as defined by the Sax Company are total traceable assets for the first measure and traceable corporate investment for the second measure.

Mr. Gess increased the numerator, income before taxes, without increasing revenues. The denominator was reduced by decreasing the assets utilized and decreasing corporate investment by the same amount. Total liabilities did not change from budgeted, although individual balances in the accounts were changed.

SUMMARY

Responsibility accounting for profit centers and investment centers is similar to that for cost centers. Additional financial factors, however, must be taken into account. While the cost center is concerned only with controllable costs, the profit center is responsible for controllable revenues and costs. The investment center is responsible for controllable capital investments as well as controllable revenues and costs. Although responsibility accounting for these additional financial factors permits considerable decentralization, it also creates new problems.

One of the problems associated with responsibility accounting for profit centers relates to the measurement of revenues when sales are made between company segments. The primary types of transfer prices used to measure such revenues are: (1) market-based price, (2) cost-based price, and (3) negotiated price. Each of these transfer prices has its advantages and disadvantages and the actual transfer price used by a firm will probably be a combination of these methods.

The procedure for evaluating the performance of profit centers includes a detailed analysis of the variances from budgeted net income. The variances generally included in such an analysis are: (1) sales volume variance, (2) sales mix variance, (3) sales price variance, and (4) cost or expense variance. The first three variances are related to revenues realized by the center and the cost or expense variance is related to costs incurred by the center.

Responsibility accounting for investment centers also requires a method for evaluating performance. One common performance evaluation technique is to relate income to the assets utilized to earn that income. This relationship is determined by calculating the return on investment (ROI). However, the return on investment calculation requires that the amount of assets utilized be known.

The performance evaluation of an investment center may include more than one ROI calculation since "assets utilized" may be defined several ways. For instance, the actual rate of return on total traceable assets may be calculated in addition to the usual calculation of the rate of return on corporate investment. Budgeted ROI and actual ROI are compared and an analysis of any differences between the two is made. In addition, a firm may wish to analyze the various components of the ROI figure to determine if the desired ROI is being met in an acceptable manner.

This chapter concludes the discussion of responsibility accounting systems. Chapter 14 discusses the various accounting approaches to planning special decisions.

KEY DEFINITIONS

Control budget—a flexible budget prepared at the end of an accounting period using the actual quantity and mix sold at the standard selling prices and costs.

Cost-based transfer price—a transfer price which may be based on the actual, standard or variable costs of the supplying segment.

Expense variances—the differences between the standard and actual costs or expenses at the actual volume and mix.

Market-based transfer price—a transfer price based on the external market price less any savings in cost; it is the closest approximation to an arm's length transaction that segments can achieve.

Negotiated transfer price—a transfer price which is established by agreement of both the selling and buying segments of the firm.

Return on investment—measures the ability of a firm, or segment within a firm, to utilize available resources effectively by expressing profit or income as a percentage of invested assets.

Sales mix variance—occurs when the contribution margin percentage at the forecasted mix and standard prices and costs (forecast budget) differs from the contribution margin percentage at actual mix and standard prices (control budget).

Sales price variance—the difference between standard prices at actual volume and mix (control budget) and actual prices at actual volume and mix.

Sales volume variance—occurs when the actual sales volume of products sold at the standard prices (control budget) differs from the forecasted sales volume of products sold at the standard prices (forecast budget).

Transfer price—the price that one segment of a firm pays to another segment of the same firm for the output or service of the supplying segment.

QUESTIONS

13-1 What does decentralization attempt to do?

13-2 What is a transfer price and why does it pose certain problems in performance measurement by segments?

13-3 What are the shortcomings of a market-based transfer price? A cost-based transfer price?

13-4 The return on investment formula is made up of two components: margin on sales and turnover of capital. Explain what each of these respective components signify.

13-5 Name two problems which are encountered in defining capital utilized in an investment center.

13-6 What is the reason for a sales mix variance? Does volume affect this variance?

13-7 What is the difference between a sales price and expense variance?

13-8 What causes a fixed cost variance when the variable costing approach is used? What impact does this variance have on actual income?

13-9 How can a responsible manager meet his budgeted return on investment if his actual margin on sales is below that budgeted? Give one example.

13-10 What specific method can a manager use to reduce his current assets in order to increase his actual asset turnover ratio? What is a disadvantage of this method?

EXERCISES AND PROBLEMS

13-11 The James Bay Company had sales of $1,000,000 and income of $450,000. It employed capital of $15,000,000.

Required:

Determine the return on investment.

13-12 Sleeper, Inc. forecasted sales of 500,000 mattresses at $150 per mattress. At the end of the year, the company determined that it had sold 498,000 mattresses at an average price of $158 per mattress. The forecasted contribution margin percentage was 42 percent.

Required:

Determine the sales volume variance and the sales price variance.

13-13 The Rubber Tire Company forecasted that 200,000 tires would be sold at a price of $60 per tire for the year. After checking figures at the end of the year, it was discovered that 210,000 tires were sold at a price of $59. The company had forecasted a contribution margin of 30%.

Required:

Determine the sales volume variance and the sales price variance.

13-14   Variable expenses for Jackson, Inc. are based on direct labour hours. They are $4.80 per direct labour hour. Last period 654,860 direct labour hours were worked. The variable costs were $4.83 per hour.

Required:

Determine the variable cost variance.

13-15   The Thomson Company has two divisions. Division 1 normally sells 75% of its output to Division 2 for $10, the same price as it sells to other customers.

Given below are the results for the year:

	Division 1	Division 2
Sales to outsiders	$15,000	$200,000
Sales to Division 2	45,000	–0–
Total	$60,000	$200,000
Transfer costs	–0–	45,000
Other variable costs	15,600	35,000
Contribution margin	$44,400	$120,000
Fixed costs	25,000	80,000
Net income before taxes	$19,400	$ 40,000

Required:

a. Prepare a report consolidating the two divisions.
b. If Division 2 could purchase the product from an outside source for $9.00 by purchasing their total needs from that source, should Division 1 meet this price? Assume that Division 1 can sell no more than 75% of their production to outsiders. (Consider this from the viewpoint of the overall company.)

13-16   Division C of the Glaser Company has the following budget for the year:

	Forecast Budget
Sales @ $10/unit °	$40,000
Variable costs @ $5/unit °	20,000
Contribution margin	$20,000
Fixed costs	10,000
Net income before taxes	$10,000

° Weighted average based on forecast sales mix.

The weighted average contribution margin on the control budget is $15,000, which is a 48 percent contribution margin. Actual sales for the year were $35,000, variable costs were $16,000 and fixed costs were

$11,000. Total assets for Division C were budgeted at $30,000 but were actually $35,000.

Required:

Prepare a variance worksheet in good form for the year assuming that Division C is a profit center.

13-17   You have been hired by East Money Inc. to work in their cost accounting department. Your first job is to calculate the ROI. Unfortunately, the sales figures for the past year have been lost. Eager to show your technical skill you state that you can still calculate ROI with only the income of $60,000 and the investment of $720,000 being known.

Required:

Calculate the ROI and show how the volume of sales has no effect.

13-18   Department A of the Stonewall Company has been purchasing the rods it uses in concrete slabs from Department B of the same company for $50 per ton. Department A purchases about 90% of the production of B. In the current year, B expects to have sales of about 1,600 tons. The remaining 10% of B's sales are to outside customers for $51 with terms of 2/10, N/30. Approximately 60% of the outside sales are paid within ten days, and about 3% of the outside sales are never paid.

A has been negotiating with several other suppliers for these rods and finds its can purchase them from an outside supplier for $48 per ton. Unless Department B lowers its price, A will use the outside supplier.

After doing some market research, B feels that it can sell 90% of its present capacity to outside customers for $51 @ 2/10, N/30, or 95% for $50 @ 2/10, N/30. Under these two arrangements, Department A will buy all purchases from outsiders.

Variable costs for the rods are $20 per ton and fixed costs are $21,000 per year. Selling expenses are $1.50 per ton if sold to outside customers.

Required:

If Department B does not consider the rest of the firm, what should it do?

13-19   Alcorn, Inc. has 2 divisions, R and S. R sells approximately 80% of its output to S for $15, but charges outside customers $15.50 because Alcorn must pay its salesman 3% of the selling price on sales to outside customers.

Given below are the results for the year:

	Division R	Division S
Sales to outsiders	$ 9,300	$72,000
Sales to Division S	36,000	–0–
Total	$45,300	$72,000
Transfer costs	–0–	36,000
Variable costs	9,000	9,600
Salesman's commission	279	2,160
Contribution margin	$36,021	$24,240
Fixed costs	23,000	10,000
Net income before taxes	$13,021	$14,240

Required:

a. Prepare a report consolidating the two divisions.

b. If Division S could purchase the product for $14.25 from an outside source, should R meet this price? Assume R could sell 90% of their production to outsiders for $15. If R sells to S, it can still sell 20% of its production to outside customers for $15.50. (Consider this from the viewpoint of the overall company.)

13-20 The following data pertain to the hardware division of Hogan Incorporated. The company has set a 20 percent return on investment as the profit objective of the hardware division.

Sales revenue	$200,000
Net income	$ 50,000
Capital used	$333,000

Required:

Was the hardware division successful in meeting its profit objective of 20 percent ROI? If the answer is no, give two suggestions for increasing the ROI to the desired number.

13-21 From the information listed below, calculate the sales mix variance for the Mondale Company.

	Forecast Budget	Control Budget
Sales revenue	$360,000	$320,000
Variable costs:		
Cost of goods sold	223,200	192,100
Salesmen's commissions	18,000	16,000
Selling expenses	3,600	3,100
Fixed costs:		
Salaries	18,000	18,000
Rent	8,000	8,000

13-22 The following data pertain to three investment centers of Alpha Enterprises for the year.

	I	II	III
Net income before taxes	$100,000	$ 150,000	$ 80,000
Sales revenue	800,000	1,000,000	700,000
Total assets	500,000	625,000	300,000
Corporate investment	300,000	500,000	200,000

Required:

a.   Calculate the margin on sales, turnover of total assets, and the ROI on total assets for the three investment centers.

b.   Calculate the turnover of total corporate investment and the ROI on corporate investment for the three investment centers.

c.   For "A and B" above, rank the three investment centers in order, highest return listed first.

13-23   The following information relates to the assembly division of the Omega Corporation for the year. The budgeted ROI on total assets was set at 20 percent and the budgeted ROI on corporate investment was set at 25 percent.

Net income before taxes	$100,000
Sales	800,000
Total assets	600,000
Corporate investment	400,000

Required:

a.   Compute the actual ROI on total assets and the actual ROI on corporate investments.

b.   Name two ways that the ROI on total assets may be improved, and two ways the ROI on corporate investment may be improved if necessary for this situation.

13-24   You are presently trying to encourage people to invest in your new company that manufactures an automatic dirty diaper washer. Potential investors are constantly asking what ROI can be expected. Unfortunately, you have not been in business long enough to know what the actual ROI is. However, you do expect one-third of all sales to equal income before taxes. The volume of sales is completely dependent on the corporate investment, sales always being one-half of the corporate investment.

Required:

a.   Calculate the ROI on corporate investment that is expected.

b.   If you are able to get investors to contribute $420,000, what will be the income before tax?

13-25   The manufacturing division of the Marple Corporation produces two products, Y and Z. The following data refer to the two products:

	Y	Z
Selling price	$6	$10
Variable costs:		
Cost of goods sold	$3	$ 4
Sales commissions	$0.60	$ 1

Total fixed costs were budgeted at $56,000 for the year.

Sales revenue was budgeted (forecast) as follows:

	Amount	Units
Product Y	$ 60,000	10,000
Product Z	$100,000	10,000

Given below is the income statement for the year reflecting the actual data.

Sales revenue		$160,000
Less: Variable costs		
Cost of goods sold . .	$80,000	
Sales commissions . . .	16,000	96,000
Contribution margin		64,000
Less: Fixed costs		48,000
Income before taxes		$ 16,000

Actual units sold . . . . . . 13,000(Y)   7,000(Z)

Required:

a. Prepare a variances worksheet for the manufacturing division. Determine the income before taxes for the forecast budget and the control budget. Determine the volume/mix and price/expense variance.

b. Prepare a performance report for the manager of the manufacturing division in which the forecast budget income is reconciled with the actual income before taxes.

13-26 The following data refer to the production division of the Gypsy Company which produces two products, C and D.

1. General information:

    Selling price of C and D was $10 per unit
    Standard variable costs were:
       60% of sales for C
       40% of sales for D
    Fixed costs were budgeted at $40,000

2. Sales for the year were forecast budgeted as follows:

Product C	$ 40,000	4,000 units
Product D	60,000	6,000 units
	$100,000	

3. The actual income statement is presented below:

Sales revenue:		
Product C (5,000 units)	$50,000	
Product D (5,000 units)	50,000	$100,000
Less: Variable costs		51,000
Contribution margin		49,000
Less: Fixed costs		34,000
Income before taxes		$ 15,000

Required:

Prepare a performance report for the production division in which the forecast budget income is reconciled with the actual income. Show all variances on the report.

13-27   The following data pertain to a division of the Oxford Manufacturing Company which produces and sells two products, A and B.

Forecast Budget
  Sales were budgeted as follows:
    Product A—10,000 units @ $5 per unit = $50,000
    Product B—20,000 units @ $10 per unit = $200,000
  The standard variable costs are:
    Product A—$2.00 per unit
    Product B—$6.00 per unit
  The total fixed costs were budgeted at $90,000.

Actual data
  Sales revenue:
    Product A—sold 15,000 units @ $6 = $ 90,000
    Product B—sold 16,000 units @ $12 =   192,000
                                          $282,000
  Variable costs totaled $150,000
  Fixed costs totaled $100,000

Required:

a. Compute the following variances:

1. Sales volume
2. Sales mix
3. Sales price
4. Expense-variable and fixed

b. Prepare a performance report for this division of the Oxford Manufacturing Company which reconciles the forecast budget income with the actual income.

13-28   The following information is available:

	X Division	Y Division
Total assets.	25,000	125,000
Net annual earnings.	5,000	18,750

Cost of capital for each division is 12%.

Required:

a.   Using return-on-investment as a measure of management success which is the more successful division? Why?

b.   Using residual income as a measure of management success which is the more successful division? Why?

(SMA, adapted)

13-29   You have been assigned the task of resolving a dispute between two divisional general managers (DGM) of the Span Company. Span is a large company with decision-making highly decentralized and each division is treated as a profit center.

DGM's receive a substantial part of their remuneration in the form of a bonus based on the return-on-investment of their divisions. Each DGM is free to purchase and sell outside the company. However, it has been traditional over the years for buying divisions to purchase within the company when possible. Selling divisions have always given a high priority to meeting intra-company orders and many selling divisions have set aside substantial proportions of capacity (over 50% in many cases) to meet the needs of buying divisions.

Each fall the DGM's meet with the president to discuss profit plans and to confirm inter-divisional transfers of goods for the next year. The president is concerned about the growing volume of these internal transfers as a potential area of disputes among the DGM's.

At the current annual profit plan discussions, a dispute has occured between the DGM's of the Lumber and the Furniture Divisions. For the past four years over 60% of Lumber's output has been sold to Furniture with the balance sold to outsiders. Last year's operating data for Lumber illustrate this relationship:

Lumber Division

	To Furniture Division	To Outsiders
Sales:		
5,000 thousand board feet (TBF) at $115. per TBF*.....................	$575,000	
3,000 thousand board feet (TBF) at $125. per TBF.....................		$375,000
Variable costs at $75 per thousand board feet..	375,000	225,000
	$200,000	$150,000
Total costs.........................	150,000	90,000
Gross profit........................	$ 50,000	$ 60,000

*This price is based on market price, less an allowance for selling and administrative costs normally incurred on outside sales.

The Furniture DGM can purchase his requirements for next year outside the company at a price of $105 per thousand board feet (TBF) and he refuses to pay a higher price to the Lumber Division. The Lumber DGM, who cannot sell the 5,000 TBF elsewhere, states that if he sells to Furniture at $105 per TBF he makes no gross profit for his Lumber Division. In addition, the capacity in the Lumber Division has been increased over the years to ensure a steady supply for Furniture's requirements.

Required:

a. Recommend to the president whether or not the Furniture Division should continue to purchase material from the Lumber Division. (Support your recommendation with appropriate figures to the extent possible).

b. Discuss briefly the limitations of using ROI for evaluation of DGM's in this situation. What changes in the bonus system and/or the organization would you recommend which might avoid or minimize future conflicts over internal prices?

(SMA, adapted)

13-30   The Westville Company manufactures a soft drink. The company is organized into two divisions, Glass and Filling. The Glass Division makes bottles and sells them to the Filling Division. Each division manager receives a bonus based on the division's net income.

In the market, bottle producers are charging as follows:

Number of Cases Per Month	Total Charge	Average Price Per Case
11,000	$135,300	$12.30
12,000	144,000	12.00
13,000	152,750	11.75
14,000	158,900	11.35
15,000	165,000	11.00

The costs per case in the Glass Division are as follows:

Volume Per Month	Glass Division Cost Per Case
11,000	$10.71
12,000	10.52
13,000	10.35
14,000	10.18

The Filling Division's costs (excluding bottle purchases) and selling prices are:

Volume Per Month	Selling Price	Cost Per Case
11,000	$38.00	$24.32
12,000	37.55	24.09
13,000	37.20	23.91
14,000	36.80	23.76
15,000	36.20	23.57

The current capacities of the divisions are 15,000 cases per month for Filling and 14,000 cases per month for Glass.

Required:

a. If market prices are used as transfer prices, what is the most profitable volume for each division and for the company as a whole? Show calculations to support your answer. Assume that *transfers and sales are made in units of one thousand* and that the Glass Division is unable to sell its production in the outside market.

b. Under what conditions should market prices *not* be used in determining transfer prices?

(SMA, adapted)

13-31   The C and P Packing Company has two divisions. Division 1 is responsible for slaughtering and cutting the unprocessed meat. Division 2 processes meat such as hams, bacon, etc. Division 2 can buy meat from Division 1 or from outside suppliers. Division 1 can sell at the market price all the unprocessed meat that it can produce. The 19x2 income statement for the company is as follows (in thousands):

Total sales...................................		$1,800
Cost of goods:		
Beginning inventory........................	$ 0	
Manufacturing costs:		
Raw materials, Division 1..................	$500	
Labour, Division 1........................	300	
Overhead, Division 1......................	200	
Processing supplies, Division 2.............	150	
Labour, Division 2........................	200	
Overhead, Division 2......................	100	
Cost of goods available for sale..............	$1,450	
Ending inventory at cost:		
Division 1..............................	0	
Division 2..............................	100	1,350
Gross profit.............................		$ 450
Operating expenses:		
Selling and administrative, Division 1........	$110	
Selling and administrative, Division 2........	120	
Head office overhead.....................	140	370
Net income before taxes....................		$ 80

The ending inventory of $100,000 is at the cost of production incurred in Division 1. This inventory is as yet unprocessed. The market value unprocessed is $120,000. The sales for the year can be broken down as follows:

Division 1............................	$ 400,000
Division 2............................	1,400,000
	$1,800,000

The market value of the unprocessed meat actually transferred from Division 1 to Division 2 (exclusive of the ending inventory) was $1,000,000.

Required:

a. Prepare division income statements designed to evaluate the performance of the two division managers.

b. Explain the transfer pricing policy you have used in preparing the statements.

c. Discuss any possible conflict in the policy you have used if this same transfer price is to be used for decision making.

13-32   The Hanbury Manufacturing Company Limited produces two products, Alma and Dafes, using the same equipment for the production of each product. The company uses a responsibility accounting system for both cost control and performance evaluation purposes.

R. Robins, who is in charge of the production department, schedules each week's production based on a sales forecast for the following week. The forecasts are received from M. Margo, vice-president of marketing.

On Monday morning, Robins received a sales forecast of 2,400 units of Alma and 1,000 units of Dafes. Since the equipment has already set up for the production of Dafes, his department produced those units on Monday and Tuesday. Tuesday afternoon was spent resetting the equipment for Alma, with production starting Wednesday morning.

On Thursday morning, Margo came into Robins's office and said that a new customer wanted 1,600 units of Dafes by Friday, but that the units were not in stock. Margo felt that the customer was too valuable a future prospect to lose and therefore requested that the production be switched back to Dafes to fill the order. Robins rescheduled the production as he was required to fulfill the requirements of the marketing department.

The change in production to fulfill this new order caused the following additional costs to be incurred:

1.	Costs of resetting for Dafes (Thursday)............	$ 2,800
2.	Costs of resetting for Alma (on Saturday, in order to complete regular orders)............	2,800
3.	Costs of employees working on Saturday and Sunday to fulfill regular orders (at 1½ times regular wages)...................	7,800
	Total additional cost........................	$13,400

Required:

a. Indicate on whose performance report (Robins's or Margo's), if any, that each cost, or any portion of it, should appear. Give your reason for each cost allocation decision.

b. For each of the costs, explain why it will or will not give rise to a variance on the performance report. Briefly explain the usefulness in management decision making of each specific variance that would arise in the above situation.

13-33   Mr. Ringo operates a chain of retail sporting goods stores, and has encountered difficulties in using his accounting data for decision-making. At present, there are five sporting goods stores in the chain. Each store carries the major product lines; e.g., tennis equipment, bicycles, sport clothing, shoes, guns, fishing tackle, etc. Orders from each store are sent to the central warehouse which does all buying and warehousing for the chain.

Sales at all stores are by cash or credit-card, the latter being processed centrally by a small office staff located in the central warehouse.

The chain publishes a catalogue once a year, showing all products carried in each of its stores. Prices are listed in the catalogue for each product, and each store sells items at the published price. Catalogues are provided in sufficient quantities to the stores and are available to customers by mail. All mail-order business is handled directly by the warehouse.

All purchasing is done centrally by one purchasing agent, and payables and payroll are handled by the central office staff.

At the present time, each store deposits cash daily and forwards copies of deposit slips and credit-card sales slips to the central office. The stores keep records daily (from cash register tapes) of sales by product line. At month-end the central office prepares one income statement for the chain with supporting schedules of sales by stores and sales by product line. Costs of goods sold are based on sales less the average mark-up by product lines. Quarterly, the warehouse and all stores take physical inventory, and the cost of goods sold figure is adjusted.

Profits have declined during the last 18 months in spite of increased sales volume. Mr. Ringo is concerned and wishes to change the accounting system so that he can obtain more relevant data necessary to determine the causes for declining profits.

Required:

You have been assigned to design a new accounting system which will provide Mr. Ringo with better performance reports for each store, as well as for the centralized warehouse operations.

a.   What costs should be included in each performance report?
b.   Explain whether the following costs should or should not be included in the performance reports:

    i.   cost of catalogue.
    ii.   cost of advertising.
    iii. central purchasing costs.
    iv.   central office costs.

    c.   How should the profitability of central warehousing and central purchasing be measured?

    d.   If Mr. Ringo decides to provide performance rewards, what basis should be used to calculate bonuses for store managers?

    e.   What other yardsticks or control devices could be built into the system to measure performance and profitability?

(SMA, adapted)

13-34   The executives of World Accord multi-national corporation are concerned over the lack-lustre performance of Kingcraft, one of World's divisions. The executives rely almost exclusively upon periodic "corporate accounting analysis" of divisional performance, which highlights sales, profits and investment performance.

Kingcraft manufactures navigational devices in the price-sensitive marine industry. The uniquely designed devices are considered to be of superior quality, giving Kingcraft a competitive edge in the marketplace. In part, the marketing success of the navigational device is due to the specially built electronic range-finder component supplied to Kingcraft by a sister division known as Tectron.

The per unit selling price and standard manufacturing cost of the navigational device are set out below:

Selling price....................................	$2,600
Standard manufacturing cost:	
Direct materials, direct labour and variable	
overhead, including $900 for the electronic	
range-finder component........................	$1,660
Fixed manufacturing overhead.....................	390
Total standard manufacturing cost....................	$2,050

Fixed manufacturing overhead is allocated on the basis of direct labour hours. The latter is used as a measure of Kingcraft's plant capacity. Each navigational device requires 26 standard labour hours to produce. Over the past year, Kingcraft has been operating at a level of 70% of its practical capacity.

Tug McPhail, the General Manager of Kingcraft, was formerly head of Tectron. While with the sister division, he had a reputation for "getting the job done" and had enjoyed substantial profit-sharing bonuses. Profit-sharing bonuses are based on the excess of divisional pre-tax profit (less corporate service costs) over a specified base. Due to the modest growth in profits of Kingcraft, Tug's bonuses had been dramatically reduced since leaving Tectron. Tug's frustrations were compounded due to serious quality control problems in his new division. The rejection rate for imperfect navigational devices has increased. This increased rejection rate is, in some cases, due to faulty electronic range-finder components. The costs of the re-work programs for repairs of faulty electronic range-finders are costs which must be absorbed by Kingcraft.

Albert Syms, formerly Assistant General Manager of Kingcraft, is the present General Manager of Tectron. His move to Tectron two years ago coincided with the appointment of Tug McPhail as head of Kingcraft as a result of the sudden death of the previous General Manager. Albert considered his "promotion" a lateral move; however, he decided to "make the best" of his situation. Since Albert joined Tectron, the division's earnings had increased at a rate of approximately 15% per year. Consequently, Albert had been receiving considerable incentive bonuses.

Sales by Tectron to Kingcraft are significant, although not considered essential to its survival. Gross profit margin percentage of costs by product line in Tectron vary only to a minor degree and have remained relatively unchanged for several years. Sales to Kingcraft in recent years have shown only modest increases when compared to the growth in sales by Tectron to its other major customers.

A corporate accounting analysis of World Accord's most recent five-year performance, together with that of two of its divisions, Kingcraft and Tectron, is set out in Exhibit I. Profits are stated on a pre-tax basis, with divisional profits reported "after allocation of corporate service costs." Annual corporate service costs to the division amount to 10% of the net book value of divisional investment. A significant portion of the divisional investment is in fixed assets which are depreciated on a straight-line basis at rates averaging 12% per annum. Investment is reported at net book value as at the end of each accounting period.

The transfer prices for goods and services exchanged between divisions is based on the actual full cost of the selling division (including a provision for corporate service costs, divisional administrative costs) plus a "reasonable profit margin." World Accord requires its divisions "to deal internally" to protect industrial secrets.

In an effort to improve profit and investment performance, the President of World Accord is considering combining the two divisions. The President requested that Tug McPhail and Albert Syms present their points of view on this matter. In brief, Syms had reacted positively, stating . . ."the benefits to be gained from combining the divisions would be to improve administration, enhance quality control and reduce costly and redundant divisional overheads." On the other hand, McPhail was not receptive to the proposal. He felt that combining the divisions would be . . ."demotivational, reduce divisional effectiveness and would result in the long-term in a reduction of existing levels of profitability." Further, he believed "that quality control is an issue which should be addressed separately."

Subsequently, the President of World Accord discussed the problems of the two divisions with a member of his executive staff, John Marks, a chartered accountant. The President had requested that John prepare a report in which he will evaluate the divisional performance, review the transfer price system and comment on the corporate reporting system. In his report, he should also consider the potential long-term impact of the proposed combination or other possible alternative solutions.

Required:

Assume the role of John Marks, Chartered Accountant, and prepare the requested report for the President of World Accord.

Exhibit I

Five-Year Performance Analysis
(All figures are stated in thousands of dollars)

Year	World Accord			Kingcraft			Tectron		
	Invest- ment	Profit*	Sales	Invest- ment	Profit*	Sales	Invest- ment	Profit*	Sales
1979	$11,000	$1,800	$15,600	$2,200	$270	$2,600	$800	$145	$1,750
1978	9,800	1,675	14,300	2,050	260	2,500	850	126	1,600
1977	9,400	1,500	13,900	1,800	255	2,550	900	110	1,450
1976	8,900	1,375	12,900	1,850	255	2,450	850	90	1,300
1975	8,300	1,275	12,000	1,750	260	2,350	750	80	1,200

*Profits are stated on a pre-tax basis with divisional profits reported after allocation of corporate service costs.

(CA, adapted)*

---

*Reprinted with permission from *Uniform Final Examination Handbook: Second Edition, 1980* (@ 1981) published by The Canadian Institute of Chartered Accountants, Toronto, Canada.

Chapter 14

Chapter 14 discusses the cost concepts and accounting approaches which are related to the planning of special decisions. Studying this chapter should enable you to:

1. Provide examples of the types of decisions which are commonly referred to as special decisions.
2. Discuss the concept of relevance as it relates to the planning of special decisions.
3. Describe how the accounting records may provide useful information for the special decision-making process.
4. Identify the two characteristics which are common to all costs used for decision making.
5. Define and give examples of the various classifications of decision-making costs.
6. Discuss and apply the general formats for presenting relevant information for special decision making.
7. Identify those factors that should be considered in pricing a product.
8. Discuss and apply the use of a learning curve when costs are not linear.

Planning Special Decisions: Accounting Approaches

ACCOUNTING records and the accounting information system serve as the basic means for accumulating information on a historical cost basis for financial accounting purposes. Accounting also plays an important role both in the normal and recurring aspects of budgeting and in the control and performance evaluation functions. For financial accounting purposes, the role of record keeping is basically historical in nature. With regard to managerial accounting, record keeping is a combination of both forward looking projections and, on a selected basis, historical accumulations for purposes of comparison. In both of these instances, the accounting system is designed to capture and communicate recurring information.

The focus of this chapter emphasizes the accounting approaches which may be used for accumulating and presenting the information required for use in making decisions that are neither recurring nor routine. Examples of the type of decisions that fall into the non-recurring or special decision category include:

1. Accept or reject decisions for a special customer order.
2. Make or buy decisions for a specific component of the firm's products.
3. Continuance or discontinuance of an operating segment, such as a sales territory or a product line.
4. Pricing decisions.

**RELEVANCE:
THE KEY TO
DECISION-MAKING**

The key to selecting an alternative in any decision-making process is to focus attention on the relevant information. Relevant information for decision-making purposes is that information which differs among the various alternatives under consideration. For example, if you were considering the purchase of a candy bar from a vending machine and all of the candy bars available cost 25 cents, the decision would not be based on the cost of the candy bar since all bars have the identical price. However, if you decided that you wanted a candy bar with peanuts and only two of the candy bars available met this criterion, then this is relevant information. The decision is now narrowed to only two alternatives, but additional relevant information is necessary in order to make the final choice. Thus, if you were allergic to chocolate and one of the two bars with peanuts contained chocolate, then this fact is also relevant to you in making the decision to select the candy bar that contains peanuts but no chocolate. The concept of relevance in the planning of special decisions is identical to the relevance considered in the candy bar example. The relevant factors analyzed in the candy purchasing decision were those factors that differed among the alternatives.

**IMPORTANCE OF
BOTH QUALITATIVE
AND QUANTITATIVE
FACTORS**

The desire for a candy bar with peanuts but no chocolate is an example of the use of a qualitative factor in a decision-making process. Qualitative factors are not expressed in either numerical or monetary terms, yet for any particular decision, a qualitative factor may be the most important consideration. In fact, for many management decisions, qualitative factors are of primary significance and concern.

Accounting concepts play an important role in developing the quantitative factors which are considered in special decisions. Quantitative factors are those factors that can be expressed in numbers. In some instances, the quantitative factors are estimates or forecasts based on the subjective judgments of knowledgeable people or on specific studies designed to develop the estimates. The only quantitative factor in the candy bar example was the price of 25 cents, which was irrelevant to the decision since all of the available bars cost 25 cents.

**DECISION-MAKING
COST CONCEPTS**

Decision making is, by definition, a process of selecting among various alternatives. The availability of all relevant information for each possible alternative would greatly facilitate this process. However, the cost of gathering all potentially useful information for each alternative is extreme. Therefore, although the accounting information system is not designed in terms of providing special decision-making information, accounting records often serve as a basis for accumulating the data which must be considered in making a special decision. For example, if a company is considering producing (with its existing equipment) a subassembly that it is presently buying, then accounting records could play a major role in developing the data required for the analysis. The cost of using the existing equipment to produce current products can be determined from the accounting records. This cost is then adjusted to reflect the different specifications required for the subassembly. The adjusted data serves as the basis for estimating the costs of manufacturing the subassembly.

Costs applicable to the decision-making process are classified differently than those costs which were defined for income determination purposes and for purposes of planning, control, and performance evaluation. Analysis of costs which are relevant to the decision-making process need not follow particular rules or special formats. These costs may be either product costs or period costs, fixed costs or variable costs, controllable costs or noncontrollable costs, common costs or traceable costs. However, all costs used for decision making do have two common characteristics:

1. They are relevant, i.e., the costs will differ under the various alternatives.
2. They are costs which are anticipated in the future under each of the various alternatives.

The cost definitions and the discussions of these definitions which follow are the basic concepts required in developing the accounting approaches used to analyze special decisions.

Relevant Costs

As previously indicated, relevant costs are those future costs that differ under the various alternatives that the firm is considering. Precision and accuracy are not always primary factors in determining relevance. Many relevant costs must be estimates since the precise cost may be known only after a particular alternative is selected and implemented.

The concepts of relevancy and accuracy are illustrated by the following example. Assume that during the next spring break you intend to visit a resort area. This resort is 1,800 kilometers from your university and you have decided either to drive alone or to fly tourist class. A three hour direct flight is available at a round-trip cost of $400. Driving time is two days each way, thus time spent at the resort will be curtailed if this alternative is chosen. Regardless of whether you fly or drive, 14 nights and 15 days of vacation are available to you. Motel accommodations will cost $20 per day, and you expect to stay at a motel every night, including those nights spent on the road if you choose to drive. Food will cost $9 per day, and your car averages 10 kilometers per litre of gasoline at an average cost of $.40 per litre. Your best estimate of the other costs such as oil, repairs, etc., total approximately $50. If you do not take your car, you do not anticipate renting a car during your stay at the resort. The resort has a courtesy car available that provides airport transportation at no cost. We will assume that the decision, as far as you are concerned, is strictly one of minimizing your vacation costs.

A summary of the total cost for each alternative follows:

By Car		*By Airplane*	
Oil, repairs, etc.	$ 50	Air fare.	$400
Motel—14 nights @ $20	280	Motel—14 nights @ $20	280
Food—15 days @ $9	135	Food—15 days @ $9	135
Gasoline: $\dfrac{2 \times 1{,}800 \text{ Km.}}{10 \text{ Km. per litre}} \times \$.40$	144		
Total cost by car	$609	Total cost by airplane	$815

As the above analysis indicates, you can save $206 ($815 — $609) by driving instead of flying. Note that in order to make this decision, all the costs do not have to be considered. Only those costs that differ between the alternatives should be considered. Motel and food costs are identical under each alternative; therefore, these costs are irrelevant to the decision. If only relevant costs are considered, the cost data can be presented as follows:

By Car		*By Airplane*	
Oil, repairs, etc.	$ 50	Air fare.	$400
Gasoline: $\dfrac{2 \times 1{,}800 \text{ Km.}}{10 \text{ Km. per litre}} \times \$.40$	144		
Relevant cost by car	$194	Relevant cost by airplane	$400

The difference between the two alternatives is still $206—the difference between the relevant costs. Eliminating costs which are common to both alternatives has no bearing on the difference between alternatives.

The degree of accuracy in the accumulation of relevant costs is questionable. Numerous factors, such as accidents or breakdowns of the car, could alter the cost of driving. The price of gasoline could increase or decrease, and the air fare could also change.

This example considered only quantitative decision factors. In addition to these factors, there are numerous qualitative factors to consider: the additional time that might be spent at the resort, the personal inconvenience of driving 3,600 kilometers, the countryside that can be seen by driving, and the safety factors of flying versus driving. None of these factors can be easily quantified and used as direct inputs in the decision-making process. Accounting approaches to decision making emphasize the quantitative factors and, at most, can only aid in identifying the qualitative factors.

Opportunity Costs

An opportunity cost is a measure of benefits that could have been derived had an alternative choice been made. For example, an opportunity cost could be the income foregone by not choosing the next best alternative which was under consideration. An opportunity cost may not always be measured with a high degree of certainty.

The concept of opportunity cost is related to every activity an individual or a firm undertakes, because an alternative course of action always exists. An opportunity cost is always associated with the commitment of scarce resources. For example, assume that you could work this evening for three hours and earn a total of $10. Instead, you choose to go out on the town and spend $15. You chose an alternative, and the income foregone or the opportunity cost associated with your decision was $10. The fact that you actually spent $15 does not affect what you gave up by choosing to go out rather than to work.

Another example of opportunity cost is illustrated by the decision to scrap defective products instead of reworking these units and selling them in the usual market. If a company had defective products that could be sold for 25 cents per unit as scrap or which could be reworked at an additional cost of 10 cents per unit and sold for 50 cents, then there is an opportunity cost involved for either alternative selected. The opportunity cost of the reworking alternative is the scrap value of 25 cents per unit. The opportunity cost of scrapping is 40 cents (the selling price of 50 cents less the reworking cost of 10 cents per unit). Note that the original production cost is not mentioned in either case as it is irrelevant in measuring opportunity cost. The production cost resulted from the initial decision to produce the units; it had already been incurred under either alternative.

Incremental or Differential Costs

An incremental or differential cost is the difference between the total costs of the various available alternatives. In practice, the term "incremental cost" is often used to describe the difference in costs incurred by producing at two different levels of activity. To illustrate the concept of incremental cost, assume that you decide to rent a car at a fixed charge of $15 a day plus a charge of 20 cents per kilometer. The rental agency will reimburse you for any gasoline and similar expenses which you might incur. If you drive the car 800 kilometers in a four-day period, your rental cost is calculated as follows:

Rental Cost for 4 days and 800 Kilometers

Fixed Costs—4 days @ $15.00.................	$ 60
Variable Costs—800 kilometers @ $.20.........	160
Total Rental Costs..........................	$220

Assume that you decide to keep the car an additional day in order to make a 150-kilometer side trip. The incremental costs of keeping the car and making this trip are calculated as follows:

Rental Costs—4 Days Versus 5 Days

	4 Days and 800 Kilometers	5 Days and 950 Kilometers	Incremental Costs
Fixed Costs—$15.00/Day....................	$ 60	$ 75	$15
Variable Costs—$.20/Kilometer................	160	190	30
Totals	$220	$265	$45

It should be obvious that incremental or differential costs are always relevant costs when making a selection between or among alternatives.

Escapable or Avoidable Costs

As the term implies, escapable or avoidable costs are those costs which are saved or eliminated by making a particular decision or selecting a certain alternative. The concept of escapable costs is useful for decision-making purposes because, in many instances, certain costs may be avoided when one alternative is selected over another. This cost definition is frequently used in discussing the elimination of a division or a segment of a business.

If elimination of a segment of a firm is an alternative under consideration, escapable costs are limited to those costs that are directly traceable to that segment. Any arbitrarily allocated costs will still be incurred even if the segment is eliminated, and the remaining segments of the firm will be required to absorb these costs. An example of this concept is discussed later in this chapter when the elimination of segments is illustrated.

Out-of-Pocket Costs

Out-of-pocket costs are those costs that require a definite outlay of funds. Relevant out-of-pocket costs are those costs which differ among the various alternatives being considered. Expenses such as depreciation or allocated costs are not considered out-of-pocket costs.

Sunk Costs

Sunk costs are costs which have already been incurred and which cannot be changed regardless of the selected alternative. Sunk costs are irrelevant as far as deciding among alternatives is concerned. An investment in fixed assets is a common example of a sunk cost. Once an asset is acquired, its original cost or net book-value is not considered in making future decisions. A relevant cost is a future cost which differs among the alternatives available. Costs which have already been incurred are neither future expenditures nor do these costs differ under the various alternatives under consideration.

If one alternative calls for the sale of an existing asset, the cash received for that asset and any tax implications of a gain or loss on the sale are relevant to that alternative. The net cash received from the sale of an asset, not the original cost or net book value of the asset, is the relevant information. The cost of retaining an asset is the net selling price of the asset because the cash received could be reinvested. It is impossible to reinvest the original cost or the net book value of a retained asset in another alternative; it is a sunk cost. The original cost is relevant only for purposes of calculating depreciation expense for the income statement, for calculating net book values for the balance sheet, and for determining tax implications regarding a sale.

GENERAL ACCOUNTING FORMATS FOR ARRANGING RELEVANT INFORMATION

Any format used for arranging decision-making information should emphasize those factors that differ among the available alternatives. Two general accounting formats used to arrange relevant information for the use of decision makers include:

1. Incremental cost and/or incremental revenue approach.
2. Contribution margin approach.

Neither of these general formats is applicable to every decision. For example, the contribution margin format requires that both revenues and the related variable costs be known in order for the contribution margin to be computed. In addition, the contribution margin format does not explicitly consider fixed costs; therefore, it is valid only when fixed costs are irrelevant. It should be noted that the contribution margin approach is not a "full" costing approach. Both formats are illustrated in the following special order decision-making process.

SPECIAL ORDERS:
AN EXAMPLE

The Karson Company has idle capacity available in its manufacturing operations. A buyer outside Karson's usual marketing area has made an offer to purchase 50 units of a standard product, Edd, at a price of $1 per unit. Edd is normally sold by the Karson Company for $2. The Karson Company does not currently sell this product in the buyer's geographical area nor does the company plan to sell it in that area in the future. This is essentially a one-time purchase by this potential customer. Any freight expense will be paid by the buyer. If Karson Company sells to this buyer, it will have no impact on its current customers.

The *current* budget for Karson Company is as follows:

Karson Company
Budget for Product
Line-Edd

Relevant Range of Production	400-750 Units
Basis for Fixed Overhead Allocation	500 Units
Budgeted Sales 500 Units @ $2.00	$1,000
Variable Costs 500 Units @ $.75	375
Contribution Margin	$ 625
Fixed Production Costs 500 Units @ $.50	250
Fixed Selling and Administrative Costs	300
Budgeted Income Before Taxes	$ 75

Any approach to the decision to produce the special order for sale at $1 per unit which is based on full or absorption costing would result in a recommendation to reject the order since the proposed selling price is less than the full cost. The current full cost of the product (with the fixed overhead allocated over production of 500 units) is $1.25 per unit [($375 + 250)/500]. Even with fixed overhead of $250 allocated over 550 units of production, the full cost of the product on a per unit basis would be in excess of $1.20 [($412.50 + $250)/550].

However, the additional order of 50 units has come at a time when idle capacity is available and when this additional production will not affect the total fixed overhead costs incurred. A production level of 550 units is well within the relevant range of activity for the firm. Quantitatively, both formats for analyzing this special decision will agree, since fixed costs are not relevant to the decision.

Contribution Margin

	Per Unit	Total for 50 Units
Revenues	$1.00	$50.00
Variable Costs	.75	37.50
Contribution Margin	$ .25	$12.50

The above analysis provides the information necessary to make a decision using the contribution margin approach. The additional sales provide a contribution margin of $12.50 or $.25 per unit, which can be applied to the recovery of the unchanged fixed costs. Thus, given the existence of idle capacity, the decision to sell the additional 50 units of Edd appears to be financially sound.

The following analysis presents the information required to make a decision using the incremental income approach:

Incremental Costs and Revenues

	Budget Without the Order	Budget With the Order	Incremental Costs and Revenues
Budgeted Sales:			
500 units @ $2.00	$1,000.00	$1,000.00	–0–
50 units @ $1.00	–0–	50.00	$50.00
Variable Costs:			
500 units @ $.75	375.00	375.00	–0–
50 units @ $.75	–0–	37.50	37.50
Contribution Margin	$ 625.00	$ 637.50	$12.50
Fixed Production Costs	$ 250.00	$ 250.00	–0–
Fixed Selling and Administrative Costs	300.00	300.00	–0–
Budgeted Income Before Taxes	$ 75.00	$ 87.50	$12.50

If the special order is accepted, the incremental budgeted net income before taxes will be $12.50. Given that all other cost factors remain the same, management should accept the order. Remember, there was idle capacity available. Without this idle capacity, the decision may have been to reject the order.

MAKE OR BUY: AN EXAMPLE

In the short-run, for a firm to consider making component parts for products rather than purchasing those parts from vendors, the firm must have available idle capacity and the ability to make the parts. The question is one of using the idle capacity to produce the parts, using the capacity for other purposes, or allowing the capacity to go unused.

If only quantitative factors are considered in the decision to make or buy a part, the current purchase price must be known. The cost to make the part must also be determined. The only relevant costs for this decision are those costs that would be incurred if the part is made. Any arbitrarily allocated costs that could not be avoided if the part were not made are irrelevant. These costs are incurred by the firm under either alternative.

The accounting department made a study and developed the following cost of manufacturing the part. The normal demand for this part is 25 units per year.

Costs to Manufacture a Component Part

	Per Unit	Total at 25 Units
Direct materials	$ .20	$ 5.00
Direct labor	1.10	27.50
Variable overhead	.30	7.50
Avoidable fixed overhead	.40	10.00
Total	$2.00	$50.00

According to the quantitative data, if the purchase price of the part exceeds $2.00, then the firm should make the part itself.

There are also qualitative factors which should be considered in a make or buy decision. Examples of these qualitative factors include the following:

1.   What quality is necessary? Can the firm make a better quality part?
2.   Will the idle capacity be available? For how long will it be available?
3.   Will current vendors of the part be willing to sell to the firm in the future if the supply of raw materials becomes limited?
4.   Will future opportunities be lost because of the lack of idle capacity resulting from a decision to make the part?

The make or buy decision may be used in a number of contexts. For example, should a firm use a service bureau for computer work or establish its own facility? Should in-house salesmen be used or should commissioned factory representatives who sell for a number of firms be used? Should employees be used on special jobs or should consultants be employed?

ELIMINATION OF SEGMENTS: AN EXAMPLE

Elimination of a segment of a business such as a product line, division, or sales territory is based on the incremental (or differential) revenues which are lost and the incremental (or differential) costs which are avoided if the segment is dropped. Recall that conventional financial reports are based on full costs which include the arbitrary allocations of common costs.

Assume that a firm has one plant and three products. The firm prepares financial reports on the basis of full costs by product line. The actual performance for the previous year is presented in the following income statement.

Income Statement by Product Lines

	Product Line #1	Product Line #2	Product Line #3	Total
Net Sales	$200	$400	$400	$1,000
Cost of goods sold:				
Direct labor	64	48	48	160
Direct material	60	90	150	300
Variable overhead	20	40	40	100
Fixed overhead:				
Property taxes	8	6	6	20
Property insurance	4	3	3	10
Depreciation	32	24	24	80
Other	8	6	6	20
Total cost of goods sold	$196	$217	$277	$ 690
Gross margin	$ 4	$183	$123	$ 310
Expenses:				
Selling	12	24	24	60
Advertising	24	48	48	120
Interest	12	12	12	36
General and administrative	15	15	15	45
Total expenses	$ 63	$ 99	$ 99	$ 261
Net income (loss) before taxes	($ 59)	$ 84	$ 24	$ 49

It appears that Product Line #1 is somewhat undesirable because it is operating at a loss. Because of this it might be erroneously inferred that if this line were dropped, the total net income before taxes for the firm would increase. Before any decisions can be made, however, each cost and expense item must be analyzed to determine which costs and expenses actually would be eliminated if the product line were dropped. To accomplish this it is necessary to know the basis used to determine each cost and expense. Obviously all revenues from Product Line #1 would be lost if the line were discontinued.

Analysis of the cost of goods sold section reveals that while the variable costs (direct labour, direct material and variable overhead) would be eliminated if Product Line #1 were dropped, the same would not be true for the fixed overhead items (property taxes, property insurance, depreciation and other). Additionally, it can be seen that whereas the variable costs are directly traceable, the fixed costs have been allocated arbitrarily on the basis of the cost of direct labour used.

Selling and advertising expenses have been charged to the various product lines on the basis of sales volume while interest and general and administrative expenses have been divided equally among the three product lines. Thus, we must investigate further to discover what portion, if any, of these expense items would be eliminated if Product Line #1 were dropped. In this example, assume that we find that sales commissions of $3 and administrative expenses of $5 could be saved if the decision were made to eliminate Product Line #1.

If a new income statement were prepared for the firm for the prior year, assuming that Product Line #1 was dropped, the results would be as follows:

	Total Before Dropping Product Line #1	Incremental Costs and Revenues on Product Line #1	Total Without Product Line #1
Net sales	$1,000	($200)	$800
Cost of goods sold:			
Direct labor	160	(64)	96
Direct materials	300	(60)	240
Variable overhead	100	(20)	80
Fixed overhead:			
Property taxes	20	–0–	20
Property insurance	10	–0–	10
Depreciation	80	–0–	80
Other	20	–0–	20
Total cost of goods sold	$ 690	(144)	$546
Gross margin	$ 310	($ 56)	$254
Expenses:			
Selling	60	(3)	57
Advertising	120	–0–	120
Interest	36	–0–	36
General and administrative . . .	45	(5)	40
Total expenses	$ 261	($ 8)	$253
Net income before taxes	$ 49	($ 48)	$ 1

Without product Line #1, income before taxes is only $1, not $49. If only the incremental revenues and costs are considered, product Line #1 provides a contribution margin of $48 that is available to cover common fixed costs which would not be eliminated if the product line were eliminated.

If a similar analysis were applied to product Lines #2 and #3, it would demonstrate that each of these lines provide substantial funds from operations to cover common costs and contribute toward profits. As long as a segment of the organization provides incremental revenues in excess of incremental costs, the segment is contributing to the recovery of common fixed costs and thus making a contribution toward profit. The firm would reduce its total net income by eliminating such a segment.

PRODUCT PRICING TECHNIQUES

The factors affecting a pricing decision cannot be completely defined as there is neither a consistent theoretical nor practical approach that is appropriate for every situation that a firm might encounter. While the pricing decision is viewed by many firms as a short-run decision, the long-run implications are substantial. In the long-run, the prices charged for the entire line of products sold by a firm must first cover the fixed costs and then provide an acceptable margin of profit. Certain products will never be acceptable on a profit-making basis, but must be carried in order to provide a complete product line. Also, a product in the initial stages of market entry may not generate profits in the short-run.

The factors considered in a pricing decision include the following:

1. The economic considerations of supply and demand at different prices in a given time period.
2. The economic considerations of competition and substitute products.
3. The nature of the product and any competitive advantage which may result from unique capabilities or legal protection such as a patent.
4. Marketing considerations associated with selling and related to factors such as brand name, advertising, promotion, service capabilities, special applications, etc.
5. Legal implications of a given price in a specific market such as the General Agreement on Tariff and Trade (GATT) and other international treaties which prohibit the "dumping" of goods in other countries, as well as various national and local laws and regulations which restrict "unfair" competition.
6. The investment which is required to produce the volume of product required.
7. The cost of producing the product.

From an accounting standpoint, the emphasis is on the last two items (6 and 7 above). In the short-run, the emphasis in accounting may focus on basic manufacturing costs rather than on the investment required to produce the product. However, it is obvious that the investment required directly affects the cost of producing a product in any given time period.

In some instances, it is possible that the investment should never have been made.

The discussion of pricing in this chapter considers two basic short-run cost approaches to pricing: (1) the contribution margin approach and (2) the cost-volume-profit approach. Chapter 15 discusses the long-range implications of whether or not the investment in assets should be made by the firm.

The Contribution Margin Approach to Product Pricing: An Example

The contribution margin approach is a short-run technique which may be used for product pricing. This method identifies the minimum price that can be charged for a product, assuming fixed costs do not change, without affecting the firm's profit. The minimum cost, and therefore price, is the total of all variable costs incurred in manufacturing and selling the product. Obviously, if the price charged for all products is equal to the variable costs of producing those products, the firm would operate at a loss. The total mix of products must cover all variable and fixed costs, and must provide a profit which allows the firm to obtain a satisfactory return on its investment.

Assume that a firm has developed a product that it wishes to introduce to the greatest potential market. The firm decides that the introductory price should be the lowest possible price that will neither increase nor decrease current profits. Management does not believe that fixed costs have been affected by this product. After reviewing the cost of making the product, the accounting department developed the following cost summary on a contribution margin format for management's use.

Pricing Decision—Using
The Contribution Margin Approach

Direct materials	$ .50
Direct labor	.75
Variable overhead	.30
Distribution costs	.05
Total variable cost	$1.60

If no other costs are involved, the minimum selling price of the product could be set at $1.60. At this price, the current profits from the sale of other products are not eroded. This approach has some merit in bidding situations, where the minimum price based on variable costs can be established and fixed costs do not change. After this absolute minimum is established, management can establish a price that provides a positive contribution margin.

Directly Traceable Costs and the Cost-Profit-Volume Approach to Product Pricing: An Example

When a pricing approach based on costs is made, and fixed costs of any kind are considered, the question of volume must also be considered because the fixed cost per unit decreases as the volume increases. If the firm discussed in the contribution margin approach to pricing example was required to rent a warehouse for one year at a cost of $260 and anticipated an advertising campaign of $500 in addition to the variable costs already considered, the minimum price calculation to allow cost recovery becomes somewhat more complex. The new cost structure for the product would be as follows:

Pricing Decision—Using the Directly
Traceable Costs and the Cost-Profit-Volume Approach

Variable Costs:
Direct materials	$ .50
Direct labor	.75
Variable overhead	.30
Distribution costs	.05
Variable costs per unit	$1.60

Managed Fixed Costs:
Warehousing	$260
Advertising	500
Total managed fixed costs	$760

The minimum price the firm must charge is greater than $1.60 per unit if the $760 of managed fixed costs are to be recovered. The problem of volume is now introduced. Management must determine an anticipated volume in order to determine the absolute minimum price possible. The minimum price is

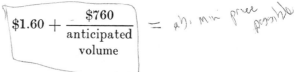

$$\$1.60 + \frac{\$760}{\text{anticipated volume}} = ab. \ min \ price \ possible$$

If the anticipated volume were 1,000 units, the absolute minimum price would be

$$\$1.60 \ + \ \frac{\$760}{1,000 \ \text{units}} = \$2.36 \ \text{per unit}$$

At a price of $2.36, the profits of the firm would neither be increased nor decreased by the sale of this specific product, assuming that other products sold and other costs incurred remain constant.

**LEARNING
CURVE ANALYSIS**

We have treated direct labor as a proportionately variable cost in most of our analysis because the firm was operating in the relevant range of activity where costs are approximately linear (see Illustration 14-1). Certain industries, such as the aerospace industry, never reach those volumes of activity that would put them in the relevant range. Therefore, when estimating costs they must deal with the problem that as the same job is repeated labor becomes more efficient. Since there is an observed regularity in the rate of improvement, we can apply the rule that as the cumulative output doubles there is a constant rate of reduction in average labor hours per unit. A commonly used rate is eighty percent. The effects of an eighty percent learning curve is presented in Illustration 14-2.

Because the eighty percent rule gives the average time it is very useful for many accounting reports or for estimating the cost of total production. But, if the analysis is an attempt to forecast the cost of only certain units in the cumulative production quantity, a certain amount of caution is necessary to derive the incremental time for those units. Refer to Illustration 14-2, the first unit produced required 100 hours. If we want to estimate the incremental time to produce the second unit by applying the learning curve rule we need to follow this procedure:

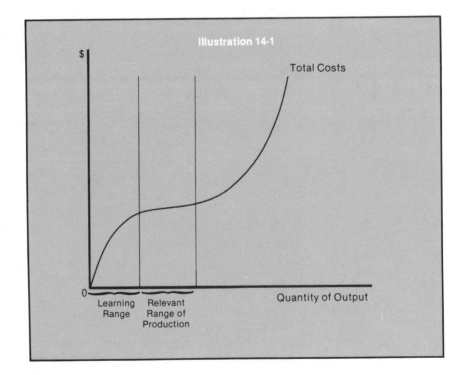

$$\text{Time of First Unit} = 100 \text{ Hours}$$
$$\text{Learning Curve Rate} = \underline{80\%}$$
$$\text{Cumulative Average Time} = 80 \text{ Hours}$$

The cumulative average does not tell us the incremental time to produce the second unit, but is used to determine that the total time for both units is 160 hours:

$$\text{Total Time} = \text{Average Time} \times \text{Total Number of Units}$$
$$= 80 \times 2 = 160 \text{ Hours}$$

Because we know that the first unit required 100 hours, the incremental time of the second unit is 60 hours.

$$\text{Incremental Time} = \text{Total Time} - \text{Time of Previous Units}$$
$$= 160 - 100 = 60 \text{ Hours}$$

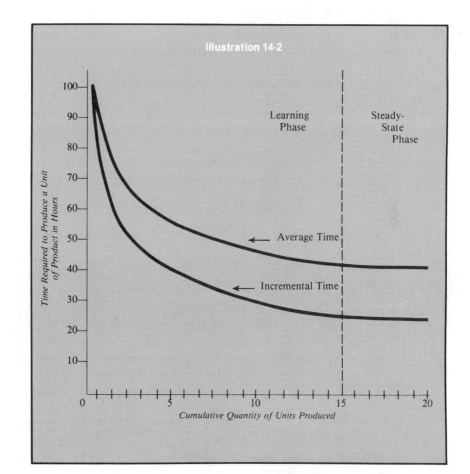

Illustration 14-2

The incremental time for units 3 and 4 (this is another doubling of cumulative production) is 96 hours.

Average Time of Units 1 and 2 =		80 Hours
Learning Curve Rate =		80%
Cumulative Average Time =		64 Hours
Total Time =	64 × 4 =	256 Hours
Incremental Time =	256 − 160 =	96 Hours

There are also other rules for estimating the incremental labor hours. One is that, utilizing an 80 percent learning curve, the average incremental time of the added cumulative production is 75 percent of the cumulative average time.

SUMMARY

The management of a firm is often called upon to make special decisions of a non-recurring nature. Information used for special decisions may include historical data obtained directly from the accounting records as well as future projections based upon this data. In addition, a firm may find it necessary to conduct special studies to generate information which is not generally accumulated in the accounting records but which is required to make a given special decision.

Although both qualitative and quantitative factors are considered in the decision-making process, the accountant is generally concerned with providing only quantitative data; that is, data that can be expressed in numbers. Cost data for special decision making is a primary type of quantitative data provided by accountants.

All costs used for special decision making have two common characteristics. First, they must be relevant costs; that is, the costs must differ among the available alternatives. Second, the costs must be costs that are anticipated or expected in the future if one of the available alternatives is selected.

An opportunity cost measures the benefits that could have been derived had an alternative choice been made. Incremental cost, also referred to as differential cost, is the difference between the total costs of available alternatives. Escapable or avoidable costs are those costs that will be eliminated by selecting a given alternative. Costs that will require a definite outlay of funds, as opposed to depreciation or allocated costs, are often referred to as out-of-pocket costs. Any of the above costs may be relevant costs for special decision-making purposes. Sunk costs, on the other hand, are irrelevant for decision making because they represent past expenditures that cannot be changed regardless of the alternative chosen.

Examples of special decisions include decisions to: (1) accept or reject a special order from a customer, (2) make or buy a component part, (3) continue or eliminate a segment of the business, and (4) determine a price to charge for a product. No single special format exists for presenting information for special decision-making purposes. However, among the formats in general use are the incremental cost and/or revenue approach and the contribution margin approach. Although either format may be used in the analysis of a special decision, the incremental approach is more appropriate in cases where fixed costs are relevant.

This chapter has discussed many of the factors which must be considered in making special decisions. Chapter 15 discusses an additional factor, the investment of the firm's resources used in the long-range operations of the business.

KEY DEFINITIONS

Contribution margin approach—a general format for arranging relevant decision-making information showing additional revenues and related variable costs to be incurred under various alternatives in determining a contribution margin.

Escapable or avoidable costs—costs which may be eliminated by making a particular decision or selecting a certain alternative.

Incremental cost and revenue approach—a general format for arranging relevant decision-making information which considers total costs and revenues to be incurred under various alternatives in determining an incremental net income or loss.

Incremental or differential cost—the difference between the total costs of available alternatives.

Opportunity cost—a measurement of benefits that could have been derived had an alternative choice been made.

Out-of-pocket costs—costs requiring a definite outlay of funds.

Relevant costs—future costs which differ under the alternatives under consideration in a decision-making situation.

Sunk costs—those costs which are irrelevant for future decisions because the expenditure has already been made and cannot be changed regardless of the alternative selected.

QUESTIONS

14-1 What information should be considered relevant in making a non-recurring or special decision?

14-2 What is the difference between qualitative and quantitative factors used in making a decision? Which factor(s) do accounting records play an important role in developing?

14-3 Define opportunity costs and explain when they are most likely to be incurred.

14-4 What is an incremental cost and when is it relevant in making a decision?

14-5 What classification of cost might be an escapable cost when one considers eliminating a segment of a firm?

14-6 Why is depreciation not considered an out-of-pocket cost?

14-7 For what purposes is the original cost of an asset relevant in making a decision?

14-8 Give two examples stating decision-making situations in which the contribution margin approach would not be appropriate.

14-9 When a pricing decision is being made, on what factors is the emphasis placed from an accounting standpoint?

14-10 How is the contribution margin approach used in setting the minimum price for a product?

EXERCISES AND PROBLEMS

14-11 Company A, a manufacturing firm, wants to know if it should manufacture or purchase part #29.

	Manufacture	*Purchase*
Direct materials	9,800	–0–
Purchased parts	–0–	20,000
Direct labor	6,300	–0–
Power	2,000	–0–
Other costs	1,500	–0–

14-12 In 19x4 and 19x5 the Chipper Company overproduced its Product L because of an increasing demand for this product. In 19x6 another company began to produce an improved model of this product which made Chipper Company's Product L obsolete. After inventory was counted in 19x6, they found they had $50,604 of Product L. After considering many alternatives, it was determined that they could sell the product for scrap for $6,850 or recycle it into another product. It will cost $12,500 to rework the product, and it will sell for $20,500. In addition to the additional cost, salesmen will receive 3 percent of the selling price.

Required:

What should be done with Product L?

14-13 The Squeak-E Tennis Shoe Company sells 20,000 pairs of tennis shoes annually. They have fixed costs of $38,000 and direct costs of $6.00 per pair. The shoes sell for $9.00 per pair. Squeak-E has a capacity of 5,000 in excess of the 20,000 pairs of shoes they sell annually. They have just received an offer from a company outside their present sales territory to buy 4,500 pairs of tennis shoes for $6.25 per pair.

Required:

a. Should they accept this order?
b. If Squeak-E did not have the excess capacity, should they accept the order?

14-14 The Easy Sleep Company is a large manufacturer of waterbeds. Unfortunately, due to the current water shortage, waterbeds have been forbidden by law. Easy Sleep has a $60,000 inventory of waterbeds at the present time. Easy Sleep must make a decision to sell the waterbeds as scrap for a total of $5,000, or modify the beds to be sold as life rafts. The modification will cost a total of $12,000, which includes the purchase of a special machine. (This machine will be sold after the modifications are finished for $3,000.) The total sales expected from the life rafts are $16,000 less 10% sales commissions.

Required:

Should Easy Sleep modify the beds or sell them as scrap?

14-15 The following income statements were prepared by the accounting department for Russel Company. Assume all fixed expenses are allocated on an arbitrary basis to each department.

	Department J	Department K	Department L
Sales	$130,000	$200,000	$145,000
Variable cost of goods sold	90,000	120,000	70,000
Contribution margin from manufacturing	$ 40,000	$ 80,000	$ 75,000
Operating expenses:			
Fixed expenses	25,000	40,000	35,000
Variable selling expenses	5,000	8,000	4,000
Fixed selling expenses	10,000	16,000	12,000
Net income	–0–	$ 16,000	$ 24,000

Required:

The president of Russel Company feels department J should be eliminated. How would you advise her?

14-16   Tipton, Inc. manufactures automobile parts. Last year the company had a large turnover in management. The new management decided to take a physical count of inventory. When they were finished, they found they had an excessive supply of parts for fifteen year old automobiles totaling $95,000. After checking further into the matter, it was decided the parts could be remachined for $25,000 and sold for $37,000, or they could be sold for scrap for $7,000.

Required:

What should Tipton, Inc. do?

14-17   The following information was made available concerning the 4 departments of the Roast Company.

	Dept. A	Dept. B	Dept. C	Dept. D
Sales	$100,000	$20,000	$50,000	$70,000
Variable cost of goods sold	70,000	10,000	30,000	45,000
Contribution margin from manufacturing	$ 30,000	$10,000	$20,000	$25,000
Operating expenses:				
Fixed expenses	20,000	4,000	10,000	15,000
Variable selling expenses .	10,000	3,000	6,000	12,000
Net income (loss)	–0–	$ 3,000	$ 4,000	($ 2,000)

Chuck Roast, the president of the company, has decided that one department must be dropped. Fixed expenses have been arbitrarily assigned according to the sales of each department. No matter which department is dropped the fixed expenses will be reduced one-fourth.

Required:

Which department should be dropped so as to give the greatest benefit to the company? What will be the company's income?

14-18   The Z Company makes saws; last year it sold 30,000 saws at a price of $5.00 and produced them at an average cost of $3.00. The sales manager thinks 40,000 units could be sold at a price of $4.30. The plant manager estimates that 40,000 units could be produced at a cost of $2.80 each.

Required:

What effect will this have on profit?

14-19   Ralph Company sells three products. Product B has yielded a net loss of $10,000 for the past three years, and there is no reason to expect a change in the future. Company officials also feel that the sales of the three products are not interrelated. Fixed expenses are allocated equally among the products in determining product profitability. Company records show:

	Product A	Product B	Product C
Contribution margin per unit	$6.50	$4.00	$7.00
Net income (loss)	$13,000	($10,000)	$16,000
Total annual fixed expenses are:	$42,000		

Required:

Based on the information given, should Product B be dropped?

14-20 Allen Tool Company is making plans for the coming year. Management feels that a target profit of $425,000 before income taxes would represent a satisfactory continuation of their growth pattern of earnings, which has been a steady 7% over the last 6 years. Marketing management has studied the market for the coming year and predicted the following sales possibilities.

	Selling Price	Advertising	Unit Sales
Alternative A	$5.00	No change	1,000,000
Alternative B	5.00	Up $60,000	1,120,000
Alternative C	5.50	No change	700,000
Alternative D	5.50	Up $60,000	810,000

Estimated fixed expenses for next year are $825,000 and estimated variable expenses are $3.75 per unit of product. These expense estimates do not include any changes in advertising. Note: In your answer show any necessary computations.

Required:

a. What should the marketing strategy be?

b. Suppose that management decided to change the selling price to $5.25 and raise advertising $45,000. If this will give unit sales of 775,000, will the target profit be achieved?

14-21 The Davis Company has been producing 20,000 units per month but wants to begin producing 25,000 units per month (capacity is 28,000 units per month) because of an increase in demand for their product. Davis has the following cost structure:

Selling price = $1.60 per unit
Variable manufacturing costs = $.35 per unit
Fixed manufacturing costs = $15,400
Variable selling expense = 5% of selling cost
Fixed selling expense = $2,000

Required:

a. Determine the incremental revenues and costs.

b. Should Davis produce the additional units?

14-22 Russel, Inc. has been purchasing a component part from another company since it began operations five years ago. Russel now has a steady demand for its product and feels it has the capacity to produce the component part itself. Russel purchased 120,000 units at a cost of $1.10 per unit last year and feels it will purchase 10% more this year for the same price. If Russel produces this part, its costs will be:

Direct materials	= $.45 per unit
Direct labor	= $.30 per unit
Variable overhead	= $.20 per unit
Avoidable fixed overhead	= $33,000

Required:

Should Russel Company purchase this part or produce it itself?

14-23   The Shelby Company normally produces and sells 50,000 units per year, but has the capacity to produce 75,000 units per year. Last year the company had the following income:

Sales		$450,000
Variable costs:		
Material	$100,000	
Labor	140,000	
Overhead	70,000	
Selling	13,500	
Shipping	25,000	348,500
Contribution margin		$101,500
Fixed overhead		30,000
Fixed selling and administrative expenses		42,000
Net income before taxes		$ 29,500

Shelby Company does not expect these relationships to change this year.

Another company that is not within Shelby's selling area has offered to buy 20,000 units at $6.90 per unit. Since there will be no salesmen involved, Shelby will not have to pay the sales commissions.

Required:

Determine whether Shelby should sell these units at $6.90. Give the incremental profit or loss if the extra units are sold.

14-24   Woodville, Inc. has been buying one of its component parts for $6.47 per unit. The management of Woodville feels that the company could make this part with an increase in fixed costs of $27,000. They expect to need about 18,000 units per year. Variable costs per unit will be:

Direct materials	$2.00
Direct labor	1.80
Variable overhead	1.28

Required:

Determine whether the company should make the part or continue to purchase the part.

14-25 The Silsbee Company has three products. Product #2 has incurred a loss for the past two years; therefore, management would like to drop this line. Given an income statement for 1980, you are to determine whether the company should drop this product. All "Fixed Overhead" items are allocated to the products as are all items under "Expenses" except selling expenses. Selling expenses are 2% of sales plus an allocated amount.

	Product Line #1	Product Line #2	Product Line #3	Total
Net sales	$280,000	$220,000	$300,000	$800,000
Cost of goods sold:				
Direct labor	$ 21,000	$ 34,500	$ 20,000	$ 75,500
Direct materials	25,000	24,600	24,000	73,600
Variable overhead	14,000	19,300	15,200	48,500
Fixed overhead				
Property taxes	28,000	22,000	30,000	80,000
Depreciation	56,000	44,000	60,000	160,000
Other	24,500	19,250	26,250	70,000
Total cost of goods sold	$168,500	$163,650	$175,450	$507,600
Gross margin	$111,500	$ 56,350	$124,550	$292,400
Expenses:				
Selling expenses	$ 26,600	$ 20,900	$ 28,500	$ 76,000
Advertising	28,000	22,000	30,000	80,000
General and Admn. Expenses	42,000	33,000	45,000	120,000
Total expenses	$ 96,600	$ 75,900	$103,500	$276,000
Net income before taxes	$ 14,900	($ 19,550)	$ 21,050	$ 16,400

14-26 Rick Rock, a well-known criminal, was considering the future revenues he could generate from two possible jobs. Due to risk and capital requirements, Rick can choose only one of the 2 possible alternatives. The breakdown of costs for each job was as follows:

Liquid Liquor Store (Job #1)

1 gun	$ 50
1 get-a-way bicycle	$ 100
1 ski mask	$ 10
1 day's observation	$ 70
1 laundry bag	$ 3
Expected payoff	$ 800

Easy Money Bank (Job #2)

3 guns	$ 240
2 accomplices	$2,000
1 get-a-way car	$1,000
Floor plans	$ 150
1 ski mask	$ 10
1 week's observation	$ 350
1 attache case	$ 60
Expected payoff	$4,400

Both jobs will be charged $150 for plane tickets to get Rick out of the country.

Required:

a. Which alternative is best for Rick assuming risk is the same?
b. Which cost(s) is irrelevant in making this decision?
c. What is the opportunity cost of the best alternative?

14-27   Samuelson, Inc. is considering making a new product. The company has excess capacity on its machinery with which it can make the product. Since only minor adjustments to the machinery will be necessary in order to make the product, fixed costs will not increase. Variable costs per unit include:

Direct materials...................... = 5 kilograms @ $.89 per kilogram
Direct labor.......................... = 1½ hours @ $4.20 per hour
Variable overhead..................... = 1½ hours @ $1.50 per hour
Distribution costs.................... = $.25 per unit
Sales commissions..................... = 2% of selling price

The company wants to introduce this product at the lowest possible price in order to induce customers to use their product rather than the competitor's product.

Required:

Determine the selling price of the product using the contribution margin approach.

14-28   Harrington, Inc. plans to introduce a new product. The company would like to make 10 percent profit on the sales. They feel that they will be able to sell from 9,000 to 12,000 units. Variable costs per unit associated with the new product are:

Direct materials................ = 2 kilograms of X @ $.32 per kilogram
                                  = 3 kilograms of Z @ $.62 per kilogram
Direct labor.................... = 1¼ hours @ $5.20 per hour
Variable overhead............... = 1¼ hours @ $2.60 per hour
Selling and distribution expense.... = $.35 per unit

In order to make this product, fixed production costs will increase by $34,000 per year. An advertising campaign costing $20,000 will also be initiated to promote the product.

Required:

Determine the range of selling prices for sales from 9,000 to 12,000 units.

14-29   The Three Musketeer's Company is trying to decide whether they should spend $30,000 on an advertising campaign which will be in effect from

May to December. Below are the cost and production data for the first four months of the year.

Months	Costs	Units Produced
1	$65,000	10,000
2	$70,000	12,000
3	$55,000	8,000
4	$60,000	9,000

The selling price is $7.50 per unit.

If the company maintains their present advertising strategy (no advertising), they expect sales to average 10,000 units a month for the last eight months of the year. However, if they contract for the $30,000 advertising expenditure, they expect sales per month to increase to an average of 12,000 units for the last eight months of the year.

Required:

Using the method of semi-averages to separate costs into their fixed and variable components, decide whether this $30,000 advertising expenditure should be made.

14-30   The Phono Company has a rather stringent attitude toward allowing credit to risky customers. The sales manager, however, believes that it would be more profitable to give the credit in the expectation that enough of these "high-risk" customers will pay their bills to allow the company to earn a contribution to fixed costs.

Presently, a decision must be made on this matter. Eight "high-risk" customers have each asked to purchase a television set on credit. The TV's sell for $350 apiece. Experience in the past shows that 75% of all "high-risk" customers will pay and 25% will not. Assume a total loss on any merchandise not paid for. The variable cost per T.V. set is $250.

Required:

Assuming that fixed costs will stay the same regardless of whether the TV's are sold to these eight customers, decide if Phono Company should sell the TV's.

14-31   The Acre Company is in the business of spraying potato fields for weeds. It has recently been offered two large jobs, but since they must be performed at the same time, only one of them can be chosen. Below are data relating to both jobs.

Job No. 1

Contract price	$ 9,250
Materials	$ 2,000
Labor	$ 3,600
Maintenance	$ 500
Insurance	$ 350
Depreciation	$ 1,700

Job No. 2

Contract price $15,350

Materials	$ 3,360
Labor	$ 5,100
Maintenance	$ 750
Insurance	$ 410
Traveling expenses (This job is located	
50 kilometers from the main office) · · · ·	$ 150
Depreciation	$ 1,700

Both jobs are charged with the depreciation on two spray-planes which were purchased three. years earlier for $100,000.

Required:

a. Which alternative is best?
b. What cost(s) is irrelevant in making this decision?
c. What is the opportunity cost of the best alternative?
d. Identify the sunk costs in this decision.

14-32   Chinwin Limited manufactures stereo radios. An outside supplier has approached management with a proposal to provide cabinets for the radio sets at a price considerably lower than the cost determined from company records for making cabinets of the same design and quality.

At the present time, the Chinwin Limited factory is operating at maximum capacity; however, about one-third of the operations are devoted to the manufacture of cabinets for the stereo sets.

You, as Chief Cost Accountant of Chinwin Limited, have been asked to determine whether it would be advisable for the company to obtain future requirements of cabinets from outside sources.

Required:

List the points which you would consider in order to make a recommendation as to whether or not the purchase of cabinets from the outside supplier would be to the company's advantage.

(SMA, adapted)

14-33   The following information summarizes the cost and revenue structures for Ace Sporting Goods manufacturer. Three products, racketball rackets, golf clubs, and lawn darts, are produced by the Iron Rod Division.

The Controller has given you the assignment of determining the following: (a) minimum pricing policy for short-run and long-run operations, (b) which product should be increased if there is excess capacity—assuming no additional fixed costs, and (c) which product, if any, should be dropped if demand increases 10 percent for racketball rackets, 6 percent for golf clubs, and 50 percent for lawn darts and the products are sold at their current sales price. Fixed costs are allocated to each product: (Assume that these fixed costs are directly related to the products as indicated. Thus, if a product is dropped, so are its fixed costs.) 26 percent to racketball rackets, 57 percent to golf clubs, and 17 percent to lawn darts. (Note—the company will not suffer a loss in plant and equipment if a product is dropped from the Iron Rod Division.)

	Racketball Rackets	Golf Clubs	Lawn Darts
Demand (in Units)	150,000	225,000	500,000
Current sales price	$15.95	$78.75	$7.95
Variable costs	$7.88	$51.25	$2.25

Fixed Costs:
Plant and equipment depreciation	$5,750,000
Manufacturing overhead	2,225,000
Selling and administrative	1,780,000
Total	$9,755,000

14-34 Geminik Limited manufactures and sells three different products —"GEM", "INI," and "NIK." Projected income statements by product line for the next fiscal year are as follows:

	GEM	INI	NIK	Total
Unit sales.	10,000	500,000	125,000	635,000
Revenue.	$925,000	$1,000,000	$575,000	$2,500,000
Variable cost of units sold.	(285,000)	(350,000)	(150,000)	(785,000)
Fixed cost of units sold.	(304,200)	(289,000)	(166,800)	(760,000)
Gross margin.	$335,800	$ 361,000	$258,200	$ 955,000
Variable general and administrative expenses.	(270,000)	(200,000)	(80,000)	(550,000)
Fixed general and administrative expenses.	(125,800)	(136,000)	(78,200)	(340,000)
Net income (loss) before provision for income taxes. . .	$(60,000)	$ 25,000	$100,000	$ 65,000

The fixed general and administrative expenses are allocated to products in proportion to revenues. The fixed cost of units sold is allocated to products by various allocation bases, such as square feet for factory rent and machine hours for repairs, etc.

Geminik management is concerned about the loss for product "GEM" and is considering two alternative courses of corrective action:

Alternative A — The company would purchase some new machinery for the production of product "GEM." This new machinery would involve an immediate cash outlay of $650,000. Management expects that the new machinery would reduce variable production costs so that total variable costs and expenses (production, and general and administrative) for "GEM" would be fifty-two percent (52%) of "GEM" revenues. The new machinery would increase total fixed costs and expenses (production, and general and administrative) allocated to "GEM" to $480,000 per year. There would be no additional fixed costs and expenses allocated to products "INI" and "NIK."

Alternative B — The company would discontinue the manufacture of product "GEM." Selling prices of products "INI" and "NIK" would remain constant. Management expects that product "NIK" production and revenues would increase by fifty percent (50%). Some of the present machinery devoted to product "GEM" could be sold at scrap value which equals its removal costs. The removal of this machinery would reduce fixed costs and expenses allocated to product "GEM" by $30,000 per year. The remaining fixed costs and expenses allocated to product "GEM" include $155,000 of rent expense per year. The space previously used for product "GEM" can be rented to an outside organization for $157,500 per year.

Required:

a. Prepare a schedule analyzing the effect of Alternative A and Alternative B on projected net income before provision for income taxes.

b. Assume the immediate cash outlay for the new machine in Alternative A is $700,000 and all other data remains unchanged. What effect will this have on your analysis? Explain.

c. Explain the term *relevant costs*. How do historical costs pertain to decision-making when using the relevant costs approach?

(SMA, adapted)

14-35   Leanne Rose operates a small machine shop. She manufactures one standard product available from many similar businesses as well as manufacturing products to customer order. Her accountant prepared the annual income statement below:

	Custom Sales	Standard Sales	Total
Sales	$50,000	$30,000	$80,000
Expenses:			
Direct material	$10,000	$ 9,000	$19,000
Direct labour	20,000	11,000	31,000
Depreciation	6,300	3,600	9,900
Power	700	400	1,100
Rent	6,000	1,000	7,000
Heat and light	600	100	700
Total expenses	$43,600	$25,100	$68,700
Net income	$ 6,400	$ 4,900	$11,300

The depreciation charges are for machines used in the respective product lines. The power charge is allocated based on the estimate of power consumed. The rent is for the building space which has been leased for ten years at $7,000 per year. The rent, heat, and light are allocated to the product lines based on amount of floor space occupied.

Leanne is planning operations for the coming year and faces a problem. A valued custom-order customer has asked Leanne if she would produce 5,000 special units for her. Leanne has contracts with her other customers requiring delivery of the same number of custom and standard units as last year. Leanne is working at capacity and would have to reduce other production in order to manufacture the special units. She cannot reduce production of custom units but could purchase 50% of the required standard products for $14,000 from another machine shop, allowing sufficient capacity for the special order. The customer is willing to pay $8 for each special unit. The direct material cost will be $2 per unit and the direct labour will be $3.40 per unit.

Total power usage will increase by 20% if the special order is accepted. Leanne will have to spend $4,000 for a special device which will be discarded when the special job is done. These are the only extra costs of the special order.

Required:

a.   Calculate total company net income if Leanne accepts the order. Based on profitability should Leanne accept?
b.   Briefly discuss three other factors that should be considered before Leanne decides to accept or reject the special order.

(SMA, adapted)

14-36   The Feel Better While You Live Company produces a high protein drink and vitamins A, C, and E. With changing market conditions, the company has hired you to evaluate the current pricing strategy for these products. The following information is available.

	High Protein Drink	Vitamins A	C	E
Demand (in packages) . .	1,000,000	1,250,000	2,500,000	750,000
Current sales price (per package)	$7.98	$2.95	$1.95	$3.95
Variable costs (per package)	$2.45	$ .51	$ .65	$ .74

Fixed Costs	
Plant and equipment depreciation	$ 2,450,000
Manufacturing overhead	3,950,000
Selling and administrative	3,780,000
Total	$10,180,000

Note—Fixed costs are distributed as follows: 56 percent to protein drink, 12 percent to Vitamin A, 15 percent to Vitamin C and 17 percent to Vitamin E. (Assume that these fixed costs are directly related to the products as indicated. Thus, if a product is dropped, so are its fixed costs.)

Required:

a. What would be the minimum price for short-run and long-run operations?
b. Which product, if any, should be dropped if demand increases 30 percent for the high protein drink and 12 percent for each of the vitamins? (Assume there is no loss in disposing of fixed assets.)
c. What is your evaluation of the *current* pricing strategy, given the available information?
d. Given the current pricing policy, how much profit will this company make?

14-37   Sun Inc. manufactures cabinets for its own radios and for sale to outsiders in a plant which is separate from the radio operation. Management expects that during the third quarter—the three months ending September 30th—the cabinet facility will be operating at 80 percent of normal capacity. Because a higher utilization of plant capacity is desired, acceptance of a special order would be considered. Cost data for the Sun Inc. cabinets now being manufactured are as follows:

Regular selling price to outsiders............	$9.00
Cost per unit:	
Raw materials.........................	$2.50
Direct labour—½ hours @ $6.00..........	3.00
Overhead—¼ machine hour @ $4.00......	1.00
Total costs..............................	$6.50

Sun Inc. has received special order enquiries from two companies, as follows:

a. Pluto Ltd. would like to order a cabinet similar to that of Sun's. The Pluto cabinet requirement is for 25,000 to be shipped by October 1 for a price of $6.00 each. The cost data for this order would be similar to that of the Sun cabinets, with one exception. According to the specifications provided by Pluto Ltd., the special cabinet requires less expensive raw materials. These will cost only $2.25 per cabinet. It is estimated by management that the remaining costs, labour time and machine time will be the same as the Sun Inc. cabinet.

b. Saturn Inc. has submitted another special order to Sun Inc. for 8,000 cabinets at $7.50 per cabinet. These too would have to be shipped by October 1. However, the Saturn cabinet is different from any cabinet in the Sun line. The estimated unit costs of this cabinet are:

Raw materials.............................	$3.25
Direct labour—½ hour @ $6.00...........	3.00
Overhead—½ hour @ $4.00...............	2.00
Total costs.............................	$8.25

In addition, Sun Inc. will incur $1,800 in additional set-up costs and will have to purchase a special device costing $2,600 to manufacture these cabinets; this device would be discarded once the special order is completed.

Sun Inc.'s manufacturing capabilities are limited to the total machine hours available. The maximum plant capacity available under normal operating conditions is 87,000 machine hours per year or 7,250 machine hours per month. The budgeted fixed overhead amounts to $208,800. All manufacturing overhead costs are applied to production at the predetermined rate of $4.00 per hour.

Sun Inc. will have the entire third quarter—July 1 to September 30—to work on the special orders. It is not expected that any repeat business will be generated from either special order.

It is Sun Inc.'s company practice not to subcontract any portion of an order when special orders are not expected to generate repeat sales.

Required:

Should Sun Inc. accept either special order? Justify your answer and show your calculations.

(SMA, adapted)

14-38 The management of the Forth Company is examining various alternatives for the production and distribution of its single product, a packaged fertilizer. The results of last year's operations are:

	Eastern Plant	Central Plant	Western Plant	Total
Sales ($5 per unit)........	$500,000	$600,000	$700,000	$1,800,000
Variable expenses........	250,000	300,000	350,000	900,000
Fixed expenses...........	80,000	100,000	90,000	270,000
Allocated home offices expenses*	20,000	24,000	28,000	72,000
Total expenses...........	$350,000	$424,000	$468,000	$1,242,000
Net income before tax.....	$150,000	$176,000	$232,000	$ 558,000

*Allocation is based on sales dollar value.

The lease renewal for the Central plant calls for an increase of $50,000 in the annual rent. In addition, a 10 percent wage increase for direct labour at the Central plant was effective on January 1 of this year. Based on the Central plant's production last year, the wage increase will cost $12,000.

The Central plant is used to supply the export market. If the Central plant is closed, export sales could be met by one of the following alternatives:

I.   *Expansion of capacity at the Eastern plant.*   Fixed costs would increase by 50 percent and shipping costs on exported sales would increase by $.50 per unit.

II. *A long-term agreement with a competing manufacturer.*   A competitor would agree to fill Forth's export commitments and to pay Forth a commission of 18 percent of the gross export sales value.

Required:

a.   A schedule showing Forth's net income before tax if the Central plant is closed under each of the two alternatives given.

   Notes: 1.   A formal income statement is not required. You may start your schedule with the reported net income before taxes for last year and make the necessary adjustments to arrive at the revised net income for each alternative.

   2.   Assume that the costs of shut-down of the Central plant are exactly offset by the proceeds of disposal of the plant.

b.   Management is considering a third alternative. Keep the Central plant operating this year and increase export selling prices. Looking at the operations of the Central plant and allowing for this year's cost increases, what selling price per unit would yield an income of 30 percent of sales before taxes and allocated home office expenses for the Central plant.

(SMA, adapted)

14-39   The Bellance Company has designed a new airplane. They have already completed two planes (for demonstration purposes only) at the following costs:

Direct Material.....................	$2,000,000
Direct Labor.......................	3,000,000
Set-Up Costs.......................	400,000
Overhead*	900,000
Total...........................	$6,300,000

*Overhead is assigned as a percentage of labor cost for purposes of bidding on contracts. While fixed overhead is independent of any particular contract, variable overhead has been observed consistently at ten percent of labor cost.

Required:

A. Prepare an estimate of costs for bidding on a contract for six more airplanes. Assume that the direct labor hourly rate will be unchanged and that the set-up costs can be reused. You should use an 80 percent learning curve as a basis for forecasting pertinent costs.

B. If this were a special order for a foreign customer, would you analyze overhead differently than you did for requirement number A?

14-40 The P&R Company has received an order from a large department store chain to manufacture 10,000 lawn chairs. P&R is a highly successful manufacturer of prestige garden furniture. Budget amounts at various activity levels are:

	75%	100%
Sales	$900,000	$1,200,000
Direct material.................................	255,000	340,000
Direct labour...................................	307,500	410,000
Foremen's salaries.............................	45,000	45,000
Supplies	9,000	12,000
Rent	20,000	20,000
Depreciation, machine hour basis.................	66,000	88,000
Power for machinery............................	1,500	2,000
Heat and light.................................	3,000	3,000
Other expenses.................................	172,500	180,000
	$879,500	$1,100,000
Net income before taxes........................	$ 20,500	$ 100,000

P&R Company is operating at full capacity. If the department store chain order is accepted, regular production will have to be cut back 20%.

The department store chain has offered a price of $20 per chair which is $5 less than P&R's selling price for the model. However, the chain is willing to accept lighter weight materials thus reducing P&R's cost.

P&R had previously calculated its costs for chairs of this particular quality (i.e., lighter weight), based on a volume 25,000, as follows:

Direct materials..................................	$125,000
Direct labour....................................	145,000
Other direct variable costs........................	25,000
Costs of special jigs (to be discarded after the job).......	5,000
Total cost for 25,000 chairs.......................	$300,000

Required:

a. Prepare a schedule showing the effect of the order on income before taxes, allowing for any cutback in regular production.

b. Should the order be accepted? Explain.

(SMA, adapted)

A 14-41 The Western Company produces and sells three product lines. Below is an income statement in summary form for a six month period:

Amounts in Thousands of dollars	Totals	A	B	C
Sales	500	200	220	80
Cost of goods sold	332	148	136	48
Gross margin	168	52	84	32
Selling expenses	82	26	42	14
Administrative	60	20	20	20
Total	142	46	62	34
Profit before taxes	26	6	22	(2)

Additional information:

i.   Cost of goods sold include $120,000 of fixed manufacturing overhead which has been allocated to the product lines as follows:

A = 40%, B = 40%, C = 20%.

ii.   Selling expenses have been allocated to the product lines on the basis of sales orders. However, the variable selling expenses for each product line amount to 10% of sales dollars.

iii. Administrative expenses are all fixed.

During a discussion with the sales manager, the president expressed dissatisfaction about the loss on Product Line C. The following alternatives were suggested:

Plan I

Eliminate Product Line C and reduce sales of Product B by 10%. The production facilities so released could be used to increase the production output of A by 50%. In order to market the extra volume of A, the sales price of A would have to be lowered by 5%.

Plan II

Eliminate Product Line C, maintain the present volume for lines A and B, and rent the unused production facilities for $6,000 a month.

Required:

Evaluate each of the above plans and recommend whether either should be adopted.

(SMA, adapted)

Chapter 15

LEARNING OBJECTIVES

Chapter 15 discusses the basic steps of the capital budgeting process, with special emphasis on evaluating and choosing among alternative long-term investments. Studying this chapter should enable you to:

1. Identify constraints affecting a firm's use of capital.
2. Discuss the principal types of data used to make capital budgeting decisions.
3. Explain how income tax considerations may affect the capital budgeting decision.
4. Describe the basic steps in developing a capital budget on a project-by-project basis.
5. Apply the various techniques of evaluating and/or ranking alternative investment possibilities.
6. Discuss sensitivity analysis and the cost of prediction errors.

Long-Range Planning: Capital Budgeting

IN THE PREVIOUS chapter, the emphasis was on making a choice from among two or more alternatives when only revenues, cost savings, and costs are relevant to the decision. In that context the commitment of resources was not a relevant financial factor. In this chapter, however, the long-term investment of the firm's resources is a major consideration in the decision-making process.

Long-range investments imply a use of capital by the firm. Suppliers of capital demand an acceptable return on this resource. Management must balance the firm's demand for capital necessitated by new investments with the available supply of capital. The process of managing the supply and demand of capital and making decisions with regard to the use of available capital is referred to as capital budgeting. The capital budget is a list and analysis of all the long-range investments in which the firm is considering investing its available supply of capital. Acceptable capital investments must be consistent with the goals and objectives of the firm.

A capital budget may be regarded as both short and long-term. The capital budgeting decision considers both the firm's financial ability to provide acceptable returns on current and future capital and the degree to which the investment meshes with the firm's other short and long-range goals.

Once management has committed the firm's capital to specific long-term investments, the firm may have limited its potential investment alternatives for some time into the future. Once a capital investment is made, it is normally difficult to modify at a later date without incurring considerable losses. Usually, the original outlay for any investment can only be recovered through the use of the asset involved.

513

TYPES OF ACCOUNTING INFORMATION NECESSARY FOR CAPITAL BUDGETING DECISIONS

Accounting information which may prove useful in capital budgeting decisions includes both accrual and cash flow data. Accrual accounting information is based on generally accepted accounting principles which normally have a tendency to average the various financial factors involved in determining revenues, costs, and investments. Therefore, analysis based on accrual accounting information will reflect this averaging approach.

Generally accepted accounting principles are not considered in estimating cash inflows and outflows. Thus, the cash flows from an investment proposal will not necessarily coincide with either the income or the accrual accounting cost savings from an investment. For example, an investment in an asset usually requires an immediate cash outlay for the acquisition cost of the asset. From an accrual accounting standpoint, this cost is allocated to the appropriate time periods over the asset's projected life through the process of depreciation.

INCOME TAX IMPLICATIONS FOR CAPITAL BUDGETING DECISIONS

There are numerous income tax implications that should be considered in the capital budgeting decision. Certain of these tax considerations are beyond the scope of this text because of their complexity and/or limited applicability. Likewise, changes to the federal *Income Tax Act* are enacted every year thus making it impractical to provide complete detail in this text without the risk of presenting obsolete material. Nevertheless, it is quite important for students to become familiar with the principal features of the *Income Tax Act* and to make due allowance for the impact of taxes when preparing a capital budgeting analysis.

The net operating expenses, revenues and cost savings associated with a capital expenditure are significantly influenced by the magnitude of the combined federal and provincial income taxes. For several decades the general tax rate for most medium and large size corporations has approximated half of taxable income.[1] Thus, revenues or cost savings represent an after tax inflow of only about half of the gross amount before taxes (100 percent less tax rate). Likewise operating expenses requiring a cash outlay

---

[1] At the time of writing, the general corporate tax specified by the federal *Income Tax Act* is something less than 50 percent with approximately three-quarters of the total going to the federal government and the remainder to the province concerned. However, each province has the authority to increase this rate within its jurisdiction and most have done so. Further, it should be noted that Alberta, Ontario and Quebec collect their own corporate taxes while the federal government performs this task on the behalf of the other seven provinces and the territories.

Corporations classified as Canadian-controlled private companies are taxed at something in the vicinity of half of the general corporate rate on their taxable income below an amount specified in the *Income Tax Act*. They pay the full rate on any income over this limit.

It should also be noted that the tax on "Canadian manufacturing and processing income" is less than would otherwise be the case.

have an after tax cost of approximately one-half of the amount actually paid.

Another important tax aspect to be considered in making capital budgeting decision is the magnitude and timing of the asset's Capital Cost Allowance (CCA). CCA is the statutory allowance for depreciation expense specified for each class of assets in the *Income Tax Act*. Although annual depreciation is a non-cash expense and, therefore, does not affect cash flow directly, CCA does have an important effect on the calculation of net *taxable income* and, hence on the amount of income tax which must be paid (in cash) for the year. For most classes of assets CCA is calculated using the declining balance method as shown in Table 15B at the end of this chapter[2]. To illustrate its effect, assume that a company purchases a certain type of auxiliary electrical generator (asset class 8, CCA 20%) for $10,000. The Capital Cost Allowance will be $1,000 for the first year (half[3] of the specified rate of 20% times $10,000). If the firm's effective tax rate is 46 percent it will realize a $460 reduction in income tax payable (46% of $1,000). The CCA for the second year will be $1,800 (20% of the $9,000 undepreciated capital cost (UCC) remaining after deducting the first year's CCA of $1,000) and the saving in income tax will be $828 (.46 of $1,800). For the third year, the CCA will be $1,440 (20% of the $7,200 UCC remaining after deducting the cumulative CCA from the original cost) and so on.

Still another important tax consideration is the investment tax credit. In its continuing attempt to influence the nation's economy, the government often allows favourable tax treatment to capital investments of a certain type and/or in certain geographic locations. A sometime used technique for accomplishing this is the Investment Tax Credit. If a firm purchases an asset eligible for such credit, it may deduct from the income tax which would otherwise be due for the year in which the asset is acquired, the percentage of the cost of the asset which is specified in the *Act* for the type and geographic location of the asset.[4] Thus, the investment tax credit effectively reduces the firm's net cash outflow for the asset by the amount of the investment tax credit allowed. In addition to this tax credit, which is a direct

---

[2] Though in the interest of simplicity they will not be included in the examples used in this book, it should be noted that there are a few instances wherein the *Income Tax Act* permits the entire cost of an asset to be written off over a period of a few years using the straight line method of calculating depreciation. In such cases, appropriate allowance must be made for the effect on cash flow resulting from smaller than otherwise tax payments.

[3] The half-year convention for first year CCA was first announced in the Budget-Speech of November 12, 1981 and became effective for all assets acquired after that date. See Income Tax Regulations 1100 (2) through (2.4).

[4] The investment tax credit was introduced in 1975 and in some form has been a part of the *Income Tax Act* since that time. While it was announced in the Budget Speech of February 26, 1986 that some investment tax credits would be phased out by 1989, it was also revealed that others would be continued, including the 60 percent credit (up to certain limits) for qualified investments in the Cape Breton area.

reduction of the amount of income tax liability (*not* the cost of the asset), the firm can claim Capital Cost Allowance (CCA) in the normal manner on the remainder of the adjusted basis of the asset (cost less allowable investment tax credit) when calculating taxable income. (The importance of the investment tax credit is obvious, but in the interest of simplicity it is ignored in the examples used in this chapter.)

THE CAPITAL BUDGET

Proposals for capital expenditures may be initiated by any group within the organization. Employees may propose an idea via suggestions to management; the research and development department may develop new products or alter current products so as to require capital outlays; technological change may introduce new methods; product demand may necessitate additional plant, equipment, warehouses, offices or other assets; or assets may simply wear out and necessitate replacement.

The process of developing the capital budget on a project-by-project basis may be divided into five steps: [5]

1. Initiating the idea and specifications.
2. Reviewing the request.
3. Making a decision regarding the request.
4. Controlling the project's progress and funds.
5. Conducting a post-audit of the results of the decision.

The five steps are presented here in order to structure the coverage and discussion of long-range capital investments. In practice, the distinction among these steps may not be as apparent or clear-cut as the above listing would lead one to believe.

INITIATION OF THE IDEA AND SPECIFICATIONS

In firms where numerous capital expenditure requests must be considered, the format of the request and the channels through which the request must be routed or directed are normally identified in the firm's policy manual. The sponsor of the request usually develops the basic idea with the aid of the appropriate supporting personnel from accounting, management, industrial engineering, the legal department, etc. If a specific department has the responsibility for developing the specifications and the capital expenditure request form for projects, the input of the original sponsor may be limited to developing the idea and basic estimates of the benefits and costs. An example of a request for a capital expenditure is presented in Illustration 15-1.

---

[5] Six steps might be more appropriate if the firm wishes to consider the available alternative financing techniques.

Illustration 15-1
Capital Expenditure Request

Sax Company
Capital Expenditure Request

Project Title _____   Date _____

Project No. _____

Proposal Overview (Attach Detail)
  Direct Capital Required _____   Depreciation Technique _____

  Working Capital Required _____

  Project Life _____

  Average Revenues or Cost Savings _____

  Average Period Expenses _____

  Net Added Profits Before Taxes _____

  Net Added Profits After Taxes _____

  Average Annual Cash Flow _____

Justification:
  Cash Payback _____   Present Value Index _____

  Accounting Rate of Return _____   Internal Rate of Return _____

  Net Present Value _____

Comments:

(Division)	Approval Date	(Corporate)	Approval Date
Project Sponsor _____		_____	
General Manager _____		_____	
Division Controller _____		_____	

REVIEW OF THE REQUEST

If a firm is large and has numerous capital budgeting proposals, the request is normally reviewed by the sponsor's supervisor. The decision to accept or reject the proposal may be made at a lower level of management provided that the request is within the manager's capital budget limit. For example, department heads may have the authority to approve projects with a cost of up to $4,000 on an individual basis, with a maximum total of $15,000 in expenditures established for a given year. A division manager may be able to approve expenditures of up to $30,000 with an aggregate limit of $150,000 in any given year. The president may be authorized to approve expenditures of up to $500,000 with an annual aggregate of $5,000,000. Normal procedures indicate that major capital expenditures should be approved by the board of directors.

The basis for establishing the various limits on expenditures at different levels within the organization is developed at the annual budget review session with top management. At this session, current proposals and related estimates are reviewed, combined and coordinated with ongoing projects from prior years and with projects in other segments or divisions of the organization. As might be expected, the forms and procedures for capital budgeting decisions in smaller firms are usually not as clearly developed or as formal as they are in larger firms.

MAKING A DECISION REGARDING THE REQUEST

There are numerous tools or techniques available to aid management in making capital budgeting decisions. Each of these techniques has strengths and weaknesses. Management normally employs several of these techniques. The most difficult part of the capital budgeting decision may well be obtaining quantifiable input data, i.e., the information and forecasts surrounding the project. After the initial proposal is prepared, making additional calculations to develop an unbiased perspective regarding a decision does not usually require significant effort or cost. If the firm has a computer facility or access to a computer service bureau, a program is usually available which will handle the basic techniques discussed in this chapter.

The techniques used to analyze proposed capital budgeting decisions may be classified into two general categories: (1) those techniques that ignore the time value of money and (2) those techniques that consider the time value of money.

Techniques That Ignore Time Value

There are several project evaluation techniques which do not consider the time value of money. While none of these methods should be used exclusively, they do have the advantages of being simple and easy to compute. They provide management with a quick method to facilitate a review of project feasibility. However, if the project involves large cash flow streams, the unadjusted evaluation techniques should generally be used as additional information to supplement a time value adjusted technique. Four project evaluation techniques which ignore the time value of money are discussed in the following section of this chapter.

No Choice or Urgency—Making the Decision

The distinguishing characteristic of the no choice or urgency technique is the real or implied need to make a decision immediately because of the particular circumstances at hand. This approach is the least desirable of the various capital budgeting techniques because, due to the urgency of the situation, profitability considerations are not analyzed, but rather are left to chance.

Urgency implies quick remedial action rather than deliberative action undertaken after a careful analysis of the available alternatives. If the potential resources involved are not great, the urgency criterion is probably justified. An effective planning scheme and a limitation on the amount of investment involved reduces the probability of large expenditures being made using the no choice or urgency plea as the basis for the decision.

Qualitative Reasons— Making the Decision

A second capital budgeting technique which does not consider the time value of money is based on qualitative rather than quantitative reasoning. In every capital budgeting decision, there are certain qualitative aspects that must be considered in addition to the available quantitative information. However, a capital budgeting decision based solely on qualitative criteria should be made only when the qualitative statements can be made with some degree of accuracy and when there is no quantifiable information available.

Qualitative reasoning is considered in many decisions made in areas such as organizational behavior or social commitment of resources. For example, if a firm chooses to install a lunchroom for its employees, this decision cannot be evaluated solely on its monetary returns. The lunchroom may have positive social value for the company which in and of itself justifies the investment. Although an investment in an employee lunchroom may produce quantifiable benefits for the firm in the form of increased revenues, decreased costs, increased productivity, lower employee turnover, or more satisfied employees, these benefits can only be measured indirectly in relation to the capital investment.

Qualitative reasons involved in capital budgeting decisions range from such factors as employee incentive plans to community relations activities for profit-oriented companies. In these decisions, it is frequently difficult to specify and quantify the benefits attributable to the investment except by comparing some aspect of the firm or its activities before and after the decision to see if a change appears to have taken place.

Payback Period— Making the Decision

The payback period is the amount of time required to produce net cash flows sufficient to recover the initial investment outlay. The payback technique does not consider the timing of the receipt of money, but is based totally on an analysis of cash flows. Moreover, the payback method does not measure the profitability of a project. This method is a simple calculation which determines the amount of time required to recover, in cash flows, the initial net investment in an asset.

The payback technique is widely used for a rough analysis of small investments that do not justify or warrant in-depth study or analysis. Despite its simplicity, the approach does have merit in the following situations:

1. If a company-wide policy requires payback within a stated time period for all capital investments below a selected dollar limit, the payback technique can effectively and efficiently screen small investment proposals before a formal request for expenditure is prepared.
2. If there is an element of uncertainty with regard to the estimates of future cash inflows or cost savings, the payback calculation provides a measure of how soon the firm can expect to recover its initial investment.
3. If cash flow is a major problem for a firm, timing of the cash returns from an investment may be considered crucial; thus the payback technique may provide relevant information.

The payback approach may be applied in several ways. The general formula is as follows:

$$\text{Payback period} = \frac{\text{Net Original Investment}}{\text{Annual Cash Inflows or Cost Savings}}$$

As long as the annual cash inflows are equal in amount, this general formula is applicable. If unequal cash inflows are expected, average cash inflows may be used or the projected unequal cash inflows for each year may be reviewed in order to determine the payback period.

To illustrate the use of the payback technique, assume that Sax Company is considering a labor-saving device that costs $1,000 and provides the following cash flow savings:

Year	Cash Flow Savings	Cumulative Cash Flow	Cumulative Cash Flow Net of Investment
1	$ 400	$ 400	($600)
2	300	700	(300)
3	300	1,000	0
4	300	1,300	300
5	200	1,500	500
Total	$1,500		

The average cash savings is $300 ($1500/5 years). Using this average cash savings, the payback period is calculated as follows:

$$\text{Payback} = \frac{\$1,000}{\$300} = 3\frac{1}{3} \text{ years}$$

If the cash savings are reviewed by specific years, the payback period is three years because $1,000 is recovered in the first three years.

The major weakness of the payback method is the disregard for the timing of the receipts and therefore the time value of money. A managerial decision which demonstrates the problem caused by a disregard for the time value of money is shown below:

	Investment A	Investment B
Cash Outflow	$1,000	$1,000
Cash Inflows		
Year 1	$ 200	$ 700
Year 2	300	200
Year 3	500	100
Payback Period	3 Years	3 Years

Alternative Investments A and B have the same investment outlays, same payback periods and are equally important to the firm. However, because capital available for investment is limited, only one investment can be selected. Since the payback period is the same for both Investment A and Investment B either alternative is equally desirable if the payback method is used as the sole criterion in choosing between these investments. An analysis of the timing of the cash flows expected under Investment B, however, points out that this investment provides a greater cash flow in the first year than does Investment A. Because there is a time value associated with future cash receipts (that is, a dollar today is of greater value to the firm than a dollar to be received next year), investment B is the better choice. The payback technique ignores the time value of money and thus is not an effective gauge of an investment's worth. The payback calculation is useful as a ranking technique in that it provides an index of the cash recovery period for an investment being contemplated. Payback should not be considered a comprehensive criterion in a capital budgeting analysis.

Accountant's Rate of Return— Making the Decision

The accountant's rate of return (ARR, also referred to as the unadjusted rate of return or accounting rate of return) also fails to consider the time value of money. Accrual accounting income is used as the basis for benefit measurement. Since income is considered in the formula, the technique does give some recognition to profitability.

The formula used for the accountant's rate of return is:

$$\frac{\text{Average Incremental Increase in Annual Net Income}}{\text{Net Original Investment Outlay}}$$

The accountant's rate of return may also be computed using the average investment outlay as the denominator. The formula then becomes:

$$\frac{\text{Average Incremental Increase in Annual Net Income}}{\frac{(\text{Original Investment} + \text{Salvage Value})}{2}}$$

The payback example can be used to illustrate the use of the accountant's rate of return, if certain additional assumptions are made. The labor-saving device considered in the payback example will be depreciated using the straight-line method over an expected life of five years. The salvage value of the asset at the end of five years is estimated to be $100. Sax Company wishes to make the analysis on a before-tax basis using both the original investment and the average investment.

$$\text{ARR Using Original Investment} = \frac{(\$1,500/5 \text{ years}) - \$180 \text{ Depreciation}}{\$1,000}$$

$$= \frac{\$300 - \$180}{\$1,000} = 12\%$$

$$\text{ARR Using Average Investment} = \frac{(\$1,500/5 \text{ years}) - \$180 \text{ Depreciation}}{\frac{(\$1,000 + \$100 \text{ Salvage})}{2}}$$

$$= \frac{\$300 - \$180}{\$550} = 21.8\%$$

The accounting rate of return, like the payback technique, is a ranking technique. Alternative investments may be ranked in the order of their profitability to provide another measure to be used in making the capital budgeting decision.

TIME VALUE OF MONEY TECHNIQUES

Capital budgeting techniques which consider the time value of money are referred to as discounted cash-flow methods. A dollar today has a greater value than does a dollar one year from now; moreover, a dollar to be received one year from now has a greater value to a firm today than a dollar to be received five years from now. Money has value over time because it can be invested and a return on the investment can be realized.

The emphasis of capital budgeting techniques that consider the time value of money is on the timing and magnitude of cash flows. Two general discounted cash flow techniques available to assist in making capital budgeting decisions are the net present value method and the internal rate of return method. These two techniques and a variation of the net present value technique, the present value index, are considered in this chapter.

The concept of present value is discussed in the Appendix to this chapter. One must understand the Appendix and must be able to use Tables 15A-1 and 15A-2 prior to considering the net present value and the internal rate of return techniques. If you are unfamiliar with this concept you should go to the Appendix before continuing with the chapter material.

The techniques that employ the concept of the time value of money usually consider the impact of income taxes on cash flows utilized in the analysis. If income tax implications are not considered, the analysis of cash flows is incomplete and inaccurate. Two similar pre-tax investment alternatives may produce entirely different results on an after-tax basis. For this reason, after-tax cash flows should be used in an analysis in which income taxes are a relevant factor.

Net Present Value— Making the Decision

The net present value technique requires that the management of a firm specify the minimum desired rate of return on an after-tax basis which must be earned on capital investments in order to make them acceptable to the firm. This minimum acceptable rate is usually referred to as the cost of capital. In essence, the net present value technique discounts all projected outflows and inflows of cash back to the present period using the cost of capital as the discount rate. If the present value of anticipated cash inflows exceeds the present value of anticipated cash outflows, the project is acceptable because the investment is earning an after-tax return which is greater than the cost of capital. If the present value of projected cash inflows is equal to the present value of projected cash outflows then the net present value of the project is zero, and the project is earning exactly the cost of capital. If the net present value is negative, the project is earning less than the cost of capital because the present value of anticipated cash outflows is greater than the present value of anticipated cash inflows.

More than one of the alternatives under consideration may be capable of earning a return greater than the minimum return acceptable to management. When more than one alternative is acceptable using the net present value criterion, management will further compare the acceptable alternatives and then make its decision. The following example illustrates the use of the net present value technique and the alternative means of approaching an investment decision.

Trembley Enterprises is considering the purchase of a new item of equipment at a cost of $200,000. This equipment is expected to have a useful life of five years and an estimated salvage value equal to the undepreciated capital cost at the end of the period. For income tax purposes it has a capital cost allowance of 30 percent (asset class 28).   During its useful life, this asset will result in a savings in operating costs of $50,000 per year but will require an overhaul costing $20,000 (considered a maintenance expense) at the end of the third year. Trembley has alternative investment possibilities for the $200,000 that will yield a return of 16 percent after taxes. Because this alternative exists, the management of Trembley has decided to use a rate of 16 percent as the cost of capital in evaluating the possible purchase of the equipment. In the past, Trembley has averaged a 45 percent tax rate on its earned income. Management anticipates that a similar tax rate will be incurred in the future. If the equipment does not earn a projected return of 16 percent after taxes, Trembley Enterprises does not wish to invest its resources in this project.

Part A of Illustration 15-2 identifies the cash flow impacts of the equipment on an annual basis. The discounting factors used are taken from Table 15A-1, Present Value of $1.00. Part B of Illustration 15-2 uses the annuity table, Table 15A-2, Present Value of Annuity of $1.00 per Period. For purposes of illustration, assume that all inflows or outflows of cash, with the exception of the initial investment, take place at the end of the year.

In Part A of Illustration 15-2, the present value of the initial outlay of $200,000 is $200,000, because the money is paid out immediately. The cost savings realized each year are discounted to reflect their current dollar value

Illustration 15-2
Net Present Value Technique

Part A: Year by Year Discounting

Year	Description	Before Tax	After Tax	P.V. Factor 16%	Present Value
Outflows					
0	Equipment purchase	$200,000	$200,000	1.000	$200,000
3	Overhaul	20,000	11,000 [a]	.641	7,051
	Total outflows				$207,051
Inflows					
1	Operating Savings	50,000	27,500 [a]	.862	$ 23,705
	CCA	30,000	13,500 [b]	.862	11,637
2	Operating Savings	50,000	27,500	.743	20,433 [c]
	CCA	51,000	22,950	.743	17,052 [c]
3	Operating Savings	50,000	27,500	.641	17,628
	CCA	35,700	16,065	.641	10,298 [c]
4	Operating Savings	50,000	27,500	.552	15,180
	CCA	24,990	11,246 [c]	.552	6,208 [c]
5	Operating Savings	50,000	27,500	.476	13,090
	CCA	17,493	7,872 [c]	.476	3,747 [c]
	Salvage Value	40,817	40,817	.476	19,429 [c]
	Total inflows				$158,407
	Present value				($48,644)

Part B: Using the Annuity Table and declining balance Capital Cost Allowance tax shield formula for the same outflows occurring in multiple years.

Year	Description	Before Tax	After Tax	P.V. Factor	Present Value
Outflows	(Same as Part A)				
0	Equipment purchase	200,000	200,000	1.000	200,000
3	Overhaul expenses	20,000	11,000	.641	7,051
	Total outflows				$207,051
Inflows					
1-5	Annual operating savings	50,000	27,500	3.274 [d]	$ 90,035
	CCA				48,946 [c]
5	Salvage value	40,817	40,817	.476	19,429 [c]
	Total inflows				$158,410
	Net present value				($48,641)

---

[a] Savings or Operating expenses are multiplied by 1 − the tax rate (in this example: 1.00 − .45 = .55).

[b] Annual CCA is multiplied by the tax rate.

[c] Present values and CCA are rounded to the nearest whole dollar.

[d] From the annuity table.

[e] Calculated using the Canadian declining balance CCA tax shield formula, see page 528.

if the rate of return on the funds is 16 percent. The cost savings are also multiplied by 55 percent (100 percent minus the income tax rate of 45 percent) to reflect the related income tax implications. If the asset is purchased, the reductions in costs cause income to rise by $50,000 per year. At a 45 percent income tax rate, an additional $22,500 in income taxes is incurred annually. Therefore, the $50,000 reduction in costs is worth only $27,500 to Trembley after taxes.

The capital cost allowance for the asset is $30,000 (half of 30% of $200,000) for the first year and $51,000 for the second year (30% of the $170,000 UCC remaining after deducting CAA for the first year that the asset is owned, i.e., $200,000 less $30,000). In the three subsequent years the allowance will be $35,700, $24,990 and $17,493, respectively. Though no cash is paid or received for capital cost allowance it is a tax deductible expense used in arriving at taxable income for the period. Thus, the amount of income tax that otherwise would be paid (in cash) is reduced by 45 percent of the capital cost allowance. For the first year the tax savings amount to $13,500 (45% of $30,000). In the second year the savings are $22,950 (45% of $51,000) and so on. Since the tax savings resulting from CCA reduce the outflow of cash required to pay income taxes, it is considered a cash inflow just as a cost savings is considered an inflow.

The overhaul expense at the end of the third year will not increase the life of the asset. This expense represents a cash outlay that will be incurred and which will be deductible at the end of year three for income tax purposes. With a 45 percent tax rate, the effective cost of the overhaul is 55 percent of the cash outlay of $20,000, or $11,000. Without this overhaul, the net income before taxes for the period would be $20,000 higher and additional taxes of $9,000 (.45 × $20,000) would have to be paid. Thus, the net cost of the overhaul is $11,000.

Note the difference between the treatment of capital cost allowance, a tax deductible item, and the overhaul which is also a deductible item for tax purposes. If no cash is paid for a tax deductible item, the amount of the effective cost savings is the tax rate multiplied by the amount of the tax deduction. If cash is paid for a tax deductible item, the effective cost (not the cost savings) of the item is 100 percent minus the tax rate. As shown in Illustration 15-2, the capital cost allowance tax saving is considered an inflow and the overhaul cost is considered an outflow in the analysis.

The salvage value of $40,817 at the end of year five represents an inflow that has no tax implications, because Trembley Enterprises believes that the salvage value will approximate the undepreciated capital cost (UCC) at the time of the disposal of the equipment. Thus from an income tax standpoint there will be no gain or loss on the disposal of the equipment. If the asset were the only one in its asset class at the time of its disposal, any proceeds in excess of the undepreciated capital cost (up to the amount of the original cost of the asset) would be considered as a recapture of capital cost allowance and would be taxed in the year of disposition at the ordinary tax rate. Should the proceeds be less than the undepreciated capital cost, the difference would be treated as additional capital cost allowance in the year of disposition.

If other assets remain in the asset class after disposing of the asset in question, no previously granted capital cost allowance will be recaptured in the year of disposition should salvage value exceed undepreciated capital cost. Such recapture will take place when (if ever) all assets in the class are disposed of. In the event that undepreciated capital cost exceeds the proceeds of disposition, capital cost allowance would continue to be authorized each year until all assets in the class have been disposed of (conceivably to infinity).

In the event that a used capital asset were to be sold for more than its original cost, the capital gains rate would apply to the difference between original cost and the proceeds from the disposition of the asset regardless of the number items in the asset class.

The same principles underlying the calculations in Part A of Illustration 15-2 are also applicable to Part B. By using the annuity table to calculate the present value of the inflows from cost savings, the time required to perform the calculations on a year by year basis has been reduced. Time also has been saved by the use of the Canadian declining balance CCA Tax Shield formula[6] to calculate the present value of the tax shield provided by the capital cost allowance relating to the asset. This formula[7] is:

$$P = \frac{CT}{R + C} \left[\left(\frac{2 + R}{2(1 + R)} \right) I - \frac{S}{(1 + R)^Y} \right]$$

---

[6] This formula is based on that explained in Robert Welch "The Effect on Capital Budgeting Decisions of Recent Changes in the CCA Calculation," *Cost and Management*, Volume 56 Number 3 (May/June, 1982), pp. 52-53.

[7] Note that the present value of the declining balance CCA tax shield which is given up ("lost") upon the disposition of an asset is the product of the terms:

$$\frac{CT}{R + C} \quad \bullet \quad \frac{S}{(1 + R)^Y}$$

EXCEPT that:

a.   If the asset is the last remaining item in the asset class at the time of disposition, use the balance remaining in the UCC pool for the asset class rather than the salvage value in those cases where there is a difference between the two amounts.

b.   If the asset is not the last remaining item at the time of disposition *and* it is sold for more than its original cost, use the *lower* of: (1) original cost *or* (2) the balance remaining in the UCC pool in lieu of the salvage value. (The reason for this is that the deduction can be no higher than the original cost as all proceeds above original cost are taxed as capital gains).

OR if the present value table (15A – 1) is used:

$$P = \frac{CT}{R + C} \left[\left(\frac{2 + R}{2 (1 + R)} \right) \; I - \text{Present Value of S in Year Y} \right]$$

Where:

P   is the present value of the tax shield provided by the CCA.
C   is the CCA rate.
T   is the tax rate.
R   is the required rate of return.
I   is the incremental investment (after deducting any investment tax credit).
S   is the salvage value.
Y   is the year of disposal.

Substituting the appropriate values in the formula, the present value of the capital cost allowance in this situation is equal to:

$$P = \left(\frac{(.30) (.45)}{(.16) + (.30)} \right) \left[\left(\frac{2 + .16}{2 (1 + .16)} \right) \; (200,000) - (.476) (40,817) \right]$$

$$P = \$48,946$$

The net present value of the equipment is a negative $48,644 or $48,641 depending upon whether the year-by-year or formula method is used to calculate the present value of the capital cost allowance tax shield. (The slight difference is due to rounding.) The present value of the outflows exceeds the present value of the inflows by that amount. Therefore, this potential investment is not expected to earn the required 16 percent after-tax return. Rather, the investment will earn something less than 16 percent. Had the net present value of the inflows exceeded the net present value of the outflows, then this investment could be expected to earn a rate of return in excess of 16 percent and would, therefore, have been an acceptable project for the company.

The net present value technique is the theoretically correct capital budgeting decision guide. It is not a ranking technique nor does it provide an answer that specifies the magnitude of the projected effective return on an investment.

**Present Value Index—
Making the Decision**

The present value or profitability index converts the present value of the inflows and outflows as determined by the net present value method into an index. To derive this index, the present value of the inflows is divided by the present value of the outflows. The higher the ratio, the higher the rate of return per dollar invested in the proposed project. A ratio of less than one indicates that a proposed project is expected to earn a return less than the desired rate of return. A proposed project with a present value index of one will earn exactly the desired rate of return, while a present value index greater than one indicates a return in excess of the desired rate of return.

The previously discussed net present value technique provides an answer stated in terms of current dollars. If only net present values are considered in selecting alternative projects, large dollar projects will normally have a net present value greater than that for small projects, even though the large projects may not be earning a rate of return as great as that earned by the small projects. The usefulness of the present value index is that different projects or investments can be ranked in terms of their relative profitability. The absolute dollar values for all projects can be converted to a relative measure of the profitability through the present value index. The present value index of the offset printing press in Illustration 15-2 is:

$$\text{Present Value Index} = \frac{\text{Present Value of Inflows}}{\text{Present Value of Outflows}}$$

$$= \frac{\$158,407}{\$207,051} = .765$$

An index of .765 indicates that the project will not earn the 16 percent rate of return or stated cost of capital.

Internal Rate of Return With Equal Cash Flows— Making the Decision

In the net present value technique discussed above, the required rate of return (cost of capital) is specified and the results indicate if the project will earn that rate, a greater rate or a smaller rate. However, the actual rate the project will earn is not determined. The internal rate of return or the time adjusted rate of return method determines the effective rate of return that a proposed project *will* earn over its expected life. The internal rate of return for the proposed project is then compared to the required rate of return to determine whether to accept or reject the project. The internal rate of return is that interest rate that equates the present value of the inflows with the present value of the outflows for the investment. The following example will illustrate the calculation of an approximation of the internal rate of return when the expected cash flows from a project are equal each period and therefore approximate an annuity.

Harry's Garage is considering purchasing a wheel alignment machine costing $16,000 to be placed into service in 1984. Harry estimates that this machine will generate $10,000 annually in additional revenues and will cost $6,000 to operate on an annual basis. The machine has an estimated life of ten years with no salvage value anticipated. Harry would like to know the effective annual rate of return on this machine on a before-tax basis.

To find the internal rate of return for Harry, the initial step is to determine the net annual before-tax cash flows generated by the wheel alignment machine.

FINISH THURS P.M.

Sales revenue (cash)............................	$10,000
Less: Operating costs (cash).....................	6,000
Net annual cash flow before taxes.............	$ 4,000

The internal rate of return is the rate of interest at which the present value of the cash inflows equals the present value of the outflows. In this example it is:

$$4,000 \times \text{Present Value of a 10 Year Annuity of \$1} =$$
$$16,000 \times \text{Present Value of \$1 in Year Zero}$$

Since the present value of $1 in Year Zero (today) is $1, the above equation becomes:

$$4,000 \times \text{Present Value of a 10 Year Annuity of \$1} = 16,000$$

Or

$$\text{Present Value of a 10 Year Annuity of \$1} = \frac{16,000}{4,000} = 4$$

Next, go to Table 15A-2 and scan horizontally the ten time period row (the life of the machine) to find the table value that approximates the value sought. A table factor of exactly four does not exist, but if it did, it would fall somewhere between 4.192 and 3.923, the amounts for the 20 and 22 percent columns. The actual rate of return on the wheel alignment machine is between 20 and 22 percent. Precision may be increased by interpolation between the two rates, but given the measure of uncertainty in the initial estimates, the range of the two rates is probably adequate in this case.

A proof of the solution for the internal rate of return for the wheel alignment machine is as follows:

Discounted at 22 percent	*Inflow*	*Outflow*
Initial costs.....................................		$16,000
Sales revenues ($10,000 × 3.923 × .5).............	$39,230	
Operating costs ($6,000 × 3.923 × .5).............		23,538
Present values...............................	$39,230	$39,538
Net present value.............................	($308)	

Discounted at 20 percent	*Inflow*	*Outflow*
Initial costs.....................................		$16,000
Sales revenues ($10,000 × 4.192 × .5).............	$41,920	
Operating costs ($6,000 × 4.192 × .5).............		25,152
Present values...............................	$41,920	$41,152
Net present value.............................	$768	

If the cash inflows and outflows are discounted at a rate of 22 percent, then it can be seen that the investment has a net present value of a negative $308 and therefore earns an internal rate of return of less than 22 percent. If the investment is discounted at 20 percent, the net present value is a positive $768. The discount factor which would make the present values of the inflows and outflows equal lies at some point between those two rates.

Internal Rate of Return With Unequal Cash Flows— Making the Decision

In the foregoing example, the effects of income taxes were ignored even though these taxes have a significant impact on most capital budgeting decisions. Likewise, the cash inflows resulting from the investment were assumed to approximate an annuity. Thus, the solution was readily obtained in a relatively straight-forward manner. Unfortunately, for ease of calculation, actual situations are seldom this simple.

While it is possible to program a computer to calculate internal rate of return, it is often more convenient and hence more practical to obtain the answer by manual means.

The first step is to make an estimate of the internal rate of return. This approximation is then used to calculate a net present value figure. Based on this, a second estimate is made and the net present value computed using this rate. As appropriate, additional estimates are made and net present values calculated until the desired degree of accuracy is obtained.

Obviously, the more accurate the initial estimate, the easier it will be to complete the solution. However, the use of overly sophisticated estimating techniques which are themselves time-consuming may well require more time and effort in the long-run than is saved, particularly if they do not reduce the number of trials that must be attempted to obtain the answer desired.

To illustrate the calculation of the internal rate of return with unequal cash flows, the Trembley Enterprises example from Illustration 15-2 is used. For convenience, the basic data are reproduced here:

> Initial Cost—$200,000
> 5 Year Life
> Salvage Value—$40,817
> Asset Class 28
> CCA—30%
> Overhaul at the End of 3 Years—$20,000
> Annual Operating Cost Savings—$50,000
> Tax Rate = 45%

The major outflow in this example is a one time payment in year zero, while the largest portion of the inflow results from the operating savings of approximately equal magnitude each year. Using this information and temporarily ignoring the remainder of the data, a very rough estimate of the rate of return before tax can be calculated using the technique shown in the preceding section:[8]

$$\frac{\text{Outflow}}{\text{Annual Inflow}} = \frac{\$200,000}{\$\ 50,000} = 4.0$$

Turning to the Present Value of an annuity table (Table 15A-2). In the five time period row, the table factor of 4 years falls between 4.1002 and 3.9927, the amounts for the 7 and 8 percent columns. If taxes were not a fact of life, it would be appropriate to use one of these two percentages as our trial discount rate. However, this is not the case and therefore adjustments are made to allow for the effect of taxes.[9]

Applying the percentage of cash available after taxes (1 minus the tax rate) to these before tax discount rates, reduces them to 3.85 percent and 4.4 percent, respectively. Since the rates in this portion of the table are denominated in whole numbers, 4 percent is used for the first trial. The net present value of the investment in this case would be a positive $10,757 calculated as follows:

Discounted at 4 percent

	Year	Before Tax	After Tax	PV Factor	Present Value
Inflows					
	1-5 Operating Savings	$ 50,000	$ 27,500	4.4518	$122,425
	1-5 CCA (from formula)				64,564
	5 Salvage Value	40,817	40,817	.8219	33,547
	Total Inflows:				$220,536
Outflows	0 Equipment Purchase	$200,000	$200,000	1.000	$200,000
	3 Operating Expense	20,000	11,000	.8890	9,779
	Total Outflows:				$209,779
	Net Present Value:				$ 10,757

The present value of the tax shield provided by the Capital Cost Allowance in this case is obtained by the previously described formula:

$$\left(\frac{CT}{R + C}\right) \left[\left(\frac{2 + R}{2(1 + R)}\right)(I) - (\text{present value of S in year Y})\right]$$

Substituting:

$$\frac{(.30) \times (.45)}{(.04) + (.30)} \left[\left(\frac{2 + .04}{2(1 + .04)}\right)(200,000) - (.8219)(40,817)\right] = \$64,564$$

---

[8] An alternative approach, which will not be covered, would entail solving the formula for the discount (interest) rate that would produce a zero net present value. That specific discount rate would be the internal rate of return.

[9] If it were not for the declining balance nature of the Canadian CCA tax shield a more accurate estimate might be obtained by calculating the net after tax cash flows for each year and using this figure to help choose the trial rate of return to be first attempted.

Since the net present value using 4 percent is a positive number, the actual rate of return must be somewhat higher. How much higher is unknown at this time. Nevertheless, it would be reasonable to try either of the next two percentages listed in the present value tables. Assuming that 6 percent is chosen, a net present value of negative $1,453 results:

Discounted at 6 percent

	Year	Before Tax	After Tax	PV Factor	Present Value
Inflows					
	1-5 Operating Savings	$ 50,000	$ 27,500	4.2124	$115,841
	1-5 CCA (from formula)				61,439
	5 Salvage Value	40,817	40,817	.7473	30,503
	Total Inflows:				$207,783
Outflows	0 Equipment				
	Purchase	$200,000	$200,000	1.000	$200,000
	3 Operating				
	Expense	20,000	11,000	.8396	9,236
	Total Outflows:				$209,236
	Net Present Value:				($1,453)

The present value of the CCA tax shield is:

$$\left(\frac{(.30) \times (.45)}{(.06) + (.30)}\right) \left[\left(\frac{2 + .06}{2 (1 + .06)}\right) (200,000) - (.7473)(40,817)\right] = \$61,439$$

Now knowing that the internal rate of return lies somewhere between 4 percent and 6 percent we next try 5 percent in order to obtain a more accurate answer.

Discounted at 5 percent

	Year	Before Tax	After Tax	PV Factor	Present Value
Inflows					
	1-5 Operating Savings	$ 50,000	$ 27,500	4.3295	$119,061
	1-5 CCA (from formula)				62,971
	5 Salvage Value	40,817	40,817	.7835	31,980
	Total Inflows:				$214,012
Outflows	0 Equipment				
	Purchase	$200,000	$200,000	1.000	$200,000
	3 Operating				
	Expense	20,000	11,000	.8638	9,502
	Total Outflows:				$209,502
	Net Present Value:				$ 4,510

The present value of the CCA tax shield is:

$$\frac{(.30) \times (.45)}{(.05) + (.30)} \left[\left(\frac{2 + .05}{2 (1 + .05)}\right) (200,000) - (.7835)(40,817)\right] = \$62,971$$

At 5 percent the net present value of the investment is a positive $4,510, while using the 6 percent discount rate produces a net present value of negative $1,453. Therefore, the internal rate of return must be between 5 percent and 6 percent. Unequal cash flows require calculating with different trial discount rates until the two adjacent rates are found that identify the crossover point of the net present value. That is, one rate produces a positive net present value and the adjacent rate produces a negative net present value. The "true" internal rate of return could be found by interpolation after finding the crossover point.

CONTROLLING THE PROJECT'S PROGRESS AND FUNDS

Once a capital investment decision has been made by management, the next step in the capital budgeting process becomes important. Control must be established over the resources committed to the project and over the progress of the project. A budget and cost record is established for each project of the firm. The budget and actual costs must agree if a budget overrun is to be avoided. The original capital expenditure proposal is based on the best information available at the time the proposal is initiated. Therefore, variances are to be expected, but the variances should be explainable. As a rule of thumb, large capital expenditures should have smaller variances on a percentage basis, because they justify more in-depth planning.

The progress of the project must also be closely monitored. Many capital expenditure projects are closely related to the activities of other segments of the organization. When this interrelationship exists, a delay in the completion of one project could cause problems in other segments of the organization. Project delays usually mean increased costs. Illustration 15-3 is an example of a format which may be used for a capital expenditure budget for a firm.

When a project is significantly off budget in terms of either dollars or time, an investigation should be undertaken. It may be necessary to revise the appropriation or the date of completion in order to coordinate expenditures for the entire firm.

A review of all on-going projects should be made on a regular basis. However, it is possible that a change in circumstances, technology, or economic conditions might warrant abandoning a capital investment project before its completion. The immediate losses resulting from abandonment may be less than the anticipated losses if the project is completed.

POST-AUDIT OF THE RESULTS OF THE DECISION

A post-audit of all major capital expenditures and a sample of the smaller expenditures should be made after completion of the projects in order to determine if the benefits expected from the projects did in fact accrue to the firm. There are certain problems associated with post-audits.

Illustration 15-3
Capital Expenditure Budget

				Sax Company			
				Capital Expenditure Budget for 1981			
Project Origination	Total Budgeted	Budgeted For This Year	Actual For This Year	Under (Over) For This Year	Under (Over) to Date	Estimated Under (Over) For Total Project	Comments
Corporate:							
Project No. 9457							
Project No. 9459							
Power Turbine Shaft:							
Project No. 9425							
Project No. 9426							
Filters:							
Project No. 8567							
Project No. 8973							
Project No. 9367							
Tanks:							
Project No. 9410							
Project No. 9411							
Total ($)							

Many expenditures are not independent of other operations, and the benefits derived from such expenditures are often neither easily nor objectively measurable. In addition, it may be necessary to convert the accounting records from an accrual basis to a cash flow basis if the original decision to make the expenditure was based on cash flows.

Post-audits can assist in identifying past mistakes made in planning capital expenditures, and can, hopefully, improve future inputs into this type of decision. In addition, the individuals responsible for preparing the estimates will probably be more cautious in their treatment of the capital expenditure decision when they are aware that their estimates will be reviewed upon the completion of the project and the subsequent start of operations.

SENSITIVITY ANALYSIS AND COST OF PREDICTION ERRORS

The cash flows that we have used in our capital budgeting models are only expected values. There is always the possibility that the actual cash flow will deviate from the expected cash flow. This possibility is called risk or uncertainty.

Sensitivity analysis attempts to analyze how susceptible a decision is to the uncertainty of the expected cash flows. Conceptually this means that expected cash flows should be examined in accordance with their probability distributions. However, in business decisions we are usually confronted with subjective probabilities as opposed to the objective probabilities we are used to in many gaming decisions. Therefore, the underlying probabilities and probability distributions are not capable of direct measurement but can only be estimated by expert opinion.

Alternative ways to allow for risk apart from estimating probability distributions include using (1) pessimistic predictions of cash flows, (2) shorter expected lives, (3) higher costs of capital, and (4) sensitivity analysis and cost of prediction errors.

As a start, assume that our estimates of the cash flows will not be completely accurate (because they are just that—estimates). It also follows that if we had known the actual cash flows when we were making the decision and with this true information the same decision would have been made, then our prediction errors did not cost the company anything. But if knowledge of the true parameters would have caused us to make some other decision, the cost of the prediction errors is measured by the incremental profit that would have been earned by making the alternative decision.

For example, assume that John decided to bet on a horse because he predicted that it would win by 10 lengths. Actual results are that the horse wins by 2 lengths. John's prediction error cost him nothing because if he had known the true parameter he would have made the same decision to bet the horse to win. However, in another example, John is trying to decide how many shoes to order for his store. Assume that he buys them for $15 and sells them for $25. Based upon his estimate that there is a demand for 100 of these shoes, John places his order accordingly. Actual demand is 110 customers. In this example there is a cost to John because of his prediction error. This is the opportunity cost of the lost sales. John could have made another $100 if he had known the true demand [10 shoes $\times$ ($25 − $15) = $100].

In summary, a decision is labeled as being very sensitive if very small errors in the estimated cash flows would lead to regret that the decision was made. A decision is considered very insensitive if there could be large errors in the predictions and the same decision would still be made. Finally, we recognize that prediction errors need not have a cost to the company if the less than perfect information still leads to the correct decision.

SUMMARY

The process of managing the demand for capital and planning the use of available capital is referred to as capital budgeting. Capital budgeting includes analyzing and selecting alternative long-range investments which insure that the firm will meet both current and future profitability demands. Information required in the capital budgeting process is based on both accrual accounting and cash flow data. In addition, a firm must consider the income tax implications of any investment under consideration.

The process of developing a capital budget on a project-by-project basis is divided into five basic steps: (1) initiating the idea and specifications; (2) reviewing the request; (3) making a decision regarding the request; (4) controlling the project progress and funds; and (5) conducting a post-audit of the results of the decision.

In making the decision regarding a particular capital investment request, a firm may choose to use various financial analysis techniques. The payback technique is a simple calculation which determines the amount of time required to recover, in cash, the initial net investment in an asset. The accountant's rate of return or unadjusted rate of return method is a measure of profitability, but does not consider the time value of money. Both the payback method and accountant's rate of return are tools that can be used to rank the relative desirability of alternative investments and are useful tools when employed along with other methods of analysis.

Capital budgeting techniques which consider the time value of money are referred to as discounted cash flow approaches. Among these techniques are the net present value technique, present value index and the internal rate of return technique. These approaches place emphasis on the timing and magnitude of cash flows. Since the predicted cash flows are only expected values, there is the risk or uncertainty that the actual cash flows will be different. Sensitivity and cost of prediction error analysis attempts to assess the seriousness of this risk or uncertainty.

APPENDIX: PRESENT VALUES

The Present Value Concept

When resources, usually cash, are invested there is an opportunity cost involved. An opportunity cost is defined as the income foregone by not choosing the next best alternative investment. When projects which require the use of resources are short-term, the opportunity cost is usually not substantial because the investment is only committed for a short period of time and will soon be converted back to cash and made available for possible reinvestment. When such projects have a long life, however, the cash inflows and outflows will occur over a long time period. The value of the cash flows over a long time period are not equal in terms of the value of a cash flow today (the present value).

The present value of $1 received today is $1 because it can be invested in assets with a value of $1 or deposited in a savings account to accumulate interest. The present value of $1 to be received one year from now is less than $1 because the opportunity to invest it and earn a return is lost for one year. The rational economic person would not give up $1 today to receive $1 a year from now because he could invest or save the $1 today and receive more than a $1 a year from now.

Calculating the Present Value of a Future Single Sum

The amount that would have to be invested today in order to receive $1 a year from now can be determined by using the following formula:

$$\text{Present Value} = \frac{\text{Future Value}}{(1 + \text{Interest Rate})^N}$$

(Where N = the number of time periods to receipt or payment.)

If an interest rate of 10 percent and an annual interest compounding period* are assumed, the numerical formula for the present value of $1 to be received one year from now is:

$$\text{Present Value} = \frac{\$1}{(1 + .10)^1}$$

$$= \frac{\$1}{1.10}$$

$$= \$.90909$$

The present value of $1 one year from now with annual compounding is $.90909. If a 10 percent return on investment could be earned, the rational economic person would consider receiving $.90909 today the same as receiving $1 one year from today, given all other factors are equal. The sum of $.90909 will equal $1 one year from now at a 10 percent annual compounding as can be seen from the following calculation.

$$
\begin{aligned}
\text{Future Value} &= \text{Present Value X } (1 + \text{Interest Rate})^N \\
&= \$.90909 \ (1 + .10)^1 \\
&= \$.90909 \text{ X } 1.10 \\
&= \$1.00 \ (\text{Rounded})
\end{aligned}
$$

---

* An interest compounding period is that period over which interest will be calculated. If the compounding period is one year on bank savings accounts and interest is stated at 4%, the interest on $1 for a year would be $1 × .04 = $.04. If interest is to be compounded semi-annually, the interest on one dollar for a year would be $1 × .02 = $.02 plus $1.02 × .02 = $.0204. The total interest would be $.0404 under semi-annual compounding. The additional $.0004 in interest with semi-annual compounding is the interest on the $.02 interest from the first-half of the year.

To illustrate the calculation of the present value of a lump sum payment occurring more than one interest period in the future, assume that an investor could earn 10 percent compounded annually on his investment. The investor needs to plan his investment so that at the end of 3 years, he will have accumulated enough funds to pay a debt of $1 due the third year. To determine what sum must be invested today in order to meet the debt of $1 three years from now, the present value formula can be solved as follows:

$$\text{Present Value} = \frac{\$1}{(1 + .10)^3}$$

$$\text{Present Value} = \frac{\$1}{1.331}$$

$$\text{Present Value} = \$.7513$$

The sum of $.7513 must be deposited at 10 percent interest compounded annually in order to produce one dollar at the end of three years. The calculation of interest per year and the total interest to date is presented in the following table.

Year	(1) Beginning of Year Principal and Accumulated Interest	$\times$	(2) Interest Rate	=	(3) Interest For This Year	(1) + (3) End of Year Principle and Accumulated Interest	Interest to Date
1	$.75130	$\times$	.10	=	$.07513	$ .82643	$.07513
2	.82643	$\times$	.10	=	.08264	.90907	.15777
3	.90907	$\times$	.10	=	.09097	1.00000	.24874

Fortunately, the calculations of present values do not have to be computed manually for each individual receipt or disbursement. Tables have been developed from the formulas that provide a present value factor for $1 for any time period and at any interest rate. Table 15A-1, Present Value of $1.00, is presented at the end of this Appendix. This table provides the present value factors for computing the present value of a lump sum amount to be received in some future number of periods discounted at a given interest rate.

To illustrate the use of Table 15A-1, assume that the present value of $1 is to be calculated at a 10 percent discount rate compounded annually for a three-year period. Go to Table 15A-1 in the 10 percent column and look down the row to the present value factor for three periods. The present value factor is 0.7513; therefore, the present value of $1 to be received three interest periods from today discounted at a rate of 10 percent is $1 X .7513 = $.7513.

Calculating the Present Value of an Annuity

An annuity is a series of equal payments or receipts of cash to be paid or received over a number of equal time periods. An ordinary annuity will have equal payments or receipts at the end of each equal time period. The present value of any stream of payments or receipts can be calculated using the present value formula for a single sum or Table 15A-1 and computing the present value for each amount for each time period. Alternatively, the present value of an annuity table (Table 15A-2) may be used to find the present value of the cash stream.

Assume that $1 is to be received at the end of each year for the next three years and interest is to be calculated at 10 percent compounded annually. There are several ways that the present value of this cash flow can be computed. Two ways to compute the present value were discussed in the prior section of this Appendix when the present value of a single sum was calculated.

Alternative One:

The present value of the total stream can be calculated by using the present value formula.

$$\text{Present Value} = \frac{\$1}{(1 + .10)^1} + \frac{\$1}{(1 + .10)^2} + \frac{\$1}{(1 + .10)^3}$$

$$\text{Present Value} = \frac{\$1}{1.10} + \frac{\$1}{1.21} + \frac{\$1}{1.331}$$

$$\text{Present Value} = \$.9091 + \$.8264 + \$.7513$$

$$\text{Present Value} = \$2.4868$$

Alternative Two:

The present value can be calculated using Table 15A-1.

Inflows	×	Present Value Factors	=	Present Value
$1	×	.9091	=	$ .9091
$1	×	.8264	=	.8264
$1	×	.7513	=	.7513
$1	×	2.4868	=	$2.4868

The third alternative is to use Table 15A-2, Present Value of Annuity of $1.00 per Period, at the end of this Appendix. Table 15A-2 is a summation of Table 15A-1. To understand this look at the present value factors for 10 percent for one time period on both Tables. They are both .9091. Now look at the present value factors for two time periods at 10 percent. In Table 15A-1, the present value factor is 0.8264. In Table 15A-2, the present value factor is 1.7355; the sum of the first time period factor of 0.9091 plus the second time period factor of 0.8264 from Table 15A-1.

If the present value of a $1 annuity at the end of each year for three years is to be calculated using Table 15A-2, look at the 10 percent column and the row for the three periods to find the present value factor of 2.4869. *One* annuity payment or receipt is multiplied by the present value factor to compute the present value of the annuity, in this case $1 × 2.4869 = $2.4869. There is a slight rounding difference (at the fourth decimal point) between alternatives one and two as compared to alternative three.

KEY DEFINITIONS

Accountant's rate of return—a measure of the profitability of various capital expenditures which expresses the related incremental increases in income as a percentage of the net original or average investment outlay.

Asset class—a specified group of assets which have the same capital cost allowance.

Capital budgeting—a process of planning and managing the investment of the firm's capital on a long-term basis. A capital budget includes a listing and analysis of all investment alternatives in which the firm is considering investing its supply of capital.

Capital Cost Allowance (CCA)—the statutory allowances for depreciation specified in the *Income Tax Act* for various classes of assets.

Cost of capital—the minimum acceptable rate of return (usually on an after-tax basis) required by the management of a firm to be earned by a capital expenditure.

Cost of prediction error—is measured by the incremental profit that would have been earned by making the alternative decision.

Internal rate of return—that interest rate which, when used to discount the cash flows, will make the present value of the inflows exactly equal to the present value of the outflows of the investment.

Investment Tax Credit—a statutory percentage of the cost of an asset which may be applied as a credit against taxes that would otherwise be payable.

Net present value method—technique that discounts all projected cash outflows and inflows related to a capital project back to the present period using the cost of capital as the discount rate.

Payback method—a technique used to consider alternative capital expenditures which does not measure profitability but merely calculates the amount of time required to recover the initial net investment in an asset.

Post-audit—a review of major capital expenditures made after the completion of a project in order to determine if benefits actually accrued to the firm as planned.

Present value index—a relative measure of profitability for ranking capital investment projects which is computed by dividing the present value of inflows by the present value of outflows.

Sensitivity analysis—attempts to assess the possible effects of risk or uncertainty on predicted cash flows.

Undepreciated Capital Cost (UCC)—the balance remaining in the capital cost allowance account for each class of assets after deducting all capital cost allowances taken.

Table 15A-1

Present Value of $1.00

Periods (n)	1%	1½%	2%	2½%	3%	3½%	4%	4½%	5%	6%	7%	8%	10%
1	0.9901	0.9852	0.9804	0.9756	0.9709	0.9662	0.9615	0.9569	0.9524	0.9434	0.9346	0.9259	0.9091
2	0.9803	0.9707	0.9612	0.9518	0.9426	0.9335	0.9246	0.9157	0.9070	0.8900	0.8734	0.8573	0.8264
3	0.9706	0.9563	0.9423	0.9286	0.9151	0.9019	0.8890	0.8763	0.8638	0.8396	0.8163	0.7938	0.7513
4	0.9610	0.9422	0.9238	0.9060	0.8885	0.8714	0.8548	0.8386	0.8227	0.7921	0.7629	0.7350	0.6830
5	0.9515	0.9283	0.9057	0.8839	0.8626	0.8420	0.8219	0.8025	0.7835	0.7473	0.7130	0.6806	0.6209
6	0.9420	0.9145	0.8880	0.8623	0.8375	0.8135	0.7903	0.7679	0.7462	0.7050	0.6663	0.6302	0.5645
7	0.9327	0.9010	0.8706	0.8413	0.8131	0.7860	0.7599	0.7348	0.7107	0.6651	0.6227	0.5835	0.5132
8	0.9235	0.8877	0.8535	0.8207	0.7894	0.7594	0.7307	0.7032	0.6768	0.6274	0.5820	0.5403	0.4665
9	0.9143	0.8746	0.8368	0.8007	0.7664	0.7337	0.7026	0.6729	0.6446	0.5919	0.5439	0.5002	0.4241
10	0.9053	0.8617	0.8203	0.7812	0.7441	0.7089	0.6756	0.6439	0.6139	0.5584	0.5083	0.4632	0.3855
11	0.8963	0.8489	0.8043	0.7621	0.7224	0.6849	0.6496	0.6162	0.5847	0.5268	0.4751	0.4289	0.3505
12	0.8874	0.8364	0.7885	0.7436	0.7014	0.6618	0.6246	0.5897	0.5568	0.4970	0.4440	0.3971	0.3186
13	0.8787	0.8240	0.7730	0.7254	0.6810	0.6394	0.6006	0.5643	0.5303	0.4688	0.4150	0.3677	0.2897
14	0.8700	0.8118	0.7579	0.7077	0.6611	0.6178	0.5775	0.5400	0.5051	0.4423	0.3878	0.3405	0.2633
15	0.8613	0.7999	0.7430	0.6905	0.6419	0.5969	0.5553	0.5167	0.4810	0.4173	0.3624	0.3153	0.2394
16	0.8528	0.7880	0.7284	0.6736	0.6232	0.5767	0.5339	0.4945	0.4581	0.3936	0.3387	0.2919	0.2176
17	0.8444	0.7764	0.7142	0.6572	0.6050	0.5572	0.5134	0.4732	0.4363	0.3714	0.3166	0.2703	0.1978
18	0.8360	0.7649	0.7002	0.6412	0.5874	0.5384	0.4936	0.4528	0.4155	0.3503	0.2959	0.2502	0.1799
19	0.8277	0.7536	0.6864	0.6255	0.5703	0.5202	0.4746	0.4333	0.3957	0.3305	0.2765	0.2317	0.1635
20	0.8195	0.7425	0.6730	0.6103	0.5537	0.5026	0.4564	0.4146	0.3769	0.3118	0.2584	0.2145	0.1486
21	0.8114	0.7315	0.6598	0.5954	0.5375	0.4856	0.4388	0.3968	0.3589	0.2942	0.2415	0.1987	0.1351
22	0.8034	0.7207	0.6468	0.5809	0.5219	0.4692	0.4220	0.3797	0.3418	0.2775	0.2257	0.1839	0.1228
23	0.7954	0.7100	0.6342	0.5667	0.5067	0.4533	0.4057	0.3634	0.3256	0.2618	0.2109	0.1703	0.1117
24	0.7876	0.6995	0.6217	0.5529	0.4919	0.4380	0.3901	0.3477	0.3101	0.2470	0.1971	0.1577	0.1015
25	0.7798	0.6892	0.6095	0.5394	0.4776	0.4231	0.3751	0.3327	0.2953	0.2330	0.1842	0.1460	0.0923
26	0.7720	0.6790	0.5976	0.5262	0.4637	0.4088	0.3607	0.3184	0.2812	0.2198	0.1722	0.1352	0.0839
27	0.7644	0.6690	0.5859	0.5134	0.4502	0.3950	0.3468	0.3047	0.2678	0.2074	0.1609	0.1252	0.0763
28	0.7568	0.6591	0.5744	0.5009	0.4371	0.3817	0.3335	0.2916	0.2551	0.1956	0.1504	0.1159	0.0693
29	0.7493	0.6494	0.5631	0.4887	0.4243	0.3687	0.3207	0.2790	0.2429	0.1846	0.1406	0.1073	0.0630
30	0.7419	0.6398	0.5521	0.4767	0.4120	0.3563	0.3083	0.2670	0.2314	0.1741	0.1314	0.0994	0.0573
40	0.6717	0.5513	0.4529	0.3724	0.3066	0.2526	0.2083	0.1719	0.1420	0.0972	0.0668	0.0460	0.0221
50	0.6080	0.4750	0.3715	0.2909	0.2281	0.1791	0.1407	0.1107	0.0872	0.0543	0.0339	0.0213	0.0085

Table 15A-1 (Continued)
Present Value of $1.00

12%	14%	15%	16%	18%	20%	22%	24%	25%	26%	28%	30%	40%	50%
0.893	0.877	0.870	0.862	0.847	0.833	0.820	0.806	0.800	0.794	0.781	0.769	0.714	0.667
0.797	0.769	0.756	0.743	0.718	0.694	0.672	0.650	0.640	0.630	0.610	0.592	0.510	0.444
0.712	0.675	0.658	0.641	0.609	0.579	0.551	0.524	0.512	0.500	0.477	0.455	0.364	0.296
0.636	0.592	0.572	0.552	0.516	0.482	0.451	0.423	0.410	0.397	0.373	0.350	0.260	0.198
0.567	0.519	0.497	0.476	0.437	0.402	0.370	0.341	0.328	0.315	0.291	0.269	0.186	0.132
0.507	0.456	0.432	0.410	0.370	0.335	0.303	0.275	0.262	0.250	0.227	0.207	0.133	0.088
0.452	0.400	0.376	0.354	0.314	0.279	0.249	0.222	0.210	0.198	0.178	0.159	0.095	0.059
0.404	0.351	0.327	0.305	0.266	0.233	0.204	0.179	0.168	0.157	0.139	0.123	0.068	0.039
0.361	0.308	0.284	0.263	0.225	0.194	0.167	0.144	0.134	0.125	0.108	0.094	0.048	0.026
0.322	0.270	0.247	0.227	0.191	0.162	0.137	0.116	0.107	0.099	0.085	0.073	0.035	0.017
0.287	0.237	0.215	0.195	0.162	0.135	0.112	0.094	0.086	0.079	0.066	0.056	0.025	0.012
0.257	0.208	0.187	0.168	0.137	0.112	0.092	0.076	0.069	0.062	0.052	0.043	0.018	0.008
0.229	0.182	0.163	0.145	0.116	0.093	0.075	0.061	0.055	0.050	0.040	0.033	0.013	0.005
0.205	0.160	0.141	0.125	0.099	0.078	0.062	0.049	0.044	0.039	0.032	0.025	0.009	0.003
0.183	0.140	0.123	0.108	0.084	0.065	0.051	0.040	0.035	0.031	0.025	0.020	0.006	0.002
0.163	0.123	0.107	0.093	0.071	0.054	0.042	0.032	0.028	0.025	0.019	0.015	0.005	0.002
0.146	0.108	0.093	0.080	0.060	0.045	0.034	0.026	0.023	0.020	0.015	0.012	0.003	0.001
0.130	0.095	0.081	0.069	0.051	0.038	0.028	0.021	0.018	0.016	0.012	0.009	0.002	0.001
0.116	0.083	0.070	0.060	0.043	0.031	0.023	0.017	0.014	0.012	0.009	0.007	0.002	
0.104	0.073	0.061	0.051	0.037	0.026	0.019	0.014	0.012	0.010	0.007	0.005	0.001	
0.093	0.064	0.053	0.044	0.031	0.022	0.015	0.011	0.009	0.008	0.006	0.004	0.001	
0.083	0.056	0.046	0.038	0.026	0.018	0.013	0.009	0.007	0.006	0.004	0.003	0.001	
0.074	0.049	0.040	0.033	0.022	0.015	0.010	0.007	0.006	0.005	0.003	0.002		
0.066	0.043	0.035	0.028	0.019	0.013	0.008	0.006	0.005	0.004	0.003	0.002		
0.059	0.038	0.030	0.024	0.016	0.010	0.007	0.005	0.004	0.003	0.002	0.001		
0.053	0.033	0.026	0.021	0.014	0.009	0.006	0.004	0.003	0.002	0.002	0.001		
0.047	0.029	0.023	0.018	0.011	0.007	0.005	0.003	0.002	0.002	0.001	0.001		
0.042	0.026	0.020	0.016	0.010	0.006	0.004	0.002	0.002	0.002	0.001	0.001		
0.037	0.022	0.017	0.014	0.008	0.005	0.003	0.002	0.002	0.002	0.001	0.001		
0.033	0.020	0.015	0.012	0.007	0.004	0.003	0.002	0.001	0.001	0.001			
0.011	0.005	0.004	0.003	0.001	0.001								
0.003	0.001	0.001	0.001										

Table 15A-2

Present Value of Annuity of $1.00 Per Period

Periods (n)	1%	1½%	2%	2½%	3%	3½%	4%	4½%	5%	6%	7%
1....	0.9901	0.9852	0.9804	0.9756	0.9709	0.9662	0.9615	0.9569	0.9524	0.9434	0.9346
2....	1.9704	1.9559	1.9416	1.9274	1.9135	1.8997	1.8861	1.8727	1.8594	1.8334	1.8080
3....	2.9410	2.9122	2.8839	2.8560	2.8286	2.8016	2.7751	2.7490	2.7232	2.6730	2.6243
4....	3.9020	3.8544	3.8077	3.7620	3.7171	3.6731	3.6299	3.5875	3.5460	3.4651	3.3872
5....	4.8534	4.7826	4.7135	4.6458	4.5797	4.5151	4.4518	4.3900	4.3295	4.2124	4.1002
6....	5.7955	5.6972	5.6014	5.5081	5.4172	5.3286	5.2421	5.1579	5.0757	4.9173	4.7665
7....	6.7282	6.5982	6.4720	6.3494	6.2303	6.1145	6.0021	5.8927	5.7864	5.5824	5.3893
8....	7.6517	7.4859	7.3255	7.1701	7.0197	6.8740	6.7327	6.5959	6.4632	6.2098	5.9713
9....	8.5660	8.3605	8.1622	7.9709	7.7861	7.6077	7.4353	7.2688	7.1078	6.8017	6.5152
10....	9.4713	9.2222	8.9826	8.7521	8.5302	8.3166	8.1109	7.9127	7.7217	7.3601	7.0236
11....	10.3676	10.0711	9.7868	9.5142	9.2526	9.0016	8.7605	8.5289	8.3064	7.8869	7.4987
12....	11.2551	10.9075	10.5753	10.2578	9.9540	9.6633	9.3851	9.1186	8.8633	8.3838	7.9427
13....	12.1337	11.7315	11.3484	10.9832	10.6350	10.3027	9.9856	9.6829	9.3936	8.8527	8.3577
14....	13.0037	12.5434	12.1062	11.6909	11.2961	10.9205	10.5631	10.2228	9.8986	9.2950	8.7455
15....	13.8651	13.3432	12.8493	12.3814	11.9379	11.5174	11.1184	10.7395	10.3797	9.7122	9.1079
16....	14.7179	14.1313	13.5777	13.0550	12.5611	12.0941	11.6523	11.2340	10.8378	10.1059	9.4466
17....	15.5623	14.9076	14.2919	13.7122	13.1661	12.6513	12.1657	11.7072	11.2741	10.4773	9.7632
18....	16.3983	15.6726	14.9920	14.3534	13.7535	13.1897	12.6593	12.1600	11.6896	10.8276	10.0591
19....	17.2260	16.4262	15.6785	14.9789	14.3238	13.7098	13.1339	12.5933	12.0853	11.1581	10.3356
20....	18.0456	17.1686	16.3514	15.5892	14.8775	14.2124	13.5903	13.0079	12.4622	11.4699	10.5940
21....	18.8570	17.9001	17.0112	16.1845	15.4150	14.6980	14.0292	13.4047	12.8212	11.7640	10.8355
22....	19.6604	18.6208	17.6580	16.7654	15.9369	15.1671	14.4511	13.7844	13.1630	12.0416	11.0612
23....	20.4558	19.3309	18.2922	17.3321	16.4436	15.6204	14.8568	14.1478	13.4886	12.3034	11.2722
24....	21.2434	20.0304	18.9139	17.8850	16.9355	16.0584	15.2470	14.4955	13.7986	12.5504	11.4693
25....	22.0232	20.7196	19.5235	18.4244	17.4131	16.4815	15.6221	14.8282	14.0939	12.7834	11.6536
26....	22.7952	21.3986	20.1210	18.9506	17.8768	16.8904	15.9828	15.1466	14.3752	13.0032	11.8258
27....	23.5596	22.0676	20.7069	19.4640	18.3270	17.2854	16.3296	15.4513	14.6430	13.2105	11.9867
28....	24.3164	22.7267	21.2813	19.9649	18.7641	17.6670	15.6631	15.7429	14.8981	13.4062	12.1371
29....	25.0658	23.3761	21.8444	20.4535	19.1885	18.0358	1o.9837	16.0219	15.1411	13.5907	12.2777
30....	25.8077	24.0158	22.3965	20.9303	19.6004	18.3920	17.2920	16.2889	15.3725	13.7648	12.4090
40....	32.8347	29.9158	27.3555	25.1028	23.1148	21.3551	19.7928	18.4016	17.1591	15.0463	13.3317
50....	39.1961	34.9997	31.4236	28.3623	25.7298	23.4556	21.4822	19.7620	18.2559	15.7619	13.8007

Table 15A-2 (Continued)
Present Value of Annuity of $1.00 Per Period

8%	10%	12%	14%	15%	16%	18%	20%	22%	24%	25%	26%	28%	30%	40%	50%
0.9259	0.9091	0.893	0.877	0.870	0.862	0.847	0.833	0.820	0.806	0.800	0.794	0.781	0.769	0.714	0.667
1.7833	1.7355	1.690	1.647	1.626	1.605	1.566	1.528	1.492	1.457	1.440	1.424	1.392	1.361	1.224	1.111
2.5771	2.4869	2.402	2.322	2.283	2.246	2.174	2.106	2.042	1.981	1.952	1.923	1.868	1.816	1.589	1.407
3.3121	3.1699	3.037	2.914	2.855	2.798	2.690	2.589	2.494	2.404	2.362	2.320	2.241	2.166	1.849	1.605
3.9927	3.7908	3.605	3.433	3.352	3.274	3.127	2.991	2.864	2.745	2.689	2.635	2.532	2.436	2.035	1.737
4.6229	4.3553	4.111	3.889	3.784	3.685	3.498	3.326	3.167	3.020	2.951	2.885	2.759	2.643	2.168	1.824
5.2064	4.8684	4.564	4.288	4 160	4.039	3.812	3.605	3.416	3.242	3.161	3.083	2.937	2.802	2.263	1.883
5.7466	5.3349	4.968	4.639	4.487	4.344	4.078	3.837	3.619	3.421	3.329	3.241	3.076	2.925	2.331	1.922
6.2469	5.7590	5.328	4.946	4.772	4.607	4.303	4.031	3.786	3.566	3.463	3.366	3.184	3.019	2.379	1.948
6.7101	6.1446	5.650	5.216	5.019	4.833	4.494	4.192	3.923	3.682	3.571	3.465	3.269	3.092	2.414	1.965
7.1390	6.4951	5.988	5.453	5.234	5.029	4.656	4.327	4.035	3.776	3.656	3.544	3.335	3.147	2.438	1.977
7.5361	6.8137	6.194	5.660	5.421	5.197	4.793	4.439	4.127	3.851	3.725	3.606	3.387	3.190	2.456	1.985
7.9038	7.1034	6.424	5.842	5.583	5.342	4.910	4.533	4.203	3.912	3.780	3.656	3.427	3.223	2.468	1.990
8.2442	7.3667	6.628	6.002	5.724	5.468	5.008	4.611	4.265	3.962	3.824	3.695	3.459	3.249	2.477	1.993
8.5595	7.6061	6.811	6.142	5.847	5.575	5.092	4.675	4.315	4.001	3.859	3.726	3.483	3.268	2.484	1.995
8.8514	7.8237	6.974	6.265	5.954	5.669	5.162	4.730	4.357	4.033	3.887	3.751	3.503	3.283	2.489	1.997
9.1216	8.0216	7.120	6.373	6.047	5.749	5.222	4.775	4.391	4.059	3.910	3.771	3.518	3.295	2.492	1.998
9.3719	8.2014	7.250	6.467	6.128	5.818	5.273	4.812	4.419	4.080	3.928	3.786	3.529	3.304	2.494	1.999
9.6036	8.3649	7.366	6.550	6.198	5.877	5.316	4.844	4.442	4.097	3.942	3.799	3.539	3.311	2.496	1.999
9.8181	8.5136	7.469	6.623	6.259	5.929	5.353	4.870	4.460	4.110	3.954	3.808	3.546	3.316	2.497	1.999
10.0168	8.6487	7.562	6.687	6.312	5.973	5.384	4.891	4.476	4.121	3.963	3.816	3.551	3.320	2.498	2.000
10.2007	8.7715	7.645	6.743	6.359	6.011	5.410	4.909	4.488	4.130	3.970	3.822	3.556	3.323	2.498	2.000
10.3711	8.8832	7.718	6.792	6.399	6.044	5.432	4.925	4.499	4.137	3.976	3.827	3.559	3.325	2.499	2.000
10.5288	8.9847	7.784	6.835	6.434	6.073	5.451	4.937	4.507	4.143	3.981	3.831	3.562	3.327	2.499	2.000
10.6748	9.0770	7.843	6.873	6.464	6.097	5.467	4.948	4.514	4.147	3.985	3.834	3.564	3.329	2.499	2.000
10.8100	9.1609	7.896	6.906	6.491	6.118	5.480	4.956	4.520	4.151	3.988	3.837	3.566	3.330	2.500	2.000
10.9352	9.2372	7.943	6.935	6.514	6.136	5.492	4.964	4.524	4.154	3.990	3.839	3.567	3.331	2.500	2.000
11.0511	9.3066	7.984	6.961	6.534	6.152	5.502	4.970	4.528	4.157	3.992	3.840	3.568	3.331	2.500	2.000
11.1584	9.3696	8.022	6.983	6.551	6.166	5.510	4.975	4.531	4.159	3.994	3.841	3.569	3.332	2.500	2.000
11.2578	9.4269	8.055	7.003	6.566	6.177	5.517	4.979	4.534	4.160	3.995	3.842	3.569	3.332	2.500	2.000
11.9246	9.7791	8.244	7.105	6.642	6.234	5.548	4.997	4.544	4.166	3.999	3.846	3.571	3.333	2.500	2.000
12.2335	9.9148	8.304	7.133	6.661	6.246	5.554	4.999	4.545	4.167	4.000	3.846	3.571	3.333	2.500	2.000

Table 15B
Maximum Capital Cost Allowance Rates*

1. Classes for which declining balance method is specified and the "half rate in the first year" rule applies:

Class 1	4%
Class 2	6%
Class 3	5%
Class 4	6%
Class 5	10%
Class 6	10%
Class 7	15%
Class 8	20%
Class 9	25%
Class 10	30%
Class 11	35%
Class 12	100%
Class 16	40%
Class 17	8%
Class 18	60%
Class 22	50%
Class 23	100%
Class 25	100%
Class 26	5%
Class 28	30%
Class 30	40%
Class 31	5%
Class 32	10%
Class 33	15%
Class 35	7%
Class 37	15%

2. Classes for which straight-line method is specified and the "half rate in the first year" rule does *not* apply:

Class 13	5 years (useful life if shorter)
Class 14	useful life of asset
Class 19	2 or 5 years (depends on taxpayer's status)
Class 20	2 or 5 years (depends on taxpayer's status)
Class 21	2 years

3. Classes for which straight-line method is specified and the "half rate in the first year" rule applies unless acquired before November 13, 1981:

Class 24	50%
Class 27	50%
Class 29	50%
Class 34	50%

4. Class for which units of production method is specified:

Class 15	(timber)

5. Special situation:

Class 36

---

*This is a somewhat simplified version of the regulations and should be used for instructional purposes only.

QUESTIONS

15-1 Define capital budgeting. Is it used for short or long-term planning? Explain.

15-2 How is the investment tax credit treated on the federal income tax return? Why did the federal government place into tax law this type of credit?

15-3 Name three ways in which the initiation of a capital expenditure may come about. Who or what governs the format and channels of a capital budget request in a large firm?

15-4 Who normally makes the ultimate decision on a major capital expenditure? If the expenditure is not a major one, who may make the ultimate decision instead?

15-5 When is the "no choice" or urgency technique for making a decision justified? Why is this technique considered the least favorable of the capital budgeting techniques?

15-6 What is the primary purpose of using the payback technique in making a capital budgeting decision?

15-7 What are two similarities between the payback technique and the accountant's rate of return when used to make a decision?

15-8 Using the net present value technique, how does one decide whether the project is acceptable or not?

15-9 What are some of the ways management allows for risk or uncertainty in capital budgeting decisions?

15-10 What is meant by sensitivity analysis?

15-11 Why is the cost of prediction errors often considered an opportunity cost?

**EXERCISES
AND PROBLEMS**

15-12   Compute the net present value of these three individual cases at a rate of 10%.

	Outlay	Future Period Inflows			
	0	1	2	3	4
A	($2,000)	$1,150		$1,150	
B	($2,000)	$1,150			$1,150
C	($2,000)		$1,150	$1,150	

Required:

a. Which of these three investments is the most desirable?

b. Which is more desirable using 6% interest?

15-13   Compute the internal rate of return for each of the following independent investments.

	Outlay	Future Period Inflows		
	0	1	2	3
A	($3,000)	$1,575		$1,735
B	($3,000)	$1,500	$1,780	
C	($3,000)		$1,700	$1,690

Required:

If the investments are mutually exclusive, which one would you choose?

15-14   Compute the payback period for each of these independent cases.

	Cost of Investment	Cash Proceeds per Year
A	$20,000	$5,000
B	$15,000	$3,000
C	$24,000	$8,000

Required:

Based on this information, which of these investments is the best?

15-15   The James Company purchased a machine several years ago for $20,000. Its book value is $8,000. The company is considering purchasing a new machine for $22,500. The salvage value of the old machine at this time is $3,275. Ignoring taxes, what is the net cash outlay for the new asset?

15-16   Weido, Inc. is considering the purchase of a new machine for $2,200. The machine has a life of 5 years and a salvage value of $200. It will be depreciated on a straight-line basis. Cash inflows will be:

Year	Inflows
1	$ 600
2	800
3	500
4	750
5	650
Total	$3,300

Required:

Determine the accountant's rate of return using:

a.   the original investment
b.   the average investment

15-17   A nonprofit organization is considering the purchase of a certain depreciable capital asset. The asset costs $10,000.

It is expected that the asset will bring an incremental increase in annual net income of $3,500 for each year of its five-year life. The desired discount rate is 10%. Since it is a nonprofit organization, income taxes and depreciation are ignored.

Required:

a. What is the payback period?
b. What is the accountant's rate of return on original investment?
c. What is the net present value of the investment?
d. What is the present value index?

15-18   You are considering an outlay of X dollars which will produce an annual benefit of Y dollars per year for Z years. Your cost of capital is 10%.

Use the following alternative choices to answer *a* to *c* below:

1. 0%
2. exactly 10%
3. equal to or greater than 10%
4. equal to or less than 10%
5. greater than 10%
6. less than 10%
7. none of the above
8. cannot determine from the data given

a. If the present value of the Y dollars per year for Z years is X dollars, the return from the investment is _____.
b. If the present value of the Y dollars per year for Z years is X + 1 dollars, the return from the investment is _____.
c. If the present value of the Y dollars per year for Z years is X—1 dollars, the return from the investment is _____.

15-19   Jess, Inc. is considering purchasing a new telephone switching device for $18,000. It will have a useful life of 10 years (salvage value of $3,000).

The old machine, which cost $15,000, has been in use for 5 of its 15-year useful life. It is not expected to have any salvage value at the end of 15 years. At the present time, the machine can be sold for $9,000. Its undepreciated capital cost is $10,316.

The company's cost of capital is 12 percent. The tax rate is 40 percent. The new machine will save the company $2,500 per year. Both machines are among several in asset class 17. CCA is 8 percent.

Required:

Using the net present value method, decide whether the company should purchase the new machine.

15-20   A firm is considering the purchase of a new piece of equipment. Below are the basic data relevant to this purchase.

Initial cost—$24,000
10-year useful life
Salvage value—$2,000
Asset Class 7 (CCA is 15%). The firm has other assets in this class.
Overhaul at the end of year four—$5,000 (deductible in year 4).

Operating cost savings—$7,000 per year
Tax rate—40%

Required:

Determine this equipment's internal rate of return. Round to the nearest dollar.

15-21   A company is considering purchasing a new machine for $12,000. The new machine will have a useful life of 10 years and a salvage value of $2,000.

   The old machine, which cost $10,000, also has a useful life of 10 more years but for tax purposes the remaining UCC is only $1,500. It can be sold for $500 at the present time.

   The company's cost of capital is 10% and the tax rate is 40%. The new machine will save the company $2,000 per year. Both machines are among several in asset class 5. CCA is 10%.

Required:

Using the net present value method, decide whether the company should purchase the new machine.

15-22   The Fattening Donuts Company was deciding what size fryer to purchase. Machine A is capable of producing 120 donuts per minute while machine B can produce 180 donuts per minute. It has been calculated that Machine A will produce a cash flow savings of $400 each year for 5 years, while machine B will produce a cash flow savings of $100 the first year and that amount will double each year through the fifth year. Machine A can be purchased for $1,400 while the cost of machine B is $1,800.

Required:

a.   Calculate the payback period of both machines using the average cash inflows.
b.   Given the results of "a" above, which machine should be purchased?

15-23   Bob, the barber, was considering purchasing a new machine that would be used to stimulate the scalp and speed hair growth. Faster hair growth would mean more hair cuts and increased revenues. The machine costs $1,700 and has a useful life of 4 years with a salvage value of $100. The expected cash inflows that will be generated are:

Year	Inflows
1	$ 600
2	$ 700
3	$ 600
4	$ 500
	$2,400

Required:

Determine the accountant's rate of return using:

a. the original investment
b. the average investment.

15-24 Determine the present value of $1,000 due in five years at each of the following interest rates:

a. 6 percent
b. 8 percent
c. 10 percent

15-25 An investor wishes to have $5,000 available at the end of five years. State the amount of money that must be invested at the present time if the interest rate is:

a. 6 percent
b. 8 percent
c. 12 percent

15-26 Determine the present value of an annuity for a period of five years with annual payments of $2,000, assuming that the interest rate is:

a. 7 percent
b. 10 percent
c. 12 percent

15-27 What is the maximum amount you would be willing to pay at the present time in order to receive 10 annual payments of $1,000 beginning one year from now? The current interest rate is 10 percent.

15-28 The Acme Company is currently using a machine which was purchased three years ago at a cost of $8,000. It was assigned a useful life of 8 years and a salvage value of $600. Its UCC is now $4,618. The company is considering replacing this machine with a new machine which would cost $9,000. The new machine would have a useful life of 5 years and a salvage value of $1,000. Both machines are in asset class 8. CCA is 20 percent.

With the new machine, expected direct labour savings would be $1,250 per year for the 5 years. The old machine can be sold immediately for $3,500.

The tax rate is 40 percent. The cost of capital (or rate of discount) is 16 percent. The company owns other machines in the same asset class.

Required:

Determine the following as they relate to the purchase of the new machine.

a. Net cash flow per year
b. Present value of the net outlay
c. Pay back period
d. Advantage (or disadvantage) of the new machine (in present value)

15-29 Rental, Inc. is considering the purchase of six garden tillers to add to those in its rental fleet. The following estimates have been made:

Cost of six tillers........................	$15,000
Rental receipts (annual).................	12,000
Expenses:	
Maintenance	3,000
Advertising on U.S. television...........	800
Salvage value at end of 5 years.............	0
Asset class............................	10
Capital cost allowance..................	30%

Assume that advertising is not a deductible expense for tax purposes and that a 40% tax rate applies to all other revenue and expense items.

Required:

a. Determine the after-tax cash flow per year.
b. Find the net present value of the investment (assume a 14% cost of capital).
c. Find the internal rate of return of the investment.

15-30 The Dizzy Company is considering a new mixing machine. They have narrowed the decision down to two choices but are unsure how to arrive at a final decision. It is your job to analyze the two machines so that the management of Dizzy can make their final decision. Assume a 40 percent tax rate, and a 10 percent cost of capital. The asset class is 10. CCA is 30 percent. There are other assets in the same class.

	Machine A	Machine B
Cost	$47,000	$60,000
Useful life	5 years	5 years
Salvage value	$ 2,000	–0–
Annual before-tax cost savings	$14,500	$18,000

15-31 The Concerned Company is considering purchasing a replacement machine on January 1. The present machine was acquired a year before at a cost of $12,000 and was assigned a useful life of 6 years, no salvage value. If it is replaced, it can be sold immediately for $9,000. It has an undepreciated capital cost of $10,200.

The list price of the replacement machine is $16,000. Shipping charges are $300 and installation is $200. The new equipment will have a useful life of 5 years and a salvage value of $1,500.

Estimated cash savings before taxes and depreciation will be $2,500. The income tax rate is 40 percent and all savings are assumed to take place at the end of each year. Both of these machines and similar ones owned by the company are in asset class 10, capital cost allowance is 30 percent.

The firm's cost of capital is 12 percent.

All calculations should be in dollars only (round cents).

Required:

Decide whether the company should replace the present equipment using both the payback method and the net present value method.

15-32   The Aggie Corporation is considering construction of a new motel containing 180 rooms.

The motel will cost $3,250,600 which will be paid to the contractor on the day the motel opens for business.

Additional information:

1. Assume a 360 day operating year.
2. Half of the rooms are single rooms and half are double rooms (i.e., one and two person rooms only).
3. The daily rate is $13.00 for a single room and $24.00 for a double room.
4. The motel will operate at full capacity for all 360 days.
5. Cash operating expenses are expected to be $675,000 per year, assumed payable at the *end* of each year.
6. Assume all room rentals will be collected at end of each year.
7. Assume no income taxes, i.e., ignore taxes.
8. Assume a cost of capital of 10%.
9. Owner plans to keep the motel for 7 years and then sell it for $500,000.

Required:

You are to decide whether this is a good investment using the net present value method and the present value index.

15-33   Taylor, Inc. has hired you for all of their capital budgeting decisions. Mr. Taylor, president of Taylor, Inc. feels that payback is the best method to use. You, however, feel that net present value analysis will yield more information and allow you to make a wiser decision. The company wants to purchase some new machinery. Given the information below, you are to use both methods of analysis and make a decision on investing. Taylor, Inc. requires a ten year maximum payback. Discuss your decision.

	Old Machine	*New Machine*
Cost.........................	$10,000	$20,000
Useful life remaining............	12 years	12 years
Undepreciated capital cost.......	$ 1,000	
Scrap value at present...........	$ 400	N/A
Scrap value in 15 years..........	-0-	$ 500
Direct labor saving/year.........		$ 3,000
Additional electricity costs per year....................		$ 500
Capital cost allowance—30%		
Tax rate—40%		
Time value of money—8%		
The company has other machines in this class.		

15-34　Fritz Company is considering an investment in a new machine to improve the production of one of their products. The old machine requires a great deal of maintenance because of its age, so the company feels it will save about $10,000 per year in maintenance costs if it purchases the new machine. The power bill will increase by $.06 per unit but the company will also be saving $.48 per unit in labor costs. The machine will cost $375,000 and has a useful life of 10 years with no salvage value at that time. Production will equal sales in all years. In years 1 through 5 production will be 90,000 units but it will increase by 20,000 units in each of the remaining years. The old machine will be abandoned in a field behind the factory. It has an undepreciated capital cost of $1,000. Both machines are in asset class 8. Capital cost allowance is 20%.

Required:

If the company's minimum rate of return is 12% and a tax rate of 40%, should the investment be undertaken? Find the internal rate of return for the investment. (Round to the nearest cent.)

15-35　Franco, Inc. has been using the payback method as the sole criterion for capital budgeting decisions. You are the newest member of the Franco staff, having just graduated from the university. You realize from courses you have taken that payback is not the best criterion. You feel that the net present value method is better, but so far have been unable to convince management of this.

　　Management is preparing to purchase a new machine for their new product. The machine appears very good using payback but, again, you are not certain they are making the right decision. There are three machines to choose from; Machine 1 is the one management wants to purchase. From the information given below, prepare an analysis using both the payback method and the net present value method. Use specific cash flows for payback, not the average cash flows. Make your recommendations to management. (Round cents to dollars.)

	Machine 1	Machine 2	Machine 3
Cost	$25,000	$30,000	$28,000
Useful life	6 years	6 years	6 years
Scrap value in 6 years	$ 400	$ 600	$ 1,000
Before-tax cash flow per year:			
Year 1	$10,000	$ 6,000	$11,000
Year 2	9,000	7,000	10,000
Year 3	8,000	7,500	8,800
Year 4	4,000	8,000	7,500
Year 5	3,000	6,000	7,000
Year 6	2,000	4,000	6,000

Tax rate = 40%
Capital cost allowance = 20%
Asset class = 8.   (There are other assets in this class.)
Cost of capital = 10%
Maximum payback period 4 years

15-36   The Grahm Company is considering three mutually exclusive proposals, all of which would require an initial cash outlay of $90,000. The company has estimated that the net cash proceeds from each proposal would be:

	Proposal A	Proposal B	Proposal C
End of Year 1	$50,000	$30,000	$30,000
2	40,000	30,000	30,000
3	30,000	30,000	60,000
4	20,000	30,000	20,000
5	20,000	30,000	20,000
6	20,000	30,000	20,000

Since only one of the three proposals can be accepted, the president of the company has argued that the decision should be made on the basis of a present value analysis. However, the treasurer of the company believes that the decision should be made on the basis of a payback analysis.

Required:

Rank the three proposals as to their desirability by: (a) the present value method (cost of capital is 12%), and (b) payback method. (Note: Do not consider taxes.)

15-37   Davis, Inc. is considering purchasing a new machine. Using the data below, determine whether this venture will be profitable. (Round cents to the nearest dollar.)

1. The new machine, which will cost $40,000, will have a useful life of 6 years. At the end of that time, it is expected to have a salvage value of $1,000. The new machine is in Class 8, CCA is 20%.
2. The new machine will not be replacing an old machine. It will be used to handle an increase in demand for the company's product. There are other machines in the same asset class.
3. Net cash inflows from operations before depreciation and taxes will be $9,500 in years 1 through 3, $12,000 in years 4 and 5, and $8,000 in year 6.
4. The company's tax rate is 40% with a cost of capital of 10%.

15-38 Based upon estimated demand, Lucy Stores purchased one thousand crates of oranges at $10 per crate. Management had originally estimated that all one thousand crates would be sold at $15 per crate. Actually only eight hundred crates were sold at $13.50 per crate and the other two hundred crates were sold to a frozen juice company for $5.00 per crate.

Required:

Analyze the cost of Lucy's prediction errors.

15-39 Based upon estimated demand for the Christmas season. Ruplinger, Inc. acquired 200 diamond pendants. With a cost of $500 each Ruplinger expected a good profit with an estimated selling price of $800. After purchasing the pendants, but before any sales, the retail price rose to $1,000 each. Also, after the 200 pendants were sold, 50 customers had to be turned away because of the lack of inventory.

Required:

Analyze the cost of these prediction errors for Ruplinger, Inc.

15-40 Sampson Ltd. is considering whether or not to replace its current wrecking machine with a newer model.

The following information is available:

Original cost of old machine	$100,000
Undepreciated capital cost of old machine	36,864
Old machine can be presently sold for	30,000
Salvage value of old machine at the end of its useful life (10 more years)	1,000
Present cost of new machine	101,000
Salvage value of new machine at the end of its useful life (10 years)	1,500
Capital cost allowance rate	20%
Sampson's cost of capital rate	12%
Income tax rate	45%
Operating costs of old machine	$ 21,000
Operating costs of new machine	9,000
Annual cash inflow generated by old machine	30,000
Annual cash inflow generated by new machine	31,000

Required:

a.   If income taxes are ignored, what is the net investment value of the old machine? Of the new machine? Should Sampson replace the old machine with the new one?

b.   If income taxes are considered, what is the net present value of the old machine? Of the new machine?

15-41   A recent provincial lottery winner has the choice of receiving $2,000,000 (tax free) now or $300,000 (tax free) at the end of each year for the next ten years. Regardless of the payment chosen, this person has already decided to invest all of the winnngs, together with any (after tax) earnings from investments for at least ten years. If the ten equal payments are chosen these payments would be reinvested in interest bearing securities which pay 10 percent per year (before taxes). If the single lump sum payment is chosen, there are two viable investment alternatives:

a.   Purchase 10 percent government bonds at par (face value). These bonds mature in ten years. The interest on these bonds would be paid in cash at the end of each year and would be fully taxable at the time of payment.

b.   Purchase a fully equipped industrial plant with a capital cost allowance of 10 percent. The plant would be leased to the government for ten years at an annual rent of $250,000 payable at the beginning of each year. The lease agreement would also provide for the plant to be sold to the government at the end of the ten years for an amount equal to its undepreciated capital cost at that time.

Any cash generated by these investments would be reinvested in interest bearing securities which pay 10 percent per year (before taxes).

The winner's combined federal-provincial marginal income tax rate is 55 percent. This is the maximum rate for residents of the province.

Required:

a.   Calculate the net present value of each of the three alternatives (10 annual payments; lump sum payment and bonds; lump sum payment and plant).

b.   Based on your answer to (a), which alternative should be chosen?

15-42   The Delta Company is planning a project which is expected to last for six years. During that time, the project is expected to generate net cash inflows of $85,000 per year.

The project will require the purchase of a machine for $310,000. This new machine is expected to have a salvage value of $20,000 at the end of the six years. In addition to its annual operating costs, the machine will require an overhaul costing $55,000 at the end of year four. The company presently has a minimum desired rate of return of 12 percent. Based on this information, the accountant prepared the following analysis:

Annual net cash inflow......................		$85,000
Less: Annual depreciation.................	$48,333	
Annual average cost of overhaul........	9,167	57,500
Average annual net income...................		$27,500

$$\text{Return on investment} = \frac{27,500}{310,000} = 8.87\%$$

Therefore, the accountant recommends that the project be rejected as it does not meet the company's minimum desired rate of return.

Required:

a. What criticism(s) would you make of the accountant's evaluation of the project?

b. Use present value analysis to determine whether or not the project should be accepted. *(SMA, adapted)*

15-43 The Cord Company Limited presently sells 25,000 units per year at a price of $90 per unit. These units are produced using a machine which was purchased five years ago at a cost of $600,000. It presently has a book value of $300,000; however, due to its specialized nature, it has a market value today of only $35,000. The machine, expected to last another five years after which it will have no expected salvage value, gives rise to the following standard costs:

Direct materials (5 lbs. @ $1.50/lb.).......................	$ 7.50
Direct labour (4 hrs. @ $15.00/hr.)........................	60.00
Variable overhead (4 hrs. @ $1.20/hr.).....................	4.80
Fixed overhead, based on an annual activity level of 100,000 direct labour hours (4 hrs. @ $1.60/hr.)............	6.40
Total standard cost per unit...........................	$78.70

The company expects the following changes for next year:

1. The selling price will increase by 10 percent.
2. Direct labour rates will increase by 15 percent.
3. Sales are expected to increase to 26,000 units (within the capacity of present facilities) and remain at that level.

Management is presently considering the replacement of their old machine with a new one which would cost $750,000. The new machine is expected to last five years with a salvage value of $30,000 expected at that time. By using the new machine, management expects to cut variable direct labour hours to 3½ hours per unit, but will have to hire an operator for the machine at $45,000 per year. The company has a minimum desired rate of return of 10 percent.

Required: (Ignore Income Taxes)

a. Determine, by using the net present-value approach, whether or not the company should purchase the new machine.

b. How many units would the company have to sell to earn annual profits of $230,000 (before taxes) if it were to purchase the new machine? Ignore any gain or loss on the sale of the old machine.

(SMA, adapted)

15-44   The Selva Co. Ltd. has just completed market testing a new consumer product—Snocult. The product is a snow blower which can be converted by the consumer to a garden cultivator for spring and summer use.

Selva's president is very enthusiastic about this new product possibility and he makes the following data available for your analysis:

a.   Product development costs to date . . . . $ 45,000

b.   Cost of manufacturing equipment for a
    one-shift capacity of 600 units $300,000
    (economic life of the equipment is estimated
    to be 3 years with a salvage value of $25,000)

c.   Estimated revenue and cost data are:

Year	Sales in Units	Average Factory Selling Price Per Unit	Average Variable Cost Per Unit	Contribution Margin Per Unit
1	400	$450	$260	$190
2	1,000	475	245	230
3	1,200	500	240	260

d.   Selva's expected income tax rate is 40 percent.

e.   The equipment will be depreciated at the Capital Cost Allowance rate of 20 percent. *Selva has no other equipment in this class.*

f.   The cost of market testing Snocult was $15,000.

g.   The following additional fixed costs will be incurred each year:

	Advertising and Building Rent
1	$15,000
2	25,000
3	20,000

Required:

a.   Prepare a schedule showing cash flows resulting from the project. Use three columns, one each for year 1, year 2, and year 3.

b.   Using the net present value method do you recommend Selva proceed with this project? For this part assume:

    i.   Initial costs are paid on January 1, year 1, while all other flows occur at the end of each year; and

    ii.   Selva's minimum desired rate of return is 10 percent.

c.   State briefly two ways in which the effect of risk may be taken into account in the quantitative evaluation of a capital investment.

(SMA, adapted)

15-45 The United Polymer Co. Ltd., is evaluating two alternative machines to convert scrap into useable raw material. The machines are expected to generate the following cost-benefit streams over their expected three year lives:

		Machine A	Machine B
Initial cost		$100,000	$100,000
Net income *after* depreciation			
but *before* taxes	1	30,000	20,000
	2	40,000	30,000
	3	40,000	40,000

Due to rapid technological change in this field, the machines will be worthless after three years. The firm's after-tax cost of capital is 12 percent and their tax rate is 40 percent. Due to the differences in the processes used by the two machines, the CCA rate for Machine A allows 20 percent of the declining balance to be written off for tax purposes each year, while that for Machine B allows 30 percent of the declining balance to be written off each year. The firm intends to finance the acquisition through a private placement of first mortgage bonds at 10 percent. Depreciation recorded will equal capital cost allowance claimed.

Required:

a. What are the present values of the after-tax cash inflows from each machine?
b. What are the present values of tax shields from the capital cost allowance for each machine?
c. Based upon the above analysis, which machine (if either) should the firm acquire?

(SMA, adapted)

15-46 During a visit to Regal Shoe Manufacturing Ltd., the audit senior, Bill Swann, was approached by Peter Light, the company's controller, who said:

"Bill, the president believes we would be better off to subcontract all our repair work that comes to us from our distributors. He has asked me to prepare a schedule demonstrating whether we would be better off to subcontract this work or to continue to operate our own repair department. I'm a little rusty on this kind of analysis so I put together some information which I hoped you and I could look at.

"Apparently, we can subcontract out the repair work for a three year period during which we would be paid a fee of $5 per pair of shoes taken in by our distributors and I estimate we will take in 4,000 pairs each year. In addition, if we subcontract the work, we could dispose of our repair machinery for $35,000, which is pretty terrific since we bought it five years ago for $15,000 and we claimed an investment tax credit of $750 on our corporate income tax return. We have presently $8,000 left in our class 29 UCC pool. Even at our tax rate of

40 percent, we should get to keep a sizeable portion of the $35,000. We also have $10,000 invested in repair materials from which we could recover $2,000. This project would commence early in our next fiscal year.

"If we continue to operate for three years, the resale value of the equipment would then be $7,000 and I suspect that the only inventory which we would have on hand would be $4,500 of repair materials which are now obsolete but are still included in our current inventory.

"On the other hand, we could continue to operate our repair department which makes a contribution of $11 per pair of shoes before the following annual costs:

Supervision . . . . $8,000 (20% of production fore-
                                                man's time)
Depreciation . . . . $3,000 (based on a 5 year life)
Power costs. . . . . $5,000 (based on an engineer's pro-
                                                jections)
Overhead . . . . $5,000 (allocated based on floor
                                                space).

"The president told me he has another project in mind for the use of the repair department's space. He didn't say what it was, but it must be a good one, because we can borrow at an after tax cost of 10 percent and he won't accept any project which yields less than 15 percent after tax. He did mention that to rent space for the project he had in mind would cost 4,000 per year."

Required:

Prepare the schedule for the president showing how much better or worse off Regal Shoe Manufacturing Ltd. would be if it subcontracts its repair work. For any cost you exclude from your schedule, briefly note the explanation you would give for doing so.

(CA, adapted)

Index

W